ABSTRACTS
from the
PENNSYLVANIA GAZETTE
1748-1755

By
Kenneth Scott
&
Janet R. Clarke

CLEARFIELD

Copyright © 1977
Genealogical Publishing Co., Inc.
Baltimore, Maryland
All Rights Reserved

Library of Congress Catalog Card Number 77-85267

Reprinted for Clearfield Company by
Genealogical Publishing Company
Baltimore, Maryland
2015

ISBN 978-0-8063-0786-2

INTRODUCTION

The present volume of abstracts concerns individuals mentioned in the *Pennsylvania Gazette* from January 12, 1748 (when Benjamin Franklin formed a partnership with David Hall, who took over "all care of the printing office") through April 10, 1755 (the last date in the tenth volume of the reprint edition of the newspaper).* Lists of persons who had letters in various post offices have been omitted, since these will be found in the book entitled *Buried Genealogical Data,* published in September, 1977, by the Genealogical Publishing Co., Inc. Names of captains in shipping lists have also been omitted. On the other hand, names of all masters of ships that appear in news items are included.

During the years 1749-1755 Pennsylvania and the neighboring colonies grew rapidly in population, as is shown by frequent notices of the arrival of Palatines and other immigrants. News items and advertisements provide a wealth of genealogical information—ages, family connections, occupations, places of residence, real estate transactions, and settlements of estates (normally with names of executors or administrators). The abstracts give a vivid picture of the times, and it is hoped that the researcher will turn to the original paper or reprint for greater detail.

During the period, New Jersey and the Three Lower Counties on Delaware had no newspaper, so the *Gazette* gave extensive coverage of these areas, as well as of Maryland. The Philadelphia newspaper, moreover, abounds in items extracted from Boston, New York, and Annapolis papers, as well as frequent notices from the press of the southern colonies.

The compilers of this volume wish to express their gratitude to the New-York Historical Society for making available the reprint edition of the *Gazette* and to Mrs. Joan Sanger for invaluable assistance in the preparation of the manuscript.

Kenneth Scott
Janet R. Clarke

---

*A previous volume of abstracts, commencing with the founding of the *Gazette* in 1728 and continuing through 1748, was published by the Genealogical Publishing Co., Inc. in 1975. Another volume, consisting mainly of death notices which appeared in the *Gazette* during the Revolutionary War, was published in 1976.

1748

Minutes of Council - 13, 14, 16 Nov. 1747 - Anthony Palmer, president, Thomas Lawrence, William Till, Robert Strettell, Joseph Turner, Samuel Hassell, Abra. Taylor, Benj. Shoemaker, William Logan, Indian: old Scaiohady, with mention of James Logan, Mr. Weiser, Richard Peters, secretary, and John Kinsey, speaker (12 Jan.)

Privateer snow Dreadnaught, Capt. Mayberry, cast away on Cape Cod (12 Jan.)

New York item mentions Capt. Heysham from Newcastle, Capt. Grenall from Cape Francois, the privateer Catherine, Capt. Obline, of New York (late Capt. Perkins, who died a few days after the privateer sailed) and Capt. Troup (12 Jan.)

Adv. of James Read, bookseller, in Second St. (12 Jan.)

Accounts with estate of Mary Halloway, late of Phila., widow, dec'd. to be settled with Jacob Cooper, exec. (12 Jan.)

For freight or passage to Barbados in the brigantine Sally, John Austin, master, at Oswald Peele's wharf, agree with Peter Keen or the master (12 Jan.)

Judith, Mulatto, age c. 25, runaway from John Cresson in Strawberry Alley (12 Jan.)

Irish servant girls to be sold by Dennis Flood in Pewter-Platter Alley (12 Jan.)

Forge on Black Creek, about ½ mile from Burden's Town, for sale; enquire of Andrew Reed and Joseph Yard in Trenton or Francis Bowes and David Davis in Phila. (12 Jan.)

Adv. of Edward Dowers in Water St., who sells cloth (12 Jan.)

Tickets in the Phila. Lottery are sold by William Allen, Joshua Maddox, William Masters, Samuel M'Call, Sr., Edward Shippen, Thomas Leech, Charles Willing, John Kearsley, William Clymer, Sr., Thomas Lawrence, Jr., William Coleman, Thomas Hopkinson and B. Franklin (12 Jan.)

Accounts with estate of Samuel Powell, Jr., late of Phila., merchant to be settled with William Coleman and James Pemberton, execs. (12 Jan.)

Adv. of Evan Morgan, cooper, in Front St., who sells wine, rum, gin, etc. (12 Jan.)

Plantation in Oxford Twp., late property of Jacob Hall, mason, dec'd. for sale; apply to Edward Collins and Abraham Leech, execs. (12 Jan.)

Mares strayed from Hugh Hall and Joseph Candour in Conewago, Lancaster Co. (12 Jan.)

Margaret Barnes (alias hopping Peg), breeches-maker by trade, born in Exeter, England; she went from Norfolk as waiting-maid to Annapolis and thence to the head of Sassafrass in Md.; she is runaway from John Langdale of Norfolk, Va., reward if brought to Langdale or to William Hudson in Phila. (12 Jan.)

For freight or passage to London in the ship Beulah, James Child master, apply to Benjamin or Samuel Shoemaker or said master (12 Jan.)

1748

House in Northern Liberties for sale by John and Jacob Naglee, execs. of Jacob Naglee, shopkeeper, dec'd. (12 Jan.)

Richard Farmar at the Unicorn in Second St. sells cloth and medicines (12 Jan.)

Accounts with estate of Joseph Richards, merchant, dec'd, to be settled with Mary Richards, exec. (12 Jan.)

Tract called Green's Manor in St. George's Hundred, Newcastle Co., for sale; enquire of John Inglis, merchant, in Phila., or John Moland of the Northern Liberties Twp. (12 Jan.)

Accounts with estate of Jasper M'Call, late of Phila., merchant, dec'd, to be settled with Magdalene, Samuel and George M'Call, admins. (12 Jan.)

Horses strayed from plantation of Samuel Preston Moore near Frankfort (12 Jan.)

John Hawksford (*alias* Hawkins or Oxford), Irish servant, age c. 28, and Catherine Dunn, Irish servant, age c. 20, runaways from Amos Garrett, of Baltimore Co., Md. (12 Jan.)

Accounts with estate of Joseph Harper, of Oxford, dec'd, to be settled with Matthias Keen of Lower Dublin, execs. (12 Jan.)

Adv. of Francis Bowes in Water St; he has store on Robert Ellis's wharf (12 Jan.)

Accounts with estate of Ebenezer Currie, dec'd, to be settled with Samuel M'Call, Sr; and John Groves, admins (12 Jan.)

Lots in Phila. for sale; enquire of Anthony Wilkinson, carver (12 Jan.)

Plantation in Manor of Moreland, Phila. Co., for sale; enquire of John Nelson in Phila. or Edmund Nihill (12 Jan.)

New York item mentions privateer *Antilope*, Capt. Amory and brigantine *Catherine*, Capt. Albine (19 Jan.)

Letter from Annapolis, Md; mentions the *Winchelsea*, Capt. Comish, the *Britannia*, Capt. Hutchinson, and Admiral Hawke (19 Jan.)

The following were chosen Officers of the Regt. of Associators raised in the townships of East and West Nantmel, Uwchland, West Caln and Charlestown, Chester.: William Moore, col.; Samuel Flower, lt. col.; John Mather, major; Capts.: David Parry, Roger Hunt, George Asheton, William M'Knight, John M'Coole, George Taylor, James Graham; lieuts.: Isaac Davy, Guyan Moore, Robert Morrel, Robert Anderson, John Cuthbertson, John Vaughan, Jr., and William Darlington; ensigns: Nathaniel Davis, William Litler, Edward Pierce, Samuel Love, James Scot, Robert Awl and Francis Gardiner (19 Jan.)

James Lownes of Passyunk Twp. has taken up cattle (19 Jan.)

Hugh Bradford, Irishman, supposed to have stolen 114 dollars from Thomas England at Robert Davis's in Water St.; reward if thief is taken to Thomas England at Joseph Osborn's in Second St. (19 Jan.)

Time of servant for sale; enquire of Archibald Anderson in Second St. (19 Jan.)

Log house and land in Kingcess Twp., adjoining Carpenter's Island,

1748

to be sold or let; enquire of Thomas Williams, shopkeeper, in Second St. (19 Jan.)

St. Eustatia ginger sold by Nathaniel Magee at the Sign of Admiral Warren in Arch St. (19 Jan.)

Warning by W. Shirley about forged bills of exchange, all signed W. Shirley, Cha. Knowles (19 Jan.)

For freight or passage to Dublin in brigantine *Pembroke*, Arthur Burroughs commander, apply to Norris and Griffiths or the master (19 Jan.)

Elizabeth, wife of Thomas Catthringer, of Phila., stay-maker, has eloped (19 Jan.)

Benjamin Davis, sheriff, has in Chester Goal Cato, a Negro, who says he ran away from John Bale, or Bailey, in Va. (19 Jan.)

Peter Fitzpatrick, an Irishman, run away from his bail, Patrick Conner in Newcastle Co. (19 Jan.)

William Henderson offers reward for recovery of strayed horse if the animal is brought to Peter Robeson's at the Sign of the Indian King (19 Jan.)

Christian Steinman, 3 miles from Lancaster, will pay reward for recovery of strayed or stolen mares (19 Jan.)

Tract of land in Limerick, Phila. Co., part of the plantation late of Edward Nicholas, dec'd, for sale; apply to William Currie or Thomas Bull, execs. (19 Jan.)

Thomas Stamper in Arch St. sells green tea (19 Jan.)

Negro woman for sale; enquire of Marcus Kuhl in Market St. (19 Jan.)

The *Scarborough*, that carried the Lady Warren to England, is arrived at Plymouth (26 Jan.)

Officers chosen by the Associators (for Phila. Co.): capts. Thomas York and John Hughes; lieuts. Jacob Leech and Matthias Holstein; ensigns John Barge and Frederick Holstein - (for Chester Co.) capts. Robert Grace, Richard Richison and Moses Dickie; lieuts. John Kent, John Cuthbert and John Boyd; ensigns Jacob Free, John Hambrith and James Montgomery - (for Lancaster Co.) capt. Hugh Patrick; lieut. Thomas Macdowell; ensign Thomas Grubb - (for Newcastle Co.) capt. William M'Crea; lieut. Alexander Moody; ensign Francis Graham (26 Jan.)

Six prizes were taken by Capt. Frankland in the *Dragon*; Capt. Adamson of Phila. from Lisbon is in the river; Capt. Dunn in a brigantine from Phila. for Dublin is ashore on Reedy Island (26 Jan.)

On night of 17 Jan. William Carson was frozen to death in his flat in Mantua Creek (26 Jan.)

Accounts with estate of John Harding, dec'd, to be settled at house of John Harding, Jr., by John Harding and George Adams, admins. (26 Jan.)

For freight or passage to Charles-Town, S.C., in the ship *Phoenix*, John Mason commander, agree with Mason or with Benjamin and Samuel Shoemaker (26 Jan.)

Leather, tanner's tools, etc. will be sold by Nicholas Scull, late
Sheriff, at the late dwelling in Phila. of John Howell, tanner
(26 Jan.)

Associators will meet at house of Nathaniel King in Kennet Twp.
to chose officers (26 Jan.)

Accounts with estate of John Barkley, late of Phila., shopkeeper,
dec'd, to be settled with Nathaniel Magee and Elizabeth Barkley,
execs. (26 Jan.)

Pocketbook dropped in the street in Phila.; reward offered by owner,
Timothy Matlack, living near the Post Office in Market St. (26 Jan.)

Adv. of John Clifton in Second St. (26 Jan.)

Plantation in Whitemarsh, whereon Samuel Irwin now lives and
George Harkness lately dwelt, being part of estate of Edward
Farmer, dec'd, to be sold at house of Christopher Robins in
Whitemarsh by Jonathan and Peter Robeson and Edward Farmer (26 Jan.)

Adv. of Henry Schleydorn, sugar-baker, in Norris's Alley (26 Jan.)

Accounts with estate of William Martin, late of Whipton Twp., dec'd
(he had a store in "Upper Dublin" and was a tailor), to be
settled with Abrahan Dawes, Richard Waln and Benjamin Davis
(26 Jan.)

French prize ship take by privateer _Antilope_, Capt. Amory, arrived
24 Jan. at N.Y. (2 Feb.)

Officers commissioned by the Associators, (for Bucks Co.) capt.,
George Bennet; lieut., Garret Wynkoop; ensign, Ralph Dunn; (for
Newcastle Co.) capts. George Gano, Edward Fitzrandolph, Henry
Dyre, Alexander Porter; lieuts., James Egbertson, Alexander Chance,
Paul Alfree, James King; ensigns, Thomas Bennet, Joseph Holtham,
Jerrard Rothwell, Samuel Alrichs (2 Feb.)

Capts. Morrison and Worsdale of Phila. are captured and taken to
Trinidad (2 Feb.)

Sermon by Rev. Gilbert Tennent and also answer to his sermon on
The Lawfulness of War soon to be published (2 Feb.)

Adv. of Godhart Armbruster, German printer in Arch St. (2 Feb.)

Negro named Greenwich, runaway from David Franks in Phila. (2 Feb.)

Apply to Isaiah Worrell, living on premises, to purchase plantation
about 6 miles from Phila. (2 Feb.)

Thomas White in Market St., opposite Sign of the Dutch Waggon,
offers imports for sale (2 Feb.)

Lynford Lardner gives notice as to when and where quitrent is to
be paid (2 Feb.)

Property in Chester to be let, apply to Isaac Howell on premises
or Joseph Howell in Phila. (2 Feb.)

Plantation in Cheltenham Twp. offered for sale by Thomas Nesmith
on premises (2 Feb.)

1748

Cloth for sale by John Parkinson at Capt. Thomas Charlton's in Chestnut St., Phila. (2 Feb.)

Houses at Christine Bridge to be let or sold by Dr. Rees Jones (2 Feb.)

Reward to be paid by Owen Roberts in Black Horse Alley or John Jones of North Wales (2 Feb.)

Accounts with estate of John Hyat, dec'd, to be brought to widow to be adjusted by execs. Thomas Lawrence, Joshua Maddox, Thomas Leech (2 Feb.)

Sugar for sale by John Morgan in Market St. Wharf (2 Feb.)

Dennis Ryan, Irish servant, age c. 18 runaway from John Miller of Lampeter Twp. (2 Feb.)

At house of Christopher Robins in Whitemarsh will be sold plantation where Samuel Irwin lives and plantation where George Harkness lately dwelt; all part of estate of Edward Farmer, dec'd; apply to Jonathan and Peter Robeson and Edward Farmer (2 Feb.)

Mention of plantation of Joseph Lownes in Passyunk Twp. (2 Feb.)

Thomas England, at Joseph Osborn's in Second St., was robbed of 114 dollars, supposedly by Hugh Bradford, an Irishman, at Robert Davis's in Water St. (2 Feb.); not Hugh Bradford the tailor (16 Apr.)

Last week Capt. Budden came passenger with Capt. Burk from London to Phila. (9 Feb.)

Officers chosen by the Associators; (for Phila. Co.) capts. Henry Pawling and Jacob Hall, lieuts. Robert Dunn and Joseph Lewis, ensigns Hugh Hamilton and William Finney; for Bucks Co., capt. Alexander Graydon, lieut. Anthony Denormandie, ensign, James Barber;(for Chester Co.) capts. Andrew M'Dowell, Hugh Kirkpatrick, John Williamson, John Mather, lieuts. John Cunningham, William Buchannan, James Macken, James Mather; ensigns, George M'Cullough, William Cumming, John Johnson, Joseph Talbert; (for Newcastle Co.) capt. David Bush; lieut. John M'Kinly; ensign, Charles Bush (9 feb.)

Sermon by Gilbert Tennent to be published next Thu. (9 Feb.)

Michael Coleman Shaghnesey will teach Latin and French at his lodgings at Thomas Davis's in Water St. (9 feb.)

Plantation in Passyunk Twp., to be let by Bartholomew Penrose on premises (9 Feb.)

Grist mill, formerly of John Bond, dec'd, in Southampton Twp., Bucks Co., for sale; apply to William Duncan, near mill (9 Feb.)

William Callender, in Front St, will sell his plantation at Richmond, alias Point-no-point (9 Feb.)

Dutch servant named Elizabeth Stormer, age c. 15, runaway from Elizabeth Weekes, of Phila., shopkeeper (9 Feb.)

Officers chosen by the Associators: (for Phila. Co.) Capt., Samuel Shaw; lieut., Isaac Ashton; ensign, John Roberts: (for Bucks Co.) capts., Richard Walker, Langhorne Biles, Joseph Inslee, lieuts, Robert Walker, Garret Vanzant, Anthony Teate; ensigns, William Davis, John Severns, David Lawell - (for Chester Co.), capt. James Hunter; lieut., Charles Moore; ensign, Benjamin Weatherby -

(for Newcastle Co.) capts., David Stuart, John Vance; lieuts., Jerome Dushane, John Vandyke; ensigns, Isaac Dushane, William Harraway (16 Feb.)

Just published; sermon by Gilbert Tennent, sermon preached at Radnor by Rev. Currie, Manual Exercise by Gen. Blakeney, Evolution of Foot by Gen. Bland (16 Feb.)

Plantation in Sadsbury Twp. (formerly of John Minshall, dec'd., late in possession of William Boyd, tavernkeeper) offered for sale by John Kinsey; bounded by land formerly of William Howell and land late of Philip Howell (16 Feb.)

Plantation in Kensington to be let,; apply to Mary Ball on premises (16 Feb.)

Plantation in Haverford for sale; apply to Henry Lewis on premises (16 Feb.)

Plantation in the Great Valley in Whiteland Twp. for sale; apply Rees Pritchard on premises (16 Feb.)

Plantation in Bensalem Twp. for sale; apply to James Baldwin on premises or to Jacob Cannon in Phila. (16 Feb.)

Mill and plantation in Upper Dublin, near John Trump's, late property of John Burk, to be sold by Huse and Edward Burk, execs. (16 Feb.)

Officers chosen by the Associators: (for Phila. Co.) capt., Edward Jones; first lieut. Griffith Griffith; second lieut., William Coates; ensign, James Richy - (for Bucks Co.) capts., Simon Butler, Henry Croson, James Huston; lieuts., James Meredith, Isaiah Vanzant, Archibald Finley; ensigns, Benjamin Butler, Joseph Hart, William Walker (1 Mar.)

Bills of credit dated 1724 to be sent to John Allen, Esq., or Treasurer, by order of Lawrence Van Buskirk and Joseph Cooper, for the House (1 Mar.)

George Okill intends for England (1 Mar.)

Accounts with estate of William Crosthwaite, late of Phila., perukemaker, dec'd, to be settled with George Okill, exec. (1 Mar.)

Daniel Cunningham, at the Indian King, has undertaken business of messenger between Phila. and Chestertown, Md. (1 Mar.)

Thomas Cathringer, staymaker in Arch St., continues in business (1 Mar.)

Plantation in Oxford Twp. to be sold by Isaiah Worrell (1 Mar.)

Joseph Kerby, at John Morgan's store on Market St. Wharf, sells muskets, sugar, etc. (1 Mar.)

Land adjoining Peryomen Church-land for sale by Edward Lane on premises (1 Mar.)

Mill and 2 plantations in Newcastle Co. for sale; enquire of Abraham Enos at the mill or George Stevenson at Blackbird's Bridge (1 Mar.)

Plantation in Wilmington Twp; Chester Co., for sale; apply to David Jones near said plantation or George James of Haverford (1 Mar.)

1748

Plantation in Cheltenham Twp. to be sold by Thomas Carvell (1 Mar.)

House in Germantown, lots and dwelling of Jacob Vonderwite to be sold by said Vonderwite and John Frederick Ax (1 Mar.)

Two houses in Lancaster., both lately belonging to Edward Edwards, one in Carnarven Twp., the other in Earl Twp., are to be sold by order of Sheriff James Sterrat (1 Mar.)

Accounts with estate of John Scoggin, late of Phila., bricklayer, dec'd., are to be settled with Mary Anne Scoggan, admin. (1 Mar.)

Plantation in Radnor Twp. for sale; apply to John Moore on premises (1 Mar.)

Accounts with estate of Jeremiah Allen, late of Phila., tavern-keeper, dec'd, to be settled with Susanna and James Allen, admins. (1 Mar.)

Adv. of Joseph Scull, keeper of pound in Phila. (1 Mar.)

Imported cloth for sale by Alexander Forbes in Second St. (1 Mar.)

Two plantations near Conestogoe road; apply to George Aston, living on one of them (1 Mar.)

Officers chosen by Associators: (for Phila. Co.) capts., Abraham Dehaven, Christopher Robbins; lieuts., Roger North, Peter Knight; ensigns, John Pawlin, Benjamin Davis - (for Bucks Co.) capt. Griffith Owen; lieut. Thomas Kelly; ensign, William Williams - (for Chester Co.) capt. William Bell; lieut., Robert Macmullin; ensign, Rowland Parry - (for Newcastle Co.) capt., William Armstrong; lieut. James Morris; ensign, Thomas Philips - (for Lancaster Co.) capt. Gabriel Dairs; lieut., Robert Ellis; ensign, Edward Davis (8 Mar.)

Capt. Lisle arrived Phila. from Antigua; Capt. Carr, attacked by enemy privateers, got safe into Antigua; the brigantine *Samuel*, Capt. Bowers, of Phila., taken by Spanish privateer, was retaken (8 Mar.)

Samuel Robeson in Vine St. makes pewter worms (8 Mar.)

Four tracts of Lottery Lands on Forks of Delaware will be sold by Thomas Graeme at house where Robert Eastbourne lately dwelt near Bethleham and two more tracts will be sold at house of John Lefaver; apply to Thomas Craig or said Lefaver living on the Forks (8 Mar.)

Colliers seeking work may apply to John Abraham Denormandy, Esq., at Bristol, Henry Mitchell at Mountholly iron-works, or to Peter Bard, John Pass or Evan Morgan in Phila. (8 Mar.)

Plantation in North Wales, late estate of Rees Nanna, dec'd, will be sold by Abraham and Jacob Nanna, living on premises (8 Mar.)

Adam Wever in Water St. sells bran and salt (8 Mar.)

Hugh Bradford, Irish servant, has run away from John Inskape, of Evesham Twp., Burlington Co. (8 Mar.)

Accounts with estate of Thomas Tatnell, late of Chester Co., dec'd, to be settled with John Knowles of Wilmington and Elizabeth his wife (sole executrix); plantation near Darby and house in Darby for sale; apply to said Knowles or to Anne Tatnell in Riley Twp. (8 Mar.)

1748

Reward for recovery of colt will be paid by Samuel Powell or Anthony Morris, Jr., of Phila. (8 Mar.)

Plantation in Blockley Twp. for sale by Richard Pearne on premises (8 Mar.)

Capt. Lloyd has lately arrived at Norfolk, Va., from Jamaica (15 Mar.)

Officers chosen by Associators: (for Bucks Co.) Col. Alexander Graydon, Esq., lieut.col. Matthew Hughes, Esq., major, John Denormandie, Esq., - (for Lancaster Co.) capt., James Gillespie; lieut. James Gilcreast; ensign, Samuel Jamison - (for Newcastle Co.) capt., Jacob Gooding; lieut., Jacob Vanbebber; ensign, David Howell (15 Nov.)

Cloth and other items, imported in the brigt. *Richa* from London, Benjamin Burk commander, are to be sold by George Emlen, Jr., in Market St. (15 Mar.)

Daniel Benezet in Front St. sells goods imported from London in the brigantine *Richa*, Benjamin Burke commander (15 Mar.)

Land on Petty's Island to be sold by Michael Biggar in Kinsington (15 Mar.)

Dutch servant, Anthony Rietz, age c. 19 or 20, runaway from Henry Klein of Phila. (15 Mar.)

John Frew, owner of a mill, offers for sale plantation in New London Twp., near mill of Job Ruston, Esq. (15 Mar.)

Tract in Warminster Twp., near land called Moore's land, for sale; apply to John Noble on York Road, near premises (15 Mar.)

Plantation in Bensalem Twp. upon Shamminy Creek for sale; apply to Abraham Griffith in Mountholly (15 Mar.)

Capt. Stamper, of Phila., arrived there from Lisbon (22 Mar.)

Officers chosen by the Associators; (for Lancaster Co. between Susquehannah and line of Pa.) col., Benjamin Chambers, Esq., lieut.-col., Robert Dunning, Esq.: major William Maxwell, Esq., capts., Richard O'Cain, Robert Chambers, James Carnaghan, John Chambers, James Silver, Charles Morrow, George Brown, James Woods, James M'Seer, Matthew Dill, Benjamin Chambers, Robert Dunning, William Maxwell, Samuel Crawford; lieuts., William Smith, Andrew Finley, James Jack, Jonathan Holms, Tobias Hendricks, James Dyssard, John Potter, John Maccormick, William Kindle, Andrew Miller, Charles M'Gill, Jack Wartin, John Mitchell, William Rowland; ensigns, John Millibell, John Lesar, John Thompson, Walter Davis, Joseph Erwin, John Anderson, John Randell, Samuel Fisher, Moses Starr, George Brennar, Robert Meek, James Wilkey, Adam Hayes, Richard M'Donald - (for Bucks Co.) capt., Alexander Hunter; lieut., James Martin; ensign, John Miller - (for Chester Co.) capts., Job Ruston, Joseph Wilson, Henry Glasford, William Boyd; lieuts., Joseph Smith, James Cochran, Robert Allison, John Culbertson; ensigns, James Dysart, Joseph Park, John Emmit, John Donall - (for Newcastle Co.) capt., William Patterson; lieut. John Reid; ensign, Thomas Montgomery (22 Mar.)

The privateer that took Capt. Mesnard of Phila. has been captured (22 Mar.)

Adv. of Thomas Meule, joiner, in Front St. (22 Mar.)

1748

Horse of Nathan Yarnall of Edgmont Twp., Chester Co., has been stolen from plantation of Jacob Caulk near Sassafras River, Md. (22 Mar.)

Horse is taken up by Edward Jones, ranger, at Vineyard plantation in Northern Liberties (22 Mar.)

Thomas Robinson of Naaman's Creek seeks a good miller (22 Mar.)

Captains and subalterns of Phila. Co. county companies are to meet at Reuben Bonner's in West-Chester Twp. (22 Mar.)

Negro named Dick or Harry, age c. 40, runaway from Valentine Dushan, Jr., of Phila. (22 Mar.)

Adv. of Simon Siron, shopkeeper, at the Sign of the Amsterdam Arms in Second St. (22 Mar.)

Plantation and malt-house in Christine Hundred for sale; apply to Joseph Nichols on premises (22 Mar.)

Adv. of Isaac Griffiths in Water St. (22 Mar.)

House in Trenton for sale; enquire of Thomas Marriott, sadler, in Bristol (22 Mar.)

Plantation in Cheltenham Twp. near mill late Richard Martin's, to be sold by Joseph Paul (22 Mar.)

House adjoining land of Israel Pemberton in Germantown for sale by John White (22 Mar.)

Mary Ball will sell plantation where she lives in Northern Liberties (22 Mar.)

Plantation in Penn's Neck, formerly belonging to William Van Culin, to be sold by Samuel Shiters, John Parrock and John Van Culin (22 Mar.)

Patrick Hopkins, Irish servant, age c. 30, who was formerly servant of Andrew and Richard Bandy, has run away from Andrew M'Clement of Kent Co. on Delaware (22 Mar.)

Houses and land in Germantown to be sold; apply to John Frederick Ax (22 Mar.)

Land on Chester road and house in Darby for sale; enquire of Thomas Preston on premises (22 Mar.)

Privateer brigantine Catherine and Edy, lately commanded by Capt. Abline, has arrived in New York (29 Mar.)

Capt. Smyter from London has arrived at Phila. (29 Mar.)

Officers chosen by the Associators; (for Bucks Co.) capts., William Craig, George Hughes, William Ramsay; lieuts., George Gray, Jacob Bogart, Hugh Miller; ensigns, Thomas Armstrong, Bernard VanHorne, James Adams - (for Chester Co.) capts., Andrew M'Dowell, William Reed, William Porter, John Millar; lieuts., John Frew, Thomas Hope, Robert Macky, George Bentley; ensigns, John Miller, Thomas Clarke, John Smith, Thomas Brown; col. Andrew M'Dowell; lieut-col., John Frew; major, John Miller - (for Newcastle Co.) capts., William Danford, David Wetherspoon, James M'Mechen; lieuts., Henry Coleberry, Alexander Armstrong, Abel Armstrong; ensigns, Peter Jacquet, Anthony Golden, Thomas Ogle (29 Mar.)

1748

Plantation in Passyunk Twp. to be let; apply to Andrew Rambo on premises (29 Mar.)

Andrew Elliot in Front St., next door to Nathaniel Allen's, sells goods imported in ship *Burlington*, Capt. Charles Smyter (29 Mar.)

Adv. of Charles Willing in Third St. (29 Mar.)

James Sacket, at house of Mr. Callender in Water St., sells goods imported in snow *Charlotte*, William Vesey master (29 Mar.)

Eight lots in Northern Liberties near Germantown for sale; apply to Thomas Yorke (29 Mar.)

Samuel Neave in Front St. has imported goods for sale (29 Mar.)

Ann Fortey, servant, has run away, supposedly with blacksmith named Samuel Collear; reward for her capture will be paid by her master, John Fortey, in Baltimore Co. or by Capt. Robert North (29 Mar.)

Plantation in Lower Dublin Twp. for sale; apply to Thomas Crispin on premises (29 Mar.)

House near that of Anthony Hinkels in German Twp. for sale; apply to John Rudolph, living near John Shepherd on Chestnut Hill (29 Mar.)

Plantation in Abington, adjoining forge of Thomas Fletcher, Esq., for sale; apply to Joshua Thomas (29 Mar.)

Adv. of merchant Abraham Claypoole, opposite Post-Office in Market St. (29 Mar.)

Plantation in Northampton Twp., Burlington Co., for sale; enquire of Revell Eaton (29 Mar.)

D. Hall at the Post-Office has for sale imported books (5 Apr.)

Ann Scoten in Third St. makes stockings and mittens (5 Apr.)

Accounts with estate of Edward Nicholas, late of Limerick, dec'd, to be settled with George Evans of Limerick; William Currie is exec. (5 Apr.)

Land in borough of Bristol for sale; apply to Caleb Emerson in Phila. or Alexander Graydon in Bristol (5 Apr.)

Neate and Smith, next door to Townshend White's in Front St. sell imported goods; they intend for England (5 Apr.)

Nathaniel Chew, at head of Timber Creek, Gloucester Co., publishes his wife Anne (5 Apr.)

Michael Cario, jeweller, has removed to house in Chestnut St. where Mr. Gillelyn lately dwelt (5 Apr.)

James Burd, opposite John Bringhurst's in Front St., sells European goods (5 Apr.)

Foresail was carried off from sloop *Philadelphia*, John Stinson master, at Mr. Allen's wharf; reward offered by Stinson or John Smith (5 Apr.)

Accounts with estate of Thomas Redmon, bricklayer, late of Phila., to be settled with Penelope Redmon (5 Apr.)

1748   11

Horse stolen from Conrad Rafeur of Charles Town, Md. (5 Apr.)

Hugh Gallaspy, Irish servant, runaway from Robert Grace at Coventry Forge (5 Apr.)

Mare gone from Samuel Cochran's plantation in Tinicom Twp., Bucks co. (5 Apr.)

Robert Cooke, English servant, age c. 30, runaway from Charles Ridgely near Potapsco Ferry (5 Apr.)

Plantation in Manner-head Twp., Phila. Co., for sale by Peter Lycan (5 Apr.)

Drums made and sold by John Woolsey at Queens-Town, near Trenton, and by John Clifton at the Sign of the George in Phila. (5 Apr.)

Plantation on Delaware near Newcastle, part of estate of George Yeates, late of Newcastle Co., Gent., dec'd, for sale by order of Orphan's Court, Richard M'William, deputy clerk (5 Apr.)

Janet Condon, Irish servant, age c. 28, runaway from John Dobbin of Phila., blacksmith (5 Apr.)

Adv. of John Harrison over the Draw-bridge in Phila. (5 Apr.)

Officers chosen by Associators: (for Bucks Co.) capt. Robert Jamison; lieut. John Board; ensign, Samuel Martin - (for Chester Co.) capt. William Clinton; lieut. Morris Thomas; ensign, William Karr - (for Newcastle Co.) capt. William Armstrong, Evan Rice, John Allmond; lieuts. William Patterson, James Walker, Lulof Peterson; ensign, William M'Crea, Charles Bryan, Sr., Luke Mounce; col. William Armstrong; lieut.col., William Patterson; major, William M'Crea (16 Apr.)

Accounts with John Howell, late of Phila., tanner, to be settled with John Mifflin, Reese Meredith and John Stamper (16 Apr.)

Adv. of Samuel M'Call, Sr., in Water St. (16 Apr.)

Horses taken in at Peter Robeson's in Market St. will be pastured by John Bleakley (16 Apr.)

Saddle with name Daniel Pistorus on paper on the tree of the saddle was stolen from horse at door of Nathaniel Goodman on Society Hill, reward for recovery of saddle offered by James Dogharty at Widow Leech's in Cheltenham Twp. (16 Apr.)

Tickets for Burlington Lottery disposed of by managers, John Allen, Esq., Stephen Williams, Revel Elton, Esq., and Nathaniel Thomas, or by Paul Miller, Esq., at Brunswick, Elijah Bond at Trenton, Joseph Borden, Jr., at Bordentown, Samuel Rogers at Allentown and Dr. John Budd at New York (16 Apr.)

Thomas Robson, Joseph Smith, John Jefferis, Henry Jones and James Boyle, seamen, runaways from ship *Rachel*, of London, Isham Randolph, commander (16 Apr.)

Cesar, Negro, runaway from Jonathan Ingham of Solebury, Bucks Co. (16 Apr.)

Adv. of Christopher Marshal in Chestnut St. (16 Apr.)

Thomas Raw (Englishman, age c. 27), George Salmon (Scotchman, age c. 23), and John Garner (Scotchman, age c. 21), servants

1748

belonging to Accokeek Furnace in Stafford Co., Va., runaways from Aquia Creek, Potomac; reward offered by Nathan Chapman (16 Apr.)

Mary Muckleroy, Irish servant, runaway from Samuel Lippincott of Northampton, Burlington Co. (16 Apr.)

House in Borough of Wilmington to be sold by Sarah Downing in said borough (16 Apr.)

Pedlars and retailers of liquor who keep booths at fair at Fredericktown, Md., shall pay 5 shillings to Francis Lee (16 Apr.)

Accounts with estate of Thomas Mayburry, dec'd, are to be settled with Sophia Mayburry, admin. (16 Apr.)

The brigantine <u>Revenge</u>, Capt. Troup, of New York, has taken a French snow; the ship <u>Widow</u>, Capt. White, of Phila., has been taken (21 Apr.)

Tue. last Alexander Urie shot and killed Arthur M'Ginness (21 Apr.)

John Newland, Irish servant, age c. 26, runaway from John Hance, living in Dragon's Neck, Newcastle Co. (21 Apr.)

House in Germantown for sale; apply to Dominicus Gassner in Germantown (21 Apr.)

Amos and Robert Strettell purpose to leave Pa. (21 Apr.)

Grace M'Swain, Irish servant, age c. 25, runaway from Manaseth Logue of Bohemia Manor (21 Apr.)

James Bigley, Irish servant, age c. 18 runaway from Jonathan Wilks of Radnor (21 Apr.)

William Gray, baker, in Anthony Norris's Alley, will sell tenement where he now lives (21 Apr.)

Nathaniel Allen, Jr., in Front St. has Carolina reed for sale (21 Apr.)

Katherine has eloped from her husband, Cornelius Lary, of Waterford Twp., Gloucester Co. (21 Apr.)

Cornelius Sullivan, Irish servant, age c. 20 runaway from John Roberts of Chester Twp., Burlington Co. (21 Apr.)

William Moode offers reward for recovery of mare strayed or stolen from his pasture near Phila. (21 Apr.)

Accounts with estate of William Darvil, late of Phila., baker, dec'd, are to be settled with John Lassell or Evan Morgan, Jr., execs. (21 Apr.)

Adv. of James Sacket in Market St. where Mr. Dowers formerly kept store (21 Apr.)

Plantation of Philip Doyle, of Gloucester Co., dec'd, joining to John Breech's grist-mill, for sale; apply to Robert and Isaac Stephens, execs. (21 Apr.)

House and fulling mill in Radnor to be let; apply to Evan Baird or Margaret or Thomas Thomas (21 Apr.)

1748

Accounts with estate of Daniel Wills, late of Burlington Co., merchant, dec'd, to be settled with Margaret Wills, exec. (21 Apr.)

Adv. of William Logan in Second St. (21 Apr.)

Goods of David Davis, dec'd, to be sold at his house in Sassafras St. by Lydia Davis and James Murgatroyd, admins. (21 Apr.)

Capt. Holland from Madeira has arrived at Annapolis (28 Apr.)

The <u>Massachusetts</u> frigate, Capt. Bennet, has arrived at Boston from Annapolis-Royal (28 Apr.)

Capt. Austil from Boston has been taken and carried into Guadaloupe (28 Apr.)

The snow <u>Dragon</u>, prize taken by privateer <u>Le Trembleur</u>, of Phila., Capt. Bowne, arrived Sat. at Phila. (28 Apr.)

Officers chosen by the Associators: (for Bucks Co.) capts., Anthony Wright, James Maclaughlin; lieuts, Lewis Rue, James Devies; ensigns, Richard Vanhorne, John Hall - (for Lancaster Co.) Samuel Anderson, Jedediah Alexander, James Galbraith, John Smith, Adam Reed, John M'Known, John Galbraith, David M'Clure, James Armstrong, Thomas M'Kee, James Graham, Robert Baker, James Patterson, Thomas Harris; lieuts. John Woodside, Hugh Whiteford, James Sample, William Cunningham, John Crawford, James Anderson, William Allison, Thomas Foster, Alexander Armstrong, Robert Smith, John Purriers, William Mitchell, James Smith; ensigns, John Bark(l)ey, James Smith, John Harris, Joseph Candor, John Young, James Finney, Nathaniel Little, Andrew Rog(g)es, John Dougherty, William Baskell, William M'Mullen, Henry Rennicks, Thomas Mitchell, John Wilson; col. Thomas Cookson; lieut.-col. James Galbraith; major, Robert Baker - (for Newcastle Co.) capts., Rev. Timothy Griffith, Archibald Armstrong; lieuts. William Faris, Thomas M'Cullough; ensigns, David Rowland, Robert Pierce - col. John Gooding, Sr.; lieut.-col., Thomas James; major, Jacob Vanbebber - (for Kent Co.) capt., John Vining; lieut., Thomas Parke; ensign, Dr. Richard Wells (28 Apr.)

Account with estate of Joseph Duffield, late of Phila., dec'd, to be settled with Ebenezer Kennersley and Samuel Swift, exec., who will sell a lot adjoining a lot of Richard Peters (28 Apr.)

Abraham Usher sells Irish linens at Thomas Charlton's in Chestnut St. (28 Apr.)

Adv. of Mordecai Yarnall at Sign of the Band-Saw in Market St. (28 Apr.)

Joshua Mullock sells European and India goods at house of James Stuard, where Capt. Mason kept store, in Water St. (28 Apr.)

Hugh Braslam, Irishman, blacksmith, age c. 25, runaway from his bail, Peter Widdifield, at Poole's Bridge, Phila. (28 Apr.)

Plantation in Dublin Twp., for sale by John Atkins, Sr., and John Atkins, Jr. (28 Apr.)

Time of servant, a stone mason, for sale; enquire of Isaac Roberts in Third St. (28 Apr.)

Samuel M'Call, Sr., in Water St, sells sugar (28 Apr.)

1748

Adv. of Charles and Alexander Stedman in Water St., under Mr. Sobert's (28 Apr.)

Adv. of Thomas Lightfoot in Water St. (28 Apr.)

James Casey, convict servant, age c. 23, runaway from Christopher Divers of Gunpowder Neck, Baltimore Co., Md. (28 Apr.)

Swain Peterson, (Swedish carpenter), George Powell, William Barnet, Samuel Cox and Thomas Boswell, runaways from ship Thistle, Hugh Coulter master; these sailors carried off a boat of Capt. Samuel White; if they are brought to David M'Cullough at Joppa or to Coulter on his ship in Bush River, Md., reward will be paid (28 Apr.)

Serjeant Hawke met a party of French and Indians within 15 miles of Montreal (5 May)

Snow Nancy, Capt. Young, and Capt. Aitkins from Boston have been taken (5 May)

Officers chosen by Associators; (for Kent Co.) capts. John Hunn, Robert Blackshire; lieuts. William Hirons, John Rees; ensigns, Mark Hirons, William Rees (5 May)

Charles Smyter offers reward for recovery of long-boat (5 May)

James Bird has removed his store to that lately possessed by George Mifflin, opposite to William Coleman's store on Carpenter's Wharf (5 May)

Accounts with Conyngham and Gardner, of Phila., merchants, to be settled promptly (5 May)

Benjamin and Samuel Shoemaker in Phila. seek information about Thomas Bourne, dec'd, who came from England to Pa. about 1670 (5 May)

Charles Willing in Third St. intends for England (5 May)

Adv. of Isaac Jones at store in Arch St. (5 May)

Joseph Sleigh, on Society Hill, next door to John Bealey's, teaches the three R's (5 May)

Mary, wife of Samuel Dyer, of Plumstead Twp., Bucks Co., has eloped from her husband (5 May)

Plantation in Blockley Twp. for sale; apply to Richard Pearne on premises (5 May)

Pnilip Whinemore, of Phila., drayman, offers reward for recovery of strayed cow (5 May)

Horse taken up by John Martin, of Warwick, Bucks Co. (5 May)

Horse has strayed from Morris Eschullion of Lower Merion; reward if returned to owner or to Robert Jones of Merion (5 May)

Ironmongery for sale by William Jevon, next door to John Mifflin's in Market St. (5 May)

Horse has been stolen, supposedly by Benjamin Gould, from William Clayton's pasture in Upper Chichester; reward offered by Thomas Clayton (5 May)

Thomas Francis, next door to Capt. John Philips in Water St., sells English and Scotch goods (5 May)

Robert M'Clew offers reward for horse strayed or stolen from yard of Nicholas Zisland in Moravian Alley (5 May)

Richard Jolly, Richard Kent and Charles Widmore, sailors, runaways from ship *St. George*, James Dobbins master, in Patapsco River; they took along a young Welsh convict servant, William Williams, (*alias* Broughton) and stole long-boat of Capt. Hamilton; reward will be paid by Alexander Lawson at Nottingham iron-works, Robert Swan at Annapolis, David Ross at Bladenburgh or John Nelson in Phila. (5 May)

Adv. of Abraham Claypoole in Market St. (5 May)

Negro named Cato, age c. 20, runaway from Philip Syng of Phila., silversmith (5 May)

Capt. Samuel Lowder of Boston, killed in engagement with enemy ships (12 May)

French snow has been taken by Rhode Island privateer, Capt. Carr (12 May)

Capt. Arnold in Rhode Island privateer sank enemy privateer (12 May)

Letter from on board privateer *Revenge*, of NY. Capt. Alexander Troup, at St. Christophers (12 May)

French Indians fire on people assisting Johannes Scherp in Manor of Livingston; a French Indian wounds son of Johannes Kool between Claverack and Kinderhook; wife of John Scott carried off by the enemy (12 May)

Snow *Molly and Sally*, Capt. Perry has arrived at Phila. from Barbados; in her passage she took the ship *Aurora*, Capt. Macarty (12 May)

Mrs. Mary Norris, relict of Isaac Norris, Esq., late of Fairhill, a daughter of Thomas Lloyd, formerly Gov. of Pa., died 1 May in her 75th year (12 May)

Jonathan Mifflin has removed to house in Market St. (12 May)

Adv. of Peter Bard and Henry Elves, of Phila. (12 May)

List of books for sale by D. Hall at the Post Office (12 May)

Cloth for sale by Edward Dowers in Water St. (12 May)

Windmill on island fronting Phila. for sale; apply to George Adams at Christine Bridge or John Harding on Society Hill; accounts with estate of John Harding, dec'd, to be settled with George Adams and John Harding, admins. (12 May)

D. Dulany of Annapolis will sell tract of land near Conicochieg; apply to Peter Reuch, Dutchman, near the place, or George Poce on the place (12 May)

Two houses for sale; enquire of Dinah Bard in Burlington (12 May)

William Whitebread of Phila. offers reward for recovery of mare strayed from plantation of William Currie in Plymouth (12 May)

1748

Adv. of Warren and Stalker, whose store is opposite the Tun Tavern in Water St. (12 May)

Michael Brown, silk-dyer from London, in Front St. in middle of alley from Edward Warner's to Joseph Oldman's; Brown claims passage and water course through property of William Maugridge, fronting Race St. (12 May)

Mare strayed from Jervis Burgess at Norris's mill in Norriton; mare was seen at William Miller's in Warwick Twp., Bucks Co.; reward will be paid by owner or Thomas Burgess in Phila. (12 May)

John Ridgeway, English servant, age c. 35, runaway from Nathaniel Grubb in Willistown, Chester Co. (12 May)

Margaret Kane, Irish servant, runaway from Joseph Reed of Trenton (12 May)

Land adjoining borough of Bristol for sale; apply to Caleb Emerson in Phila. or Alexander Graydon in Bristol (12 May)

Capt. Davis in flag of truce arrived in Phila. from Havana (19 May)

The *Phoenix*, Capt. Pyramus Green, was taken by a French privateer; the prize crew, when the ship was at anchor in Hoarkill Road, boarded the brigantine *Tinker*, Capt. M'Carter, from Providence; Green escaped with his ship and arrived at Phila. (19 May)

Officers chosen by Associators: (for Phila. Co.) capt., John Hall; lieut., Joshua Thomas; ensign, Philip Thomas; col. Edward Jones; lieut.-col., Thomas Yorke; major, Samuel Shaw - (for Bucks Co.) capt., John Wilson; lieut., Thomas Blair; ensign, George Overpack - (for Kent Co.) capt., George Martin; lieut., Jacob Allee; ensign, John Vanwinkle (19 May)

Parchment made by Joseph Wood in Kensington is sold by David Hall at the Post Office (19 May)

Engraving is done by Lawrence Herbert from London at Philip Syng's, goldsmith, in Front St. (19 May)

Linens for sale by Abraham Usher at Thomas Charlton's in Chestnut St. (19 May)

John Belden, of Norwalk, Conn., offers reward for recovery of stolen horse (19 May)

Time of servant lad for sale by Thomas Murray on Society Hill at house where Joseph Scull formerly lived (19 May)

Horse for sale by Edward Evans in Sassafrass St. (19 May)

Dougal Cameron and Andrew Smith, rebel servants, runaways from Robert Horner at Newport, Charles Co. (19 May)

Deborah, wife of John Shippey, of Middlesex Co., East N.J., has eloped from her husband (19 May)

Thomas Barton, who formerly lived on Andrew Rambo's plantation, has moved to Nathan Gibson's in Kingsess (19 May)

Jacob Sharts of Strasburgh Twp., Lancaster Co., has taken up a horse (19 May)

Two cows have strayed from Jacob Hagie, of Wissahykon in Germantown Twp. (19 May)

Scipio, Negro, age c. 25 or 30, runaway from Marcus Kuhl, of Phila., baker (19 May) and James, Negro, age c. 20, also runaway from said Kuhl (9 June)

1748

Colt strayed from plantation of Widow Rebecca Leech in Cheltenham (19 May)

The **Triumph**, Hilton master, from New York arrived in London and the **Monmouth**, Mann master, from New York arrived at Haverford west (26 May)

Privateer **Trembleur**, of Phila., Capt. Bowne, has taken six prizes; Capt. Pocock has taken a ship (26 May)

Gov. James Hamilton of Pa. is about to embark for his government (26 May)

Capt. William Greenway, of Phila., taken by a privateer, has been retaken (26 May)

Col. Taylor's regt. of Associators in Phila. was reviewed on Tue. (26 May)

Capt. Burk of brigantine **Riche**, was taken; George Porteous, one of the owners of the **Three Brothers**, retook the vessel (26 May)

Companies of Col. Edward Jones, Lt.-Col. Yorke, Major Shaw, Capt. Jacob Hall and Capt. John Hall are to be reviewed at Germantown; companies of Capt. Pawlin, Capt. Dehaven, Capt. Robins and Capt. Hughes will be reviewed at Norris's mill, Norrington Twp. (26 May)

Notice of John Smith, Clerk of Council of Proprietors of East N.J. (26 May)

House of late Joseph Bowman in lane adjoining property of Benjamin Morgan in Germantown for sale; accounts with Bowman's estate to be settled with Margaret Bowman, Christopher Meng and Derrick Keyser, execs. (26 May)

Nathan Levy, of Levy and Franks in Phila., intends for England (26 May)

Arthur Boradill in Chester Twp., Burlington Co., has taken up a stray horse (26 May)

Arthur Haines, apprentice lad of Jonathan Ellis of Waterford Twp., Gloucester Co., runaway, supposedly to his brother Hugh Haines at Opekon (26 May)

William Greenway, in Norris's Alley, next door to Mr. Schleydorn's, sugar-baker, has Negro for sale (26 May)

Negro named Dick (**alias** Harry), age c. 40, runaway from Valentine Dushane, living near St. George's, Newcastle Co. (26 May)

Share in forge to be sold at Bordentown, taken in execution at suit of admin. of Mary Yard, dec'd, and at suit of Andrew Read against admin. of David Davis, dec'd; remainder may be bought from William Yard (26 May)

Reward for lost horse will be paid by John Becktel in Germantown or William Nixon in Sassafrass St. in Phila. (26 May)

John Knowles of Phila. offers reward for recovery of strayed horse (26 May)

Friends of Peter Painter, age c. 18, born in Germany, who came to America about 4 years ago and was bought by Peter Knot, seek news of him; information may be given to Cornelius Tanner in Lancaster Co.; letter for Tanner may be left with Mrs. Mary Lawler, tavern-keeper at Newtown (26 May)

Adv. of Francis Bowes in Water St. (26 May)

Prize ship **Aurora** for sale at Nixon and Edgar's wharf (26 May)

Jacob Huber of Conestogo seeks forgemen (26 May)

1748

Stray horse at plantation of John Lloyd in Horsham Twp. (26 May)

Mills lately belonging to John Shaw, dec'd, in Freehold, Monmouth Co., for sale; accounts with estate of said Shaw to be settled with William Hankinson, Robert Cumming and John Henderson (26 May)

George Proctor swam ashore at Elsingborough, Salem Co., from a Spanish privateer (2 June)

Brigantine King George, Capt. Stuart, arrived 26 May at New York from Belfast (2 June)

William Crippen, of the sloop Success, and Andrew Haskell, of the sloop Burgess, both from Boston were turned adrift in a small boat by a Spanish privateer (2 June)

Sloop Joseph and Mary, of Phila., Capt. Ambler, at Reedy Island was taken by the privateer St. Michael, Capt. Vincent de Lopez (2 June)

Capt. White, of the Mary, of Phila., was taken by Spanish Privateer (2 June)

Schooner Martha, Capt. Blake, Capt. Edwards in a sloop, Capt. Thompson and Capt. Roberts were taken by the enemy (2 June)

Capt. Outerbridge has arrived at New York from Turks Island (2 June)

Parts of the privateer Trembleur will be sold at Roberts's coffee-house by William Allen and Joseph Turner, execs. of Andrew Hamilton, dec'd (2 June)

Accounts with estate of John Jones, tavern-keeper, late of Third St., Phila., dec'd, to be settled with John, Thomas and Sara Jones, execs. (2 June)

Michael Israel, on Society Hill, offers reward for recovery of horse stolen from the Indian King in Market St. (2 June)

Time of a servant lad for sale by Thomas Robinson in Spruce St. (2 June)

William Parker, intending to leave Phila., has property for sale, including kiln and mill now in occupation of Jonathan Durell (2 June)

Cornelius Sullivan, Irish servant, age c. 20, runaway from John Roberts of Chester Twp., Burlington Co. (2 June); runaway 14 June from Joseph Biddle of Burlington (23 June)

Mare has strayed from Jacob Rieger at Pineford in Derry Town (2 June)

A packet of rings, buckles and clasps dropped by Anne Church in Lewes; reward offered by Daniel Church in Lewes (2 June)

Accounts with estate of John Bood, dec'd, to be settled with Gertrude Bood and Robert Greenway, execs. (2 June)

Reward offered for recovery of cows strayed from Peter Gardner's plantation in Blockley Twp. (2 June)

Plantation for sale at Rackoon Creek, Gloucester Co.; apply to Gabriel Friend on premises or Evan Morgan in Water St., Phila. (2 June)

Capt. Keith has arrived at Boston from Jamaica (9 June)

Account of cruize of Capt. Burgess (9 June)

Capts. Dreson, Scurlock and Palmer have arrived at Phila. (9 June)

1748

Sermons by David Evans, minister formerly at Tredyffryn and now of Piles Grove, are for sale (9 June)

Treatise by William Currie for sale (9 June)

John Huston offers reward for capture of the following deserters from H.M.'s service: Patrick Burk, born in Ireland, age 27, lately servant to William Moore, Esq., in Chester Co.; George Savage, born in England, tailor, age c. 25, who formerly worked in Burdentown; Thomas Murray, born in Ireland, weaver, age c. 35; Edward Smith, born in Ireland, age c. 27; Richard Dowdle, born in Ireland, age 25; William Goodman, born in Ireland, age c. 30; William Scanlin, born in Ireland, age c. 35; Patrick Karney, born in Ireland, age c. 28, who lived near Salem; Manchester Holaway, born in Pa., blacksmith (9 June)

Accounts with estate of John Harrison, late of Manor of Moreland, dec'd, to be settled with Joshua Potts and Cornelius Corsan, admins. (9 June)

James Moore, Irish servant, age c. 22, runaway from Thomas Harris of Reden's-town, Hunterdon Co. (9 June)

Horses strayed from pasture of Israel Pemberton in Northern Liberties (9 June)

Horse strayed from Charles Jenkins, living at Ashetons Ferry, Blockley Twp. (9 June)

Privateer *Trembleur*, Abraham Matthews commander, is fitting out for a cruize (9 June)

Jane, wife of Peter Henry Dorsius, of Phila. Co., daughter of Derrick Hogeland of Bucks Co., has eloped from her husband (9 June)

Richard Richison, Chief Ranger of Chester Co., lists strays (9 June)

Horse strayed or stolen from James David, of Charlestown, Chester Co. (9 June)

Henry Harry, of New Britain, Bucks Co., has taken up a horse (9 June)

James Greenwood, English servant, runaway from James Vahan of Upper Freehold, Monmouth Co., N.J. (9 June)

Plantation in New London Twp., Chester Co., for sale; one road from it leads to mill of Job Ruston, Esq.; apply to John Frew (9 June)

David Hughes (*alias* Luellin), convict servant, blacksmith, age c. 40, who formerly belonged to Vincent Askin, late of Charles Co., dec'd, runaway from Peter Wagener, of Prince William Co., Va.; runaway has pass signed by Capt. Robert Vaulx, justice of Westmoreland (9 June)

Irish convict servants, James Daley, weaver, age c. 40, and Owen M'Vey, age c. 25, laborer, runaways from Hugh Coupland, living on Gunpowder River, Baltimore Co. (9 June)

Report that Capts. Stephens, Moor and Williams have been taken by a Spanish privateer (16 June)

Shallop from Norfolk, with Capt. Bogle's second mate on board, has been taken by a privateer (16 June)

Capt. John Seager in the sloop *Bohemia* has arrived at Annapolis (16 June)

Prize taken by the *Phoenix*, Capt. Martin Bicker, has arrived at New York (16 June)

1748

Horse strayed from Joseph Oldman of Phila.; reward offered by Oldman will be paid by him or David Faris of Wilmington (16 June)

Officers chosen by the Associators: (for Phila. Co.) capt., Jacob Leech; lieut., John Barge; ensign, Jacob Naglee - (for Bucks Co.) capt., Bernard Vanhorn; lieut., Robert Cummings; ensign, Ralph Dean - (for Chester Co.) capt., Thomas Hubbert, Jr.; lieut., John Rees; ensign, Ralph Dean - (for Lancaster Co.) capts., Andrew Gregge and James Snodgrass; lieuts., William Crawford and John Alexander; ensigns, Samuel Simpson and John Snodgrass; col., James Gillespy; lt.-col.Samuel Anderson; major, James Whitehill - (for Kent Co.) capts., John Catton and James Edwards; lieuts., Robert Catlin and James Lewis; ensigns, Joseph Hodson and James James (16 June)

Benjamin Britton, baker, in Chestnut St., will sell time of a servant lad (16 June)

Cows strayed from plantation of Peter Gardner in Blockley Twp. (16 June)

Tom, Mulatto, age c. 21, runaway from Peter Kemble of N. Brunswick, probably with Samuel Ryalls, servant to William Plain (16 June)

For freight or passage to Bristol on brigantine Hope, Thomas Lloyd master, apply to master or Charles Willing (16 June)

Accounts with estate of Barefoot Brunson, dec'd, late High Sheriff of Sommerset Co., to be settled with Mrs. Mary Brunson or Thomas Lawrence, of Phila., merchant, execs. (16 June)

James Cavanach, convict Irish servant, runaway from William Bennet, living in Baltimore Co. on Deer Creek (16 June)

Horse taken up at plantation of John Jones (16 June)

David Dundas, Scotch servant, age c. 35, runaway from Jonathan Hough, of Springfield Twp., Burlington Co. (16 June)

Patrick Mitchell, Irish servant, age c. 24 or 25, runaway from Andrew Ball, living in Manington Twp., Salem Co. (16 June)

Harry Wells (alias Bond's Harry), Negro, age c. 35, runaway from John Ridgely, living near Baltimore (16 June)

Province ship Massachusetts, Capt. Bennet, is about to sail in quest of enemy privateers (23 June)

Capt. Frankland in H.M.S. Dragon has taken 5 prizes, Capt. Tyrrel 2, Capt. Emey 2, Capt. Strawbridge 1 (23 June)

Capt. Wilson, bound from Belfast to Barbados, was taken (23 June)

Sloop Industry, Capt. Thomas Jenkins, from Boston, was plundered by Don Joseph Hannoteau (23 June)

Capt. William Clymer, Jr., from Charles-Town, S.C., went ashore with his men when chased by a privateer (23 June)

Capt. Frith from Antigua arrived at Phila. (23 June)

Companies that marched to defend Newcastle were Col. Armstrong's, Lt.-Col. Patterson's, Major M'Crea's, Capt. Grey's, Capt. M'Mechan's, Capt. Bush's, Capt. Crow's, Capt. Danford's, Capt. Reese's, Capt. Porter's, Capt. Clinton's (23 June)

Col. Armstrong reviewed his regiment at Newcastle; Col. Gooding's will be reviewed there after the harvest (23 June)

Yesterday H.M.S. Otter, Capt. Ballet, fell down on a cruize (23 June)

1748

Plantation on Delaware for sale; apply to Nathaniel Johnson at the Widow Howell's in Market St., Phila., or Joseph Sims (23 June)

Barbara, wife of Jacob Snider, of Vincent Twp., Chester Co., has eloped from her husband (23 June)

Reward offered for return of horse to Joseph Cockburn at the Three Tuns in Chestnut St. (23 June)

James Reynolds and Archibald Weathers, deserters from the regt. of Col. Edward Trelawney; reward if they are brought to Lt. Ninian Wisehart at Roberts's Coffee-house, Phila. (23 June)

Adv. of Henry Wright, whipmaker from London, last from Annapolis, Md., now in Chestnut St. (23 June)

John, Spanish Negro, age c. 30, runaway from John Potts, of Colebrookdale, Phila. Co., Esq.; reward will be paid by Potts or Thomas Yorke (23 June)

James Scott has removed his store from Walnut St. to Water St. to store lately possessed by Capt. Martin (23 June)

Account of clash at sea between Capt. Haddon and Capt. Green, both from Providence (30 June)

Ship Antilope, Capt. Amory, has arrived at New York with three prizes (30 June)

Capt. Kip, arrived at New York from Georgia, reports that a Spanish privateer was taken by the Heron, Capt. Seamour, of Georgia (30 June)

The following have been taken and carried into Martinico: Capts. Shevers and Combes from Boston; Capt. Tyrant from New London; Capt. Turner from R.I.; Capt. Frasey from N.Y.; Capt. Martin from Barbados; Capt. Farler from Barbados; Capt. Jolly from England; Capt. Allen from Belfast; Capt. Bruce from Gibraltar (30 June)

Capt. Gass, of Phila., has come in from Newry, with news of ship Betty, of Glasgow, Capt. Aiking (30 June)

Privateer Trembleur, Capt. Matthews, is fallen down to proceed on a cruize (30 June)

Time of Irish servant girl for sale; enquire of John Stinson of Walnut St. (30 June)

Accounts with partnership of Neat and Smith to be settled, as they intend for England (30 June)

Adv. of John Burey of Phila., tailor (30 June)

Stills, still-house of Benjamin Morgan, dec'd, to be sold by Evan Morgan, John Ross and Katharine Morgan; also for sale woodland adjoining ground of Thomas Carvil and house on the bank in Front St. wherein Capt. Budden dwells (30 June)

Carberry Cloath, Irish servant, age c. 17, runaway from Alexander Watson of Phila. (30 June)

House in Trenton for sale by Enoch Anderson in Trenton or Samuel Hazard, merchant, in Phila. (30 June)

Ralph Sawer offers reward for recovery of cattle strayed from plantation of Anthony Nice near the Rising Sun on Germantown Road (30 June)

Burlington Lottery is managed by Peter Kemble, James Lyne, John Berrian and John Broughton (30 June)

1748

Thomas Bentley, servant, country born, runaway from James Smith of Donnegal, Lancaster Co. (30 June)

Conrad Weiser, Ranger of the N.E. corner of Lancaster Co., lists strays (30 June)

Report from Louisbourg that Capts. Glover and Edingwood have been taken and Lt. Glazier carried off by the enemy (7 July)

Vincent de Lopez in the privateer St. Michael has taken a schooner, Capt. John Ingram, the snow Pearl, Robert Jeffries master, and the ship Margaret, William M'Cunn master (7 July)

The ship Rose, Peter Huston master, from London, the sloop Sarah, Capt. Goodridge of Boston, the ship Mercury Galley, Capt. Hargrave of London, and the snow Speedwell, Capt. Harris from Whitehaven, have been taken by the enemy (7 July)

Capt. Mesnard was to leave Gravesend for Phila. on 27 April (7 July)

Joseph Sims is removed to house near Samuel Powell's wharf (7 July)

James Pemberton in Phila. offers reward for recovery of horse strayed or stolen from pasture at Horsham (7 July)

Real estate for sale by Thomas Yorke (7 July)

Laughlin Tracey, Irish servant, age 21, runaway from Robert Boyle of Fallowfield Twp., Chester Co. (7 July)

Accounts with estate of Edward Rockhill, late of Aimwell, dec'd, to be settled with Ann Rockhill at late dwelling of the dec'd or William or Parnell Clayton of Trenton, execs. (7 July)

Imported goods for sale by Joshua Mulock in house of James Steward, where Capt. Mason kept store in Water St. (7 July)

Accounts with Francis Johnson, of Phila., butcher, are to be settled, as he intends to leave the province (7 July)

Apollo, Negro, age c. 36, block-maker, runaway from Samuel Austin of Phila. (7 July)

Katherine Anderson, Irish servant, age c. 23, runaway from Martin Bickham of Greenwich Twp., Gloucester Co. (7 July)

House late of Peter Baynton, Esq., in Burlington, lately possessed by the Widow Hunlocke, to be sold or let; enquire of Mrs. Mary Baynton in Burlington or John Baynton, of Phila., exec. (7 July)

Hugh Montgomery, servant, age c. 20, runaway from John Kell; reward will be paid by Kell or by Walter Denny (7 July)

Francis Hamilton, apprentice, age c. 19, runaway from Charles Williams, living near Tohikan, Bucks Co. (7 July)

Daniel M'Keddie, Scotch servant, age c. 18, and Swilli, a Negro, age between 30 and 40, runaways from Benjamin Duvall, of Caroline Co., Va. (7 July)

William Boat, Irish servant, age c. 20, shoemaker, runaway from John Baldwin, of Neshaminy Ferry (7 July)

Lots of ground adjoining Evan Morgan's new buildings for sale; for plan of the lots apply to Michael Hellegas (14 July)

Samuel Foyle, miller, and John Smith (alias Knowles), deserters from regt. of Lt.-Gen. Philipps; reward if brought to George Cottnam in Phila. (14 July)

Francis Le Blanc, wig-maker, late from France, and Anthony Noel, doctor, will set up at the Sign of the Bear and Highlandman in Front St. (14 July)

1748

Windmill on the island opposite Phila. for sale by John Harding on Society Hill (14 July)

Tickets in Phila. Lottery for sale by Joseph Turner, Abraham Taylor, Tench Francis, John Inglis, Samuel Hazard, John Sober, William Plumsted, Patrick Baird, Philip Syng, Evan Morgan, Jr., Jacob Duché, Augustine Hicks, Samuel M'Call, Jr., Joseph Sims and Richard Nixon (14 July)

Adv. of Preserve Brown in Water St. (14 July)

Plantation in Whiteland Twp. in the Great Valley, joining the tavern late of James Trigo, dec'd, for sale; apply to Richard Richison on the premises or John Biddle in Market St. (14 July)

On 26 June in encounter with Indians Capt. Hobbs of Mass. had three men killed, Samuel Gunn, Eben. Mitchell and Ely Scott (21 July)

John Fitch of Lunenburgh, his wife and 5 children are supposed to have been carried off by Indians (21 July)

Privateer Dragon, Capt. Waynman, arrived Sat. at New York; the Massachusetts Frigate, Capt. Bennett, of Boston, is at Sandy Hook (21 July)

Notice concerned with the General Loan Office, signed by John Kinsey (21 July)

Cuzzins & Smyter in Phila. offer reward for capture of Henry Foster, a sailor, who ran away from the ship Macclesfield, taking a new Moses (21 July)

Reward for recovery of boat stolen from the sloop Francis, Benjamin Styles commander (21 July)

Books by George Fisher, Rev. Whitefield and Rev. John Lewis for sale (21 July)

Negro woman for sale; enquire of Richard Smith, "minor," or John Pole, merchant, in Phila. (21 July)

John Clifton, at the George Inn, offers reward for two strayed or stolen horses (21 July)

Tom, Mulatto, age 22, runaway from Peter Kemble, of New Brunswick, N.J. (21 July)

Edward Shippen offers for sale real estate, including a lot near George Emlen, Jr's summer-house and garden, a plantation at Tulpehocken where Henry Smith lives, a plantation on west side of Susquehannah River where John Proby lives and another near Shippensburgh where Thomas Eastland lives (21 July)

Joseph Wharton, at lower end of Second St., offers for sale a meadow at Moyamensing; colliers, forge-men, quarry-men may find employment by applying to John Wharton at Rock-forge in Aston Twp., Chester Co., or to Joseph Wharton in Phila. (21 July)

Charles O'Neill, clerk, certifys that Tarver Artis, a prisoner in gaol if Salem Co. for debt, took oath before William Hancock, Esq. (21 July)

Horse stolen from plantation of Benjamin Rounsavall of Hopewell, N.J. (21 July)

Mare is taken up at plantation of Samuel Martin, Warwick Twp., Bucks Co. (21 July)

John Burn, Irish servant, age c. 20, runaway from Henry Mitchell of Bristol Twp. (21 July)

Thomas Jacob revokes adv. that his wife Martha has eloped (21 July)

Dove, Negro, age c. 30, and Kate, Mulatto, age c. 16, runaways from David Lindsay, of Northampton, Bucks Co. (21 July)

Party marching from Col. Hinsdale's fort to Fort Dummer was attacked by Indians (28 July)

On Arrosick Island the Indians on 23 June shot Adam Mack, Henry Bookins and a son of Joseph Whitcom (28 July)

Vessel carried into Hampton, Va., is supposed to be the schooner *Mary*, late commanded by Capt. White (28 July)

Horse has been stolen from Matthew Hazell of Chester- town, Kent Co., Md. (28 July)

Accounts with estate of Vioeall Chubb, dec'd, who kept store on Rees Meredith's wharf, are to be settled with Sarah Chubb and Joseph Saunders, admins. (28 July)

Ned, Negro, age c. 18, and Mona (a Spanish Negro man), age c. 28 or 30, runaways from Sophia Maybury, who lives at Green Lane Forge and is the widow of Thomas Maybury; reward for the capture of the runaways will be paid by Sophia Maybury or by Michael Hillegas, merchant, in Second St. (28 July)

Plantation in Newtown Twp., Gloucester Co., where John Breach lately lived will be sold by Simon and Peter Breach, execs. (28 July)

Thomas Palmer in Horsham Twp., Phila. Co., has taken up a mare (28 July)

House in Arch St., next door to Alexander Parker's, for sale; apply to Humphrey Day, living in said house (28 July)

Mary, wife of John Boyden, of Uuchland Twp., Chester Co., has eloped from her husband (28 July)

Timothy Scannell, Irish servant lad, runaway from William Spafford of Phila. (28 July)

People from H.M.S. *Fowey*, Capt. William Francis Drake, were carried to South Carolina by Capt. Keteltas, of New York, and Capt. John Collins of Jamaica (4 Aug.)

Details about the snow *Concord*, Capt. Macklereath, the *Royal Catherine*, Capt. Bill, and the brigantine *Hester*, Capt. Robert Troup (4 Aug.)

The following were killed by Indians on 18 July about 3 miles from Schenectade: Daniel Tol; Francis Vanden Bogart, Jr.; Jacob Glen, Jr.; Daniel Van Antwerpen; J.P. V. Antwerpen; Cor. Vielen, Jr.; Adrian Van Slyke; Peter Vroman; Klaas A. De Graaf; Adam Conde; John A. Bradt; Johan Marines; the following persons are missing: Isaac Truax; Ryer Wemp; John S. Vroman; Albert John Vedder; Frank Canner; also others who belonged to the forces posted there with Lt. Dearn of Conn. are dead or missing (4 Aug.)

Sun. last Capt. Hall arrived at Phila. and reported that the ship *Griffin*, of Phila., Capt. Arthur, was struck by lightning; Capt. Stovell reported that the ship *Tetsworth*, Capt. Cornish, was taken (4 Aug.)

Samuel Kennedy, servant, born in North of Ireland, age c. 23, runaway from Richard Richison of Whiteland Twp. in the Great Valley (4 Aug.)

Joseph Oborn, tallow chandler in Second St., Phila., wishes to settle all his accounts (4 Aug.)

Edward Hendrick, Irish servant, age c. 25, runaway from Benjamin Heritage, of Chester Twp., Burlington Co. (4 Aug.)

Teddy O'Lanshahin, Irish servant, age c. 21, runaway from Joseph Gavin of Phila., shoemaker (4 Aug.)

William Brown, English servant, runaway from Robert Erwin of Phila. (4 Aug.)

Bernard Macclue, Irish servant, age c. 16, runaway from Rebecca Leech, of Cheltenham Twp., Phila. Co. (4 Aug.)

Adv. of Charles Batho whose store is on Meredith's wharf (4 Aug.)

Emanuel Rouse, clock- and watchmaker, is removed from Elias Boudinot's in Second St. to Michael Koyl's in Front St. (4 Aug.)

Negro woman for sale; enquire of Samuel Hasell (4 Aug.)

Tar-water is sold by Sarah Murry in Third St. (4 Aug.)

Abraham Lone, Irish servant, age c. 18, and Duncan Campbell, Scotch servant, age c. 16, runaways from Robert Arthur of Little Creek Hundred, Kent Co. (4 Aug.)

Tue. last Capt. Day arrived at Boston from Lisbon (11 Aug.)

On 3 July Indians killed Aaron Belding in Northfield Town (11 Aug.)

The snow **Speedwell**, David Harris master, arrived at New York; another snow, retaken by the **Royal Catherine** privateer, Capt. Bill, has arrived at Phila.; it is reported that Capt. Menzie of the **Brave Hawk** privateer has been killed (11 Aug.)

News of Capts. James, Green, Dracy, Joy, Stamper, Cornish, Vance and Norbury (11 Aug.)

Nicholas Wyrick, a German, in or near Hanover Twp., Lancaster Co., has been committed to goal for the cruel murder of his little daughter; jury brought in verdict of manslaughter against him (11 Aug.)

Horse of Andrew Bartholomew strayed or stolen from stable in Black Horse Alley, Phila. (11 Aug.)

Dr. Spitzer is removed to house of Thomas Gretell's in Arch St., Phila. (11 Aug.)

Daniel Wormelsdorf at Manhatawny, Phila. Co., wishes to employ a fuller (11 Aug.)

William Rise, born in England, age c. 26, escaped from prison in Phila.; reward for his capture offered by Joseph Scull (11 Aug.)

Margaret Kelly, Irish servant, age c. 18, runaway from Samuel Hodge, peruke-maker, of New York City; reward will be paid for her return to her master or John Stoop, tailor, in Second St., Phila. (11 Aug.)

Adv. of Thomas Lloyd at house where Joseph Sims lately lived near the Coffee-house (11 Aug.)

Accounts with estate of Thomas Marriott, late of Bristol, dec'd, to be settled with the execs., Thomas Marriott, William Paxton and Mahlon Kirkbride (11 Aug.)

Adv. of Smith and James in Water St. (11 Aug.)

Mare stolen from plantation of Samuel Brown of Falls Twp., Bucks Co. (11 Aug.)

Fulling mill to be let; apply to Isaac Dushane at St. George's, Newcastle Co. (11 Aug.)

1748

Plantation at Gwynedd Twp., Phila. Co., for sale; apply to Thomas Yorke of Germantown (11 Aug.)

Bristow, Negro, age c. 20, runaway from Wilson Hunt of Hopewell (18 Aug.)

News of Capts. Vance, Anthony, Arnold, Lawson and Mesnard (18 Aug.)

Adv. of Andrew Elliot next door to Nathaniel Allen's in Front St. (18 Aug.)

Cloth sold by Henry Harrison, next door to Samuel Shoemaker's in Front St. (18 Aug.)

Adv. of William Wallace in Front St. and Buckridge Sims at house of Joseph Turner (18 Aug.)

Adv. of Capt. Joseph Redmond in Front St. (18 Aug.)

For freight or passage to Belfast in the snow *Lord Russell*, John Martin commander, apply to the master or Alexander Lang opposite Fishbourne's wharf (18 Aug.)

For freight or passage to London in the ship *Delaware*, Stephen Mesnard commander, apply to James Pemberton or the master (18 Aug.)

Servants and Whitehaven coal, imported in the brigantine *Pembroke*, Arthur Burrows master, from Dublin, to be sold by Norris and Griffiths in Front St. (18 Aug.)

Neate and Smith intend for England (18 Aug.)

Land in Newcastle Co., late property of Nathaniel Bryan, for sale by Joseph Henderson (18 Aug.)

Adv, of Thomas White in Market St. (18 Aug.)

William M'Donald offers reward if strayed or stolen horse is brought to Thomas Woolley's in Strawberry Alley (18 Aug.)

Time of servant woman for sale; enquire of Anthony Whitley at the Ship a-ground in Front St. (18 Aug.)

Land in Waterford Twp., Gloucester Co., for sale by Isaac Burrows (18 Aug.)

Adv. of John Wilcox, below the drawbridge in Phila. (18 Aug.)

Negro wench, rum, sugar cocoa, olives and powder for sale by John Harrison, over the drawbridge (18 Aug.)

A merchant mill in London Grove Twp., Chester Co., to be sold or let by William or John Culberson (18 Aug.)

Joseph Gray, at the Sign of the Conestogoe Waggon in Market St., offers reward for recovery of strayed or stolen horse (18 Aug.)

James Hagan, Irish servant, runaway from Benjamin Engle of Germantown (18 Aug.)

David Chambers is removed from Walnut St. to Plumb St., where he makes Windsor chairs (18 Aug.)

Catherine Deyerman, Irish servant, runaway from Alexander Scott of Hempfield Twp., Lancaster Co. (18 Aug.)

Adv. of James Sackett, whose store is in Market St., under Capt. William Spafford's (18 Aug.)

Accounts with estate of Ebenezer Currie, late of Phila., merchant, dec'd, to be settled with John Groves on Hamilton's wharf, by order of John Seton of London, merchant, and Samuel M'Call, Sr., execs. (18 Aug.)

For freight or passage to London in ship <u>Myrtilla</u>, Richard Budden commander, agree with Levy and Franks or the master (18 Aug.)

Reward for recovery of mare stolen from plantation of John Antram of the twp. and co. of Burlington (18 Aug.)

Plantation in Manor of Moreland for sale by Joseph Comly (18 Aug.)

Benjamin Beal, country born, age c. 23, runaway from his bail, Josiah Wilkinson of Bucks Co. (18 Aug.)

House a little beyond Germantown to be sold or let by Dominicus Gesner, comb-maker (18 Aug.)

Evan Morgan, cooper, is removed to house where his father Benjamin dwelt, between Thomas Lawrence and William Allen in Water St; accounts with estate of late Benjamin Morgan to be settled with Evan Morgan, John Ross and Katherine Morgan, execs; house in Front St. in which Capt. Budden lives, over against Joseph Tumey's, Esq. house and lot in Germantown in Bowman's lane, and woodland adjoining ground of Thomas Carvil, are for sale; accounts with estate of William Darvil, late of Phila., baker, to be settled with John Lassell and Evan Morgan, Jr. (18 Aug.)

Time of Irish servant girl for sale by Mary Johnston at Wicacoa (25 Aug.)

Accounts with estate of John Howell, late of Phila., tanner, to be settled with John Mifflin, Rees Meredith and John Stamper (25 Aug.)

Real estate in High St., Phila., bounded on E. by tenement of Jacob Shoemaker and on W. by tenement of John Mifflin, for sale; apply to George Heap in Third St. (25 Aug.)

Anne Watkins of Marple has taken up three stray mares (25 Aug.)

Adv. of Joseph Sims at his house where Samuel Powell, Jr., dec'd, lived (25 Aug.)

Adv. of James Burd at his store on Carpenter's wharf, opposite to William Coleman's, and formerly possessed by George Mifflin (25 Aug.)

Advs. of Peter Turner in Market St., opposite the Post-Office, Isaac Jones in Arch St., Daniel Benezet in Front St., at the corner of Morris's Alley (25 Aug.)

James Stant offers reward for arrest of William Taylor, who broke into storehouse of William Banks, of Queen Ann's Co., Md. (25 Aug.)

Advs. of William and David M'Ilvaine in Front St., and Christopher Marshall at the Sign of the Golden Ball in Chestnut St. (25 Aug.)

N.Y. item mentions Capts. Arrowsmith, Foster and Freeman (1 Sept.)

Capt. Dowell of the privateer <u>Pandour</u> has arrived at Phila. (1 Sept.)

Tickets of the New Lottery are available at houses of Nixon, Sims and Hicks (1 Sept.)

Advs. of James Benezet and of Samuel Neave, both in Front St. (1 Sept.)

Horse strayed from Jonas Kholer on plantation of William Moore; reward if horse is brought to Kholer or to Henry Schleydorn in Phila. (1 Sept.)

Time of servant for sale; enquire of Patrick Ferguson, next door to the London Apprentice in Second St. (1 Sept.)

Lots of land sold at Kensington by John Baker of Phila., carpenter, living in Sassafras St. (1 Sept.)

Rebecca Edgill of Phila. offers reward for recovery of a horse (1 Sept.)

Thomas Claborne, apprentice, age c. 18, runaway from Nehemiah Allen of Phila. (1 Sept.)

For freight or passage to Jamaica in ship *Lynch*, Thomas White commander, agree with Samuel M'Call, Sr., or John Groves (1 Sept.)

House on west side of Callowhill Market for sale by John and Jacob Naglee, execs. of Jacob Naglee, shopkeeper, dec'd (1 Sept.)

Lydia, wife of John Rue, of Phila., has eloped (1 Sept.)

House in Sassafras St. for sale by Enoch Story (1 Sept.)

Archibald Campbell, Irish servant, age c. 28, runaway from Edward Means, of Middleneck, Cecil Co., Md. (8 Sept.)

Thomas Middleton, Irish servant, nailor and blacksmith, runaway from Joseph Oldman of Phila. (8 Sept.)

Medicines sold by Samuel Emlen at the Sign of the Golden Heart (8 Sept.)

Adv. of William Logan at his store in Second St. (8 Sept.)

Tract of land in Darby Twp. for sale; apply to Solomon Humphrys in Darby or John Parker in Phila. (8 Sept.)

Prizes taken by Capt. Isaac Freeman, of the *Bethel Frigate*, owned in Boston (15 Sept.)

News of Capt. Connoly brought by Capt. Morton from Cape Breton (15 Sept.)

Capts. Arnot, Brown and Tate have arrived at Phila. from Holland with Palatines (15 Sept.)

Advs. of Charles and Alexander Stedman in Second St., opposite to Richard Sewell's, and of John Pemberton at the store on Chestnut St. wharf, lately in tenure of Smith and James (15 Sept.)

Ship *Esther*, William Hall commander, will sail for St. Christopher's (15 Sept.)

Ship *Pandour* to be sold at Mr. Plumsted's wharf; inventory available at Mrs. Roberts's Coffee-house (15 Sept.)

Ship *Hampshire*, Thomas Cheeseman master, will sail for Charles Town, S.C. (15 Sept.)

House in Bowman's Lane, part of estate of Benjamin Morgan, dec'd, for sale (15 Sept.)

Stray horse taken up at plantation of Edward Inhaven of Whippin Twp., Phila. Co. (15 Sept.)

Household goods for sale by Lucy Bowling at Sign of the Rose and Crown in Arch St. (15 Sept.)

Land in Northern Liberties for sale; apply to Robert Meade, living in Isaac Norris's Alley, or to Andrew Farrell, tanner, in Phila. (15 Sept.)

Elizabeth, wife of Thomas Sugar, of Phila., house-carpenter, has eloped from her husband and has made over some of his property to her son, David Lynn (15 Sept.)

Plantation in Buckingham, Bucks Co., late property of Jacob Holcombe, dec'd, to be sold by Mary Holcombe, exec. (15 Sept.)

M'Mechen's mills upon Whiteclay Creek for sale by William M'Mechen (15 Sept.)

Accounts with estate of Joseph Kirkbride, late of the Falls, Bucks Co., dec'd, to be settled with Nicholas Austin, Mark Watson and Sarah and Mahlon Kirkbride (15 Sept.)

Real estate in Germantown, next to the house of Joseph Shippen, to be sold and also lot of land to be let at house of Jacob Bowman, dec'd; apply to the Widow Bowman, Derrick Keyser or Christopher Ming, execs. (15 Sept.)

House and tanyard on Borough of Lancaster, formerly belonging to estate of John Faulk, dec'd, to be sold by Edward Smout on the premises (15 Sept.)

Adv. of John Stow, brass-founder, in Third St., Phila. (15 Sept.)

Malt- and brew-house in Chesterfield Twp., Burlington Co., West N.J., for sale; apply to Nicholas Farnsworth (15 Sept.)

Report of capture of ship *Triton*, Capt. Askew, of the *Louisa*, Capt. Seires, and of Capt. Perrin (22 Sept.)

Eleanor, wife of Christopher O'Brian, has eloped from her husband (22 Sept.)

Amwell Lottery is managed by Martin Ryerson, Esq., Peter Prall, Michael Henry and Emanuel Croyal; tickets are sold by William Bradford (22 Sept.)

Robert Millby, convict servant, born in Ireland, formerly dragoon in regt. of Lord Stair, runaway from Lawrence Washington; he went off in company with an Irish servant of Mr. Darrell of Fairfax Co.; Millby was first bought by Mr. Blackstone of St. Mary's Co. (22 Sept.)

Richard Farmar, at the Unicorn in Second St., sells medicines imported in the ship *Mary*, Capt. Lawson (22 Sept.)

Ephraim Seely, near Salem, Cumberland Co., West Jersey, seeks a journeyman fuller (22 Sept.)

Dr. Roan, near Marcus Hook, seeks a miller (22 Sept.)

Toney, Negro, slave of Charles Hinson, of Kent Co., Md., 10 miles below Newtown, is in custody of Sheriff Joseph Hollinshead (22 Sept.)

John White in Fifth St. has drugs for sale (22 Sept.)

Tom, Negro, age c. 40, who formerly belonged to Samuel Swift of Smithfield, runaway from James Coultas at the Middle Ferry on Schuylkill (22 Sept.)

Real estate on north side of Lombard St., Phila., for sale by Thomas James, exec. of estate of Richard Harris, dec'd (22 Sept.)

Report of death of Col. Gorham proves to be groundless (29 Sept.)

Capt. Freeman has arrived at Boston (29 Sept.)

Account of the adventures of Capt. Robert Troup of the privateer *Hester* (29 Sept.)

News of Capt. William Clymer of the sloop <u>Victory</u>, Capt. Green and Capt. Haddon (29 Sept.)

Margaret Ingram has opened the West-India Coffee-House at the corner of Market and Front Sts. (29 Sept.)

Ship <u>Prince William</u>, John Peel commander, now at John Smith's wharf, will sail for Londonderry (29 Sept.)

William Chapman, stay-maker, is removed to the house of Ebenezer Tomlinson in Walnut St. (29 Sept.)

Joshua Mulock lately removed to the house next door to James Benezett, where Capt. Mackey formerly kept store (29 Sept.)

Land known as Dr. Dinsdale's farm in Burlington Co., West New Jersey, for sale; apply to Abraham Farrington and Thomas Budd in Mountholly (29 Sept.)

George Fling has Negro for sale; enquire of Thomas Campbell, shopkeeper in Phila. (29 Sept.)

Richard Sewell is candidate for sheriff of Phila. Co. (29 Sept.)

Thomas Cash offers reward for horse strayed or stolen from pasture of George House near Phila. (29 Sept.)

Ship <u>Duke of Bedford</u>, Ephraim Gilbert commander, at Mullin's wharf, will sail for Jamaica (29 Sept.)

House near the courthouse in borough of Chester for sale; apply to William Preston in Phila. or Thomas Morgan in Chester (29 Sept.)

Goods of Owen Gwin, dec'd, will be sold by Hannah Gwin, admin.; tenement and land in East Nantmell Twp., near Mrs. Nutt's ironworks, will be sold by order of the Orphan's Court, Henry Hall Graham, deputy clerk (29 Sept.)

Mare stolen from plantation of Robert Gordon, near Allen-Town, East Jersey (29 Sept.)

Francis Nealis, servant, age c. 18, runaway from James Allison of Donegal (29 Sept.)

Catherine, wife of Umphry Ellis, of East-town, Chester Co., has eloped from her husband (29 Sept.)

House in Haddonfield, Gloucester Co., to be sold or let; enquire of Letitia Mickle, living in said house, or John Mickle or David Cooper, execs. (29 Sept.)

Jane and Thomas Hatton will sell the house where they now live between Front St. and Duck St. (29 Sept.)

Boston item mentions Capt. Freeman (6 Oct.)

Representatives elected for Phila. Co.: Isaac Norris, John Kinsey, Owen Evans, Hugh Evans, Edward Warner, Joseph Trotter, James Morris, Oswald Peele; commissioner, William Callender; assessors, Abraham Levant, John Morris, William Foulke, James Jones, Robert Thomas, Jonathan Zane - for Bucks Co., representatives, Derick Hogeland, Mahlon Kirkbride, Cephas Child, Joseph Hampton, Abraham Chapman, John Watson, Richard Mitchell, George Logan; sheriff, Amos Strickland; coroner, John Hart; commissioner, John Woolston; assessors, Giles Knight, William Murry, Thomas Paxton, William Edwards, Abraham Vastine, Daniel Palmer - for Chester Co., representatives, Thomas Worth, George Ashbridge, Francis Yarnall, John Davis, John Owen, Joseph James, Thomas Chandler, Joseph Gibbons; sheriff, Benjamin Davis; coroner, Isaac Lee; commissioner, Isaac Davis; assessors, Elisha Gatchell, Jr., Robert Isaac Pearson, Robert Mendinghall, Joseph Bartholomew, Phineas Lewis, John Ray - for Lancaster Co., representatives, John Wright, Arthur Patterson, James Webb, Peter Worrall; sheriff, Joseph Pugh; coroner, Isaac Saunders - for Newcastle Co., representatives, William Armstrong, John M'Cool, Jehu Curtis, James M'Meken, John Vance, John Edward; sheriff, John Vandyke; coroner, Samuel Silsby - for Kent Co., representatives, James Gorrell, Andrew Calwell, Robert Wilcocks, Abraham Allee, John Brinkle, John Clayton; sheriff, John Hunter; coroner, William Blackstone - for Sussex Co., representatives, Jacob Kollock, Woolsey Barton, Ryves Holt, John Clowes, John Neill, Bethel Watson; sheriff, Peter Clowes; coroner, William Shankland (6 Oct.)

Mon. last Israel Pemberton, Sr, and Thomas Leech were chosen burgesses for Phila., and as assessors William Moode, Joseph Fox, Edward Catherall, Jacob Duche, Samuel Morris and John Clifton; on Tuesday Charles Willing was elected mayor (6 Oct.)

For freight or passage to London in the ship *Beulah*, James Child master, apply to Benjamin or Samuel Shoemaker or the master (6 Oct.)

Accounts with estate of Samuel Powell, Jr., dec'd, to be settled (6 Oct.)

Time of servants for sale on the *Dolphin* on Capt. Coodman's wharf (6 Oct.)

Accounts with estate of John Hunt, late of Hopewell, dec'd, to be settled with Wilson and Jonathan Hunt, execs. (6 Oct.)

Warning not to accept bond of James Macelhaga payable to Matthew Chain (6 Oct.)

Advs. of Robert Ramsay in Water St., next door to Capt. John Philips's, and of Capt. Francis and Thomas White (6 Oct.)

Edward Collins, gardiner in Phila., offers reward if strayed mare and colt are brought to him or to Peter Robeson at the Sign of the Indian King in Market St. (6 Oct.)

Brigantine to be sold by Joseph Henderson (6 Oct.)

Mary Burk, Irish servant, age c. 18, runaway from William Scott, of Province Island, formerly of East Jersey (6 Oct.)

Mare stolen or strayed from George Taylor at French-Creek-Forge in Chester Co. (6 Oct.)

Reward if horse strayed from Norriton mill in Chester Co. is returned to John Eastbourne at Norriton, Phila. Co., or Joseph Gray in Phila.; horse was bred at Thomas Chandler's, near Brandywine, Chester Co. (6 Oct.)

Bryan O'Murry, Irish servant, runaway from Joseph M'Farlan of Tenicum Twp., Bucks Co. (6 Oct.)

Inhabitants of Cape-Fear, led by Capt. Dry, attack men of two Spanish privateers (13 Oct.)

Lewis Evans is engraving map of Pa., N.J., and N.Y. (13 Oct.)

H.M.S. *Otter*, Capt. John Ballet, and Capt. Moore, from Londonderry have arrived at Phila. (13 Oct.)

Richard Sewell was elected Sheriff of Phila. Co., and Henry Pratt coroner (13 Oct.)

Accounts with estates of Thomas and Ann Waterman, dec'd, to be settled with John Jones, admin. (13 Oct.)

Adv. of Thomas Lightfoot in Water St. (13 Oct.)

1748

Land in Limerick Twp., Phila. Co., part of estate of Edward Nicholas, dec'd, to be sold by George Evans (13 Oct.)

For freight or passage to Jamaica in ship *John*, George Matthews master, apply to Henry Harrison, next door to Samuel Shoemaker in Water St., or to Robert Greenaway (13 Oct.)

Andrew Lamb, at corner house of Chestnut and Second Sts., over against Mr. Stretch's, clockmaker, teaches mathematics (13 Oct.)

Joseph Coburn of Phila. has lost purse containing gold coins (13 Oct.)

Plantation in Gwynedd Twp., Phila. Co., for sale; apply to Thomas York of Germantown (13 Oct.)

Chocolate sold by James Humphreys at house in Second St. where the Widow Newman formerly lived (13 Oct.)

William Price, English servant, age c. 19, runaway from Samuel Coles of Gloucester Co. (13 Oct.)

Colt has strayed from Valentine Boyer, butcher, in Race St. (13 Oct.)

Irish linen for sale by Alexander Johnston at Capt. William Blair's in Second St. (13 Oct.)

Lt.-Col. Heron and Major Horton went to defend Fort William against the Spaniards; some Creek Indians attacked party of Spaniards and Yamasee Indians about 15 miles beyond Capt. Carr's and killed Chillawlee, headman of the Yamasees (20 Oct.) Mention of Capt. Mackey from Jamaica and Capt. M'Daniel (20 Oct.)

A few billets of the first class of the Phila. Lottery may be bought from Abraham Taylor, Esq. (20 Oct.)

Goods imported in ship *Delaware*, Stephen Mesnard commander, and in the *Mary Galley*, George Lawson commander, and the snow *George*, George Rankin commander, to be sold by Edward Dowers in Water St., near Samuel Shoemaker's house (20 Oct.)

Accounts with estate of John Howell, late of Phila., tanner, dec'd, to be settled with John Mifflin, Rees Meredith and John Stamper (20 Oct.)

Adv. of John Hughes, baker, at house where the late Mr. David lived, near the Indian King in Phila. (20 Oct.)

Edward Olive, Irish servant, age c. 18, runaway from Alexander Morgan of Waterford Twp., Gloucester Co. (20 Oct.)

Adv. of George Armbruster, printer, in Arch St. (20 Oct.)

Mare stolen from James Arbuckle of Newtown, Bucks Co. (20 Oct.)

Hugh Kelly, Irish servant belonging to Samuel Hodge of New York, periwig-maker, runaway from the *Morning Star* privateer of New York; reward for his capture offered by William Cannon, tailor, in Front St., and S. Hodge in New York (20 Oct.)

Boss, Negro, age c. 20, for sale; enquire of George Harding, leather-dresser, in Market St. (20 Oct.)

Michael Collins, Irish servant, age c. 22, runaway from John Grant, of Basking Ridge, Sumerset Co., East Jersey (20 Oct.)

Adv. of John Fleming, who kept school in Dublin and later in Md. for almost 12 years, is recommended by William Moore, Esq., at Moore Hall (20 Oct.)

Five pastures to be sold at John Ashton's in Moyamensing; plan of pastures to be seen at Surveyor General's office, at John Cross's, at George Hidner's in Market St., at Michael Israel's, at the Sign of the Lion in Wiccacoe (20 Oct.)

Crew of the Princess of Orange privateer, Capt. Davidson, ordered to be sent to England to stand trial for piracy (27 Oct.)

Ship Patience and Margaret, Capt. John Govan, has arrived at Phila. from Rotterdam with Palatines (27 Oct.)

John Fleming will open school at house of Mrs. Chapman in Chestnut St. (27 Oct.)

Plantation in Oxford Twp. for sale; enquire of Joseph Sims near the drawbridge (27 Oct.)

For freight or passage to St. Christopher's in brigantine Jane, Isaac Hardtman commander, now at Samuel M'Call, Jr's wharf, agree with Joseph Sims or the master (27 Oct.)

For freight to Potomack River, Va., in the snow Diligence, Thomas Francis commander, agree with the master at his lodgings at Jonathan Evans's in Front St. (27 Oct.)

Adv. of Capt. Redmond in Front St. (27 Oct.)

Grist mill in Lower Dublin Twp. on Pennypack Creek for sale; apply to John Atkins (27 Oct.)

Partnership dissolved between Robert and Amos Strettell (27 Oct.)

Cloth sold by John Norwood at corner of Pewter-platter Alley (27 Oct.)

Horse stolen from plantation of William Moore, Esq., of Moyamensing; reward will be paid by Jonas Kebler on premises (27 Oct.)

Horse strayed from pasture of Benjamin Franklin; reward will be paid by J. Kent (27 Oct.)

Horse strayed or stolen from William Moore in Nantmill Twp., Chester Co. (27 Oct.)

James Lane in Sadsbury, Bucks Co., has taken up a mare (27 Oct.)

Accounts with estate of Joseph Ellis, late of Plymouth, dec'd, to be settled with Eve Ellis and Charles Humphreys, execs. (27 Oct.)

Negro, age c. 40, this country born, miller and bisket-maker, for sale; enquire of Jacob Eversley, smith, at Sign of the Lock in Third St. (27 Oct.)

Patrick Allison has lost watch, Herring of London the maker, perhaps on road to Capt. Coultas's ferry; reward if watch is brought to John Meas in Front St. (27 Oct.)

Francis Nellis, servant, age c. 18, runaway from James Allison in Donnegal (27 Oct.)

Letter from Capt. Bradbury at St. George's Fort concerning the Penobscot Indians (3 Nov.)

Engagement between Admiral Knowles and the Spaniards off the Havanna (3 Nov.)

News of the privateer Trembleur, Capt. Matthews (3 Nov.)

Adv. of Charles Willing in Third St. (3 Nov.)

Dr. John Denormandie designs for Europe in the spring (3 Nov.)

1748

Dr. Adam Thomson, originally from Edinburgh, is settled at the house of Mrs. Mary Andrews in Water St. (3 Nov.)

Adv, of James Sackett, lately removed to the house next to the Jersey ferry (3 Nov.)

James Boucher, Irish servant, age c. 18, runaway from Samuel Evans, of Ridley, Chester Co. (3 Nov.)

Cornelius Bower, indented servant, age c. 30, runaway from Thomas Potts, Sr., of Colebrookdale, Phila. Co. (3 Nov.)

Plantation in Passyunk Twp. to be let; enquire of Dr. John Kearsley, Andrew Haney or Bartholomew Penrose (3 Nov.)

John Justice in the Northern Liberties has taken up a horse (3 Nov.)

James Thompson, Irish servant, weaver, runaway from Edmund Conoly of Kennet Twp., Chester Co. (3 Nov.)

For freight or passage to Charles-Town, S.C., in the ship *John*, Joseph Woolcomb commander, agree with Cuzzins and Smyter (3 Nov.)

Adv. of Arnold Custard, opposite to Joseph Gray's in Market St. (3 Nov.)

John Costeloe, Irish servant, age c. 23, shoemaker, runaway from Obadiah Bonsall of Birmingham Twp., Chester Co. (3 Nov.)

James Knox, Irish servant, blacksmith, runaway from Thomas Fitzwater, of Whitpain, Phila. Co. (3 Nov.)

John Ryley, Irish servant, age c. 20, runaway from John Michener, of Manor of Moreland, Phila. Co. (3 Nov.)

Schooner *Two Sisters*, Capt. Roney, of Phila., is taken by a privateer (10 Nov.)

Account of bequest of Thomas Marriott, late of borough of Bristol, dec'd, to his son Isaac; the execs. are Thomas Marriott, William Paxton and Mahlon Kirkbride (10 Nov.)

Accounts with Dr. Thomas Bond, late of Phila., but now gone beyond sea, are to be settled with his attorneys, Phineas Bond and Jonathan Zane (10 Nov.)

Schooner *Elizabeth*, now at Samuel Parr's wharf, for sale; agree with Robert Gill on board (10 Nov.)

Thomas Murnahan, living on plantation of Anthony Tunis in Merion, offers reward for recovery of strayed or stolen horse (10 Nov.)

William Price, English servant, age c. 19, runaway from Samuel Coles of Gloucester Co. (10 Nov.)

Adv. of James Steward, tailor, in Front St. (10 Nov.)

Horse has strayed from plantation of John Holmes of Pennypack; reward will be paid by John Quinton if said horse is brought to Holmes or to the Sign of the Buck in Franckford (10 Nov.)

Expired paper money of the Three Lower Counties on Delaware will be exchanged by Jacob Kollock (10 Nov.)

Reward for recovery of strayed or stolen mare will be paid by John Clifton if mare is brought to Sign of the George in Second St. (10 Nov.)

William Wyerman on Permuchian Creek, Lancaster Co., has taken up a stray horse (10 Nov.)

1748

For freight or passage to Dublin in the snow *Jenny*, William Gregg commander, agree with Cunningham and Gardner (17 Nov.)

Plantation in Caln Twp., Chester Co., for sale; apply to Thomas Pim, living near it, or the owner, Patrick Miller, living in Chestertown, near William Moore's, Esq. (17 Nov.)

Richard Blackham in Front St. has lost a horse (17 Nov.)

James Steward, of Phila., tailor, will sail for London in ship *Beulah*, Capt. James Child (17 Nov.)

Thomas Lewis in Montgomery Twp., Phila. Co., has taken up a horse (17 Nov.)

Mare has been stolen from William Moode of Phila. (17 Nov.)

John Purfield, Irish servant, age c. 35, runaway from John M'Call of Warminster Twp., Bucks Co. (17 Nov.)

Jack, Negro, brought up in Kent Co., who formerly belonged to Andrew Hamilton, runaway from Thomas Collins, of Thoroughfare Neck, Apoquiminy Hundred; Jack has a brother who lives with John Palmer, of Phila., bricklayer (17 Nov.)

James Harris offers reward for return of horse strayed or stolen out of New London, Chester Co. (17 Nov.)

Reward for recovery of horse strayed or stolen from Philip French of New Brunswick (17 Nov.)

Mare and colt strayed from Richard Thomas of Pencador Hundred, Newcastle Co. (17 Nov.)

John Scarlet in Robertson Twp., Lancaster Co., has taken up a mare (17 Nov.)

Gloucester, Negro, age 21 or 22, runaway from Luke Morris of Phila. (17 Nov.)

Michael, Mulatto, country born, age c. 17, runaway from Anthony Morris, Jr., of Phila. (17 Nov.)

Gov. James Hamilton arrived in Phila. on 23 Nov. (24 Nov.)

Time of servant for sale by Hathorn Taylor in Front St. (24 Nov.)

For freight or passage to London in ship *Griffin*, Joseph Arthur commander, agree with Norris and Griffith in Front St. (24 Nov.)

For freight or passage to Cape Fear in schooner *Stork*, Philip Stevens commander, agree with John Durborow or the master at Dickinson's wharf (24 Nov.)

Stephen Williams on Neshaminy in Bucks Co. seeks a miller (24 Nov.)

Hannah Swainy, Irish servant, who has been in the country 7 or 8 years and served former time with David Haistins at Ochterara, runaway from James David of Charles-town, Chester Co. (24 Nov.)

House in New Castle Town on Delaware for sale; apply to Ezekiel Boggs of New-Castle (24 Nov.)

James Ray, servant, age c. 21, runaway from John Stokes, near Ley-cock, Bucks Co. (24 Nov.)

Samuel Kennedy, servant, age c. 23, who speaks French and Dutch, runaway from Richard Richison, of Whiteland, Chester Co. (24 Nov.)

Mare has been taken up at plantation of Robert M'Curdy in Springfield Twp., Phila. Co. (24 Nov.)

Accounts with estate of Thomas Hake, late of Rocksborough Twp., Phila. Co., schoolmaster, dec'd, to be settled with Thomas Davis, exec., in Metachen, Phila. Co. (24 Nov.)

Schuylkill Mill in Blockley Twp. to be sold or rented; apply to Lewis Jones, living on the premises (24 Nov.)

Advs. of James Trotter in Water St., John Wallace at house in Front St. where Ebenezer Currie formerly lived, and Alexander Hamilton in Water St., who sell goods imported in the Loyal Judith, Capt. James Cowie (1 Dec.)

John Huston offers reward for capture of the following deserters from H.M.'s service: Richard Simons, William Gilliam, Manchester Holloway, William Scanton, Patrick Kearney, William Goodman, Thomas Murray, Edward Smith, John Clark (age c. 28, born in Ireland), John Marheal (age c. 30, born in England), John Dixson (age c. 23, born in Ireland), Frederick Crest (age c. 40, born in Germany, huntsman), John Cunningham (age c. 22 born in Ireland, cordwainer), Robert Jemison (age 21, born in Ireland), James Nagle (age 23, born in Ireland, tailor) and Hugh Reed (age 18, born in Ireland) (1 Dec.)

Margaret Philips, servant, age c. 30, runaway from John Eglington of Gloucester Co. (1 Dec.)

Two horses, owned by John Bodine, strayed from Germantown; reward if they are returned to owner or to Conrad Gehr or Thomas Carvel in Germantown (1 Dec.)

Joseph Bourgoin, John M'Dearmon or Matthias Lamey offer reward for arrest of John Murphy, late of Whiteland, Chester Co., who ran away from his bail (1 Dec.)

Reward if horse strayed or stolen from John Hunt's pasture is brought to Thomas Blackwell in Hopewell Twp., Hunterdon Co. (1 Dec.)

Time of a servant, carver by trade, for sale by Bryan Wilkinson of Phila. (1 Dec.)

Dr. Matthias a Brackel Vander Krüyt, who arrived from Holland Sept. last, sells medicines at his house in Fourth St. (1 Dec.)

Ship Burlington, Capt. Smyter, has arrived at London, and the brigantine Hope, of Phila., Capt. Lake, has arrived at Bristol (8 Dec.)

Dr. John Rowan, who intends for Ireland, has an invoice of his medicines at John Erwin's (8 Dec.)

Adv. of Philip Benezet in Water St., opposite Carpenter's wharf, where Thomas Hopkinson lately kept store, adjoining William Coleman (8 Dec.)

Plantation in Lower Dublin Twp., Phila. Co., for sale; apply to Hans or Nicholas Lycan on the premises or Septimus Robinson or James Petty in Phila. (8 Dec.)

John Steward, Irish servant, age c. 15, runaway from James Eldridge of West Caln, Chester Co, (8 Dec.)

Thomas Craven, near the courthouse in Burlington, teaches writing and arithmetic (8 Dec.)

Robert Evans of Merion has taken up stray colt (8 Dec.)

1748   37

Real estate in Worcester Twp., Phila. Co., for sale by Peter
Spyeker on the premises (8 Dec.)

Accounts with estate of Evan Morgan, late of Phila., merchant,
dec'd, to be settled with Samuel Hazard and Thomas Morgan,
execs.; among items to be sold are a house in Water St., next
door to Peter Bard, and a pasture adjoining Robert Ellis's
pasture; Morris Morgan, son of Evan, will sell ironware at
house late of Evan Morgan (8 Dec.)

Adv. of Nathaniel Bowser, tailor, from London, whose store is
on Hamilton's wharf (8 Dec.)

Jacob Leyering in Roxburgh Twp. has taken up a stray horse
(8 Dec.)

A mare has been stolen from John Hyde of Hopewell, Hunterdon
Co. (8 Dec,)

News from Boston of Capts. Preble, Coffin, Gorham and Davis
and of death of William Croxford, shot by Indians (13 Dec.)

Capts. Neven and Cale have sailed for Louisbourgh (13 Dec.)

Thu. last Capt. Lyon arrived at Phila. from Jamaica (13 Dec.)

Henry Waugh, sadler, came to America in 1738 and is supposed
to be in Va. or N.C.; he will hear something to his advantage by applying to Alexander Moore, peruke-maker, in Phila.
(13 Dec.)

Horses have strayed from John Compton at upper end of Third St.
(13 Dec.)

Michael, Dutch servant, age c. 25, runaway from John Femel of
Phila., baker (13 Dec.)

Michael Inglehart, Dutch servant, age c. 19, runaway from Jacob
Asleman in Conestogoe (13 Dec.)

Wendle Staltz seeks news of his brothers Matthias and Abraham
from whom he has not heard for 7 years; notice of them may be
sent to the Post-Office in Market St. or at Capt. Ulrick's
in Second St. (13 Dec.)

Horse strayed or stolen from Thomas Cooch, miller, in Christine (13 Dec.)

Peter Righter, in Roxburgh Twp., near Robeson's mill, has taken up a cow (13 Dec.)

Plantation in Haverford for sale; apply to Henry Lewis, living
thereon (13 Dec.)

Deed drawn by Arthur Forster (late clerk to Charles Brockden)
near Michael Hillegas's in Second St. (20 Dec.)

History of the Late Rebellion in Great-Britain, by John Marchant, is for sale (20 Dec.)

Mayor Charles Willing forbids barbers and peruke-makers to
work on Sunday (20 Dec.)

James Steward, of Phila., intending to decline following his
trade, has appointed Isaac Norris and William Griffiths to
settle his affairs (20 Dec.)

David Lewis in Third St. has a horse that was left in his stable (20 Dec.)

Christopher Marshal in Chestnut St. has some pieces of gold
lately found in Phila. (20 Dec.)

Robert Steward, Irish hired man, age c. 23, runaway from Leonard Keffer of Morris Co., N.J. (20 Dec.)

George Gibson will sell his house in Borough of Lancaster (20 Dec.)

William Allison, born in North of Ireland, age c. 28, who formerly raised hemp in Conestogoe, runaway from his bail; reward for his capture offered by George Smith of Lancaster (20 Dec.)

Capt. Hasty reported at Williamsburg that the ship *Endeavour*, Capt. John Simpson, from Glasgow, was taken by a privateer commanded by John Ferdinando (27 Dec.)

Capt. Ritchie has arrived at Phila. from Jamaica (27 Dec.)

Alexander Forbes sells cables and rigging on William Masters's wharf (27 Dec.)

Derrick Tyson in Upper Dublin Twp., Phila. Co., has taken up a mare (27 Dec.)

Land in Hopewell Twp., Lancaster Twp., at a corner of Robert Black's land, for sale; apply to Patrick M'Carmish at Marple, Chester Co., or Samuel Rhodes in Phila. (27 Dec)

Accounts with estate of Samuel Coates, shopkeeper, dec'd, to be settled with Mary Coates, exec., next door to Thomas Campbell's in Second St. (27 Dec.)

1749

Address of Gov. Shirley of Mass. (3 Jan.)

Capts. Dubois and Hageman are in goal at Leoganne (3 Jan.)

Information on eclipse by Theophilus Grew (3 Jan.)

Accounts with estate of Andrew Robeson, late of Roxburgh Twp., dec'd, to be settled with Magdalene Robeson, admin., in Sassafrax St. (3 Jan.)

Mare and colt have strayed from Zebulon Hollingsworth in Cecil Co., Md. (3 Jan.)

Adv. of Thomas Lloyd, two doors below Widow Roberts's Coffeehouse (3 Jan.)

Accounts with estate of Joseph Beddome, who intends for England, are to be settled; he has for sale a house at Christine Bridge in Newcastle Co. (3 Jan.)

Speech of Gov. James Hamilton of Pa. (10 Jan.)

Mention of Capt. Schermerhorne from South Carolina (10 Jan.)

Accounts with estate of Dr. Benjamin Morris, late of Phila., who is now gone beyond sea, are to be settled with Joseph Morris, his attorney (10 Jan.)

A Mulatto has run away from the sloop *Tryal*, Joseph Dickinson commander (10 Jan.)

Accounts with estate of Richard Stanley, late of Phila., dec'd, to be settled with Volantine and Mary Stanley, execs. (10 Jan.)

Real estate of William Parker of Phila., blacksmith, is for sale (10 Jan.)

Bryan, or Barnabe, M'Glew, Irish servant, age c. 18, runaway from John Vernor of Leacock Twp., Lancaster Co. (10 Jan.)

Tract of land on north side of Rariton River, opposite Perth Amboy, for sale by George Leslie, who lives thereon (10 Jan.)

Two horses strayed or stolen from John Macklevain, of Norrington, Phila. Co. (10 Jan.)

House and lot in Fifth St. for sale; apply to Col. Thomas White in Market St. (10 Jan.)

Henry Shafter, born in England, shoemaker, runaway from his master in Wilmington, Newcastle Co.; reward for his arrest will be paid by John Chamberlin or Goldsmith Edward Folwell (10 Jan.)

John Weynant, Dutch servant, age $\underline{c}$. 20, runaway from Henry Damood of Lampiter Twp., Lancaster Co. (10 Jan.)

Capt. Blair has arrived in Md. (17 Jan.)

Capt. Ellwell in a sloop from Boston is cast away on Sinepuxant Bar (17 Jan.)

Lot in Northern Liberties, late part of estate of Joseph Lynn, dec'd, will be sold at house of William Nicholson in Arch St.; it was taken in execution at suit of Thomas Whitten, exec. of Benjamin Duffield, dec'd (17 Jan.)

Household goods will be sold at house of late George Miller, tavern-keeper, in Chestnut St., dec'd, by order of William Blair, exec. (17 Jan.)

Abraham Wood, apprentice, age $\underline{c}$. 19, runaway from Jacob Lewis of Phila., carpenter, supposedly in company of a Mulatto who is named George Shirley, servant to Samuel Rowland of Lewestown (17 Jan.)

Wagon for sale by Abraham Carpenter, near the drawbridge in Phila. (17 Jan.)

Richard Murray will sell all his Chestnut St. ground-rents; enquire of Benjamin Franklin (17 Jan.)

Dr. Walter Porter, formerly doctor of the privateer <u>Trembleur</u>, runaway from his bail, John Anderson, living in Salem, N.J. (17 Jan.)

Land for sale by Sheriff Ananias Sayre; part is in Fairfield Twp., Cumberland Co., belonging to estate of Edmond Kiff, dec'd, adjoining land belonging to Hezekiah Lowring; also for sale is a tract near the road from John Ogden's to Maurice River (24 Jan.)

For freight or passage to Jamaica in the snow <u>Strange-Wish</u>, Thomas Caton master, apply to Israel Pemberton, Jr. (24 Jan.)

Will, Mulatto, age $\underline{c}$. 25, son of an Indian mother and Negro father, runaway from plantation of Dr. Graeme in Horsham, Phila, Co. (24 Jan.)

Accounts with Jacob Naglee, late of the Northern Liberties, dec'd, to be settled with John and Jacob Naglee, execs. (24 Jan.)

Accounts with estate of Thomas Howard, late of Phila., dec'd, to be settled with John Howard, exec., in Second St. (24 Jan.)

Joseph Gray has taken down his Sign of the Conestogoe Waggon; he will sell wine, sugar and brandy at his house in Market St. (24 Jan.)

John M'Ghee, Irish servant, age $\underline{c}$. 20, runaway from Samuel Reed, of Piles Grove, Salem Co. (24 Jan.)

James Muirhead, Irishman, lately a servant, has run away with a coat which he stole from Isaac Lemon, of Lampiter Twp., Lancaster Co. (24 Jan.)

Tract of land in Wright's-town Twp., Bucks Co., for sale; apply to John Leadlie, living on the premises (24 Jan.)

Plantation in Northern Liberties for sale; apply to Andrew Farrell in Chestnut St. (24 Jan.)

John Davis, Welsh servant, age c. 25, runaway from James Galbreath, Esq., of Lancaster Co. (24 Jan.)

Accounts with estate of Enoch Story, hatter, dec'd, to be settled with Elizabeth Story, exec. (24 Jan.)

Mention of arrival at Boston of Capt. Ryan and at Rhode Island of Capt. Richards (31 Jan.)

Sometime ago died in Queens Co., N.Y., Col. Thomas Hicks, who left above 300 descendants; Jacob Blackwell, who died there at age of 52, weighed 429 lbs. (31 Jan.)

Capt. Witter from Coracoa reported at New York the murder by four Spanish Negroes of William Johnson, master of the sloop *Polly*, and all on board, including Capt. Hall of New York (31 Jan.)

In Dec. last died in Westchester Co., N.Y., John Hadden, age 96, and his wife Abigail, age above 90 (31 Jan.)

Jan. 30 arrived at Phila. Capt. Aylmer Gravell from New York (31 Jan.)

Two horses strayed or were stolen from Samuel M'Call, Jr. (31 Jan.)

Accounts with estate of Ebenezer Currie, dec'd, to be settled with John Groves (31 Jan.)

Accounts with estate of Richard Hayes, late of Phila., dec'd, to be settled with John Hallowell, admin. (31 Jan.)

Accounts with estate of Sylvanus Jones, of Phila., cooper, dec'd, to be settled with Hugh Forbes, admin. (31 Jan.)

Servant girl for sale; enquire of James Whitehead, Keeper of the Workhouse (31 Jan.)

Mathematical instruments made by Anthony Lamb in New York (31 Jan.)

House in Second St. to be let by Joshua Emlen (31 Jan.)

If Joseph and Jacob Wall and their kinsman, John Wall (supposed to have been born in Worcester and lately arrived in America), apply to Ebenezer Large in Burlington, they will hear something to their advantage (31 Jan.)

Richard Holland, English servant, shoemaker, age c. 23, runaway from Benjamin Kendall of Phila. (31 Jan.)

House in Passyunk Twp. for sale; apply to John Cox in Phila. (31 Jan.)

House in the alley near Charles Willing's, Esq., to be sold by John and Jedediah Snowden (31 Jan.)

John Grace, *alias* John Jones, servant, born in Md., ironworker, runaway from John Pennill in Chester (31 Jan.)

John Bourne, Irish servant, age c. 20, runaway from Henry Mitchell of Bristol Twp., Bucks Co., supposedly in company with Dutchman, a freeman, one Henry Anks (31 Jan.)

Adv. of John Inglis at Hamilton's wharf (31 Jan.)

1749

Letter from St. Thomas mentions Capts. Daniel Harriot, Alex. Martin, Stephen Bowen, Robert Hessy, Joseph Lunt, Tho. Jadcocks and George Roundtree (7 Feb.)

Ship Salisbury, Capt. Breme, left the Downs for Phila. (7 Feb.)

Jacob Baker, on Fisher's Island, will sell shad during the season at Schuylkill Mouth (7 Feb.)

Notice about quitrent signed by Lynford Lardner (7 Feb.)

Colt strayed from Andrew Hodge of Phila. (7 Feb.)

Shop in Chestnut St. lately belonging to Caleb Emlen, Jr., dec'd, to be sold by two of the execs., Joshua Emlen and John Armitt (7 Feb.)

Request that person who took a letter from Jamaica from Peter Furnell, Esq., addressed to John Clifton, take the same to the Post Office; it was brought in the ship of Capt. Thomas Stamper (7 Feb.)

Plantation in Merion Twp., Phila. Co., for sale; apply to Lewis Jones at Schuylkill Mills (14 Feb.)

Accounts with estate of Alexander Lang, late of Phila., merchant, dec'd, to be settled with Redmond Conyngham and Theophilus Gardner, execs. (14 Feb.)

Adv. of John Pole in Phila. (14 Feb.)

Two cows strayed from plantation of Samuel Preston Moore near Oxford Church (14 Feb.)

M. a Brakel Van der Kluyt, M.D., in Fourth St. plans to return to Holland (14 Feb.)

Francis Grimes, Irish servant, age c. 22, runaway from Hugh Rendels of Mill-creek Hundred, Newcastle Co. (14 Feb.)

Tavern in Center-town, Middlesex Co., N.J., for sale by Stephen Warne, innkeeper, living on the premises (14 Feb.)

Ship Pearl, of Bristol, Capt. Ingelado, was lost on Barbuda; many persons were then saved by the assistance of William Byam, Esq. (21 Feb.)

Engraving of Lewis Evans's map of Pa. is finished (21 Feb.)

Capts. Katter and Morrison have arrived at Phila. (21 Feb.)

Tickets for the lottery for building a church and parsonage in New Brunswick, N.J., are to be obtained from Peter Kemble, John Berrian, John Broughton and James Lyne; also from Dirck Schuyler and Benjamin Franklin in Phila.; also from William Bradford, Jr., and James Napier in New York (21 Feb.)

Tract of land in Worcester Twp., Phila. Co., for sale; apply to John Jones on premises (21 Feb.)

Real estate in Phila. for sale; apply to Joseph Davis in Sassafras St. (21 Feb.)

Shad fishery, formerly carried on by Jonathan Jones, now dec'd, and John Towers in partnership, is now conducted by his son-in-law, William Jones, and John Towers (21 Feb.)

Three lots in Market St. for sale; enquire of Dr. John Wright in Chestnut St. (21 Feb.)

For freight or passage to Barbados in ship Hawk, Patrick Vance master, apply to Jonathan Mifflin or Thomas Lightfoot (21 Feb.)

Capt. John Brame, late commander of the Salisbury, died on Reedy Island (28 Feb.)

Capt. Anderson arrived at Phila. from Barbados (28 Feb.)

New England rum sold by Peter Franklin on the Charming Molly at Mr. Pole's wharf (28 Feb.)

Subscriptions for Lewis Evans's map taken by James Parker in N.Y., Caleb Weiser in Tulpahoccon, Rev. Timothy Griffith in Newcastle Co., Ebenezer Miller, Jr., in Couhanzy, and Lewis Evans in Arch St., Phila. (28 Feb.)

Imported goods for sale by Andrew Elliott, next door to Nathaniel Allen's in Front St. (28 Feb.)

Samuel M'Call, Sr., offers reward for ship's Moses that broke loose (28 Feb.)

James Pummell, apprentice, born and bred by French Creek, runaway from Thomas Green of Phila. (28 Feb.)

House at the Vineyard to be let by Edward Jones (28 Feb.)

Accounts with estate of Benjamine Canby, late of Solsbury, Bucks Co., dec'd, to be settled with William Hill, William Yardley and Thomas Yardley, execs. (28 Feb.)

Sawmill in Merion to be let; apply to David Davis, living near the mill (28 Feb.)

Plantation in Concord Twp., Chester Co., to be let; apply to Joseph Cloud on the premises or William Hughes, living in Phila. Co., near the Lower Ferry, upon a plantation of George Gray (28 Feb.)

Accounts with estate of William Plasket, late of Trenton, dec'd, to be settled with Nathan Beaks, exec. (28 Feb.)

Sloop commanded by one Poor was forced on rocks near mouth of Piscataqua harbor (7 Mar.)

Sloop of Capt. Wade foundered on coast of Va., but all men were saved (7 Mar.)

Adv. of William Edgell in Market St. under Capt. William Spaffords, who sells goods imported in the Salisbury, Capt. Hunter (7 Mar.)

Adv. of Myles Strickland in Market St. (7 Mar.)

Adv. of Isaac Jones in Arch St. (7 Mar.)

William Doughty, late of Phila., blacksmith, leased ground on Pool's Hill in the Northern Liberties (leased of Benjamin Mifflin for 7 years) to Alexander Lang, late of Phila., dec'd; lease to be sold by Conyngham and Gardner, execs. (7 Mar.)

Evan Morgan has removed from house near the drawbridge to house in which his late father Benjamin Morgan lived, between Thomas Lawrence and William Allen, Esqrs., in King St.; accounts with estate of William Darvil, late of Phila., baker, dec'd, are to be settled (7 Mar.)

House in Lower Dublin Twp. where George Bale lives, part of estate of Ralph Sandiford, dec'd, for sale; apply to Matthias Aspden, exec., in Phila. (7 Mar.)

Piece of cloth was left at house of Griffith Jones, skinner, in Market St., next door to John Kinsey, Esq. (7 Mar.)

Plantation in Whiteland Twp., Chester Co., for sale; apply to Matthias Lamey (7 Mar.)

1749   43

Andrew Liburt has mare and horse that came to plantation called Rhodes's (now Hainey's) in Passyunk Twp. (7 Mar.)

It is reported from Piscataqua that Mr. Austen of Dover, N.H., was drowned (14 Mar.)

Barn of Jonah Rodes of Jamaica, L.I., was struck by lightning and burned (14 Mar.)

Snow *Jane*, Capt. Abraham Keteltas of N.Y., was driven ashore at Sandy Hook by the ice (14 Mar.)

News of Capts. Davis and Richie who sailed from N.Y. in Dec. (14 Mar.)

Capt. Phoenix has arrived at New York from the West Indies (14 Mar.)

For freight or passage to Newport, R.I., in sloop *Charming Molly*, Peter Franklin commander, agree with the master at Pole's wharf (14 Mar.)

Advs. of Joseph Trotter and Hunn Roberts in Phila. (14 Mar.)

Adv. of Charles Stow, sadler, in Second St., next door to John Ross's (14 Mar.)

Adv. of Mordecai Yarnall in Market St. (14 Mar.)

European goods sold by Marcus Kuhl in Market St. (14 Mar.)

Amwell, N.J., Lottery tickets sold by William Bradford in Phila. (14 Mar.)

Dan, Mulatto slave, age c. 25, runaway from Cornelius Eltinge, living near the Great Falls in Potomack, Prince George's Co., Md. (14 Mar.)

Accounts with estate of Margaret Nanna, late of Germantown, dec'd, to be settled with Thomas and Rees Peters, execs. (14 Mar.)

Persons indebted to Thomas James, now in Barbados, are to settle with Thomas James, Jr., and James Coultas in Phila. (14 Mar.)

Steer has come to plantation of Isaac Garrett in Willistown, Chester Co. (14 Mar.)

Adv. of Arent Hassert in Letitia Court (14 Mar.)

Red lead for sale by James Clulow at the Widow Stanley's in Market St. (14 Mar.)

Plantation in borough of Bristol, Bucks Co., late of Thomas Sisom, dec'd, for sale by William Atkinson and Ennion Williams, execs. (14 Mar.)

On Mar. 20 Capt. Faulkner arrived at Phila. from Cadiz (21 Mar.)

Ship *Leostoff*, Capt. Fielding, sank on the rocks at Jamaica (21 Mar.)

Accounts with estate of Andrew Edge, late of the Northern Liberties, tanner, dec'd, to be settled with Richard Hall and Robert Shewell, execs.; lot fronting road to Mr. Masters's mill for sale (21 Mar.)

Adv. of John Beals, music master from London, in Fourth St., joining to Mr. Linton's, collar-maker (21 Mar.)

House at Landaw in Germantown for sale by Dominicus Gasner, comb-maker (21 Mar.)

1749

- Two horses came to plantation of Richard Mitchell in Wrightstown, Bucks Co. (21 Mar.)
- Deed of Henry Van Bebber to Fredrick Antes (lately recorded in office of Charles Brockden) has been lost; reward offered (21 Mar.)
- Negro for sale; enquire of the printers or Joseph Saul, wheelmaker (21 Mar.)
- Accounts with estate of Robert Jewell, late of Phila., ropemaker, dec'd, to be settled with Sarah Jewell, widow and admin. (21 Mar.)
- William Reynolds, living at Sinking Springs, Cumrie Twp., Lancaster Co., offers reward if strayed horse is brought to Richard Richison (chief ranger for Chester Co.) or James David of Charlestown, Chester Co., or Edward Smout, Conrad Weiser of James Calbreth, chief rangers for Lancaster Co. (21 Mar.)
- A certain Deeing of Black Point is committed to York Goal in Mass. for murder of his wife (28 Mar.)
- House, stable, wharf and stores of Walter Goodman in Phila. to be let (28 Mar.)
- Anthony Morris, Jr., has taken up two stolen pieces of cloth (28 Mar.)
- Philip Syng in Phila. has for sale a turner's wheel and lath (28 Mar.)
- Adv. of Benjamin Rawle in Water St. (28 Mar.)
- James Lynch, lately from St. Christopher's and designing to return there, desires to settle his accounts (28 Mar.)
- Accounts with estate of John Kinnard, late of Moreland Twp., Phila. Co., dec'd, to be settled with John and Anthony Kinnard, execs. (28 Mar.)
- John White, who has removed from Fifth St. to the Sign of the Dove, next door to George Plumley's, cutler, has medicines for sale (28 Mar.)
- Renard Fosset, English apprentice lad, calker by trade, runaway from Margaret Pocklenton of Phila. (28 Mar.)
- Real estate in Germantown and Northern Liberties for sale; apply to Thomas Tilbury at Robeson's mill (28 Mar.)
- Matthew Potter, living on James Logan's plantation near Germantown, offers reward for recovery of strayed bull (28 Mar.)
- Real estate for sale by public vendue at house of John Biddle in Elbow Lane; for particulars enquire of John Wright in Chestnut St. (28 Mar.)
- John Bell, servant, born at Albany of Dutch and Swedish parents, age c. 33, runaway from Joseph Gray at the Sign of the Conestogoe Waggon (28 Mar.)
- Ship *Mermaid*, Capt. Woodrop, was driven ashore on Cape Charles (5 Apr.)
- Sloop from New York, Capt. Bourjeau, was taken and carried to Leoganne (5 Apr.)
- A snow, Capt. Styles, is lost (5 Apr.)
- Accounts with estate of Samuel Faris, miller, late of Warwick Twp., Bucks Co., dec'd, to be settled with Helen Faris and Andrew Hodge, admins. (5 Apr.)

1749

Real estate to be sold by Joseph Wharton at David Cowpland's in Chester; some lots join upon Joseph Parker's lots; upland meadow in Borough of Chester joins on S. a lot of Edward Russel and on the N. a lot of Jacob Howell (5 Apr.)

On 27 Mar. before William Allen, Esq., appeared Michael Hillegas, of Phila., shopkeeper, bringing Moses Thomas and Joseph Rush, both of Phila., house-carpenters, who deposed that Hillegas was in good health and sound of mind (5 Apr.)

Mare strayed or stolen from John Lawrence of Maxfield Twp., Bucks Co., near Thomas Yarly's; reward if mare is brought to owner or to Thomas Rush in Lower Dublin (5 Apr.)

William Mooney, Irish servant, age c. 20, carver, runaway from Brian Wilkinson of Phila., ship-carver (5 Apr.)

For freight or passage to Madeira in brigantine Hawk, James Brown commander, now at Kock's wharf, agree with the master or George Bascum, merchant, at his lodgings at the Widow Evans in Market St. (5 Apr.)

Two-thirds of mills in Chester Twp. for sale; apply to Rees Williams (5 Apr.)

House, many years a tavern, in Market St., Borough of Wilmington, Newcastle Co., to be sold; apply to Sarah Downing on the premises (5 Apr.)

Ship Sea-flower, of N.Y., Capt. Elberson, on 13 Feb. overset near Atwood's Key in the Bahamas; all on board were rescued by Capt. Cale (13 Apr.)

Persons murdered on the sloop Vulcan, Capt. Bergeau, were Abraham Bergeau (master), James Filling (mate), John Mercy, Nicholas Little and Samuel Brookman (sailors); the man who escaped is Philip Steuart (13 Apr.)

Capt. Devereux from the Havanna reported at New York that the brigantine Sarah, Capt. Harris, of New York, was seized at the Havanna (13 Apr.)

Brigantine Pembroke, Capt. Burrows, of Phila., has arrived at Cork (13 Apr.)

Timothy Matlack in Market St. offers reward for lost pocketbook; it contained a bond to Francis Collins (13 Apr.)

Accounts with estate of William Cotes, Sr., late of the Northern Liberties, brick-maker, dec'd, to be settled with Thomas Say, admin.; the execs. of the estate of William Cotes, Jr., also late of the Northern Liberties, dec'd, are Thomas Say and John Cotes, Jr. (13 Apr.)

The windmill on the island opposite to Phila. will be sold; apply to George Adams and John Darding (13 Apr.)

William Grey will sell tenement where he lives, along with the bakehouse and granary, all in Morris's Alley (13 Apr.)

Land, part of estate of Jacob Casdorp, late of Phila., shipwright, dec'd, is for sale; one piece of land was bought of William Cotes, Sr., dec'd; one lot at Fair-hill meeting-house was bought of James Holt; a lot on Delaware was bought of Benjamin Shoemaker; apply to Thomas Say or Henry Casdorp, son and admin. of the decedent (13 Apr.)

Horse has been taken up at plantation of John Davis in Plymouth (13 Apr.)

1749

Accounts with estate of Joseph Linton, late of Southampton, Bucks Co., dec'd, to be settled with Cuthbert Hayhurst and Benjamin and John Linton, admins. (13 Apr.)

Plantation in Providence, 21 miles from Phila., for sale; apply to Joshua Maddox (13 Apr.)

A certain Hunt, a lime-seller in Boston, has wounded two boys, one the only son of Capt. Cussens (20 Apr.); Hunt hanged himself in prison (27 Apr.)

Mention of Capt. Kip from Coracoa (20 Apr.)

Tract of land in Moyamensing, late estate of Andrew Hamilton, dec'd, for sale by William Allen and Joseph Turner, execs. (20 Apr.)

Cask of merchandize, imported in the Mary-galley, George Lawson commander, was left at store of Smith and James (20 Apr.)

R. Croxall seeks a hammer-man and refiner at the Baltimore Ironworks on Patapsco, Md. (20 Apr.)

William Blows, English servant, age c. 28, runaway from John Hirst, of Buckingham, Bucks Co. (20 Apr.)

Thomas Johnson, English convict servant, age c. 30, and Richard Prestwood, English convict servant, age c. 40, runaways from the Nottingham Ironworks in Baltimore Co.; reward for their capture is offered by Alexander Lawson (20 Apr.)

For freight or passage to London in ship Desire, William Clark commander, agree with Cuzzins and Smyter in Water St. (20 Apr.)

Dick, Negro, country born, age c. 28, runaway from Abraham Humphries, tanner, of St. George's Hundred, Newcastle Co. (20 Apr.)

M a Brakel Vander Kluyt, about to depart, has left his arcanum antevenereum with Peter Nygh, M.D., in Second St. (20 Apr.)

Jacob Johnston, servant, born in England, age 24, runaway from James Graham, of West Nantmell Twp., Chester Co. (20 Apr.)

John Haines, English servant, age c. 30, and Thomas Welch, Irish servant, age c. 18, runaways from Joseph Ellis, of Newtown, Gloucester Co. (20 Apr.)

Adv. of Conrad Swichehauser, living next door to Septimus Robeson in Arch St.; he makes and gilds frames for pictures (20 Apr.)

Negro, age c. 40, runaway from Valentine Dushane, Jr., of Redlion Hundred, Newcastle Co. (20 Apr.)

John Welch, Irish servant, age c. 21, shoemaker, runaway from John Brown of Pequa, Lancaster Co. (20 Apr.)

House in Germantown, between Samuel M'Call's house and bakehouse of Leonard Stoneburner, for sale (27 Apr.)

John Morgan, servant, born in Ireland, age c. 18, runaway from Thomas Pryor in Solbury Twp., Bucks Co. (27 Apr.)

Horse strayed from pasture of George David Seekel at upper end of Market St. (27 Apr.)

Plantation in Thornbury Twp., Chester Co., late estate of John Willis, Jr., where John Smith now dwells, for sale; apply to William Webb, Esq., in Kennet, or to Amos Brown and Benjamin Gibbs, Jr., at Christine Bridge (27 Apr.)

House and tanyard, late of Barrack Wright of Germantown, tanner, dec'd, in Germantown, opposite to Thomas Carvell's; apply to Dirk Keyser and Thomas Carvell, admins., to buy (27 Apr.)

Plantation near the Frankford meeting-house ground will be sold by public vendue at the Sign of the Indian King, being the house of John Biddle in Market St.; sale is by the executor of John Bood, dec'd (27 Apr.)

Capt. Stevens has arrived at Boston from Louisbourgh; the snow *Irene*, Capt. Garrison, has arrived at Sandy Hook with 100 Moravians on board; Capt. Barnes has arrived at New York from Cape Breton (4 May)

Capt. Stupart in the ship *Macclesfield* has arrived at Phila. from London (4 May)

Adv. of George Smith, next door to Townsend White's in Front St. (4 May)

Mrs. Jane Noyer will open school in Phila. to teach French and writing to young ladies (4 May)

House in Lombard St. for sale; enquire of James Pillar, almost opposite Lyn-Ford Lardner's in Second St. (4 May)

Sloop *Robert*, Robert Bascome commander, will sail for Bermuda (4 May)

Mare has been stolen from pasture of David Reynolds of Springfield Twp., Phila. Co. (4 May)

Frank, Negro, who formerly belonged to William Macneell of Phila., runaway from Richard Bevan of Upper Merion, Phila. Co. (4 May); reward will be paid by his master or by William Rakestraw of Phila. (18 May)

Real estate in Phila. for sale, property of Richard Allen, late of Phila. but now of Lower Dublin Twp., Phila. Co., brass founder (4 May)

John Fitzgerald, Irish servant, age c. 20, runaway from Daniel Howell, living in the Welsh Tract, Newcastle Co.; a shipmate, age c. 23, of said Fitzgerald, runaway from David John of the Welsh Tract (4 May)

Thomas Dene, hired man, born in Ireland, silversmith by trade, age c. 30, runaway from George Fling of the Northern Liberties; reward will be paid by Fling or by John Clare at the Goldenfleece in Second St. (4 May)

Capt. Craigie reports plans to transport settlers to Nova Scotia under convoy of Capts. Lloyd and Rous (11 May)

Advs. of George Smith, James Trotter, James Burd and Thomas Maule (11 May)

Booner (alias Mooner), Spanish Negro, runaway from Mrs. Maybury of Cushahopen in Marlborough Twp., Phila. Co. (11 May)

Plantation in Roxburgh Twp. to be let; enquire of Rudeman Robeson in Race St., Phila. (11 May)

Accounts with estate of David Sandelands, dec'd, late of Tinnachum Island, to be settled with William Smith and James Claxton, admins. (11 May)

William Cunningham, shipwright, offers reward for recovery of a horse (11 May)

Mention of Capt. Fones, Otis Little (appointed Surveyor-General of Nova Scotia), Eliakim Palmer (agent for Conn.) and Richard Partridge (agent for Pa. and R.I.) (18 May)

Mr. Bonnin plans to show eight prospects of London (18 May)

Samuel Robeson of Phila. makes pewter still-worms; warning(as to danger in the use of copper worms) by the following doctors in Phila.: John Kearsley, Thomas Graeme, Christopher Witt, Lloyd Zachary, Samuel Preston Moor, William Shippen, Peter Sonmans, Richard Farmar, Phineas Bond and John Kearsley, Jr. (28 May)

For freight or passage to Cork or Dublin in ship <u>Bendall Galley</u>, James M'Elveney master, apply to Conyngham and Gardner (18 May)

Two horses of John Shaw and a cow of Benjamin Corsen, both of Northampton Twp., Bucks Co., have been shot (18 May)

Race horse called the Tinn Grey, formerly belonging to Anthony Waters, has strayed or been stolen from George Ryall (18 May)

John Hudson of Phila. offers reward for recovery of mare stolen or strayed from pasture of Mary Eves, Burlington Co., West New Jersey (18 May)

Hugh Williams, Irish servant, age c. 19, runaway from Samuel Read of Phila., baker (18 May)

John Gilespy, Irish servant, age c. 21, runaway from Robert Nivin of Whiteclay Creek Hundred, Newcastle Co. (18 May)

Notice signed by Fra. Lee, Register, Cecil Co., Md., that commissioners will meet at house of Richard Norton to renew forfeited titles to lots in Charles-Town (18 May)

Horse strayed or stolen from plantation of Abel Armstrong, near Whiteclay Creek, Newcastle Co. (18 May)

John Sheppard will sell lots at the Sign of the Swan on Chestnut Hill in Germantown Twp. (18 May)

Real estate in Northern Liberties, lately property of Andrew Edge, dec'd, for sale; enquire of Joseph Watkins in Mulberry St. (18 May)

Advs. of Fisher and Fussell in Water St. and George Okill in Front St. (25 May)

Real estate in Northern Liberties, adjoining plantation of Lloyd Zachary, property of William Parker, of Phila., blacksmith, for sale (25 May)

House of Jeremiah Piersal, of West Nantmel, Chester Co., was robbed, supposedly by Patrick Higgins; reward if Higgins is taken to Dennis Wellen at the Three Tuns in Nantmell Twp., or James Way, tavern-keeper in Caln Twp. (25 May)

Real estate on west side of Front St., Phila., late estate of William Crosthwaite, to be sold by George Okill, exec. (25 May)

Accounts with estate of Hugh Young, late of Wright's-town, Bucks Co., dec'd, to be settled with Robert and Eleanor Young, admins. (25 May)

Five lots on Society Hill in Lombard St. to be sold at the coffee-house of Thomas James, Jr.; for details apply to James Burd, merchant, in Phila. (25 May)

May O'Donnel, Irish servant, age 22, runaway from Dennis Cunrads of Lower Merion, Phila. Co. (25 May)

Stephen Greenleaf, servant, age c. 23, runaway from Jonathan Ingham of Solbury, Bucks Co. (25 May)

Robert Moore, house-carpenter, runaway from his bail, Joseph Hubbs, living in North Wales, Phila. Co. (25 May)

1749   49

Reward if horse strayed from plantation of George Logan in
   Makefield, Bucks Co., is brought to the Red-lion tavern in
   Newtown or to Robert Heaton's in Northampton; reward will
   be paid by Joseph Insley, Robert Heaton or John Roney in
   Makefield (25 May)

Pasture in Moyamensing to be sold by Widow Mary Lownes, living
   near the premises (25 May)

Sloop *Morning Star*, Capt. Holmes, has arrived at New York from
   Cape Breton (1 June)

Gabriel Nesman, minister at the Swedish Church in Wicacoa,
   will preach in French (1 June)

Adv. of Stephen Potts, bookbinder, who has removed from Market St. to Third St. (1 June)

Jacob Schoonmaker, Jr., offers reward for recovery of mare
   strayed from commons of Phila. (1 June)

Bag of money taken up near Germantown; apply to John Phipps
   of Abington (1 June)

Isaac Cromwell, Mulatto servant, age 40, and Anne Green, English servant, age c. 45, runaways from Thomas Cresap, living
   in old town Potomack, Frederick Co., Md.; reward if servants
   are brought to Cresap or to James Whitehead, Keeper of the
   Phila. Workhouse (1 June)

Adv. of John Kidd, next door to Capt. John Philips's on Fishbourne's wharf (1 June)

Two mares strayed from plantation of John Ellit in Mill-creek
   Twp., near Bethlehem, Bucks Co. (1 June)

Horse strayed from Matthew Young of Fogg's Manor, Chester Co.,
   has been seen at plantation of Nathaniel Grubb in Goshen;
   reward if horse is returned to owner or to John Biddle in
   Market St. (1 June)

Accounts with estate of George Shiers, late of Phila., merchant,
   dec'd, to be settled with Daniel Durborow and Hannah Shiers,
   exec. (1 June)

House, late of Dominicus Gasner, in Creesam, Germantown Twp.,
   and lot in Springfield Twp., near William Ottinger's, for
   sale; apply to Anthony Newhouse at the paper-mill on Sandy
   Run or to Christian Lehman in Germantown (1 June)

Accounts with estate of Thomas Parry, late of Manor of Moreland, Phila. Co., dec'd, to be settled with Jane, John and
   Stephen Parry, execs. (1 June)

Two Negroes for sale; apply to John Mifflin in Market St. (1
   June)

Margaret Brown, Irish servant, age c. 36, runaway from John
   Leadlie of Wright's Town, Bucks Co. (1 June)

Borax for sale by James Benezet at house where Richard Hockley
   formerly lived (8 June)

Adv. of Alexander Hamilton in Water St., fronting house of
   Capt. John Philips (8 June)

Cordage, cables, rigging for sale by Samuel M'Call, Sr., or
   Nehemiah Allen, cooper, below the drawbridge in Phila. (8
   June)

Plantation in Marlborough, Chester Co., for sale; apply to
   Lewis Davis in Haverford (8 June)

James Steell, servant, New England born, age c. 23, runaway from William Pennell, of Middletown, Chester Co.; runaway was seen at George Gray's ferry (8 June)

Mare broke into pastures of William Bell; apply to William Bell, innkeeper, in White-horse-alley (8 June)

List of strays in custody of George Boone, ranger (8 June)

Nicholas Cowalt, servant, born in Holland, age c. 25, runaway from Alexander Murray at the Union Ironworks in Hunterdon Co., West New Jersey; reward if Cowalt is brought to the ironworks or to Allen and Turner in Phila. (8 June)

John Lowe, servant, age c. 23, and Hugh M'Laughlin, native Irishman, runaways from Robert Stewart of Leacock Twp., Lancaster Co., and Peter Worrel, Esq. (8 June)

James Mackelliek, servant, born in Ireland, age c. 29, weaver, runaway from Patrick Heany of Little Conewago, Lancaster Co. (8 June)

Daniel Macdonald, Irish or Highland servant, age c. 18 or 20, runaway from Patrick Brown of Lebanon, Hunterdon Co., West New Jersey (8 June)

Robert Carroll, Irish servant, age 22 or 23, runaway from George Polley, of Phila., shoemaker (8 June)

Mare came to plantation of Jonathan West of Warwick Twp., Bucks Co. (8 June)

Real estate upon Salem Creek and in Maidenhead upon Assancunk Creek for sale; apply to William Morris, Jr., in Trenton (8 June)

James Wickrey, servant, this country born, age c. 28, runaway from Swan Boon, of Darby Twp., Chester Co. (8 June)

Peter, Negro, age c. 19, runaway from Elizabeth Biles of Trenton (8 June)

Mare strayed or stolen from William Douglas of Earltown, Lancaster Co.; reward if mare is brought to Squire Edwards in Lancaster Co. or John Hambrygt at the Sign of the White Horse (8 June)

Jack, Mulatto, runaway from Hugh Mathews of Hartsborough, Phila. Co. (8 June)

For freight or passage to Barbados in the brigantine Dolphin, Moses Minshell commander, at Wilmington, agree with Griffith Minshell, Robert Lewis or the master (8 June)

Sloop Vulcan, Capt. Smelt, has arrived at Nantasket with news of Gov. Hobson of Nova Scotia (15 June)

Ship Desire, William Clark, will sail for London (15 June)

James Robinson, Scotch servant, lately brought over by Capt. Stupart, age c. 37 or 38, runaway from Samuel M'Call, Sr. (15 June)

Time of English servant for sale; enquire of Anthony Whitley at the Ship Aground on Chestnut St. wharf (15 June)

Adv. of John Harris at house where John Harding formerly lived on Market St. wharf (15 June)

Mare strayed from John Goodshius of Germantown, sadler (15 June)

For freight or passage to Barbados in schooner Bredah, John Gilbert commander, agree with the master at Powell's wharf (15 June)

Adv. of Benjamin Britton, baker and boulter, in Chestnut St. (15 June)

Hutton and Gordon in Norris's Alley, Phila., sell tobacco and snuff (15 June)

Indented servants, just imported in the snow *Jenny and Sally*, Brice M'Clelland commander, to be sold by Conyngham and Gardner; for freight or passage to the West Indies apply to the master at William Spafford's (15 June)

Land in and adjoining the Borough of Bristol, Bucks Co., for sale; enquire of Alexander Graydon in Bristol or William M'Ilvaine in Phila. (15 June)

Cow strayed from Joseph Marks's place near Germantown (15 June)

Edward Pare intends for Barbados (15 June)

Real estate, including lots in Second St., opposite to Mr. Halbert's, will be sold in Second St., near Peter Snow's; enquire of Andrew Farrell, tanner, in Chestnut St. (15 June)

Negro man and girl for sale; enquire at Benjamin Gomez's, next door to Charles Edgar (15 June)

Horse strayed or stolen from Widow Ball's plantation in the Northern Liberties; reward if horse is brought to John Francis in Arch St., Phila., or to Samuel Roberts in New Providence (15 June)

Capt. John Mackey, late clerk of Newcastle Co., dec'd, had purchased the house in Wilmington wherein Capt. James Chambers, since dec'd, lived; said James was brother of John Chambers, merchant of Antigua (15 June)

Horse strayed or stolen from James Russel, of Phila., coachmaker (15 June)

Adv. of William Rush in Front St. (15 June)

Adv. of John and Christopher Carnan in Water St. (15 June)

Reward for recovery of horse strayed or stolen from plantation of John Spruce in Whiteland Twp., Chester Co., if the horse is brought to Spruce or to William Richards at the Plough and Harrow in Third St., Phila. (15 June)

Several officers of Col. Shirley's regiment have arrived at Boston (22 June)

Capt. Wall in a snow of Phila. is cast away on Port-Morant Keys (22 June)

Last week at Newcastle John Gillespie and John Roach were sentenced to death for burglary and John Slain for rape (22 June)

Real estate in Kensington in the Northern Liberties for sale; enquire of John Baker, of Phila., carpenter (22 June)

Thomas Mullan, at the Sign of the Tun in Water St., offers reward for recovery of a 53-pound turtle that broke out of Carpenter's dock (22 June)

Adv. of George Guion at Archibald Montgomery's in Chestnut St. (22 June)

Land in Passyunk Twp., leading to George Gray's ferry, for sale; enquire of Daniel Dupuy, goldsmith, in Second St. (22 June)

Cows strayed from John Ragennas of the Northern Liberties (22 June)

William Rumsey in Chestnut St. sells medicines (22 June)

Real estate in Northern Liberties, property of Timothy Scarth, tanner, for sale (22 June)

Dickinson's Burnt Buildings, belonging to estate of Jonathan Dickinson, dec'd, for sale; they were taken in execution at suits of Edward Jones (admin. of Francis Jones, dec'd, Thomas Hatton (admin. of Joshua Hyam, dec'd) and Thomas Hatton (admin. of Daniel May, dec'd); Richard Sewell is sheriff (22 June)

Thomas Rabling and wife, in St. Mary's Co., Md., near the head of Jowles's Creek, were struck and killed by lightning (29 June)

Schooner *Anson* sailed for Annapolis with Col. Gorham on board (29 June)

Capt. Phenix arrived at New York from Turks Island (29 June)

Capt. Jauncey from Madeira gives account of murder at sea by four Portuguese of Capt. Alexander Kinnenmouth, John Carr (mate), John Welch and William Dudley (seamen) of the ship *Venus* (29 June)

Adv. of William Rigdon, house-, ship-, and sign-painter from London, next door to the Phenix in Front St. (29 June)

Adv. of John Erwin in Strawberry Alley (29 June)

Real estate, known as Byerley's lands, in Morris and Hunterdon counties for sale by Joseph Murray and John Kinsey, execs. of Thomas Byerley, dec'd (29 June)

George, Spanish Mulatto servant, who formerly ran away from Charles Read of Burlington, runaway from George Marple of Goshen Neck, Burlington Co. (29 June)

House in Market St. to be let by Hannah Pearson (29 June)

House belonging to William Till, Esq., in Water St. to be let; enquire of Peter Bard (29 June)

Time of man servant for sale; enquire of John Stinson in Walnut St. (29 June)

James Gordon on ship *Myrtilla* at Hamilton's wharf offers a reward for recovery of stolen silver watch (29 June)

Three cows strayed from William Brown in Walnut St. (29 June)

Land and fulling-mill, adjoining land of John Renshaw, William Palmer and Samuel Ashmead, for sale; enquire of George Harding, leather-dresser, in Market St. (29 June)

Accounts with John Norwood, late of Phila., merchant, to be settled with Peter Bard, Henry Elves and James Benezet (29 June)

Owners may claim two horses in the pound by applying to Joseph Scull, pound-keeper (29 June)

William Tucker, Irish servant, age c. 17, runaway from Samuel Read of Phila., baker (29 June)

Col. Cornwallis is appointed governor of Nova Scotia (6 July)

Major Gilman arrived at Boston with Capt. Foster; mention is made of Phillips's regiment and of Capt. Rous (6 July)

Capt. Hutchison arrived at Newcastle with servants from Cork (6 July)

Meadow known as Carpenter's Island, late in the possession of Matthew Moss, dec'd, for sale by Hannah Moss, admin. (6 July)

Frances Duffy, Irish servant, age c. 18, runaway from John Glenn, Jr., in East Nottingham, Chester Co. (6 July)

Lot of land in Market St. for sale; enquire of John Howard (6 July)

A small wherry has been taken up by Job Jacob in borough of Wilmington (6 July)

William Thompson, indented servant, born at Duck Creek, Newcastle Co., runaway from John Sparling, of corporation of New Brunswick, N.J. (6 July)

Adv. of Thomas Davies, dry-scourer, in Front St. (6 July)

Land in Chester Twp. for sale; enquire of Thomas Barton on the premises or William Humphries, merchant, in Phila. (6 July)

Accounts with estate of Gilbert Albertson, late of Gloucester Co., N.J., dec'd. to be settled with the widow, Jane Albertson, admin., now living on Society Hill, near Samuel Hall, in Phila. (6 July)

James Bryan seeks position as cook; he is to be heard of at the Duke of Cumberland in Walnut St. (6 July)

Adv. of Peter Knowlton, free fan-maker from London, in Sassafras St., near the Moravian Church (6 July)

Mare strayed from Abraham Coffing of Abington Twp., Phila. Co. (6 July)

Accounts with estate of William Crosthwaite, late of Phila., peruke-maker, dec'd, to be settled with George Okill, exec. (6 July)

William Wilkinson, servant, age c. 20, runaway from John Barclay, of Colerain Twp., Lancaster Co. (6 July)

Valentine Strong, Irish servant, age c. 20, runaway from William Robeson in Southampton, Bucks Co. (6 July)

John M'Neal (alias Oneal), Irish servant, age c. 24, who served some time in Talbot, Md., runaway from Benjamin Weatherby of Marple Twp., Chester Co. (6 July)

New ship for sale by Thomas Howell at Marcus Hook, Chester Co. (6 July)

Mare strayed or stolen from Frederick Whitely of Lancaster (6 July)

John Standly, Irish servant, who served his former time with one Martin near town of Chester, runaway from John Patrick of East Nantmell, Chester Co. (6 July)

Capt. Mudie arrived at Boston from Lisbon (13 July)

Reference to Richard Partridge, William Bollan, Peregrine Furye and Robert Charles, colonial agents in London (13 July)

Above 60 views shown by Samuel Jackson in Strawberry Alley, next door to the tavern (13 July)

Peter Allricks in Newcastle Co. has taken up a colt (13 July)

Adv. of Benjamin Gomez, below the drawbridge, next door to Capt. Edgar's (13 July)

Benjamin Bagnall in Front St. repairs and sells watches (13 July)

Plantation in Penn's Neck for sale; apply to James Barclay near said place or to James Guthery of Mill-creek Hundred, Newcastle Co. (13 July)

Elisha Bullingham, apprentice, age c. 16, house-carpenter, runaway from Matthew Forsyth of Chesterfield, Burlington Co. (13 July)

Scipio, Negro, who is said to have been seen at Mr. Harris's on Susquehannah, runaway from Capt. Thomas Prather of Prince George's Co., Md.; reward will be paid if slave is brought to George Croghan or George Gibson in Lancaster or Marcus Kuhl in Phila. (13 July)

Morgan Murphy, Irish servant, age c. 20, runaway from Reas Thomas in Pencader Hundred, Newcastle on Delaware (13 July)

Nasey, Negro, age c. 40, runaway from John Cox of Sassafras, Cecil Co., Md. (13 July)

Capt. John Martin has for sale Irish linens at Capt. Montgomery's in Chestnut St. (13 July)

Stallion stolen from stable of Rees Francis of Whiteland, Chester Co., supposedly by one Joseph Wilson; reward if horse is brought to John Hunt in Black Horse Alley, Phila., or John Hambricht at the White Horse on Conestogoe Road (13 July)

Christopher Robins in Whitemarsh has taken up a horse (13 July)

On 29 June Timothy Brown came to Boston from Canada; he gave information he obtained from Daniel Maddox (the King's interpreter); mention of Cape Cod Indians who were under Col. Gorham in 1745; captives in Canada are Jonathan Dore from Rochester, N.H., the daughter of Widow Francis taken near Casco Bay, two young women named Thompson who have a kinsman in Boston named John Bell; mention of Gov. Hobson, Col. Cornwallis and Capt. Rous (20 July)

Cornelius Macdid, born in the parish of Lake, Donegall Co., came to Pa. about 4 years ago in the ship *Happy Return* from Londonderry; his brother James asks that Cornelius come to Capt. Thomas Gray's on Ridley Creek near Newcastle (20 July)

Samuel Sommers, living on Great Egg-harbour River, offers reward for money and articles stolen from a trunk (20 July)

Patrick Kelly, Irish servant, silk-weaver, runaway from Benjamin Benson of Cecil Co., Md. (20 July)

Real estate in Northern Liberties, including lots opposite Mr. Halbert's, to be let or sold by Andrew Farrell, tanner, in Chestnut St. (20 July)

Charity, wife of William West, of Amwell, Hunterdon Co., has eloped from her husband (20 July)

Adv. of John Morgan on Market St. wharf (20 July)

Accounts with estate of Mary Davis, late dec'd, of Phila., to be settled at house of Sarah Lancaster in Blackhorse Alley; Mary and John Jones are admins. (20 July)

Adv. of Randle Mitchell, next door to Capt. Phillips's in Water St. (20 July)

Stephen, Negro, who formerly lived with Dr. Brown, runaway from William Peters, fuller, of Concord, Chester Co. (20 July)

Boston item mentions Capt. Bell from Nova Scotia, Gov. Cornwallis, Gov. Mascarene, Col. Gorham, Mr. Ramsay and Capt. Foster (27 July)

Mary Rogers pardoned at the gallows (27 July)

On 19 June died at Springfield, Mass., Samuel Bliss in his 102 year; he was born there 7 Sept. 1647; he left alive 6 children (27 July)

New York item mentions Capt. Hammond, Capt. Johnson of the sloop Polly, and a slave of Capt. Hall (27 July)

Capt. Gibbs has arrived at Phila. from Turks Island (27 July)

Real estate in Lombard St. for sale; enquire of James Peller (27 July)

Adv. of Thomas Maule, now removed from Front St. to Second St. (27 July)

Mill near Germantown where Christian Kinsing, dec'd, formerly lived will be sold by Jacob Ruch (27 July)

John Bronon, Irish servant, age c. 23, runaway from Thomas Lewis of Pikeland Twp., Chester Co. (27 July)

Plantation in Guynedd Twp., Phila. Co., property of Frederick Knodle, late dec'd, for sale by Michael Cleim and Anna Maria Knodle, execs. (27 July)

Land in Northern Liberties, adjoining plantations of Robert Wall and Elizabeth Paschall, for sale; enquire of Mary Coates in Second St., next door to Thomas Campbell's; debts to the estate of Samuel Coates to be paid promptly (27 July)

Accounts with estate of Samuel Powell, Jr., late of Phila., merchant, to be settled with William Coleman, exec. (27 July)

Thomas Seal from Norfolk, Va., was found guilty of robbery and sentenced to be hanged (3 Aug.)

Boston item mentions Capts. Foster, Rous and Pearse and Gov. Mascarene (3 Aug.)

Water lots in Northern Liberties for sale by John Baker (3 Aug.)

Horse strayed or stolen from Martin Clever; reward if horse is brought to John Behm, German printer, in Arch St. (3 Aug.)

At the house of Widow Jones, the Sign of the Three Crowns, in Second St., will be sold houses in the tenure of John Page and John Clark, another in the tenure of John Knight and the schoolhouse adjoining, now in tenure of Stephen Vidal, property belonging to James Mackey, taken in execution at the suit of Aaron Jenkins (3 Aug.)

James Claypole in Walnut St., who sells colours, also has for sale a lot of ground between the New-market and the improvements of Joseph Scull, Joseph Richards and others (3 Aug.)

Adv. of John Stow in Third St., brass-founder (3 Aug.)

At house of James Coultas will be sold tract of land in Blockley Twp., in the tenure of David Brooks, late property of the estate of Badem Davis, dec'd, taken in execution at suit of Samuel Sellers (3 Aug.)

H.M.S. Hector, Capt. Masterson, sprung her bowsprit and has returned to Hampton-road (10 Aug.)

Mention of Sir Peter Warren and William Bollen in connection with the Cape-Breton money (10 Aug.)

Eliakim Palmer, Esq. (eldest son of the late Thomas Palmer of Boston), agent for Conn., died of fever in London on 19 May (10 Aug.)

Mention of Capts. Pearse and Rous (10 Aug.)

Capt. Dorrell reports the death of Thomas Applewhaite at Barbados (10 Aug.)

Silver cadel cup, weighing 33 ounces, maker's mark P.S., has been stolen from House of James Keappock of Phila. (10 Aug.)

Negro boys for sale; enquire of James M'Cullough in Market St. (10 Aug.)

House and lot near Charles Willing's, Esq., for sale by John and Jedediah Snowden (10 Aug.)

House known as The Center, now in tenure of Robert Dixon, to be sold by Peter Robertson (10 Aug.)

Adv. of George Brooks, glazier, plumber and house painter from Londonderry, now in Market St. (10 Aug.)

Colt strayed from Michael Cassel of Berwick Twp., Lancaster Co.; reward if colt is brought to said Cassel or to Jacob Huber in same township (10 Aug.)

Land on west branch of Monockasy Creek, Bucks Co., bounding on land of William Allen and James Bingham, for sale; it lately belonged to Jeremiah Langhorne, dec'd; enquire of John Pemberton (10 Aug.)

Catherine M'Clue (*alias* Moore), convict servant, runaway from Robert Alison, living near North East, Cecil Co., Md. (10 Aug.)

Negro boy, who says he belongs to Mr. Lane of Cecil Co., Md., is in Phila. Workhouse; Thomas Lang, master of the schooner *Stork*, took the lad to New York, where the boy confessed that he belonged to Mr. Lane (10 Aug.)

Mention of Capts. Pearse and Rouse and of Col. Graham (17 Aug.)

Cornelius Quick, apprentice to Jacob Ryker, baker, of New York, fell from the garret and died (17 Aug.)

Conrad Weiser came to Phila. with deputies of 11 Indian nations (17 Aug.)

Brigantine *Chalkley*, of Phila., Capt. Anderson, is cast away (17 Aug.)

George Doude, servant, age c. 20, runaway from Ralph Whitsitt of Lebanon Twp., Lancaster Co. (17 Aug.)

Negro man, age 22, for sale; enquire of Capt. Stafford Somersall, at James Keappock's, instrument-maker, in Front St. (17 Aug.)

Samson, Negro, age c. 21, runaway from Samuel Lynch of Penn's Neck, Salem Co. (17 Aug.)

William Osbourne, English servant, age c. 22, runaway from Nathan Rigbie of Bohemia, Cecil Co., Md. (17 Aug.)

Negro girl, age c. 15, for sale; enquire of Thomas Williams in Second St. (17 Aug.)

Accounts with estate of Anthony Palmer, Esq., dec'd, to be settled with Thomasine Keith and Elizabeth Palmer, admins. (17 Aug.)

1749

James Harrison at Susquehannah Lower Ferry offers reward for recovery of horse stolen from him (17 Aug.)

M'Brid, Daniel, servant, weaver, runaway from John Rowan near Marcus Hook (17 Aug.)

A Negro butcher for sale; enquire of Edmund Stacy at Capt. Child's in Chestnut St. (17 Aug.)

House and lot in Water St. for sale by Richard Renshaw (17 Aug.)

Lots near Farmar's mill for sale by Samuel Morris (17 Aug.)

Adv. of Thomas Gordon on Powell's wharf (17 Aug.)

Adv. of Townsend White in Front St. (17 Aug.)

Water lot at Wicacoa, bounded on S. by ground of John Parham and on N. by land of William Donaldson, for sale; enquire of Joseph Donaldson at Abraham Mitchell's (17 Aug.)

James Taylor, who lived on northwest fork of Nanticoke River in Dorchester, died from bite of rattlesnake (24 Aug.)

Capt. Stevenson has arrived at Boston in ship from Fyal (24 Aug.)

At Portsmouth, N.H., Capt. John Mitchel of Londonderry, concerned with William Blair in sending threatening letters to Jotham Odiorne, Esq., was convicted and fined 1,000 pounds (24 Aug.)

Fire broke out on new ship of Capt. Thomas of Phila. at Cannon's wharf in New York; Widow Levy, of New York, died of fright (24 Aug.)

Mention of Capts. Mifflin, Ballet, Adams and Clarke and Lt. Kearney (24 Aug.)

Aaron Allen, servant, this country born, age $\underline{c}$. 17, escaped from Joseph Scull of Phila. (24 Aug.)

Forty lots of land in Woodbury Town, Gloucester Co., for sale by Abraham Chattin, living near Woodbury meeting-house (24 Aug.)

Horse strayed or stolen from George Gray's plantation in Passyunk Twp. (24 Aug.)

James Parrock in Phila. offers reward for recovery of strayed or stolen horse (24 Aug.)

George, Spanish Mulatto, who formerly ran away from Charles Read of Burlington, has run away from George Marple of Goshen Neck (24 Aug.)

Edward Dowers is removed from Water St. to the house in Front St. where Thomas Wells lately lived (24 Aug.)

Pamphlet published by William Bradford in Second St. (24 Aug.)

Twelve stills for sale by William Coleman in Phila. (24 Aug.)

Thomas Francis, English servant, age $\underline{c}$. 22, skinner, runaway from Isaac Coran of Phila. (24 Aug.)

Joseph Weaver, English servant, age $\underline{c}$. 24, runaway from Walter Comly of the Manor of Moreland, Phila. Co. (24 Aug.)

Coles Hardwich, English servant, age $\underline{c}$. 23, runaway from Alexander Parker of Phila.; he went off with a fellow named Thomas who served his time with William Morris in Trenton (24 Aug.)

Lots of ground in Kensington in the Northern Liberties for sale; apply to Hannah Boyd, widow, in Kensington, or Thomas Say in Phila. (24 Aug.)

Real estate in Phila., property of William Hawkins of Phila., innholder, for sale (24 Aug.)

Mention of the sloop *Diamond*, Capt. Hunter (31 Aug.)

Thomas Fielding and James Johnson, said to be sailors, robbed Thomas Green and Jacob Kollock; the thieves were arrested and committed; in their chests were found silver spoons marked T.F.; two men, supposedly thieves, tried to buy pistols from Mr. Rush, gunsmith; Capt. Dorrell's cabin and Peter Bard's kitchen were robbed; dogs scared away some men prowling about Mr. Allen's house (31 Aug.)

Friday George Croghan came to Phila. from the Ohio River (31 Aug.)

Capts. James, Brown and Coatam arrived at Phila. with Palatines; Capt. James brought news of Capt. Arthur of Phila. (31 Aug.)

William Lascom in Kingsess Twp. has taken up a cow (31 Aug.)

Accounts to be settled with Dr. John Kinly of Wilmington as he intends for Europe (31 Aug.)

John Wilcocks of Phila. offers reward for recovery of horse (31 Aug.)

Cornelius Sullivan, Irish servant, age c. 22, runaway from Joseph Biddle of Burlington, West New Jersey (31 Aug.)

Young Negro, painter by trade, for sale; enquire of Thomas White, chocolate-maker, in Front St. (31 Aug.)

Lot of land near Passyunk road for sale; plan may be seen at Sarah Cox's, 3rd door below Friends meeting-house in Second St. (31 Aug.)

Thomas Winey, convict servant, imported lately in the *Litchfield*, Capt. Johnson, has run away; he came from goal of Maidstone, Kent Co., Great Britain; with him went a Mulatto slave named James, age 21; reward for their capture offered by William Fitzhugh (31 Aug.)

Capt. Garretson carried home Moravian Greenlanders (7 Sept.)

Andrew Elliot intends for England in the ship *Carolina*, Capt. Mesnard (7 Sept.)

Joseph Wood has for sale real estate, including a tract adjoining the place where David Witherspoon now lives and where Andrew Patterson formerly lived (7 Sept.)

Accounts with estate of Matthew Jung of borough of Lancaster, shopkeeper, dec'd, to be settled with Ann Margaret Jung, Mark Jung and John Graeff (7 Sept.)

Plantation in Plymouth Twp., Phila. Co., for sale; apply to William Currie on the premises or John Ross, Esq., in Phila.; Currie has a Negro girl for sale; enquire at Thomas Williams's in Second St. (7 Sept.)

James Macky has for sale the house wherein he lives in the Northern Liberties and also a house in Second St., Phila., now in the tenure of John Stoops (7 Sept.)

Richard Sewell is candidate for Sheriff of Phila. Co. (7 Sept.)

James Boucher, Irish servant lad, runaway from John Leake of Rockey-Hill (7 Sept.)

Capt. Waterhouse has arrived at Boston (14 Sept.)

French and Indians have taken a sloop belonging to Boston, one Beath master, and also five men belonging to schooner of Capt. Clapham (14 Sept.)

Capt. Davis from Hamburgh reports that the ship Jacob sailed for New York with 300 Palatines and Capts. Tanner and Heysham before him; Capt. Griffiths of New York has arrived in England and Capt. Randel of New York at Amsterdam (14 Sept.)

The vagrant Tom Bell is lurking about New York (14 Sept.)

Two Dutchmen, brothers, by the name of Hawke, are jailed in Phila. on suspicion of counterfeiting doubloons and pieces of eight (14 Sept.)

Mr. Garrick of Phila. escaped from robbers (14 Sept.)

Man got in through window in back part of Capt. Dowers's house in Front St. and a thief got down the chimney into apartment of the Widow Dodd, next door to Capt. Dowers; the thieves escaped; attempts were made to break into the house of Col. White and house of Mrs. Jekyll (14 Sept.)

Sloop Dolphin, Capt. Le Gros, has arrived at Phila., as have Capts. Mason, Russell and Arnott from Holland with Palatines (14 Sept.)

For freight or passage to Charles Town, S.C., in the ship Elliott, John Adams commander, agree with Charles and Alexander Stedman (14 Sept.)

Thomas Neill, age c. 50, cordwainer, runaway from his bail, Patrick Kelly of Cecil Co., Md. (14 Sept.)

Dr. John Rowen will sell plantation where he now lives near Marcus Hook (14 Sept.)

Time of a servant, peruke-maker and barber, for sale; enquire of William Charleton, wig-maker, in Front St. (14 Sept.)

Grist mill on Red Lion Creek for sale by James Robass, of Queen Anne's Co., Md. (14 Sept.)

Bridget Gallacher, servant, age c. 30, runaway from Robert Williams, near Charlestown, Cecil Co., Md. (14 Sept.)

Land known as Dr. Monkton's lot and also ground-rent of a lot in Chestnut St., occupied by Jonathan Beers, George Sharwood, James Bambridge and George House, for sale by Susanna Asheton, widow and admin. of estate of Ralph Asheton, dec'd, and James Humphreys, by order of orphan's court (14 Sept.)

Jury in Suffolk Co., Mass., reversed decision of a former jury that had awarded 750 pounds sterling to Charles Knowles, Esq., in case between him and Dr. William Douglas (21 Sept.)

Capt. Ferguson arrived 10 Sept. at Boston from London (21 Sept.)

Brigantine of Capt. Joel was lost in hurricane at Bermuda (21 Sept.)

William Heaton, apprentice, age between 19 and 20, runaway from John Hutchinson of Bristol, Bucks Co., joiner (21 Sept.)

Adv. of John Malcom, sail-maker from London, at his loft in Kock's wharf near Market St. (21 Sept.)

For freight or passage to London on ship Crown, Michael James master, apply to John Pemberton (21 Sept.)

Dick and Sib, Negroes, runaways from John Baker of Lampeter Twp., Lancaster Co. (21 Sept.)

Horse was brought to William Gray's, the Sign of the Conestogoe Waggon, in Market St. (21 Sept.)

Negro for sale; apply at Mrs. Howell's in Market St. (21 Sept.)

If John Hunt is alive and will call at John Haword's in Kent. Co., Md., he will receive a packet from England directed to him at George William Forrester's, containing account of his uncle's death (21 Sept.)

Brick house in Fourth St., now in tenure of Gilbert Tennent, is to be sold (21 Sept.)

Capts. Falconer, Wedham, Partridge and Hussey have arrived at Boston (28 Sept.)

Gov. Cornwallis has sent armed vessels to prevent trade to Cape Breton (28 Sept.)

Indians are reported to have killed two of Col. Gorham's men (28 Sept.)

In Phila. James Johnson, Thomas Fielding and Thomas Green have been found guilty of robbery on the highway (28 Sept.)

Ferdinando Huses, tried in Phila. for murder of John Brown, has been found guilty of manslaughter (28 Sept.)

John Webster is to be tried in Phila. for breaking open the store of Smith and Jones and stealing gold and silver money (28 Sept.); he is found guilty of felony (5 Oct.)

Joseph and John Redman of Phila. offer reward for recovery of two horses (28 Sept.)

Aaron Leidenburg, English servant, age c. 31, a good scholar, runaway from John Hirst, of Buckingham, Bucks Co. (28 Sept.)

William Blows, English servant, age c. 28, illiterate, runaway from John Hirst, of Buckingham (28 Sept.)

Negro, a skinner, for sale; enquire of Stephen Anthony in Second St. (28 Sept.)

William Jones, of Lomberton, Sommerset Co., N.J., offers reward for recovery of a stolen mare (28 Sept.)

Horse has strayed or been stolen from James Webb of Lancaster (28 Sept.)

For freight or passage to Newry and Liverpool in the Earl of Holderness, John Hamilton commander, agree with Thomas Walker at Lloyd's wharf (28 Sept.)

Jeremiah Wood has made off with pilot boat owned by Thomas Holway of Phila., victualler (28 Sept.)

For freight or passage to Barbados in the snow Mary Ann, John White commander, agree with John Erwin in Strawberry Alley (28 Sept.)

Horse stolen or strayed from pasture of Jacob Shoemaker, Jr., in Kensington (28 Sept.)

Unsatisfied accounts against the First Phila. Lottery to be brought to William Coleman (28 Sept.)

Accounts with estate of Peter Baynton to be settled with John Baynton in Front St., exec. (28 Sept.)

H,M.S. Mermaid, Capt. Montague, arrived at Boston with William Bollan on board (5 Oct.)

1749

Capt. Anderson, late of the brigantine Chalkley, was accidentally killed when a passenger on board Capt. Bosworth (5 Oct.)

Monday last the following were elected: (for Phila. Co.) representatives, John Kinsey, Isaac Norris, Edward Warner, Joseph Trotter, James Morris, Oswald Peele, Owen Evans, Hugh Evans; sheriff, Richard Sewell; coroner, George Heap; commissioner, Evan Morgan; assessors, Robert Thomas, William Foulke, Abraham Levant, James Jones, John Morris, Jonathan Zane - (for Bucks Co.), representatives, John Woolston, Samuel Eastbourne, Joseph Hamton, Mahlon Kirkbride, Richard Walker, Griffith Owen, Gerret Vansant, John Hall; sheriff, John Hart; coroner, William Smith; commissioner, John Chapman; assessors, Giles Knight, Daniel Palmer, William Murray, William Edwards, Thomas Paxton, Abraham Vastine - (for Chester Co.), representatives, Joseph Gibbons, George Ashbridge, Henry Hockley, Thomas Chandler, Nathaniel Grubb, Nathaniel Pennock, Roger Hunt, Thomas Cummings; sheriff, John Owen; coroner, Isaac Lee; commissioner, Isaac Pearson; assessors, Elisha Gatchell, John Pusey, John Fairlamb, Joseph Bartholomew, Phineas Lewis, Thomas Pearson - (for Lancaster Co.), representatives, Arthur Patterson, Peter Worrall, James Wright, Calvin Cooper; sheriff, Andrew Worrick; coroner, Robert Stewart - (for Newcastle Co.), representatives, William Armstrong, John Vaunce, John M'Cool, James Macmechan, John Edwards, Jehu Curtis; sheriff, John Vandyke; coroner, Samuel Silsby. On Tue. last Israel Pemberton, Sr., and Thomas Leech were chosen burgesses of Phila.; assessors chosen were Charles Jones, Thomas Gordon, Abel James, Joseph Stretch, Samuel Morris, Joseph Redman; Thomas Lawrence was elected mayor (5 Oct.)

George Sweeney, Irish servant, age c. 20, runaway from John Wilcocks (5 Oct.)

Persons wishing employment to cut wood at Mount Holly Ironworks are to apply to John Abraham Denormandie, Esq., at Bristol, to Peter Bard and Samuel Hazard in Phila., and to John Dennis at the ironworks (5 Oct.)

Plantation in Goshen Twp., Chester Co., for sale; apply to James Serrill in Upper Darby Twp. (5 Oct.)

Plantation where Mr. Tuett lives in Nottingham Twp., Burlington Co., N.J., to be let; apply to Elizabeth Biles in Trenton (5 Oct.)

For freight or passage to Maryland in ship Speedwell, apply to James Creagh at Mr. Graham's in Front St. (5 Oct.)

Real estate for sale by Richard Renshaw or Rebecca Steel; included are two houses on Society Hill, bounded on the S. by ground belonging to the estate of William Annis, dec'd; still another house is in Germantown between Samuel M'Call's, Jr., and bakehouse of Leonard Stoneburner (5 Oct.)

Land in Plumstead, Bucks Co., and Myomensing for sale; apply to Benjamin Kendall, shoemaker, in Chestnut St. (5 Oct.)

Horse strayed from Matthias Geiger of Piles-grove, Salem Co.; reward if horse is returned to Michael Hillegas in Phila. or to the Roman minister in Cushahopen (5 Oct.)

Mare strayed from Benjamin Petton of Hopewell (5 Oct.)

Mare taken up between Middle Ferry and Phila.; owner to apply to John Eyre, tavern-keeper at the Three Stars in Phila. (5 Oct.)

New ship to be sold by Thomas Howell at Marcus Hook, Chester Co. (5 Oct.)

Horse stolen from pasture of William Cook in Maidenhead, Hunterdon Co. (5 Oct.)

Mills and plantation in and joining to Allen's-town in Upper Freehold, Monmouth Co., N.J., for sale by Sarah Allen and Robert Lawrence, execs. of estate of Nathan Allen, dec'd (5 Oct.)

John Reily is removed from Second St. to Front St.; he draws instruments in writing; Reily and Thomas Archdall sell rum, sugar, salt (5 Oct.)

John Smith and Abel James will settle their business as soon as possible; one of them intends for England (5 Oct.)

Mare that formerly belonged to Jacob Bennet has strayed from Dr. John Rowan near Marcus Hook; reward if horse is delivered to James Claxton at the Three Tuns in Chestnut St., Phila., or to Aubry Bevan in Chester or to John Kerlin at Marcus Hook (5 Oct.)

Adv. of Content Nicholson, shopkeeper, who has removed from Strawberry Alley to Chestnut St., next door to Christopher Marshall's (5 Oct.)

Horse lost from Thomas Woolley's stable in Strawberry Alley; reward if horse is taken to Woolley or to Alexander Forman, Jr., of New Britain, Bucks Co., owner (5 Oct.)

Widow in Phila. will take to board children who come from the country for schooling; enquire of Edward Shippen or Benjamin Franklin (5 Oct.)

Horse stolen from Sarah Wallace, living in London-grove Twp., Chester Co.; supposed thief is John Owen (5 Oct.)

Abraham Magee, Irish servant, tailor, runaway from Michael Hutchinson of Makefield Twp., Bucks Co.; Magee went away in company with Bartle Maquire, an Irishman (5 Oct.)

John Inglis on Hamilton's wharf sells Jesuit's bark (5 Oct.)

An Englishman, who said his name was William Thompson, on the highway in Prince George's Co., Md., stole from John Jones a horse, money, a bond against John Hope, a bill of sale from William Donaldson, and a pass from Mayor Charles Willing; reward for the capture of the thief will be paid by John Jones or Joseph Beeler in Uwlchland, Chester Co. (5 Oct.)

Boston item mentions Capt. Donnel, Capt. Joseph Gorham, M. Millard (a priest); Phila. item mentions M. Jonquiere (new Gov.-Gen.), age between 60 and 70, and M. Gallissoniere (former Gov.-Gen.) (12 Oct.)

Vain attempt of highwaymen Fielding and Johnson to escape; they were sentenced to death; Ferdinando Huses, convicted of manslaughter in the killing of John Brown, was burnt in the hand; John Webster was sentenced to be whipped for stealing money from a store; Ann Brooks, convicted of receiving stolen goods from Negroes, was sentenced to three months in prison and to pay a fine of 50 pounds (12 Oct.)

For freight or passage to Antigua in the ship *Lesley*, James Ballendine commander, apply to said commander (12 Oct.)

Christopher Hausse, age c. 22, and wife Regina (Lang), runaway servants from James Comings in Northampton Twp., Bucks Co. (12 Oct.)

Reward offered for recovery of horses strayed from pasture of William Bell, living at the White Horse in Market St., Phila. (12 Oct.)

Samuel Parr, of Phila., merchant, desires to settle all his accounts (12 Oct.)

James Adams, at the Post-Office in Phila., offers reward for recovery of strayed horse (12 Oct.)

Accounts with estate of George Harding, late of Phila., skinner, dec'd, to be settled with Elizabeth Harding, admin. (12 Oct.)

Reward offered for recovery of strayed or stolen horse of Michael Ege in Second St., Phila.; horse to be taken to him or to Lawrence Shwytser or Christoper Sauer in Germantown (12 Oct.)

For freight or passage to St. Christophers in sloop <u>Royal Ranger</u>, Samuel Brownlow commander, apply to Brownlow at the Sign of the Crown in Market St. or George Bascome in Water St. (12 Oct.)

John Mecomb offers reward for recovery of boat drifted from his landing in the Jerseys, over against Newcastle (12 Oct.)

Samuel Suther, schoolmaster, in Cherry St., teaches High German; enquire of Michael Slater, High German minister (12 Oct.)

Real estate in Passyunk, now in possession of Mr. Brotherson, for sale; enquire of Thomas Hopkinson in Phila. (12 Oct.)

Capt. Dunbibin in a brigantine and Capt. Dickinson in a sloop were both driven ashore near Sandy Hook (19 Oct.)

The following were elected for York Co., representatives, John Wright, John Armstrong; sheriff, Hance Hamilton; coroner, Nicholas Ryland - for Sussex Co., representatives, Jacob Kollock, Woolsey Burton, Ryves Holt, John Neill, John Clowes, Shepard Kollock; sheriff, Peter Clowes; coroner, William Shankland (19 Oct.)

Adv. of George Smith, now removed from his store next door to Townsend White's in Front St., to house where John Wallace lately dwelt (19 Oct.)

Adv. of Samuel Burge at house where William Till lately dwelt in Water St. (19 Oct.)

For freight or passage to Antigua in the brigantine <u>Cumberland</u>, Clement Conyers commander, agree with Joseph Conyers near the drawbridge or the master at Oswald Peele's wharf (19 Oct.)

For freight or passage to Charles-Town, S.C., in ship <u>St. Andrew</u>, James Abercrombie master, agree with Charles and Alexander Stedman or the master at Stamper's wharf (19 Oct.)

Adv. of James Lytton, next door to the Royal Oak in Lombard St. (19 Oct.)

Henry Harrison in Market St. sells goods imported in the <u>Dove</u>, Capt. Macartie (19 Oct.)

Cattle for sale at plantation late of Joseph Cooper, dec'd, in Newtown, Gloucester Co. (19 Oct.)

Land, mill and tanyard on Germantown Road for sale; enquire of Andrew Hawke (19 Oct.)

Adv. of Robert Moore in Phila. (19 Oct.)

Mare strayed from William Whitebread in Second St., Phila., innholder; reward if mare is brought to him or to the owner, Lewis Thomas in Pencader Hundred, Newcastle Co. (19 Oct.)

John Donesan, Irish servant, age c. 24, runaway from Robert Simonton of Lancaster Co. (19 Oct.)

Thomas Nicholls and one George, seamen, runaways from the sloop *Speedwell*, Nathan Solly master, in New York (19 Oct.)

Plantation in Bucks Co. for sale; enquire of Margaret Johnson on the premises (19 Oct.)

Accounts with estate of Richard Marple to be settled with Alice Marple (19 Oct.)

Shares in a grist-mill in Chester Co. for sale; enquire of Rees Williams (19 Oct)

On 8 Oct. in a gale Capt. Maxwell narrowly escaped being driven upon the rocks in Nantasket Road (26 Oct.)

Reports from Halifax concerned with Major Gilman and with Col. Gorham's Rangers (26 Oct.)

Letter from Annapolis mentions Capt. Strachan and Col. Tucker (26 Oct.)

Last week Richard Bennet, Esq., supposed to be the richest man in America, died at Wye River (26 Oct.)

John Iden, servant, age c. 19, runaway from John Hallowell, of Phila., shoemaker (26 Oct.)

Sat. next will be published *Some remarks on Abel Morgan's Answer to Samuel Finley* (26 Oct.)

Horse taken up by Henry Keppele, of Phila., tavern-keeper (26 Oct.)

Real estate for sale, including land now in tenure of the widow of Johannes Van Eeckelen, land in Muskmelon Hundred, Kent Co., near dwelling of Thomas Clark, Esq., land (part of the estate of Benjamin Shurmer, late of Kent Co., Esq., dec'd) in forest of Apoquimony Hundred, near Sapience Harris's; also land on north side of William Haman's mill-pond; likewise land in Duck Creek Hundred, Kent Co., late in tenure of Joshua Edwards; also 200 acres on both sides of the road from Duck Creek to Dover, between Nicholas Loockerman's and Nicholas Powell's; enquire of George Stevenson (26 Oct.)

William Edgell has removed his store from William Spafford's to the corner of Church Alley in Third St. (26 Oct.)

On 12 July 1736 Andrew Walker sailed from Londonderry for America and since has not been heard from by his friends in Doneraill; if Walker will apply to Thomas Jones in Lancaster, he will hear something to his advantage (26 Oct.)

A slave, age 25, runaway from Hugh Davey, of Phila., merchant (26 Oct.)

Negroes for sale by Joseph Sims, over the drawbridge (26 Oct.)

Andrew Lamb, at house of Mr. Byles near the middle of Pewter-Platter-Alley, teaches bookkeeping, navigation, etc. (26 Oct.)

Plantation in Plymouth Twp. for sale; apply to William Currie on premises or John Ross, Esq., in Phila. (26 Oct.)

Land in Northern Liberties, between land of Mr. Goodman and Mr. Parker, to be let; enquire at the Widow Bright's or at Joseph Richardson's, silversmith, in Front St. (26 Oct.)

Lot in Church Alley, Phila., late belonging to Obadiah Eldridge, taken in execution at suit of Cornelia Bradford and Buckridge Sims, is to be sold at house of the Widow Pratt in Market St. (26 Oct.)

Elizabeth Gregory, Negro, born on Long Island, who formerly served in the family of Gov. Morris at Trenton and about 18 months ago was taken out of prison by Thomas Lawrence, Esq., runaway from John Kearsley, Jr. (26 Oct.)

Services of schoolmaster or schoolmistress sought by William Foster near Mount Holly, West Jersey (26 Oct.)

David Dondorse, a Scotchman, escaped from goal of Burlington and stole horse of Caleb Shinn; reward for his capture is offered by Sheriff John Hollinshead (26 Oct.)

Steer strayed from Richard Lloyd of Darby (26 Oct.)

John Wiglay, a West-country-man, farmer, imported in the _Litchfield_ about a year ago, and Edmund Ayers (_alias_ Grievous), shoemaker, born at Luds in Yorkshire, who has been in the country about four years, and Rebecca Wooley, Irish woman, runaway servants from George and Richard Lee (26 Oct.)

Horse stolen from Jacob Shoemaker, Jr., at Kensington (26 Oct.)

Accounts with estate of Peter Baynton to be settled with John Baynton, exec. (26 Oct.)

For freight or passage to St. Eustatia in schooner _Joseph and Ann_, Michael Cranfield commander, agree with Joseph Jones in Market St. or the master in Gray's Alley; the schooner is at Oswald Peal's wharf (2 Nov.)

Samuel Spicer will give up the ferry over Cooper's Creek (2 Nov.)

Scipio, Negro, runaway from Marcus Kuhl of Phila., baker (2 Nov.)

House where Widow Jekyll lately lived to be let by Samuel Morris at lower end of Second St. (2 Nov.)

Daniel M'Daniel, Irish servant, age c. 20, and Henry Tibb, a West-country Englishman, age c. 30, runaways from John Horner, living at Princetown (2 Nov.)

John Baker has real estate in Kensington for sale and also some lots in Race St., Phila. (2 Nov.)

John Bleakly takes horses to winter (2 Nov.)

Accounts with estate of Thomasin Keith, dec'd, to be settled with Samuel Palmer and Alexander Allair, execs. (2 Nov.)

Accounts with estate of Anthony Palmer, Esq., dec'd, to be settled with Alexander Allair; Palmer's late dwelling in Kensington is to be sold (2 Nov.)

Adv. of Walter Shea at his store in Samuel Parr's house in which Thomas Charlton now dwells, fronting Water St. (2 Nov.)

Dick, Negro, runaway from Valentine Dushane, living near St. George's in Newcastle Co. (2 Nov.)

Thomas Kittera in Earltown, Lancaster Co., has taken up a horse (2 Nov.)

Land in Passyunk Twp. for sale by Andrew Haney, living in that twp. (2 Nov.)

Eleanor, wife of Andrew M'Broom, of Manor of Moreland, Phila. Co., has eloped (2 Nov.)

1749

John Hughes, Irish servant, age c. 22, runaway from Thomas
Collins, near Bombahook (2 Nov.)

Teacher of Latin and arithmetic sought for school in Phila.
apply to Israel Pemberton, Jr., or Robert Willard (2 Nov.);
name corrected to Robert Willan (23 Nov.)

For freight or passage to Jamaica in ship *Flower*, of Cork,
James Dymond commander, agree with said commander or with
Davey and Carson, merchants, in Phila. (2 Nov.)

Capts. Gallop and Blivan were taken by the Spaniards, who
were then pursued by Capts. Wanton and Dunbar; the Spaniards
ran Gallop's sloop ashore (9 Nov.)

Capt. Miller in the ship *Mary and Jane* arrived at New York;
he brought in the crew of the sloop *Seaflower*, Capt. Gross,
which he had found in a helpless condition (9 Nov.)

The ship *Beulah*, Capt. Child, and the ship *Myrtilla*, Capt.
Budden, of Phila., are both safely arrived at London (9 Nov.)

For freight or passage to St. Christophers and Nevis in the
ship *Swimmer*, William Rice commander, agree with Robert and
Amos Strettell or the commander at Turner and Massey's wharf
(9 Nov.)

Catherine, wife of George Miller, of Phila., carpenter, has
eloped from her husband (9 Nov.)

Nathaniel Scott, late of Edenderry, Ireland, but now of New
York, gives notice to his brother Henry Scott, shoemaker,
some time since resident of Phila. or parts adjacent, that
their father, Jonathan Scott, died, leaving a legacy to
Henry (9 Nov.)

Gabriel Poneo, of Evesham Twp., Burlington Co., publishes his
wife Mary (9 Nov.)

Frederick Vandyke, Low-Dutch servant, sawyer or carpenter,
runaway from Edward Hill of Dunks's Ferry (9 Nov.)

Samuel Morris offers reward for information leading to the
conviction of the person or persons who stole 1,000 pounds of
flour, which were taken from Morris's mills in Whitemarsh
to Phila. (9 Nov.)

Darby Henry (*alias* Jeremiah Henry), Irish servant, age c. 16,
runaway from James Wilson, of West Caln, Chester Co. (9 Nov.)

Mathias Lense, living on land of John Davis of Plymouth, has
taken up a mare (9 Nov.)

Sloop of Capt. Davidson from Barbados, bound to New England,
was lost 29 Oct. on beach between Egg-Harbour and Barnagat
(16 Nov.)

Accounts with estate of John Yarnall, dec'd, to be settled with
Abigail, Philip and Nathan Yarnall, execs., who will sell
real estate of the dec'd (16 Nov.)

For freight or passage to Lisbon in the snow *Hazard*, Leech
Harris commander, agree with Samuel Hazard or said commander at Warner's wharf (16 Nov.)

Richard Watson, Irish servant, age c. 18, runaway from John
Wily of Maiden Creek (16 Nov.)

William Anderson, deputy sheriff, offers reward for capture of
the following who escaped from goal of Bucks Co.: Michael
Redding, Irishman, age c. 40, Henry Ancts, Dutchman, and
John Doneson, Irish servant, age c. 24 (16 Nov.)

John Bartholomew Rieger, George Michael Weiss and John Philip Leydich (minister at N. Hanover) state that the Rev. Michael Slatter (minister in Phila.) has done what his duty required concerning money sent from Holland by Jacob Reiff (16 Nov.)

Caesar, Negro, age c. 24, runaway from David Davis of Earltown, Chester Co. (16 Nov.)

George Shriner, Dutch servant, age c. 22, runaway from Michael Brand of Hanover Twp. (16 Nov.)

William Pyewell in Second St. has leather for sale (16 Nov.)

Real estate in Middlesex Co., adjoining to Kingston, for sale by Jedediah Higgins (16 Nov.)

Two mares strayed or stolen from Jane Evans in London-Britain Twp., Chester Co. (16 Nov.)

Daniel Adams, Irish apprentice, age c. 17, runaway from Daniel Hathorn of Phila., tailor (16 Nov.)

Jacob Levering of Roxborough Twp. has taken up two cows (16 Nov.)

Thomas Bennet, English servant, age c. 40, runaway from James Clark of Windsor, Middlesex Co., East Jersey (16 Nov.)

Robert Kelly, trader, has been murdered by some French Indians (23 Nov.)

The Friend's Goodwill, Capt. Crawford, with 400 Palatines on board, is feared lost (23 Nov.)

Twenty-one Negroes owned at Port Royal escaped in a boat stolen from Capt. Mackey (23 Nov.)

Capt. Rivers, arrived at New York, reports the sloop of Capt. Kellog of New York entirely lost in a hurricane (23 Nov.)

Gabriel Nesman (minister at Wicacoa) will preach in Swedish and English; he soon expects a call to Swedeland (23 Nov.)

House and ground known as the Center, now in the tenure of Robert Dixon, will be sold by Peter Robertson (23 Nov.)

James Powell, Negro, runaway from Peter Brotherton (23 Nov.)

For freight or passage to London in the ship Brothers, William Muir commander, agree with Charles and Alexander Stedman - in the snow Amphitrite, James Young commander, agree with Levy and Franks (23 Nov.)

Joseph Chapman of Wright's-Town has taken up two mares (23 Nov.)

John Coleman has taken up a strayed bull at his plantation in Plymouth Twp. (23 Nov.)

Dr. Rees Jones is about to depart for Europe (23 Nov.)

Bartholomew Maguire, Irish servant, runaway from George Enterkin of East Bradford, Chester Co. (23 Nov.)

John Campbell, Irish servant, runaway (supposedly in company with Stephen Hill, a soldier) from Prince Snow of Warwick Twp., Cecil Co., Md. (23 Nov.)

Biscuits are sold by Josiah Davenport, baker, in Gray's Alley (23 Nov.)

Messuage and lot in Phila., the estate of Adam and John Lewis, dec'd, now in tenure of John Morrison, taken in execution at suit of Isaac Norris & al., will be sold at house of the Widow Pratt in Market St. by Sheriff Richard Sewell (23 Nov.)

Accounts with estate of Thomas Hart, late of Phila., bricklayer, dec'd, to be settled with Mary and Thomas Hart, execs. (23 Nov.)

Joseph Wilson and Isaac Wright have been committed to prison in Annapolis on suspicion of counterfeiting (30 Nov.)

Accounts with estate of Michael Koyl, late of Phila., dec'd, to be settled with Thomas Leech and Benjamin Franklin, execs. (30 Nov.)

John Roche, Irish servant, runaway from James Moore of East Caln Twp., Chester Co. (30 Nov.)

Joseph Scull has a horse in the pound of Phila. (30 Nov.)

Thomas Harper at Frankford has taken up a horse (30 Nov.)

John M'Coy, servant, age c. 17, runaway from Thomas Carney of Penn's Neck, Salem Co.; the runaway left a gun at house of Mr. Trueaxe at Bomba Hook and was later seen at William Ellis's plantation in Cecil Co., Md., with William Dessner and wife, shipmates of said servant (30 Nov.)

Two horses strayed from house of William Jenkins in Abington, Phila. Co.; reward if they are brought to Jenkins or to Ephraim Harker in Bethlehem, West Jersey (30 Nov.)

Notice of Mayor Thomas Lawrence concerning cord-wood (30 Nov.)

Joseph Ashbridge of Chester offers reward for recovery of a mare (30 Nov.)

Plantation in Newberry Twp., York Co., for sale; apply to Nathan Hussey on premises (30 Nov.)

Notice of Thomas Colvill that Joseph Wilson, middle aged, a schoolmaster in Newcastle Co., under sentence of death in goal of Cecil Co. for counterfeiting money of Md., has broken out of goal; Michael Earle, sheriff, offers reward for his capture (30 Nov.)

Plantation and grist-mill on Great Conestogoe Road to be sold or let by Jacob Bayerley, miller, on the premises (30 Nov.)

Time of a servant, tailor by trade, for sale by John Cotringer, tailor, in Arch St. (30 Nov.)

Alexander Johnston gives notice that Samuel Aston, miller, his wife and five children, who came in with Johnston in the Catherine, Capt. Henderson, master, are to go to Capt. Blair in Phila. to pay for their passage; otherwise reward will be paid for arrest of Aston and his family (30 Nov.)

John Dunnoghon, Irish servant, age c. 24, runaway from Robert Siminton of Conestogoe, Lancaster Co. (30 Nov.)

James Hayes, Irish servant, age c. 20, runaway from William Williams of New-Britain Twp., Bucks Co. (30 Nov.)

Land at Passyunk, now in possession of Mr. Brotherton, for sale; enquire of Thomas Hopkinson in Phila. (30 Nov.)

Obituary of Richard Bennett, Esq,, who died 11 Oct. at his seat in Queen Anne's Co. in his 83rd year; by his will he forgave more than 150 of his poor debtors (5 Dec.)

Account of "terrible gale" in letter from Capt. Tingley of the ship *Indian King*, of Phila., from Bay of Honduras (5 Dec.)

Patrick Kirk, Irish servant, age c. 21, runaway from Luke Morris of Phila., rope-maker (5 Dec.)

James Dundass, Scotch servant, age c. 24, runaway from William Bogden, living near Queen Anne (5 Dec.)

Managers of the Phila. Lottery are William Branson, George Spafford, Samuel Smith, Samuel Hazard, William Shippen, Joseph Redman, Andrew Read and William Patterson in Pa.; James Hude, James Nelson and Samuel Woodruff in the Jerseys; tickets will also be sold by Peter Vanbrugh Livingston and William Peartree Smith in New York (12 Dec.)

Accounts with estate of William Roberts, of Worcester, late dec'd, to be settled with Owen Roberts and Edward Hughes, execs. (12 Dec.)

Roger Flanagen, Irish servant, runaway from Samuel Swift of Bustletown (12 Dec.)

Negroes, household goods, etc., at plantation of Peter Kock, dec'd, to be sold by William Clymer and Charles Edgar, admins. (12 Dec.)

George Okill intends to leave Pa. (12 Dec.)

Accounts with estate of Morris Lewellin, late of Merion, dec'd, to be settled with Evan Evans, Alexander Cruikshanks, James Truman and Isaac Taylor, execs. (12 Dec.)

Peter Bard, Henry Elves and James Benezet, auditors appointed upon an attachment issued against John Norwood, will sell messuage and lot in Front St., bounded on N. by Joseph Knight's brick house (12 Dec.)

List of strays at plantation of John Bleakley in Kingsess; horses to be wintered there should be sent to John Bittle's at the Sign of the Indian King in Phila. (12 Dec.)

George Gibson will sell house in Lancaster where he lives; it has been a tavern for several years (12 Dec.)

Capt. Craige of Boston has arrived at Martha's Vineyard from London (19 Dec.)

Last week died in Phila. Thomas Godfrey, inventor of the New Reflecting Quadrant (19 Dec.)

Accounts with estate of Thomas Kenton, late of Oxford Twp., Phila. Co., to be settled with Thomas and William Kenton, execs. (19 Dec.)

Plantation in Oxford Twp., near Jacob Hall's, late belonging to James Boyden, dec'd, taken in execution at suit of William Jackson, will be sold by Richard Sewell, sheriff, at the house of Thomas Harper in Franckfort (19 Dec.)

Plantation in Mansfield, five miles from Burlington, for sale; apply to William Clayton at Trenton or George Nicholson at Croswicks (19 Dec.)

Accounts with estate of John Linton, late of Phila., harnessmaker, dec'd, to be settled with Martha Linton, exec. (19 Dec.)

Peter Conter, of Lancaster, offers reward for recovery of a mare strayed or stolen from pasture next to fence of Michael Myer (26 Dec.)

Edward Dowers is removed from house in Water St. to house in Front St. where Thomas Wells lately lived (26 Dec.)

House below the drawbridge to be let; enquire of Robert Warren or Ebenezer Tomlinson; also lot below Wicacoa to be let by John Nicholls, Samuel Rhoads or Ebenezer Tomlinson (26 Dec.)

On board brigantine Charming Polly, Capt. Keteltas, in New York harbor, minute guns were being fired for funeral of Mrs. Provost; a lad of c. 15, apprentice to Capt. Riven, attending on the gunners, was badly injured when a cartridge exploded; his right arm and the thumb of his left hand were amputated (2 Jan.)

Lewis Evans is removed to the house next the pump in Arch St. (2 Jan.)

Mare stolen from James Watson, living on plantation of the Reading Furnace Co., Chester Co. (2 Jan.)

Plantation in Newcastle Co., three miles from Christine Bridge, for sale by James King (2 Jan.)

Robert Warren in Phila. has lost a silver stay-hook and a gold sleeve button, marked R W, the maker's mark C. B. (2 Jan.)

Lot of ground at Wicacoa in Passyunk and Moyamensing, in the tenure of Widow Bood, late belonging to estate of John Bood, dec'd, taken in execution at suit of Mary Andrews will be sold (2 Jan.)

James Humphreys is removed from his house in Second St. to the house where Benjamin Price, attorney-at-law, lately lived in Second St. (2 Jan.)

Two colts have been taken up at plantation of Isaac Ashton in Lower Dublin, Phila. Co. (2 Jan.)

Accounts with estate of John Marshall, late of Darby, Chester Co., dec'd, to be settled with Lewis Thomas, Thomas Pearson and Isaac Pearson, execs., all living in Darby (2 Jan.)

Reese Gwin, servant, age c. 20, shoemaker, runaway from John Jones of East Caln, Chester Co. (2 Jan.)

Thomas Curry, shoemaker, has absented himself from his bail (2 Jan.)

Sixteen sheep have strayed from pasture of Adam Cantz; reward will be paid if they are brought to Ralph Sarver, at the Rising Sun (2 Jan.)

Annapolis item of 29 Nov. 1749 states that a shallop loaded with oysters and a schooner are ashore on Eastern Neck Island; owners are to apply to Mr. Weeks or Mr. Hynson on said island; item of 6 Dec. 1749 reports that a sloop with pig iron to be taken aboard Capt. Thompson at Wiccocomico was lost in a storm; item of 13 Dec. 1749 states that warrant is issued for execution of John Murphy of Frederick Co., Md. (9 Jan.)

Capt. Trotter has come to Phila.; Capt. Currie from Antigua in a sloop belonging to Wilmington has arrived there (9 Jan.)

On 9 Jan. the malt house of Preserve Brown, Jr., in Second St., Phila., was consumed by fire (9 Jan.)

Real estate at Wilmington, belonging to the estate of Lucas Stridham of Crane-hook, Newcastle Co., dec'd, is to be sold by Peter and Jonas Stridham, admins. (9 Jan.)

Ground and house in Front St., now in tenure of John Clare, late belonging to estate of Jonathan Dickinson, dec'd, taken in execution at suits of Edward Jones (admin. of Francis Jones, dec'd), Thomas Hatton (admin. of Daniel May, dec'd) and Thomas Hatton (admin. of Joshua Hyam, dec'd), are to be sold at Roberts's coffee-house (9 Jan.)

Real estate in Front St., now in tenure of Ralph Loftus, taken in execution at suit of William Parker, to be sold at James's coffee-house (9 Jan.)

Plantation in Charles-town, Chester Co., taken in execution at suit of sundry persons against David Jones, Jr., to be sold at house of Aubrey Bevan in Chester (9 Jan.)

Stone bridge to be built over Christine Creek; persons who desire to do the work or supply stone are to apply to William Patterson, John Read, Thomas Montgomery and Joseph Rotheram (9 Jan.)

Thomas Aspay of Kennet, Chester Co., offers reward for arrest of William Sim, age 21, of Londonderry Twp., Chester Co., who on 6 Dec. 1749 murdered Thomas Aspay's son John (9 Jan.)

Joseph Lownes of Passyunk Twp. has taken up a cow; Lownes has for sale a tract of land over against Israel Pemberton's plantation in Passyunk Road (9 Jan.)

Accounts with estate of William Hartley, late of Reading Twp., Phila. Co., dec'd, to be settled with Hannah Hartley, widow and exec. (9 Jan.)

Peter, Negro, age c. 19, this country born, runaway from Wilson Hunt, of Hopewell, Hunterdon Co. (9 Jan.)

Boston item gives account of murder of an Indian named Saracy and wounding of two others, Captains Job and Andrew, by some white men, who are now apprehended (16 Jan.); protest made by 20 young men led by Madockawando, in the name of their chief, Toxus, to the garrison at Richmond (30 Jan.)

New York item of 1 Jan. gives account of the loss of the ship Jane, Capt. Keteltas, and the arrival at New York of Capt. Daveraux from St. Eustatia and of Capt. Hutchings from Virginia (16 Jan.)

Two Negro men for sale by Thomas Hart in Second St.; one is a mason, the other a chocolate-grinder (16 Jan.)

James Claypole in Walnut St. sells window glass (16 Jan.)

Mention of Capts. Child, Budden, Gibson and Alison (23 Jan.)

George Bootman of Abington, Phila. Co., publishes his wife Mary (23 Jan.)

Thomas Thornbrugh of the borough of Lancaster has taken up a horse (23 Jan.)

Edward Hill, hired man, runaway from Leonard Vandegrift of Bensalem Twp., Bucks Co. (23 Jan.)

Woman named Pendergrass in Boston is suspected of murdering her infant (30 Jan.)

John Petty of Northfield is drowned in Conn. River (30 Jan.)

Young man named Taylor, at Rutland in Worcester, when hunting, accidentally shot and killed a young man named Heaton (30 Jan.)

The St. John's Indians have taken prisoner Lt. Hamilton, Bill Handfield and Alex. Winniet; Capt. Gorham marched against the Indians but they were gone before he reached Minas (30 Jan.)

Sloop Pidgeon, Capt. Givin, from Barbados has arrived at New York (30 Jan.)

Capt. Langdon spoke with Capt. Knox from London (30 Jan.)

Stone tenement in Germantown, belonging to Richard Renshaw, taken in execution at suit of Theobald End and others, is to be sold (30 Jan.)

House in Water St., late belonging to Francis Bowes, dec'd, bounded on N. by Thomas Say's lot and on S. by Joseph House's lot, is for sale; also seven lots in Trenton, between Thomas Lawrence, Esq., and Elijah Bond's lots, are for sale by John Kinsey and Thomas Lawrence, Esqrs., Peter Delage, Andrew Read and Rachel Bowes, execs. (30 Jan.)

Ferdinando Hughs, Irish servant, age c. 23, tailor, runaway from Nathaniel Bowser, tailor, in Front St., Phila. (30 Jan.)

Accounts with estate of William Murrell, late of Mount Holly, Burlington Co., dec'd, to be settled with Henry Paxson, exec. (30 Jan.)

Anne Boyd of Phila. offers reward for capture of thief who broke into her house and stole money and articles of silver and gold (30 Jan.)

Land in Kingsess, being part of Boone's Island, and two houses in Wiccacoa, one in Water St. between Jacob Duche's garden and ground of John Stevens, for sale; enquire of Thomas Williams, hatter and shopkeeper, in Second St. (30 Jan.)

Horse strayed from James Webb of Lancaster (30 Jan.)

Reward for recovery of mare and horse, strayed or stolen, if brought to Thomas Pearse in Pewter-Platter-Alley or to Jenkin Philip in Rockhill Twp., Bucks Co. (30 Jan.)

Mention of ship Brave Hawke, Capt. Bill, of New York (6 Feb.)

Capt. Brad, arrived at Phila. from Barbados, reports that Capt. Mortimer has arrived safe at Boston (6 Feb.)

Real estate, now in tenure of James Stewart, in Water St., taken in execution at suit of Mary Plumsted and others, will be sold at James's Coffee-house (6 Feb.)

Real estate on Center Square, now in tenure of Robert Dixon, lately belonging to estate of Peter Evans, dec'd, taken in execution at suit of William Plumsted, Esq., will be sold at Roberts's Coffee-house (6 Feb.)

Peter Garragan, Irish servant, age c. 20, runaway from George Middleton in Nottingham Twp., Burlington Co. (6 Feb.)

Honor Yerack Grumble, Dutch servant, age c. 28 or 30, runaway from William Albertson in Newtown, Gloucester Co. (6 Feb.)

Log house and lot at the Four Lane Ends in Middletown, Bucks Co., for sale by David Wilson, Jr. (6 Feb.)

Snow Friendship, Walter Stirling commander, at Hamilton's wharf, will sail for Barbados; for freight or passage agree with the commander or Mr. Bell (6 Feb.)

Adv. of Christopher Marshall at the Golden Ball in Chestnut St., who intends for Europe (6 Feb.)

Thomas Webster in the borough of Chester has a brick house for sale (6 Feb.)

Ground in Front St., part of estate of John Fisher, dec'd, will be sold at James's Coffee-house by John and Jonathan Paschall (6 Feb.); accounts with estate of Joseph Newberry, dec'd, to be settled with Jonathan Paschall, admin. (6 Feb.)

Houses in Ammon St. on Society Hill for sale; enquire of Samuel Hill in same street or John Nicholls in Arch St. (6 Feb.)

1750

Martin Wall at Passyunk has taken up a stray cow (6 Feb.)

Margaret Simkins, wife of Daniel Simkins of Stow Creek, Cumberland Co., from time to time elopes from her husband (6 Feb.)

Edward Oliff, Irish servant, age c. 19, runaway from Alexander Morgan of Waterford Twp., Gloucester Co., West Jersey (6 Feb.)

Arrival at Phila. of ship Beulah, Capt. Child, and at Va. of the ship Brothers, of Phila., Capt. Stewart (13 Feb.)

Ship Crown will sail for London; for freight or passage agree with Capt. James on board or Isaac Greenleafe (13 Feb.)

Catherine Davidson, convict servant, imported in the Thames Frigate, John Dobbins master, runaway from George Buchanan, living near Baltimore; she was induced away by John Greek (Italian or Greek by birth), foremastman of said ship (13 Feb.)

Adv. of Parker and Garrett in Third St. (13 Feb.)

Adv. of Joseph Ogden in his store at Benjamin Kendall's at corner of Chestnut and Third Sts. (13 Feb.)

Anthony Stocker, at his store under the house of John Sober in Water St., sells goods imported in brigantine George, James Kennedy master (13 Feb.)

Plantation in Oxford Twp., late the estate of Jacob Hall, dec'd, for sale by Edward Collins and Abraham Leech, execs. (13 Feb.)

Brick house in borough of Wilmington, estate of Thomas Brown, dec'd, being the tavern that Peter Ganthony now inhabits, is for sale; apply to James Brown and Peter Ganthony, execs. (13 Feb.)

Mark Lolor and John Beady, Irish servants, runaways from Hugh Clark and Walter Theadford of Mill-Creek Hundred, Newcastle Co. (13 Feb.)

Goods and chattels of James Paul Heath, late of Cecil Co., Md., gentleman, dec'd, are assigned to James Calder, of Chester-Town, gentleman, in trust for creditors and children of the dec'd; Rebecca Hedges (wife of William Hedges of Cecil Co.) is only acting executrix (13 Feb.)

Notice of meeting signed by James Trotter, Clerk of St. Andrew's Society (13 Feb.)

Jack (alias John Powell), Negro, cooper, runaway from Mordecai Moore of Phila.; reward if slave is brought to William Whitehead, keeper of the city workhouse (13 Feb.)

Joseph Steer, of Lampeter Twp., Lancaster Co., has taken up two horses (13 Feb.)

House on south side of Cedar St., late in tenure of Adam Lasher, and lots in Cedar St., adjoining house of Thomas Stewart, belonging to Richard Renshaw, taken in execution at suit of Mary Plumsted and others, are for sale (20 Feb.)

Ground, Mifflin's wharf and stores in Water St. for sale; enquire of Morris Morris near the premises or Samuel Morris at White-marsh, Phila. Co. (20 Feb.)

Real estate, tanyard, mill- and beam-house in Northern Liberties, late property of Andrew Edge, dec'd, to be let; enquire of Joseph Watkins in Phila. (20 Feb.)

Plantation in Blockley Twp., 4 miles from Phila., late the property of Isaac Warner, dec'd, to be sold; apply to Thomas Tilbury in Phila. or Veronica Warner, admin. (20 Feb.)

Mill in Millcreek Hundred at Whiteclay Landing, Newcastle Co., for sale by Owen Williams (20 Feb.)

Jonathan Belcher, Gov. of N.J., has ordered strict suppression of riots (27 Feb.)

Sloop of Capt. Kip from the Bay of Honduras was driven ashore on south side of the East Bank, near Sandy Hook (27 Feb.)

Capt. Riddle from New York took up at sea one Brown from Egg-Harbour, belonging to Conn. (27 Feb.)

Accounts with Capt. John Sim, late of Island of Jamaica, are to be settled with William Charles, his admin. (27 Feb.)

Plantation in Middletown, Bucks Co., near the Four-Lane-Ends, late property of Benjamin Field, dec'd, for sale; apply to Sarah Field, exec., living on the premises (27 Feb.)

Plantation in Upper Chichester, Chester Co., for sale by William Hewes, living at Marcus-hook (27 Feb.)

Mare strayed from John Bose, at Benjamin Davis's in Upper Dublin; reward if mare is brought to Bose at Deep-run or to John Kelly at Perkasey (27 Feb.)

Linens for sale by William Gamble in Mrs. Andrew's house in Water St., next door to Capt. Phillips's (27 Feb.)

Time of Dutch servant for sale; enquire of Caleb Kuisey, deputy sheriff in Newcastle (27 Feb.)

James Boyd in Sadsbury Twp., Chester Co., has taken up a mare (27 Feb.)

George Spriggs, sawyer, was run down by a sley in Boston and died 24 hours later (6 Mar.)

Praise of the *Boston*, man-of-war, built in Boston by Benjamin Hallowell (6 Mar.)

New free schoolhouse kept in New York by Joseph Hildreth, clerk of Trinity Church, caught fire and burned to the ground (6 Mar.)

Group of commedians from Phila. have taken a room in a building lately belonging to Rip Van Dam, Esq., dec'd, in Nassau St. in New York (6 Mar.)

Joseph Freemiller, Dutch servant, age c. 17 or 18, runaway from Samuel Burrows in the Jerseys (6 Mar.)

Plantation of Joseph Jackson in London Grove Twp., Chester Co., for sale; apply to Jackson, living on the premises (6 Mar.)

Tract of land with grist-mill in Bethlehem, adjoining land of Mr. Allen, to be sold or let by Jonathan Stark in Bethlehem (6 Mar.)

Edward Houton, servant, age c. 35, sawyer and sailor, runaway from Jacob Giles at Susquehanna; Houton was transported for 7 years from London in ship *Barwick*, John Malger commander, on 12 June 1743 and was sold to Norton Groves, baker; Houston ran away but was caught, and Graves sold him to Richard Deaver to row in the ferry-boat; after Deaver's death he became property of Widow Mary Deaver, from whom he ran away; Mary got him back and sold him to Michael Webster, who eventually sold him to Jacob Giles (6 Mar.)

Time of a servant lad for sale; enquire of Capt. John Andrews on his sloop at Peter Bard's wharf (6 Mar.)

Hans Yerrick Haase, Dutch servant, age c. 24, shoemaker, runaway, in company with Hans Michael Calvin, a free man, from Thomas Jones of Hilton Twp., Bucks Co. (6 Mar.)

John Pole intends for London (6 Mar.)

For freight or passage to Dublin in ship Boyne, Henry Ash commander, at Capt. Goodman's wharf, agree with commander or John Erwin in Strawberry Alley (6 Mar.)

House in Sassafras St. for sale; apply to Edward Evans, living in said house (6 Mar.)

Persons indebted to Henry Lewis, late of Haverford, Chester Co., are to pay what they owe (6 Mar.)

Plantation in Pilesgrove, Salem Co., for sale by Andrew Tranberg in Wilmington (6 Mar.)

Letter from Capt. Badger, of the brig Sarah of New York, from Lisbon mentions the ship from Boston commanded by Andrew Dewer (13 Mar.)

Sloop Success, Oliver Shourt master, of New York, is cast away near Cape Hatteras (13 Mar.)

Sloop Derborough, Capt. Coger, lost its rudder in going through Hellgate (13 Mar.)

Ship Carolina, Capt. Mesnard, has arrived at Dover, and sloop Dolphin, Capt. Le Gros, has arrived at London (13 Mar.)

Three men are in goal in Gloucester Co. for murder of Joseph Young of that county (13 Mar.)

Two mares have been taken up at plantation of William Deweese in Whitemarsh (13 Mar.)

William Burrman, servant, from West of England, runaway from Lyde Goodwin, near Baltimore town, Md. (13 Mar.)

Adv. of Henry Schleydorn, sugar baker, in Norris's Alley (13 Mar.)

House and land in West Marlborough Twp., Chester Co., for sale; apply to Joshua Pennock, Sr., living near said land, or Samuel Pennock in Phila. (13 Mar.)

Twp plantations in Paxton Twp., Lancaster Co., for sale; apply to John Fisher in Phila. (13 Mar.)

Bryan Doron, Irish servant, age 35, runaway from Bartholomew Tims in Thornbury Twp., Chester Co. (13 Mar.)

House and ground in Third St., lately belonging to the Widow Parker, now in the tenure of Stephen Potts, is to be sold by Abraham Potts on the premises; enquire of George Plumley in Third St., Phila., or said Parker in Wilmington (13 Mar.)

Plantation in Middletown Twp., Chester Co., to be sold by Joseph Colbourn in Market St., opposite to Strawberry Alley (13 Mar.)

Money due Samuel Parr, of Phila., merchant, to be paid promptly (13 Mar.)

John Donnoghon, Irish servant, age c. 24, and Thomas M'Donough, Irish servant, runaways from Theophilus and Robert Siminton of Conestogo, Lancaster Co. (13 Mar.)

1750

Articles have been stolen from house of Michael Israel on Society Hill at the Sign of the Blue Lion (13 Mar.)

Charles Hunt, servant, age c. 25, runaway from Alexander Parker of Phila.; Hunt had lived with one Cheaseman on Timber Creek (13 Mar.)

Capt. Dowell from the Havanna has arrived at Phila., and with him as passenger Capt. Cuffy of New York, whose vessel was seized at the Havanna (20 Mar.)

Two Negroes, age c. 12, for sale; apply to William Henderson in Church Alley (20 Mar.)

Bartholomew M'Guire, Irish servant, runaway from Thomas Evans of Uuchland, Chester Co. (20 Mar.)

David Pew, English servant, age c. 36, runaway from Hinson Wright of Queen Anne's Co., Md. (20 Mar.)

Accounts with estate of Christopher Taylor, of Tinicum Island, dec'd, to be settled with Benjamin Taylor and Enoch Elliot, execs. (20 Mar.)

John Bleakley has let his plantation and will not pasture horses after 25 Mar.; owners to pick them up by that time and pay John Smith at the pasture (20 Mar.)

Accounts with estate of John Hannis, dec'd, to be settled with Andrew Hannis, exec., living in Phila. (20 Mar.)

Tract of land in East Marlborough Twp., Chester Co., now in tenure of James Chaffen, to be sold; apply to Lewis Davis in Haverford (20 Mar.)

Water lot in Kensington for sale; enquire of William Shippen at his house in Market St. or shop in Fourth St., at the Sign of the Paracelsus Head (20 Mar.)

From Antigua comes list of captains whose vessels were distressed since 23 Nov. last: David Lindsay, John Underwood, George Giddens, John Jones, John Churchill, Christopher Lushing, Gideon Smith, Elisha Patting, James Cobb, Reuben Chandler, Askins, Woodside, Tasker, John Lee and Tillage (27 Mar.)

Sloop, Capt. White, built at Newbury, was driven ashore on Plumb Island and lost (27 Mar.)

Parish house at Hampton Falls, N.H., where Rev. Mr. Whipple lived, caught fire on 18 Mar. and burned to the ground (27 Mar.)

Capt. Ruggles, on voyage from Boston to Jamaica, took up an Indian who belonged to Nantucket in a small whale boat (27 Mar.)

Letter from St. Thomas, dated 29 Jan., lists the following then at that island: Capts. Lewis, Baker, Phaenix, Hope, Mesnard and Hill, all belonging to New York; also Capt. Bill; Capt. Hill arrived at St. Thomas 25 Jan. (27 Mar.)

Sloop *Aletta*, Capt. Richards, in going through Hellgate, struck on the rocks and bilged (27 Mar.)

Person desiring work as schoolmaster is to apply to John Barge in Germantown (27 Mar.)

Copper stills for sale may be viewed at Alexander Forbes's in Second St. (27 Mar.)

John White sells medicines at Sign of the Dove in Third St., next door to George Plumley's, cutler (27 Mar.)

1750

Rent charge arising from a lot on west side of Frankford Road, belonging to William Clem, is for sale; also lot in Kensington in tenure of Jacob Maag, at lower end of Vienna St.; also lot in tenure of Adam Clampfer in Kensington; plan is to be seen at Alexander Allaire's in Kensington or at Lewis Evans's in Phila.; the rent charge and lots, the estate of the late Anthony Palmer, Esq., dec'd, were taken in execution at suit of Mary Leech (27 Mar.)

Tract of land in Morris Co., West Jersey, for sale by John Jenkins, living in Trenton (27 Mar.)

Accounts with estate of Samuel Dunlope, dec'd, who in 1746 and 1747 was a lodger in house of Arthur Graham in Nantmill Twp., Chester Co., are to be brought to William Bell at the White Horse in Phila., where the execs. and John M'Michael will meet (27 Mar.)

Adv. of John Vavasor at his store in Mrs. Andrews's house in Water St. (27 Mar.)

Eighth part of Durham Ironworks and land belonging thereto, late property of Robert Ellis, Esq., taken in execution at the suits of Edward Shippen and William Logan, Esqrs., and James Murgatroyd, will be sold at Joseph Insley's in Newtown; also to be sold at same time is a tract in Newtown, late belonging to Joseph Walley, dec'd, taken in execution at suit of John Strickland, by Sheriff Joseph Hart (27 Mar.)

Notice of Samuel Hazard and Thomas Morgan, execs. of Evan Morgan, late of Phila., merchant, dec'd (27 Mar.)

Thomas Dawson, apprentice, age c. 20, runaway from Peter Bufinton, of East Callen Twp., Chester Co. (27 Mar.)

Grist- and saw-mills on White Clay Creek, Newcastle Co., to be sold or let; apply to Edward Miles at the mills (27 Mar.)

Patrick M'Guire, Irish servant, age c. 17, runaway from Thomas Wills, of Middle-town, Chester Co. (27 Mar.)

Report of William Clymer, Hugh Roberts, John Smith, Thomas Lloyd, John Mifflin and Abel James, arbitrators in dispute between Michael Slatter (minister in Phila.), Valentine Bayer, Michael Baker, Jacob Wiedman, Christian Erden and John Baiser of the one part, and Daniel Bouton, Michael Diel, Jacob Maag, John Gool, Bernard Laufersweiler and Leonard Melchior of the other part; sums were due to William Allen, Esq., Benjamin Loxley, William Waugh, Melchior Crator, John Gebbard, Adam Strickler, Leonard Melchior, Hugh Roberts, Daniel Steinmitz, Michael Diel, John Gool and Jacob Maag (5 Apr.)

At Worcester, Mass., on 5 Mar. Moses Morse, age c. 60, fell 20 feet into a stream and died (5 Apr.)

Mention of Capt. Barclow, who brought in M. Gerard, a French priest (5 Apr.)

On 25 Mar. the mate and a boy of the sloop <u>Jenny</u>, Capt. Arrowsmith, were drowned off Staten Island (5 Apr.)

On 27 Dec. 1749 the brigantine <u>Alida and Catharine</u>, Joseph Baily master, overset but the men were rescued (5 Apr.)

A brigantine belonging to Amboy, Thomas Crowell master, was cast away near Barnagat; all men were saved (5 Apr.)

The three men tried at Gloucester for the murder of Joseph Young were found guilty (5 Apr.)

Lot on S. side of M'Coombs's Alley to be sold or let by Benjamin Trotter in Arch St. (5 Apr.)

Position of schoolmaster open; apply to Edward Tomkins in Springfield or Jonathan Thomas in Burlington (5 Apr.)

Edward Roach, a young fellow, escaped from Thomas Brown, brickmaker of the borough of Lancaster (5 Apr.)

Adv. of Thomas Yorke, next door to Peter Bard's in Water St. (5 Apr.)

John Hopkins, of Phila., merchant, claims title to part of the Durham Ironworks in Bucks Co., taken in execution as the property of Robert Ellis, late of Phila., merchant (5 Apr.)

Aaron Allen, servant, age c. 17, belonging to Joshua Wood of Newcastle Co., runaway from James M'Connell, of Sadsbury Twp., Lancaster Co. (5 Apr.)

Evan Price, of Cymru Twp., Lancaster Co., offers reward for capture of man who stole goods from his house, Dennis Carroll, an Irishman, who served as a private under Capt. John Deimer against the French and then under Col. William Moore of Charles-Town, Chester Co. (5 Apr.)

Tracts of land for sale by James M'Connell, living in Sadsbury Twp., Lancaster Co. (5 Apr.)

Real estate in Lower Dublin Twp. for sale; enquire of Septimus Robinson, Esq., or John Petty in Phila., or Hance Lycan, Sr., and Nicholas Lycan, living on the premises (5 Apr.)

James M'Fall, Irish servant, age between 40 and 50, runaway from Nathaniel Bowser, tailor, in Front St., Phila. (5 Apr.)

Real estate in Uwchland Twp., Chester Co., to be let or sold; enquire of John Prigg on the premises or Peter Ashton (the owner), next door to James Morris's in Second St., Phila. (5 Apr.)

Land at mouth of Stowe Creek, part of the estate of Edmund Iliff, dec'd, taken in execution at suit of Robert Moore, is for sale (5 Apr.)

Letter from Annapolis Royal mentions Col. Warburton, Gov. Hobson, Gov. Cornwallis (12 Apr.)

Capt. Waddel reports that the ship Joseph, Capt. Bryant, had arrived at London from New York; Capt. Cornee, bound for New York was in the Downes; Capt. Gifford from New York arrived at Bristol (12 Apr.)

Capt. Haselton from Jamaica arrived at Phila. (12 Apr.)

Man was committed to goal in Phila. for robbing house of William Douglas at Trenton Landing, and another man was committed for being found in the house of James Benezet in Phila. (12 Apr.)

Three men are to be executed at Gloucester for murder of Joseph Young (12 Apr.)

House of Elisha Smith at Great-Egg-Harbour was struck by the lightning (12 Apr.)

House in Wicacoa, late of John Bood, dec'd, is for sale; enquire of Nicholas Scull in Arch St. (12 Apr.)

Jonathan Belcher accepts surrender of the charter of the borough of Trenton (12 Apr.)

Parcel of furniture to be sold at the house of the Widow Hawkins at the Sign of the Jolly Sailor in Front St. (12 Apr.)

Samuel Emlen, at the Sign of the Golden Heart in Phila., sells Schwanberg's liquid shell (12 Apr.)

Gregory Readington, Irish servant, age c. 20, runaway from Samuel Mendenhall in Concord, Chester Co. (12 Apr.)

House at corner of High and King Sts. in Wilmington is for sale by Richard Richardson (12 Apr.)

William Gray will sell tenement, with bakehouse and granaries, in Anthony Morris's Alley; apply to said Gray or Edward Shippen (12 Apr.)

Adv. of Henry Wright, whip-maker, in Chestnut St. (12 Apr.)

Horse strayed or stolen from stable of Cuthbert Hayhurst in Middletown, Bucks Co. (12 Apr.)

Time of Dutch servant girl for sale; enquire of Owen Fling, in Chestnut St., next door to Israel Pemberton, Jr. (12 Apr.)

Anne, wife of John Quick, of the Forks of Delaware, has eloped from her husband (12 Apr.)

Accounts with estate of Benjamin Field, late of Middletown, Bucks Co., dec'd, to be settled with Sarah Field, exec. (12 Apr.)

Land, wharf and stores in Water St. where Edward Hicks now dwells is for sale by Jacob Kollock; for terms apply to John Swift of Phila., merchant (12 Apr.)

Two horses have strayed from plantation of Anthony Pritchard in Charles-town, Chester Co. (12 Apr.)

House and lot on west side of Second St., now in possession of David Franks, for sale by William Allen, Edward Shippen and Samuel M'Call, Sr., attornies to execs. of John Moore, Esq., dec'd; also to be sold is plantation in Moyamensing Twp., late estate of John Moore (12 Apr.)

Samuel Fail, servant, miller, age c. 25, runaway from Joseph Dixon, of New Garden, Chester Co. (12 Apr.)

Letters from Halifax mention Col. Gorham and his company of rangers (19 Apr.)

Hannah Gertrude Flemer is in custody in Lancaster on suspicion of having murdered her bastard child (19 Apr.)

John Smith, Irish servant, age c. 23, runaway from William Patterson, of East Caln Twp., near Presbyterian meetinghouse (19 Apr.)

David Davis, fuller, in Darby, takes in work at the Sign of the White Horse in Elbow Lane; some work was delivered to Thomas Woolley (19 Apr.)

Reward if horse strayed or stolen from the Commons is brought to John Biddle at the Indian King (19 Apr.)

Accounts with estate of Stephen David, dec'd, to be settled with Hannah David, exec. (19 Apr.)

Daniel James, who pretends to be a Quaker, took position in Germantown as schoolmaster but left at noon of the first day (19 Apr.)

Mare strayed or stolen from John Shepard, living on Chestnut Hill in Germantown (19 Apr.)

William M'Cay, servant, runaway from James West (19 Apr.)

Brick house in Second St., contiguous to Samuel Nickle's, for sale by Alexander Stedman (19 Apr.)

Real estate in Northern Liberties for sale; apply to William Palmer on the premises (19 Apr.)

House in Second St., next door to Capt. Blair's, to be let; enquire of John Mifflin, Jr., living in house where Ann Coombs lately dwelt in Water St. (19 Apr.)

Land in Kent Co. for sale; apply to John Mifflin, Jr., or to Vincent Lockerman in town of Dover (19 Apr.)

Letter from Cadiz mentions Capt. Arbuthnot of the <u>Nightingale</u> man-of-war (26 Apr.)

Letter from River St. Croix mentions Capts. Gorham, St. Lo, Clapham, Rous and Cobb and General Philips (26 Apr.)

Capt. Mesnard has arrived at Phila. from London (26 Apr.)

Ship <u>Brothers</u>, Capt. Stewart, is cast away in Chesapeek Bay (26 Apr.)

Plantation in Oxford Twp., Phila. Co., for sale; enquire of Joseph Lewis, living on the premises, or Robert Waln, baker, in Front St., Phila. (26 Apr.)

James Steel, servant, born in New England, age c. 22, runaway from William Pennell, living in Middletown, Chester Co. (26 Apr.)

John Malcom, of Phila., sail-maker, has stopped a piece of stolen sailcloth (26 Apr.)

Horse strayed or stolen from George Baker of Kensington (26 Apr.)

Real estate on Gunner's Run on the Frankfort Road for sale at vendue at Thomas Harper's in Front St.; enquire of Joseph Oldman and Abel James (26 Apr.)

Joseph Donaldson, redemptioner, age 50, runaway from schooner <u>Prince George</u>, William Woodside commander; reward for his capture will be paid by said Woodside or by William Humphreys, merchant, in Phila. (26 Apr.)

Partnership between John Smith and Abel James has expired (26 Apr.)

Accounts with estate of John Lewis, formerly of Phila., cord-wainer, to be settled with John Lewis, admin. (26 Apr.)

Darby Henry, servant, age between 20 and 30, runaway from James Wilson of West Caln, Chester Co. (26 Apr.)

Persons indebted to estates of Benjamin Morgan or William Darril, dec'd, are to pay debts promptly to Evan Morgan and the other execs. (26 Apr.)

Real estate in Germantown will be sold by John Rudolph at the house of Anthony Hinckel in Germantown (26 Apr.)

Mare has been taken up by John Bear, living on plantation of John Goods in Leacock Twp., Lancaster Co. (26 Apr.)

Plantation in Conestogoe Twp., Lancaster Co., late property of John Postlethwaite, dec'd, for sale by Thomas Cookson, exec. (26 Apr.)

Plantation at Richmond, commonly called Point-no-Point, for sale by Robert Hopkins (26 Apr.)

1750

Capt. Shirley reports that the snow <u>Volunteer</u>, Capt. Chace, of Boston put into Dover on 1 Mar. (3 May)

Capt. Edwards from Liverpool informs that the ship <u>Happy</u>, Capt. Wilson, of New York, was cast away Feb. last (3 May)

John Forder, servant, born in London, age <u>c</u>. 17, runaway from Brian Wilkinson, of Phila., carver (3 May)

John Smith, Irish servant, age <u>c</u>. 22, runaway from Dr. John Diemer, of New-Providence; reward if runaway is brought to Diemer or Nathaniel Magee in Arch St. (3 May)

Heifer taken up by John Meas of Phila. (3 May)

Adv. of Reily and Archdall in Water St. (3 May)

House in Water St., opposite Joshua Emlen's Alley and next to John Jones, merchant, to be sold at the Widow Davis's in Front St.; apply to Benjamin Mifflin at the north end of Phila., who also has for sale real estate on Poole's hill, Kensington and Dover Square in Kent Co. (3 May)

Several lots of land for sale in Kensington; apply to Samuel Palmer (3 May)

John Lovegrove, servant, cooper, runaway from Stephen Sturgiss of Chester town, Kent Co., Md.; reward will be paid by Sturgiss or by Benjamin Brittin, baker, in Phila. (3 May)

Adv. of Samuel Spofforth, at Hamilton's wharf (3 May)

Patrick Dougherty, Irishman, runaway from his bail, Edward Lane of New-Providence (3 May)

Andrew Kimpler, next door to the Harp and Crown in Third St., offers reward for recovery of mare strayed or stolen from Richard Thatcher's in Kennet, Chester Co. (3 May)

Thomas Ellet offers reward if horse strayed from Richard Pearsell's in Nantmell Twp., Chester Co., is brought to Joseph Long's in said twp. (3 May)

Tract of land in Blockly Twp., about one mile and a half from Scull's ferry, for sale; enquire of Veronica Warner on the premises or Thomas Tilbury in Phila. (3 May)

Grist mill, house and barn in Cheltenham Twp., Phila. Co., for sale; apply to Mary and Susannah Martin, both living on the premises (3 May)

Train-oil sold by Thomas Clifford in Water St., near the ferry-house (3 May)

Lawrence Growdon, in Trevose, Bucks Co., has a Negro for sale (3 May)

Peter Bellec, a Frenchman, committed to goal in Boston for theft, claims he had a partner, Julian Giraudet (10 May)

Boston item of 30 Apr. reports that Robert Auchmuty, Esq., died there Sat. last (10 May)

Letter from Halifax mentions Major Lawrence, Capts. Rous, St. Loe, Bartelo, Scott and Clapham, Lieuts. Gorham, Paschall, Winslow, Watmaugh and Arbuthnot, Mr. Mitchell and Gov. Cornwallis (10 May)

For freight or passage to Charles-Town, S.C., in the snow <u>Strong</u>, Thomas Culbin commander, at Turner's wharf, agree with James Wallace at his store in Water St. (10 May)

1750

Tract of land close to Asheton's ferry, bounded to N. by John Warner's land, to be sold by James Humphreys; plan may be seen at Roberts's and James's coffee-houses, at Reese Meredith's, etc. (10 May)

Time of Dutch servant for sale; enquire of Jacob Henke, turner, in Second St. (10 May)

Accounts with estate of John Dilwyn to be settled with Susanna Dilwyn, admin. (10 May)

Accounts with estate of William Hawkins, dec'd, to be settled with Phebe Hawkins, admin. (10 May)

Francis Garrigues offers reward for recovery of boat that went adrift in the Delaware River (10 May)

Tanyard and house on west side of King St. to be sold by Benjamin Biles in Trenton (10 May)

John M'Guire, Irishman, runaway from George Taylor, of Middletown, Monmouth Co.; M'Guire took with him an Irish servant, Catherine Carroll, age c. 30 (10 May)

Real estate in Trenton and a plantation where William Douglas now lives, about 2 miles south of Trenton, adjoining plantation where Mr. Tuite lately lived, for sale by Thomas Cadwalader at Trenton (10 May)

Owen Daley, Irishman, age c. 25, runaway from William Hamilton of Cheltenham Twp., Phila. Co. (10 May)

Adv. of William Moode in Chestnut St. (10 May)

For freight or passage to Coracoa in sloop Sea-flower, Patrick Fitzsimons commander, agree with the commander or with William Moode (10 May)

James Erwin, servant, born in England, age c. 14, runaway from Samuel Fisher, of East Caln, Chester Co. (10 May)

Malt- and brew-house at the ferry on Schuylkill, late belonging to Ralph Ashton, dec'd, now in tenure of Joseph Scull, to be let (10 May)

John Dunbar, Irish servant, age c. 20, runaway from Calvin Cooper, of Sadsbury Twp., Lancaster Co. (10 May)

Horse strayed or stolen from Cook's Orchard in Oxford Twp.; reward offered for its recovery by George Bale, near William West's, at the Sign of the Sun, on Bristol Road (10 May)

Accounts with estate of John Stevens, late of Phila., tavernkeeper, to be settled with Margaret Stevens, exec. (10 May)

Dry goods for sale by Isaac Rodriguez Santino at his store in Chestnut St. (10 May)

Enos Carty was executed in Cecil Co. for being concerned in the murder of his late master, Hugh Machaffy, Jr.; Margaret Machaffy, widow of the dec'd, is to be tried for the murder of her husband (17 May)

William Green has been elected Gov. of Rhode Island, and Robert Hazard has been elected Deputy Gov. (17 May)

On 29 Apr. the schooner commanded by Capt. Crowningshield was driven ashore at Cape Ann (17 May)

Daniel Smith, convicted in New York of theft, was whipped at the cart's tail and stood in the pillory (17 May)

Fri. last John Kinsey, Chief Justice of Pa. and Speaker of the Assembly, died at Burlington (17 May)

1750

The snow <u>Wansworth</u>, Capt. Smith, arrived 16 May at Phila. from London (17 May)

Foundation of the Rev. Tennent's New Meeting-House is laid in Mulberry St. (17 May)

Drawing of lottery for New Jersey College will begin 28 May at Samuel Hazard's (17 May)

Plantation in Oxford Twp. to be sold; plan of the lots to be seen at Robert Waln's in Front St. or Joseph Levis's, on the premises (17 May)

Meadow, part of Boon's Island, adjoining Carpenter's Island, to be sold at Andrew Cox's on Boon's Island in Kingsess by Thomas Williams, hatter, in Second St., Phila. (17 May)

Evan Griffith of Lower Merion has taken up a mare (17 May)

James M'Donnald, Irish hired servant, age c. 24, runaway from John Valentine, of New Providence Twp., Phila. Co. (17 May)

Horse strayed or stolen from Isaac Feree of Leacock Twp., Lancaster Co. (17 May)

Plantation in Kensington to be sold by Henry Miller (17 May)

Tobey, Negro, age between 40 and 50, runaway from James Mackey, living in Wood St. at north end of Phila. (17 May)

Beef and pork for sale; enquire in Second St. at house where Thomas Hart, dec'd, formerly lived, next door to Thomas Craeme, Esq. (17 May)

Plantation of William Noblit in Middletown, Chester Co., to be let or sold (17 May)

Jacob Parrot, convict servant, age c. 21, born in west of England, who has been a footman, runaway from Hugh Jones, of Cecil Co., Md.; he left in company with James Jones, age c. 16 or 17, born in Ireland, servant of Dr. Bradford (17 May)

Mary Conolly, Irish servant, age c. 23, runaway from David Wilkin, of Noxonton, Newcastle Co.; reward for her capture will be paid by John Jones in Noxonton (17 May)

Capt. Phillips has sailed from Boston for London (24 May)

Richard Crawford, Irish servant, and John Pritchard, servant, born in England, runaways from Charles Foreman, living near Chestertown, Kent Co., Md. (24 May)

Estate of Thomas Griffith, late dec'd, in King St., for sale (24 May)

Tract of land in Bristol Twp., Bucks Co., late estate of John Johnson of Bucks Co., dec;d, but since conveyed by Giles Lawrence to William Allen and Robert Strettell, for sale; enquire of Allen and Strettell in Phila. or Samuel Carey in Bucks Co. (24 May)

Real estate adjoining Christine Bridge in Whiteclay-Creek-Hundred, Newcastle Co., the place where John M'Mechen, dec'd, lately lived, opposite to the house of Thomas Montgomery, merchant, to be sold by James M'Mechen (24 May)

Adv. of James and Joseph Morris in Front St. (24 May)

Mare strayed from plantation of Edward Barwick, Esq., in Lancaster Co. (24 May)

Adv. of Randle Mitchell in Water St., opposite to Alexander Hamilton's and next door to Capt. Phillips (24 May)

A silver watch was lost on Conestogoe Road, between David George's and the Merion Meeting-house; reward if brought to Musgrave Evans at Thomas Hoodt's in Water St. or to William Gray's at the Sign of the Conestogoe Waggon; the watch is supposed to have been taken up by Daniel Crosby (24 May)

Accounts with estate of Thomas Holcomb, miller, late of Abington, to be settled with Jacob Leech, Walter Moore and Robert Thomas, auditors (24 May)

Adv. of Arent Hassert in Laetitia Court (24 May)

Adv. of Stephen Carmick in Market St. (24 May)

Thomas Lanphier, late teacher in H.M.'s navy, teaches navigation, astronomy, etc.; enquire at James White's, shopkeeper, near the drawbridge in Phila. (24 May)

Irish servants, just imported in the ship Catherine, for sale at house of Thomas Williams, at the Sign of the Hat in Second St.; apply to said Williams or to Abraham Shelley at the Widow Dawson's, next door to the Friends Meeting-house (24 May)

Adv. of Alexander Modie and James Hood, tailors from London, at the Sign of the Thistle in Second St. (24 May)

Adv. of Peter Galloway, living opposite to the prison in Market St., and Asher Mott, near the New-market on Society Hill (24 May)

Thomas Cummings, English servant, blacksmith, runaway from George Rock, living at the head of North-East River, Md. (24 May)

Hanis Yarick Grumley, Dutch servant, middle-aged, runaway from William Albertson of New-town Creek, Gloucester Co. (24 May)

Time of Irish servant, plaisterer by trade, for sale; enquire of Thomas Penrose, ship-carpenter, or James Milne on Society Hill (24 May)

Black horse has been taken up by David Morgan of New-Britain, Bucks Co. (24 May)

Horse stolen from Edward Hill, living at Dunk's Ferry, by John Miller, alias John Stogdal (24 May)

John Maycum, indented Indian or Mulatto servant, age c. 25, runaway from John Chick, Jr., of Cecil Co., Md. (24 May)

Henry Dixon, English servant, age c. 19, born in Manchester, runaway from Abraham Chattin, Jr., of Timber Creek, Gloucester Co. (24 May)

Two convict Irish servants, James O'Bryan, age c. 22, and Catherine, age c. 30, runaways from John Ashford, of Cecil Co., Md., near Warwick Town (24 May)

Brick house within a mile of Capt. Hopper's inspecting-house in Queen Anne's Co., Md., to be let; apply to Matthew Dockery, living near the premises (24 May)

Real estate in Phila., part of a lot adjoining Isaac Zeans's present dwelling, for sale at the Widow Roberts's Coffeehouse; plan to be seen at John Durborow's (31 May)

John Donnohon, Irish servant, age c. 24, runaway from Robert Siminton, of Conestogoe, Lancaster Co. (31 May)

George Gordon, Sheriff of Frederick Co., offers reward for capture of the following, all committed for debt, who have broken out of the goal of Frederick Co.: William Snowden, tailor; William Jenkins, labourer; George Tarr, carpenter, lately come to Pa.; John Hack, labourer; the two last are Dutchmen (31 May)

John Valentine, Chief Ranger at Gilbert's Manor, Phila. Co., lists strays that he has taken up (31 May)

Horse has strayed from pasture of Thomas Gordon on Society Hill (31 May)

Tract of land in Lower Dublin Twp., now in tenure of Hance and Nicholas Lycan, taken in execution at suit of John Petty and others, to be sold at house of Richard Allen near Pennypack (31 May)

Lots of ground in Kensington, belonging to William Parker, taken in execution at suit of Robert Greenway and others, execs. of John Bood, dec'd (31 May)

House at corner of Sassafras and Second Sts. in which Benjamin Franklin now dwells is to be let; enquire of Sarah Dillwyn (31 May)

For freight or passage to Charles-Town, S.C., in schooner Betsy, John Strachan master, agree with Robert and Amos Strettell (31 May)

Thomas Katera in Earl Twp., Lancaster Co., has taken up a horse

John Winter, landskip painter, next door to George Heap's in Third St., teaches drawing and painting (31 May)

Adv. of Morgan and Elkins at the Sign of the Ship a Ground in Front St. (31 May)

Benjamin Britton gives terms of the will, dated 2 Nov. 1721, of John Johnson, who left his estate to his seven children (31 May)

Lilly, Negro, age 35, born in Bermudas, who formerly belonged to Mr. Bailey of Lewiston, pilot, runaway from John Gilleylen, of Southampton Twp., Bucks Co.; reward if runaway is brought to Francis Manny, sail-maker, in Chestnut St. (31 May)

Derrick Rappalie offers reward for return of two horses that were stolen from him near New Brunswick, supposedly by Thomas Francis, said to have come from New-town, Md. (31 May)

House (an inn) where Peter Ganthony now lives in Wilmington, belonging to estate of Thomas Broom, dec'd, to be sold by James Broom and Peter Ganthony, execs. (31 May)

House in Wilmington, lately belonging to Elizabeth Broom, dec'd, to be sold by James Broom, admin. (31 May)

William Grace, convict servant, age c. 23 or 24, runaway from William Davis, living at Boyd's Hole, Stafford Co., Va.; with him went a hireling, Alexander M'Quillin, a north-country Irishman, who served his time with Col. Thomas Lee (31 May)

James Cregg, servant, age c. 11, stolen, supposedly by his mother, from James Blair, of Westmoreland Co., Va. (31 May)

Mary, wife of John Morgan, of Whiteland Twp., Chester Co., has eloped from her husband (7 June)

For freight or passage to London in ship Lydia, Peter Reeve commander, agree with James Pemberton (7 June)

Cornelius Stevens, apprentice, age c. 18, shop joiner, runaway from William Attmore (7 June)

Mary Crosby, Irish convict servant, age c. 20, runaway from Timothy Brannin, of Warwick, Cecil Co., Md. (7 June)

Plantation, late in possession of Alexander Lockhart, Esq., three or four miles from Trenton, N.J., adjoining plantation of Charles Clark, Esq., for sale; enquire of John Cox in Trenton (7 June)

House between Phila. and the Lower Ferry, late John Kinsey's, Esq., dec'd, to be let (7 June)

Adv. of Abraham Carpenter, at the Sign of the Duke of Cumberland, over Pool's bridge; said Abraham has a shop by the dock, at the back of Hugh Cordrae, to be let or sold (7 June)

Grist mill and land in Cheltenham Twp., Phila. Co. to be let; apply to Mary and Sarah Martin, both living on the premises (7 June)

Adv. of Charles Batho, whose store is on Fishbourn's wharf and whose house is on Society Hill, next door to William Peters, notary public (7 June)

John Shoppley, alias Williams, servant, country born, shoemaker, runaway from Marmaduke Tilden, living in Kent Co., Md. (7 June)

Mare strayed from Derrick Cleaver, living in Douglass Twp., Phila. Co., near Thomas Potts's Ironworks; reward if mare is brought to Reiner Tyson or Richard Waln in White-marsh, or Peter Cleaver in Upper Dublin or to the owner (7 June)

New York item of 11 June reports how a shot fired from H.M.S. Greyhound, Capt. Roddam, then lying in the North River, killed the nurse to a child of Col. William Rickets of Elizabeth-town, who was going home from New York in Col. Rickets's boat (14 June)

House and lot in High St., Phila., now in tenure of John Linn, for sale (14 June)

Lot in Spruce St. to be sold at the Widow Roberts's Coffee-House by John Ord (14 June)

Accounts to be settled with Charles Willing, who intends for England in the ship Macclesfield, Capt. Stupart (14 June)

English servants, just arrived from Bristol in the Golden Fleece, Richard Symes master, to be sold by Robert and Amos Strettell (14 June)

William Benning, stay-maker, has removed from Front St. to the house where William Jevon lived, next door to John Mifflin in Market St. (14 June)

Accounts with estate of Thomas Burgess, dec'd, to be settled with Thomas Shaw and Samuel Sansom, execs. (14 June)

For freight or passage to Bristol in the snow Batchelor, George Noarth master, agree with the master (14 June)

Francis Feghan, servant, who speaks English, Dutch and French, age c. 27, who has resorted frequently about Roger Hunt's in Water St., runaway from David Watson, living near great Connewagoe, York Co. (14 June)

Robert Dugall, Scotch servant, age c. 35, who says he worked in the King's Yard in Gibraltar, runaway from Henry Baker in Cecil Co., Md. (14 June)

Daniel Dupuy, William Ghislin and Philip Syng have stopped two large spoons (makers' marks P.S. and E.B.) and three teaspoons (makers' marks P.S. and D.D. and one illegible but with the Irish sterling mark); Joseph Richardson has a silver-hilted sword, owner unknown (14 June)

Dennis Madden, <u>alias</u> Duncan Woods, born in Dublin, age c. 25, who served his first time in Chester Co. and went a soldier to Cape Breton, runaway from Joseph Tate, minister in Dunnegill, Lancaster Co.; reward if brought to said Tate or to Samuel Scott or Robert Thompson (14 June)

Hugh Hall, apprentice, age c. 18, runaway from John Catheringa, tailor (14 June)

Some Indians were killed or wounded about Pisquit in a skirmish with Capt. John Rouse and Capt. Philips (21 June)

Capt. Kierstede arrived at New York from Jamaica with account of a terrible fire at Port Royal which started in the house of a Mr. Sullivan (21 June)

H.M.S. <u>Hector</u>, Capt. Maisterson, at New York, fell down from Turtle Bay to the Watering Place (21 June)

Accounts with estate of George Fitzwater, late of Phila., merchant, dec'd, to be settled with William Coleman and Francis Richardson, execs. (21 June)

Nicholas Curran, servant, age c. 20, runaway from Joseph Frazer, living in Little Britain Twp., Lancaster Co. (21 June)

House and lot (subject to rent payable to Edward Warner) in Third St., late dwelling of Sebastian Murry, dec'd, for sale by Sarah Murry, admin. (21 June)

Adv. of John Bell, whose store is on Hamilton's wharf (21 June)

Mare strayed or stolen from William Pearson, of Chester Twp., Chester Co. (21 June)

Parcel of servants for sale by John Erwin in Strawberry Alley (21 June)

Thomas Griffitts, hatter, near the drawbridge, has a schooner, the <u>Flying Fish</u>, for sale (21 June)

Grist mill in Nottingham Twp., Burlington Co., N.J., for sale by William Morris (21 June)

Andrew Tate, living in Gloucester, has found a snuff box and two pocketbooks in the woods near Gloucester (21 June)

Abraham Taylor, intending to go to England with his family, wishes to settle all his accounts (21 June)

Mare strayed from John Morris of French-Creek-Fords; reward if brought to the Widow Christie in Strawberry Alley (21 June)

Real estate in Willis Twp. and Whiteland Twp. to be sold by George Aston, of Whiteland Twp., Chester Co. (21 June)

Land in Pickering, Chester Co., will be sold by Nathaniel John at William Goldsmith's, tavern-keeper, in Pickering; for information apply to Daniel John in Pickering (21 June)

A Negro, a block-maker, for sale by Daniel Benezet in Front St. (21 June)

1750

Valentine Strong, Irish servant, who used to follow soap-boiling in Ireland but now pretends wampum-making, and Bartholomew Logan, servant, this country born, wampum-maker, runaways from William Spear of Donnegall Twp., Lancaster Co. (21 June)

Adv. of George Robotham on Hazard's wharf (21 June)

Adv. of John Stevens, next door to Dr. Zachary's in Walnut St. (21 June)

Adv. of Richard Farmar, at the Unicorn in Second St. (21 June)

On 6 June 1735 tract of 400 acres in Orange Co., Va., was by deed granted to Edward and John Dougherty; if they do not pay off quit-rents within three months, Thomas Lord Fairfax will grant said land to Dr. William Lynn of Fredericksburgh, Va. (21 June)

Adv. of Joseph Beddome on Samuel Hazard's wharf (21 June)

H.M.S. the Hound, Capt. Dove, the Tryal, Capt. Le Cras, and Albany, Capt. Rous, have arrived at Boston, whence H.M.S. Success, Lord Colvil, has sailed for Nova Scotia (28 June)

Mortgages, wills, notes, etc. drawn by Paul Isaac Voto (late clerk to Charles Brogden) at his office at John Jervis's, hatter, in Black-horse-alley, Phila. (28 June)

Adv. of Samuel Hasell, next door to the Bible, in Front St. (28 June)

Horse of William Stanley in Market St. strayed or stolen from the Commons in Phila. (28 June)

Hugh Kelly, Irish servant, age c. 21, runaway from George Monro of Newcastle (28 June)

Accounts with estate of Matthew Moss, late of Carpenter's Island, dec'd, to be settled with Hannah Moss, admin. (28 June)

Plantation on the Delaware, within a mile of Trenton, for sale; apply to Joseph Worrell near the premises or Joseph Wharton or John Jenkins at William Plumsted's in Phila. (28 June)

Josiah Ellis, of Byberry, Phila. Co., intends for England; persons with demands on him are desired to meet him at the house of John Biddle, the Sign of the Indian King (28 June)

The schooner Anne and Rebecca, Oswald Eve master, now at Shoemaker's wharf, will sail for Antigua (28 June)

Cloth for sale by Matthew and Abraham Usher in Front St., opposite James's Coffee House, next door to Mr. Peters's, notary public (28 June)

John Clark, Irish servant, age c. 40, runaway from John Mortemor of Fallowfield (28 June)

Horse strayed or stolen from Thomas M'Kean, innholder, of Chester Co., on Conestogoe road (28 June)

Horse strayed from Alexander Graydon of Bristol, Bucks Co.; reward if horse is brought to Graydon or to Joseph Marks in Phila. (28 June)

Horse came to plantation of Isaac Abraham in Upper Merion, Phila. Co. (28 June)

Hugh Glasgow, servant, age c. 35, runaway from Joseph Chick, living in Bohemia Manor, Cecil Co., Md. (28 June)

John Eugene, servant, age c. 30, runaway from Robert Young of East Nottingham, Chester Co. (28 June)

House and lot in Sassafras St., belonging to estate of Samuel Spencer, for sale; enquire of John Spencer in Front St. or Benjamin Lee in Second St. (28 June)

Mare strayed from plantation of Samuel Scott; reward if mare is brought to the owner, Hugh Pedin, or Samuel Scott, tavern-keeper, at Big Chickie's Creek, Lancaster Co. (28 June)

Account of arrest and trials of Margaret Mahaffy, suspected of being an accessory to the murder of her husband, Hugh Mahaffy, Jr., by Enos Carty; she was examined by Justices Rock and Baker and was tried and acquitted; she was again arrested on a warrant issued by Justice Roberts but the Grand Jury at Annapolis found no bill and she was discharged (28 June)

Caesar, Negro, born in Guinea, runaway from David Davis, living in Earlstown, Lancaster Co. (28 June)

Capt. Sweeting has arrived at Rhode Island (5 July)

On 21 June at Amboy the wife of Obadiah Ayres was shot dead by her own Negro; said Negro and another, his accomplice, confessed and are to be executed (5 July)

Adv. of Joseph Saunders at his store on Rees Meredith's wharf (5 July)

Robert Callow, of Hemiock, Devonshire, England, about nine years since sailed to Pa. and there lived with Owen Owen, at the Sign of the Indian King in Phila.; later Callow removed to Bucks Co.; if he will apply to Joseph Williams at Concord, Chester Co., he will hear something to his advantage (5 July)

Jacob, Negro, age c. 28, runaway from Job Ruston, living in Fogs Manor, Chester Co. (5 July)

Timothy Matlack is removed to his brew-house in Market St. (5 July)

Property in Market St., bounded on E. by the tenement and ground late of the Widow Glover and on W. by the house and ground of Marcus Kuhl, is for sale; enquire of Hannah Pearson, living on the premises (5 July)

Two servants, both aged about 30, Edward Foster and Richard Mitchell, runaways from John Lovering of Sassafras, Cecil Co., Md. (5 July)

Caleb Pusey, Deputy Sheriff of Newcastle on Delaware, gives notice of the three following men taken up and committed to goal: William Davis, age c. 40; George Griffin, age c. 22; James Burns (5 July)

Tract of land in the Northern Liberties, known as Oxley's plantation, adjoining the seat lately belonging to Thomas Chalkley, to be sold by Benjamin Callender, at William Callender's in Front St. (5 July)

Two lots in Almond St., between William Preston's and the house where Joseph Richards lately dwelt, bounded on the W. by a lot of Cadwalader Morgan's, are for sale by Joseph Durborow (5 July)

Mare stolen from Samuel Smith, of Maidenhead (5 July)

Mare strayed or stolen off Province Island; reward offered by John Banes if mare is brought to John Biddle's at the Sign of the Indian King (5 July)

Copper stills are sold at the house of Michael Hillegas in Second St. (5 July)

Lot in Phila., belonging to estate of John Marshall, late of Darby, Chester Co., dec'd, to be sold by Lewis Thomas and Thomas and Isaac Pearson, execs. (5 July)

William Hogan, Irish servant, blacksmith, runaway from Alexander Alexander, of Phila. (5 July)

Capts. Hill and Watson, arrived in York River, report the death on 1 Apr. of William Parker, printer of the <u>Virginia Gazette</u> (12 July)

Lot in Sassafras St., belonging to estate of Thomas Redman, dec'd, to be sold by Penelope Redman, admin. (12 July)

Adv. of John Priest in Water St., opposite the store of Levy and Franks (12 July)

For freight or passage to London in the ship <u>Forrest</u>, Patrick Ouchterlony master, agree with Alexander Hamilton or said master (12 July)

Lot in Chestnut St., belonging to Jasper Carpenter, taken in execution at the suit of Luke Morris and wife, execs. of Joseph Richards, dec'd, will be sold at James's Coffeehouse (12 July)

Plantation in Oxford Twp., belonging to Robert Harper, taken in execution at the suit of Edward Hill, will be sold at the house of Thomas Harper in Frankfort (12 July)

House and lot in Front St., belonging to William Hillier, taken in execution at the suit of Walter Goodman, will be sold at the house of William Nicholson (12 July)

Plantation in Blockley Twp., belonging to John Warner, taken in execution at the suit of Rebecca Edgell, will be sold at the house of Joseph Scull (12 July)

James Carr, Irish servant, age <u>c</u>. 16 or 17, runaway from George Lownes of Springfield, Chester Co. (12 July)

Plantation on Delaware River in Oxford Twp. for sale; apply to Joseph Sims near the drawbridge (12 July)

Medicines imported in the ship <u>Swift</u>, Capt. Le Gros, are for sale by John M'Kinly (12 July)

Item about John Thomas, exec. of estate of Thomas Sharp (12 July)

Accounts with estate of Thomas Holcomb, late of Abington, Phila. Co., miller, to be settled at the house of Thomas Fletcher, Esq., in Abington, with Jacob Leech, Walter Moore and Robert Thomas (12 July)

Octavo Bible of the King family about three years ago was sent by the then post rider from Maryland to Phila. to be rebound; it has not been heard of, and the rider has gone away; it had marginal notes with names and ages of persons in the family (12 July)

Two houses belonging to James Steward in Lombard St. are for sale; enquire of Isaac Norris and William Griffitts (12 July)

New York item mentions Capts. Vardil and Ross of New York, Capt. Tucker of Bermuda, Capts. Heysham and Kattur (19 July)

Richard Richison, Chief Ranger of Chester Co., lists strays (19 July)

House in Kensington, lately belonging to Anthony Palmer, Esq., to be sold or let; enquire of Alexander Allaire, living on the premises (19 July)

Adv. of Charles Dawson in Arch St., where Mr. Vanderspeigle lately lived (19 July)

Adv. of Thomas Ellis, glazier, in Front St. (19 July)

Mary M'Creary, convict servant, age c. 47, and her son, James M'Creary, convict servant, age c. 24, runaways from Thomas Ebthorp and Thomas Money, living on Bohemia Manor in Cecil Co., Md. (19 July)

John Wright, servant, shoemaker, and William Cherryhome (a Yorkshire-man), servant, and Sam (a Negro), runaways from John Hammond on Elkridge, Anne-Arundel Co., Md. (19 July)

John Davis, servant, who served his time with Peter Stretch in Phila. and went with Capt. Trent on the expedition to Canada, runaway from Thomas James of borough of Lancaster (19 July)

Robert Kid, English servant, blacksmith, runaway from William Rush of Phila., blacksmith (19 July)

Horse and mare strayed from Commons of Phila.; reward if they are brought to Thomas Cateringer at the Sign of the Green Stays in Arch St. (19 July)

Tract of land in New-town, Bucks Co., late belonging to Joseph Walley, dec'd, taken in execution at the suit of John Strickland, to be sold at Joseph Insley's in New-town (19 July)

Adv. of John Davis at Francis Trumble's, joiner, in Second St. (19 July)

John Smith, at pasture formerly known as Carpenter's Island, pastures horses and cows; enquire of John Bleakley in Phila. (19 July)

Mare strayed or stolen from Parson Melenbergh's plantation in Providence Twp., Phila. Co.; reward if brought to said Melenbergh or to Bernard Hubley in Lancaster (19 July)

Tract of land in Whiteland Twp., Chester Co., late property of James Rowland, dec'd, to be sold by Lewis James (19 July)

Frederick Vandyke, Dutch servant, age c. 30, runaway from John Juquat, of Swannack, Newcastle Co. (19 July)

Vendue will be held at house of Isaac Williams, next door to the Quakers Meeting-house in Market St. (26 July)

H.M.S. America, Capt. Barnsley, has arrived at Boston (26 July)

James Honymin, Episcopal minister at Newport for 46 years, died on 2 July (26 July)

Shop- and household goods, late belonging to Thomas Williams, hatter, in Second St., will be sold; demands against his estate to be brought to John Kidd, Peter Turner and John Wallace to be settled (26 July)

Lots of land in Smithfield, late belonging to estate of John Bood, dec'd, taken in execution at suits of Thomas Bond and others, will be sold at the house of John Keen at Smithfield (26 July)

Accounts with estate of Rebecca Edgell, widow, dec'd, to be settled with Jonathan Mifflin, exec. (26 July)

Real estate in township of North Wales, belonging to John Jones, taken in execution at the suit of John Trump, will be sold at the house of Benjamin Davis in Upper Dublin (26 July)

Real estate in Horsham Twp., belonging to John M'Comb, taken in execution at the suit of Thomas Green, will be sold at the house of Benjamin Davis in Upper Dublin (26 July)

Horse strayed from the Commons; reward if horse is brought to James Green, victualler, in Fourth St., Phila. (26 July)

If the following apply to Jonathan Thomas, postmaster in Burlington, they will hear something to their advantage: Daniel Philips (from Kingsbridge in England, supposed to reside in New Jersey); Mark Casey, sailor or shoemaker, who seven years ago came from Cork to Pa.; Michael Casey (brother of Mark), a shoemaker, who also came from Cork to Pa. seven years ago; any persons named Place who had an uncle named Aaron Place in England (26 July)

Peter Garagan, Irish servant, age c. 21, runaway from Bennet Bard of the city of Burlington (26 July)

Accounts with estate of Michael Koyl, late of Phila., dec'd, to be settled with Thomas Leece and Benjamin Franklin, execs. (26 July)

Money has been stolen from James Way of West Caln, Chester Co. (26 July)

Plantation in Haverford Twp., Chester Co., for sale; apply to James Day, living on the premises (26 July)

Tract of land, lying part in Frederick Co., Md., part in York Co., near Marsh-Creek, for sale; apply to Sarah Brown, who lives on the premises (26 July)

Capt. Benjamin Stoddert arrived at Albany from Canada (30 July)

Bar iron for sale by Thomas White in Market St. (30 July)

Register for the academy of Phila. with the Rector, Mr. David Martin (2 Aug.)

Goods imported by Capt. McCarthy for sale by Randle Mitchell, opposite Mrs. Mary Andrews,and next door to Alexander Hamilton, in Water St. (2 Aug.)

Reward offered by James Carr, shopkeeper, for the return of a watch and spoons (2 Aug.)

Time of Irish servants, brought in the brig. *Dove*, Capt.Daniel McCarthy, for sale by James Pemberton (2 Aug.)

Plantation for sale in Newcastle Co.; apply to Obadiah Elliot (2 Aug.)

Horse missing from plantation of George Rock of North-east,Md.; reward will be paid by Rock, Joseph Colbourn of Phila., or James Mather of Chester (2 Aug.)

Irish apprentice, Daniel McKneel, runaway from the *Prince George*, William Woodside, Commander (2 Aug.)

Adv. of Richard Wagstaffe, London peruke-maker, in Third St. (2 Aug.)

Mare strayed from John Bliler of the Great Swamp; return to said Bliler or to Jacob Siegel, in Arch St. (2 Aug.)

Adv. of Andrew Lamb, navigation teacher in Abraham Taylor's Alley, near Second St. (2 Aug.)

For sale or rent, property of Sebastian Murry, dec'd., on Third
St.; rent payable to Edward Warner; Sarah Murry, admin.(2 Aug.)

Land bounded by property of Joseph Wharton, to be auctioned at
Anthony Whiteley's, on Society-hill (2 Aug.)

Plantation to be sold, in Middletown, Chester Co., at the home
of Samuel McCrea (2 Aug.)

Phil, Negro, age c.25, and Bess, Mulatto, age e.20, runaway from
Job Ruston in Fog's Manor, Chester Co. (2 Aug.)

Frank, Negro, lived in NY with Frederick Bekers of York, baker
and butcher, runaway from Isaac Shano of Falis Twp., Bucks
Co. (2 Aug.)

William Fell, convict English servant, runaway from James Dimmitti, Baltimore Co.,Md. (2 Aug.)

Adv. of Alexander Huston, in Market St. (2 Aug.)

For sale, property near Charles Willing's, Esq; apply to John
and Jedediah Snowden (2 Aug.)

For freight or passage to St. John's, brig. Gregg, John Allen,
Commander; apply to said commander or Capt. William Blair,
(9 Aug.)

For freight or passage to Barbados, ship Molley and Salley, at
Dickinson's wharf, Thomas Perry, Master; apply to Anthony
Stocker at his store beneath John Steber's house in Water St.
(9 Aug.)

For freight or passage to London, ship Beulah, John Richey,
Commander,; apply to Benjamin or Samuel Shoemaker (9 Aug.)

Plantation for sale, Charles Twp; apply to William Reilly, Whiteland Twp. (9 Aug.)

Lost, ferry boat; reward offered by William Vaughan and Benjamin Howell of Marcus Hook (9 Aug.)

Reward offered by Richard Sewall, sheriff, for capture of James
Murphy, hammerman (9 Aug.)

Mary, wife of Thomas Hunt of Hopewell, Hunterdon Co, New Jersey
has eloped (9 Aug.)

Medicines and imported goods for sale by Levy and Franks (9 Aug.)

John Wallace has removed his store from Second St. to Chestnut
St. (9 Aug.)

Accounts with the estate of Dr. Thomas Shaw, dec'd, of Burlington, may be settled with Samuel Shaw and Anne Shaw, execs.
(9 Aug.)

House for sale, Sixth St, bounded north with Jonathan Zanes's
lot, west with land of Isaac Zanes, and south with Thomas
Tilbrey's lot; enquire of Jacob Shoemaker, blacksmith (9 Aug.)

Edward Tyler, English, age c. 25, from Worcestershire, runaway
from Richard Brookbank, baker, Laetitia-court (9 Aug.)

Effects and estate of Thomas Holcomb, dec'd, for sale at his
grist-mill in New-Britain Twp, Bucks Co, by Amos Strickland,
Samuel Cary, William Crosdale, auditors (9 Aug.)

Runaway from the ship Prince Frederick, James Cawley, Commander,
two servants: Henry Potter, Irish, age c.30, and Matthew Burk,
Irish, weaver, age c.24; return to Capt. Darby Lux, merchant
Baltimore, Md. (9 Aug.)

Adv. of Robert Moore, shopkeeper, in Front St. (9 Aug.)

1750

Malashiah or Melchior, Colpen or Calvin, age c.21, runaway from Jacob Ove of Pepaek, Somerset Co, East-Jersey (9 Aug.)

Lot, Negro, once lived in Great Egg-harbor with Joseph Sooy, runaway from Thomas Hooton of Trenton Ferry, Burlington Co. (9 Aug)

For sale, land; enquire of Alexander Graydon in Bristol, or William McIlvaine in Phila. (9 Aug.)

For sale, tavern; enquire of George Gibson, on the premises (9 Aug.)

Accounts with the estate of William Hartley, Reading Twp, Phila. Co; settle with Hannah Hartley, widow and exec. (9 Aug.)

For sale or rent, property at Christine Bridge; apply to Dr. Rees Jones, who intends for Europe (9 Aug.)

Land for sale; apply to Thomas Cadwalader at Trenton; also, a plantation occupied by William Douglas adjoining property late of Mr. Tuite (9 Aug.)

Goods for sale by Stephen Carmick, shopkeeper, in Market St. (9 Aug.)

For sale, Oxley's plantation in the Northern Liberties, next to land late belonging to Thomas Chalkley; enquire of Benjamin Callender at William Callender's, in Front St. (9 Aug)

Property for sale on Mifflin's Wharf; enquire of Morris Morris, or Samuel Morris, at White-marsh, Phila. Co. (9 Aug.)

Tanyard for sale by Benjamin Biles, living on the premises at Trenton (9 Aug.)

Gristmill and plantation in Nottingham Twp., Burlington Co., to be sold by William Morris of Trenton (9 Aug.)

Adv. of Thomas Gordon, below the Drawbridge, on Powell's wharf (9 Aug.)

The partnership between John Smith and Abel Jones is dissolved (9 Aug.)

Imported goods for sale by Mordecai Yarnall, at the sign of the Handsaw, in Second St. (9 Aug.)

Adv. of Joseph Sims, below the Drawbridge, and Buckridge Sims, at the house of Joseph Turner (9 Aug.)

Silver watches, etc. for sale by Daniel Benezet at his store in Front St. (9 Aug.)

Adv. of Edward Weyman, upholsterer, at Jacob Legay's, in Arch St. (9 Aug.)

Reward offered by James Green, victualler, in Fourth St., for the return of a stray horse (9 Aug.)

Negro for sale; enquire of widow Linton, in Chestnut St. (9 Aug.)

Goods and medicines, imported in the Ship **Speedwell**, Capt. Stevenson, from London, for sale by Charles Dawson, in Arch St., where Mr. Vanderspeigle lately lived (9 Aug.)

The General Assembly of Phila. unanimously chose Isaac Norris, Esq. as Speaker in room of John Kinsey, Esq., dec'd. (16 Aug.)

Property, next to Thomas Bond's ground, for sale at widow Gregory's in Kensington (16 Aug.)

The estate, late of Isaac Williams, to be sold at Thomas Carvill's at the Tun, in Germantown, by John Reynell, Abel James, Isaac Jones, and James Benezet (16 Aug.)

To be sold, plantation, formerly belonging to Ebenezer Large, late Samuel Large's dec'd; apply to William Murfin, exec. (16 Aug.)

Benjamin Bagnall,Jr. has two clocks for sale at his house in Front St. (16 Aug.)

For freight or passage to Jamaica on the brig. Cumberland, Joseph Conyers,Commander; apply at his house, over the Drawbridge, or on board the vessel at Powell's wharf (16 Aug.)

Household and shop goods to be sold by Richard Sewell, sheriff, at the house of Judah Foulke, in Market St. (16 Aug.)

Plantation to be sold at Thomas Clayton's in Chichester, Chester Co.; also, land in West Bradford between that of Edward Brinton, William Pimm, and John Leard, to be sold at the house of Thomas Park in Caln, Chester Co.; plantation on Brandywine creek, next to lands of Samuel Taylor and Jonathan Park, to be sold at Matthias Kerlin's, Concord; all are to be sold by John Taylor (16 Aug.)

William Vaughan and Edward Whitaker give notice of the annual fair to be held at Chichester (16 Aug.)

James Love, Irish, runaway from Patrick Miller at the sign of the Buck, Conestoga Rd., Chester Co. (16 Aug.)

Philip Harrison, age c.23, Irish, runaway from William Kendall, Limerick Twp., Phila. Co. (16 Aug.)

For freight or passage to South Carolina in the ship Patience, Hugh Steel, Commander; apply to said Steel or to Charles and Alexander Stedman (16 Aug.)

Elizabeth, wife of George Hart of West Bradford, Chester Co., has eloped (16 Aug.)

William Mearns, English, age c.30, pretends to be a mason, and, Will, Negro, age c.25, runaways from Isaac Whitelock, in Lancaster borough (16 Aug.)

James Ward, Irish, age c.23, served six years to John Hannams, runaway from John Hanly of Chester, Chester Co. (16 Aug.)

Goods for sale by Matthew and Abraham Usher at their store in Front St., opposite Norris's Alley, in the house where Mr. Monnington lives, Also, rum and sugar for sale at their store on Hamilton's wharf (16 Aug.)

William Farrell, Irish, runaway from Joseph Jackson of London Grove, Chester Co.; with Thomas Collard, Irish, runaway from Samuel Ramsay, of Londonderry, Chester Co. (16 Aug.)

Plantation in Tryduffryn, Chester Co., to be sold by Mathusalah Davis, on the premises (16 Aug.)

Goods imported in the snow Wantworth, Capt. Smith, for sale by George Smith at his store between Norris's Alley and Gray's Alley (16 Aug.)

Goods for sale by Charles Batho at his store on Fishbourne's wharf or at his house on Society Hill, next door to where Robert Ellis formerly lived (16 Aug.)

Goods from London imported in the snow *Triton*, Capt. Shirley, to be sold by James Trotter at his store next door to Townsend White, in Front St; Trotter intends for England (16 Aug.)

Land for sale in Fredericks Co., Md.; apply to Sarah Brown, living on the premises (16 Aug.)

Goods imported from Liverpool in the snow *Strong*, Capt. Thomas Cubbin, to be sold by James Wallace at his store where James Steward, tailor, formerly lived, in Water St.

Capt. Ion was brought to Phila. to his trial (23 Aug.)

Isaac Griffitts is a candidate for the office of Sheriff for the city and county of Phila. (23 Aug.)

James Trotter, Sec'y. of the St. Andrew's Society, calls the Quarterly meeting at the Tun tavern (23 Aug.)

To be sold or let by Edward Shippen, a water lot near William Attwood, Esq's. stores and wharf (23 Aug.)

Joseph Redman, appointed collector of the excise for the city and county of Phila., desires all retailers of spirits to account quarterly to him instead of to Judah Foulke, late collector (23 Aug.)

Accounts to be settled with Judah Foulke, shopkeeper; see John Smith, Richard Hockley, or Isaac Jones, at the widow Evan's, in Market St. (23 Aug.)

Workshop and lot for sale by Anthony Yeldhall; borders the messuage and lot late of William Fishbourn, dec'd. (23 Aug.)

George Aston, Irish, age c.20, runaway from Robert Boyle, tanner, of Fallowfield Twp., Chester Co. (23 Aug.)

Horse came to the plantation of Joseph Sackett of Wrightstown, Bucks Co. (23 Aug.)

Household goods and smith's tools to be sold at the late dwelling-house of George Kelly, dec'd; apply to James White and John Reardon, admins. Said White sells European goods, near the Drawbridge (23 Aug.)

English servant's time for sale; apply to William Sellers in Laetitia Ct. (23 Aug.)

Mark Lelar, Irish, and Morris Welch, runaway from Hugh Clark of Miln Creek hundred, Newcastle Co. (23 Aug.)

Horse taken up by John Valentine, chief ranger of Gilbert's manor, Phila. Co. (23 Aug.)

Reward offered by John Allen of Trenton, or William Dewees of Whitemarsh for the return of a mare (23 Aug.)

Stray horse came to the plantation of Jonathan Jones of Merion (23 Aug.)

Daniel Henman, Irish, lately bought out of the **Dublin** vessel, Capt. McCarthy, Commander, runaway from Samuel Allen of West Nantmill Twp. Chester Co. (23 Aug.)

Barn of James Richards of Dedham, Mass., was struck by lightning and consumed (30 Aug.)

John Colden, Esq., third son of the Honorable Cadwalleder Colden, died at Ft. Hunter, Albany Co. (30 Aug.)

Bill, age c.30, and Robin, age c.40, **Negroes,** runaway from the Union Iron Works in Hunterdon Co., West Jersey; reward offered by William Bird, at the works, or by Allen and Turner, in Phila. (30 Aug.)

Salt, Cheshire Cheese, etc. for sale by George Duncan, on the snow Ross, at Turner's wharf (30 Aug.)

For freight or passage to S. Carolina on the ship **St. Andrew**, John Brown, commander; apply to said Brown, or Charles and Alexander Stedman (30 Aug.)

Henry Schleydorn, in Norris's Alley, has sugar and spices for sale (30 Aug.)

Two servants from Dublin, Matthew Kinchlow, age c.19, and Edward Edwards, age c.26, who has been in Virginia and Carolina, runaway from James Bennet and Robert Warburton of Middletown, Chester Co. (30 Aug.)

James Morris notifies all persons with outstanding mortgages to pay them promptly to the trustees of the general loan office (30 Aug.)

Household furniture to be sold at widow Bell's house next door but one to John Inglis, over the Drawbridge (30 Aug.)

Mare stolen from the pasture of Thomas Evans, living near the sign of the White Horse on Lancaster Rd., Chester Co. (30 Aug.)

Servant girl's time for sale; enquire at John Stinson's, at the sign of the Three Mariners, in Water St. (30 Aug.)

For freight or passage to S. Carolina on the ship Edinburgh, James Russel, Commander; apply to said Russel, or Benjamin and Samuel Shoemaker (30 Aug.)

Horse, stolen or strayed, from Joseph Leech, at the widow Leech's Phila. (30 Aug.)

Darby Hendry, Irish, runaway from James Wilson, West Caln, Chester Co. (30 Aug.)

Lucy Hatton and two sons perished in a fire in their home in Annapolis, Md. (6 Sept.)

Madeira wine for sale by John Cox and Nathaniel Allen at their store on William **Masters'** wharf, near Market St. (6 Sept.)

Samuel Fisher, hatter, in Second St., has servant's time for sale (6 Sept.)

Imported goods and sugar for sale by Alexander Hamilton at his store in Water St, fronting Fishbourn's wharf (6 Sept.)

For freight or passage to London or Rotterdam on the ship Nancy, Capt. Thomas Coatam; apply to Charles and Alexander Stedman, or said capt. at Samuel McCall's wharf (6 Sept.)

For freight or passage to London on the ship Myrtilla, Richard Budden, Commander; apply to said Budden or to Levy and Franks (6 Sept.)

For freight or passage to Jamaica on the sloop Minerva, Enoch Hobart, Commander; apply to said Hobart or to James Peller, who has rum, ginger, and mahogany for sale (6 Sept.)

Catherine, wife of John Slaughter of Germantown, has eloped (6 Sept.)

Adv. of Samuel Burge in Water St. (6 Sept.)

Fyall wine and a Negro for sale by George McCall at his house over the Drawbridge (6 Sept.)

William Wallace, in Front St., and Buckridge Sims, at Joseph Turner's house, have sugar and molasses for sale (6 Sept.)

Patrick McCamish, mason, of Chester Co., has land for sale; apply to Samuel Rhoads, carpenter, Phila., or to Standish Forde, inn-keeper, Phila. (6 Sept.)

Francis Farrel, Irish, runaway from John Hammond, near Potapsco ferry; and Robert Wood, runaway from Charles Porter (6 Sept.)

Horse, stolen or strayed, from the plantation of Eleazar Evans, near the Sinking Spring (6 Sept.)

Silver watches, clocks, etc. imported in the Speedwell, Capt. Stevenson, for sale by John Davis at Francis Trumble's, joiner, in Second St.; said Trumble has ready made furniture for sale (6 Sept.)

Adv. for Dr. Benjamin Godfrey's general cordial; available at Christopher Marshall's, at the Golden Ball, Chestnut St. (6 Sept.)

Rum, mackrell, etc. for sale by John Mifflin, where Ann Combes lately dwelt, on Fishbourn's wharf, opp. Fisher's and Russell's store (6 Sept.)

Ambrose Moore, Irish, age c.19, lately arrived on the Dove, Capt. McCarthy, Commander, runaway from William Fullerton of Pequay, Salisbury Twp., Lancaster Co. (13 Sept.)

Tom, Negro, runaway from Silas Parvin (13 Sept.)

Imported English goods for sale by Joseph Ogden at his store at Benjamin Kendall's, corner of Third and Chestnut St.(13 Sept.)

European and East Indian goods for sale by Charles Willing at his new store in Front St. (13 Sept.)

Jacob Walter has horses for sale at Anthony Morris's plantation, Moyamensing Twp. (13 Sept.)

Land for sale in Soles-berry Twp. LancasterCo., near Branson's iron works; apply to George Gibson, tavern keeper, Lancaster town, or Thomas Bourtchier, Water St. (13 Sept.)

Goods imported in the ship Myrtilla, Capt. Richard Budden, from London; to be sold by Parker and Garrett at their store in Third St. (13 Sept.)

Sam, Negro, age c.30, runaway from James James, near St. George's, Newcastle Co. (13 Sept.)

Land, between Joseph Oldman's and Edward Warner's, to be sold at the house of Jeremiah Smith (13 Sept.)

Land belonging to Ebenezer Tomlinson, taken at the suit of Charles Willing, to be sold by Richard Sewell, sheriff, at the house of Michael Israel (13 Sept.)

James McCullough will depart the province in Oct. (13 Sept.)

Imported goods for sale by George Smith at his store between Norris's and Gray's Alley (13 Sept.)

For freight or passage to S. Carolina on the ship <u>Bennet-Galley</u>; apply to John Wadham, Commander, at Capt. Goodman's wharf (13 Sept.)

Samuel Pearson, age c.17, runaway apprentice to Patrick Ogilby, tailor, in Chestnut St. (13 Sept.)

House and lot in Market St., taken at the suit of Richard Hockley from Judah Foulke, to be sold at the house of widow Pratt, in Market St.(13 Sept.)

Imported goods to be sold by John Priest at his store at the widow Griffin's, Water St.; and by Robert Priest, in the **Jerseys** (13 Sept.)

Christopher Major, English, age c.25, runaway from Thomas Boutchier, shoemaker, in Water St. (13 Sept.)

Thomas Mathias has snuff and shells for sale in Arch St., next door to John Peel and over against Nathaniel Walton's schoolhouse (13 Sept.)

Grist mill and land of the estate of Swethen Justice, late of Newcastle Co., carpenter, dec'd; for sale by Neils Justice and Mary Justice, admins. (13 Sept.)

Joshua Way in Wilmington has imported goods for sale (13 Sept.)

Plantation in Newtown Twp. for sale; apply to Charles Hubs, on the premises (13 Sept.)

Plantation for sale in the Northern Liberties, lying between those of Tench Francis and Dr. Thomas Bond; apply to John Justice, living on the premises (13 Sept.)

William Smith has spermacety oil for sale; opp. the Three Tuns, in Chestnut St. (13 Sept.)

William Merone, age c.17, shoemaker, apprentice to Augustine Stillman, has run **away with an apprentice of Robert Worrall's** (13 Sept.)

Accounts with the estate of Capt. George Dickinson, dec'd, to be settled with George Stevenson, admin., at Capt. George Spofford's. George Stevenson will sell property situated on Market St.,between the house of George Fitzwater, dec'd, and that of Abraham Claypole, now in the tenure of Jonathan Mifflin (13 Sept.)

Evan **Roberts,** Welsh, age c.25, shoemaker, runaway from Abraham Dehaven, of New Providence Twp. (13 Sept.)

Will, Mulatto, cooper, runaway from Elizabeth Griffin (13 Sept.)

John Hill, age c.30, dyer, runaway from Thomas Cookson (13 Sept.)

Andrew Tress, age c.25, runaway from George Gibson (13 Sept.)

John McDaniel, age c.35, mason, runaway from Thomas Thornbrough (13 Sept.)

Reward offered by George Rock for return of Thomas Cummings, English runaway, age c.35, blacksmith, formerly servant to Thomas Marsh, Kent Island (13 Sept.)

Broke out of Lancaster Co. Goal: William Freeborn, age c. 21; Jacob Heflikefer, Dutch; Nicholas Curains, Irish; John Davis and John Wise, English; reward offered by John Jones, sub-sheriff (13 Sept.)

Adv. of William Biddle, candidate for office of sheriff of Phila. (13 Sept.)

Mill, brew- and malt-house for sale; apply to Jane Grevill, who lives on the premises in Coates's Alley (20 Sept.)

Owen Sullivan and John Tias have been convicted and sentenced for counterfeiting in Boston (20 Sept.)

Land, late in tenure of John Meldrum, dec'd, located near mill of John Vance in Newcastle Co., for sale by John Williams, joiner, in Phila. (20 Sept.)

Dennis Fitzpatrick, Irish, age c. 35, and Sheeley Macarty, age c. 36, runaways from William Hitchman of Cecil Co., Md. (20 Sept.)

James McBride, Irish, age c. 40, runaway from James Moore, storekeeper near Reading, Chester Co. (20 Sept.)

The following members of present or past assemblies in which Peter Worrall was representative for Lancaster Co. vouch for his honesty and private character: Israel Pemberton, Thomas Leech, Joseph Trotter, James Norris, Edward Warner. The bretheren and friends of Sadsbury Meeting wish to clear said Worrall of scandalous action relating to a bond of Joseph Jones, namely Andrew Moore, James Moore, William Evans, John Griffith, Thomas Musgrave, Nicholas Steer, John Kirk, James Love, Moses Brinton, Joseph Steer, Thomas Poultney and Thomas Bullert (20 Sept.)

Adv. of Robert Ragg at his store, the corner house of Chestnut St. Wharf (20 Sept.)

For freight or passage to Jamaica in the ship *Richmond*, William Lawson commander, apply to Alexander Hamilton or said Lawson at Hamilton's wharf (20 Sept.)

Joseph Richardson, goldsmith, has stopped a silver tankard lid (20 Sept.)

For freight or passage to Barbados in the snow *Ross*, George Duncan commander, apply to William Blair or to Duncan at Turner's wharf (20 Sept.)

William Kidney has a Negro girl for sale at Capt. Murrell's on Society Hill (20 Sept.)

John Macwhan, servant, runaway from Katherine Child of Water St. (20 Sept.)

Property near Isaac Zean's to be sold at coffee house of the Widow Roberts; apply to Mary Durborow, widow, near Thomas Penrose, shipwright (20 Sept.)

House, next door but one to Thomas Griffiths, to be let; enquire of John Cresson (20 Sept.)

House and lot, now in the tenure of Maurice and Edmund Nihill, to be sold at Roberts's coffee house; enquire of Samuel Carpenter at Emanuel Josiah's near Powell's wharf (20 Sept.)

For freight or passage to Newry in snow *Jenny and Sally*, Archibald Stewart master, apply to Conyngham and Gardner, who have for sale imported linen (20 Sept.)

For freight or passage to Belfast in brig *Stadtholder*, John Johrston master, apply to Wm. Humphries in Walnut St. (20 Sept.)

- Mr. Batter, French physician received 55 lashes for taking money, goods and clothing from a warehouse and sugar house (27 Sept.)
- Robert Watts, of New York, merchant, died at age of 73 and was buried at Trinity Church (27 Sept.)
- Thomas Williams, of King George Co., Va., died at age of 120 (27 Sept.)
- Supreme Court of Pa. appointed William Allen chief justice of the province and Lawrence Growdon and Caleb Cowpland assistant judges (27 Sept.)
- Goods stolen from store of Joseph Saunders in Water St. have been recovered (27 Sept.)
- Mention of Mr. Cunningham at the Sign of the Rising Sun in Market St. (27 Sept.)
- George Heap will run for another term as county coroner (27 Sept.)
- Josiah Davenport, baker, in Gray's Alley sells biscuit and Boston loaf sugar (27 Sept.)
- Money and plate have been stolen from house of William Clemm, shopkeeper, in Second St., near the Sign of the Trumpet (27 Sept.)
- Adv. of John Bell, storekeeper, on Hamilton's wharf (27 Sept.)
- Adv. of Potts and Yorke, storekeepers, in Water St. (27 Sept.)
- For freight or passage from Phila. to New York by boat and stage apply to Joseph Borden, Jr. (27 Sept.)
- Property for sale or rent; enquire of Philip Syng (27 Sept.)
- Isaac Freeborn, apprentice, age c. 19, runaway from Matthew Atkinsen, fuller, in Lampeter Twp., Lancaster Co. (27 Sept.)
- Joshua Davis, apprentice, age c. 18, of Welsh extraction but country born, son of Ann Davis, near John McKelvain's, tavern-keeper, runaway from John Byars, shoemaker, of Lancaster Co. (27 Sept.)
- Horse stolen from plantation of John Channel of Germantown to be returned to said Channel or Samuel Aston of Phila. (27 Sept.)
- Run and pace races to be held at John Holtham's at Back Creek Mill; plantation for sale at Cecil Co. Court House; apply to said Holtham (27 Sept.)
- Horse stolen from pasture of Widow Richardson; reward if returned to Benjamin Armitage on York Road or to Ralph Sarver (27 Sept.)
- Reward for return of letter come from Liverpool by Capt. Rees for Randle Mitchell (27 Sept.)
- Real estate of Gabriel Wilkinson, dec'd, for sale; apply to Sarah Wilkinson, admin. (27 Sept.)
- House in Third St. for sale by Christian Van Erden, living on premises (27 Sept.)
- Catherine, wife of Thomas Carroll, plasterer, has eloped (27 Sept.)
- Thomas Williams sells broadcloth at Elizabeth Hammer's, next door to Dr. Bond's in Front St., and rum at his store on Lloyd's wharf (27 Sept.)

1750

Goods imported from London in ship <u>Samuel</u> and <u>Jenny</u>, Capt. Smith, for sale by John Clifton at store in Second St., between Arch and Race Sts. (27 Sept.)

Daniel Lee, Irish servant, age c. 16, runaway from John Alison of Little Britain Twp., Lancaster Co. (27 Sept.)

For freight or passage to Cork in ship <u>Phoenix</u>, John Mason commander, agree with Mason or with Benjamin or Samuel Shoemaker (27 Sept.)

Elected for Phila. Co., representatives: Isaac Norris, Edward Warner, Joseph Trotter, Hugh Evans, Owen Evans, Israel Pemberton, Jr., Evan Morgan, John Smith; sheriffs: Isaac Griffitts, Edward Collins; coroners: William Trotter; George Heap; commissioner: John Norris; assessors: Samuel Golden, Joseph Stretch, Owen Jones, Robert Thomas, Richard George, Derrick Keyser - for Bucks Co., representatives: Mahlon Kirkbride, Joseph Hamton, John Woolston, Griffith Owen, John Hall, Garret Vansant, Richard Walker, Abraham Chapman; sheriff: Joseph Hart; coroner: William Smith; commissioner: John Hart; assessors: Giles Knight, Daniel Palmer, William Edwards, Abraham Vastine, Peter Traxler, Alexander Brown - for Chester Co., representatives: Joseph Gibbons, George Ashbridge, Thomas Cummings, Thomas Chandler, Henry Hockley, Nathaniel Grubb, Nathaniel Pennock, Peter Dicks; sheriff: John Owen; coroner: Isaac Lee; commissioner: Edward Brinton; assessors: Phineas Lewis, John Ferlon, Thomas Pearson, James Miller, Randle Mellin, Jeremiah Brown - for Lancaster Co., representatives: Arthur Patterson, James Wright, Calvin Cooper, James Webb; sheriff: Andrew Work; coroner: Robert Stewart - for Newcastle Co., representatives: William Armstrong, **Jehu** Curtis, James M'Mechen, John Edwards, John M'Cooll, John Vance; sheriff: John Vandyke; coroner: Samuel Silsby - for the City of Phila., burgesses: Joseph Fox, William Clymer; assessors: Samuel Morris, Abel James, Jacob Cooper, Thomas Gordon, William Hedge, Thomas Saye; mayor: William Plumsted; recorder: Tench Francis (4 Oct.)

William Jones, Irish servant, runaway from Robert Hartshorne of Middletown, Monmouth Co., N.J. (4 Oct.)

Plate of ten pounds to be run for at John Williams's ferry in Falls Twp., Bucks Co.; horses to be entered at Elijah Bond's, tavern-keeper in Trenton, or William Douglas's, tavern-keeper at Trenton Landing (4 Oct.)

Imported olives for sale at house of Capt. Arthur in Walnut St. (4 Oct.)

Two parcels of land for sale in Bristol Twp.; one adjoins land of Thomas Roberts, the other that of Griffith Griffith; apply to Erasmus Stevens or William Branson (4 Oct.)

Stallion, strayed or stolen from Thomas Gray, of Mill Creek Hundred, Newcastle Co. (4 Oct.)

Property in Cheltenham Twp., late belonging to Edward Collings, dec'd, seized at the suit of George House, to be sold at the house of Thomas Harper at Frankford (4 Oct.)

For freight or passage to Antigua in sloop <u>Polly</u>, Clement Conyers commander, agree with Conyers at Charles Edgar's wharf (4 Oct.)

Edward Jones at the Vineyard or the workhouse in Phila. has the time of servants for sale (4 Oct.)

Mills and plantation of Nathaniel Ware in West Jersey for sale; apply to Thomas Clarke in New York, Andrew Smith in Hopewell Twp., Hunterdon Co., or William Pigeon in Trenton (4 Oct.)

For freight or passage to Belfast in snow Durham, David Blair commander, agree with William Blair or the commander on Dickenson's wharf; William Blair has imported goods for sale at his store in Water St., next door to Mary Andrews (4 Oct.)

Elected for Kent Co., representatives: James Gorrell, Andrew Caldwell, James Train. John Clayton, Jr., Abraham Allee, Benjamin Chew; sheriff: Thomas Parke; coroner: William Blakiston - for Sussex Co., representatives: Woolsey Burton, Jacob Kollock, Abraham Wynkoop, John Clows, Ryves Holt, Shepard Kollock; sheriff: William Shankland; coroner: Robert M'Ilvaine - for Cumberland Co., representatives: Joseph Armstrong, Hermanus Alrichs; sheriff: John Potter; coroner: Adam Hoops (11 Oct.)

Plantation late belonging to Daniel Roberts, taken in execution at suit of Richard Peters, and land in Northampton Twp., late belonging to John Price, taken in **execution at suit of Evan** Jones, will be sold at Joseph Insley's at Newtown (11 Oct.)

Plantation lately surveyed to Joseph Stedman, dec'd, taken in execution at suit of Israel Pemberton, and land in Buckingham Twp., late estate of Joseph Jackson, dec'd, taken in execution at suits of Enion Williams and Thomas Buckley, to be sold at Patrick Poe's in Plumsted Twp., Bucks Co. (11 Oct.)

Plantation of Peter Walbert in Upper Milford Twp., a tavern late belonging to Nicholas Walbert, taken in execution at suit of Rebecca Steel, to be sold (11 Oct.)

Plantation where Andrew Macgill formerly lived, at head of Pipe Creek, Baltimore Co., for sale; apply to Thomas Parke, Dover, Kent Co. (11 Oct.)

Horses have been stolen from Rev. John Hamilton, of Charlestown, Md., supposedly by John Egonsons, a forge carpenter, who has run away with his family (11 Oct.)

Tom, Negro, runaway from Silas Parvin (11 Oct.)

Grist mill in New Britain Twp., Bucks Co., late the property of Thomas Holcomb but now in possession of Joshua Morris, is to be sold (11 Oct.)

Johannis Weis of Lancaster seeks his daughter Anna, who was sold as a servant to Richard Parks (11 Oct.)

Daniel Sullivan, Irish servant, and John Dunn, Irish convict servant, runaways from Joseph Wood and Adam Vanbebber, of Back Creek, Cecil Co., Md. (11 Oct.)

Two plantations, one in Whiteland Twp., Chester Co., and the other in Willistown Twp., to be sold by George Aston (11 Oct.)

John Ashton, innholder in Moyamensing Twp., has tenement and a lot for sale (11 Oct.)

Horse stolen from Richard Bull; reward if brought to said Bull or Henry Pawling, of Providence Twp., or William Gray, at the Sign of the Connestogo Waggon (11 Oct.)

Horses strayed from Thomas Kendall in Huntingdon Twp., York Co.; if they are located, notice to be sent to Richard M'Allister's mill in York Co. (11 Oct.)

Isaac Norris is chosen Speaker of the Pa. Assembly (18 Oct.)

John Jerman's almanack for 1751 for sale (18 Oct.)

Property, goods and land in Upper Dublin, adjoining land of Ezekiel Davis, taken at suit of George Emlen, Jr., to be sold at house of Thomas Thomas in Horsham Twp. (18 Oct.)

Abraham Magee, Irish servant, age c. 25, tailor, and John Clarke, a New England man, age c. 25, carpenter and joiner, runaways from Philip Marot of Bordentown (18 Oct.)

Elizabeth Morris, English servant, age c. 24, runaway from Robert Montgomery, of New Providence Twp. (18 Oct.)

House and lot lately belonging to Jacob Casdorp, dec'd, taken at suit of Cuzzins and Smyter, to be sold at house of Jeremiah Smith, the Sign of the Queen of Hungary, in Front St. (18 Oct.)

Land of Ebenezer Tomlinson, bounded on N. and W. by lots of Joseph Wharton, taken at suit of Charles Willing, to be sold at Roberts's coffee house (18 Oct.)

Real estate of Thomas Shugar, taken at suit of James Tipper, to be sold at house of William Gray, the Sign of the Conestogo Waggon, in Market St. (18 Oct.)

William Hackett, whose right name is Brian Doron, Irishman, age c. 35, runaway from his bail, Ebenezer Brown of Gloucester (18 Oct.)

Richard M'Cree, Irish servant, age c. 23, runaway from Robert M'Kee in the Manor of Moreland, near Fletcher's mill, Phila. Co. (18 Oct.)

Improvements of new mill and land, late the estate of Thomas Holcomb, in Manor of Moreland, Phila. Co., for sale; attendance given by Jacob Leech, Robert Thomas and Walter Moore (18 Oct.)

Boy, age c. 4, has been taken by his mother, Sarah Butler, from Lott Evan, of Nantmel Twp., Chester Co. (18 Oct.)

Accounts with estate of Henry Miller, of Kensington, dec'd, to be settled with Henry Kepple, **David** Sackel, Leonard Herman and Lawrence Bast, execs. (18 Oct.)

Horse strayed or stolen from Philip Weinemer, porter, of Phila. (18 Oct.)

John M'Mechen, Irishman, age c. 25, and William Stewart, age c. 17, runaways from Robert Adams, of Londonderry, Chester Co. (18 Oct.)

Hance Ulrich Seiler, a Switzer, has been found guilty of the murder of his mistress, the wife of David Shultz, of Upper Hanover (25 Oct.)

Vidonia wines for sale at store of James Burd on Carpenter's wharf (25 Oct.)

Accounts with estate of Cornelius Kollock, Jr., dec'd, to be settled with John Swift, admin. (25 Oct.)

John Clifton intends to depart from the province (25 Oct.)

A baker's time for sale; enquire of William Sellers in Laetitia Court, Phila. (25 Oct.)

Michael Chapman, age c. 16, apprentice, runaway from Thomas Rickey, shoemaker, of Maxfield Twp., Bucks Co. (25 Oct.)

Jane, wife of Henry Johnston, of Pilesgrove, Salem Co., has eloped from her husband (25 Oct.)

Bake house, now in possession of John Spafford, to be let; enquire of Mary Lisle (25 Oct.)

Mare, strayed or stolen from house of Andrew Engelhart in Upper Market St.; reward if returned to owner or Jacob Schlaugh in Macongee (25 Oct.)

Subscribers to the Life of the Rev. David Brainard are to apply to Samuel Hazard at his store on Arch St. wharf (25 Oct.)

Pictures painted on glass and servants' time for sale by John Denyce, opposite the Baptist meeting in Second St. (25 Oct.)

Mare taken up at plantation of Thomas Chandler in Newcastle Co. (25 Oct.)

Real estate next to Richard Allen's, now in tenure of Andrew Boore, late belonging to Joseph Boore, dec'd, seized at the suit of Septimus Robinson, exec. of the will of John Parrott, dec'd, will be sold at house of Richard Allen, near Pennypack in Lower Dublin (25 Oct.)

Joseph Fitzwater, English convict servant, age c. 20, runaway from Jacob Hite, of Frederick Co., Va. (25 Oct.)

David Dunblass, Scotch servant, and Abington Nicholls, servant, born in Virginia, runaways from Dr. Adam Stephens, of Frederick Co., Va.; reward if brought to master or to William Mitchell's in said county (25 Oct.)

Kersey great coat, lost or lent, to be returned to Jeremiah Elfreth (25 Oct.)

Land to be sold at house of Samuel Lamplugh in Marcus Hook, Chichester Twp., Chester Co. (25 Oct.)

Nicholas Welsh, age c. 40, and wife Mary, age between 20 and 30, servants, together with their baby, runaways from Archibald Little, of Wilmington, Newcastle Co.; reward if returned to Joseph M'Dowell, of East Marlborough Twp., Chester Co. (25 Oct.)

Report from Chinecto of murder of Capt. How, with mention of M. Le Corne, Capt. Foss and Capt. Robinson (1 Nov.)

Boston item reports arrival of Capt. M'Cunn from Glasgow and prints excerpt from letter of S. Denny, Esq., of Arrowsick (1 Nov.)

House of Benjamin Franklin, printer, robbed (1 Nov.)

Land for sale; enquire of Richard Peters and Lyn-Ford Lardner, Esqrs., in Phila. (1 Nov.)

Open boat to be sold by William Tremble at the public wharf on the drawbridge (1 Nov.)

Mare strayed from John Eyre of Elbow Lane (1 Nov.)

Household goods for sale at Thomas Gordon's on Powell's wharf (1 Nov.)

John Wamsley, Irish servant, age c. 25, runaway from Benjamin Morgan, of Towamensing Twp., Phila. Co. (1 Nov.)

Horse taken up at plantation of Thomas West in Warwick Twp., Bucks Co. (1 Nov.)

Maria Fisher, servant, sold on 23 Sept. 1743 to John Smith; anyone knowing their whereabouts is to contact Daniel Stonemat in Second St., Phila., or Melchior Fisher, father of the girl, at Neshaminy Ferry (1 Nov.)

Anti-paedorantism Defended by Abev. Morgan, of Middletown, East Jersey, has just been published (1 Nov.)

Horses have been taken up at plantation of Nicholas Aston, of Abington, Phila. Co. (1 Nov.)

For freight or passage to Jamaica in ship Martha, Robert Rait commander, apply to Rait at William Plumsted's wharf or to John Cappes at James's coffee house (1 Nov.)

Land for sale by James Chattin, of Passyunk Road (1 Nov.)

Real estate in Merion Twp., adjoining property of John Bevan, David Price, Sr., and Daniel Thomas, mortgaged to the Loan Office by Morris Llewelin, is to be sold at house of Richard Pearn in Merion Twp.; notice signed by James Morris (1 Nov.)

Mare taken up at plantation of John Renshaw in the Northern Liberties (1 Nov.)

Mention of Mr. Greenville, governor, and M. Deligny, provisional commander of Barbados (8 Nov.)

For freight or passage to London in ship Carolina, Stephen Mesnard commander, apply to said Mesnard or James Pemberton (8 Nov.)

Daniel Reaverdy, age c. 18, weaver, runaway from William Graham, of Rockhill Twp., Bucks Co. (8 Nov.)

Joseph Lyon, Irish servant, age c. 20, heel-maker, runaway from Thomas Overend (8 Nov.)

Plantation for sale; enquire of Crispin Collett or Alexander Edwards, of Biberry Twp., Phila. Co. (8 Nov.)

Mare has come to plantation of Henry Miller, late of Kensington, dec'd; apply for the same to Henry Kepple, tavern-keeper in Market St. (8 Nov.)

For freight or passage to Jamaica in snow Jane, Thomas Caton commander, apply to Israel Pemberton, Jr., or to Caton at Peel's wharf (8 Nov.)

Heifer taken up at plantation of Charles Cookson at Pequay in Solsbury Twp., Lancaster Co.; enquire of Thomas Dun (8 Nov.)

William Crasswell of York Co. will not pay debts incurred in future by his wife Anne (8 Nov.)

Edward Jones, ranger, has strays at the Vineyard Plantation in the Northern Liberties (8 Nov.)

Dry goods, imported in the snow Baldwin from Liverpool, for sale by Greenway and Rundle at the middle store on Reese Meredith's wharf (8 Nov.)

Annapolis item mentions case in which Thomas Chase, of Baltimore Co., clerk is **plaintiff, and Jonas Green, of Annapolis,** printer, is defendant (15 Nov.)

Schooner belonging to Capt. Major of Halifax has been set on fire by the enemy (15 Nov.)

John Hines, age c. 18, Irish servant, plasterer, and John M"Cullough, Irish servant, runaways from John Wilson and Adam Menely, of Tenicum Twp., Bucks Co. (15 Nov.)

Land in Cresham, near Anthony Hinckes, at the Sign of the Black Horse, on Whitemarsh Road and opposite property of William Allen, Esq., to be sold by Jonathan Livezey, Jr. (15 Nov.)

House in Darby for sale by Obadiah Johnson on the premises (15 Nov.)

William Milne, in the first house next the west end of the bridge on the **south** side of Walnut St., keeps night school and also posts books and draws accounts (15 Nov.)

Plantation for sale by Philip Fields, of Dover, Kent Co. on Delaware (15 Nov.)

Accounts with estate of Mary Philpot, dec'd, to be settled with Philip or William Tillyer, of the Manor of Moreland, Phila. Co. (15 Nov.)

Joannah Griffin, Irish servant, age c. 28, runaway from Thomas Faulkner, of Bethlehem Twp., Bucks Co. (15 Nov.)

William Welch, Irish servant, age c. 25, runaway from James Anderson, of Donegall, Lancaster Co. (15 Nov.)

Mill and plantation in Darby Twp., 3 miles from ferry of Capt. Coultas, for sale; apply to Abraham Marshall, of Wilmington, Newcastle Co. (15 Nov.)

Adv. of John Dagworthy at Peter Bard's in Water St. (15 Nov.)

Remainder of time of Thomas Wright, apprentice lad, bred to the business of skinning, gloving and leather breeches making, is to be sold by Peter Hodgson in Market St. (15 Nov.)

For freight or passage to Newry on ship Ruby, Cony Edwards commander, agree with Richard Edwards, William Corry, Thomas Lightfoot or the **commander** at Carpenter's wharf (15 Nov.)

Thomas Trotter, secretary, notifies members of the St. Andrew's Society of the Anniversary Assembly to be held at the Tun Tavern in Water St. (15 Nov.)

William Handley, cooper, runaway from Capt. John Fitz, of Dorset Co., Md; reward if returned to owner or to Thomas Williams in Water St. (15 Nov.)

James Hood and Alexander Moodie, tailors from London, are removed from the Sign of the Thistle in Second St. to Thomas White's in Front St. (15 Nov.)

On 16 Oct. Capt. Judd and Jeremiah Chase on Petapsco road were robbed by highwaymen (22 Nov.)

At Pelham, N.H., on 12 Oct. the house of Henry Richardson was consumed by fire and his son, aged 10, and one John Wright perished in the conflagration (22 Nov.)

Capt. Cobb in the sloop York attacked a French schooner which was a-ground at Cheparta (22 Nov.)

It is reported that Zebulon Wade of Scituate has made off with 150,000 dollars in silver and with cochineal to the value of 100,000 dollars from the wreck of a Spanish ship off the coast of Carolina (22 Nov.)

A New York item reports the arrival there of Capt. Tingley with 340 Palatines (22 Nov.)

Margaret Henley, Irish servant, age c. 30, runaway from Nathan Lewis, of Newtown Twp., Chester Co. (22 Nov.)

Time of a Dutch servant and a Negro, age c. 26, a skinner, for sale by John Correy in Market St. (22 Nov.)

Horses have strayed or been stolen from Walter Williams, of Bethlehem, West Jersey, near John Coats's, at the Sign of the Hart; reward for their return to Williams or to Moore Furman in Trenton (22 Nov.)

Mare strayed or stolen from Adam Linn of Plimouth Twp., Phila. Co. (22 Nov.)

Accounts with estate of George Wood, late of Darby, dec'd, to be settled with Hannah, Ann and George Wood and John Pearson, execs. (22 Nov.)

House, late property of Thomas Powell, dec'd, to be sold by his execs., George Spafford and David Chambers (22 Nov.)

Adv. of Samuel Burge, in Water St., near Market wharf (22 Nov.)

Colt taken up at plantation of Stephen Goodman in Lower Merion (22 Nov.)

Real estate of Thomas Williams, taken at suit of Andrew Elliot, to be sold at house of John Cross, below the drawbridge (22 Nov.)

Negro woman and man (a fiddler) for sale; apply to Robert Warren, over the drawbridge (22 Nov.)

William Hollyday gives notice that two stray cows are with John Miller, tavern-keeper, on Conestogo Road (22 Nov.)

John Jones, English servant, runaway from Joseph Moore, of Hopewell (22 Nov.)

Tanyard and house at Trenton to be sold or let by Benjamin Biles, living on premises (22 Nov.)

Adv. of Conrad Swikehauser, near Second St. (22 Nov.)

Frame house and lot in borough of Bristol, adjoining land of Samuel Cary, Anthony Burton and Samuel Stackhouse, taken in execution at suit of John Abraham Denormandie, and also 114 acres in Solebury, Bucks Co., late belonging to Benjamin Canby, dec'd, taken in execution at suit of William Atwood, are to be sold by Sheriff Joseph Hart (22 Nov.)

Thomas Lee, President of H.M.'s Council in Va., gives notice of the escape of Edward Rumney, age c. 40, from goal of Fairfax Co.; Rumney assisted Low Jackson in counterfeiting. Under suspicion as accessories are John Jackson, watchmaker, and James Jackson, age c. 20, a blacksmith (22 Nov.)

Gov. Jonathan Law of Conn. died on 6 Nov. (29 Nov.)

To be published: A Discourse on the preparation of the body for the small pox by Adam Thompson, physician in Phila. (29 Nov.)

Mare taken up by William Bell, at the Sign of the White Horse, in Phila. (29 Nov.)

Rum, shot, snuff, etc. for sale by Robert and Amos Strettell (29 Nov.)

House, rented to Francis Johnson, and lots for sale; apply to said Johnson or John Nicholas, carpenter (29 Nov.)

Irish servants imported in the ship Boyne, Henry Ash commander, for sale by John Erwin at his house in Strawberry Alley (29 Nov.)

James Wilson, age c. 23, imprisoned for debt, has escaped from John Redford, High Sheriff of Monmouth Co., N.J. (29 Nov.)

Christiana Treasury, Dutch servant, age c. 21, runaway from Benjamin Sharpless, of Middletown, Chester Co. (29 Nov.)

Horse strayed or stolen from Richard Jones of Goshen, Chester Co. (29 Nov.)

Lot of land in Third St., a bark-house, mill-house, curryingshop and other buildings, being the tanyard of John Langdale, late of Phila., to be sold at the Three Tuns in Chestnut St.; enquire of Philip Syng (29 Nov.)

Mare and colt have strayed and a fiddle and stick have been stolen from Abraham Carpenter, at the Sign of the Duke of Cumberland, near Poole's bridge, in the Northern Liberties (29 Nov.)

Plantation in Whitpin Twp., Phila. Co., belonging to estate of William Martin, dec'd, for sale; enquire of Abraham Daws, Richard Waln, Jr., and Benjamin Davis, admins. (6 Dec.)

Subscriptions for a course in experimental philosophy are taken in by David James Dove, at Mr. Duche's in Chestnut St. (6 Dec.)

John Neglea in Second St. stables horses (6 Dec.)

Plantation in Falls Twp., late property of Mark Watson, dec'd, to be sold by Mahlon Kirkbride and William Paxson, execs. (6 Dec.)

Pocketbook lost in Second St. by Cesar Godfrey (6 Dec.)

William Coxe, at his house in Front St., next door to Conyngham and Gardiner's, has for sale goods imported in the *Triton*, Capt. Shirley (6 Dec.)

Horse taken up on the Commons can be had again from William Gray, at the Sign of the Conestogo Waggon (6 Dec.)

For freight or passage to London in the ship *Prince William*, John Mitchell master, agree with John Smith, Abel Jones or the master (6 Dec.)

Mare stolen, supposedly by Thomas O'Bryan, from the plantation of James O'Bryan in Little Bohemia, Cecil Co.; reward if returned to James or John O'Bryan (6 Dec.)

James Sackett is removed from Mrs. Lloyd's house on Lloyd's wharf to Francis Rawles's in Water St., next to the Jersey ferry (6 Dec.)

Mary Watt, over the drawbridge, has a Negro boy for sale (6 Dec.)

Catherine, wife of Samuel Humphres of Pilesgrove, Salem Co., has eloped from her husband (6 Dec.)

The following carried off goods from John Macilvaine of Earl Twp., Lancaster Co.: John M'Fall, age c. 25, and James Sieven, age c. 23, both Irish (11 Dec.)

Account of loss of sloop *Jubile*, Capt. Fry, of New York, on 22 Oct. at Seal Island, near Cape Anne (11 Dec.)

Report that Capts. Hutchinson and Brooks, both from Phila., put into Bermuda for repairs (11 Dec.)

Plantation in Horsham Twp., Phila. Co., for sale; apply to Joseph Barns, living on premises (11 Dec.)

Accounts with estate of Samuel Cooper, late of Manor of Mooreland, to be settled with William Brittin, Sr., John Boucher and Samuel Swift, execs. (11 Dec.)

The following broke the goal of Gloucester Co.: Henry Bate, an Englishman, David Parks and William Cully, Irishmen, all three committed for felony, and John Langly, an old man, this country born, committed for assault and battery; reward offered by Samuel Harrison, sheriff (11 Dec.)

Thomas Lee, President of Va., died on 13 Nov. (18 Dec.)

Annapolis item of 21 Nov. reports that Capt. Meshech Botfield of Talbot Co. was accidentally thrown from his chaise about a fortnight before; his wife was injured but recovered; he has two brothers, Shadrach and Abednego (18 Dec.)

Letter from Dr. Adam Thompson regarding item in Bradford's paper concerning address about small pox delivered by Thompson before the trustees of the Academy; Benjamin Franklin certifies address was delivered (18 Dec.)

Imported goods for sale by James Louttit at his store on Hamilton's wharf (18 Dec.)

Two Negroes for sale by Standish Ford at the Sign of the George in Second St. (18 Dec.)

Persons indebted to William and David M'Ilvaine are desired to make prompt payment (18 Dec.)

House, for several years an inn, in Second St., between Sassafras and Mulberry Sts., for sale; apply to Michael Hillegas, living next door (18 Dec.)

Plantation late belonging to Joseph Davis of Darby, dec'd, now in tenure of Henry Chafin, to be sold in Marlborough Twp., Chester Co., by Lewis Davis, John Davis, John Levis and William Parker, execs. (18 Dec.)

Shop goods and household furniture for sale at the house of the late Charles Connor, dec'd, by Samuel Neave and Atwood Shute, admins. (18 Dec.)

John M'Daniel has stolen a horse from Ambrose Reily, of Colebrook Twp., Phila. Co. (18 Dec.)

Horse strayed or stolen from Esther Kinnard in the Manor of Moreland, Phila. Co., near the Billet on York Road (18 Dec.)

John Turner, Irish servant, age c. 21, runaway from Edward M'Farland; if runaway is captured, notice to be sent to Samuel **Flower at Reading Furnace (18 Dec.)**

Susanna, wife of John M'Cunn, ship-corker, has eloped from her husband (18 Dec.)

Accounts with estate of John Parham, of Wicacoa, Phila. Co., dec'd, to be settled with Margaret Parham and Francis Garrigues, admins. (18 Dec.)

Report from Kingston, Jamaica, that one Dobbins, in a sloop of Messrs. Lawrence and Godden, has turned pirate, according to a letter from Black River (25 Dec.)

Charles-Town, S.C., items mention Capts. John Powell, Kattur, John **Brigs, Rench, Woolford and William Whittal (25 Dec.)**

Boston item mentions Capts. Wait, Becket, De Jersey and How (25 Dec.)

New York item mentions Capts. Haviland, Peter Newgar, Henderson and Sawyer (25 Dec.)

Thu. last a trunk with items to the value of 30 pounds was stolen from the shop of James Kerr in Market St. (25 Dec.)

Wed. night the house of Mr. Bevan, tavern-keeper, in Walnut St., was broke open and robbed (25 Dec.)

<u>History of the Five Indian Nations of Canada</u> by Cadwallader Colden is for sale at the Post-Office (25 Dec.)

Thomas Maule sells dry goods at the Sign of the Cross-cut Saw in Second St. (25 Dec.)

Christina Pau seeks her son, Hans Michael Pau, age c. 14, who last year was sold for seven years (25 Dec.

Mare strayed from Peter Goff on Society Hill (25 Dec.)

Anchovies and capers sold by Capt. Sibbald (25 Dec.)

Cocoa, coffee, etc. for sale by Benjamin Rawle, next door but one below the Ferry House (25 Dec.)

Accounts with estate of Michael Cline, late of Whitpin Twp., Phila. Co., dec'd, to be settled with Susannah Cline and George Kastner, execs. (25 Dec.)

Daniel Foy, Irish servant, age c. 26, runaway from Abraham Lord of Piles-Grove, Salem Co. (25 Dec.)

Horse stolen from Samuel Taylor of Chesterfield, Burlington Co. (25 Dec.)

Horse belonging to John Morris stolen or strayed from house of Francis M'Coy (25 Dec.)

Accounts with estate of John Rush, late of Springmill, Phila. Co., dec'd, to be settled with Barbara Rush and Thomas Rose, admins.; Rose will be at his dwelling in Bristol Twp, near Germantown (25 Dec.)

1751

Ship *Charlotte*, Richard Farish late master, now commanded by Robert Bishop, put in at Antigua to refit after storm (1 Jan.)

Attempt made to **break** into store of Messrs. Fisher and Fussell in Water St. (1 Jan.)

Boston item mentions James Ford, captain of a schooner, and James Davidson, the owner, both captured by the Indians (8 Jan.)

New York item of 24 Dec. reports that the sloop *Catherine*, Capt. Ramadge, was driven ashore at the point of Nutten Island (8 Jan.)

New York item of 24 Dec. records the death on Fri. last of Mrs. Lucy Roddam (wife of Robert Roddam, commander of H.M.S. *Greyhound*, and eldest daughter of our governor) (8 Jan.)

Part of presentment of Grand Jury of Phila., John Searle foreman (8 Jan.)

The several schools of the Academy in Phila. will meet at the large house of Mr. Allen in Second St. (8 Jan.)

House (a former tavern) in York-Town, on west side of Sasquehana, where George Mendenhall, dec'd, lately dwelt, for sale; enquire of William Pim in Chester Co. or Sarah Mendenhall, widow and admin., living on premises (8 Jan.)

Isaac Greenleafe, of Phila., at his store in Second St., near Stretch's corner, has imported goods for sale and also the plantation, late of Peter Collins, in Bradford Twp., Chester Co., as well as land in Hunterdon Co., West Jersey, adjoining Jonathan Robinson's forge (8 Jan.)

Land in Lower Dublin, late property of Samuel Worrell, taken in execution at suit of Robert Worrell and others, will be sold at house of Thomas Harper in Frankford, at order of Isaac Griffitts, sheriff (8 Jan.)

Accounts with estate of David Livesey, late of Lower Dublin Twp., Phila. Co., dec'd, to be settled with Jonathan and Thomas Livesey, execs. (8 Jan.)

House in Second St., against the Baptist Meeting House, now in the tenure of William Biddle, to be let; enquire of Samuel Hasell (8 Jan.)

House, with shop and lots, in Albany St., New Brunswick, for sale by Jacob Kemper, living on premises (8 Jan.)

1751

Gabriele Nesman, Swedish minister, teaches Latin, German, English and French in upper room of Mr. Vidall's schoolhouse in Second St. (1 Jan.)

House (a tavern) where Peter Ganthony now lives in borough of Wilmington, late estate of Thomas Broom, dec'd, for sale by James Broom and Peter Ganthony, execs. (8 Jan.)

Edward Edwards, English servant, age c. 30, runaway from Robert Walburton of Middletown Twp., Chester Co.; reward for his capture will be paid by his master or by John Stinson, at the Sign of the Three Mariners in Water St., Phila. (8 Jan.)

Plantation in Trydufrin, tavern known as the Sign of the Ball, for sale by Thomas M'Kean, living on premises (8 Jan.)

Richard Pritchard, Welsh servant, age c. 25, runaway from James M'Knight, of Packston Twp., Lancaster Co.; reward will be paid by master or Jeremiah Warder, hatter, in Phila., or by John Harris, ferryman (8 Jan.)

House of Abigail Pederow, shopkeeper, in Water St. has been robbed (15 Jan.)

Accounts with estate of Samuel Parr, merchant, dec'd, late of Chestnut St., are to be settled with William Parr, John Reynell and Joseph Trotter, execs. (15 Jan.)

Horse strayed from John Armitt (15 Jan.)

For freight or passage to Dublin in the snow _Three Friends_, John Troy commander, agree with Troy or with Randle Mitchell, in Burlington (15 Jan.)

Lots of land between road to Moyamensing and that to Gloucester, **meadow** land in Moyamensing, and bar iron for sale at Carpenter's wharf or at his forge in Aston Twp., Chester Co., by Joseph Wharton (15 Jan.)

Plantation near Burlington, now renting to Gov. Belcher, and a lot formerly belonging to estate of Peter Banton in Burlington, for sale; apply to Joseph Oldman or Isaac Conarow in Burlington (15 Jan.)

Roger Wolcott has been chosen Gov. of Conn. and Thomas Fitch Deputy Gov. (22 Jan.)

Letter by Eleazer Phillips concerning the silk worm (22 Jan.)

It appears that the culprits in the robberies at Abigail Pederow's, Mrs. Steel's, Mr. Delage's and John Ross's were, upon information from Edmund Nihil, brewer, found to be one John Crow, Betty Robinson, John Morrice or Morrison, a certain M' Hugh and wife, one M'Coy and wife, and Joseph Cooper (a servant belonging to a turner; Morrison was apprehended at the house of John Stinson, a tavern-keeper in Water St. (22 Jan.)

John Jones, an outlaw of Va., a suspected coiner, has been apprehended in a haystack (22 Jan.)

New York item states that the ship _John_, Capt. Deane, is being repaired at New York (22 Jan.)

Shop and household goods and a Negro woman for sale by Thomas Hood in Water St. (22 Jan.)

Matthew Howard, convict English servant, age c. 30 or 40, horsefarrier, runaway from John Sheerwood of Talbot Co., Md. (22 Jan.)

Accounts with estate of Joseph Paxton, dec'd, to be settled with Mary Paxton, exec. (22 Jan.)

Charles Connor, Irish servant, age c. 20, runaway from John
   Henderson, of Welch-Track, Newcastle Co. (22 Jan.)
Matthew Richmond, Irish servant, age c. 24, runaway from John
   Smith, living in Lancaster Co. (22 Jan.)
John Hagan, Irish servant, runaway from Robert M'Kee, living at
   the Cross-road in New London, Chester Co. (22 Jan.)
Mr. Kemp, of Talbot Co., Md., has been bitten by a mad dog (29
   Jan.)
Edward Taylor of Cecil Co. at beginning of Dec. last was shot
   and killed by his runaway Mulatto slave Joe (brother to the
   man hanged some years ago for shooting Aquila Hall in Balti-
   more Co.); Col. Colvill, Mr. Veazy, Mr. Nathan Baker, Mr. Bax-
   ter and Mr. Rock are to hold a court for trial of said Joe
   (29 Jan.)
Annapolis item of 19 Dec. reports that on Sat. last two Negroes,
   Bob and Dick, both born in this country, were executed at Port
   Tobacco for robbing the store of Mr. Mitchell (19 Jan.)
Annapolis item of 2 Jan. reports that Mr. Middleton of Annapolis
   came up in a small vessel from Norfolk and got into Rappahan-
   nock River (19 Jan.)
Annapolis item of 2 Jan. reports arrival there of the ship Fal-
   con, Capt. Thomas Spencer, from Biddeford, after passage of
   12 weeks (29 Jan.)
Capt. Appowin brings news to Phila. from St. Christophers (29
   Jan.)
Capt. Leak of Phila. arrived there on 28 Jan. from Cadiz (29
   Jan.)
A Dutch woman in Phila. falsely accused Samuel Noble, tanner,
   before the Mayor of Phila., of beating her; her deceit was
   discovered and she has been imprisoned (29 Jan.)
Land for sale within tract to north of the Blue Hills lately
   purchased from the Indians; apply to the Land Office, Richard
   Peters, secretary (29 Jan.)
Snow Warren to be sold at coffee-house of the Widow Roberts;
   inventory to be seen there or at house of William Humphrey
   (29 Jan.)
Cow strayed from stable of Samuel M'Call in Water St. (29 Jan.)
Accounts with estate of James Scott, merchant, to be settled
   with Joseph Sims, Townsend White and Samuel M'Call, Jr. (29
   Jan.)
John Mifflin, Jr., is removed from Fishbourn's wharf to house
   in Second St., near Walnut St., next door to Capt. Blair's
   and opposite Mary Lisle's (29 Jan.)
Delage and Read have ship bread to be seen at store of John
   Spafford, baker, over the drawbridge in Water St. (29 Jan.)
James Wilson, better known as Scotch James, has received a 30
   shilling bill instead of one for 3 shillings (29 Jan.)
Horses taken up at plantation of Hezekiah Anderson of Lower
   Maxfield, Bucks Co. (29 Jan.)
Christopher Cooney, Irish servant, age c. 26, for some time
   hostler at Jonathan Thomas's in Burlington, runaway from
   Nathan Watson of Mountholly (29 Jan.)

1751

Christopher Major, English servant, age c. 30, runaway from Matthias Holstein, of Phila. Co., near the Gulph mill (29 Jan.)

Bartholomew M'Guire, Irish servant, age c. 25, runaway from Francis Graham, of Mill-Creek Hundred, Newcastle Co. (29 Jan.)

James M'Carty, Irish servant, weaver, age c. 21, runaway from Thomas Martin of Uwchlan, Chester Co. (29 Jan.)

Horse taken up at plantation of Isaac Ellis, of Whitpain Twp., Phila. Co. (29 Jan.)

Plantation on Rackoon Creek in Greenwich Twp., Gloucester Co., West New Jersey, for sale; on it is dwelling wherein Morris Connor keeps tavern; apply to Morris Morgan (29 Jan.)

Wood boat for sale by Thomas Green or John Parrock (29 Jan.)

Speech of Lt.-Gov. S. Phipps of Mass. (5 Feb.)

Letter from Enoch Titcomb from Newbury described wreck on 7 Jan. of the sloop Dolphin, Simeon Mirick master and Thomas Noyes of Stonington owner, at Plumb Island in Newbury; Mirick, John Sadler (the pilot) and Benajah Bill were frozen to death after they got ashore (5 Feb.)

Mr. Canada and a young man named Deming perished on 11 Dec. last when a well in Hartford East Precinct caved in (5 Feb.)

On 7 Jan. a brigantine from Lisbon, Capt. Calley, was cast away near Cohasset (5 Feb.)

At Phila. on Tue. last John Morris, Elizabeth Robinson, Francis M'Coy and John Crow were sentenced to death for breaking into and robbing the house of Philip Pederow of Phila., shopkeeper, on 13 Jan.; John Stinson was burnt in the hand; Mary M'Coy was acquitted (5 Feb.)

Land called Scults Level in Baltimore Co., formerly belonging to Archibald Douglass, and other tracts in Baltimore and Ann Arundel Counties for sale by William Hedges of Cecil Co. (5 Feb.)

Plantation in Trediffryn Twp., Chester Co., for sale by Richard Pearne, living in Merion Twp., Phila. Co. (5 Feb.)

Accounts with estate of John Packer, late of New-Garden, dec'd, to be settled with Thomas Lightfoot at his store, three doors above the Tun Tavern in Water St. (5 Feb.)

House wherein Mr. Burd lives, a brewhouse in Mr. Logan's alley and a water-lot near Mr. Woodrope's store are to be let by Edward, Joseph and William Shippen (5 Feb.)

Horse taken up at house of Amos Jones, living at the Sign of the Brig and Snow in Strawberry Alley (5 Feb.)

Items from Antigua mention Gov. Gilbert Fleming and Capts. Henderson, Wadley and Duchar (12 Feb.)

Laws of the Province of New Jersey to be published under the editorship of Samuel Nevill. Subscriptions are taken in Middlesex Co. by James Smith and John Wetherill; William Ouke in New Brunswick; Thomas Bartow in Perth Amboy and Francis Braiser at the Upper Landing. Monmouth Co., Robert Lawrence in Upper Freehold; John Taylor in Middle-Town; and John Redford in Shrewsbury. Essex Co., John Crane and Joseph Camp; David Ogdon in Newark, and Robert Ogdon in Borough of Elizabeth. Sommerset Co., John Van Middlesworth and Hendrick Fisher; and Robert Lettice Hooper at Rockey-Hill. Bergen Co., Lawrence Vanbuskirk and Derrick Dey; and David Provost at Hackinsack. Burlington Co., Richard Smith, Jr., and Daniel Smith in Burlington; William Hook in Croswicks; John Rispham in More's-Town; Samuel

1751

Woodward at Croswicks Bridge. Gloucester Co., William Mickle and Samuel Harrison. Salem Co., William Hancock and Nicholas Gibbon. Cumberland Co., John Brick, Sr., and John Brick, Jr. Cape-May Co., Aaron Leaming and John Spicer. Hunterdon Co., William Mott and John Emley, and Elisha Bond at Trenton. Morris Co., Jacob Ford and John Keney. Subscriptions will also be taken by the editor and by James Parker, living at New York (12 Feb.)

For freight or passage to Newburn, N.C., in ship Hope, Thomas Lake commander, agree with Willing and Lloyd or with said Lake at Dickinson's wharf (12 Feb.)

Accounts with estate of James Morris, dec'd, to be settled with Anthony Morris, Jr., and John Morris, execs; all persons indebted to James and Joseph Morris when in partnership are to settle with Joseph Morris (12 Feb.)

A plantation, animals, goods and house of Martin Bickham, dec'd, in Greenwich, Gloucester Co., N.J., for sale by Sarah Bickham, exec. (12 Feb.)

Imported goods and servants for sale at store of Hugh Donaldson and John Troy in Front St., next door to Thomas White, chocolate- maker, opposite Morris's Alley (12 Feb.)

Shallop for sale by Peter Grubb, of Wilmington, Newcastle Co. (12 Feb.)

Accounts with Patrick Baird, late vendue master, to be settled with Alexander Forbes (12 Feb.)

New York item of 21 Jan. mentions Capts. Mortimore and Oliver Jones (19 Feb.)

A schooner, one Holland master, was wrecked in harbor at Portsmouth, N.H. (19 Feb.)

One Stroap, a country farmer, living near the Catskill Mt., struck and killed his wife about 10 days ago (19 Feb.)

New York item of 4 Feb. reports that Thu. last a man going by the name of William Broughton (alias Evans) was committed to goal (19 Feb.)

Rev. Thomas Arthur, Pastor of Presbyterian Church in New Brunswick, died there 2 Feb. in his 27th year; his wife died a few days before him (19 Feb.)

Wed. last John Morris, Francis M'Coy and Elizabeth Robinson were executed at Phila.; John Crow was reprieved; one Sweat and a certain M'Kneel and his wife, supposedly concerned in the late robberies in Phila., are in goal in Chester (19 Feb.)

Messuage, plantation and land near the Gulph mill in Merion, late in possession of George Warmer, taken in execution at suit of William Coleman and James Pemberton, execs. of the will of Samuel Powell, Jr., dec'd, to be sold at the house of Richard Hughes in Lower Merion (19 Feb.)

Robert Davis at the Queen's Head in Water St. has time of a **Scotch weaver for sale (19 Feb.)**

Negro for sale by Mary Hartt in Second St., nearly opposite the church (19 Feb.)

James Whitehead, work-house keeper, has found a silver watch and silver buckles (19 Feb.)

Benjamin Bagnall has watches and clocks for sale at his house in Front St. (19 Feb.)

Sarah, Negro slave, age c. 30, brought up at Amboy in family of Col. Hamilton, runaway from Judah Hays of New York (19 Feb.)

Accounts with estate of Tobias Griscom, house-carpenter, dec'd, to be settled with William Clymer, Joseph Fox and William Fisher, auditors (19 Feb.)

Three plantations in Towamensing Twp., Phila. Co., late the estate of William Tennis, dec'd, for sale; apply to Samuel and John Tennis, admins. (19 Feb.)

Two horses taken up at plantation of Michael Baughman in Manham Twp., Lancaster Co. (19 Feb.)

Kingston, Jamaica, item of 5 Jan. reports that two Negroes who murdered Elisha Rogers in a ship at sea were executed on Wed. last at Port Royal (26 Feb.)

On 13 Nov. H.M.S. *Ferret*, Capt. Scroop, arrived at Black River on the Musquita Shore (26 Feb.)

On 1 Feb. the Mulatto Joe was executed in Cecil Co. for the murder of his master (26 Feb.)

Letter from Antigua on 21 Nov. states that a few days ago Commodore Holborn sailed for Barbados and that on 20 Nov. Capt. Falkingham in the sloop *Shark* sailed for the same place (26 Feb.)

Capt. Alex. Brown, upon his arrival at New York on 17 Feb., reported that the sloop *Prosperity*, Capt. Manchester, is cast away upon Port Morant Keys (26 Feb.)

Capt. Conyers, upon arrival at Phila. last week, reported that he spoke the ship *Bentham*, Jacob Brown master, in distress (26 Feb.)

Persons inclined to serve on the nightly watch for Phila. are to apply to the following wardens: William Callender, Jonathan Zane, Thomas Crosby, Joshua Fisher, Philip Syng and Hugh Roberts (26 Feb.)

Farm on Wishahickon Road and a house in Arch St., wherein Nicholas Scull dwells, to be let; enquire of Joshua Maddox (26 Feb.)

Managers of the Borough of Lancaster lottery are: Adam Simon Kuhn, Lodowick Stone, George Gibson, Isaac Whitelock, John Hart, Valentine Crook, Michael Groce and Robert Thompson (26 Feb.

Andrew Robinson, Irish servant, who came last summer from the north of Ireland, age c. 20, and Edward Fling, native Irishman, age c. 30, runaways from Peter Dicks and Humphrey Johnson, of Chester Co. (26 Feb.)

Patrick O'Neil, Irish servant, age c. 19, runaway from Marks Conner of Whitemarsh (26 Feb.)

Manus Harly, Irish servant, age c. 25, runaway from John Edwards of Newcastle Co. (26 Feb.)

House, wherein Mr. Ellis lived, on east side of Front St. and the adjoining house, now in occupation of Charles Batho, to be let by William Peters (26 Feb.)

Thomas Dennis has for sale a plantation **in Radnor, Chester Co.**, adjoining the estate of Samuel Harry on one side and the Plough Tavern on the other (26 Feb.)

The Blue Anchor, a public house in High St., Burlington, wherein Mary Bickley formerly lived, is to be sold or let by William Skeeles of Burlington (26 Feb.)

Demands against John Stinson, late of Phila., tavern-keeper, to be settled with Isaac Griffitts, sheriff (26 Feb.)

Accounts with estate of James Steel, late of Phila., dec'd, to be settled with Rebecca Steel and others, execs. (26 Feb.)

Negroes for sale; apply to Robert Warren, over the drawbridge (26 Feb.)

Charles-Town, S.C., item of 28 Jan. reports that a ship from Antigua, one Allen master, was driven ashore on Sullivant's Island, and Capt. Boyd's sloop was driven ashore at Port Royal (5 Mar.)

Admiral Boscawen is expected at Halifax early in the spring (5 Mar.)

Boston item of 4 Feb. reports that on 2 Feb. Jeremiah Morriel in Salisbury was struck dead by falling under the iron work wheel (5 Mar.)

Boston item of 11 Jan. reports that on Fri. last Capt. Benjamin Blany of Malden died when thrown by his horse (5 Mar.)

Boston item of 11 Jan. reports the death by drowning of Mr. M'Intyre (owner of a sloop, one M'Kown master) and a mate and a boy in George's River (5 Mar.)

New York item of 25 Feb. gives account of apprehension of one Elizabeth Herbert near Elizabeth-Town Point; she is thought to belong to a gang of thieves (5 Mar.)

Records of Supreme Court of Pa. are removed to office in the western wing of the Stadthouse, where attendance will be given by James Read, prothonotary (5 Mar.)

John Kearsley, medico-chirurgus, has just published remarks on Dr. Adam Thompson's <u>Discourse</u> (5 Mar.)

House, bake-house, cooper's shop, wharf, etc. to be let in Bristol; enquire of Anthony Wilson in Middletown, Bucks Co., or Patrick Hanlin in Bristol (5 Mar.)

Plantation in the Northern Liberties, late belonging to John Oxley, dec'd, adjoining plantation late of Thomas Chalkley on the road leading from Point-no-Point to Frankford, will be sold at house of Thomas Harper in Frankford; plans may be seen at George Heap's, serveyor, in Third St., at Joseph Saunder's office on Carpenter's wharf, at John Reily's, conveyancer, in Front St., and at William Callender's in Front St. (5 Mar.)

Copper stills for sale at house of John Holmes in Second St. (5 Mar.)

Gold buttons lost between Philip Syng's and Pewter-platter-alley; reward if found and brought to Mr. Franklin's (5 Mar.)

Elizabeth Morris, English servant, age c. 24, who can talk broken French, runaway from John Robinson, of New Providence, Phila. Co. (5 Mar.)

Tanyard to be let by Samuel Morris in Second St. (5 Mar.)

Accounts with estate of Robert Shewell, dec'd, to be settled with Elizabeth, Stephen and Joseph Shewell, execs.; plantation in New Britain, Bucks Co., to be let by the execs.; Elizabeth and Joseph continue bisket baking (5 Mar.)

Plantation in Northern Liberties wherein Thomas Venable lately lived to be let; apply to Edward Jones, ranger, at the Vineyard in the Northern Liberties (5 Mar.

1751

Apply to Charles Allen, at Timothy Matlack's in Market St., for title and terms of sale of seven tracts of land in Londonderry Twp., Chester Co., now in the tenure of the following: Alexander M'Cashen, Samuel Sproule, John Little, James Green, William Crosby, William Robertson and John Carrick (5 Mar.)

Partnership of Norris and Griffitts is terminated, and William Griffitts intends to leave the province (5 Mar.)

Robert Jones, servant, runaway from Hugh Meredith, of Newtown, Chester Co. (5 Mar.)

On 4 Feb. wife of Meverell Lock of St. Mary's Co. gave birth to a son and two daughters (12 Mar.)

Annapolis item of 27 Feb. reports that schooner from Cherry Point, Va., one Smith formerly master, was abandoned at Clement's Bay in St. Mary's Co. by two men going by the names of Newton and Jones (12 Mar.)

William Davis, Irish servant. who belonged to William All, age c. 30, runaway from John Roe, of Queen Anne's Co., near Tulley's Neck, Md. (5 Mar.)

Dry goods for sale by Anthony Stocker at his store under the dwelling of John Sober in Water St. (5 Mar.)

Philip Laughlen, Irish servant, age c. 25, runaway from James Martin, living in Baltimore Co., near Deer-Creek meetinghouse (5 Mar.)

Thomas Francis, an old forge man, runaway from Joseph and Jacob Carter and his bail, at Kingsberry forge, near Chester, Chester Co. (5 Mar.)

Plantation in Buckingham Twp., Bucks Co., for sale by Matthew Hall, on the premises (5 Mar.)

Ship *Dragon*, Capt. Nicoll, from Jamaica, reported in New York to have been lost upon Portland Keys (12 Mar.)

Ship *Forrest*, Capt. Ochterlony, from Phila., reported to have arrived at London (12 Mar.)

Real estate in Northern Liberties, late the property of Henry Miller, dec'd, taken in execution at suit of Jonathan Mifflin, exec. of Rebecca Edgell, dec'd, to be sold at the house of Jeremiah Smith in Front St. (12 Mar.)

House and lot on Society Hill, late the property of Thomas Griffith, taken in execution at suit of Joseph Sims and some others, to be sold at Roberts's coffee-house (12 Mar.)

House and lot in Passyunk and Moyamensing, late the property of Edward Devereux, taken in execution at suit of Andrew Farrell, to be sold at house of John Biddle (12 Mar.)

One quarter part of the ship *Charming Polly*, Joseph Greenway master, lying next to Samuel Powell's wharf, over the drawbridge, is for sale; inventory may be seen at John Durborow's or at Roberts's coffee-house (12 Mar.)

Joseph Greenway has for sale a bank house near Market St. (12 Mar.)

Property has been lost off a horse; reward if brought to James Wagstaff, tinman, in Phila., or to Thomas Hughes, in Exeter, Phila. Co. (12 Mar.)

Abraham Carpenter, at the Sign of the Duke of Cumberland, over Pool's bridge, near the sugar house, sells indigo seed (12 Mar.)

Pasture lots in the Northern Liberties, part of Coates's land, adjoining lots of Samuel Burge, William Cox, Stephen Paschall, Robert Shewell and William Masters, subject to ground rent belonging to Judah Foulke, taken at suit of Richard Hockley and others, to be sold at house of Jeremiah Smith, at the Sign of the Queen of Hungary in Front St. (12 Mar.)

Two servants, Joseph Savage and Edward Reace, runaways from Roger Coleman and Thomas Slipper, of Kent Co., Md. (12 Mar.)

Plantation in Germantown Twp., Phila. Co., for sale by Anthony Tunes, living in Lower Merion Twp. (12 Mar.)

House and lots in Borough of Wilmington, Newcastle Co., late of Hester Bishop, dec'd, to be sold by John Stapler, exec. (12 Mar.)

Thomas Kelly, Irish servant, runaway from Samuel Scott, of Rapho Twp., near Lancaster (12 Mar.)

Kingston, Jamaica, item of 29 Dec. reports that in a duel Dr. Parker Bennet was killed by Dr. John Williams (19 Mar.)

Boston item of 18 Feb. reports a fire in the keeping-room of Rev. Mr. Gray (19 Mar.)

Boston item of 25 Feb. records the accidental death of two of the crew of Capt. Mackey's ship (19 Mar.)

Boston item of 25 Feb. reports that three deserters from the French gave details about the murder of Capt. How; Col. Lawrence has sent the deserters to Annapolis to Capt. Cobb (19 Mar.)

Boston item of 25 Feb. reports the death at Pemequid of Capt. William Phipps, eldest son of the lt.-gov. (19 Mar.)

New York item of 11 Mar. notes the arrival there of Capt. Jones from the Bay of Honduras (19 Mar.)

Capt. Dowers, arrived at Phila. from Lisbon, reports the arrival at London of Capts. Ritchie and Flint, both from Phila.; Capt. North has arrived at Bristol from Phila. (19 Mar.)

Meadow in Passyunk Twp. to be let; enquire of Joseph Sims (19 Mar.)

Stable in M'Combs's Alley, between Arch and Market Sts., near the corner of Second St., to be let; enquire of David Franks or Evan Evans (19 Mar.)

Nails for sale at John Pole's wharf (19 Mar.)

For freight or passage to Jamaica in the ship Richmond, William Lawson commander, apply to Alexander Hamilton or to the commander at Lloyd's wharf (19 Mar.)

For freight or passage to Antigua in the snow Mary, Humphry Clase commander, apply to John Reynell or to the master at Peele's wharf (19 Mar.)

Francis Richardson intends for London this spring (19 Mar.)

Plantation in Bethlehem Twp., Hunterdon Co., whereon William Gammon formerly lived, for sale; apply to John Beaumont in Bucks Co. or John Allen or William Pidgeon in Trenton (19 Mar.)

Lot, a Negro, age c. 24, runaway from Elijah Bond (19 Mar.)

Plantation in Marple Twp., Chester Co., for sale by John Morris in Newtown (19 Mar.)

Persons indebted to office of surveyor general in Burlington, formerly kept by Isaac De Cow, dec'd, are to settle with Joseph De Cow in Trenton or Isaac De Cow in Burlington (19 Mar.)

John Bartholomew has for sale a plantation in Montgomery Twp., Phila. Co. (19 Mar.)

Garrat Dewees has for sale land on Chestnut Hill; plans are at house of John Shephard, near the premises (19 Mar.)

Heifer came to stable of Alexander Alexander in Phila. (19 Mar.)

New York item of 18 Mar. states that on Thu. last Capt. Carlisle arrived from Barbados (28 Mar.)

Account of duel at Kingston, Jamaica, between Dr. Bennet (who was born at Montserrat, was educated in Great Britain and practiced in France) and Dr. Williams (28 Mar.)

Stray mare in custody of Widow Steen in West Nantmill, Chester Co. (19 Mar.)

Joseph Weaver, English servant, age c. 26, runaway from Walter Comly, of the Manor of Moreland, Phila. Co. (19 Mar.)

Public house, the Sign of the White Horse, on King's high road between Darby and Chester, for sale; apply to Isaac Gleaves (19 Mar.)

Michael M'Guire, age c. 18, lately servant to George Stevenson of York, runaway from John Abbitt, near York (19 Mar.)

Walter Dougherty, of Chester-town, Kent Co., Md., intends to leave the province and has for sale a house on Main St. (19 Mar.)

Mare came to the plantation of William Hamilton, where Jonathan Liddle lives, in Leacock Twp., Lancaster Co. (19 Mar.)

In pursuance of letters patent granted by Jonathan Belcher, Gov. of N.J., two fairs are to be held annually at Princetown in Windsor Twp. (19 Mar.)

Joshua Babcock, Chief Justice of Superior Court of R.I., seeks relatives of William Jackson (supposedly a Virginian), who was murdered, it is believed, by Thomas Carter, also believed to be a Virginian (28 Mar.)

Joseph Pratt, admin., will sell goods and chattels of Thomas Moore, Jr., dec'd, and also real estate formerly belonging to Mordecai Maddock of Springfield Twp. (28 Mar.)

Real estate in Front St., late property of Peter Lloyd, dec'd, taken at suit of Israel Pemberton, will be sold at Roberts's coffee-house (28 Mar.)

Real estate in Fourth St., late the property of Jacob Kroft, taken in execution at suit of Thomas Maule and others, will be sold at house of William Gray in Market St. (28 Mar.)

Lot in Wicacoa, late the property of Lawrence Algerus, taken in execution at suit of Thomas Hurst, will be sold by Sheriff Isaac Griffitts at James's coffee-house (28 Mar.)

Real estate on the Passyunk Road for sale; enquire of James Chattin, living on the premises (28 Mar.)

Accounts with estate of Joseph Boor, dec'd, to be settled with Thomas Hopkinson, exec., in Walnut St. (28 Mar.)

John Reily, in Front St., opposite Norris's Alley, sells rum, shot, seeds, etc. and draws deeds and other writings (28 Mar.)

Accounts with estate of Charles Connor, late of Aston Twp., Chester Co., to be settled with Samuel Neave and Attwood Shute at Aubrey Bevan's in Chester (28 Mar.)

John Cely, age c. 30, servant, who pretends to be a barber and wig-maker, runaway from David Jones of London Britain Twp., Chester Co. (28 Mar.)

Plantation in Bensalem Twp., Bucks Co., contiguous to lands of Samuel Hasell, Gilbert Hix and Daniel Seaverns, for sale; apply to Henry Enochs on the premises (28 Mar.)

Thomas Donaldson, Irish servant, age c. 35, and Thomas Ryan, Irish servant, age c. 22, runaways from Uriah Blue and Henry Bishop, near White-Clay-Creek in Mill Creek Hundred, Newcastle Co. (28 Mar.)

John Hughes, baker, of Phila., has plantation to be let (28 Mar.)

Thomas Anslow, Dutch servant, bred in England, age c. 25, runaway from James James, near St. George's in Newcastle Co. (28 Mar.)

Roger Noland, Irish servant, who served four years in the province and then went on expeditions to Cape Breton and Canada, runaway from Mounce Keen, of Pilesgrove Twp., Salem Co. (28 Mar.)

For freight or passage to London in ship _Grampus_, Robert Lee master, apply to Rees Meredith or to the master at Meredith's wharf (28 Mar.)

On 14 Mar. a ship belonging to Newport, R.I., Benjamin Carr master, was cast away on the back of Long Island (4 Apr.)

A schooner from Boston, Capt. Potts, was spoke with on 14 Mar. in latitude of Cape Hatteras (4 Apr.)

New York item of 1 Apr. reports arrival there on 31 Mar. of the brig _Hester_, Capt. Troup, from the Bay of Honduras; Capt. Heysham of the ship _Antilope_ died there the day before the _Hester_ sailed (4 Apr.)

New York item of 1 Apr. records the escape from goal on Fri. last of John M'Lean, John Douning, Francis M'Neal and Elizabeth Harborth (4 Apr.)

Accounts with estate of Abraham Claypoole, dec'd, to be settled with Deborah Claypoole, William Coleman and John Swift, execs. (4 Apr.)

Third part of Mountjoy forge in Upper Merion for sale; enquire of Daniel Walker, living near the premises (4 Apr.)

Isaac Roberts in Arch St., opposite the Quaker burying ground, has three Negroes for sale (4 Apr.)

Benjamin Alburtis, an apprentice, age c. 20, cooper, runaway from John Evans, living in Trenton (4 Apr.)

House (a tavern) in Yorktown, where George Mendenhall lately dwelt, to be sold by Sarah Mendenhall, admin. (4 Apr.)

At the house of Daniel Pistoras in Germantown the following real estate will be sold: lot in tenure of Richard Rose; lot in Trout's lane, between the lands of Derrick Keyser and Samuel M'Call, Jr., late the property of Matthew Ingels, dec'd, taken in execution at suit of Evan Morgan and others (4 Apr.)

William Taylor, English servant, age c. 20, runaway from John Davis, of Earltown, Lancaster Co. (4 Apr.)

House and lot in Lombard St., late belonging to Edmund Beach, taken in execution at suit of Mark Kuhl, will be sold at the house of Widow Jones in Second St. (4 Apr.)

Accounts with estate of James Albin, dec'd, to be settled with James Hunter, of Newtown, and James Bennet, of Middletown, Chester Co. (4 Apr.)

For freight or passage to Barbados in the brigt. Rebecca and Mary, Daniel England commander, apply to Joseph Oldman or to the commander at Morris Morris's wharf (4 Apr.)

Patrick Baird, intending for England, wishes to settle all his accounts (4 Apr.)

Horse taken up at house of Abraham Cowardin, living at the Sign of the Sun in Kent Co. (4 Apr.)

John Clark, age c. 35, servant, runaway from Catherine Kirkpatrick (4 Apr.)

Real estate for sale at the house of John Cross, below the drawbridge, all the property of Thomas Williams, taken in execution at suit of William and David M'Ilvaine (4 Apr.)

John M'Caulefd, Irish servant, tailor by trade, age c. 18, runaway from Adam M'Nelly, of Tinnecum Twp., Bucks Co. (4 Apr.)

Passengers on stage boat of Joseph Borden, Jr., will meet with a stage wagon of Joseph Richards in Bordentown and then proceed to John Cluck's opposite Perth Amboy; a stage boat of Daniel Obryant will next proceed to Whitehall Slip in New York (4 Apr.)

Annapolis item of 20 Feb. reports that John M'Michael, a Portuguese sailor, at a court held at Cambridge in Dorchester Co., was convicted of murder; at the same court a Negro named Sharper was sentenced to death for a rape (11 Apr.)

Annapolis item of 20 Feb. states that the schooner Aurora, John Lovit commander, of Salem, Mass., was filling with water at sea when on 2 Feb. Capt. Kinney in a brigantine took up the master and crew and on Sat. last brought them into Annapolis (11 Apr.)

According to Annapolis item of 6 Mar. on Thu. last Mary Stedman was found dead in bed; it is suspected that her husband murdered her (11 Apr.)

Commission is set up in Cecil Co. to try Sarah Bevers, suspected of murdering her bastard child. At the same court will be tried a person supposed to have been concerned in the murder of Hugh Mahaffy, for which Enos Carty was executed; one Mary Baker, on whom Mahaffy's sleeve buttons and pocketbook were found, has lately made a confession (11 Apr.)

Letter from Va. gives account of attempt by Spaniards to seize Mr. Harbury's ship the Jubilee (11 Apr.)

Annapolis item of 20 Mar. reports that last week two young Negro wenches were sentenced to death for burning a tobacco-house of Joseph Galloway (11 Apr.)

Annapolis item of 20 Mar. reports that on Thu. last Jeremiah Swift, age c. 21, convict servant of John Hatherley of Elk Ridge, murdered two sons (ages c. 11 and 9) and a daughter (age c. 14) of Mr. Hatherley (11 Apr.)

On 19 Mar. a boat owned by Mr. Sutton of Kent Island, coming from there to Annapolis, overset, and Nathaniel Conner (the ferryman) and Mr. Sutton's eldest son (age c. 19) were drowned (11 Apr.)

It is reported from Chinecto that the Indians have taken a sloop from Boston, one Harbottle master (11 Apr.)

New York item of 8 Apr. notes the arrival there of Capt. Ramadge from Leoganne and of the sloop *Moses*, Capt. Ireland, from the Musquito Shore; Capt. Ramadge reports that the French took a Capt. Dickinson, confined him for 30 days and then released him (11 Apr.)

New York item of 8 Apr. reports that Capt. Bennet, in a sloop from the bay, was cast away (11 Apr.)

News from Bucks Co. that John M'Caulefd, a convict servant, who robbed several houses, has been imprisoned (11 Apr.)

On 10 Apr. at the Supreme Court in Phila. Samuel Saunders was tried for the murder of Simon Girtie and convicted of manslaughter (11 Apr.)

House where Robert Meade dwells, next door to Anthony Morris, Jr., in Water St. is where household furniture of the late Dr. John Michael Brown will be sold by public vendue (11 Apr.)

David Jones, a sail-maker from Dublin, is open for business at his sail room on Arch St. wharf, where Rowland Monrow formerly had his sail room (11 Apr.)

House and lot in Frederick-town to be sold or let; apply to Peter Bayard at Bohemia River, John M'Dermott, next door to said house, or Thomas Williams in Phila. (11 Apr.)

For freight or passage to Cork and Dublin on the brig. *Prince William*, Edward Snead commander, apply to Randle Mitchell at his store in Water St. (11 Apr.)

Sheriff Joseph Hart of Bucks Co. will sell property late belonging to Daniel Wright, dec'd, at Patrick O'Hanlin's in the Borough of Bristol, taken at suit of Robert Harvey and Richard Smith; also at Joseph Insley's in Newtown land in Springfield Twp., late the property of Robert Ellis, taken at the suit of James Morgatroyd; also real estate in Middletown Twp., late belonging to Thomas Gurney, dec'd, taken at suit of Septimus Robinson (11 Apr.)

John Murphey, Irish servant, age c. 25, runaway from Amos Strickland, of Newtown, Bucks Co. (11 Apr.)

William Young of Phila., shoemaker and shopkeeper, intends for Va. (11 Apr.)

Land in the Northern Liberties for sale by Benjamin Callender at the house of John Biddle in Market St. (11 Apr.)

John Rees, cooper, age c. 19, runaway from Phineas Roberts of Phila. (11 Apr.)

Plantation in Buckingham Twp., Bucks Co., for sale; enquire of Matthew Hall, living on the premises (11 Apr.)

Plantation in the Falls Twp., late the property of Joseph Hutchinson, dec'd, for sale; apply to Michael and Randel Hutchinson, execs. (11 Apr.)

Daniel Gardy, apprentice, age c. 17, runaway from Jacob Hagy in Germantown (11 Apr.)

Capt. Phineas Stevens has arrived in Boston from Quebec, after seeking to redeem the English captives there (18 Apr.)

William Carter to be executed in R.I. for the murder of William Jackson, who leaves a wife and seven children in Va. (18 Apr.)

Timothy Wheaton (whose brother Solomon died in Canada, as did one Philip Jenkins), taken prisoner at Swan Island, near Richmond, was brought to Boston from Quebec by Capt. Stevens (18 Apr.)

Ship _Myrtilla_, Capt. Budden, of Phila., is believed to have arrived in London (18 Apr.)

John Black at Strausburgh Twp., Lancaster Co., has taken up a white mare (18 Apr.)

D. Hall has for sale at the Post-Office _The Natural History of Barbados_ by Rev. Griffith Hughes, Rector of St. Lucy's Parish on Barbados (18 Apr.)

Household furniture and looking glasses are for sale at the house of James Sackett (18 Apr.)

Accounts with estate of Hennretta Allaire, dec'd, to be settled with Alexander Allaire, admin. (18 Apr.)

Francis Cannon, born in Ireland, runaway from Adam M'Cool, a blacksmith, of West Nantmell Twp., Chester Co. (18 Apr.)

Real estate in the Northern Liberties, near Frankford, late the property of Henry Hartman, will be sold at the house of Thomas Harper in Frankford (18 Apr.)

House to be sold or let; enquire of Isaac Roberts in Arch St., opposite the Quakers' burying ground (18 Apr.)

Land in Dromore Twp., Lancaster Co., for sale; apply to James Siddal, of Middletown, Bucks Co. (18 Apr.)

Real estate in Kensington, a plantation in Bucks Co., a house and tanyard on Germantown Road, about a mile from Phila. (being the house where Timothy Scarf now lives) and lots in Phila., all for sale; enquire of Thomas Green, living on Germantown Road, or George Heap, coroner and surveyor (18 Apr.)

Reuben Jones, servant, this country born, runaway from John French at Mount Holly (18 Apr.)

Lots in Germantown in the lane leading from the market place to Robeson's mill, adjoining land of Samuel M'Call, Sr., and a lot at the upper end of Germantown, adjoining John Johnson's land, to be sold by George Bringhurst in Germantown (18 Apr.)

Mare came to the house of Samuel Lewis in Leacock Twp., Lancaster Co. (18 Apr.)

Land on the Beaverdam branch of Goose Creek in Fairfax Co., Va., for sale; apply to Lovell Jackson, the owner, living on the premises (18 Apr.)

Boston item of 11 Apr. reports that on Fri. last Phillis, a Negro girl, was found guilty of the murder of her master's child (25 Apr.)

Letter from South Kingston, R.I., written in answer to an adv. of Thomas Bows of Newark, reports confession made by Thomas Carter, murderer of William Jackson of Va. (25 Apr.)

Horse stolen from the field of Christina Hains, widow of Henry Hains of Lampeter Twp., Lancaster Co. (25 Apr.)

Sturgeon for sale at Anthony Wilkinson's in Water St. (25 Apr.)

Negroes for sale; enquire of Trent Denny at Samuel Gray's in Market St. (25 Apr.)

Land in Caln Twp., Chester Co., and in Warwick, Bucks Co., for sale by Deborah Claypoole, William Coleman and John Swift, execs. of Abraham Claypoole, dec'd (25 Apr.)

Notice from Gilbert Fleming, Lt.-Gen. and Commander-in-chief of Leeward Caribbee Islands, is published by Gov. James Hamilton (25 Apr.)

Persons indebted to Peter Aston are to settle accounts with Samuel Hazzard, John Bell or Edmund Kearny; shop and household goods will be sold at the house of Peter Aston in Second St. (25 Apr.)

Plantation in Southampton Twp., Bucks Co., purchased of John Eastburn, will be sold at the dwelling of John Gilleylen (25 Apr.)

The following real estate in or near Phila., belonging to the estate of Abraham Claypoole, dec'd, is to be sold at James's coffee-house: lots between Passyunk Rd. and land of Joseph Wharton; ground at Wicacoa, bounded on south by land of the Widow Johnson and on north by land late of John Cadwalader, dec'd; land on Lower-ferry Rd., opposite to house late of John Kinsey, dec'd; lot on east side of Second St., adjoining Philip Halbert's ground, now in tenure of Hannah Lloyd; lot on Society Hill, between grounds of William Plumsted and Samuel Wetherell; plans may be seen at house of John Swift (25 Apr.)

Frederick Hasser will sell land at the upper end of Germantown (25 Apr.)

John Hughes, of Phila., baker, has land for sale near Mr. Branson's forges in Lancaster Co. (25 Apr.)

If William Probart, who lived in St. Mary's Co. in the year 1739, will apply to Dr. David Ross at Bladensburg, he will hear of a legacy left him in England (25 Apr.)

Horse strayed from plantation of Samuel Lightfoot near Chester; reward if horse is brought to Benjamin Lightfoot ot to William Gray's tavern in Market St. (25 Apr.)

Land for sale in Creesham Twp., opposite William Allen's; enquire of Jonathan Livezey (25 Apr.)

Thomas Bibbing, English servant, age c. 30, mason and bricklayer, and William Coombs, West Country Englishman, age c. 18 or 20, bricklayer, runaways from Gamaliel Butler and Patrick Doaren of Annapolis, Md.; they have been seen at the house of Col. Benjamin Chambers in Canogogige (25 Apr.)

Boston item of 22 Apr. gives news from Halifax that Gov. Cornwallis was preparing to visit Chignecto (2 May)

On 28 Apr. Capts. Tucker and Foster arrived at New York (2 May)

Sarah Brown, widow of Michael Brown, silk-dyer from London, will continue the business at her late husband's house in Sassafras St. (2 May)

Steer came to plantation of John Houston in Strasburgh Twp., Lancaster Co. (2 May)

Moses Tharp, born at Woodbridge in East Jersey, servant, age c. 21, runaway from Edward Hill of Duncks's Ferry (2 May)

Joseph Norris, servant, this country born, age c. 30, runaway from John Rees of Whitpain Twp. (2 May)

Samuel Hasell has a horse for sale (2 May)

1751

Time of servant man for sale; enquire of Andrew Bartholomew in Chestnut St. or Thomas Maule in Second St. (2 May)

William M'Gee, Irish servant, age c. 18, runaway from William Boyd of Sadsbury Twp., Chester Co. (2 May)

Horse strayed or stolen from the Borough of Wilmington; reward if brought to Elizabeth Dowdle or John Crampton at Brandywine mill (2 May)

Land on Oldman's creek in Piles-grove, Salem Co., for sale by Joshua Wright or Samuel Atkinson (2 May)

Thomas Renshaw offers reward for recovery of horse strayed or stolen from the plantation of John Renshaw at the Northern Liberties (2 May)

Horse stolen from stable of Joseph Moore in Hopewell (2 May)

Mare strayed from George Wampalt in Rockhill Twp., Bucks Co.; reward if returned to owner or to Walter M'Cool (2 May)

Daniel Cooper in the Jerseys has for sale a Negro fellow; enquire of William Cooper in Market St. (2 May)

Account of rude behavior of a Spanish commander to Capt. Scroope of H.M.S. Ferret (9 May)

Kingston, Jamaica, item of 23 Feb. describes a fire which broke out Mon. last at Port Royal in the back house of Drs. Webb and Dodson (9 May)

Sun. last Capt. Slade arrived at Phila. from Liverpool; Capt. Mesnard has arrived at London; Capt. Edwards has arrived at Newry (9 May)

Annapolis item of 27 Mar. gives account of boat that overset in the bay on Thu. last and of the remark of Conner, one of those drowned (9 May)

Annapolis item of 27 Mar. relates that Francis Linthicum, two of his children and two of his Negroes were poisoned (9 May)

At court in Cecil Co. Sarah Bevers was convicted of the murder of her bastard child (9 May)

Annapolis item of 10 Apr. reports that the house of Widow named Wooden, near West River, was burnt to the ground on Mon. last (9 May)

Details of trial and conviction of Jeremiah Swift, servant of Mr. Hatherly of Elk Ridge; Swift murdered John (age 12) and Elizabeth (age 14) and wounded two other children of his master, Benjamin (age 10) and Benedict Leonard (age c. 9) (9 May)

Annapolis items of 17 Apr. report drowning of Abraham Woodall of Annapolis, conviction of John Owen for horse staling, conviction of Sharper, a Negro, for rape, conviction of Jane Sewell and John Hart, both for stealing, conviction of John Stedman, a Scotchman, age 54, for murder of his wife, and conviction of David (alias Daniel) Sullivan, age c. 23, who murdered Donald M'Kennie (overseer of Mr. Digges) in Baltimore Co. (9 May)

About two weeks ago 6 or 7 men broke into the house of Mr. Bennet in Chestertown but were timely discovered and fled; the same night they robbed the store of Mr. Connor (9 May)

Hue and cry in Virginia after Edward Davis, a rogue who speaks broad North Country English and pretends to be a well digger; he is supposed to have robbed the store of Mr. James Dunlap (9 May)

A person who called himself Chamberlain on Thu. last came to Messieurs Levy and Franks, merchants in Phila., with a forged order pretended to be drawn by Mr. Wardrop, a Maryland merchant; the forger has been imprisoned (9 May)

The house of Mr. Lievezey, near Leech's Mill, was lately robbed (9 May)

Sheriff Isaac Griffitts gives notice of election to be held to choose a burgess for Phila. in place of William Clymer, dec'd (9 May)

Robert Steell, from the London brew-house in Walnut St., now at the Edinburgh brew-house in Second St., formerly kept by Mrs. Mary Lisle, brews beer and ale (9 May)

Negroes and Barbados rum for sale by Thomas Gilbert at Jonathan Evans's in Front St. (9 May)

Dry goods and English beer, imported in the snow **Recovery**, Capt. Jonathan Slade, for sale by James Wallace at his store where James Steward, tailor, formerly lived, opposite the Queen's Head in Water St. (9 May)

Francis Garrigues is selling the ferry where he now lives; it was formerly George Gray's (9 May)

If Margaret Davis can prove herself to be the sister of the late Edward Davis of Virginia, she will hear something to her advantage (9 May)

Daniel Cooper has found a barrel of pork on the Jersey shore (9 May)

For freight or passage to Jamaica in the sloop **Three Friends**, George Eacles commander, apply to Garraway and Wright at the Widow Montgomery's or to said commander at Powell's wharf (9 May)

Imported goods for sale by John Priest, who is removed from his store in the house of Widow Griffin that was, into the store that Philip Benezet kept on Carpenter's wharf in Water St. (9 May)

Lottery tickets for sale by Samuel Watts, John Quincy, Joseph Richards, Harrison Gray and James Russel, managers, and Benjamin Branklin (sic!) in Phila. (9 May)

Adv. of William Fitzgerald and William Hussey, tailors, at the Sign of the Hand and Shears, near the drawbridge in Front St. (9 May)

Adv. of Daniel Rundle, who has moved his store to Water St., opposite Dickinson's Burnt Buildings (9 May)

Wherry belonging to Richard Renshaw went adrift from the ferry at Greenwich-point (9 May)

For freight or passage to London in the ship **Sally**, Joseph Stiles master, apply to William Edwell or said master (9 May)

Real estate in Marcus Hook, Chichester Twp., Chester Co., that is bounded on west by ground of Benjamin Howell and on the east and north by land of Thomas Howell, is for sale; enquire of William Vaughan, ship-carpenter in Marcus Hook, or Jacob Worrel, ship-carpenter in Phila. (9 May)

Abraham Griffith, Jr., in Northampton Twp., Bucks Co., has for sale a wagon, horses and a Mulatto wench (9 May)

Tom, Mulatto, age c. 37, runaway from Nicholas Everson of East N.J., near Perth Amboy ferry; he was seen enquiring for John and Thomas Nutus, Indians, at Susquehanna (9 May)

William Dobin, Irish servant, age c. 18, runaway from Thomas James of Upper Merion, Phila. Co. (9 May)

John Rodman, a New Englander, age c. 25, a shoemaker, has escaped from William Bradshaw, constable of Christine Hundred, Newcastle Co. (9 May)

John Cowan, servant, bred near Biberry, age c. 23, runaway from Peter Dicks of Providence, Chester Co. (9 May)

George Monrow, age c. 30, and James Tracy, age c. 28, Irish servants, runaways from William and John Roberts of Manington, Salem Co. (9 May)

Horse strayed or stolen from the plantation of Hugh Roberts in Lower Merion (9 May)

Williamsburg, Va., item of 18 Apr. gives news of the following persons tried: Low Jackson of Nansemond Co. has been found guilty of counterfeiting; John Hill (*alias* Seale) from Southampton Co. has been convicted of horse stealing; John Markham from Northumberland has been found guilty of stealing tobacco and John Boah of receiving it; John Birk from King George has been convicted of stealing tobacco and John Ashwell from Essex of stealing wigs; Thomas Smith from Northumberland was convicted of the manslaughter of Robert Knowles; William Maniffee from Spotsylvania was indicted for manslaughter and Thomas Alley from York for felony but both were acquitted; the trial of Samuel Carr from Nansemond for the murder of Samuel Milner is continued to October (16 May)

Annapolis item of 1 May reports that on Wed. last Jeremiah Swift was executed at Elk Ridge (16 May)

Body of Capt. Smith, murdered by Newton and Jones, has been driven ashore; the two murderers have been apprehended at George's River and committed to prison (16 May)

Some persons suspected of being concerned in the murder of Donald M'Kennie (for which Sullivan has been executed) have been committed to goal (16 May)

Annapolis item of 1 May reports that on Sun. last two little Negro boys belonging to Mr. Creagh of Annapolis were drowned (16 May)

Annapolis item of 3 May reports the arrival at Patuxent of Capt. Adam Spencer from London (16 May)

Capt. Fones has brought news to Boston about a grant for the settling of Nova Scotia, the payment of bills drawn by Gov. Cornwallis and the raising of recruits by Capt. John Winslow (16 May)

Capt. Grigg from Turks Island informs in New York that a Spanish privateer has captured Capt. Dickinson in his sloop (16 May)

Mr. Dove, professor of English at the Academy, has taken a house for the reception of young gentlemen (16 May)

Mordecai Yarnall and Isaac Greenleafe are appointed assignees to Peter Aston by Samuel Hazard (16 May)

George Risler at Elizabeth George's in Blockley found a basket on the Conestogo Road (16 May)

Two English servants, William Blumefield, carpenter, age c. 35, and James Morgan, wheelwright, age c. 27, runaways from Patrick Renalds of Mount Holly, West N.J., and Peter Bard of Phila. (16 May)

Two country born Negroes, George (a carpenter) and Will (a plantation worker), runaways from Joseph Milburn Semmes, of Charles Co., Md., supposedly in company with two Irish servants of William Tate of Northumberland Co., Va. (16 May)

Horse stolen from the stable of Theophilus Hartman, glazier, in Lampeter Town, Lancaster Co. (16 May)

Matthew Williams, English servant, age c. 25, belonging to William Keepers of Baltimore Co., Md., runaway from Cornwall iron-works in Lancaster Co.; reward if brought to Amos Garret at said works (16 May)

Adv. of Charles and Alexander Stedman at their store, next door to Samuel Neave's in Front St. (16 May)

Edward Shippen has the following property to let: the house in Walnut St. where Mr. Burd lately lived; lots on Society Hill, near Capt. Attwood's and Woodrope's stores; a dwelling, bakehouse, granary and cooper's shops, belonging to William Gray, now in the tenure of Josiah Davenport, bisket baker, in Mr. Morris's alley (16 May)

Property on Turner's Lane for sale; enquire of Thomas Say or Richard Blackham (16 May)

Charles Elliott, Irish servant, age c. 25, runaway from John Baker, house-carpenter, in Kensington (16 May)

Andrew Cleara, Irish servant, age c. 30, runaway from Daniel Crawford of Leacock Twp., Lancaster Co. (16 May)

John Bacchus, servant, runaway from George Hooke of York Town, York Co. (16 May)

Neal M'Mullen of Londonderry, N.H., age c. 22, wigmaker, has failed to return a horse borrowed from Robert Perkeson; reward if news of M'Mullen is sent to said Perkeson or to the Rev. Muirhead in Boston (16 May)

Thomas Morgan, age c. 30, born in East N.J., and Adam Somers, a Palatine, age c. 60, a collier, broke out of the goal of Gloucester Co.; reward for their capture offered by Sheriff John Mickle (16 May)

London item of 6 Feb. reports the death there on Mon. last of Mrs. Freame (widow of Capt. Thomas Freame, who died at the siege of Carthagena), daughter of William Penn, late proprietor of Pa. (23 May)

In April near Chignecto, Nova Scotia, Indians fired upon a sloop, one Miller master (23 May)

Phila. item mentions Capts. Mitchell, Dunn, Shirley, Davis, Moore, Johnston, Hamilton, Boggs, Falls and Smith (23 May)

Request that observations of eclipse be sent to Theophilus Grew, professor at the Academy in Phila. (23 May)

Edward Jones, ranger, gives notice of stray horses at the Vineyard Plantation in the Northern Liberties (23 May)

Accounts with estate of Frederick Taylor, dec'd, late of Charles Town in Chester Co., to be settled at the house of Daniel Goldsmith in Charles Town; Arons Raff Snyder, admin., will sell the property and household goods (23 May)

Accounts with estate of Aubrey Richardson, dec'd, to be settled with Richard Richardson, exec., at Samuel Lane's in New-Providence Twp; also for sale is property adjoining the road between Norris's mill and Lewis's mill (23 May)

Nathan Durant, at Capt. Morrell's on Society Hill, has Negroes for sale (23 May)

Hannah Moss, living in Fourth St., has land in the Northern Liberties for sale (23 May)

William Nicholas, English servant, age c. 30, runaway, in company with two others, John Fox and one M'Murray, from William Jones, of Kingsess Twp., Phila. Co. (23 May)

Household goods to be sold by Mary Roberts at the Crooked-billet in Front St. (23 May)

Judah Hays seeks information about his Negro Sarah, who is suspected of being harbored by some white person in Phila. (23 May)

Real estate in Front St., opposite the new buildings of William Allen, late belonging to Abigail Morton, dec'd; apply to John Hood or Joseph Scattergood, execs., or to John Koster in Second St. (23 May)

Horses for sale by Jacob Walter at Anthony Morris's plantation in Moyamensing Twp. (23 May)

James Sackett intends shortly to leave the province (23 May)

Adv. of Arent Hassert in Laetitia Court (23 May)

Adv. for Dr. Benjamin Godfrey's general cordial, sold by Christopher Marshall at the Golden Ball in Chestnut St. (23 May)

Land for sale by Samuel Morris at the house of William Nicholson in Arch St.; title and terms at Samuel Mifflin's in Market St. (23 May)

Bay mare has been taken up by Thomas Thomas of Robeson Twp., Lancaster Co. (23 May)

Real estate for sale at the house of Nathaniel Jones in Uuchland Twp., Chester Co., by Richard Goucher and Evan John (23 May)

Jonathan Everston, Irish servant, runaway from Joseph Lusby in Baltimore Co. (23 May)

On 22 Apr. Samuel Hall and wife were carried off by Indians (30 May)

On 19 May Newton and Jones (who now call themselves Wilson and Brown) were committed to prison in Boston by Justice Philips (30 May)

New York item of 27 May mentions Capts. Badger, Richards, Pell, Randle, Furlong and Miller (30 May)

Phila. item mentions Capts. Cuthbert and Slade, who arrived from Dublin with servants (30 May)

John Malcomb, sail-maker, next door to Benjamin Rawle's in Water St., has a pair of coach horses for sale (30 May)

James Connaly, Irish servant, age c. 21, runaway from James Hart, of Plumsted, Bucks Co. (30 May)

John Kidd is removed from his store on Fishbourne's wharf in Water St. to the store where Norris and Griffitts lately lived in Front St. (30 May)

Hans William Kabe, age c. 16, thought to be with Frederick Isen and Philip Shout, runaway from George Miller, of Lebanon, Hunterdon Co., N.J. (30 May)

Adv. of Joseph Pattison, turner, from London, whose shop is between Black Hose Alley and Roberts's coffee-house in Front St. (30 May)

Israel Morris in Second St., next door to the Sign of the Chest of Drawers, makes and repairs horse-whips (30 May)

Daniel Carty, apprentice, age. c. 17, runaway from Jacob Hagie, paper-maker, of Germantown Twp. (30 May)

Joseph Marks has for sale rum, ginger and Negro boys and gurls (30 May)

Horse strayed from Thomas Bowen, of Whiteland Twp., Chester Co.; reward will be paid by Bowen or John Hembryght, living at the Sign of the White Horse (30 May)

Adv. of John Clifton at the Two Lamps in Second St. (30 May)

John Ashton has real estate for sale at Moyamensing (30 May)

Sheriff Hance Hamilton of Phila. Co. reports escape of George Griffin and Henry Wills, tailors from Baltimore, Md., and also William Braken, former schoolmaster; all three are accused of passing counterfeit money, and it is thought they will join a counterfeiter named John Lyon (30 May)

Plantation on Iron Hill in Pencader Hundred, Newcastle Co., for sale; apply to Timothy Griffith at the plantation where Peter Sigfridus Allrichs lately lived, near Christine Bridge (30 May)

Property for sale at Duck Creek in Kent Co., Salisbury Town; apply to David Witherspoon in Newcastle Co. or George Griffin in Kent upon Delaware (30 May)

Accounts with estate of John Renshaw, late of York, York Co., attorney-at-law, dec'd, to be settled with James Smith, admin. (30 May)

Plantation in Northampton, Bucks Co., for sale; apply to Robert Heaton, living on the premises, John Carver of Biberry or John Plumley of Southampton (30 May)

Martin Reardon, sadler, in Chestnut St., offers reward for the apprehension of an Egyptian woman called Mary, who robbed the house of Mary Clayton, widow, in Chichester, Chester Co. (30 May)

James Humphreys in Second St. has for sale a large assortment of mourning, since he intends to follow the business of undertaker (30 May)

Thomas Green, dyer and printer from England, has set up his business in Sassafras St. in the house where Michael Brown, dec'd, lately lived (30 May)

Halifax item of 13 May reports that some of Capt. Joseph Gorham's Rangers were attacked at Minas and that Lt. Arbuthnott was wounded (6 June)

Boston item of 27 May reports arrival of Capt. Folger from London and of Capt. Proctor from Halifax; also that Newton and Jones have confessed their guilt and admitted that their real names are W. Sutton and G. Wilson (6 June)

New York item of 3 June reports arrival there on Thu. last of the schooner *Trial*, Capt. Duthy, with William Bull, Jr., from South Carolina as passenger (6 June)

W. Sutton and G. Wilson will be sent from Boston to Maryland to be tried for murder (6 June)

Act. of Pa. Assembly mentions Lt.-Gov. James Hamilton and Thomas and Richard Penn (6 June)

Notice from John Lawrence, clerk of Court of Quarter Sessions, warning Public housekeepers of Phila. to renew licenses (6 June)

Mare strayed from William Crabb of Marcus Hook (6 June)

Merchandize for sale at house of Charles Dawson in Water St. (6 June)

Adv. of Peter Partridge, from Bristol, England, now at Joseph Saul's, near the Rising Sun in Market St. (6 June)

Accounts with estate of George Jones, late innholder at the Black Horse in Phila., dec'd, to be settled with Jonathan Robeson, Capt. Lawrence Anderson and Jacob Duche, execs. (6 June)

Edward Kite, Englishman, age c. 30, cooper, runaway from his bail, Samuel Jaques and James Marshall, of Elizabeth Town, Essex Co., N.J. (6 June)

Richard Fitzpatrick, Irish servant, age c. 19, runaway from Joseph Smith, of Londonderry Twp., Chester Co. (6 June)

Real estate, part of it adjoining the lot of Samuel Powell, for sale by James Mackey, Jr.; apply to James Mackey, Sr., in Church Alley, next door to Hugh Roberts's new house (6 June)

Plantation in the Jerseys for sale; apply to Samuel Boggs, who lives on the premises, back from Cooper's Ferry, near Haddonfield (6 June)

William Harrison, convict Irish servant, age c. 28, runaway from David Logan, of Frederick Co., Va. (6 June)

John Graham, Irish servant, age c. 25, and William Seers, apprentice, country born, age c. 20, both weavers, runaways from Boaz Boyce, of St. George's Hundred, Newcastle Co. (6 June)

Elliott Benger, sole Deputy-Post-Master-General in America, has died in Va. (13 June)

Capt. James Dobbins arrived at Annapolis from London in the Thames Frigate with 120 convicts (13 June)

According to New York item of 10 June on Thu. last Catherine Pemberton (wife of Rev. Ebenezer Pemberton of New York) died and was interred Sat. in the Presbyterian Church (13 June)

Mare stolen from pasture near Phila.; reward if mare is brought to Thomas Jervis at the Sign of the Indian Queen in Market St. (13 June)

Real estate in Quarry St., Phila., belonging to estate of Philip Fehl, to be sold by Catherine Fehl, admin. (13 June)

William Melchoir, in Treadiffrin, Chester Co., will sell a plantation in Upper Dublin and North-Wales, Phila. Co.; apply to Melchoir or to Daniel Morrice and Benjamin Davis, living near the premises; he will also sell plantation in Trediffrin on which he now lives, plantation formerly in possession of Abel Walker (13 June)

John Crow, now in goal in Phila., claims to have a mare belonging to John Scogan, of Salem Co., N.J. (13 June)

William Coxe, at his house in Front St., where Charles Norris lately lived, has Negroes for sale (13 June)

Following Negroes runaways from William James, founder, at Grubb's iron-works in Lancaster Co.: Cuff (former slave of Isaac Roberts, bricklayer); James (once slave of C. Humphis); Dick (13 June)

Property in Third St., late belonging to the widow Parker, dec'd, now in the tenure of Stephen Potts, for sale; enquire of Abraham Parker in Kennet Twp., Chester Co., or George Plumley in Third St. (13 June)

James Lewis, Welshman, age c. 24, farmer, has taken away a horse belonging to Thomas Green, living on the Germantown Rd. (13 June)

House in Second St., opposite Stephen Armitt's dwelling, to be let or sold; enquire of Joseph Marshall, next door (13 June)

Thomas Smith, Sheriff of Cape May Co., has in custody Jupiter Hazard, a runaway Negro, age c. 27, well-travelled, who says his master's name is John Bannister, who lives at Piscataway, R.I. (13 June)

Malt house, brew-house and dwelling, now in tenure of Maurice and Edmund Nihell, to be sold at John Biddle's, the Sign of the Indian King; enquire of Samuel Carpenter at Emanuel Josiah's, near Powell's wharf (13 June)

Mare and horse strayed or stolen from James Carruthers; reward if they are returned to owner or to Thomas Craig in the forks of Delaware (13 June)

Adv. of Robert Meade, next door to Anthony Morris, Jr., in Water St. (13 June)

Lot in Third St., being the back end lot late of Henry Cliffton, dec'd, to be sold by John Cliffton, living near the Swedes Church (13 June)

Land in Woodbury Creek, Gloucester Co., for sale; apply to James or David Cooper, living on the land, or to Timothy Matlack in Phila. (13 June)

William M'Carter in Front St. has imported stays for sale (13 June)

House in Second St., next door to the Sign of Amsterdam, for sale; apply to John Marl on the premises (13 June)

House in Water St., Trenton, near the mills, for sale by John Allen (13 June)

Thomas Lane, alias Lyons, servant, age c. 30, shoemaker, runaway from Daniel Goldsmith, living in Charlestown, Chester Co., near William Moore, Esq. (13 June)

Land on Franckford Rd. in the Northern Liberties, adjoining land of John Moland, for sale; enquire of John Philip Told, next door to William Branson's in Second St. (13 June)

John Dixey, master of a Marblehead fishing schooner, tells of his encounter with a French man-of-war (20 June)

Col. Lawrence, commander of the English troops at Chignecto, has received a reinforcement (20 June)

New York item of 17 June mentions Capt. Manly, whose sloop has been wrecked, and Capts. Burger, Ingham, Witter and Tucker (20 June)

Hercules Roney, of Horsham, weaver, and Benjamin Gilbert, blacksmith, have been committed to goal in Phila. for counterfeiting (20 June)

Brewhouse in Sixth St., near the State House, for sale; apply to Edmund Nihell, living on the premises (20 June)

Land for sale by Richard Crosby at house of John Crosby in Ridley Twp., Chester Co. (20 June)

Robert Warren intends to leave the province (20 June)

Information is sought in England as to whether John Jones, a stone mason, native of Ross in Herefordshire, supposed to be dead, has left any children (20 June)

Miles Strickland has moved from Market St. to Fourth St., between Dr. Shippen's and the wheelwright's, opposite Timothy Matlack's brewhouse (20 June)

John Leacock, goldsmith, is removed from Second St. to the Sign of the Cup in Water St. (20 June)

Information is sought in England as to whether Mary Collison or any of her family are still alive; she is eldest daughter of Capt. Robert Collison of Dunbarton's Regiment by his wife Margaret Dugud, daughter to Dugud of Achinhoove in Scotland; she left England about 50 years ago with her husband, who was supposed to have been a sheriff in Pa. in or about 1715 (20 June)

Standish Forde has three Negroes for sale at the Sign of the George, at the corner of Second and Arch Sts. (20 June)

Francis Johnson, baker, has moved to the upper end of Front St, near Morris Morris's brewhouse (20 June)

Mare strayed from Abraham Meyer, living between Lancaster and Christian Stoneman's mill (20 June)

Mare strayed or stolen from Henry Gilbert of the Northern Liberties (20 June)

Drawing of the Trenton Lottery will be at the house of Nathaniel Parker in Bucks Co., under management of Robert Pearson, David Dunbar, Robert Lettice Hooper, John Allen, Elijah Bond, Daniel Byles, John Dagworthy, Jr., and William Pidgeon; tickets are sold by them and by David Martin, Andrew Read, William Coxe, William Franklin and David Hall in Phila.; by John Garrison in Amwell; by Peter Kimble and Francis Costigin in Brunswick; by Daniel Coxe in Hopewell; by John Berrian in Rocky-Hill; by Lewis Ashfield and Elisha Lawrence in Monmouth; by Joseph Borden, Jr., in Bordentown; by John Stevens in Amboy; by James Parker in New York (20 June)

Reward offered by Israel Jacobs for recovery of mare strayed from plantation of John Jacobs of New Providence, Phila. Co. (20 June)

Charles and Alexander Stedman, attornies of Dr. Patrick Baird, will sell real estate in Fourth St., lying northward of land of Samuel Preston Moore and Richard Hill (20 June)

If Thomas Pickford of Congleton in Cheshire be living, he may hear of a considerable estate left him; he is said to have worked some years in Phila. as a bricklayer or labourer (20 June)

William Russell, servant, a West Country man, runaway from Sutton Burgan, of Kent Co., Md. (20 June)

The following servants are runaways from the ship *Anna*, Nathaniel Chew master: William Downes, weaver, age c. 33; Edward Jones, shoemaker; John Starr, a German; John Johnston, a Weat Country man, a gardiner, age c. 25 (20 June)

Books and calf- and sheep-skins for book-binding, imported in the *Wandsworth*, Capt. Smith, are for sale by David Hall (20 June)

Annapolis item of 12 June reports that Jacob Windsor on Wed. last was executed in Queen Anne's Co. (20 June)

Annapolis item of 12 June reports that Thomas Poney, found guilty
of felony, is sentenced to be burnt in the hand; Onesiphorus
Lucas, convicted of burglary, is to be hanged (27 June)

Boston item mentions Lord Colvill, who has sailed for Halifax,
and Col. Lawrence, commander in Chignecto (27 June)

John Bartram, botanist of Pa., has written a preface and notes
to the third edition of Medicina Britannica, to be published
by B. Franklin and D. Hall (27 June)

Irish servants in the ship Sally are to be sold by John Erwin
in Strawberry Alley (27 June)

Levy and Franks have removed from their store in Front St. and
Water St. to the house of Isaac Norris, where the governor
lately lived, in Second St. (27 June)

Ground in Sassafras St., opposite house of Nicholas Castle, to
be sold or let; enquire of Thomas Campbell in Phila. (27 June)

Mare came to the house of William Barclay in Little Britain Twp.,
Lancaster Co. (27 June)

Horse belonging to William Peters strayed or stolen out of a
stable in Mr. Taylor's Alley (27 June)

John Wallace has a Negro man and woman for sale (27 June)

Real estate late belonging to John Gebhard, taken at the suit
of Daniel Stonemetz, is to be sold by Isaac Griffitts, sheriff,
at the house of Jeremiah Smith in Front St. (27 June)

Negro and a horse for sale by Joseph Sims, below the drawbridge
(27 June)

Edmund M'Donald, Irish servant, age c. 35, runaway from Thomas
Evans, of New Britain Twp., Bucks Co. (27 June)

For freight or passage to Jamaica in the snow Batchelor, George
Noarth master, agree with said Noarth in Front St. or on the
snow at Child's wharf (27 June)

A gelding belonging to Joshua Crosby has strayed from a pasture near Phila. (27 June)

Property to be sold by the administratrix of Thomas Lacy, dec'd,
and Benjamin Britton at the house of Joseph Colbourn (27 June)

Mare stolen from Jacob Eicholtz, living in the Borough of Lancaster (27 June)

John Boyce, servant, age c. 25, runaway from Onion's iron-works
in Baltimore Co. Md.; reward will be paid by Stephen Onion or
by Israel Pemberton, Jr., in Phila. (27 June)

Joe, a Negro, age c. 28, runaway from Valentine Bryant of West
Jersey (27 June)

Horse is in custody of Edward Barwick in the Borough of Lancaster (27 June)

Francis Fagen, Irish servant, mason, his wife Mary and John
Pankes, a Low-Dutchman, runaways from George Hooke of York-
town (27 June)

Capt. Philips arrived 23 June at Boston from London (4 July)

On 1 July contributors to the Pa. Hospital chose as managers
Joshua Crosby, Benjamin Franklin, Thomas Bond, Samuel Hazard,
Richard Peters, Israel Pemberton, Jr., Samuel Rhodes, Hugh Roberts, Joseph Morris, John Smith, Evan Morgan and Charles Norris; John Reynell was chosen treasurer (4 July)

House in Market St. to be let; enquire of B. Franklin (4 July)

Land in Front St., adjoining land of Edward Warner, being part of the estate of Isaac Griffitts, taken at the suit of Nathaniel Marston, will be sold by George Heap, coroner, at the house of William Nicholson in Arch St. (4 July)

James Holland, white-smith, in Front St., near Black-horse Alley, has time of a servant, a white-smith, for sale (4 July)

Persons with accounts to be settled with Susanna Rutter are desired to bring them to Caspar Ulrick's (4 July)

Edward Dowers, at the upper end of Race St., has anchovies for sale (4 July)

George M'Cartney, English servant, age c. 19, runaway from Daniel Bates of Gloucester Co. (4 July)

John Websley, a criminal, and George Adams, a servant, age c. 19, broke out of Somerset Goal; reward offered by Sheriff Francis Hollinshead (4 July)

Samuel Farmar was lately discharged from confinement for debt; his plantation in White-marsh, Phila. Co., is to be let; all accounts with him are to be settled with William Barge and Peter Robeson (4 July)

The boat that formerly belonged to Thomas January on Tuesdays will leave from Carpenter's wharf in Phila. for Newcastle; for freight or passage agree with John Funston (4 July)

Jeremiah Chichester, Iriah servant, age c. 21, imported in the ship *Sally*, Capt. Dunbar, runaway from Arnold Francis in the Northern Liberties (4 July)

Gelding stolen from the stable of Joseph Moore in Hopewell (4 July)

Hugh Matthews, *alias* M'Mahon, Irishman, age between 40 and 50, has escaped from Chester Goal; reward offered by William Hay, sub-sheriff (4 July)

Capt. John Sibbald has Madeira wine and citron for sale at his house in Second St. (4 July)

Joseph Greenway has Negroes for sale (4 July)

Horse came to the plantation of Nicholas Kasel in Warwick Twp., Lancaster Co. (4 July)

Any gentleman wanting a schoolmaster qualified to teach Latin and Greek may apply to David Hall at the Post-Office (4 July)

Horse stolen from Benjamin Miller of Conestogoe Manor, 6 miles from Lancaster (4 July)

Accounts with estate of Zeanus Savage, late of Rocksborough Twp., to be settled with Deliverance Savage and Anthony Newhouse, execs. (4 July)

The sloop *Hunter Galley*, Clement Conyers commander, now at Bard's wharf, will sail for Barbados directly (4 July)

Edward Stiles has cotton, sugar, salt, etc. for sale on board the sloop *Benjamin* at Market St. wharf (4 July)

Mare strayed from William Hamilton of Cheltenham Twp., Phila. Co.; reward will be paid by said Hamilton or by George Hughes of Buckingham Twp., Bucks Co. (4 July)

William Peters has a brew-house, malt-house, and mill for sale; persons having empty barrels from Pierce and Fisher are desired to contact Jane Grevell at her house in Second St., at the Sign of St. Andrew (4 July)

Onesiphorus Lucas was executed at Annapolis on 26 June (11 July)

On 25 June two thieves attempted to rob the house of Charles Cole, merchant in Annapolis; they were frightened by John, Cole's servant (11 July)

On 13 June at Halifax a new brig, the *Osborne-Galley*, owned by Col. Gorham and commanded by Capt. Samuel Appleton, was launched (11 July)

On June 11 Benjamin Ledite was tried at York for the murder of an India woman at Wiscasset (11 July)

On Sun. last the house of Thomas Harper in Frankford was robbed (11 July)

The snow *Ann*, lying at Hasell's wharf, will be sold at James's coffee-house; accounts with estate of Samuel Hasell, dec'd, to be settled with Ann Hasell, exec. (11 July)

Two Negroes and sugar for sale by Stanford Verhulst at Mrs. Mary Roberts's in Front St. (11 July)

Charles Stow in Market St. has the time of Dutch servant girls for sale (11 July)

Cow has strayed from Stephen Armitt (11 July)

Daniel Macartie, Irish apprentice, age c. 17, runaway from Jacob Hagie of Germantown Twp. (11 July)

Land for sale in Wicacoa; apply to William Donaldson at Wicacoa or Joseph Donaldson, hatter, in Market St. (11 July)

Mare, strayed or stolen from Stephen Carpenter at Point-No-Point (11 July)

An exact model of Christ Church steeple in Bristol, Great Britain, and a mechanical woman can be seen at the house of John Baker in Kensington (11 July)

James Lenox, about to move to West Jersey, has a plantation in York Co. for sale; enquire of Samuel Underwood (11 July)

Daniel Swan, coach-maker, has moved from Chestnut St. to Market St. (11 July)

Williamsburgh, Va., item of 8 July mentions Capts. Camney and Wallace (18 July)

H.M.S. *Success*, Lord Colvill commander, has arrived at Boston (18 July)

On 22 June two men were executed at Albany for the murder of Johannes Smith, who lived about 8 miles above Albany (18 July)

New York item of 15 July mentions William Bull of S.C. and Capts. Richards, Crosby and Machet (18 July)

Phila. item mentions Capt. Mesnard (18 July)

The four following runaways from William Bird and James Keemer of Amity Twp., Phila. Co.: William Burchell, Englishman, age c. 30; George Brooks, Englishman, age c. 25; Patrick Wall, Irishman; Joseph Moore, Irishman (18 July)

For freight or passage to London in the ship *White-Oak*, apply to Charles Lyon commander or to Jeremiah Warder (18 July)

William Standley is giving up his business of shop-keeping and is moving to a house in Market St. (18 July)

Joseph Beddome, intending shortly for England, will sell real estate and possessions at his house in Arch St. (18 July)

John Rawlinson, at his store in Water St., opposite to John Hopkins's, has for sale sugar and cotton imported in the Henry, Richard Smith commander (18 July)

James Wallace has removed from his store opposite the Queen's Head to a new store, also in Water St., next door to Capt. George Spafford's and opposite to John Aris's, at the Sloop (18 July)

Isaac Shoemaker in Germantown has a house for sale (18 July)

Negro for sale; enquire of Thomas Smith (18 July)

A gelding was taken from the pasture of John Vancleave, of Maidenhead in the Jerseys (18 July)

Henry M'Cormick, Irish servant, formerly servant of John Parry, Esq., dec'd, runaway from Richard Evans, of Tredyffrin Twp., Chester Co. (18 July)

Joseph Steell, servant, age c. 28, and a Negro boy named Caesar, runaways from William Oakford, of Alloway's Creek, Salem Co. (18 July)

Peter Spycker will give attendance at the sale of property at the market-place in the Borough of Lancaster (18 July)

Mare strayed or stolen from Harmon Gregg, of Christiana Hundred, Newcastle Co. (18 July)

Annapolis item of 17 July discusses crime wave, with mention of the attempt made at Mr. Cole's and murders committed by Jones and Newton (25 July)

Nathaniel Fales of Norwich, Conn., after passing a great number of counterfeit dollars, has gone to Halifax (25 July)

Boston item of 15 July mentions Capts. M'Carthy and Snow (25 July)

House of the Widow Ten Eyck in Broad St. in New York was broken into and robbed (25 July)

Capt. Edwards of Phila. has arrived there from Newry and Capt. Leiths from Waterford (25 July)

Lightning struck the house of John Guy, carter, near Society Hill in Phila. (25 July)

A man from Virginia, going by the name of Thomas Riggaby, is in goal in Phila. for attempting to break into the house of one Robert Dixon (25 July)

Clerks of the fire companies are to meet at the Widow Pratt's in Market St. (25 July)

Two Negro men for sale; enquire of John Biddle or Thomas Bartholomew in Phila. (25 July)

Land in York-town, York Co., for sale; apply to John Spencely, living in said town (25 July)

Michael Brannen, Irish servant, age c. 20, runaway from Daniel Britt of Newcastle Co. (25 July)

Richard Bevan, living near the Gulph mill in Upper Merion, intends to let his plantation; he has two Negroes for sale (25 July)

Patrick Connolin, Irish servant, age c. 17, runaway from George Bratten of Brandywine Hundred, Newcastle Co. (25 July)

Gelding strayed or stolen from plantation in Trenton; reward offered by John Allen and William Pidgeon (25 July)

1751

Land, late the property of Thomas Rush, taken at the suit of John Holme, exec. of James Holme, dec'd, is to be sold at the house of Thomas Harper in Frankfort (25 July)

Land, late the property of David Davis, dec'd, is to be sold at the house of Daniel Pistoras in Germantown (25 July)

Mare strayed or stolen from the plantation of David George, of Blockley, Phila. Co. (25 July)

Parker and Garrett intend to terminate their partnership (25 July)

Adv. of Samuel and Thomas Smith, on Market St. wharf (25 July)

Two servants are runaways from Isaac Whitelock of Lancaster (25 July)

Walter M'Cool, Ranger of Bucks Co., has in his custody several horses and meres (25 July)

Adv. for freight or passage each week between Phila. and New York by stage-boat, kept by Patrick Cowan, living in Burlington; mention of Fretwell Wright at the Blue Anchor in Burlington, John Predmore at Cramberry, James Wilson at Amboy and Matthias Iselstine and Obadiah Ayrs, innkeeper at Amboy Ferry (25 July)

Adv. of James Thornton in Bristol, Bucks Co. (25 July)

Lot between the ground of John Shoemaker and John Johnson and another lot in Division St., between the lots of Peter and John Shoemaker, late the property of Isaac Shoemaker, will be sold at the house of Daniel Pistorus in Germantown (25 July)

Effects of Owen Owens, blacksmith, dec'd, will be sold in Whiteland Twp., Chester Co., at the house of Richard Thomas (25 July)

Martha, wife of William Sweating of Phila., has eloped from her husband (25 July)

For freight or passage to Corocoa in the sloop Little Benjamin, Edward Stiles commander, apply to said Stiles at Market St. wharf (25 July)

Land on Petty's Island near Kensington, adjoining land of Daniel Cooper and Robert Moore, to be let or sold by Benjamin Loxley in Kensington (25 July)

Joseph Harvey of Ridley, Chester Co., has land with several mills for sale (25 July)

Accounts with estate of Thomas Sharp, late of Phila., merchant, dec'd, to be settled with William Whitebread, exec. to John Thomas, dec'd, who was exec. to the said Sharp (25 July)

John Dougherty, servant, runaway from Henry Lawrence of Marple Twp., Chester Co. (25 July)

Robert Wisenden, servant, age c. 28, ship-carpenter, born in Deptford, England (who was imported Dec. last in the Rachel, Capt. Armstrong), and William Hose, servant, age c. 45, whose business was to drag ballast in the Thames and has been about three years in Virginia, runaways from Fairfax Co., Va.; reward for Wisenden will be paid by Thomas Fleming and Anthony Ramsay, for Hose by Sampson Darrell, near Belhaven; these men ran away in company with three other servants, Selkirk, Parker and Macnamara (25 July)

Joseph Shippen has a Negro for sale (1 Aug.)

1751

Capt. Sohier, late master of a brigantine which was wrecked and then burnt by Indians at Chignecto, has returned to Boston (1 Aug.)

Boston item of 22 July mentions Capt. Snow (1 Aug.)

Jonathan Woodman of Narraganset has been committed to goal in New York for uttering counterfeit bills (1 Aug.)

Edward Duffield in Arch St. sells capers and lemons (1 Aug.)

Thomas Clifford in Water St., near the ferry-house, has for sale Rhode Island cheese and rum (1 Aug.)

John Clifton at the Two Lamps in Second St. sells drugs and medicines (1 Aug.)

Public answer to John Ludgate by Peter Delage and John Harrison, making mention of Hugh Roberts, Evan Morgan and Townsend White, auditors, and Samuel Parr (1 Aug.)

Samuel Neave and Attwood Shute, admins. of the estate of Charles Connor, late of Aston, Chester Co., will give attendance at Aubrey Bevan's in Chester (1 Aug.)

David Hall has for sale time of English servant girl (1 Aug.)

James Mosson, Irish servant, age c. 23, skinner, runaway from Amos Strickland in Newtown, Bucks Co. (1 Aug.)

Edmund Megound, Irish servant, age c. 40, hammerman, runaway from Samuel Barnes of Cohanzy, Cumberland Co. (1 Aug.)

Time of servants of various trades, just imported from Waterford in the snow *Three Friends*, John Leiths commander, to be sold; apply to Abraham Shelley or said commander or to Abel James, merchant, in Phila. (1 Aug.)

Horse strayed or stolen from the plantation of Edward Collins, between Leech's and Martin's Mill; reward will be paid by Francis Hamilton (1 Aug.)

James Carway, Irish servant, age c. 27, who served his time in Merion, Phila. Co., with Daniel Davis, now runaway from Richard Flower of Marcus Hook, Chester Co. (1 Aug.)

The lease of the ferry at Schuylkill, now in the tenure of James Coultas, will soon expire; for the lease apply to Mayor William Plumsted of Phila. (1 Aug.)

Jacob Hagie, paper-maker in Germantown Twp., has time of an Irish servant for sale (1 Aug.)

Persons with demands on Lawrence Hebert, engraver, are to settle with Peter David in Second St. (1 Aug.)

Horse has been taken up at plantation of Abel Parke in East Caln, Chester Co. (1 Aug.)

George Wescott, brazier, in Third St., has a Mulatto woman for sale (1 Aug.)

John Malone, Irish servant, age c. 16, runaway from Nehemiah Baker of Edgmont Twp., Chester Co. (1 Aug.)

Negro named Lot, age c. 24, runaway from Elijah Bond, living near Trenton (1 Aug.)

Real estate in Burlington, late property of James Verree, dec'd, for sale; enquire of Rachel or James Verree, execs., or Moses Thomas in Phila. (1 Aug.)

Michael Foely, Irish servant, age c. 21, in goal in Perth Amboy, claims to have served time with Daniel Britt at St. George's; apply to Sheriff William Deare to have him or prove him free(1 Ag

Annapolis item of 31 July reports the finding in Frederick Co. of a horse stolen from Mr. Raitt (8 Aug.)

Boston item of 29 July mentions Capt. James Gilbert of Phila. and also Capts. Dogget and Arthur Perry (8 Aug.)

Some 40 Irishmen on George's Island deserted to the enemy; one of their leaders, a certain Ryan, has been captured and is now in irons (8 Aug.)

On 18 June at Halifax Lt. Pateshall had three malefactors executed; Rev. Dr. Tutte had prayed with them (8 Aug.)

James Bill, *alias* Bradford, a Narraganset man, was apprehended in N.J. as concerned with Jonathan Woodman in counterfeiting bills of credit in New York (8 Aug.)

Capt. Fowle at New York reported that the following captains have been taken by the Spaniards: Ja. Dickinson, R. Dickinson, Chase, Shortes, Tucker and Appleton (8 Aug.)

Phila. item mentions Capts. Mitchell, Macilvaine and Lee (8 Aug.)

William Jones, Welch servant, a plaisterer, who came in last year from Liverpool, runaway from Samuel Vallacot (8 Aug.)

Thomas Archdall in Front St. (next door to Mr. Richardson, silversmith) sells sugar, coffee, tea, chocolate, etc. (8 Aug.)

House and lot on Society Hill, late the property of Thomas Griffith, taken in execution at suit of Joseph Sims and others, will be sold at James's coffee-house (8 Aug.)

John Rockhill, living at Dr. Cadwalader's in Phila., has real estate for sale in Morris Co., West Jersey; apply to owner or to Maurice Robeson at Oxford Furnace or Joseph Clayton at Trenton (8 Aug.)

Conyngham and Gardner have for sale servants imported from Ireland in the ship *Cumberland*, Capt. Macilvaine (8 Aug.)

Richard Richison, Chief Ranger of Chester Co., list strays in his custody (8 Aug.)

House where Nathan Levy lately lived is to be let; enquire of Joseph Sims (8 Aug.)

Morris Gwin has for sale a merchant-mill in Lower Dublin Twp. (8 Aug.)

Charles Stow, Jr., admin. of estate of Sarah Mitchell, dec'd, will settle all accounts and will sell land extending from Market St. westward with George Emlen's property (8 Aug.)

Reward will be paid by Anthony Morris, Jr., or Samuel Rhoads in Phila. for recovery of a horse, stolen or strayed (8 Aug.)

Anne, wife of Fortunatus Woods, has eloped from her husband (8 Aug.)

John Griffin, Irish servant, born in Dublin, blockmaker, lately come in the snow *Batchelor*, George Noarth master, from Bristol, runaway from James Child (8 Aug.)

Peter Clearwater, this country born, age c. 34, runaway from Ephraim Oliphant of Amwell, Hunterdon Co. (8 Aug.)

Horse has been stolen (for the second time) from Theophilus Hartman, glazier, of Lampeter Twp., Lancaster Co. (8 Aug.)

Withers Conway, of Stafford Co., Va., has been robbed; he suspects John Churchill, schoolmaster, who lived in his house (8 Aug.)

Charles Conner, Irish servant, age c. 20, runaway again from John Henderson of Welch Tract, Newcastle Co. (8 Aug.)

Item from Nova Scotia reports the splitting of a cannon on board ship of Capt. Cobb (15 Aug.)

New York item of 12 Aug. mentions Capts. Holly, Langdon, M'Cleve, Dickinson, Briggs and Everson (15 Aug.)

John Palmer, living in Chestnut St., and Thomas Penrose, living in Wicacoa, execs. of the estate of Margaret Smith, late of Wicacoa, dec'd, will sell land at the house of Anthony Whiteley, at the Sign of the Ship Wilmington and George on Society Hill (15 Aug.)

Roger Connor, of Lancaster, has property in York-town for sale (15 Aug.)

James Carr, Irish servant, runaway from John Robinson of New Providence (15 Aug.)

Annuity upon lot on west side of Fourth St. in Phila., the estate of Jonathan Price, taken at suit of William Coleman and James Pemberton, execs. to the estate of Samuel Powell, Jr., dec'd, to be sold at the house of William Gray in Market St. (15 Aug.)

Lot in Vine St., adjoining land of Jonathan Zane, and lots in Kensington, all late property of George Ryall, taken at suit of William Coleman and James Pemberton, execs. to estate of Samuel Powell, Jr., dec'd, to be sold at house of Jeremiah Smith in Front St. (15 Aug.)

Land in Whitemarsh, late the property of Nicholas Knight, taken at suit of Thomas Bartholomew, to be sold at house of Richard Waln in Whitemarsh (15 Aug.)

Samuel M'Call, Sr., has lost a spying-glass between Phila. and Germantown (15 Aug.)

Persons indebted to James Burd are to make speedy payment to James Louttit (at his store on Hamilton's wharf), attorney to said Burd (15 Aug.)

William Gray, baker, has assorted properties for sale; one house is in the occupation of Josiah Davenport, baker; another is in the occupation of Patrick Farrel, cooper; ground-rent is payable to Anthony Morris (15 Aug.)

Mare has been stolen out of a pasture belonging to Mrs. Stevens at the Harp and Crown in Third St. (15 Aug.)

Rachel, wife of Gordon Howard, of Donnegall Twp., Lancaster Co., has eloped from her husband (15 Aug.)

House in South St. to be sold at the house of Amos Jones in South St., at the Sign of the Brigantine (15 Aug.)

Robert Dunwiddie is appointed Gov. of Va. (22 Aug.)

W. Sutton and G. Wilson have escaped from goal in St. Mary's Co., Md. (22 Aug.)

John Connor, convict servant at Elk Ridge, has confessed that he and Thomas Bevan were the ones who tried to rob Mr. Cole on 2 July (22 Aug.)

Capt. Nathaniel Skelden of Jamaica, while moving his goods from his store in Montego Bay to one at Dry Harbour, had them stolen by a mutinous crew (22 Aug.)

Capt. Mauger, of Halifax, and Mr. Prescott, of Boston, are erecting a distillery at Halifax (22 Aug.)

Ten men, women and children, captured by the Indians and sold into slavery to the French, have arrived in Boston by virtue of the application made by Capt. Stevens (22 Aug.)

Kingston, Jamaica, item of 13 July mentions Capt. James Pollock (22 Aug.)

Halifax item of 29 July mentions Col. Warburton and Capt. Huston (22 Aug.)

New York item of 19 Aug. mentions Capts. Gifford, Machet, Ryan, Petty, Troup, Garrison and Deane (22 Aug.)

Mon. last the ship <u>Anderson</u>, Capt. Campbell, from Holland, arrived at Phila. with Palatines (22 Aug.)

Third of the snow <u>Isabella</u>, late the property of Alexander Boyd, dec'd, now at James West's wharf, to be sold at the coffee-house; accounts with estate of said Boyd or of William Stocks, mariner, dec'd, to be settled with Theophilus Gardner, admin. (22 Aug.)

Land in Cheltenham Twp., late the property of Edward Collings, dec'd, taken at the suit of Mary Martin, exec. to estate of Richard Martin, dec'd, will be sold at the house of Thomas Harper in Frankford (22 Aug.)

At the house of Timothy Matlack in Market St. will be sold his shop and household goods, seized at the suit of Charles Willing and others (22 Aug.)

Household furniture to be sold at the house of Edward Dowers in Race St. (22 Aug.)

Shop and household goods of Alice Burn, dec'd, for sale; accounts with her estate to be settled with John Clifton (22 Aug.)

John Piercy, convict servant, who passes for a sailor, runaway from John Simkin at the house of Thomas Williams at Christine Bridge in Newcastle Co. (22 Aug.)

Effects of Philip Henning, late of York-town, shopkeeper, attached at the suit of Jost Mahr, are to be sold at the house of John Read in York-town, York Co.; the auditors are John Wright, George Stevenson and Daniel Kenly (22 Aug.)

Contributors to the Pennsylvania Hospital may apply to John Reynell, treasurer (22 Aug.)

Land in Chestnut St., now in the tenure of Isaac Williams, bounded by the house of Charles Meredith and that of James Tipper, for sale; enquire of Thomas Miller in Front St., opposite Key's alley, at the Sign of the City of Dublin (22 Aug.)

John Bell, secretary, gives notice of a meeting of the St. Andrew's Society (22 Aug.)

Property in Germantown for sale; apply to John Mock, living on said place (22 Aug.)

Time of a servant woman for sale; enquire at Mary Coffy's, opposite the Sign of the Boar's Head in Pewter Platter Alley (22 Aug.)

Michael Dardis, who came into this country 5½ years ago from Dublin and served his time with Capt. Flower and worked last at Branson's Iron-works, is sought by his wife Catherine, lately come over; word of him may be sent to Mr. Erwin's, merchant, in Strawberry Alley; Michael, a millwright, is supposed to have gone to York or Cumberland Co. with Arnold Pender, a German millwright (22 Aug.)

House to let in Market St., opposite distillery of John Harrison; apply to John Mill, joiner, opposite Stretch's corner (22 Aug.)

Boston item of 19 Aug. gives excerpt from journal of Capt. William Otten concerning discovery of an island, in search of which Capt. Rodney, Gov. of Newfoundland, has gone (29 Aug.)

House of Robert R. Livingston, merchant in New York, has been robbed (29 Aug.)

Capt. William Seamour from Coracoa brings news of an encounter between the Dutch and Spaniards (29 Aug.)

House of Joseph Price of Shrewsberry was struck by lightning (29 Aug.)

Capt. Flower reports that the brigantine Sea-Flower, John Bristow commander, from R.I., was cast away on Cape Florida but the captain and crew are safe in Charles-town (29 Aug.)

Isaac Griffitts, sheriff, seeks votes in conjunction with Judah Foulke at the coming election (29 Aug.)

Mr. Dove proposes to open a school at the Academy for young ladies (29 Aug.)

Plantation where Joseph Harlan formerly dwelt, in Kennet, Chester Co., near Benjamin Taylor's mill, is for sale (29 Aug.)

John Connor, age c. 30, has stolen money from Andrew Hays, of Alloway's Creek, Salem Co. (29 Aug.)

Nathan Levy offers reward for apprehension of the sportsmen who use the wall of the Jewish burying-ground for target practice (29 Aug.)

Medicines for sale by Peter Sonmans, at his house in Front St., near the Sign of the Platter (29 Aug.)

John Baynton has land for sale in West New Jersey; part of it adjoins the land of James Logan (29 Aug.)

Land for sale in Germantown; enquire of John Bartlet, sadler, living on the premises (29 Aug.)

John Lawless, Irish servant, age c. 35, runaway from John Bowen, of Whiteland, Chester Co. (29 Aug.)

Adv. of Mungo Campbell from Dublin, pewterer, at the corner of Second and Chestnut Sts. (29 Aug.)

Patrick White, Irish servant, age c. 23, runaway from John Clark of St. George's Hundred, Newcastle Co. (29 Aug.)

Land for sale in and near Borough of Bristol, Bucks Co.; enquire of Alexander Graydon in Bristol or William M'Ilvaine in Phila. (29 Aug.)

Boston item of 26 Aug. mentions Rev. Dr. Sewall, Major Luttrel, commander of the British troops at Chignecto, and Capt. Cosby of H.M.S. Centaur (5 Sept.)

Capt. Walker, who arrived at New York from the Bay of Honduras, tells of the capture by the Spaniards of the following: Capt. Battagen of Jamaica; Capt. Serjeant of R.I.; Capt. Groves of Boston; Capt. Broadhurst of New York. Capts. Broadhurst and Saltus of New York and Capt. Bailey of Bermuda have been released (5 Sept.)

Letter from St. Thomas mentions Capts. Falkingham and Carpenter (5 Sept.)

Letters mentions Perkins, Newton and Jones, criminals in Va. (5 Sept.)

John Cisti, the Annapolis post-rider, can be spoke with at specified times and places, one being the house of Mr. Claxon, at the Sign of the Three Tuns in Chestnut St. (5 Sept.)

Thomas James, Jr., a candidate for the coroner's office, desires votes in conjunction with William Gray (5 Sept.)

Horse strayed or stolen from Mark Morris, of East-town Twp., Chester Co. (5 Sept.)

James Maloney, Irish servant, age c. 20, runaway from John Gourley of Wright's Town, Bucks Co.; reward if news of his capture is given to William Gray at the Conestogoe Wagon (5 Sept.)

Two stray mares have been taken up by Joseph Scull at Ashton's Ferry on Schuylkill (5 Sept.)

Robert Stephens in Newtown, Gloucester Co., has taken up a raft that was adrift (5 Sept.)

Catherine Diemer of Germantown, at the house of Isaac Will, can relieve persons afflicted with scald heads (5 Sept.)

Henry Redman, age c. 24, runaway from James Campbell of Plimouth Twp., Phila. Co.; Redman has been in Coracoa and Cape Breton (5 Sept.)

Three silver spoons were found in an out-house belonging to Thomas Parke, living at Dover, Kent Co. (5 Sept.)

Neal M'Fall, Irish servant, age c. 45, runaway from William M'Concky of Freehold Twp., Monmouth Co., East Jersey (5 Sept.)

Mare belonging to Nicholas Walber has strayed from William Clemm's stable; reward if mare is returned to Clemm in Phila. or to Titer Bauman in Cushahoppen (5 Sept.)

John Henry Sickman, Low Dutch servant, runaway from John Potts of Colebrook Dale; reward if runaway is returned to said Potts or to Thomas York in Phila. (5 Sept.)

For freight or passage to Charles-Town, S.C., in the ship Hallifax, Thomas Coatam commander, agree with Charles and Alexander Stedman or Samuel M'Call, Jr. (5 Sept.)

For freight or passage to Eustatia and Tortola in the sloop Cartmale, John Rawlison master, apply to said master on the sloop or at Augustine Stilman's in Market St. (5 Sept.)

Horse has been taken up at plantation of Andrew Cox in East Caln, Chester Co. (5 Sept.)

Accounts with estate of Anthony Nicholas, dec'd, John Nicholas and Attwood Shute (at his house in Walnut St.), execs. Household goods of Anthony Nicholas to be sold at his house in Church Alley; tools to be sold at the smith's shop, late of said Anthony, in Market St. (5 Sept.)

Edward Swinny, Irish servant, weaver, runaway from John Thomas, of Cheltenham Twp., Phila. Co. (5 Sept.)

Accounts with estate of Miles Strickland, late of Phila., shopkeeper, to be settled with John Strickland in Bucks Co., exec., or to be brought to the widow Hillbourn in Market St. (5 Sept.)

John Ginnens, apprentice tailor, age c. 19, country born, runaway from Bryan Murphy of the Borough of Lancaster; he is supposed to keep about John Holston's, sawyer, on Society Hill, who is an uncle of his (5 Sept.)

Susanna, wife of Andreas Kempler of Phila., has eloped from her husband (5 Sept.)

Mare strayed from Christian Good in Brackteneck Twp., Lancaster Co.; reward if returned to owner or to Michael Grose in Lancaster (5 Sept.)

Elizabeth Shewell has two pastures to be sold or let (5 Sept.)

Charles J. Dutens, jeweller from London, settled in New York, will be in Phila. and any customers may be informed where to meet with him at John Sayre's, late from New York (5 Sept.)

Jacob Cossar, who came two years ago from Holland and sold his daughter Margaret to a person who said he lived about 15 miles from Phila., seeks news of his daughter; word of her may be sent to Caspar Wistar (5 Sept.)

Boston item of 2 Sept. reports arrival there of Capt. Sanders (12 Sept.)

Jonathan Woodman, in goal in New York for uttering counterfeit bills, has hanged himself (12 Sept.)

Phila. items mention Capts. Steel, Stamper, Abercrombie, Coatam, Muir, Mason, Russel and Spurrier (12 Sept.)

George Spofford desires votes as candidate for office of sheriff (12 Sept.)

William Trotter, candidate for office of coroner, desires votes in conjunction with John Jervis (12 Sept.)

James Claypole, candidate for office of coroner, requests votes (12 Sept.)

The schooner *Ruth* (now lying at John Pole's wharf) to be sold at James's coffee-house ; apply to Pole and Howell (12 Sept.)

Empty hogsheads for cider are sold by John Harrison in Market St. (12 Sept.)

Wines are sold by Nathaniel Allen and John Cox at their store on the south side of Market St. wharf (12 Sept.)

Even Morgan in Water St., between Thomas Lawrence and William Allen, has wines, medicines and corks for sale; he also has for sale a house in Bowman's Lane in Germantown, belonging to the estate of Benjamin Morgan, dec'd (12 Sept.)

For freight or passage to Barbados in the ship *Molly*, apply to Robert Ragg, who is removed from his store at the corner of Chestnut St. wharf to a store in Water St., next door to Samuel Austin (12 Sept.)

A silver watch (maker's name W. Josephson, London) has been stolen from Benjamin Bagnall (12 Sept.)

Timothy Regan, Irish servant, age c. 20, runaway from William Marshall of Kennet Twp., Chester Co. (12 Sept.)

Patrick Wall, Irish servant, age c. 21, plaisterer, runaway from William Bird of Robeson Twp., Lancaster Co. (12 Sept.)

Thomas Ryan, Irish servant, runaway from Henry Bishop, living near White-Clay Creek, Newcastle Co. (12 Sept.)

Mills and plantation, late in Timothy Roberts's tenure are for sale; apply to Timothy Griffey, near Christine Bridge, or Jacob Van Bibber, near St. George's in Newcastle Co., or John Passmore, living near the premises (12 Sept.)

Thomas Connoly, Irish servant, age c. 24, runaway from Thomas Miller, near Charles-town in Cecil Co. (12 Sept.)

Jeremiah Sullivan, servant, age c. 22, runaway from John Logue, of Christine Hundred, Newcastle Co., supposedly with Timothy Regan (12 Sept.)

New York item of 16 Sept. mentions Capts. Pye and Hutchinson (19 Sept.)

Captains Abercrombie, Jeffrey, Muir, Coatam and Russel have arrived at Phila. with Palatines; Capts. Smith and Kerr have arrived there with servants from Ireland (19 Sept.)

George Hatton, born at Nansemond, Va., said to have been a soldier under Bacon, died the latter end of Aug., aged 103, at Amwell in the Jerseys (19 Sept.)

George Heap requests votes for office of sheriff (19 Sept.)

Dudley Hanley, Irish servant, age c. 20, runaway from James Moore of Millcreek Hundred, Newcastle Co. (19 Sept.)

Adv. of Bartholomew Rowley, schoolmaster in Burlington (19 Sept.)

Moses Dicky, of Newcastle Co., fraudulantly obtained a carry note of Mary David, the wife of Evan David of Tredyffrin in Chester Co., with Thomas Cross as security (19 Sept.)

The schooner *Betsey* at Arch St. wharf is for sale; apply to Robert Ragg (19 Sept.)

Adv. of Henry Harrison, storekeeper in Market St. (19 Sept.)

James Williams (*alias* Symes), age c. 40, who pretends to be a cooper and has been a soldier in Port Mahon, runaway from John Carsson, of Paxton, Lancaster Co.; reward will be paid by his master or by William Pyewell in Second St. (19 Sept.)

The brigantine *Sally* is for sale; her inventory may be seen at the house of Capt. James Hazelton (19 Sept.)

Accounts with the estate of John Stevens, dec'd, late of Phila., baker, to be settled with Josiah Davenport, admin. (19 Sept.)

Mare and colt, strayed or stolen from plantation of Robert Lloyd at North-wales; also a horse from John Heathcoat in Fourth St.; reward if animals are brought to Moses Peters in North-wales or John Heathcoat in Phila. (19 Sept.)

Joshua Bispham gives notice of sale of land on Oldman's Creek which belonged to Mahlon Stacy, dec'd; sale to be held at Joseph Wood's, at the Sign of the Seven Stars in Pilesgrove, Salem Co. (19 Sept.)

William Graves, dec'd, entered bail for Thomas Hanlin at the suit of Joseph Bennet of Chester-town, Md.; Hanlin, a West Country man, age c. 40, has run away, with his wife, age c. 50, and two daughters; it is likely that Patrick Carney and his wife and child are with them; reward offered by Sarah Graves, exec. (19 Sept.)

New York items of 23 Sept. mention Capts. Ramadge and Daniel Seymour (26 Sept.)

Phila. item mentions Capts. Arnot, Wier, Mason and Spurrier who have arrived from Holland with Palatines; also Capt. Breading from Lochswilly, Capt. Marshall from Londonderry and Capt. Matthews from Bristol, all with servants (26 Sept.)

At Phila. Charles Rothwell was tried and acquitted for the murder of his master, Benjamin Moore, an Indian trader (26 Sept.)

The snow *Warwick*, Capt. Manypenny, of Phila., is cast away on Attwood's Keys (26 Sept.)

George Okill has dry goods for sale at his house in Water St., next door to Samuel Shoemaker (26 Sept.)

Michael Slainey, Irish servant, professed collier and miller, runaway from John White, near Joppa, Baltimore Co., Md. (26 Sept.)

Mare strayed or stolen from James Miles, tavern-keeper, on Connestogoe Rd. in Radnor Twp., Chester Co.; reward if brought to John Ayres in Elbow Lane, Phila., or to said Miles (26 Sept.)

A person understanding the business of fuller may apply to Ephraim Seely of Cohanzy in Cumberland Co., West Jersey (26 Sept.)

House where Erasmus Stevens now lives, at the corner of Front and Pine Sts., to be let by Francis Richardson (26 Sept.)

John Moore (or Morn), Irish servant, age $\underline{c}$. 20, for some years in the rope-making business, runaway from John Inglis of Phila. (26 Sept.)

A baby was found in the alley fronting the dwelling of Edward Shippen, Esq. (26 Sept.)

Real estate on Passyunk Rd., bounded by land lately belonging to John Cox, dec'd, and by land of George Emlen, to be sold by James Burd; plan to be seen at Burd's house in Fifth St. (26 Sept.)

David Jones, Welch servant, runaway from Joshua Humphreys of Merion; Joseph Thompson, Irish servant, age $\underline{c}$. 22, runaway from David Lawrence of Haverford, Chester Co.; Walter Tudor, Welch servant, age $\underline{c}$. 30, runaway from William Lawrence of Haverford (26 Sept.)

Adv. of Samuel Palmer at his house opposite the Academy in Arch St. (26 Sept.)

Ellis Roberts, Welshman, a debtor, has escaped from Sheriff Joseph Hart at Newtown, Bucks Co. (26 Sept.)

Meadow in Moyamensing, near John Ashton's, for sale; enquire of said Ashton, who lives on the road leading to the lower parts of Joseph Turner's plantation (26 Sept.)

Plantation of Barefoot Brunson, dec'd, situated at Millstone River Bridge on the Brunswick Rd., and also land in Middlesex Co. for sale; enquire of Mary Brunson and Thomas Lawrence, execs. (26 Sept.)

A forge, saw-mill and real estate near the mouth of Valley Creek for sale; apply to Stephen Evans and Joseph Williams (26 Sept.)

Alexander Steel, Irish servant, age $\underline{c}$.19, formerly a drummer in the army, runaway from Hugh Kelly and Walter Thetford at Rariton in Millcreek Hundred, Newcastle Co. (26 Sept.)

Daniel Headon, Irish servant, age $\underline{c}$. 28, blacksmith, runaway from John Cox of Chester Twp., Burlington Co. (26 Sept.)

Gordon Howard of Donnegall Twp., Lancaster Co., has received back his wife Rachel into her former place of credit and esteem (26 Sept.)

Annapolis item of 18 Sept. states that Thomas Bevan pleaded guilty to attempting to rob the house of Mr. Cole (3 Oct.)

Annapolis item of 25 Sept. states that George Wilson (one of the murderers of Capt. Smith) has been sentenced to death; one of his accomplices is thought to have fled to Perkins and his gang (3 Oct.)

Letters from London brought in Capt. Troup's ship advise that Robert Hunter Morris, Chief Justice of N.J., is appointed Lt.-Gov. of New York (3 Oct.)

New York item mentions Capts. Amory, Bryant, Cornee and Machugh (3 Oct.)

Capt. Budden in the ship *Myrtilla* has arrived at London (3 Oct.)

The following have been elected: (for Phila. Co.) representatives, Isaac Norris, Edward Warner, Joseph Trotter, Henry Pawling, Hugh Evans, Evan Morgan, John Smith, Joshua Morris; sheriffs, Isaac Griffitts, Judah Foulke; coroners, Thomas James, William Trotter; commissioner, Thomas Say; assessors, Derrick Keyser, Robert Thomas, Daniel Williams, Morris Morris, Isaac Jones, Isaac Levant - (for Bucks Co.) representatives, Mahlon Kirkbride, Joseph Hamton, Abraham Chapman, John Woolston, Griffith Owen, Richard Walker, Samuel Brown, Garrett Vansant; sheriffs, Joseph Hart, William Yardley; coroners, Evan Jones, William Smith; commissioner, William Paxson; assessors, Giles Knight, Daniel Palmer, Peter Traxler, Alexander Brown, Samuel Foulke, Samuel Dupue - (for Chester Co.) representatives, Joseph Gibbons, Thomas Cummings, George Ashbridge, Nathaniel Grubb, Peter Dicks, Nathaniel Pennock, Henry Hockley, Thomas Chandler; sheriffs, John Owen, Aubrey Bevan; coroners, Joshua Thomson, John Taylor; commissioner, William Lewis; assessors, Thomas Pearson, Phineas Lewis, Randal Malin, James Miller, Jeremiah Brown, Jr., John Fairlamb; Robert Strettell was elected Mayor of Phila.; Benjamin Franklin and Hugh Roberts were chosen Burgesses of Phila.; assessors for the city are Bartholomew Penrose, Charles Jones, Joseph Lownes, Jacob Lewis, Joseph Watkins, Samuel Shoemaker; wardens elected are Joseph Stretch, Jacob Cooper (3 Oct.)

Houses and plantations where John Clove, dec'd, lately lived, situated on Chester River in Md., for sale; enquire of John M'Neil, exec. (3 Oct.)

Goods imported from London in the ship *Peak-Bay*, Walter Stirling master, to be sold by John Bell on Hamilton's wharf (3 Oct.)

Notice signed by Richard Hill, Jr., and Andrew Elliot, directors, about admission to the Philadelphia Assembly, opening the evening of 3 Oct. (3 Oct.)

For freight or passage to Belfast in the ship *Daniel*, Edward M'Cormick commander, now at Capt. Edgar's wharf, apply to James Blair, merchant, in Second St. (3 Oct.)

Negroes for sale by John Strutton, at Spencer Trotter's in Front St.: they may be seen at a free Negro woman's in Chestnut St., opposite Anthony Benezet's (3 Oct.)

Tract of land in Ulster Co., N.Y., for sale; apply to Philip Livingston or John Aspinwall in New York (3 Oct.)

Zach. Butcher has invented an instrument for use in surveying and navigation (3 Oct.)

Adv. of Thomas M'Janett at his store in Water St., opposite John Hopkins's (3 Oct.)

Parcel of men servants to be disposed of by James Pemberton or Peter Reeve, commander of the *Lydia* (3 Oct.)

Iron sold by Thomas Yorke at his store in Water St., next door to Peter Bard (3 Oct.)

Benjamin Franklin seeks a manager for a steel-work (3 Oct.)

Mare has been taken up by James Hope, of the Forks of Delaware, Bucks Co. (3 Oct.)

Servants and furniture for sale by Isaac Shano at his house near Nicholson's tavern in Arch St. (3 Oct.)

Two houses in Market St., one in tenure of Capt. William Allison, the other in that of Mrs. Grames, for sale; apply to James Polgreen at Mrs. Mary Roberts's in Front St. (3 Oct.)

William Bowen, born in Wales, a tailor, age c. 22, runaway from on board the snow Baldwin, George Matthews commander; reward will be paid by Greenway and Rundle (3 Oct.)

Phila. item reports the arrival in Phila. of Capts. Parish and Cunningham from Holland with Palatines and also of Capt. Shirley (3 Oct.)

The following have been elected: (for Lancaster Co.), representatives, Arthur Patterson, James Wright, Calvin Cooper, Peter Worrall; for sheriff, Robert Stewart; coroner, Joseph Howard - (for Newcastle Co.) representatives, Jehu Curtis, John M'Cooll, William Armstrong, John Vance, James M'Mechan, Evan Rice; sheriff, George Monro; coroner, Thomas Brown - (for Kent Co.) representatives, Benjamin Chew, Andrew Caldwell, James Train, Robert Wilcocks, John Vining, John Caton; sheriff, Thomas Parke; coroner, James Gray - (for Sussex Co.) representatives, Jacob Kollock, Ryves Holt, Benjamin Burton, Abraham Wyncoop, Shepard Kollock, John Neill; sheriff, William Shankland; coroner, Robert Macilvaine - (for York Co.) representatives, John Wright, John Witherow; sheriff, Hance Hamilton; coroner, Alexander Love - (for Cumberland Co.) representatives, William Trent, Daniel Williams; sheriff, Ezekiel Dunning; coroner, Tobias Hendricks (10 Oct.)

Michael Burrows, Irish servant, age c. 24, lately arrived from Dublin in the snow Jenny and Sally, Archibald Stewart master, runaway from Robert Jessop (10 Oct.)

House between Poole's Bridge and the Sugar-house to be let; enquire of Anthony Wilkinson (10 Oct.)

Horse strayed from John Harris's at Sweatarra; if found, word to be sent to Samuel Scot, tavern-keeper, near Lancaster; reward will be paid by Harris, Scot or Arthur Blair (10 Oct.)

Two silver spoons have been stopped by Philip Syng and one has been found by a girl belonging to John Greenway (10 Oct.)

Daniel Macarty, Irish servant lad, and Johannes Lantzell, Dutch servant, age c. 17, runaways from Jacob Hagie of Germantown Twp., paper-maker; reward will be paid by Hagie or by John Goodshius, sadler, in Phila. (10 Oct.)

Adv. of Edward Cathrall at his store in Water St., next door to Smith and James (10 Oct.)

Tenement in Sassafras St., bounded by property late of Edward Evans, now of Jos. Gross, and by Dilwyn's ground, for sale; apply to George Moschell in Second St., near Dr. Graeme's (10 Oct.)

For freight or passage to Glasgow in the ship Neptune, James Wier master, apply to the master or to James Pemberton (10 Oct.)

Livestock for sale at the house of Lawrence Growdon in Bucks Co. (10 Oct.)

Dry goods imported in the Peak-Bay, Capt. Stirling, from London for sale at his store on Hamilton's wharf (10 Oct.)

Plantations and livestock for sale by Thomas Ogle of Ogle-town in Newcastle Co.; Martha, wife of said Thomas Ogle, has eloped from her husband (10 Oct.)

Adam Massacre, Low Dutchman, age c. 23, country born, bred up a farmer, who was on the Canada expedition, and James Marier, an Italian, bred up a sailor, runaways from Sheriff Hance Hamilton of York Co. (10 Oct.)

English servants, just imported, to be sold by Denyce and Mason, opposite the Baptist meeting in Phila. (10 Oct.)

Thomas Thornton of Joppa and Mrs. Sarah Ramsay, at the head of Severn in Md., offer reward for capture of John Mitchell, late miller to George Brown, on Gunpowder forest, who stole a mare from Mrs. Ramsay's orchard (10 Oct.)

George Saunderson, English servant, age c. 19, runaway from Nathaniel Potts of Mansfield Twp.; also Samuel Butcher, English servant, runaway from Edward Rockhill of Chesterfield; also Mary Newel, Welsh servant, age c. 22, runaway from Stophel Longstreet of Allenstown (10 Oct.)

Cuff, Negro, age c. 30, who belonged nearly two years ago to Anthony Morris, Jr., runaway from Daniel Cooper, at the ferry opposite to Phila. (10 Oct.)

Col. Tasker has arrived at Annapolis from Lord Baltimore in London with a commission to Samuel Ogle (17 Oct.)

Boston item mentions Capt. Samuel Gallop, late master of the brigantine *Polly*, and gives account of his rescue by Capt. Parker (17 Oct.)

Phila. item mentions Capts. Churchman, Stiles and Montpelier (17 Oct.)

Isaac Norris was unanimously chosen speaker of the General Assembly of Pa. (17 Oct.)

At a court in Lancaster a father and son, both named Sigismund Hainly, were condemned to death for counterfeiting (17 Oct.)

For freight or passage to Barbados in the ship *Fame*, Henry Churchman commander, apply to Charles Willing and Son or to the master at Lloyd's wharf (17 Oct.)

Capt. Richard Jeffery, on board the ship *Duke of Bedford*, desires to purchase a Negro man (17 Oct.)

Negro man, age c. 24, for sale; enquire at Thomas Bartholomew's in Market St., at the Sign of the White Horse (17 Oct.)

Night school is kept by William Milne in his room in Alridge's alley, at the Sign of St. Andrew, opposite the shop of Nathan Trotter, blacksmith, in Second St. (17 Oct.)

Robert Lettis Hooper, now living in Trenton, has for sale three plantations in Somerset Co., N.J. (17 Oct.)

Thomas Irons has a house to let in Dover, Kent Co. on Delaware (17 Oct.)

A merchant mill and forge for sale by George Rock on the premises in North East, Cecil Co., Md. (17 Oct.)

Land in Penn St., Phila., for sale; apply to Samuel Rhodes or Jacob Lewis (17 Oct.)

Morgan Murfey, Irish servant, runaway from David Lawell of Newtown, Bucks Co.; reward will be paid by Lawell or by William Anderson (17 Oct.)

Edward Dean, servant, age c. 17, runaway from Jonathan Crathorn, commander of the snow *Sea-horse*, now at Woodrop's wharf; reward will be paid by Crathorn or by Davey and Carson, merchants in Phila. (17 Oct.)

Land, late the property of John Bood, dec'd, and land, late the property of John Norwood, dec'd, both items taken at the suit of Alexander Allair and wife, execs. of Anthony Palmer, dec'd, to be sold at the house of the widow Gregory in Kensington (17 Oct.)

Land, late the property of John Costard, seized at the suit of John George Arnold, to be sold at the house of Daniel Pastorius in Germantown (17 Oct.)

Jacob Coozar, Dutch servant, age c. 24, runaway from George Cowin of Pensborough, Cumberland Co. (17 Oct.)

New York item of 21 Oct. notes the arrival there from Ireland of Capt. Duncan, who had rescued Capt. William Vass of London and his crew (24 Oct.)

Phila. item reports news from Jamaica that Capt. Elphinston was cast away on the Hogsties and Capt. Richards on Henneago (24 Oct.)

Catalogue of books to be sold at Mr. Vidal's Long Room in Second St. (24 Oct.)

Plantation in the Jerseys for sale; apply to Timothy Rain (24 Oct.)

Real estate on Passyunk Rd., bounded by land late of John Cox, dec'd, and land of George Emlen, to be sold by James Burd at William Gray's, at the Sign of the Waggon in Market St.; plans are to be seen at Burd's house in Fifth St. or at Charles Brockden's (24 Oct.)

Accounts with the estate of John Rush, gunsmith, dec'd, to be settled with William Rush, blacksmith, and Hannah Rush, execs. (24 Oct.)

Anthony Porter seeks information about Victor Knox, pedler, who lived in the Borough of Lancaster for nearly a year past (24 Oct.)

Richard Ion, Englishman, convicted of murder on the high seas, late commander of a schooner from S.C., where his family now dwells, has escaped from Edward Collins, keeper of the goal in Phila. (24 Oct.)

Land in Cheltenham Twp., late belonging to Edward Collins the elder, dec'd, taken at the suit of Mary Martin, exec. of Richard Martin, dec'd, to be sold at the house of Thomas Harper in Frankford (24 Oct.)

Mare stolen from the plantation of Daniel Harman of Lampeter Twp., Lancaster Co. (24 Oct.)

Land about four miles from Trenton, now in the possession of Thomas Sutton, for sale; apply to Andrew Reed in Phila., next door to the Jersey Ferry, or Joseph Reed and Moore Furman at Trenton or said Sutton (24 Oct.)

Quality of the work of Charles Dutens, jeweller, at Mrs. Elizabeth Green's in Second St., can be attested by John Sayre, late from New York (24 Oct.)

Ferdinand Hughes, tailor, age c. 25, runaway from Robert Savage of Middletown Point, Monmouth Co.; reward will be paid by Patrick Hanlon at Bristol, Bucks Co., or by said Savage (24 Oct.)

Hardware for sale by William Mason, at John De Nyce's in Second St. (24 Oct.)

Annapolis item mentions John Matthews of Baltimore Co. (31 Oct.)

Ezekiel Eldred, convicted of polygamy at a court in Salem, Mass., was burnt in the hand (31 Oct.)

Negro man belonging to Charles Beekman of New York was convicted of burglarizing the house of John Peterson and that of Isaac Deirs (31 Oct.)

H.M.S. Centaur, Capt. Cosby, has arrived at New York (31 Oct.)

William Wilson, of Chester Co., farmer, was robbed and killed (31 Oct.)

Chairs and chaises are sold by Joseph Carbutt at a store on House's wharf; enquire at Benjamin Bagnall's, watchmaker in Front St. (31 Oct.)

Plantation near Buckley's mill in Sadsbury Twp., Lancaster Co., formerly belonging to James Ogilvie, now to James Burd, adjoining the plantations of David Elder, Robert Tweed and John Matthews, and at present occupied by John Jones, for sale (31 Oct.)

James Knox of Lancaster Co., brother of Victor Knox, now dec'd, wishes to contact Anthony Porter regarding his advertisement (31 Oct.)

Accounts with the estate of Elizabeth Woodward, shopkeeper, to be settled with John Bell, Alexander Hamilton or James Louttit (31 Oct.)

Isaac Morris, whip-maker, has removed from Second St. to the house of Joseph Saul, chair-maker, in Market St. (31 Oct.)

House in Market St., now in tenure of Capt. William Allison, for sale; apply to Thomas Bickley Polgreen, at the house of Jonathan Evans in Walnut St. (31 Oct.)

For freight or passage to Newry and Irvine in the snow Grizie, John Cameron master, apply to James Blair or to the master on Lloyd's wharf (31 Oct.)

William Bamber, Irish servant, runaway from John De Nyce, opposite the Baptist Meeting House (31 Oct.)

Mares strayed or stolen from Isaac Cooper in Newtown Twp., Gloucester Co.; reward if returned to said Cooper or to Samuel Noble in Second St. (31 Oct.)

Goods and money have been stolen from Archibald M'Curdy, pedlar, out of George Little's house in Earltown Twp., Lancaster Co.; if discovery is made, news is to be sent to Justice Edwards or to George Little, near Mr. Branson's Iron-works (31 Oct.)

William Bromwich, staymaker, intends for England; Jacob Carver, who has worked five years with him, has taken over his house. (31 Oct.)

Accounts with the estate of John Naglee, dec'd, to be settled with Catherine, John and Jacob Naglee and Alexander Forbes, execs., by whom the following properties are to be sold: one in Germantown, opposite James Logan's; another in the Northern Liberties, now in the tenure of John Striker, tavern-keeper (31 Oct.)

Mare came to the plantation of Benanuel Lownes of Springfield, Chester Co. (31 Oct.)

Daniel Lee, Irish servant, age c. 19, and Christopher Lennord, Irish servant, age c. 18, runaways from John Alison and Benjamin Galey of Little Britain Twp., Lancaster Co. (31 Oct.)

Reward offered by Thomas Tilbury in Phila. or Robert Roberts in Gwynadd for return of a stray horse (31 Oct.)

Patrick Sullivan, Irish servant, age c. 50, runaway from John Moor of New London Twp., Chester Co. (31 Oct.)

Maurice Smith, Irish servant, age c. 20, who professes to be a wig-maker and barber, runaway from Richard Sedgwick of Cecil Co., Md. (31 Oct.)

Land in Oley, Phila. Co., bounded by the lands late of Abraham Ashman, George Hunter, George Shiers, John Bartolett and Caspar Wister, for sale; enquire of Richard Hockley in Third St. (31 Oct.)

For freight or passage to Cork and Rotterdam in the ship Duke of Wirtemberg, Daniel Montpelier master, apply to Christian Henry Curtius in Second St., next door to Dr. Graham's (31 Oct.)

Jacob Heselgaser, Dutch servant, age c. 21, runaway from Joseph Inslee of Newtown, Bucks Co. (31 Oct.)

Alexander Scheetz, Dutch servant, runaway from Christopher Robins of Whitemarsh Twp, at the Sign of the Three Tons (31 Oct.)

Jonathan Zane has real estate and merchandize for sale (31 Oct.)

Ground in Chestnut St., now in tenure of Isaac Williams, bounded by the house in the tenure of Charles Meredith and by that in the tenure of James Tippar, will be sold at the house of Jeremiah Smith, the Sign of the Queen of Hungary, in Front St. (31 Oct.)

Thomas Green, living on Germantown Rd., has several properties for sale, one being the house where Timothy Scarf now lives; plans may be seen at office of Charles Brockden, office of George Heap (coroner), or at Standish Ford's, at the Sign of the George (31 Oct.)

In Nov. or Dec. 1749 James Lewis, a Welshman, age c. 24, farmer, without leave took the horse from Thomas Green; reward if the horse or thief is taken (31 Oct.)

New York item of 4 Nov. mentions Capts. Amory, Corne and Bryant (7 Nov.)

Boston item of 21 Oct. gives report brought by James Minot from both houses of the Pa. Assembly about the western tribes of Indians, with mention of Mrs. Sergeant, Mr. Hollis, Mr. and Mrs. Ashley, Sir Peter Warren and Capt. Kellogg (7 Nov.)

At Portsmouth, N.H., Samuel Dusten was tried for uttering counterfeit bills and acquitted (7 Nov.)

Capt. Partridge arrived 27 Oct. at Boston from London (7 Nov.)

Thu. last James Logan died in Phila. in his 77th year (7 Nov.)

At the Mayor's Court in Phila. last week Anna Magdalena Stamer was sentenced to be carted and whipped; her accomplice, Daniel Worms, was fined; the woman had brought false accusation against Mr. Noble (7 Nov.)

Nanny Gardner, a poor old woman, living in Petticoat Lane in New York, fell into the fire on Sat. last and was burnt to death, according to New York item of 4 Nov. (7 Nov.)

The American Country Almanack for 1752 has just been published; the author is Thomas Moore (7 Nov.)

Pastures adjoining meadow of Charles Brockden to be sold at John Ashton's in Moyamensing (7 Nov.)

Land bounded by a lot of Benjamin Loxly and property of Thomas
Stuart and John Church, late belonging to Thomas Shute, taken
at the suit of Benjamin Loxly, John Church and John Ware,
will be sold at the house of John Biddle in Market St. (7
Nov.)

Gelding stolen from John Montgomery at Christine-bridge, Newcastle Co. (7 Nov.)

Two Negroes for sale; enquire of Patrick M'Alister in Arch St.
(7 Nov.)

Plantation in White-clay-creek Hundred, Newcastle Co., part of
the estate late of Richard Nivin, yeoman, dec'd, will be sold;
attendance will be given by Margaret Nivin, Robert Evans and
James M'Mechen, execs.; sale by order of Richard M'William,
clerk of the Orphans Court (7 Nov.)

William Jenkison, English servant, age c. 14, who served part
of his time with George Stevenson in Phila., runaway from
Samuel Lamb at Pennsborough Twp., Cumberland Co.; reward will
be paid by Samuel Lamb, mason, at Carlisle-Town (7 Nov.)

Brigantine Shirley, Oswall Eve commander, at Shoemaker's wharf,
will sail for Lisbon (7 Nov.)

Real estate in Third St., bounded by workshop of John Rouse,
lot late of Thomas Rutter and ground of John Snowden, late
the property of Thomas Rutter, dec'd, to be sold at the house
of John Biddle (7 Nov.)

John King, born in England, age c. 40, weaver, runaway from
Thomas Hallam, living near Joppa, Baltimore Co., Md. (7 Nov.)

Horses strayed from Jos. Lyndvil of Cymrn, Lancaster Co.; reward if creatures are secured and notice is sent to Thomas
Edwards in Lancaster Co. or David Edwards in Cymrn (7 Nov.)

House and goods of Joshua Way, dec'd, to be sold by Elizabeth
Way, Joseph Hews and David Ferriss, execs. (7 Nov.)

Horse came to the plantation of James Ingles of Coventry, Chester Co. (7 Nov.)

Hannah, wife of James Stewart of East-Town Twp., Chester Co.,
has eloped from her husband (7 Nov.)

On 25 Oct. the house of Mr. Hersey, of Hingham, Mass., was consumed by fire; Hersey, his wife and his children are safe (14
Nov.)

Gulian Verplank, of New York, merchant, died there 10 Nov. (14
Nov.)

Capt. Hinton reports the marriage of Thomas Penn to Lady Juliana Fermor, youngest daughter of the late Earl of Pomfret
(14 Nov.)

Phila. items mention Capts. Ritchie, Lauderdale and Whitefield
(14 Nov.)

Obituary of Thomas Hopkinson of Phila., Judge of the Admiralty,
who died last week (14 Nov.)

Theophilus Grew, Prof. of Mathematics, will board students for
the Academy in Arch St. (14 Nov.)

Thomas Archdall has moved his store from opposite Mr. Richardson's, silversmith, in Front St., to opposite Gray's alley
(14 Nov.)

Servants, imported in ship Phila, Capt. Hinton, for sale by
Levy and Franks (14 Nov.)

William Ghiselin, goldsmith, is removed from Second St. to the house in Second St. where the widow Bright lately lived (14 Nov.)

Thomas Fitzsimons, at William Fitzsimon's, baker, next door to the Easy Chair in Second St., has wigs and linens for sale (14 Nov.)

Jacob Barnet, Dutch servant, runaway from Michael Cougler, of Ducklinger Twp., miller; reward if he is brought to Christian Sneider, tavern-keeper in Second St. (14 Nov.)

John Baker has a variety of curiosities to show at his house in Kensington; the proceeds are to go to the poor (14 Nov.)

Mare came to the plantation of Robert Holloway in Robertson Twp., Lancaster Co. (14 Nov.)

Dr. Thomas Sackett of Newtown, Bucks Co., intends to leave the province (14 Nov.)

Real estate in Willis-Town, Chester Co., for sale; apply to David Jones, living on the premises (14 Nov.)

For freight or passage to Belfast in the ship _Dursly_, William Hamilton master, apply to John Roan on Society Hill or to the master (14 Nov.)

Last week Richard Smith, Esq., of Burlington, West New Jersey, was buried there in the Friends Burying Ground (21 Nov.)

Sigismund **Hainly, the father,** has been executed but his son of the same name has been reprieved (21 Nov.)

Phila. item mentions Capts. Carlile and Dulby (21 Nov.)

Andrew Bartholomew has a house to let in Carter's Alley (21 Nov.)

The following servants are runaways from the ship _Phila_, Caot. Hinton: Michael Jacobs, born in **Denmark,** a caulker; James Fitzgerald, Irishman, a sawyer; Alexander M'Donald, Irishman, a sawyer; William Crompton, Englishman, a hatter; Edward Cross, Englishman, a gardiner; John Stevens, Irishman; James Bourne, Irishman, a weaver; John Nugent, Englishman, a wheelwright; a reward will be paid by Levy and Franks (21 Nov.)

John Cameron or **James** Blair will offer a reward for Cuddie Cockren, sailor, age $\underline{c}$. 24, runaway from the snow _Grizie_ (21 Nov.)

Nicholas M'Daniel, servant, age $\underline{c}$. 20, runaway from a sloop at Poughkeepsie, N.Y.; he came lately from Ireland with Capt. Anderson; he says that Henry Mulhall in Amboy is his uncle; he has a brother in Poughkeepsie who also is a servant to James Isaiah Ross of New York, merchant; said Ross offers reward for capture of M'Daniel (21 Nov.)

John Brooks, born in Essex, England, age $\underline{c}$. 28, butcher, imported in the ship _Speedwell_, Nicholas Stephenson commander, runaway from Jacob Giles of Baltimore Co. (21 Nov.)

Accounts with the estate of John Harrison, dec'd, to be settled with Peter Bard, admin. (21 Nov.)

Adv. of Joseph Davis, leather craftsman, next door but one to George Plumley's **and adjoining the shop of John Stow,** brassfounder, in Third St. (21 Nov.)

Benjamin Ashton, age $\underline{c}$. 20, runaway from Matthias Keen, of Oxford Twp., Phila. Co. (21 Nov.)

John Noah, Welchman, age $\underline{c}$. 15, runaway from James Roberts, blacksmith, near Nutt's Iron-works in Vincent Twp., Chester Co. (21 Nov.)

Robert Walker, Irish servant, age c. 20, who served four years in Va., runaway from John Kelly of Donegall Twp., Lancaster Co. (21 Nov.)

Horse stolen from the pasture of Edward Adair, of Bristol, Bucks Co.; reward will be paid by Adair or by Standish Ford, at the Sign of the George, in Phila. (21 Nov.)

On 7 Sept. a brig belonging to Col. Saltonstall was wrecked; all on board were drowned except Capt. Leeds and one of the crew (28 Nov.)

On 10 Nov. Daniel Bailey, age 68, married Elizabeth Waters, age 78, in Kingston, East New Jersey (28 Nov.)

The ship Joseph, Capt. Bryant, and the snow Jupiter, Capt. Amory, have arrived at New York (28 Nov.)

Horse that formerly belonged to Mr. Swan, joiner, has strayed from James Lindsay in Front St. (28 Nov.)

Sloop to be sold at James's Coffee House; inventory may be seen at Peter Bard's or Henry Elves's in Water St. (28 Nov.)

George Tonat of Springfield Manor has taken up two stray horses (28 Nov.)

Adv. of Hugh and Randle Mitchell at their store in Water St. where Levy and Franks formerly lived; they still keep their store opposite Mary Andrews; persons concerned with Benjamin Fuller, late clerk, are to apply to Randle Mitchell, his brother Alexander, or Charles Jones, clerks to the company (28 Nov.)

Samuel White of Marticks Twp., Lancaster Co., has taken up a stray gelding (28 Nov.)

Plantation near Trenton for sale; apply to Elizabeth Biles, who lives on the premises (28 Nov.)

Robert Crocket, Scotch servant, shoemaker, runaway from John Jackson of Phila., shoemaker (28 Nov.)

Benjamin Heathbourn, Scotch servant, age c. 21, runaway (it is supposed in company with Robert Crocket) from Robert Parrish of Phila., carpenter (28 Nov.)

Plantation in Lancaster Co. to be sold by Matthew Brown, living on the premises (28 Nov.)

Mare stolen from John Vandever at Brandewyne Bridge (28 Nov.)

Hercules Roney, of Horsham Twp., weaver, was convicted of counterfeiting; he was sentenced to stand in the pillory and be whipped on 18 Dec. (5 Dec.)

House and lot in Sassafras St., bounded by land late of Edward Evans (now of Joseph Groff) and by Dilwin's ground, for sale; apply to George Moschell in Second St., near Dr. Greams's (5 Dec.)

House of George Adams at Christine Bridge, Newcastle Co., was robbed on 18 Nov.; Adams surprised the thief in his shop; the thief left his shoes behind; later the suspect bought shoes from Adam Marley, shoemaker, in Newport (5 Dec.)

Henry Harrison, John Kidd and Abel James, merchants in Phila., have for sale a plantation adjoining land of Thomas Livezey, near Robert Thomas's mills, late in the possession of Samuel and Robert Worrall (5 Dec.)

Richard Farmer has a Negro woman for sale (5 Dec.)

Drugs and medicines, prepared by Corbyn and Clutton in London, are sold by John White at the Sign of the Mortar and Dove in the house in Second St. out of which Dr. Thomas Bond lately removed (5 Dec.)

John Welch, servant, age c. 25, weaver, formerly servant to John Cooper, of Chester Co., weaver, runaway from Arthur M'Ilveen of Deptford Twp., Gloucester Co., West New Jersey (5 Dec.)

Christiana mills, land and effects of John Parkinson, dec'd, to be sold by William Patterson and Jane Parkinson, exec. (5 Dec.)

A letter directed to Samuel M'Call, Sr., by Capt. Hinton has not come to hand (5 Dec.)

Edward Pennington has for sale at his store on Israel Pemberton's wharf goods imported in the snow Melling, John Matthews commander (5 Dec.)

Horse has been taken up at the house of Isaac Cleave, at the Sign of the White Horse between Darby and Chester (5 Dec.)

Adv. of Samuel Howell at the Sign of the Beaver at the end of Strawberry Alley in Chestnut St. (5 Dec.)

John Dunnivin, Irish servant, age c. 19, runaway from Henry Counsill, living in Tulley's Neck, Queen Ann's Co., Md. (5 Dec.)

Reward will be paid by William Whitebread, in Second St., or Robert Austin, miller, of Abington Twp., Phila. Co., for the return of a horse strayed from the yard of John Howard of Phila., joiner (5 Dec.)

Plantation in Providence Twp., Phila. Co., late the estate of Awbray Richardson, dec'd, to be sold by Richard Richardson (5 Dec.)

Samuel Fisher, hatmaker in Second St., intends to move to the house where William Standley lately dwelt (5 Dec.)

Archibald Young, at the Province Island, takes in horses to winter; he receives them at John Biddle's (5 Dec.)

Medicines, shop and household goods to be sold at the late dwelling of Dr. John Wright, dec'd, at Christine Bridge; attendance will be given by Elizabeth Wright, admin. (5 Dec.)

The following persons were tried at the General Court in Williamsburg, Va.: George Kerr from Norfolk for murder, guilty, death; Richard Burk from Norfolk for murder, acquitted; Anne Gray from Stafford for felony, acquitted; William Johnson from Spotsylvania for stealing a watch, guilty, death; John Brown from King William for stealing a watch, acquitted; Edward Stokes from Frederick for horse-stealing, acquitted; Henry Stanworth from York for murder, guilty, death; Nicholas Dernin from Amelia for burning the prison, guilty, death; John Holt from Stafford for felony, guilty; Robert Howles from Hanover for breaking goal, imprisoned one year; Moses Rawlings from Norfolk for counterfeiting coin, acquitted (10 Dec.)

Sarah Clark in Baltimore Co. was murdered and her husband John injured in a plot conceived by his son-in-law, John Berry, who planned to marry an orphan named Sarah Catcham; also involved were two servants, Pat and Martha (10 Dec.)

John Webster, suspected of robbing the stores of Smith and James and John Read and George Adams, was committed to goal in Phila.; Susannah M'Connell, his accomplice, was committed to the workhouse (10 Dec.)

Miles Reily, Irish servant, age c. 17, runaway from Robert Miller of Leacock Twp., Lancaster Co. (10 Dec.)

James Nealey of East Nantmell, Chester Co., has received no consideration for several notes of hand payable to John and William Gibson of Mountjoy Twp., York Co. (10 Dec.)

Land in Charlestown, Md., for sale; apply to Philip Cazier, Jr., in said town (10 Dec.)

David Martin, Rector to the Academy in Phila., died Wed. last (17 Dec.)

Thomas Cadwalader has real estate in Trenton for sale (17 Dec.)

Adv. of John Hall from London, jack-maker, near the Pewter Platter in Front St. (17 Dec.)

William Freeman from Birmingham has imported hardware for sale at his store, next to George Plumley's, in Third St. (17 Dec.)

Coffee, ginger, etc. are sold by William Moode at his house in Chestnut St. (17 Dec.)

Thomas Lister has snuff and English garden seeds for sale at his store in Third St., next to George Plumley's (17 Dec.)

Imported dry goods for sale by Joseph Ogden at his store in the house of Thomas Cash, at the Sign of the Last, in Chestnut St. (17 Dec.)

Adv. of John Jennings at his store in the house of Peter Bard in Water St. (17 Dec.)

James Alexander, gardiner, has imported seeds for sale (17 Dec.)

Accounts with John Frew of East Nottingham, Chester Co., to be settled with William and David M'Ilvaine, merchants (17 Dec.)

Mare came to the plantation of James Skerrett of Blockley Twp., Phila. Co. (17 Dec.)

Plantation in Trydufrin to be sold by Thomas M'Kean, living on the premises (17 Dec.)

The *Robert and Mary*, Thomas Tucker master, was wrecked 17 Sept. on the coast of North Carolina (24 Dec.)

Rev. Mr. Whitefield has arrived in Charles-Town from Georgia (24 Dec.)

Esther M'Connell (mother of Mary M'Connell) was committed to goal in Phila. for harboring John Webster (24 Dec.)

Capt. Flower's vessel from South Carolina has got up to Marcus Hook (24 Dec.)

Real estate in Front St., bounded by the house of Jacob Jones and that of Isaac Bolton, to be sold by David Linn; enquire of Thomas Lawrence, Esq. (24 Dec.)

Philip Kieve, servant, age c. 20, runaway from Hugh M'Clelent, living near Pequa meeting-house in Lancaster Co. (24 Dec.)

William M'Crackan, who came from London last summer, may hear something to his advantage by applying to Lewis Gordon in Norris's Alley (24 Dec.)

A colt has been stolen out of the stable belonging to Thomas Slemons of Salisbury Twp., Lancaster Co. (24 Dec.)

John Atkinson, staymaker, at the Sign of the White Stays in Second St., desires prompt payment of all debts due him (24 Dec.)

Accounts with the estate of William Paschall, dec'd, sadler, to be settled with John Knight, admin. (24 Dec.)

Negro lad to be sold by Joseph Richardson, silversmith, in Front St. (24 Dec.)

The partnership between Fisher and Fussell is expiring (24 Dec.)

Two Negroes for sale; enquire of Isaac Jones in Arch St. (24 Dec.)

Adv. of Green and Whitlock at their store at Mrs. Howell's in Front St. (24 Dec.)

Land in Caln Twp. in Chester Co. and in Warwick Twp., Bucks Co., for sale by Deborah Claypoole, William Coleman and John Swift, execs. of Abraham Claypoole, dec'd (24 Dec.)

Capt. Flower from South Carolina reports that the Rev. George Whitefield designs to sail for Phila. in the spring (24 Dec.)

Daniel Goodman, baker, in Second St. has a cure for the bite of a mad dog and, as he is a seventh son, a cure for the King's evil (31 Dec.)

Accounts with the estate of Samuel Hasell, Esq., late of Phila., dec'd, to be settled with Alexander Huston, next door to the Sign of the Spinning-Wheel in Market St. (31 Dec.)

Horse has come to the plantation of Thomas Terry in the Falls Twp., Bucks Co. (31 Dec.)

Horse has strayed from the stable of Joseph Sims (31 Dec.)

Accounts with the estate of John Knox, late of Phila., merchant, dec'd, to be settled with John Bleakley and James Magill, admins. (31 Dec.)

Adv. of William and David M'Ilvaine, who have for sale goods imported in the snow _William_, Alexander Katter commander (31 Dec.)

1752

Annapolis item of 4 Dec. reports the arrival there Mon. last of Capt. Lorain from Bristol with about 50 servants, chiefly convicts (7 Jan.)

Annapolis item of 4 Dec. reports that one Solomon Sharp of Talbot Co. has caught a porpoise in a shallow creek (7 Jan.)

On 8 Nov. at Springfield, Long Meadow, the house of John Hall burned to the ground (7 Jan.)

On 4 Dec. a brig, one Church master, belonging to Newport, R.I., was cast away at Point Judith (7 Jan.)

John Macknab died on 8 Dec. in Dedham, Mass. (7 Jan.)

Boston item of 16 Dec. reports that on Tue. last a young seafaring man named Ross, born in North Britain, died when he fell from the mast of a vessel at the Long Wharf (7 Jan.)

New York item of 30 Dec. reports that on Wed. last a boat with three men aboard, two of whom were brothers named Parker, overset near Red Hook; one of the brothers got ashore; the other two men were drowned (7 Jan.)

Phila. item reports the arrival at the Capes of Capt. Gass from Dublin with servants (7 Jan.)

Sermon was preached at the Academy in Phila. on 6 Jan. by the Rev. Peters (7 Jan.)

Goods saved from brig _Prince William_, Edward Snead master, for sale (7 Jan.)

Sugar, pewter, etc. sold by James Peller on Powell's wharf (7 Jan.)

Real estate in Front St., bounded on west by an alley extending to Coombs's alley, to be sold by David Linn at the house of William Nicholson in Arch St.; enquire of Thomas Lawrence (7 Jan.)

Plantation in Lower Merion, late the property of William Havard, taken at the suit of Charles Meredith, assignee of Mary Andrews, to be sold at the house of Richard Hughes in Lower Merion Twp. (7 Jan.)

Lot between Third and Fourth Sts., adjoining land of Clement Russel and Joseph Shippen, and also land on Society Hill, bounded by property of Edward Shippen, to be sold by James Burd at the coffee house (7 Jan.)

John Newcomb, Irish servant, age c. 22, runaway from Thomas Blair of Bethlehem Twp., Hunterdon Co., West Jersey (7 Jan.)

Mr. Dove, professor of English at the Academy, has moved into Rock Hall to accomodate the number of his boarders (7 Jan.)

Colt came to the plantation of Eunus Lewis of Guinnop Twp., Phila. Co. (7 Jan.)

Mare has been stolen from William Tussey of Brandywine Hundred, Newcastle Co.; suspected thief is Alexander Davis, formerly a servant in the area (7 Jan.)

Land at the south end of Phila., bounded by land late of Anthony Noble, late of John Faris, and ground of William Faris, in the tenure of Anthony Whitely, late the property of John Faris, taken at the suit of Charles Edgar, will be sold at the house of Anthony Whitely on Society Hill (7 Jan.)

Real estate in Sassafras St., now in the tenure of Rev. Michael Slayter, late the property of John Boude, taken at the suit of Henry Elves, to be sold at the house of John Biddle in Merket St. (7 Jan.)

David Chambers, stone-cutter, in Arch St., has lost a silver watch, marked Robert Wilson on the dial plate and within Samuel Gerrard (7 Jan.)

Tract of land in New London and West Nottingham Twps., Chester Co., late belonging to John Frew, taken at the suit of John Richardson and others, will be sold by Sheriff John Owen (7 Jan.)

Horse strayed or stolen from Alexander Barclay in Second St. (7 Jan.)

Sampson, a Negro, runaway from John Philips of Phila. (7 Jan.)

Advertisements for the German and English Gazette, printed at Lancaster by Miller and Holland, are taken at the Post Office (14 Jan.)

Reward if lost pocket-book is returned to David Hall at the new Printing office (14 Jan.)

Time of a Dutch girl to be sold; enquire of Anthony Yaldmall, opposite James's Coffee-House in Front St. (14 Jan.)

Mary Ball in Front St. has a Negro girl for sale (14 Jan.)

William and David M'Ilvaine, who have an assignation to the lands, etc. of John Frew, of East Nottingham, Chester Co., have substituted John Hamilton of Londonderry Twp. as their attorney (14 Jan.)

Jane Bennet, in Carter's Alley, joining to Mr. Sewell's, late sheriff, intends to follow the business of baking pound cake (14 Jan.)

Mare came to the plantation of Matthias Hole in Kensington (14 (Jan.)

Michael Hunt, servant, from Waterford in Ireland, age c. 25, who served 4 years with David Rees, runaway from William Vogan, weaver, of Sadbury Twp., Lancaster Co. (14 Jan.)

Horse came to Richard Renshaw's at Greenwich Point, opposite Gloucester (14 Jan.)

Accounts with estate of Archibald Poak, late of Abington, dec'd, to be settled with Thomas Fletcher, William Adams and Matthew Wilson, execs. (14 Jan.)

Adv. of Anthony Duche, dyer, in Chestnut St. (14 Jan.)

Adv. of Thomas Gibbons, watchmaker from London, next door to Mr. Inglis's, over the drawbridge; his wife makes manteels and stays (14 Jan.)

Two pocket-books have been lost by John Priest, who lives in Front St., two doors below Pewter-Platter Alley (14 Jan.)

Adv. of Jonathan and John Mifflin at their new store, opposite Hamilton's wharf (14 Jan.)

Henry Wardrop, Scotch servant, age c. 24, who has been commander of a vessel, runaway from Edward Realy of Phila. (14 Jan.)

Boston item of 23 Dec. mentions Capt. Waldo from Jamaica (21 Jan.)

Boston item of 30 Dec. reports that on Tue. last the ship _Bumper_, Capt. Cussens, was driven on the rocks near Pull-in-Point; the men were saved except a Mr. Mason, a passenger, who died from cold on the beach ; the same day the sloop of Capt. Morton ran upon the rocks near Cape Anne (21 Jan.)

New York item of 6 Jan. mentions Capts. Bennet, Shoals and Bruen (21 Jan.)

Letter from Jamaica reports that the sloop _Freemason_, Capt. Perkins, overset on 5 Sept.; the captain and three others were drowned; the rest of the crew rescued by Capt. Corlop (21 Jan.)

New York item of 13 Jan. reports that last week a young woman stole clothing from the house of William Peartree Smith in New York (21 Jan.)

House of James Rutherford in Trenton was broken into and robbed in the night between 6 and 7 Jan. (21 Jan.)

Tue. last John Webster made an attempt to hang himself in jail in Phila. but was cut down (21 Jan.)

Reward offered by William Bell for capture of William Harley of Phila., a coach-maker, an Englishman, who has run away from his bail (21 Jan.)

Adv. of James Humphreys, notary public, whose office is in the house of John Reily, conveyancer, in Front St.; Humphreys has imported goods for sale in his store in Second St.; he also intends to follow the business of undertaker (21 Jan.)

Accounts with the estate of Thomas Potts, late of Colebrookdale, dec'd, to be settled with Magdalene Potts, John Potts, Thomas Potts and Thomas Yorke, execs. (21 Jan.)

James Boucher, Irish servant, shoemaker, with old indenture, runaway from John Lettimore of Pencader Hundred (21 Jan.)

Real estate now in the possession of Michael Halling, bounded by a tenement of Daniel Puttin, property late of Michael Brown, dec'd, and real estate of Edward Warner, late the property of Anthony Noble, dec'd, taken at the suit of Michael Halling, to be sold at the house of John Biddle, the Sign of the Indian King (21 Jan.)

Real estate for sale, one item joining the mill of Thomas Busby, being part of the plantation of William Philpot, dec'd, and another item a public house in Busseltown; enquire of the owner, John Atkins, innholder (21 Jan.)

Accounts with the estate of Mary Shewbart, late of Phila., dec'd, widow, to be settled with Richard Hockley, Isaac Zane and Sarah Brown, execs.; household goods to be sold at the house of the dec'd in Tenth St. (21 Jan.)

New York item of 20 Jan. mentions Capts. Sheldon, Jefferson, Shourt and M'Connell (28 Jan.)

Archibald Cunningham and wife Alice on 6 Jan. at Dover in Kent Co. were convicted of the murder on 25 Dec. of Eleanor Gollohar (?) in Duck Creek Hundred (28 Jan.)

Richard Price was found guilty of stealing from Simon Hirons of Motherkill Hundred (28 Jan.)

Hay and fresh limes for sale at the plantation of William Callender at Point-no-Point (28 Jan.)

Plantation at Whitehill, West New Jersey, to be let; enquire of Robert Field, living on said plantation (28 Jan.)

Horse stolen out of the stable of Joshua Howel in Amwell, N.J. (28 Jan.)

Lot in Wicacoa, near the battery, to be sold; it bounds upon a lot of Joseph Wharton; apply to John Meredith on the premises (28 Jan.)

Andrew Head, Dutch servant, age c. 22, runaway from Benjamin Morgan of Waterford Twp., Gloucester Co. (28 Jan.)

George Fling has for sale livestock, farm implements and time of servants at the plantation on Frankford Rd. that belongs to Mr. Norris (28 Jan.)

Lot in Cedar St., bounded by ground of Edward Shippen, Swanson and William Shippen, late the property of Conrad Waltaker, to be sold at the house of John Biddle (28 Jan.)

At the house of Daniel Pastorious in Germantown will be sold a lot and messuage, bounded by the Northwales Rd., land of K. Weas and land now or late of Ulrick Pednore, late the property of William Antig, taken at the suit of Dominicus Gasner (28 Jan.)

Gold- and silversmith's tools, late the property of Bouman Hunlock, taken at the suit of John Ord and others, will be sold at the house of John Biddle (28 Jan.)

Adv. of William Mason, glover, from London, now in Second St., over against the Baptist Meeting (28 Jan.)

Part of lots in Chestnut St. and part of the house wherein Joseph Cobourn now lives, at the Sign of the One Tunn, are for sale by Nathaniel Broughton '28 Jan.)

Lucy Hubbs, exec. of Robert Hubbs, dec'd, will sell the plantation where said Robert lived in Gloucester Co. (28 Jan.)

Mare stolen from Thomas Moore, near Newcastle, is supposed to have been taken by Henry Francis Sherwood, who has lived in Md.; Francis stole clothing from John Eves in Newcastle; reward will be paid by John Read, merchant, or Thomas Moore, near Christine Bridge (28 Jan.)

Annapolis item of 18 Dec. states that a Negro man of James Maccubbin was found frozen and dead on the road beyond South River (4 Beb.)

Annapolis item of 25 Dec. reports that Wed. last the persons concerned in the murder of Mrs. Clark on 20 Nov. were tried at a court held at Joppa; one, a boy, was acquitted; the following four were sentenced to death: Martha Basset (otherwise Catcham); John Berry; Mary Powell; Edward Evans, who was subsequently pardoned (4 Feb.)

At the same court Elizabeth Jenkins (charged with the murder of her bastard child) was acquitted; Stephen Rose and Samuel Mitchelson were found guilty of stealing and of prison-breaking (4 Feb.)

New York item of 27 Jan. mentions Capts. King and Everson (4 Feb.)

New York item of 27 Jan. reports that Mary Clarke was there condemned to be executed on 14 Feb. for stealing (4 Feb.)

Capt. Magee of Phila. has arrived at the Capes from Barbados (4 Feb.)

Adv. of Jacob Shoemaker, at the Sign of the Spinning-wheel, in Market St. (4 Feb.)

James Wallace is removed from his store in Water St. to the house where the Sign of the Trembleur formerly was kept, commonly called Bourne's Corner, next door to where Samuel Burge kept store, and opposite Mr. Masters's new buildings on Market St. wharf (4 Feb.)

Plantation and grist mill, late belonging to Jacob Leech, dec'd, to be let by the Widow Leech in Arch St. (4 Feb.)

Accounts with the estate of John Owen, late of Chester, dec'd, to be settled with George Owen and James Rhodes, execs. (4 Feb.)

Schooner Friendship, Benjamin Flower master, will sail for South Carolina; apply for passage to Willaim Branson or the master (4 Feb.)

Sheriff John Mickle offers reward for capture of the following men who broke out of the goal of Gloucester Co.: Sylvanus Gosling (son of John Gosling) of Greenwich, blacksmith, and Morgan Rorke, Irishman (4 Feb.)

John Harvey, English servant, runaway from John De Nyce, opposite the Baptist Meeting-house (4 Feb.)

Gelding strayed from Jonathan Paschall's in Kingsess, Phila. Co. (4 Feb.)

Isaac Cooper has two properties to let, one being where he formerly dwelt in Newtown Twp. (4 Feb.)

John Roberts, servant, age c. 20, runaway from Douglass Campbell, collier, at Reading Furnace (4 Feb.)

Edward Walker, age c. 21, tailor, runaway from Robert Barnes, living in Moreland, Phila. Co. (4 Feb.)

Property in Cheltenham Twp., late of Edward Collings, taken at the suit of Mary Martin, exec. of Edward Martin, dec'd, will be sold by Isaac Griffitts at the house of Thomas Harper in Frankford (4 Feb.)

Hannah, wife of Ralph Walker, mariner, has run him into debt (4 Feb.)

Boston item of 6 Jan. mentions Capt. Folger (11 Feb.)

New York item of 3 Feb. mentions Capt. Lawrence and also Capt. Shourt, late of the sloop *Success* (11 Feb.)

William Kerr, who claims to be a weaver and to live at Bethlehem in the Jerseys with one William M'Crackken, is in goal in Phila. on suspicion of counterfeiting (11 Feb.)

Jacob Stroud, country born, age 26, formerly a soldier at Albany, runaway from his bail; reward offered by Isaac Warner (11 Feb.)

Benjamin Kendall, shoemaker, intends for England (11 Feb.)

Land and other items to be sold by William Buchanan at Marsh Creek in York Co. (11 Feb.)

Plantation late of Aubrey Roberts, dec'd, in North Wales, Phila. Co., to be sold by Ellin Roberts and Isaac Jones, execs. (11 Feb.)

Joseph Mitchell, of Tryduffryn Twp., Chester Co., has two Negroes for sale (11 Feb.)

Thomas Barlo, apprentice, age c. 21 or 22, this country born, runaway from Richard Dennis, of Phila. (11 Feb.)

Pocketbook of Thomas Robbs of Phila. was stolen at the house of John Smith, tavern-keeper, at the Sign of the Lamb, about a mile from Phila. on Frankford Rd.; lottery tickets in said pocketbook, if stopped, are to be sent to George Poolley's in Chestnut St. (11 Feb.)

Plantation where Adam Archer formerly lived, in Ridley Twp., Chester Co., commonly called the White Horse Tavern, is to be let by Isaac Gleave on the premises (11 Feb.)

Archibald Cunningham and his wife Alice were executed 8 Feb. at Dover (18 Feb.)

Depositions at Jamaica of Patrick Roney, John Holt and Francis Welsh, passengers on the sloop *Diamond*, of New York, Nathaniel Lawrence commander; the sloop was taken by the Spaniards, whose commander, Don Domingo Santia, forced Roney to sign a document (18 Feb.)

Hugh Roberts intends to remove his ironmongery and tobacco from his house, at the Sign of the Pipe, in Market St., to a store in the back (18 Feb.)

Accounts with the estate of John Atkins, late of Oxford Twp., Phila. Co., dec'd, to be settled with Samuel Wells of Lower Dublin Twp., yeoman, and Benjamin Taylor, of Upper Mackfield Twp., Bucks Co., blacksmith, execs. (18 Feb.)

Cargo of the *Prince William*, Edward Snead master, to be sold on Fishburn's wharf (18 Feb.)

Lewis Gordon, secretary, calls the meeting of the St. Andrews Society (18 Feb.)

Cocoa sold by Thomas White, chocolate-maker, in Front St. (18 Feb.)

Accounts with the estate of David Martin, late of Phila., gent., dec'd, to be settled with John Jenkins, admin. (18 Feb.)

John Correy is removed from the corner of Strawberry Alley to a house next door but one to the Indian King (18 Feb.)

John Beals from London makes all sorts of nets and gives music lessons at his house in Fourth St. (18 Feb.)

Peter Swigard, chocolate grinder, in Market St., opposite the prison, has for sale the time of servants (18 Feb.)

Adv. of Richard Blackford on Reese Meredith's wharf (18 Feb.)

Ann Trotter and Mary Clary have been committed to goal in Boston by Justice Philips for stealing from shops; both are Irish, late from Phila. (25 Feb.)

Capt. Ross of New York has been taken by the Spaniards (25 Feb.)

Mary Clark has been pardoned on condition that she leave the Province of New York (25 Feb.)

Capts. Lyon and Mesnard, both from Phila., have arrived at London (25 Feb.)

William Kerr has been found guilty of counterfeiting and has been sentenced (25 Feb.)

Daniel Miller, Edward Drury and Edward Plaisted have been convicted by the Mayor's Court in Phila. and are to be whipped (25 Feb.)

Aaron Moore, Indian trader, deposes against Francis Fulton, Nehemiah Steen, Charles Poke and Andrew Steen, who seized his property and that of his dec'd father, Benjamin Moore (25 Feb.)

Livestock and household goods to be sold at the plantation where Henry Feagon, dec'd, dwelt, in Passyunk Twp., by Bartholomew Penrose, admin. (25 Feb.)

Plantation in Passyunk Twp. to be let; enquire of Dr. John Kearsley, Andrew Hannis or Bartholomew Penrose (25 Feb.)

Plantation at Point-no-Point for sale; apply to William Callendar in Front St. (25 Feb.)

John Smith at his store in Water St. sells tea, sugar and dry goods (25 Feb.)

Sugar and a bedstead for sale by Samuel Palmer at his house in Race St. (25 Feb.)

Thomas Webber, servant, age c. 21, who served three years as ship-carpenter in the King's Yard at Deptford, runaway from Randle Mitchell & Co.; he lodged with Dennis O'Farrel, porter, in Third St., near the Harp and Crown (25 Feb.)

Thomas Campbell has erected a new bleaching-green near Phila.; the bleaching is to be done in the best manner by Isaac Davenport (25 Feb.)

Thomas Brown has taken up a horse at the plantation where Francis Hickman dwelt in West Caln Twp., Chester Co. (25 Feb.)

David Wells, living in Londonderry Twp., Chester Co., has real estate for sale (25 Feb.)

Accounts with the estate of Alexander Forbes, dec'd, to be settled with Ann Forbes and John Neglee (25 Feb.)

Phila. item gives account by Capt. Marshall of his speaking Capt. Sprout in a sloop of Norfolk, Va., in distress ((3 Mar.)

Name of man to be whipped at Phila. for felony was incorrectly given in last issue as Edward Drury; it should be Edward Ruby (3 Mar.)

William Cunningham, living at the Sign of the Rising Sun in Market St., has two pilot boats for sale (3 Mar.)

For freight or passage to Antigua in the snow Betty and Peggy, William Willock master, at Oswald Peele's wharf, apply to George Okill or said master (3 Mar.)

Plantation in Whiteland Twp., Chester Co., where Peter Osborne, maltster, lately lived, to be sold by James Sellers, John Milhous, etc., owners (3 Mar.)

Horse strayed from James Chattin in Arch St. (3 Mar.)

House in Wilmington, adjoining the late dwelling of Joshua Way, for sale; apply to Edward Dawes in Wilmington or Andrew Jolley in Phila. (3 Mar.)

William Rush in Front St. follows the nailing business (3 Mar.)

Benjamin Noxon, living in Noxontown, has several properties to let (3 Mar.)

Grist mills in Darby Twp., Chester Co., late belonging to John Marshall, dec'd, to be sold by Abraham Marshall (3 Mar.)

Land in Blockley Twp., Phila. Co., belonging to the estate of John Marshall, dec'd, to be sold by Lewis Thomas, Thomas Pearson and Isaac Pearson, execs. (3 Mar.)

Plantation where Robert Field now lives, at Whitehall, West New Jersey, to be let (3 Mar.)

Land in Passyunk Twp. to be let; enquire of Joseph Sims below the drawbridge (3 Mar.)

Mary, wife of Martin Hughes of Ashton, Chester Co., has absconded from her husband; it is said she lately worked in Phila. and keeps company with one James Bryant, a skinner (3 Mar.)

John Corry, Irish servant, age c. 25, runaway from John M'Cullough of Chestnut Level, Lancaster Co. (3 Mar.)

Land in Blockley Twp. for sale; apply to William Couch, who lives on the premises (3 Mar.)

Goods and livestock at Colebrooke-dale Furnace to be sold by John and Thomas Potts, execs. of Thomas Potts, Sr., dec'd (3 Mar.)

Accounts with the estate of John Owen, late of Chester, dec'd, to be settled with George Owen of Phila. and James Rhoads of Marple Twp., Chester Co., execs. (3 Mar.)

John Berry has been executed at Soldier's Delight in Baltimore Co., near the place where he contrived the murder of Mrs. Clark (10 Mar.)

The furnace for making iron that belongs to Mr. Lawson and to others in Baltimore Co. burnt down (10 Mar.)

Two servants of John Howard (son of Gideon) of Frederick Co. have been bitten by mad dogs (10 Mar.)

Capt. George Bell of the brig Grove gives an account of Capt. Judd of the Neptune (10 Mar.)

The Greyhound, Capt. Gracey, has brought in 150 convict servants (10 Mar.)

Phila. items mention Capt. Vass of the ship <u>Catharine</u> and the loss of the ship <u>Halifax</u>, Capt. Adams (10 Mar.)

Plantation in Lower Merion Twp., late the property of William Havard, dec'd, to be sold by Charles Meredith in Phila. (10 Mar.)

The estate of Thomas Griffitts, Esq., dec'd, bounded on the N. by property of Samuel Hasell, Esq., and on the S. by that of Abel James, to be sold by the assignees of Isaac Griffitts (10 Mar.)

Land, belonging to the estate of Job Harvey, late of Darby in Chester Co., dec'd, to be sold at the house of John Scarlet in Robinson Twp., Lancaster Co., by Samuel Bunting and Isaac Pearson, execs. (10 Mar.)

Adv. of Joseph Saunders, who is removed from his store on Reese Meredith's, or Carpenter's wharf, to the house where Israel Pemberton, Sr., lately lived, in Water St., next door to James Pemberton's (10 Mar.)

Plantation in New Britain Twp., Bucks Co., some time in the possession of Archibald Finley, dec'd, to be sold by William Coleman and Francis Richardson, execs. of George Fitzwater, dec'd (10 Mar.)

Horse came to the plantation of John Baricraft of Solesbury Twp., Bucks Co. (10 Mar.)

Accounts with the estate of Joshua Wright, dec'd, to be settled with Thomas Folkes and Samuel Stokes (10 Mar.)

William Hay, Sheriff of Chester Co., will sell at Robert M'Kee's property lately possed by Robert Allen in New-London Twp.; also land in East Nottingham, late belonging to John Frew, taken at the suit of William and David M'Ilvaine; also property in Sadsbury Twp., late belonging to Malcom Hamilton, taken at the suit of Levy and Franks (10 Mar.)

House and lot in Wood St. in the Northern Liberties to be sold by Thomas Tilbury at the house of John Strickers, at the Sign of the Billet in Second St; the land adjoins Preserve Brown's brewhouse (10 Mar.)

George Chambers, Scotch servant, age c. 20, runaway from John Townsend, of East Bradford, Chester Co. (10 Mar.)

John Gregg, undersheriff in Bucks Co., informs John Kelly, of Donnegall Twp., Lancaster Co., that Robert Walker, his servant is in goal in Newtown (10 Mar.)

Andrew Miller, of Lebanon Twp., Lancaster Co., has a fulling mill to rent (10 Mar.)

John Chisholm, in Charles-town, Cecil Co., Md., will teach Latin, English and French at his school (10 Mar.)

Milford, a Negro, age c. 20, born in Antigua, runaway from William Reynolds in Annapolis (10 Mar.)

Real estate in Whiteland Twp., Chester Co., for sale; apply to Richard Thomas, living on the premises (10 Mar.)

John Hamilton, Irish servant, age c. 22, runaway from Henry Caldwell, of Newtown, Chester Co. (10 Mar.)

Christiana mills to be sold; enquire of William Patterson, near Christiana Bridge, Newcastle Co., or Samuel Hazard, in Phila. (10 Mar.)

Christian Groll's shop in York-town was broken into and robbed (17 Mar.)

York-Town item of 2 Mar. recounts the accidental shooting of Mr. Diggs's son by Jacob Kitzmiller, son of Martin Kitzmiller, who was to be arrested at the suit of Mr. Digges (17 Mar,)

On Sat. last the house of Peter Robeson in Whitemarsh burnt to the ground (17 Mar.)

Nails are made and sold by Edward Matthews in Gilbert's Alley, next door to William Rush's shop (17 Mar.)

Thomas Clear, English servant, age c. 18, who came over last fall from London, runaway from William Nicholson of Phila. (17 Mar.)

William Kennedy, English servant, age c. 25, surgeon apothecary, who came over last fall from London, runaway from Levy and Franks (17 Mar.)

Samuel Heap, servant, age c. 25, who calls himself John Fisher and passes for a carpenter, runaway from Stephen Onion in Baltimore Co. (17 Mar.)

James Reily (son of Hugh Reily), this country born, age c. 16, formerly of Bethlehem but now of Amwell, runaway from Samuel Large, of Kingwood, West Jersey (17 Mar.)

Adv. of Andrew Reed, next to the Jersey Ferry in Water St. (17 Mar.)

Samuel M'Call, Sr., in Water St., and Archibald M'Call, below the drawbridge, have for sale wines imported in the ship *Ariana*, Capt. Glentworth (17 Mar.)

Dr. Hugh Matthews intends to leave the province; he has a house in Fourth St. for sale (17 Mar.)

Mary Leech, widow of John Leech, has removed from Coombs's Alley to Market St., next door to Samuel Grisley's; she supplies mourning and also chocolate, coffee, etc. (17 Mar.)

John Stow, brass-founder, has removed from Third St. to the Sign of the Three Bells in Second St., opposite John Lawrence's and near William Whitebread's, at the Sign of the King's Arms (17 Mar.)

Henryhale Graham, deputy clerk, gives notice of a sale at the house late of Charles Conner, dec'd, of land once his, in Aston Twp., Chester Co., by Samuel Neave and Attwood Shute (17 Mar.)

Real estate in and near Bustletown for sale by John Atkins, admin. (17 Mar.)

Household furniture and a lot, bounded on the S. by a lot of John M'Cullough, to be sold by the assignees of Isaac Griffits at his late house in Water St.; to see the furniture, apply to Abel James (17 Mar.)

The drawing of the Trenton Lottery will be at the house of Nathaniel Parker in Bucks Co., being the ferry-house from the Pa. side to Trenton (17 Mar.)

Charles-Town, S,C., item of 22 Feb. describes an encounter with the Spaniards and several British captains, namely Peter Newgar of Boston, Henry Stevenson of Rhode Island, Alexander Belcher of London, David Littlejohn of Leith, Peter Griffin of Bristol and Capt. Troup of New York (24 Mar.)

Mrs. Elizabeth Child of Brookline, Mass., **died 11 Feb. at age** of 86 and has left behind 139 children, grand-children and great-grand-children (24 Mar.)

Plantation in Surinam was destroyed by Negroes, who killed the owner, a Mr. Cordava (24 Mar.)

At Surinam Mr. Crawford, a Scotchman, was killed by a Dutchman in a duel (24 Mar.)

Letter from Kingston, N.J., to Mr. Parker mentions the separation of Daniel Baley and his wife, Elizabeth Waters (24 Mar.)

Phila. items mention Capts. Ash, West, Stamper, Lyon and Shirley (24 Mar.)

Real estate adjoining meadow of Charles Brockden is to be sold at John Ashton's in Moyamensing (24 Mar.)

Cheeses imported in the ship Liverpool, Thomas Stamper master, are sold by William Lightfoot at Edward Pennington's store on Chestnut St. wharf (24 Mar.)

For freight or passage to Antigua in the snow Mary, Humphry Chase master, apply to John Reynell or the master at Lloyd's wharf (24 Mar.)

William Smith, opposite the Three Tuns in Chestnut St., has shop goods for sale (24 Mar.)

Dennis M'Auliff, Irish servant, blacksmith, runaway from Jacob Shoemaker, blacksmith; reward will be paid by Jacob Shoemaker, Jr. (24 Mar.)

Persons inclined to be city watchmen are to apply to any of the six wardens: Philip Syng, Hugh Roberts, Thomas Crosby, Joshua Fisher, Joseph Stretch and Jacob Cooper (24 Mar.)

Heifer came to the plantation of James Brown in Plimouth Twp.; apply to James Wood (24 Mar.)

John Stanaland, stone-cutter, is removed to his free-stone quarry in Roxborough, Phila. Co.; for stone, apply to Thomas Child, stone-cutter, in Fifth St. (24 Mar.)

House near the sugar-house in Phila. to be let by Anthony Wilkinson (24 Mar.)

Accounts with the estate of Miles Strickland, dec'd, to be settled with John Strickland, exec. (24 Mar.)

John Kelly, shoemaker, in Arch St. has Negro boy and girl for sale (24 Mar.)

Plantation and grist-mill, late of Jacob Leech, dec'd, for sale; enquire of the Widow Leech in Arch St. (24 Mar.)

Property in Water St., Borough of Wilmington, to be sold or let by David Bush (24 Mar.)

Charles Dutens, jeweller, has removed from the Widow Green's to John Correy's in Market St. (24 Mar.)

Benjamin Smith, in Amwell, Hunterdon Co., has several properties for sale, one being the plantation where Thomas Seant lives in Hanover Twp., Burlington Co. (24 Mar.)

Two houses on Pool's Hill and Negroes for sale; enquire of Hannah Mifflin, living on the premises, or John Mifflin, Jr., near the drawbridge (24 Mar.)

Capt. Smith reports the death of John Gorham, Esq., commander of an independant company of Rangers in Nova Scotia (2 Apr.)

Capt. Macarty, late master of the brig Lion, of Boston, was rescued by the Speedwell, John Thornton master, from Virginia (2 Apr.)

Capt. Turner reports that Capt. Sherburne of Boston was cast away on 1 Mar. (2 Apr.)

New York item of 23 Mar. gives extract of a letter from Oswego describing the suffering and cannibalism of the following deserters from the fort: John Cadogan and Michael Finn of Capt. Rutherford's Company; William Burchell, drummer; David Ray; Timothy Sullivan; Edward Burns; Corporal William Barry; James Read; Peter Egbergen; Mark Sampson; one John Coulson is also mentioned (2 Apr.)

New York items mention Capt. Bedlow, Myer, Troup, Redfield, John Hewit, William Dodsworth, Lewis and Scot Lawrence (2 Apr.)

Ephraim Moore, a farmer of Donnegall Twp., age c. 104, lately danced at a wedding there (2 Apr.)

Philadelphia items mention Capts. Williams, Falkner, Ritchie and Lyon (2 Apr.)

The following pieces of real estate will be sold by Sheriff Isaac Griffitts at the house of John Biddle in Market St.: two lots in Sassafras St, one bounded by Spencer's lot and that of Anthony Furnis, the other bounded by John Smith's lot, being late the property of Thomas Redman, dec'd; also, in the Northern Liberties, near Mr. **Masters's mill**, a lot, late the property of Thomas Rutter, dec'd, taken at the suit of John Searls; finally, a brewhouse in the Northern Liberties, late belonging to Preserve Brown, Jr., taken at the suit of Preserve Brown, Sr. (2 Apr.)

Persons indebted to Thomas Hoodt are to settle immediately with Rees Meredith, John Kidd or James Trotter, trustees for the creditors of Hoodt (2 Apr.)

Horse strayed or stolen from John Smith, at the head of Northeast, Md. (2 Apr.)

Thomas Jones, age c. 19, English servant, who served some time to plantation business with James Read of York Co., runaway from John Read of York-town; Jones was seen crossing the Sasquehannah at Mr. Anderson's ferry (2 Apr.)

Plantation in Lower Dublin Twp., adjoining land late of Thomas Livezey, near Robert Thomas's mills, late in the possession of Samuel and Robert Worrall, to be sold at the house of Thomas Harper in Frankford (2 Apr.)

Lot in Wicacoa Lane to be let by John Inglis (2 Apr.)

Adv. of Thomas Preston at his store in Water St., next door to Anthony Morris, Jr. (2 Apr.)

Charles Willing will sell the Exchange Plantation in Kent Co. on Delaware, where John Hacket lately lived (2 Apr.)

Dudley Hanley, Irish servant, age c. 20, runaway from Thomas Hastings in Salisbury Twp., Lancaster Co. (2 Apr.)

Cornelius Smith, Irishman, age c. 25, has escaped from the constable of Amity Twp., Phila. Co.; reward will be paid by Isaac Wiseman and Samuel Seely (2 Apr.)

Theophilus Severns, Secretary of the Library Company of Trenton, calls the annual election at the house of William Yard in Trenton (2 Apr.)

John Singleton, of London Britain Twp., Chester Co., has a mare that was left by a servant at the house of Standish Foard at the George in Arch St. (2 Apr.)

Joseph Simmons, Irish servant, age c. 18, who formerly belonged to John Ogburn, carter, in Kensington, runaway from Joseph Hackney of Chester Twp., Burlington Co. (2 Apr.)

Dick, a Negro, age c. 26, chocolate-grinder, lately belonging to Conrad Waltiker, butcher, in Phila., runaway from Vincent Lockerman of Dover (2 Apr.)

Articles of the coach-maker's business to be sold at the shop late belonging to William Harlee in Union St., near William Plumstead's; accounts with said Harlee may be adjusted with John Frazer, Thomas Wells and John Baley (2 Apr.)

Mare and saddles stolen from John Day and Elisha Hughes, of East Nottingham, Chester Co. (2 Apr.)

Land in Water St., adjoining a lot of Joseph Peters, late of the borough of Wilmington, dec'd, to be sold by Thomas Sloss in Wilmington, Newcastle Co. (2 Apr.)

John Cain, Irish servant, age c. 20, runaway from Thomas Martin of Uwchlan Twp., Chester Co. (2 Apr.)

Purse with gold ring in it found by John Cresson in Strawberry Alley (2 Apr.)

Accounts with estate of George Pashashee, dec'd, to be settled with Michael Ege and Michael Deal, execs. (2 Apr.)

Matthias Bondley, Register, gives notice of a meeting of the commissioners of Charles-Town, Md. (2 Apr.)

William Smith, opposite the Three Tuns in Chestnut St., has shop goods for sale (2 Apr.)

Messages of Gov. John Hamilton to the Assembly, with replies, which mention Evan Morgan, Benjamin Franklin, Richard Walker, George Ashbridge, and James and John Wright, a committee to study the paper currency and trade (9 Apr.)

Boston items of 23 and 30 Mar. recount sufferings at sea of Capts. Daniel Smith, one Rocquet, Winslow, Mitchell, Wakefield and Hunnewell (9 Apr.)

New York item mentions Capt. Betagh (9 Apr.)

Thomas Dunn, servant, runaway from Abraham Bonsall, of Darby, Chester Co. (9 Apr.)

Mon. last fire destroyed the stables and 14 horses of Elijah Bond in Trenton (9 Apr.)

Mon. last the White Oak, Capt. Lyon, arrived at Phila. from London (9 Apr.)

New York item of 6 Apr. reports the death on Mon. last of Isabella Morris, widow of the late Gov. Lewis Morris of N.J., in her 80th year (9 Apr.)

William Nixon, who left Ireland with his family and lived in Maxfield Twp., Bucks Co., may hear something to his advantage at the post office (9 Apr.)

Elizabeth, wife of William Ford of Phila., mariner, has eloped from her husband (9 Apr.)

David Hall, at the New-Printing-Office, has for sale books imported in the Beulah, Capt. Ritchie (9 Apr.)

For freight or passage to Barbados in the snow Reynolds, John Hoult commander, apply to Abel James or to the commander on board at Griffitts's wharf (9 Apr.)

Messuage in Chestnut St., late belonging to Moses Hughes, taken at the suit of James Pemberton and others, will be sold at the Widow Jones's (9 Apr,)

Imported goods for sale by Daniel Roberdeau, next door to Capt. John Philips in Water St. (9 Apr.)

Daniel Rundle will hold a weekly auction opposite the place where Forbes and Biddle held one (9 Apr.)

Brewing utensils, late the property of Robert Steel, taken at the suit of Robert Smith, will be sold at the London Brewhouse in Walnut St. (9 Apr.)

For freight or passage to Jamaica in the brigantine Cumberland, John Lownes commander, agree with said commander at White Masley's wharf (9 Apr.)

Dwelling and lot in High St., adjoining lot of Marcus Kuhl, for sale; apply to Hannah Pearson, living on the premises, or Thomas Say, next door to Dr. Graeme's in Second St. (9 Apr.)

John Halthom, tavern-keeper, in Cecil Co., Md., has fraudulently obtained two bonds from Anthony Cadman at Newport (9 Apr.)

Capt. Troup of the ship Indian King, of New York, died at the end of Feb. in Jamaica; charge of the ship was then given to Capt. Smith (16 Apr.)

Capt. Collier, of Lascelles Regt., Commander of H.M.'s Forces in Chignecto, died there at the beginning of March (16 Apr.)

M. La Janquiere, late Intendant-General of New France, has died at an advanced age in Quebec (16 Apr.)

Charles Morris is appointed First Justice of Nova Scotia (16 Apr.)

Phila. item mentions Capts. Eve and Ewing (16 Apr.)

Purse was found at Newtown, Bucks Co.; apply to Sheriff Joseph Hart (16 Apr.)

The following broke out of Lancaster Goal: William Freeborn, William Farra, Edward Boul (since taken), Michael Hunt, Edward Welsh, Patrick Allen and Henry Grimore (a Dutch lad); a reward will be paid by John Clark, sub-sheriff (16 Apr.)

Peter Sonmans has drugs and a Negro wench for sale at his house in Front St. (16 Apr.)

House in Second St., in the tenure of John Stricker, to be sold by Catherine, John and Jacob Naglee, execs. (16 Apr.)

Moses Witten, servant, this country born, age c. 22, runaway from Cornelius Quick, living in the Great Swamp, Hunterdon Co. (16 Apr.)

Corner bank house, fronting three streets, Walnut, Front and Water, where John Stinson now lives, for sale; apply to Anthony Yeldall (16 Apr.)

Walter Dougherty of Chester-Town plans to leave the province (16 Apr.)

Wines for sale by Nathaniel Allen and John Cox in William Masters's store on Market St. wharf (16 Apr.)

William Hall, West Country servant, Thomas M'Harge, Scotch servant, a tailor, and Robert Crocket, Scotch servant, a shoemaker, runaways from William Bell, at the Boatswain and Call, near the drawbridge; reward will be paid by Bell, Hussey and Fitzgerrald and John Jackson (16 Apr.)

Horse strayed or stolen from Marcus Kuhl (16 Apr.)

John Hogan, Irish servant, age c. 18, who stole money that belonged to his master and Mary Foster, runaway from William Foster, of Donnegall Twp., Lancaster Co. (16 Apr.)

Thomas Gordon has a house to let in Walnut St. (16 Apr.)

Patrick Dunn, Irish servant, age c. 30, runaway from John Michener in the Manor of Moreland, Phila. Co. (16 Apr.)

Plantation in Kingwood, Hunterdon Co., West Jersey, late the property of William Emley, dec'd, to be sold; apply to John Emley, Elisha Emley and John Emley, Jr., execs. (16 Apr.)

John Hunt has removed from Black Horse Alley to the Sign of the Ship a Ground, next to Mr. Bard's in Water St., where he keeps public house as usual (16 Apr.)

John Pepperdine, this country born, who goes by the name of John Higgins and went to Phila. last fall with one Fowler, runaway from Philip Croney, living in Queen Anne's Co. Md. (16 Apr.)

Land in Oxford Twp., Phila. Co., for sale; enquire of David Davie on the premises or Griffith Griffith in Bristol (16 Apr.)

Garret M'Daniel, a tall young man, runaway from Joseph Brick (16 Apr.)

Joseph Weaver, English servant, age c. 25, runaway from Walter Comly, of the Manor of Moreland, Phila. Co. (16 Apr.)

Alexander Davidson, age c. 24, has escaped from Chester Goal; reward will be paid by William Hay, sheriff (16 Apr.)

Duncan M'Griger, Scotch **servant,** age c. 19, who was seen crossing the Sasquehannah at Harris's Ferry, runaway from Edward Drugan, living in Kent Co., Md. (16 Apr.)

A sailor named Whitefield (related to the Rev. George Whitefield) belonging to Capt. Spencer was drowned in Patuxent (23 Apr.)

On 17 Mar. a tornado in Calvert Co. blew down the buildings of John Grover's plantation, killed his eldest daughter and a child in her arms and hurt his wife and another child. Also the house of the Widow Hall, near Lower Marlborough, was almost blown down (23 Apr.)

New York item of 20 Apr. mentions the snow William, Capt. Richards, the ship Jolly Toper, Capt. Linsey, and Capt. Ewing (whose ship foundered on a sand bank) (23 Apr.)

On Fri. last John Webster was sentenced to death in Phila. for stealing from the house of William Clemm (23 Apr.)

For freight or passage to Jamaica in the ship Anne, James Gibbon master, agree with John Bell in Water St. or the master at Hamilton's wharf (23 Apr.)

For freight or passage to Jamaica in the snow Polly, apply to Alexander Hamilton or to Robert White, master (23 Apr.)

For freight or passage to Barbados in the brigantine Addison, John M'Pherson commander, apply to Samuel Hazard or John M'Pherson at Arch St. wharf (23 Apr.)

For freight or passage to South Carolina in the schooner Industry, Anthony Whitely commander, at Edward Chew's wharf, apply to James Rennals, Alexander Alexander, or the commander, next door to Capt. Huston on Society Hill (23 Apr.)

Chester mills for sale; apply to John Pennell, living on the premises (23 Apr.)

Jane Bennet is removed from Carter's Alley up Chestnut St, near the State House (23 Apr.)

Daniel Coffey, **Irish** servant, age c. 16, runaway from John Dunnody, of West Nantmell Twp., Chester Co. (23 Apr.)

Hugh **Steward**, apprentice, cooper, age c. 18, runaway from Samuel Hart in Trenton (23 Apr.)

Arthur M'Closky, Irish servant, age c. 25, who has been a servant before, runaway from Robert Powell, in Whiteland, Chester Co. (23 Apr.)

William Adams, overseer in the Alms-house in Phila., has a plantation for sale in the Northern Liberties (23 Apr.)

Accounts with the estate of Asanus Savage, late of Roxburgh Twp., Phila. Co., to be settled with Deliverance Savage and Anthony Newhouse, admins. (23 Apr.)

Several tracts of land to be sold by James M'Manus, living on Tar River in Granvill Co., North Carolina (23 Apr.)

James Durham, age c. 18, who has a brother named Stephen in Phila. and a step-father in Lancaster named Richard Glover, brick-maker, and John Underhill, age c. 23, runaways from Nathaniel Grubb and Anthony Wayn of Willistown, Chester Co.

Andrew Culbertson, servant, age c. 23, runaway from Abner Evans in Chester Co. (23 Apr.)

Horse strayed from Abraham Carpenter, who, with his son, makes cattle bows, etc. for the West Indies, at the Sign of the Duke of Cumberland, on Poole's Hill (23 Apr.)

Adv. of Henry Schleydorn, sugar-baker, in Norris's Alley (23 Apr.)

Persons indebted to the estate of Thomas Sharp, late of Phila., merchant, dec'd, are to pay William Whitebread, exec. to John Thomas, dec'd, who was exec. to Sharp (23 Apr.)

Two Irish servants, John M'Bride and John Foy, runaways from Thomas Ebthorp of Bohemia Manor, Cecil Co., Md. (23 Apr.)

Jane Pain, English servant, age c. 20, runaway from John Roe, in Queen Anne's Co., near Tulley's Neck (23 Apr.)

On 6 Apr. Rev. Mr. Whitefield embarked from Charlestown, S.C., on board Capt. Fell for Cowes (30 Apr.)

John Webster to be executed at Phila. on Sat. next (30 Apr.)

Essays to be sold by James Chattin at the Printing-office in Church Alley (30 Apr.)

Thomas Lawrence, Jr., vendue master, will sell old Jamaica spirit on Lloyd's wharf (30 Apr.)

Judah Foulke, at the house of William Nicholson in Arch St., will sell a lot in the Northern Liberties (30 Apr.)

The sloop Dove, George Buckmaster master, from R.I., now at John Pole's wharf, will be sold at James's Coffee-house (30 Apr.)

Thomas Davis, at the corner house of Mr. Taylor's lot, opposite Mr. Sewell's in **Second** St., dry scowers gentlemen's garments (30 Apr.)

Horse strayed or stolen from pasture on Society Hill; reward offered by William M'Ilvaine (30 Apr.)

Real estate, including messuage where John Hall dwells, late belonging to John Hall, taken at the suit of Charles Reed and others, to be sold at Patrick O'Hanlon's in borough of Bristol (30 Apr.)

James Monk, born in the country, age c. 30, and Samuel Turner, born in Kent, England, age c. 21, together with John Huston, age c. 16, runaways from Michael Earle, living in Fredericktown, Md. (30 Apr.)

Accounts with the estate of Samuel Hasell, Esq., late of Phila., to be adjusted with Alexander Huston, who is removed from Market St. to the house where William Biddle lately lived in Second St. (30 Apr.)

Household furniture to be sold at the late dwelling-house of Sarah Read, next door to Franklin and Hall's printing-office in Second St. (30 Apr.)

Accounts with the estate of Edward Smout, late of the borough of Lancaster, dec'd, to be settled with Elizabeth Smout, Marcus Young and John Hobson, execs. (30 Apr.)

Moses Stanley has indigo and sugar for sale at William Stanley's opposite the Conestogoe Waggon in Market St. (30 Apr.)

Andrew Smith, of Hopewell, Hunterdon Co., West Jersey, has a plantation for sale (30 Apr.)

The following real estate to be sold at the house of John Biddle in Market St.: land in Elbow Lane, late the property of Isaac Coran, taken at the suit of Robert Towers; to be sold at the house of Daniel Pastorious in Germantown: property in Cresham Twp., late the property of Matthias Milan, taken at the suit of Cornelia Bradford; also to be sold land and furniture on the premises in Byberry Twp., late the property of Theodorus Hall, taken at the suit of Robert Thomas (30 Apr.)

On 4 Apr. a son of Col. Blackburn and five other persons were drowned in the Potowmack (7 May)

Annapolis item of 23 Apr. reports that at the Provincial Court William Grady and Thomas Hornbrook were convicted of horse-stealing; Thomas Stanley, James Dilland and Terence Swinney were acquitted of the same charge; Ebenezer Alexander of Talbot Co. was acquitted of the killing of John Campbell; John Broughton was found guilty of picking pockets; James Powell of Somerset Co. was found guilty of burglary (7 May)

Annapolis item of 23 Apr. mentions Capt. James Dobbins from London (7 May)

New York item of 4 May mentions Capts. Deane and Corne and and M'Dowal (7 May)

Prior to his execution John Webster confessed to stealing a teapot from Mr. Clemm and to robbing the store of Mr. Saunders but he denied murdering Mr. Wilson (7 May)

Contributors to the Pennsylvania Hospital chose as managers Joshua Crosby, Hugh Roberts, Israel Pemberton, Jr., John Smith, Benjamin Franklin, Joseph Morris, William Griffitts, Isaac Jones, Samuel Rhodes, Samuel Hazard, John Reynell and Thomas Lawrence, Jr., and as treasurer Charles Norris (7 May)

Thomas Lawrence, Jr., vendue master, is removed from his house in Front St. to the house of Peter Bard in Water St. (7 May)

Henry Wright, whip-maker, has removed from Chestnut St. to Market St., almost opposite the Indian King (7 May)

Accounts with Moses Hewes to be settled with James Pemberton and Samuel Sansom (7 May)

Two tracts of land in Biberry Twp., Phila. Co., in the tenure of John Carver, Jr., and Isaac Carver, to be sold at the house of John Atkins in Busseltown (7 May)

Land on Sassafras St., bounded by Spencer's lot, Anthony Furnis's lot and John Smith's lot, taken at the suit of Samuel Hazard and others, execs., against Ann Redman and others, to be sold at the house of Jeremiah Smith, at the Sign of the Queen of Hungary (7 May)

Messuage and two lots in Germantown, lying next to land of Joseph Marks, next to John Burger's lot, both in the hands of William Stadleman and Abraham Shelleberg, execs. of George Allbrecht, taken at the suit of Sarah Green, to be sold at the house of Daniel Pistorious in Germantown (7 May)

Thomas Lane, servant, country born, age c. 36, shoemaker, runaway from James Belford at Windsor Forge, Carnarven Twp., Lancaster Co. (7 May)

Twenty-one lots of land in Germantown, some fronting the road that leads to Lucken's mill, to be sold at the house of Daniel Mackenet (7 May)

Persons indebted to Richard Sewell, late sheriff, are requested to pay (7 May)

Real estate in Front St. in Newcastle for sale; apply to Isaac Janvier, admin. (7 May)

Plantation in Oxford Twp. for sale; enquire of William Parr, attorney-at-law, in Second St.; accounts with the estate of Samuel Parr, late of Phila., merchant, dec'd, to be settled with William Parr (7 May)

Edward Coffery, Irish servant, age c. 20, runaway from James Hinchman, of West N.J., about 7 miles from Cooper's ferry (7 May)

Mungo Campbell, pewterer from Dublin, has the time of a servant to sell; enquire at Thomas Overend's in Chestnut St. (7 May)

Real estate in the southern bounds of Phila.(one lot, bounded by a lot of John Palmer, opposite Capt. William Spafford's rope-walk, late in the tenure of Charles Barry) to be sold at James's Coffee-house; to view, apply to Edmund Nihell, of Phila., brewer (7 May)

Accounts with the estate of John Rush, late of Lower Dublin Twp., miller, dec'd, to be settled with Wilmot Rush, admin. (7 May)

On 21 Apr. house about 5 miles from Upper Marlborough, belonging to Benedict Calvert, Esq., was burnt to the ground, apparently a case of arson (14 May)

George Wilson (alias Newton or Jones) on 30 Apr. in Annapolis was convicted of the murder of Capt. Smith about 15 months ago (14 May)

Annapolis item of 7 May reports the death of Samuel Ogle, late Gov. of Md., on Sun. last in his 58th year (14 May)

Capts. Nelson and Gifford, both from New York, have arrived at Bristol, and Capt. M'Neal at Newry (14 May)

Fire consumed the bake-house and dwelling of the Widow Prior in Water St. and burnt the upper floor of Mr. Craddock's and the roof of Mr. Saunders's (14 May)

Deposition of the following men of the brigantine Union of Dublin: John Sargeant (master), William Thomson (mate), David Allen (boatswain), James Keoron, Abraham Penny, James M'Cann, James Hillard and John Mailey (mariners); signed by Richard Beckford, secretary; the Union was taken by a Spanish sloop, Francisco Panch commander (14 May)

Irish servants have just arrived from Cork in the snow Hawk of Belfast, John Brown commander (14 May)

Hugh Roberts has moved his shop goods from his house in Market St. to his shop in the back part of the same lot (14 May)

Land in the Northern Liberties, belonging to the estate of Thomas Shute, dec'd, for sale; apply to Joseph Fox or William Davis, execs. (14 May)

Adv. of William Grant at his store in Second St., where Dr. Cadwalader lately lived (14 May)

Accounts with the estate of Charles Cookson, late of Pequay, Lancaster Co., dec'd, to be settled with Elizabeth Cookson, admin. (14 May)

For freight or passage to Madeira and the Canary Islands in the sloop Tenerife, George Ecles commander, apply to commander at Mr. Plumsted's wharf or to Albert Nisbet, next door to the Unicorn in Water St. (14 May)

Lot in Bowman's lane, Germantown, late the property of Emanuel Kolghleser, taken at suit of Benjamin Shoemaker, to be sold at house of Daniel Pastorious in Germantown (14 May)

Two parcels of land in Gwineth Twp., Phila. Co., late property of John Jones, taken at suit of John Trump, to be sold at house of Richard Waln in Whitemarsh (14 May)

Piece of land in Cresham Twp., late property of Matthias Jacobs, taken at suit of Matthias Milan, to be sold at house of Daniel Pastorious in Germantown (14 May)

Brew-house in Wood St. in the Northern Liberties, late property of Preserve Brown, Jr., taken at suit of Preserve Brown, Sr., to be sold at house of John Butler in the Northern Liberties (14 May)

Mill, late the property of John Lasher, taken at the suit of Elias Stine, to be sold at the house of Jonas Steele, Esq., in Reading town (14 May)

Francis Vigoe, Dutch servant, shoemaker, runaway from John Metcalf at Patapsco, Md. (14 May)

Capts. Fones, Johnson, Craige and Comerin have arrived at Boston from London (21 May)

Brig Samuel, Capt. Palmer, bound from St. Christophers for London, was found abandoned at sea (21 May)

New York item of 18 May mentions Capts. Badger and Richards (21 May)

The Sally, Capt. Giddings, has arrived at Newcastle from Bristol with servants (21 May)

Notice by assignees of Elizabeth Woodward, late shopkeeper (21 May)

Mr. Whitehead at the workhouse has for sale the time of a barber and periwig-maker (21 May)

John Parry, Welch servant, runaway from Richard Parker of Phila., tailor (21 May)

Real estate in Phila. for sale by Sarah Wilkinson, widow (21 May)

Twenty acres of wheat and oats on the plantation of Michael Deato in Oxford Twp., taken at suit of James Adams, to be sold at the house of Thomas Harper in Frankford (21 May)

Two horses came to the plantation of Alexander Hunter on the Forks of Delaware (21 May)

Land in Germantown, contiguous to land of Joseph Marks and to lot of John Buzer, opposite to Baltus Reizer's, in the hands of William Stadleman and Abraham Shelleberg, execs. of George Allbrecht, taken at suit of Sarah Green, for sale (21 May)

Servants, just imported in the ship Joseph and Jane, William Wasdale commander, from Liverpool, now at Hamilton's wharf, to be sold by William and David M'Ilvaine (21 May)

Peter Papin de Prefontaine, professor of French, will open a school for ladies at his house next door to Rees Peters's, in Chestnut St. (21 May)

House in Germantown where the late Mr. Benezet lived is to be let; enquire of John Wistar in Market St. (21 May)

Robert Dugall, Scotch servant, who pretends to be a carpenter, runaway from Henry Baker (21 May)

Thomas M'Clurf has not received value for bonds passed to William Davison (21 May)

Plantation in Bristol Twp. for sale; enquire of John Marll, a cooper, living in Second St., between the Sign of Amsterdam and Vine St., or to Jacob Row, living on the premises (21 May)

A colt and gelding have strayed from the plantation of Peter Evans in Upper Merion Twp., Phila. Co.; reward offered by Edward Scull on Chestnut Hill (21 May)

For freight or passage to St. Christophers in the snow Jane, lying at Andrew Hodge's wharf, apply to James Wood, commander (21 May)

Jacob Parrott, born in the West of England, bred in a gentleman's family in Devonshire, age c. 22, runaway from Hugh Jones of Bohemia Manor (21 May)

Time of Dutch servants for sale; enquire of George or Owen Fling in Strawberry Alley (21 May)

Adv. of Samuel Powell, founder, from London, in Second St. (21 May)

Wines, imported in the brig Molly, Capt. Milton, to be sold by Samuel M'Call, Sr., in Water St. (21 May)

Accounts with the estate of John Snowdon, late of Phila., tanner, dec'd, to be settled with Isaac Snowdon in Second St., exec. (21 May)

Accounts with the estate of George Bringhurst, late of Germantown, dec'd, to be settled with Anna Bringhurst, exec.; also several properties to be sold, one in the Northern Liberties, adjoining Reiner Custard's, and another on the road to Robinson's mill, adjoining land of Mr. M'Call (21 May)

Horse, stolen from Bermudian Settlement, Cumberland Co., supposedly by Joseph Henchy, Englishman, who pretends to be a mason, age c. 50; reward will be paid by George Henry, blacksmith, near Newcastle (21 May)

1752

- Joseph Smith, English servant, age c. 35,who pretends to be a barber, seen at John Coughman's, west of Lancaster, runaway from Thomas Harris, of Donegal Twp., Lancaster Co. (21 May)
- New York item of 25 May reports the death on Sat. last of William Bradford, printer, in his 94th year; he came to America upwards of 70 years ago (28 May)
- New York items of 25 May mention Capts. Beauchar, Deane, Corne, Merseyer and Wadham (28 May)
- Map of Phila. will be published and sold by Nicholas Scull, David Hall, George Heap and William Bradford (28 May)
- Josiah Davenport, baker, is removed from his bake-house in Gray's Alley to Kay's Alley; his former house and bake-house are to be let; apply to Mrs. Wayman, widow, in Arch St. (28 May)
- Robert Ragg intends for England (28 May)
- House in tenure of Sarah Read, on Pewter-Platter Alley, bounded by lots of Thomas Byles, Thomas Hines and John Linn and by a lot in tenure of David Hall, to be sold at James's Coffee-house (28 May)
- William Acton, English servant, age c, 35, runaway from Nathan Bewley of Abington Twp. (28 May)
- Capt. Richard Stiles has Negroes for sale; enquire on board the sloop *Sarah*, at Jenkins's wharf, or at the Widow Evans's in Market St. (28 May)
- Land in Gloucester Co. to be sold by Garret and Cornelius Dewees; enquire of Edward Shippen, Esq., in Phila., or John Lad, Esq., in Gloucester, or said Deweeses on the premises (28 May)
- Goods imported in the ship *Carolina*, Capt. Mesnard, from London, to be sold by Donaldson and Fuller at their store in Walnut St. (28 May)
- Patrick Kelly will not honor debts contracted in future by his wife Elizabeth (28 May)
- Messuage in Pewter-Platter Alley, late belonging to John Norwood, dec'd, to be sold at James's Coffee-house by Henry Elves, Peter Bard and James Benezet, auditors (28 May)
- Horse strayed from William Ball, goldsmith, in Front St. (28 May)
- Annapolis items of 7 May relate the death of Samuel Ogle on Tue. last, the death by lightning of John Ray in Prince George's Co. and the loss of a vessel belonging to William Adams, near Kent Island (4 June)
- Mr. Justice Dent in Annapolis pronounced sentence of death on the following: George Wilson for the murder of William Smith, Bazaleel Foster and the Negro Cuffee; on James Powell for burglary; Thomas Hornbrook and William Grindy for horse-stealing; Grindy has been pardoned but must leave the province (4 June)
- John Broughton, pickpocket, was burnt in the hand and sentenced to servitude (4 June)
- Annapolis item of 21 May describes the execution of James Powell, born in Md., age c. 39 (4 June)
- Alexander Lord Colvil was honored by the city of Boston (4 June)
- According to Capt. Leacraft, Capt. Roome was taken by a Spanish pirate (4 June)

Five chiefs of the Catawba Indians arrived in New York in Capt. Mallam from South Carolina (4 June)

In Phila. Francis Huff was found guilty of counterfeiting and sentenced to stand an hour in the pillory and receive twenty-one lashes (4 June)

Glover Hunt, who makes and sells chocolate, has imported sadlary ware for sale at his shop next door to John Mifflin's in Market St. (4 June)

Adv. of Samuel Foster, Jr., dry-scowerer and silk-dyer, at his house in Market St. (4 June)

James Trotter intends for England (4 June)

Sugar and Negro boys and girls to be sold by Alexander Cook at Capt. Morrell's on Society Hill (4 June)

Accounts with estate of Dr. Thomas Shaw, dec'd, to be settled with Samuel and Ann Shaw, execs. (4 June)

Half of a grist-mill and saw-mill and land in Ridley Twp., Chester Co., to be sold by Jacob or Joseph Carter, living near the premises (4 June)

House formerly belonging to Richard Cantwell, Esq., dec'd, a tavern being kept there for years, to be sold by Edward Cantwell at Appoquiminy Landing (4 June)

William Palmer, this country born, age c. 21, who served some time as a weaver, of late driving a team and farming, runaway from Henry Lawrence of Marple, Chester Co. (4 June)

Public school between the branches of Elk River, formerly taught by the Rev. Francis Alison, is now continued under the Rev. Alexander M'Dowell (4 June)

Horse strayed or stolen from Hance Black; reward if brought to Zebulon Hollingsworth, at the head of Elk River in Cecil Co., Md. (4 June)

Frank, a Negro, age c. 26, runaway from Joseph James at Cohansey Bridge, Cumberland Co. (4 June)

Land and houses, formerly the estate of James Verree, dec'd, late of Burlington, joiner, bounded by land of the late Henry Ballinger, for sale; enquire of Rachel Verree, exec., or Ebenezer Large in Burlington (4 June)

Plantation in Bensalem Twp., Bucks Co., for sale; apply to Gilbert Hicks, living on the premises (4 June)

Boston item of 1 June mentions Capts. Maxwell and Hatch and Commodore Townsend (11 June)

New York item of 8 June gives Capt. Robert Troup's account of the wreck of the brig *Hester* (11 June)

Phila. item relates the sufferings of the crew and passengers of the snow *Good Intent*, late of Capt. Watson (11 June)

Notice to winners of Trenton Lottery tickets purchased from William Franklin (11 June)

House where Mrs. Mary Leech now lives, in Market St., for sale; enquire of Thomas Bickley Polgreen at Jonathan Evans's in Front St. (11 June)

William Benning, stay-maker, is removed from Market St. to William Moore's, opposite Mr. Franks's in Front St. (11 June)

Mare came to plantation of Joseph Pearson, of Plumsted Twp., Bucks Co. (11 June)

John Clark, sub-sheriff, gives notice of the escape from Lancaster Goal of James Grady, Irishman (11 June)

Messuage belonging to Ebenezer Tomlinson on the west side of Second St., bounded on the south by John Wilcox, taken in execution, to be sold by Sheriff Samuel Morris (11 June)

Gabriel Nesman, Swede minister, intends for Swedeland (11 June)

Accounts with the estate of Thomas Griffitts, Esq., dec'd, to be settled with Charles Norris, Joseph Fox, Abel James and Joseph Morris (11 June)

The insurance office for shipping and houses is kept by Joseph Saunders at his house in Water St., where Israel Pemberton, Sr., lately lived (11 June)

Horse strayed or stolen out of the pasture of Thomas Tindall in Trenton; John Sharpless offers reward if horse is brought to said Tindall or to Joseph Cobourn in Phila. (11 June)

James Byrn, Irish servant, age c. 17, supposed to have gone to Md. to his father, runaway from John Inglis (11 June)

Accounts with the estate of Enoch Story, late of Phila., hatter, dec'd, and Elizabeth Story, his widow, dec'd, to be settled with Edward Evans or Thomas Say, execs. (11 June)

William Davis, Irish servant, age c. 21, runaway from Joseph Frazier at Timber-Creek, Gloucester Co.; there went with him Mary Kelly, Irish servant, age. c. 20, runaway from Samuel Boggs of Haddonfield, Gloucester Co. (11 June)

The following persons indicted for felony at Williamsburg were brought to trail: Peter M'Guire, from Spotsylvania, acquitted; Henry Todd, from Gloucester, guilty; Thomas Wenwick, from Prince-William, guilty; Robert Milton, from Nansemond, guilty; Hannah Hopkins, from York, guilty, but pardoned; William Hoomes, from King-William, acquitted; Ambrose Bucker, from Culpepper, for murder, acquitted; Hamill Moore, from Essex, for a cheat, guilty; trial of William Flannakin, from Hanover, for rape, was put off until June Court; George Smith and John Shockley, for horse-stealing, were outlawed (18 June)

John Keef, who came to Va. in 1750 in the *Dutchess of Queensbury*, Capt. Dixon, as an indentured servant, has been committed to goal on suspicion of having stolen Dublin bank notes payable to Catherine O'Brian or bearer and signed by Richard Brewer for John Wilcox and John Dawson (18 June)

The ship *Apollo*, Capt. Joseph Richardson, arrived 3 June in Annapolis with servants and transports (18 June)

New York item of 15 June relates the adventures of four men from Goshen, N.Y., namely Robert Thompson, Anthony Car, Silas Houlse and Abraham Finch, who almost straved to death when lost in the woods (18 June)

Richard Brushford, servant, shoemaker, age c. 19, runaway from George Sharswood, shoemaker (18 June)

Hans Knage warns against accepting his bonds from Michael Tise of Tulpehoken (18 June)

Hugh Davis, Irish servant, age c. 22, runaway from John Hamilton of Carnarvon Twp., Lancaster Co. (18 June)

David Jones, Welch servant, age c. 35, runaway from Joshua Humphreys of Merion Twp., Phila. Co. (18 June)

Valentine Arnold, Dutch or German servant, age c. 18, runaway from Owen Jones of Phila., baker (18 June)

1752   183

Horses strayed from Whitemarsh; reward if returned to plantation of Mr. Francis in Whitemarsh or to William Coxe in Phila. (18 June)

Thomas Burn, Irish servant, who pretends to be a shoemaker, runaway from William Wilkins, living at Woodberry Creek in West Jersey (18 June)

Land on Society Hill, bounded by lot of Cadwalader Morgan and lot of Mary Dawson, to be sold at Anthony Whitely's, near the premises, by Mary Durborow, exec. (18 June)

Luke Whalen, Irish servant, age c. 30, miller, runaway from William Herlan, of West Marlborough, Chester Co. (18 June)

Michael Dowd, of Newtown, Bucks Co., warns against accepting bonds in his name from Moses Walker (18 June)

Thomas Campbell, of Phila., mariner, will not pay debts contracted in future by his wife Ann (18 June)

Set of clothier's tools for sale; enquire of Joseph Maule, at the Sign of the Blue Heart in Second St. (18 June)

For freight to Lisbon in the brig *Charming Molly*, Capt. Milton, apply to Samuel M'Call, Sr., or said captain on board at Allen's wharf (18 June)

Charles-town, S.C., item mentions Capt. Bestock (25 June)

Deposition (with introduction by Randle Mitchell), taken before William Till at Newcastle and made by Sylvester Morarty, commander of the schooner *Industry*, and Maurice Nihell, merchant, mentions Archibald M'Lane and Charles Garroway, both of Phila., merchants, and Robert Tatnall and William Power, mariners on said schooner (25 June)

John Atkins, convict servant, born at Bath in England, and Daniel Murphey, Irishman born, convicted at Bristol, who pretends to be a sawyer, runaways from Simon Wilmer and William Steward, of Kent Co., Md.; Atkins is a butcher (25 June)

For freight or passage to Cork in the snow *Good Intent*, John Taylor master, agree with Benjamin and Samuel Shoemaker (25 June)

John Taylor, Irishman, age c. 18, weaver, runaway from John Adamson of Horsham Twp. (25 June)

Several strays came to the plantation of Benjamin Thomas of Montgomery Twp., Phila. Co. (25 June)

Edward Pennington is removed from his store on Israel Pemberton's wharf to one next to Edward Warner's buildings near Arch St. wharf (25 June)

Accounts with the estate of Caspar Wistar, late of Phila., dec'd, to be settled with Catherine Wistar, David Deshlar, Richard Johnston and Richard Wistar, execs. (25 June)

George Monrow, Scotch servant, age c. 30, who can talk Dutch and Irish, runaway from John Brown, of Gloucester Co., West Jersey (25 June)

Messuage in Front St., lately belonging to John Read Carpenter, now in tenure of William M'Ilvaine, bounded by ground of John Baynton and that of Hugh Cardery, taken at the suit of David and William M'Ilvaine, to be sold at James's Coffee-house (25 June)

John Cain, Irish servant, age c. 21, runaway from Thomas Martin in Uwchlan Twp., Chester Co. (25 June)

Thomas Green, living in Germantown Rd., has real estate for sale on Petty's Island, formerly called Furman's Island (25 June)

Thomas Wilson, English servant, age c. 36, runaway from George Gray, brewer, in Phila. (25 June)

Thomas Hunter, only son of Benjamin Hunter, dec'd, intends to sue the heir of Daniel Smith of Burlington for land in West New Jersey that said heir claims (25 June)

Horse strayed or stolen from the commons of Phila.; reward if returned to Richard Hall, near the New-Market, or to John Eiris, at the Stars in Elbow Lane, near the Old Market, a tavern-keeper (25 June)

Mare strayed out of a pasture at Chester; reward if returned to Philip Dunn of Newtown, Chester Co. (25 June)

James Lennox has property to sell at Beaver Creek (25 June)

Mare strayed or stolen from John Blaker, of Northampton in Bucks Co. (25 June)

Francis M'Daniel, age c. 20, is suspected of stealing a horse and clothing from Thomas Lloyd in the Manor of Moreland, Phila. Co. (25 June)

Freight or passage between New York and Phila. - a stage-boat is kept by Patrick Cowan in Burlington; a stage-wagon is kept by Fretwell Wright at the Blue Anchor in Burlington, by John Predmore at Cranberry and James Wilson at Amboy Ferry; stage will proceed to Obadiah Ayrs's, innkeeper at Amboy Ferry, to a stage-passage-boat kept by Matthias Iselstine (25 June)

New York item of 29 June reports that the house of Thomas Perry, watchmaker, on the dock, near the Merchants Coffee-house in New York, was robbed; a suspect, Edward Lee, a young man from Virginia, has been apprehended (2 July)

On Wed. last Michael Renner, at Deer Lick in Bern Twp., accidentally shot and killed John Shutzman (2 July)

Wolfgang Haggan, gunsmith in Reading, accidentally ignited some gunpowder and blew up the house (2 July)

Accounts with the estate of William Edgell, dec'd, to be settled with John Mifflin and Amos Strettell (2 July)

House where Joshua Crosby now dwells, near the State-House, to be let by John Ross (2 July)

Time of a Dutch servant boy to be sold by George Fling or Owen Fling in Strawberry Alley (2 July)

Tenement in St. George's, Newcastle Co., to be sold by Isaac Dushane (2 July)

Real estate in St. George's Hundred, Newcastle Co., for sale; apply to Darby Carty (2 July)

Rafts have gone adrift from Capt. Coultas's ferry on Schuylkill (2 July)

Real estate for sale by Robert Lettis Hooper, living in Trenton (2 July)

Servants imported in the ship Sampson, Capt. May, from Bristol, to be sold by Pole and Howell (2 July)

Jehu, Mulatto slave, age c. 38, runaway from Henry Waggaman in Somerset Co., Md. (2 July)

1752

Boston item of 29 June mentions Capt. Shurtleff (9 July)

The snow **Batchelor**, Capt. Wallace, brought to Phila. the distressed vessel of Capt. Campbell from Edenton, N.C. (9 July)

Two brothers named Black and a son of one of them were struck by lightning in Chester Co. (9 July)

Snuff-boxes and imported hair are sold by Stephen Vilett at Mrs. Trotter's in Front St.; Vilett intends to leave Phila. next month (9 July)

Sugar, rum and indigo for sale by Moses Stanley on Carpenter's wharf (9 July)

Plantation in Bristol Twp., Phila. Co., for sale; enquire of William Stanley in Phila., potter (9 July)

John Anderson, native Irish hired servant, age c. 20, runaway from Anne Little, widow, and Francis Leech in Salisbury Twp., Lancaster Co. (9 July)

Messauage in Oxford Twp., adjacent to land of John Bood, late in the tenure of Samuel Parr, land of Samuel Sansom, land of Joseph King, land of John Ross, land of Thomas Kent, land of John Smith and also about ten acres of wheat and rye, late the property of Michael Deato, all to be sold at the house of Thomas Harper in Frankfort (9 July)

Land on Frankfort Rd., bounded by lands of the estate of William Ball and of George Emlen, taken at suits of Edward Warner and Joseph Jackman, late the property of Daniel Worthington, dec'd, to be sold at the house of Thomas Harper (9 July)

Charles, a Negro, age c. 21, runaway from Bryan Wilkinson, ship-carver (9 July)

Mary Baker, **alias** Rawlins, servant, who speaks Low Dutch, runaway from Andrew M'Gill at the Dugg-hill in Md. (9 July)

Reward offered by John Phillips for the return of a parcel of money lost near the Northern Liberties (9 July)

Thomas Mahar, Irishman, runaway from his bail; reward for his capture will be paid by Thomas Lewis in Pikeland, Chester Co., or Jonathan and John Mifflin, Jr., in Phila. (9 July)

Edward Proger, English servant, tailor, age c. 20, supposed to be on board a vessel bound to Rhode Island, Joseph Hadley commander, runaway from James M'Ilvaine, at Cool Spring, Sussex Co. upon Delaware (9 July)

Property in Walnut St., late belonging to Joseph Gardiner, subject to ground-rent to George House, bounded on east by by lot of Samuel Powell, to be sold at James's Coffee-house (7 July)

Land in Mulberry St., bounded by lots of William Shakleton, William Herd and Rebecca Steel, to be sold by John Wilkinson at the Sign of the George (9 July)

Annapolis item of 25 June reports the arrival there of the ship **Triton**, Capt. Thomas Askew, from London (16 July)

Annapolis item of 2 July reports that on Tue. last the house of Dr. Tootell was struck by lightning (16 July)

Boston item of 6 July reports that on Fri. last at Braintree, Mass., Mr. James Penniman was struck and killed by lightning (16 July)

Tue. last the house of William Sims on Society Hill was broken into and robbed of a watch and money (16 July)

New York item of 13 July reports that at New Brunswick, N.J., on Thu. last the still-house of Mr. Schuyler and a brew-house of Mr. Antil across the river were struck by lightning (16 July)

Letter from Chester, dated 13 July, states that on Thu. last a person using the name of Charles Hamilton, pretending to be a doctor and to have come from Topsham, England, was apprehended and found to be a woman; she now says her name is Charlotte Hamilton and claims to be aged 28 but seems to be 40 (16 July)

Last week at the Mayor's Court in Phila. the following men were convicted of felony: Michael Hogan, Michael Donnelly, Miles Cane and Patrick Tool (16 July)

Joshua North, at Daniel Benezet's, at the corner of Morris's alley in Front St., pays the highest price for genseng root (16 July)

William Peters has marble head-stones, chimney-pieces, etc. to sell; enquire of John Grant, stone-cutter, in Mr. Taylor's alley (16 July)

Silver watch and chain, with maker's name Matt. Skinner, was stolen from the house of William Sims on Society Hill (16 July)

Three servants, Richard Lightborne, convict, West-countryman, age c. 40, Alexander M'Donnell, age c. 22, and James Fitzgerald, age c. 20, both Irish and both sawyers, who call themselves half-brothers, runaways from Samuel Massey and Daniel Surrell, living at Kings-Town, Queen Anne's Co., Md. (16 July)

Michael Burrows, Irish servant, age c. 22, runaway from John Thomas of Vincent Twp., Chester Co. (16 July)

William Ryan, Irish servant, tailor, age c. 24, runaway from Robert M'Felly, living in Strasburg Twp., Lancaster Co. (16 July)

Maxwell M'Cormick, Irish servant, age c. 19, runaway from William Creighton, of Leacock Twp., Lancaster Co.; he ran away some time ago and called himself Jonathan Hawthorn (16 July)

Enoch Haines warns against accepting bonds from Samuel Barnes of Cumberland, N.J. (16 July)

John Mackbride, Irish servant, runaway from Thomas Ebtharp, who lives on Bohemia Manor in Cecil Co. (16 July)

Three plantations on Chestnut Hill in Germantown Twp. for sale; enquire of Derrick Lefferts in New York, Charles Edgar in Phila. or Christian Lehman in Germantown (16 July)

Negro woman for sale; enquire of John Hall in Biberry, Bucks Co., or the Widow Rush in Front St., Phila. (16 July)

Accounts with the estate of Andrew M'Farland, late of Bristol, fuller, dec'd, to be settled with Alexander Graydon, admin.; fulling-mill is to be let; enquire of William Buckley in Bristol (16 July)

Deputy Sheriff Caleb Pusey has in jail in Newcastle the following: Ned, a Negro, who says he belongs to John Elsey, of Summerset Co., Md.; James Coldren and an Irish woman named Ann Cortney; Coldren is from Accamack, Va.; John Phillips, age c. 24 (16 July)

Capt. Jones has arrived at Boston from Halifax (23 July)

According to New York item of 20 July John Ayscough, sheriff, in New York, offers reward for the capture of Edward Lee, age c. 21, who escaped from jail to which he had been committed for the burglary of Mr. Perry's house (23 July)

Second edition of Lewis Evans's map has been published; it is sold by Evans in Arch St., by James Parker, printer, in New York, and Samuel Holland, printer, in Lancaster (23 July)

Servants, imported from Waterford in the snow Three Friends, for sale; apply to Abraham Shelley, commander, or Abel James, merchant (23 July)

Charles Dutens, jeweller, has set up business at the Sign of the Ring and Dove in Market St. (23 July)

Mare strayed or stolen from the plantation of Joseph Garrat in Goshen, Chester Co. (23 July)

Grist-mill, land, cooper's shop and bake-house, about ¼ mile from Germantown, the estate of Caspar Myer, dec'd, to be sold by Henry Shellenberg and Rudolph Surber, execs. (23 July)

Mare came to the tavern called the Plow on Conestogoe Rd.; enquire of Richard Barry (23 July)

Messuage in Third St., bounded by lots of John Naglee, Jacob Bubb and Thomas Hart, late the property of George Miller, taken at the suit of William Allen, Esq., to be sold at the house of John Biddle (23 July)

House in Moyamensing, late the property of Conrad Waltaker, taken at the suit of Mark Kuhl, to be sold at the house of John Biddle (23 July)

Horse strayed or stolen from Daniel Williams (23 July)

Bartholomew Baker gives highest prices for gentian and snake-root; he can be met with at the Sign of the Handsaw in Second St. (23 July)

Two servants, James Wood, age c. 23, smith, and Henry Sherwood, age c. 23, a tailor, runaways from Charles Ridgley of Baltimore Co. (23 July)

Leonard Sommet, Dutch servant, age c. 23, runaway from Jacob Greff, bricklayer, in Second St. (23 July)

Daniel Coffey, Irish servant, age c. 16, runaway from John Dunwody, living in West-Nantmill Twp., Chester Co. (23 July)

William Pennel, English servant, age between 35 and 40, carpenter and joiner, runaway from James Prowell of Vincent Twp., Chester Co. (23 July)

Robert Porter, servant, born in north of Ireland, runaway from David Crawford, of Springfield Twp., Chester Co.; reward will be paid by said Crawford or James Crozier (23 July)

John Rigbee, heir-at-law, has for sale land in Md., late the property of Nathan Rigbee, dec'd, and also a tract of land in York Co., Pa., on the road from John Wright's ferry to York-Town, with the house late the dwelling of Joshua Minehex, dec'd (23 July)

John Sparks, under sentence of death at Williamsburg for the murder of James Fox, escaped, was re-captured and on 3 July was hanged; he acquitted James Trotman of the crime, who was then respited (30 July)

William Charlton, servant, runaway from James Egburts of Thoroughfare Neck, Newcastle Co. (30 July)

1752

On 28 June last the Rev. Hugh Conn, Presbyterian minister, near Bladensburg, Prince George's Co., Md., dropped dead when he was preaching about the suddenness of death (30 July)

Richard Wistar, brass-button-maker and glass supplier, is removed from his late father's house in Market St. to a house higher up (30 July)

Lawrence Hall, Dutch servant, age c. 15, who formerly lived with Mr. Catringer, in Phila., tailor, runaway from James Scott, if Newtown, Chester Co. (30 July)

House and lot in Chestnut St., late the property of Moses Hewes, for sale (30 July)

James Tolford, Irishman, who pretends to be a blacksmith and was committed for passing counterfeit coins, has escaped from David Arnett, goal-keeper of the borough of Elizabeth (30 Juny)

George Okill is removed from his store in Water St. to the house where Thomas Lawrence, Jr., lived, in Front St. (30 July)

Molasses, rum and sugar, imported from Jamaica in the sloop Deborah, Edmund Butler master, to be sold by Capt. John Hussey at his store on Edwards' wharf (30 July)

The reversion of property now in the possession of Nicholas Tucker and his wife, the reversion in fee at their death in Joseph Comely, in the Manor of Moreland, next to land of Joshua Jones, Samuel Swift and Nicholas Tucker, taken at the suit of John Hall, to be sold at the house of John Keen in Smithfield (30 July)

Property in Wicacoa Twp., one lot being bounded by ground of William Wood, Anthony Duchee and wife, George Shiers, dec'd, and Mary Knowles, taken at the suit of Charles Brockden and others, to be sold at the house of John Biddle in Market St. (30 July)

Hendrick Theodorus Tedman, High Dutch servant, runaway from Cornelius Bogart, tavern-keeper in Rariton (30 Juny)

Reward will be paid by Capt. John Leaths or Conyngham and Garner for the capture of William Pride, redemptioner, runaway from the snow Nancy from Waterford; he has been here before, using the name of Brian Doyle and is said to have served time with Archibald Beard of Newcastle Co.; he is supposed to have gone off with Robert Porter, servant to David Crawford of Chester Co. (30 July)

John Hayman, Giles Hayman and Nicholas Hayman (sons of Nicholas Hayman, late of Christiana Bridge, Newcastle Co., dec'd), who left the country some years ago, may claim their share in the estate of John Hayman, of Amsterdam, dec'd; their brother Peter is also entitled to share in the estate (30 July)

John Monrow, of New-Hanover, Burlington Co., N.J., will pay no debts incurred in future by his wife Margaret (30 July)

Grist mill on Whiteclay Creek, adjoining the town of New-Wark, for sale; apply to Edward Miles on the premises (30 July)

Brewing utensils sold by Robert Matthews, brewer, in Second St. (30 July)

John Casey, Irish servant, age c. 40, runaway from Nathaniel Parker of Trenton Ferry (30 July)

Household goods to be sold at late house of Hannah Shiers, near Sign of the Boar's Head in Pewter-Platter Alley (30 July)

Land in Haddonfield, Gloucester Co., late the property of Samuel
Mickle, dec'd, for sale; apply to John Mickle or Daniel Cooper,
execs. (30 July)

For freight or passage to London in the ship Catherine, George
Burnet master, apply to Capt. James Child, who intends for
England in said ship (30 July)

Dudley Hanley, Irish servant, age c. 20, who served part of his
time with James Thompson and James Moore in Newcastle Co.,
runaway from Thomas Hastings of Salisbury Twp., Lancaster Co.
(30 July)

Household goods and boats to be sold by Johanna Smith, admin.
of the estate of Hugh Smith, dec'd, boat-builder (30 July)

Newport, R.I., item of 24 July mentions Capts. Wilcox, Mawds-
ley and Cozens (6 Aug.)

New York items of 3 Aug. mention Capts. Furlow, Man, Jones,
Bowen, Shoals, M'Namara, Griffiths, Bogart, Burr and Giles
(6 Aug.)

Proclamation issued on 4 Aug. by Gov. James Hamilton (also
signed by Secretary Richard Peters) for the apprehension of
three men who on 1 Aug., at the house of Eleanor Davis in
Tredyffrin Twp., killed said Eleanor Davis and John Thomas
and wounded Rachel James (6 Aug.)

Last week Peter Horn was killed by the oversetting of a wagon
on Chestnut Hill (6 Aug.)

On 29 July the house of William Dennis at Springfield in the
Jerseys was robbed (6 Aug.)

Sat. last Gideon Casey from Rhode Island was committed to jail
in Phila. for uttering counterfeit dubloons (6 Aug.)

On Sat. last Morgan Murphys was committed to jail in Phila. for
robbing the houses of Matthias Keen and James Elliot near
Frankfort (6 Aug.)

The report of Richard Perot's being robbed last week in Penn's
Manor is found to be false (6 Aug.)

Samuel Morris seeks votes for election to the office of sheriff
(6 Aug.)

Time of servants, arrived at Newcastle from Ireland in the ship
Sarah and Rebecca, Peter Eaton commander, for sale; apply to
Wallace and Bryan, merchants in Phila. (6 Aug.)

Matthew and Abraham Usher, at the Green Door on Walnut St. wharf,
have linens for sale (6 Aug.)

Mare came to the plantation of Thomas Razwell in Warwick Twp.,
Bucks Co. (6 Aug.)

The house at the Indian King in Germantown to be let; enquire
of Evan Morgan in Phila. (6 Aug.)

Horse strayed or stolen from George Ashbridge in Goshen, Chester Co. (6 Aug.)

Plantation in Duck-Creek Hundred in Kent Co. on Delaware for
sale; enquire of John Pennington, living on the premises (6
Aug.)

House and bake-house in Gray's alley, late belonging to William
Gray, where Josiah Davenport lately lived, to be let; enquire
of Mrs. Weyman in Arch St. (6 Aug.)

Accounts with Robert Rollinson, victualler, to be promptly
settled (6 Aug.)

Brick house where John Hall now dwells, taken at the suit of Charles Reed and others, to be sold at Patrick O'Hanlon's in the borough of Bristol; also to be sold there is the licensed tavern where Lydia White lives, late belonging to Joseph Hough, dec'd, taken at the suit of Septimus Robinson and John Abraham Denormandie, Esqrs.; also property in Mill St., late belonging to Richard Glover, dec'd, taken at the suit of John Abraham Denormandie, admin. of David Murrey, dec'd (6 Aug.)

Boat belonging to Capt. John Hopkins, merchant, has gone adrift out of Carpenter's wharf; reward if returned to said Hopkins or to Robert Murrey (6 Aug.)

John Jebb, convict servant, born in Shropshire, England, age c. 30, shoemaker, and Thomas Robinson, convict servant, born in Yorkshire, Englsnd, age c. 30, and Peter Campbell, born in Ireland, convict servant, all runaways from John Grinef Howard, Daniel Pocock, Sr., and William Watkins, living in the Forks of Gunpowder, Baltimore Co., Md. (6 Aug.)

Horse strayed from Thomas Chestnut of Cecil Co., Md.; reward if returned to owner or Robert Morrison at Wilmington Ferry, wigmaker, or James Huston in Phila. (6 Aug.)

Hugh Davis, Irish servant, age c. 22, runaway a second time from John Hamilton of Carnarven, Lancaster Co. (6 Aug.)

Thomas Minshall warns against property dealings of James Rigbee and mentions such dealings between their fathers, Joshua Minshall, dec'd, and Nathan Rigbee (6 Aug.)

Mare strayed or stolen from George Wyshe of Rockhill Twp. (6 Aug.)

John Lannam, Irish servant, age c. 19 (supposed to be with William Newton), runaway from John Scholdfield in Plumsted Twp., Bucks Co. (6 Aug.)

Jonathan Durell, potter, is removed from Preston's Alley to his new house in Market St., back of the Conestogo Waggon (6 Aug.)

Annapolis item of 23 July reports that lightning struck the houses of Gerard Hopkins, near the head of South River, and of Mr. Homewood, on the north side of Severn, and also the houses of Mr. Inch and of Benedict Calvert, Esq., in Annapolis (13 Aug.)

Annapolis item of 30 July reports the arrival there of the ship Speedwell, Capt. Nicholas Stephenson, from London, with 40 servants (13 Aug.)

Annapolis item of 30 July reports that on Mon. last lightning struck the house of Mrs. Buchanan, widow of Dr. Buchanan, about 3 miles from Baltimore Town, killing the widow's companion, Miss Elizabeth Gill (13 Aug.)

A young man named Spear, age c.21, from Braintree, Mass., was killed by lightning at Swanzey (13 Aug.)

New York item of 10 Aug. reports that a few days ago the only son of Johannes Bradt of Schenectady was accidentally killed (13 Aug.)

New York items of 10 Aug. mention Capts. Haviland, Young, White, and Shourt, Commodore Pye, Gen. Matthews and Gov. Hopton of Nova Scotia (13 Aug.)

Matthias Ambruster, Dutch servant, age c. 36, mason, runaway from Obadiah Elliot, living at the Red Lion, Newcastle Co. (13 Aug.)

Judah Foulke seeks re-election as sheriff (13 Aug.)

John Church and Thomas Stewart, wharf-builders, have dissolved their partnership (13 Aug.)

Goods imported from Jamaica for sale by Edward Ball at his house at the corner of Walnut and Second Sts., where Augustine Hicks lately lived (13 Aug.)

Accounts with the estate of John Wheatley, late of Abington, dec'd, to be settled with James Hunter, exec. (13 Aug.)

Lot in Front St., bounded by the bank lot late of Thomas Furman, to be sold at the house of Jeremiah Smith, the Sign of the Queen of Hungary; apply to Daniel Ostley, next door to Capt. Morrell on Society Hill (13 Aug.)

Salt, imported in the ship Bendall, from Liverpool, for sale by Capt. William Hope or by Conyngham and Gardner, who have the indentures of six servants for sale on board the Rebeccah and Sarah, at Market St. wharf (13 Aug.)

David M'Ilvaine, secretary, calls a meeting of the St. Andrews Society (13 Aug.)

The famous stallion Tister, imported from Ireland, is to be sold by John Rowan on Society Hill (13 Aug.)

For freight or passage to Jamaica on the ship Dursley-Galley, apply to John Rowan, John Erwin or Capt. William Hamilton (13 Aug.)

For freight or passage to Jamaica in the brigantine Mermaid, Oliver Ring Warner master, apply to said master or to Thomas Hatton, near the drawbridge (13 Aug.)

William Henderson, opposite the Indian King in Market St., has three Negroes for sale (13 Aug.)

Tanyard and other real estate for sale by Benjamin Biles in Trenton (13 Aug.)

Mare came to the plantation of Jacob Dilworth in Bristol Twp. (13 Aug.)

Two servants, Robert Scott, age c. 30, and Lot Morrison, age c. 40, runaways from John Kirkpatrick, living in Nottingham Twp., Chester Co. (13 Aug.)

Two servants, Patrick Slevan, Irishman, age c. 25, and David Lewis, this country born of Welsh descent, age c. 18, carpenter, who speaks Dutch, Welsh and English, have broken into houses and run away from David Scott and Samuel Macferran, who live at Conacocheague in Cumberland Co. (13 Aug.)

William Hustler, hired servant, country born, who has a Scotch wife, runaway from William Ward, living at Sassafras Neck in Cecil Co., Md. (13 Aug.)

Merchant mill to be sold at the house of Thomas Lewis at Mingo Mill in New Providence, Phila. Co. (13 Aug.)

Hans Martin Whip, late of Hanover Twp., Lancaster Co., has absconded with a note payable by George Neisley (13 Aug.)

Nicholas Magahey, Irish servant, who has lately been cutting wood at Allen and Turner's works, runaway, with his wife Catherine, from William Woodward in Trenton; reward for his capture will be paid by William Woodward, of Croswicks, or John Allen, of Trenton (13 Aug.)

Williamsburg item of 17 July states that Tom Bell, who for the past 2 years has been a schoolmaster in Hanover, is in town (20 Aug.)

Gov. Gabriel Johnston of North Carolina died 17 July at Edenhouse (20 Aug.)

Boston items of 10 Aug. mention Mr. Hall, Thomas Stannard, Capt. Stevens and Nathaniel Wheelwright (20 Aug.)

New York items mention Capts. Tudor, Seamour, Stevenson and Menzie (20 Aug.)

Thomas Kelly, with a pass from Kent Co., Md., is wanted in connection with the murder of John Thomas and Eleanor Davis (20 Aug.)

The house of Amos Jones on Society Hill was broken open and robbed (20 Aug.)

John Jones has been taken up in Phila. on suspicion of housebreaking (20 Aug.)

Reward offered if lost lap dog is brought to William Dunlap at the New Printing Office (20 Aug.)

For freight or passage to Barbados in the ship Speedwell, Thomas Hogg master, now at Lloyd's wharf, apply to the master or to Thomas Lloyd (20 Aug.)

James M'Clean, servant, tailor, runaway from Thomas Lawson (20 Aug.)

Wax figures on display by Richard Brickell in Front St., next door to the Hand and Shears (20 Aug.)

For freight or passage to Jamaica in the ship Two Brothers, Timothy Coats master, apply to said master at Lloyd's wharf (20 Aug.)

Joseph Robinson, Scotch servant, tailor, runaway from George Hargroves, living near Bush River in Baltimore Co. (20 Aug.)

John M'Claughlin, Irish servant, age c. 35, runaway from Peter Bard and Co., owners of the Holly Iron-works; reward if brought to Peter Bard at Mount Holly, John Abraham Denormandie at Bristol or Morris Morgan in Phila. (20 Aug.)

James M'Guire, Irish servant, age c. 25, currier and tanner, runaway from Roger North of Providence Twp., Phila. Co.; reward if brought to said North or to George Plim in Chestnut St. (20 Aug.)

Accounts with James Wallace or with Wallace and Bryan to be settled immediately, as James Wallace intends to leave the province (20 Aug.)

Real estate in Front St., lately belonging to John Read, carpenter, now in the tenure of William M'Ilvaine, bounded by ground of John Baynton and Hugh Cordery, taken at the suit of William and David M'Ilvaine, to be sold at James's Coffeehouse (20 Aug.)

John Jones of Queen Anne's Co., Md., who has been committed to goal in Phila., has left a horse (supposed to be stolen) at the house of Abraham Carpenter on Pool's Hill (20 Aug.)

Mare stolen from William Green of Trenton (20 Aug.)

Deposition of James Adair of Falls Twp. before John Abraham Denormandie and Alexander Graydon, Justices of Bucks Co., mentions one Perot and Theophilus Severns (a magistrate in Trenton) (20 Aug.)

Adv. of Daniel Roberdeau, next door to Joshua Crosby in Front St. (20 Aug.)

James Kelly, Irish servant, age c. 18, runaway from Thomas Underhill, near the head of North-east, Md. (20 Aug.)

One Owen Sullivan has cut a plate for counterfeiting bills (27 Aug.)

New York item of 24 Aug. mentions Capts. Williams, Talbot, Carr, Jackson and Husk (27 Aug.)

Phila. item mentions Capts. Nimms, Mitchell, Stout, Morrison, Child and Budden (27 Aug.)

Michael Pugh and Isaac Pearson intend to run for the office of sheriff (27 Aug.)

John Swift intends for England (27 Aug.)

Lot near Arch St. wharf to be sold at James's Coffee-house; enquire of Sarah Wilkinson, exec. of Gabriel Wilkinson, dec'd (27 Aug.)

Servants, imported in the brig Deborah, Joseph Stout master, for sale; enquire of William Pyewell and Co. or said master (27 Aug.)

Letters that came by Capt. Child from London, directed to Emanuel Josiah, were taken up yesterday at the Coffee-house but have not been delivered (27 Aug.)

A coach and horses to be let; enquire of Jacob Byarley on Poole's bridge (27 Aug.)

Robert Davis has declined keeping a publick-house and intends to leave Phila. (27 Aug.)

Plantation to be let by Ruth Gorrell, living at John Vining's, about 2 miles below Dover in Kent Co. (27 Aug.)

Land on Blackbird Creek, Newcastle Co., late part of the estate of Thomas Hopkinson, dec'd; apply to Mary Hopkinson, Dr. Thomas Cadwalader, Richard Peters and Charles Willing, execs. (27 Aug.)

Land within a mile of Gloucester, West Jersey, adjoining plantation of William Masters, for sale; enquire of Joseph Hogg, joiner, in Race St., Phila. (27 Aug.)

Mary Moore, Irish woman, with a child of five months, runaway from her bail, Adam Jordan, of Warminster Twp., Bucks Co. (27 Aug.)

Richard Barrett, Irish servant, age between 50 and 60, house-carpenter, and William Silvene, English servant, runaways from John Bordley and Kinvin Wroth, of Chester-town, Md. (27 Aug.)

William Brambel, English servant, age c. 30, butcher, runaway from John Vernor, of Leacock Twp., Lancaster Co. (27 Aug.)

Plantation about 2 miles from Newcastle and 3 from Christine Bridge, late the estate of Samuel Rush, yeoman, dec'd, to be sold by Mary Rush, admin., by order of Richard M'William, clerk of the Orphan's Court (27 Aug.)

Gelding, left by one John M'Daniel at the plantation of David Witherspoon in Newcastle Co. (27 Aug.)

London item of 30 June announces birth of a son on Sun. last to Thomas Penn (14 Sept.)

Boston items of 24 Aug. mention Capts. Brown and Robbins and Gov. Shirley (14 Sept.)

Edward Humphreys is candidate for sheriff of Chester Co. (14 Sept.)

1752

Deposition of Hezekiah Doane, master of the sloop <u>Elizabeth</u>, concerning an attack made by Indians at Canso upon Capt. Elisha Doane (14 Sept.)

New York item of 31 Aug. mentions Capts. Collins, Bryant, White, and Capt. Dun of Phila. (14 Sept.)

The ship <u>Two Brothers</u>, Capt. Arnot, arrived at Phila. from Holland with Palatines, and Capt. Wright at Newcastle from Newry with passengers (14 Sept.)

Ground-rents in Chestnut St. belonging to Richard Murray are to be sold (14 Sept.)

Electrical experiments and lectures by Ebenezer Kinnersley in Arch St. (14 Sept.)

Joseph Lyon, servant, age <u>c</u>. 20, who came over about 2 years ago from Ireland (his shipmate lives at William Peters's over Schuylkill), runaway from Joseph Sinclair of Phila., heel-maker (14 Sept.)

House between Poole's bridge and the sugar-house and also lots in Second St., above Joshua Emlin's, to be let; enquire of Anthony Wilkinson (14 Sept.)

Hinshelwood and Gilmore, breeches-makers from London, have set up business at Zachariah Barr's, at the Horse and Groom in Strawberry Alley (14 Sept.)

Land near Christiana Bridge, late belonging to Samuel Hale, to be sold by David Finney at Newcastle (14 Sept.)

Florence M'Carty, convict servant lad, who was taken out of Trenton Goal and belongs to John Flannagan, of Cecil Co., Md., has escaped from Patrick Hamilton; reward if he is captured and word is sent to James Whitehead, Keeper of the Phila. Workhouse (14 Sept.)

Bonds, given by Jacob Hagie, Elias Schreiber and George Schreiber, were lost out of the house of Anthony Newhouse in Germantown (14 Sept.)

The late dwelling of Archibald Anderson, a noted tavern, in Mill-Creek Hundred, is to be sold (14 Sept.)

Plantation in Lower Maxfield, Bucks Co., about a mile from Thomas Yardley's ferry, for sale; apply to Henry Hough, who lives on the premises (14 Sept.)

Items relating to the Richard Perot affair and also the murder of Eleanor Davis and John Thomas, including a declaration of Ennion Williams of Bristol, a deposition of Patrick O'Hanlon of Bristol, innholder, before Alexander Graydon, J.P., and deposition of James Adair; mentioned are Mr. William Yard of Trenton and two gentlemen (sons of Mr. Morris and Mr. Powell (21 Sept.)

Annapolis item of 27 Aug. states that last week the house of George Tubb in St. Mary's Co., Md., was burnt down (21 Sept.)

Boston item of 13 Aug. states that Capt. Salter and crew, who had been taken by the Indians, have been released (21 Sept.)

Boston items of 13 Aug. mention Capts. Stoddard, Oliver and Murray (21 Sept.)

New York items mention Capts. Asa King, Ames and Gregg (21 Sept.)

Capts. Russell and Coatam have arrived at Phila. with Palatines (21 Sept.)

Phila. item mentions Capts. Appowin and Forrester (21 Sept.)

On 20 Sept. the following persons were sentenced at the Court of Quarter Sessions in Phila.: Morgan Murphy (for felony); Elizabeth Linn, alias Herbert (for felony); William Herbert (for receiving stolen goods); William Reagan (for attempting to rape a girl of 13) (21 Sept.)

Theophilus Grew and Horace Jones will open an evening school at the house of Mr. Atkinson in Second St., opposite to Mr. Boudinot's (21 Sept.)

Frances Riddle, who came about 26 years ago as a servant and supposedly married one Richard Wagstaff, a Leicestershire man, will hear something to her advantage if she is alive and will call at the New Printing Office (21 Sept.)

The dwelling-house and store of John Hamilton, near Little Conewago, York Co., was robbed by his servant, Hugh Matthews, who has run away (21 Sept.)

James Dowdall, servant, labourer, runaway from the ship Friendship, Hugh Wright commander, at William Allen's wharf; reward will be paid by Wallace and Bryan on Market St. wharf (21 Sept.)

Jewelry, lace, toys, etc. for sale by Mrs. Redmond in Chestnut St. (21 Sept.)

Spirits of turpentine, rosin and varnish are distilled by Thomas Milner in Wilmington and sold there by William Jones (21 Sept.)

Michael Kerevan, servant, age c. 18, runaway from William Huse, living in Baltimore Co., near Perkins's ferry (21 Sept.)

Negro woman and boy for sale; apply to John Jones, near the Crooked Billet in the Manor of Moreland, Phila. Co. (21 Sept.)

Mare came to the plantation of John Swift in Lower Dublin Twp., near Robert Thomas's mill (21 Sept.)

Accounts with John Faris are to be settled with John Frazer, John Bailey and Thomas Wells, auditors (21 Sept.)

William Moore, justice, at a Court of General Quarter Sessions for Chester Co, reminds tavern-keepers to take out licenses; notice is signed by Joseph Parker, clerk (21 Sept.)

Land in Chestnut St., part of the estate of Thomas Lacy, dec'd, to be sold at the house of Joseph Cobourn by Mary Britton, admin., and Benjamin Britton (21 Sept.)

John Thompson, servant boy, and Hannah Meldrum, servant girl, runaways from James Edmondston of West Nottingham (21 Sept.)

The snow Hester, Capt. Kitts, of Charles-town, S.C., is taken by the Spaniards (28 Sept.)

Charles-town items mention Capt. Baddley and Don Melchior de Navaretta, late Gov. of St. Augustine (28 Sept.)

New York items of 25 Sept. mention the sloop Diamond, Nathaniel Lawrence master, Capt. Viscount (whose ship was cast away) and Capts. Jaspar, Ritchie, Burger, Mann, Brace, Jones, Bowen and Watson (28 Sept.)

Phila. items mention Capts. Budden, Rogers, Dewar, Leak, Stirling, Abercrombie, Muir, Moore, Dunlap, Kenneway, Ewing, Morrison and Campbell (28 Sept.)

The store of Moses Standley on Carpenter's wharf was broken open and robbed of some sugar loaves (28 Sept.)

Cloak found opposite Lyn-Ford Lardner's in Second St.; apply to Charles Stow (28 Sept.)

Subscriptions for a prospect of the City of Phila. by George Heap are taken at New York by James Parker, at Phila. by Nicholas Scull in Second St. and by the author in Third St. (28 Sept.)

Plantation in Greenwich Twp., Gloucester Co., for sale; apply to James Currie on the premises (28 Sept.)

Household furniture, sadler's tools and saddles to be sold at the late dwelling of Samuel Holt, dec'd; apply to Elizabeth Holt, exec. (28 Sept.)

Plantation in Colebrook-dale, where Thomas Potts, dec'd, formerly lived, to be sold; apply to Thomas Yorke, Magdalen Potts, John Potts or Thomas Potts, execs. (28 Sept.)

For freight or passage to Barbados in the snow <u>Hannah</u>, Joseph Cornish commander, apply to Thomas Gilbert at Jonathan Evans's or said commander at Hamilton's wharf (28 Sept.)

James Smith, servant, age <u>c</u>. 24, shoemaker, runaway from William Moode (28 Sept.)

Richard Brushford, servant, shoemaker, West-country man, runaway from John Reardon, cordwainer (28 Sept.)

John Macguire, Irish servant, turner, runaway from James Terry, near the drawbridge (28 Sept.)

John Malcolm offers reward for recovery of a boat stolen by the three abovementioned runaway servants (28 Sept.)

Land on Sadbrook's Island to be sold by Joseph Brittkirll at James's Coffee-house (28 Sept.)

William Clifton, apprentice, age 17, whose mother, Sarah Clifton, lives in Dorset Co., Md., runaway from William M'Crea of Phila., ship-joiner (28 Sept.)

Land in High St. and utensils belonging to the still-house of John Harrison, late of Phila., merchant, dec'd, to be sold at James's Coffee-house; inventory can be seen at the house of Peter Delage, merchant, in Second St. (28 Sept.)

Land in the Northern Liberties between Coates's run and Masters's mill-dam, rent payable to William Coates, being the estate of John Harrison, dec'd, to be sold at James's Coffee-house (28 Sept.)

Accounts with the estate of John Norwood, late of Phila., merchant, dec'd, to be settled with Peter Bard, Henry Elves and James Benezet, auditors (28 Sept.)

Property in Phila. and a plantation near Wilmington to be sold at the house of William Poleson in the borough of Wilmington by John Staples, attorney for said Poleson (28 Sept.)

Henry Bimpson, English servant, clock-maker, age <u>c</u>. 30, runaway from George Crow of Wilmington (28 Sept.)

James M'Curry, servant, age <u>c</u>. 18, runaway from Philip Davis in Peters's Twp., Cumberland Co. (28 Sept.)

Fulling mill in Darby, late of Job Harvey, dec'd, to be sold by David Davis, fuller, living on the premises (28 Sept.)

John Burk, servant, from Dublin, Ireland, age <u>c</u>. 19, runaway from Joseph Ludlam of Cape May Co. (28 Sept.)

Annapolis item of 21 Sept. reports that George Rosse and Richard Wall, servants to Benjamin Denny, near Choptank Bridge are wanted on suspicion of murder; Mary Perry, their accomplice, has been convicted of robbery (5 Oct.)

On 20 Sept. Capt. Coward passed Annapolis on the way to Petapsco with 250 Palatines, and Capt. Lucas is expected with 250 more (5 Oct.)

H.M.S. Success, Lord Colvill commander, has sailed from Boston for England (5 Oct.)

New York items of 2 Oct. mention Capts. Cosby, Pickeman, Everson, Betagh, Garrison, Richards, Corne, Bryant and Emott and Admiral Knowles (5 Oct.)

Patrick Moore, age c. 15, stood in the pillory in New York for picking pockets and John Brady for stealing deerskins (5 Oct.)

Amos Roberds, one of the leaders of the Jersey rioters, has been committed to jail in Newark by Judge Samuel Nevill (5 Oct.)

Tom Bell, now in Va., proposes to publish an account of his adventures (5 Oct.)

A letter from Charlestown, S.C., dated 26 Aug., mentions Capt. Carr (5 Oct.)

The following persons have been elected to office: (for Phila. Co.) representatives, Isaac Norris, Joseph Trotter, Edward Warner, Hugh Evans, Evan Morgan, Joshua Morris, John Smith, Joseph Stretch; sheriffs, Samuel Morris, Judah Foulke; coroners, Thomas James, William Gray; commissioner, Jacob Duche; assessors, Derrick Keyser, Isaac Jones, Daniel Williams, Robert Thomas, Morris Morris, John Schrock; Mayor of Phila., Benjamin Shoemaker; burgesses, Benjamin Franklin, Hugh Roberts; assessors, Joseph Watkins, Joseph Lownes, Thomas Lightfoot, Jacob Lewis, Jeremiah Warder, Anthony Morris; wardens, Charles Jones, Joseph Richardson - (for Bucks Co.) representatives, Mahlon Kirkbride, Samuel Brown, Richard Walker, Griffith Owen, Abraham Chapman, Joseph Hamton, William Hoge, Derrick Hogeland; sheriffs, William Yardley, Timothy Smith; coroners, Evan Jones, Simon Butler, Jr.; commissioner, Joseph Watson; assessors, Daniel Palmer, Giles Knight, Samuel Foulke, John Kelly, Alexander Brown, William Means - (for Chester Co.) representatives, Joseph Gibbons, Thomas Cummings, Nathaniel Pennock, George Ashbridge, Peter Dicks, Nathaniel Grubb, William Peters, Jacob Howell; sheriffs, Benjamin Davis, Isaac Pearson; coroners, John Kerlin, Joshua Thompson; commissioner, John Fairlamb; assessors, Jeremiah Brown, Phineas Lewis, James Miller, Thomas Pearson, Randle Mellen, Joseph Ashbridge - (for Newcastle Co.) representatives, Jehu Curtis, William Armstrong, Evan Rice, John M'Cooll, James M'Mechan, John Vance; sheriffs, George Monro, William Golden; coroners, Robert Morrison, John Yeates - (for Berks Co.) representative, Moses Starr; sheriffs, Benjamin Lightfoot, Jacob Morgan; coroners, William Boone, Samuel Hoy; commissioners, Evan Price, Samuel Golding, Edward Drury; assessors, Abraham Levan, Nathan Evans, Thomas Wright, Jacob Warren, Joseph Millard, Michael Read (5 Oct.)

Phila. item of 5 Oct. notes the arrival of Capts. Morrison and Mason; Capt. Ochterlony is expected (5 Oct.)

John Jerman's Almanack for 1753 is on sale (5 Oct.)

Mare, formerly the property of Francis Hickman, of Westown, Chester Co., strayed or stolen from Israel Morris, at the house of Joseph Saul, chair- and spinning-wheel-maker in Market St. (5 Oct.)

Trunk lost between Arch St. and Charles Jenkins's ferry (5 Oct.)

John Campbell, Irish servant, formerly servant to Charles Bush, runaway from Capt. John Richey of Phila. (5 Oct.)

Isaac Gingle, convict servant, born in West of England, runaway from John Metcalfe at Patapsco in Md. (5 Oct.)

Seven lots on Society Hill, late the property of William Annis, dec'd, near the land of William Branson and that of Philip Herbert, to be sold at Anthony Whitley's by Abraham Mason and Susannah Lindsay, execs. (5 Oct.)

Time of four English servants to be sold at Parr's wharf (5 Oct.)

Plantation in Weston, Chester Co., for sale; enquire of Joseph James (5 Oct.)

Two plantations in Germantown and also a paper-mill in Wissahickon Creek, late the property of Peter Kock, dec'd, to be sold by order of the heirs of Derrick Lefferts and Anne Kock; apply to Charles Edgar in Phila. or Christopher Lehman in Germantown (5 Oct.)

Real estate near Wilmington for sale by Daniel Few (5 Oct.)

Land in Donnegall Twp. for sale; apply to Lazarus Lawrie, who lives in Market St., opposite the Conestogoe Waggon (5 Oct.)

Land upon Germantown Road, adjoining land of John Logan, Thomas Tilbury, John Bringhurst and John Reily, to be sold at the house of Jacob Naglee by Jacob and John Naglee (5 Oct.)

Newport, R.I., item mentions Capts. John Lance and Butler (12 Oct.)

Boston items of 2 Oct. mention Capts. Nicholls and Elisha Doane (12 Oct.)

Richard Perot has turned out to be almost another Tom Bell (12 Oct.)

New York item of 9 Oct. mentions Capt. Bennet (12 Oct.)

Nathan Smith and Richard Skinner have been committed to jail in Phila. for stealing from Isaac Ashton of Abington Twp. (12 Oct.)

James Talbot and Mary Belly, runaway convict servants belonging to Major Washington on Potomack River in Virginia have been committed to prison in Phila. (12 Oct.)

Phila. item mentions Capts. Bachop and Henderson (12 Oct.)

Will, a Mulatto, age c. 29 (in company with one Thomas Stillwell), runaway from Dr. Thomas Graeme's plantation in Horsham Twp., Phila. Co. (12 Oct.)

Last speech and confession of John Batter, who was executed 14 Aug. at Cecil Court House in Md. He was transported a convict to America and sold for 7 years; there, with Patrick Skully and Dennis Hayes, he broke open Mr. Lunan's store in Charles-Town; other criminals associated with him were John Hart, Patrick Connolly and Ned Burns; he stole various items from a church, Dr. Bradford and Mr. Baxter's people (12 Oct.)

Examination, before Caleb Coupland, of Thomas Kelly, of Kent Co., Md., age c. 22, suspected of murdering John Thomas and Eleanor Davis. Kelly was servant to Patrick Kearns in Kent Co., Md.; he also worked for one John Nemo; Kelly's criminal associates were Bryan Doran, age c. 30, and James Rice (alias Dillon), age c. 27, and Anne Jordan (whom Rice called his wife); Kelly once had a stab wound treated by Dr. Matthews (12 Oct.)

1752 199

The following persons have been elected to office:(for Lancaster Co.) representatives, Arthur Patterson, Calvin Cooper, Peter Worral, James Wright; sheriff, Thomas Smith; coroner, John Dougherty - (for Kent Co.) representatives, Benjamin Chew, John Brinkley, John Vining, Andrew Caldwell, Vincent Lockerman, John Caton; sheriff, John Clayton, Jr.; coroner, French Battelt - (for Sussex Co.) representatives, Jacob Kollock, Ryves Holt, Benjamin Burton, Abraham Wyncoop, John Clowes, David Hall; sheriff, William Shankland; coroner, John Rodney - (for York Co.) representatives, John Wright, David M'Conaughby; sheriff, John Adlum; coroner, Alexander Love - (for Cumberland Co.) representatives, Joseph Armstrong, John Armstrong; sheriff, Ezekiel Dunning; coroner, Tobias Hendricks - (for Northampton Co.) representative, James Burnsides; sheriff, William Craig; coroner, Thomas Wilson; commissioners, Robert Gregg, Peter Traxler, Benjamin Shoemaker; assessors, Frederick Shul, George Custord, John Holder, James Rawiston, John Walker, Joseph Everhart (12 Oct.)

- Mrs. Thomasine Brown, at James Bell's in Second St., next door to Rebecca Steel's, will teach needlework, reading and spelling (12 Oct.)

- Plantation in Tinnekum Twp., now in the tenure of William Mines, late belonging to George Cope, and also property in Springfield Twp., adjoining land of John Dennis and land late of James Boyd, taken at the suit of Walter M'Coole, will be sold at the house of Blass Byers in Rockhill Twp. (12 Oct.)

- Silver watch, maker's name Wall, with new crystal put in by Mr. Stretch, has been lost; reward if returned to David Cowpland (12 Oct.)

- Property in Kent Co., including the late residence of Ebenezer Hathorn, dec'd, to be sold in Dover, Kent Co. upon Delaware, by Benjamin Chew, in behalf of Samuel M'Call, Sr., of Phila. (12 Oct.)

- For freight or passage to Newry in the brigantine *Princess*, Matthew Dresson master, agree with John Hopkins or Matthew and Abraham Usher, at the Green Doors on Walnut St. wharf (12 Oct.)

- William Canise and Thomas Thornton, servants, runaways from David Davis and John Starr, in Charles-town, Chester Co. (12 Oct.)

- Gregg, a Negro, age c. 23, runaway from James Davies, living in Red Lion Hundred, Newcastle Co. (12 Oct.)

- Roger Connor, Irish servant, age c. 18, runaway from John Davis, of Whiteland, Chester Co. (12 Oct.)

- On 23 Sept. Mrs. Mary Davis died at Newton, Mass., in her 115th or 116th year (19 Oct.)

- At Providence, R.I., one Sullivan, an engraver, has been cropped and branded for counterfeiting (19 Oct.)

- At a court held in Worcester, Mass., on the second Tue. of Sept. Jonathan Fairbanks, of Douglass, Mass., was convicted of incest, and Daniel Baily and Mary Rainer, of a place adjoining Sheffield, were convicted of adultery (19 Oct.)

- Boston item of 9 Oct. reports that Ezekiel Wells has been convicted and punished for counterfeiting (19 Oct.)

- On 30 Sept. a coasting vessel, one Macky master, was cast away near Cape Ann (19 Oct.)

New York Items mention Capts. Machet, Innes, M'Clean, Pickeman and Griffiths (19 Oct.)

New York item of 16 Oct. reports that one night last week the boat of Alexander Blair of Brunswick was robbed (19 Oct.)

Capt. Henderson from Londonderry reports in Phila. the death of Sir Peter Warren (19 Oct.)

Capt. Lisle brings news of the death of General Matthews, Gov. of the Leeward Islands (19 Oct.)

Isaac Norris has been chosen Speaker of the Pa. Assembly (19 Oct.)

Tue. last James Rice, alias Dillon, one of the murderers of Eleanor Davis and John Thomas was put into the dungeon (19 Oct.)

Mon. last Capt. Barnes arrived at Phila. with Palatines (19 Oct.)

For freight or passage to South Carolina in the snow Entwistle, John Smith master, now lying at Oswald Peel's wharf, apply to George Okill or the master (19 Oct.)

For freight to Antigua in the brigantine Samuel, Francis Piesley commander, apply to Walter Shea, James and Thomas Harvey, or said commander at Andrew Hodge's wharf (19 Oct.)

Robert Cleary, Irish servant, age c. 22, who has kept a school, runaway from David Evans, of Whiteclay Creek Hundred, Newcastle Co. (19 Oct.)

William Kitchen, English servant, age c. 35, runaway from Alexander Miller, living near Conagogee, Cumberland Co. (19 Oct.)

Time of servants for sale; enquire of Phineas Roberts in Fourth St., opposite the Indian Queen, or of William Gray, opposite the Sign of the Conestogoe Waggon (19 Oct.)

An evening school will be opened by Stephen Vidall and John Jones, assistant in the Academy, in Mr. Vidall's schoolroom (19 Oct.)

Lot in Arch St., next to the lot of the late Anthony Peel, with a tenement where John Mornington lives, for sale; apply to John Mornington on the premises (19 Oct.)

Thomas Robinson, of Naaman's Creek, Newcastle Co., intends for Europe (19 Oct.)

Conrad Klingenmeyer seeks information about his son, Conrad, age c. 14, who came into this country in Oct. of 1751 in the ship Duke of Wirtemberg, Capt. Montpellier; the man who bought the lad lives about 30 miles from Phila. on the Germantown Rd.; news to be sent to David Hall (19 Oct.)

William Blake, servant, tailor and stay-maker, runaway from Jacob Chandler, living in Kingwood, Hunterdon Co., N.J. (19 Oct.)

Real estate at the head of Back Creek in Cecil Co., Md., to be sold by Joseph Wood, living on the premises (19 Oct.)

Land to be sold by the Widow Beezley in Sassafras St.; sale to be held at Standish Ford's, at the Sign of the George, in Second St. (19 Oct.)

Henry Coleman, Irish servant, runaway from John Young, of Lampeter Twp., Lancaster Co. (19 Oct.)

Williamsburg item of 21 Aug. reports that in July a Negro attempted to murder Tunstall Hacke of Northumberland Co., Va. (26 Oct.)

Annapolis item of 28 Sept. reports that Mon. last Mary Perry received sentence of death; also a Negro named Joe received the same penalty for a felony and burglary (26 Oct.)

On 27 Sept. in Md. Terence Connor was sentenced to death for the murder in Aug. last of James Boyles in Frederick Co. (26 Oct.)

Annapolis item of 5 Oct. reports that on Tue. last John Williams, a ferryman, was drowned near Kent Island (26 Oct.)

Annapolis item of 28 Sept. reports the arrival of the ship *Patiance*, Capt. Steel, in Potomack with 260 Palatines (26 Oct.)

Boston items of 16 Oct. mention Capts. Goodwin, Hoskin, Watson, Wooton, Mace, Grainger and Dotton (26 Oct.)

On 7 Oct. a daughter of the Rev. Mr. Rutherford and a daughter of the Rev. Mr. M'Clenachan were drowned near Squam Harbor when the vessel of Capt. Hoskin was wrecked (26 Oct.)

New York item of 23 Oct. mentions Capts. Coale, Wallace, Bruen and Pierce (26 Oct.)

Phila. item of 26 Oct. mentions Capts. Shirley, England, M'Fun, Montpelier and Grove (26 Oct.)

Last week in the Mayor's Court in Phila. Gideon Casey was found guilty of uttering counterfeit dubloons and was fined (26 Oct.)

Sat. last William Kerr stood in the pillory and was whipped for counterfeiting (26 Oct.)

Description of Bryan Doran, age c. 30, sought for the murder of John Thomas and Eleanor Davis (26 Oct.)

Resolution of the Pa. Assembly, signed by William Franklin, the clerk, offering 150 pounds reward for the arrest of the murderers of said Davis and Thomas (26 Oct.)

Anthony Armbruster will teach English and German at a night school in his house in Arch St. (26 Oct.)

Edward Shippen has land for sale in Moyamensing (26 Oct.)

A book about Richard Davies, reprinted in Phila., will be sold by James Chattin, next door to the Pipe in Church Alley (26 Oct.)

For freight or passage to Rotterdam in the ship *Amelia*, Charles Ross master, apply to Alexander Ray on Hamilton's wharf (26 Oct.)

A silver tablespoon, marked M.L., the maker's name P. David, has been lost (26 Oct.)

The five following sailors have run away from the snow *Katie*, Theophilus Barnes master: Thomas Lane, age c. 25; John Cook, age c. 24; Joseph Cardman, age c. 20; John White, age c. 25; John Harris, age c. 26; reward will be paid by Theophilus Barnes or George Okill (26 Oct.)

Messuage in Wicacoa Twp., bounded by Swanson's land, ground of John Tilla, land of Dorothy Gibbs and Mifflin's ground, to be sold at James's Coffee-house (26 Oct.)

Quarter of Mount-Holly Iron-works to be sold by John Abraham Denormandie, living in Bristol, Bucks Co.; inventory to be seen at his house or at Andrew Reed's in Phila. (26 Oct.)

Land and wharf in Wicacoa, bounded by land of George Allen (late of John Tilla) and ground of George Mifflin, late the property of George Allen, taken at the suit of George Mifflin, to be sold at James's Coffee-house (26 Oct.)

Messuage in Fifth St., bounded by lot of William Ireson, lot of Matthew Cummings and messuage of Edward Shippen, late the property of James Wragg, taken at the suit of James Murgatroyd, to be sold at the house of William Biddle (26 Oct.)

House where Alexander Barclay lately lived is to be sold by Samuel Morris (26 Oct.)

Plantation in Colebrook Dale for sale by John Potts, living at Potts-grove in M'Call's Manor (26 Oct.)

Real estate in the Great Valley in Tredyffryn Twp., late the property of Thomas Jones, dec'd, to be sold by Lewis Jones; for terms apply to William Griffitts, merchant, in Second St. (26 Oct.)

John Cocklin, English servant, age c. 30, runaway from John Hamilton of Londonderry Twp., Chester Co. (26 Oct.)

Francis Didger, Dutchman, age c. 36, a wigmaker, who lived with Frederick Holstein, sadler, in Upper Merion, came to James Bell's shop in Phila. and in the name of the Rev. William Currie took away valuable locks and hinges; reward for Didger's capture is offered by Holstein (26 Oct.)

Richard Edwards, Welch servant, age c. 18, who came into the country last fall, runaway from John Williams, at Blakeley's Creek in Bucks Co.; Williams formerly kept the Falls Ferry, commonly called the Trenton Ferry (26 Oct.)

Margaret Rogers, apprentice, this country born, age c. 14, who is thought to be gone to Newport in Christine, where her mother lives with John Martin, cooper, runaway from Alice Dodd of Phila. (26 Oct.)

Samuel Alison, Irish servant, age c. 30, runaway from Joseph Dixon, of New Garden, Chester Co. (26 Oct.)

For freight or passage to Belfast in the snow Hibernia, William Wallace commander, apply to Peacock Bigger in Market St. or said commander at Fishbourne's wharf (26 Oct.)

Boston item of 23 Oct. reports the death there on Sun. last of Dr. William Douglass, prominent physician (2 Nov.)

On 22 Oct. Capt. Hutchinson arrived at Boston from London (2 Nov.)

New York items of 30 Oct. mention Capts. Greenal, Miller, Dickson, Amory, Bryant, Garrison, Richards, Griffith, Davis, Tingley, Spofford and Cornee (2 Nov.)

On the basis of the confession of James Rice, alias Dillon, and the evidence of Hugh M'Guire, Patrick Karin, Philip M'Dermot and Margaret his wife have been committed to goal in Chester Town as accessories in the murder of John Thomas and Eleanor Davis (2 Nov.)

The ship Phenix, Capt. Spurrier, has arrived at Phila. from Holland with 600 Palatines, whose freights are to be paid to Pole and Howell (2 Nov.)

Horse and mare, sold last June by James Rice, alias Dillon, to Patrick Karin and supposed stolen, are in the custody of Simon Wilmore of George-Town, Kent Co., Md. (2 Nov.)

John Monrow retracts his July adv. concerning his wife's debts (2 Nov.)

Job Walker retracts his Feb. adv. concerning his wife Hannah's debts (2 Nov.)

John Clare still teaches mathematical sciences, next door to William Attwood's in Front St. (2 Nov.)

Hoses belonging to Jacob Duche broke out of pasture on the west side of Moyamensing Rd., neat Phila. (2 Nov.)

For freight or passage to Dublin in the new ship Molly, now at Mifflin's wharf, apply to Samuel Hastings, Thomas Walker or Capt. William Blair (2 Nov.)

Managers of the lottery for finishing the steeple of Christ Church and purchasing a ring of bells are Thomas Lawrence, Abraham Taylor, Benjamin Franklin, Charles Stedman, John Kearsley, Henry Harrison, James Humphreys, Joseph Redman, Evan Morgan, Thomas Leech, Henry Elves, John Baynton and Jacob Duchee (2 Nov.)

Real estate in Pewter-Platter Alley, bounded by house and lot of Thomas Byles, lot of Thomas Hyne, lot of Jacob Lynn and house and lot of Robert Grace, late the estate of Sarah Read, to be sold at James's Coffee-house (2 Nov.)

Real estate in Oxford Twp., Phila. Co., on road leading to Jacob Hall's, adjoining lands of Robert Walln and Samuel Sansom, late belonging to William Finney, taken at the suit of Richard Finney against John Bringhurst and others, execs., to be sold on the premises (2 Nov.)

Two lots, one in High St., the other in the Northern Liberties, taken at the suit of Israel Pemberton, Jr., against the admin. of Robert Greenway, to be sold at James's Coffee-house (2 Nov.)

Tract of land on branches of Blackbird Creek, part of the estate of Thomas Hopkinson, late of Phila., dec'd, to be sold; apply to Mary Hopkinson, Dr. Thomas Cadwalader, Richard Peters or Charles Willing of Phila. (2 Nov.)

Tract of land in Caln Twp., Chester Co., to be sold by John Swift, one of the execs. of Abraham Claypoole, dec'd, at the house of one Morgan, at the Sign of the Plow, on the little Lancaster Road (2 Nov.)

Six hundred acres in Warwick, Bucks Co., to be sold by John Swift, one of the execs. of Abraham Claypoole, dec'd, at the house of David Reese, at the Billet, on Old York Road (2 Nov.)

Real estate in Bucks Co. for sale; enquire of Garret Vansant (2 Nov.)

Tenement and lot in Sassafras St. to be sold by Aquila Jones (2 Nov.)

Land in Warminster Twp., bounded by land of William Noble, Abel Noble, Thomas Dungon and James Craven, late belonging to the estate of Abel Noble, dec'd, taken at the suit of Peter Turner, merchant, in Phila., to be sold at the tavern of Evan Jones in Northampton Twp., Bucks Co. (2 Nov.)

Horse has come to the house of Francis Campbell, tavern-keeper, in Shippensburgh, Cumberland Co. (2 Nov.)

Lot in Newtown, Bucks Co., for sale; apply to John Twining, who lives in Bussel-Town, Phila. Co., or John Twining, living in New-Town, Bucks Co. (2 Nov.)

Thomas Clark, Irish servant, age c. 18, runaway from Henry Chalfant, of West Marlborough, Chester Co. (2 Nov.)

Boston item of 30 Oct. reports the conviction of two counterfeiters, John and Jonathan Webber, brothers, from Wells in York Co. (9 Nov.)

Capt. Henry Cregier arrived 5 Nov. at New York from Charles-Town, S.C., and brought account of havoc wrought by a hurricane on 15 Sept.; mention is made of Capts. John Bulman, John Badley, John Babb, Walker, Richard Manley, Simmons, William James, John Tuppen, Robert Johns, George Gore, Alex. M'Gillivray and Amos Minot; also of Mr. Wright, Col. Heron, Mr. Scott, David Brown, Mr. Raper, Dr. Caw, Mr. Edwards, Thomas Smith, Mr. Price, Mr. Beresford, Thomas Elliot, Mr. Motte, Mr. Eveleigh and John Matthews (9 Nov.)

New York item of 6 Nov. mentions Capts, Coon, Corne, Bryant, Amory and Viner Leycraft and also Robert Hunter Morris, Chief Justice of the Jerseys (9 Nov.)

Phila. item mentions Capts. Dewar, Stirling, Leak, Ragg, Parish and Pitcairn (9 Nov.)

At court in Lancaster on 26 Oct. Hamilton Carson was sentenced to death for burglary, and James M'Connell and his wife Esther were convicted as accomplices after the fact to a burglary committed by John Webster (9 Nov.)

At a court in York Co. on 30 Oct. Hugh Matthews was convicted of taking a mare from John Carahan on the highway; Martin and Jacob Kitzmiller were tried for the murder of Dudly Diggs; Martin was acquitted; Jacob was found guilty of manslaughter (9 Nov.)

Household furniture to be sold at the house of Capt. William Dowell in Front St. (9 Nov.)

A large silver spoon, marked IxM, silversmith's stamp W.V., has been lost or stolen (9 Nov.)

Time of Irish servant woman for sale; enquire of John Doyle, blockmaker, in Water St. (9 Nov.)

Joseph Miller, consul in Barcelona, gives notice of the disappearance of John Padmore, master of the sloop William and Mary, age c. 35; Padmore was transporting sum of money (9 Nov.)

Land in Marcus Hook in Chichester, Chester Co., bounded by lots of Robert Moulder and George Chapman, is for sale; apply to William Clayton in Chichester (9 Nov.)

Horse came to the plantation of John Foulke in Richland, Bucks Co. (9 Nov.)

Pocketbook belonging to William Grant, of Phila., has been lost; reward if brought to Charles Stow in Market St. (9 Nov.)

Conrad Waltaker, of Phila., butcher, will pay no debts contracted in future by his wife Margaret (9 Nov.)

Adv. of Edward Dowers, who is removed from his house in Water St. to a house in Carter's Alley (9 Nov.)

Imported goods are sold by M'Janet and M'Murphy at their store in Water St., opposite Messers. Pole and Howell (9 Nov.)

Various properties to be sold by Thomas Green, living on Germantown Road; enquire at Charles Brogden's office or at Standish Ford's, at the Sign of the George Tavern in Second St. (9 Nov.)

House at the Indian King in Germantown and house and lot in Bowman's Lane, belonging to the estate of Benjamin Morgan, dec'd; enquire of Evan Morgan in Water St. (9 Nov.)

Frederick Fisher, Dutch servant, age c. 17 or 18, runaway from Joseph Sears of the Northern Liberties (9 Nov.)

Horse (formerly stolen by Bryan Doran, one of the murderers of John Thomas and Eleanor Davis) has now been stolen from Henry Kendrick, of Strasburgh Twp., Lancaster Co. (9 Nov.)

William Taylor, English servant, runaway from John Carman of Northampton, Burlington Co. (9 Nov.)

Thomas Elliot, late tavern-keeper at the Sign of the Red-lion in Market St., Charles-town, Cecil Co., Md. is now moved to the Sign of the Indian King in said street (9 Nov.)

Horse has been stolen from the plantation of Henry Lewis, of Hilton, Bucks Co. (9 Nov.)

Land in Uwchland, Chester Co., adjoining lands of David Owen and John Evans; also a tract, adjoining lands of Joseph Phipps, Jr., and of Benjamin Jackson; also another tract in the same twp., late the property of Peter Ashton and Arnold Pendor, taken at the suit of Isaac Greenleafe and Mordecai Yarnall, all to be sold at the house of John Vaughan in Uwchland (9 Nov.)

James Jackson, Scotch servant, age c. 21, runaway from James Moore, in West Sadsbury, Lancaster Co. (9 Nov.)

Charles-Town, S.C., items mention Capts. Bulman, Feartlough, Timothy M'Daniel, Moreland, Edward Carleton, Parsons, Copythorne, Connor, Robert Rankin, Dorrington, Tucker, Gore, Babb, M'Gillivray, Baker, Robert Jones, Arthur Tran, Rodger, John Mills, Waldron, Isaac Colcock, Tedar, Parsons, M'Daniel, Boyd, Hutchins, Spencer, Philip White and Harvie; also Messers Rattray, Mortimore, Child, Cattell, Purry and Beresford (16 Nov.)

Halifax items mention Capt. Piggot and the Hon. Edward Cornwallis (16 Nov.)

New York item mentions Capts. Herring and Adams (16 Nov.)

Mon. last Daniel Hurley received sentence of death in Phila. for the murder of James Clarke (16 Nov.)

Phila. items mention Capts. Stirling, Dewar and Budden (16 Nov.)

David M'Ilvaine, secretary, announces meeting of the St. Andrew Society to be held at William Biddle's, at the Bull's Head in Market St. (16 Nov.)

Horse has strayed from Thomas Hope, of Sadsbury Twp., Chester Co. (16 Nov.)

Mare has been stolen (supposedly by John Jones) from Morris Gwin of Abington (16 Nov.)

For freight or passage to Newport, R.I., in the sloop *Polly*, Eleazer Nicholls master, apply to said master at Market St. wharf (16 Nov.)

For freight or passage to Londonderry in the *City of Derry*, Archibald M'Ilwain commander, apply to Samuel Corsan, merchant, or to said commander (16 Nov.)

Nathaniel Parr will sell all his shop goods at his house in Market St. (16 Nov.)

John M'Laughlin, Irish servant, runaway from Joseph Alison, of New-London, Chester Co. (16 Nov.)

Tavern called the Bell, in Tredyffrin Twp., Chester Co., for sale; apply to Thomas M'Kean (16 Nov.)

Tracts of land in the Great Valley in Tredyffrin Twp., late the property of Thomas James, dec'd, for sale; apply to Lewis James on the premises (16 Nov.)

Christopher Marshall, at the Golden Ball in Chestnut St., sells medicines and paints (16 Nov.)

Two servants, James Boyle and John Clarke, runaways from Constable Samuel Pritchard, near the head of Opecken, Va. (16 Nov.)

Item of 20 Oct. from Williamsburgh, Va., gives an account of attack made by party of French and Indians (23 Nov.)

New York item of 20 Nov. gives Capt. Hill's account of a fight **between Spaniards and ships of Capts. Hall and Crowel; also** of attack made by Spaniards on Capt. Arnold, in course of which Don Palmo, the Spanish commandant, was killed; Capt. Hill gives news of Capts. Fones, Ruff, Winthrop, Sluman, Waynman, Adams and Johnson (23 Nov.)

New York item of 20 Nov. mentions Capts. Richards, Miller and Bryant (23 Nov.)

Charles-Town, S,C., items mention Capts. Davis, Mills, Colcock, Boyd, Harvie, Nicholson, Amos Minot, Holwell, Charles Cookson and William James (23 Nov.)

Newbern, N.C., item of 20 Oct. reports that on Mon. last the following were executed: William Jillet and David Johnston, both for coining; David Smith, *alias* Griffith, for robbery; Patrick Moore had turned evidence against the coiners; Peter Matthews, at whose house the coiners were taken, was acquitted (23 Nov.)

Phila. items mention Capts. Lusk, Stevens and Honnor (23 Nov.)

Account of fire on Tue. last at the seat of Joseph Turner, Esq., in Moyamensing (23 Nov.)

Mon. next a court will be held at Chester for the trial of James Rice and Thomas Kelly for the murder of John Thomas and Eleanor Davis (23 Nov.)

Wed. next Daniel Hurley is to be executed (23 Nov.)

Negro woman for sale by James Whitehead at the Work-house (23 Nov.)

Several Negroes to be sold by Allen and Turner at Joseph Turner's wharf (23 Nov.)

William Peshley and William Crossman, seamen, runaways from the ship *Whitehill*, Gurnay Wall master; reward will be paid by Andrew Oswald or David Hall (23 Nov.)

Yawl has been taken from Thomas Lawrence's wharf by some Jersey people; reward will be paid by Andrew Oswald or Joseph Warner, boat-builder (23 Nov.)

Samuel Maccoy, age c. 19, apprentice tailor (son of John Maccoy, at the Great Swamp, Bucks Co.), runaway from Michael Hutchinson, tailor, in Lower Makefield, Bucks Co. (23 Nov.)

Several strays have come to the plantation of William Boggs in Warwick Twp., Bucks Co. (23 Nov.)

James Dowdall, servant, runaway from Adam Hoope, of Antrim Twp., Cumberland Co. (23 Nov.)

The following sailors are runaways from the brigantine Molly, in Hampton River, Va.: David Aiken, Scotchman, age c. 35; John Evans, Welshman; Robert Ford; they took a boat whose canvas has the maker's name on it, Robert Ouchterlony and Co., Montrose; reward will be paid by James Graham (23 Nov.)

Green and Whitlock, who keep store at Capt. Brown's on Market St. wharf, intend to break up store; William Freeman, at the same store, intends to leave Phila. (23 Nov.)

Andrew Reed is removed to the house of Peter Bard in Water St., where Thomas Lawrence, Jr., lately lived (23 Nov.)

Salt and dry goods, imported in the snow George, Joseph Arthur commander, are sold by Wallace and Bryan on Market St. wharf; they also sell limes, imported from Barbados in the brigantine Greyhound, Capt. Falkner (23 Nov.)

John Gardner, Irish servant, age c. 18, runaway from the sloop Endeavour, James Nicholls master; reward if brought to said master or to Samuel and Thomas Smith (23 Nov.)

For passage to Cowes in the ship Queen of Denmark, George Parish commander, apply to Henry Keppley or said commander (23 Nov.)

Horses stolen from Thomas Holloway, of Phila., who offers a reward (23 Nov.)

Plantation in Lower Merion Twp., Phila. Co., near the Gulph mill and mill of John Roberts, for sale; apply to John Cuthbert of Whiteland or Michael Wills, shoemaker, of Tredyffrin Twp., execs. to the estate of Michael Wills, dec'd, or to Thomas Wills, living on the premises (23 Nov.)

Williamsburgh, Va., item of 19 Oct. reports that on Mon. and Tue. last the following were tried there: Henry Bates, from King William, for felony, guilty; Moses Thomson, from Frederick, for horse-stealing, guilty, death; Thomas Kelly, from Fairfax, for shooting Thomas Davis (a robber and horse-thief), acquitted (30 Nov.)

Annapolis item of 26 Oct. reports that on Fri. last Terence Connor, born in Ireland, was executed at Annapolis for the murder of James Boyles in Frederick Co. (30 Nov.)

Boston item of 20 Nov. reports that some seamen were attacked there by some boys and young men; one seaman, John Crabb, was beaten to death; one Chubb (a white boy) and a Negro have been committed to goal (30 Nov.)

Boston item of 20 Nov. reports that on Thu. last Nathaniel Lloyd, from Long Island, was drowned when going from Boston to his brother's on Long Island (30 Nov.)

Newport, R.I., item of 16 Nov. reports that a sloop belonging to Boston, one Gordon master, was cast away at Cormorant Rock; all perished save two foremast men, Emerson and Miller (30 Nov.)

Capts. Bryant and Garrison have arrived at New York; with Capt. Bryant came John Penn, grandson of the late William Penn (30 Nov.)

Richard Roach and John Kennedy are in goal in New York for picking the pocket of Theophilus Elsworth (30 Nov.)

John Tharp, sea-faring man, has been committed to goal in New York for stealing (30 Nov.)

On 29 Nov. Daniel Hurley was executed in Phila. (30 Nov.)

New York item of 27 Nov. mentions Capts. Gordon and Reese (30 Nov.)

New York item of 27 Nov. reports that on Tue. last William Bishop, convicted of stealing linen, was whipped round the city (30 Nov.)

Phila. item mentions Capts. Lake and Dewar (30 Nov.)

Mon. last a court at Chester found Thomas Kelly and James Rice guilty of the murder of John Thomas and Eleanor Davis (30 Nov.)

A clerk seeks employment; he can be heard of at Paul Isaac Voto's office in Second St. (30 Nov.)

Real estate, including a sixteenth part of Durham Iron-works; land below Francis Garrigue's Ferry; a water lot near Woodrope's and Attwood's wharf; a city lot, with a cooper's shop thereon, now in the tenure of Joseph Brown, between Mr. Jackson's and Mr. Claypoole's lot in Walnut St.; a lot near Charles Willing's in Third St.; tracts of land in Gloucester Co., West N.J., belonging to Col. Alford in Boston, all for sale by Edward Shippen (30 Nov.)

Mare strayed from Christine Ferry; reward if brought to Joseph Scull at Ashton's Ferry (30 Nov.)

Haberdashery, cutlery, pewter for sale by Thomas Davis at his house in Market St. where Hugh Roberts lately lived (30 Nov.)

John Baker has on display at the Ship-a-ground in Water St. a new steeple and set of bells (30 Nov.)

Robert Croxall at the Baltimore Iron-works offers a reward for the capture of two convict runaway servants, imported this fall in the ship **Biddeford**, John Knill commander: John Platt, born in Staffordshire, age c. 24, belonging to Dr. Charles Carroll, and John Wakefield, age c. 35 or 40, an Englishman, belonging to the Widow Buchanan (30 Nov.)

William Moody, English servant, tailor, runaway from Joseph Duer, of Makefield, Bucks Co. (30 Nov.)

Mare, strayed or stolen from the pasture of Joseph Bell, a tavern-keeper in Third St., at the Harp and Crown; reward if brought to said Bell or to James Perry, living at Doe-run (30 Nov.)

Joseph Joslyne, servant, plaisterer and painter, runaway from Henry Feddemon, of Queen Anne's Co., Md.; Joslyne stole a horse from John Carr, of Talbot Co. (30 Nov.)

Accounts with estate of Samuel Parr, late of Phila., dec'd, to be settled with William Parr, attorney-at-law in Second St. (30 Nov.)

Examination of James Rice (<u>alias</u> Dillon), labourer, before Chief Justice William Allen: Rice states that last spring Bryan Doran suggested that they rob a wealthy tinker in Amwell; later he met Doran at Maybury's Iron-works; Rice, Doran and Thomas Kelly met at house of Patrick Kearn; account of murder of Eleanor Davis; Kelly goes to Dr. Hacket in Talbot Co.; Rice was hired by Hugh M'Guire to go to one Woolford's in Dorset Co. to fetch M'Guire's wife; one Jarvis of George-Town offered reward for capture of Doran; James M'Neil and Philip M'Dermot and wife were accessories; Rice was apprehended at Union Iron-works by Jonathan Robison and John Hacket (7 Dec.)

New York item mentions Capts. Miller, Richards, Alexander Sloan, Barnes, Cooper, Ogilsby and Lyell (7 Dec.)

New York item of 4 Dec. reports that on Tue. last John Tharp was whipped at the cart's tail through the city (7 Dec.)

House of Thomas Doughty of New York, merchant, was broken into on the night of 3 Dec. (7 Dec.)

Letter of 23 Nov. from Chester, Md., informs that on Mon. last at a court held there Peter Ball was sentenced to death for the murder of his Negro slave; Philip M'Dermot and his wife Margaret were indicted for concealing James Dillon; Patrick Kearn is to appear at the next court (7 Dec.)

John Penn (son of Richard Penn) arrived Fri. last in Phila. (7 Dec.)

Bryan Doran has been taken up in Baltimore Co., Md. (7 Dec.)

Thomas Kelly and James Rice are to be executed Sat. next (7 Dec.)

Thomas Brabston has been sentenced for attempted rape (7 Dec.)

Richard Skinner has been sentenced to receive 21 lashes for stealing (7 Dec.)

A long-boat has gone adrift from Goodman's wharf; reward if brought to Capt. Spurrier of the ship Phoenix or to Samuel and Benjamin Shoemaker (7 Dec.)

Persons indebted to Peacock Bigger, lately removed to Charles-Town, Md., are to make payment to Conyngham and Gardner (7 Dec.)

Gelding has strayed from George Bullock's in Walnut St.; reward if brought to John Twining in Bussel-town or Edward Cowgill in New-Town, Bucks Co. (7 Dec.)

Mare has strayed from the stable of John Naglee in Second St. (7 Dec.)

Merchant mill and bake-house at the head of Bohemia River to be let by William Rumsey, who is called abroad on business (7 Dec.)

Michael M'Cartney, Irishman, tailor, who has stolen goods from Francis M'Connell, runaway from his bail, James Hamilton, of West-Nantmell Twp., Chester Co.; Lawrence White, an Irishman, also went with him; reward for capture of the runaways will be paid by said Hamilton and M'Connell or by Bryan M'Cune or James Walker (7 Dec.)

Anthony Newhouse of Germantown will not pay debts contracted in future by his wife Mary (7 Dec.)

William Bromwich, staymaker, now returned from England, is removed to the house where Capt. Burrows lived (7 Dec.)

Accounts with the estate of Ephraim Leech, late of Warrington Twp., Bucks Co., dec'd, to be settled with Archibald M'Clean and William Birney, of Horsham, execs. (7 Dec.)

The ship Peggy and Nancy, Capt. Isaac Johns, on 22 Oct. was wrecked on Willoughby Point, Md.; the people were all saved (14 Dec.)

Mary Perry has been delivered of a boy in goal of Queen Anne's Co. (14 Dec.)

Phila. items mention Capts. Rees, Cox, Edwards and M'Dougall, all of whom suffered in storms (14 Dec.)

Sat. last James Rice was executed for the murder of John Thomas
and Eleanor Davis; Thomas Kelly was reprieved until Sat. next
in order that he may identify the third murderer (14 Dec.)

Accounts with the estate of John Leacock, dec'd, who lived in
Arch St., to be settled with Mary Leacock, admin. (14 Dec.)

James Smith, brass founder, has moved from over against the
Baptist Meeting-house to Second St., at the Sign of the Founders Arms (14 Dec.)

Two lots in Phila. to be let or sold; enquire of the Widow Shaw
in Arch St. (14 Dec.)

John Leech, of Warrington, Bucks Co., has absconded; his creditors are to meet at the house of Richard Walker, Esq., in
Warrington (14 Dec.)

Negro girl for sale; enquire of William Jackson in Walnut St.
(14 Dec.)

Chest of Samuel Ellis, mariner, was broken open on the schooner
Deptford, and a watch was stolen; reward if brought to Benjamin Bagnall, watchmaker, in Front St. (14 Dec.)

David Moore and Janet his wife, who came this fall in the ship
Holderness, Capt. Simpson, from Leath, Ireland, are sought by
Margaret Lennox, sister to Janet; Margaret lives at John
Mick's, in Nottingham, Pa. (14 Dec.)

Cow strayed or stolen out of the pasture of William Allen, Esq.,
on Germantown Road; reward will be paid by James Coultas at
the Corporation Ferry (14 Dec.)

George Monro, sheriff, gives notice of three servants in goal
of Newcastle: James Caddle, age c. 35, who says he belongs
to James Chestnut at Susquehanna; John Campbell, age c. 30,
who says he belongs to Capt. John Richey; J. Thomson, weaver,
who says he came in with Capt. Archibald Stewart from Newry
(14 Dec.)

Servants, just imported in the ship Dolphin, Capt. Dewar, for
sale; apply to Joseph Marks in Walnut St. or Joseph Redmond
in Chestnut St. (14 Dec.)

Rachel Mahorne, alias M'Cormick, Irish servant, age c. 25, runaway from Matthias Keane, of Oxford Twp., Phila. Co. (14 Dec.)

Abraham Carpenter claims he has been cheated by one Michael
Dowling, who recovered a false debt (14 Dec.)

New York items of 11 Dec. mention Capts. Styles and Davis (19
Dec.)

Sat. last Thomas Kelly was executed at Chester (19 Dec.)

Laws of the Province of New-Jersey, prepared by Samuel Nevill,
is sold by Nevill in Perth Amboy and by Joseph Scattergood in
Burlington (19 Dec.)

Finder of a lost blue cloak is desired to send it to William
Coxe's (19 Dec.)

Joseph Borden's shallop, Charles Vandike master, will run again
next March; the stage-schooner, Nicholas George master, will
continue (19 Dec.)

Horse came to the plantation of John Best, of Cumry Twp., Berks
Co. (19 Dec.)

Tavern, near the Market-house in the borough of Wilmington, Newcastle Co., to be let; apply to Robert Hannum, living on the
premises (19 Dec.)

Six-sevenths of a lot of land at the corner of Walnut and Third Sts., late the property of Francis Knowles, dec'd, to be sold (19 Dec.)

William Sims, Scotch servant, age c. 25, runaway from the ship Industrious Bee, Thomas Beare commander (19 Dec.)

Horse came to the plantation of George Enterkin, of East Bradford, Chester Co. (19 Dec.)

New York item of 18 Dec. mentions Capt. Williams (26 Dec.)

New York item of 18 Dec. reports that Peter Vallet, born in France, an eminent merchant of New York, died there Sun. last; his corpse was interred in the Stuyvesant vault (26 Dec.)

The following three servants are runaways from the ship Dolphin, Capt. David Dewar: Stephen Gom, Englishman, who pretends to be a gardner; John M'Donald, Scotchman, age c. 24, a baker; Matthew Green, Englishman, age c. 20, who pretends to be a printer; reward if they are brought to said Dewar or to Joseph Marks in Walnut St. (26 Dec.)

Tract of land in Whitemarsh Twp., adjoining land of John Morris, late the estate of John Harry, to be sold by Samuel Morris at the house of Christopher Robins in Plymouth Twp. (26 Dec.)

Translation from German of document concerning Rev. Michael Slatter (Minister of the Reformed Congregation in Phila.); it is witnessed by the Rev. Jacob Lischy (Minister of the Reformed Congregation at the other side of Sasquehanna) and the Rev. John Philip Leidich (Reformed Minister of the Congregation in Falckner Swamp); Henry Bastler and Jacob Walther certify that the translation is correct (26 Dec.)

William Hay, keeper of the goal of Chester Co., gives notice that the following runaways are now in his custody: Andrew Dun, Irishman, bought by Joshua Roberts, of West N.J., and sold by him to William Walker in Northampton Twp.; Thomas Wood, Englishman, age c. 19, who says that his master is John Smith, who lives within 4 miles of Patapsco; Joseph Simmonds, born in Norwich, England, brickmaker, age c. 20, runaway from John Boham, of Lancaster Co.; David Greenwood, born in England, age c. 60, weaver (26 Dec.)

Thomas Browning, living near George-Town in Kent Co., Md., makes and sells hats (26 Dec.)

Rebecca Leech declines carrying on the tanning business (26 Dec.)

John Moore, a Protestant, age c. 24, a weaver, runaway from Thomas Robertson, living in Fogg's Manor, Chester Co. (26 Dec.)

For freight or passage to Jamaica in the brigantine Addison, Daniel Denormandie master, agree with Adam and William Clampster (26 Dec.)

Thomas Rogers, Irish servant, wigmaker, runaway from Andrew Crawford, living in Plymouth Twp. (26 Dec.)

Andrew Bears has absconded; creditors are to appear before John Scott before 24 Feb. next (26 Dec.)

Frenchmen from Perigord may find plantation work by applying to John Crevet in St. George's Hundred, Newcastle Co. (26 Dec.)

John Crevet, surgeon, announces the establishment of a school for poor children (26 Dec.)

1753

New York items of 25 Dec. mention Capts. Bayne, Palmer, Lowrie, White, Davis, M'Dougall, Deane, Bogart, Stephens, Waynman, Sluman, Winthrop, Phoenix, Man and Albouy (2 Jan.)

At the north branch of Rariton on 13 Dec. Jacob Vaneste, when on his way home from Dr. Van Wagenen's, was murdered by two Negroes (2 Jan.)

Walter Gordon was whipped round New York for stealing a barrel of flour (2 Jan.)

Gov. Trelawny has left Jamaica for home (2 Jan.)

Phila. item of 2 Jan. mentions Capt. Allison and Capt. John Green of Kent Co. (2 Jan.)

Eleanor Morris, Irish servant, age c. 23, runaway from Lydia Morgan of Phila. (2 Jan.)

Francis Caulfield, servant, age c. 19, a tailor, runaway from Joseph Clarke, tailor, of Bucks Co. (2 Jan.)

George Orr, brazier, is removed from Front St. to the house in Market St. where Peacock Bigger lived (2 Jan.)

William Prosser, apprentice, age c. 18, shoemaker, runaway from Thomas Witherill, Jr., of Burlington (2 Jan.)

William Richardson, age c. 24, born in Amwell in the Jerseys, was paid to flat wood to Phila. by James Baldwin but has not been heard of since (2 Jan.)

Richard M'Manemen, Irish servant, runaway from John Buffington, living in West Bradford, Chester Co. (2 Jan.)

Mare stolen from Jacob Warrick, of Springfield, Burlington Co., is supposed to have been stolen by John Jones, who stole a mare from Morris Gwin in Abington and sold her to Robert Chambers, near Trenton (2 Jan.)

Joseph Wilson, country born, age c. 30, sadler, runaway from Thomas Lewis in Wilmington; reward if returned to Edward Davis, tavern-keeper, in Wilmington, Newcastle Co., or Joseph Cobourn in Phila.; reward will be paid by Thomas Lewis or Griffith Minshell (2 Jan.)

Negro girl for sale; enquire of Samuel Jacobs in Market St. (2 Jan.)

New York items of 1 Jan. mention Capts. Tuder, Creighton, Barnes, Smith and Hunt (9 Jan.)

Capt. Stephen Tuder has died of smallpox in the Bermudas (9 Jan.)

New York item of 1 Jan. reports that on Tue. last the barn of Abraham Duryee, at New Bushwick on Long Island, was burnt down (9 Jan.)

New York item of 1 Jan. reports that the Negro who murdered Mr. Van Neste, his master, in N.J., was burnt at Millstone on Wed. last (9 Jan.)

Capt. Falkner of the brigantine Polly is feared lost (9 Jan.)

Mr. Hideggar, Gov. of St. Eustatia, has died (9 Jan.)

Three daughters of Mr. Lawson of Baltimore Co., Md., Miss Betsy Read, and a schoolmaster were drowned on Christmas Eve last, when the ice gave way (9 Jan.)

The following persons in Phila. were ordered to be whipped: (for felony) William Davis, Timothy Hussey, Luke Kelly, Cornelius Maclaughlin and John Hamilton; (for receiving stolen goods) Peter Power (9 Jan.)

Barbary, wife of Matthew Graff, of Phila., baker, has eloped from her husband (9 Jan.)

Stray cows have come to the plantation of Simeon Powell in Salisbury Twp., Bucks Co. (9 Jan.)

John Ormsby, lately arrived from London, teaches fencing and dancing at the house of Mr. Fowler in Market St. (9 Jan.)

A gelding has been stolen from the Sign of the Black Horse in Lower Merion, supposedly by Timothy Linch; reward will be paid by Gerard Jones (9 Jan.)

Cornelius Collins, Irish servant, age c. 22, runaway from Abel Harris, living in Manington Twp., Salem Co. (9 Jan.)

A filly has strayed from the plantation of John Hambright, in Whiteland, Chester Co.; reward will be paid by Henry Hambright (9 Jan.)

Henry Callister has established a new ferry across Chester River, 8 miles south of George-Town (9 Jan.)

John Baynton, living in Phila., has several tracts of land to sell in West N.J.; one in Hunterdon Co. adjoins land of James Logan (9 Jan.)

Real estate in the Northern Liberties to be sold or let; apply to Preserve Brown at his mills in Nottingham, Burlington Co., or Benjamin Mason in the Northern Liberties or Thomas Clifford in Phila. (9 Jan.)

Mr. Hallam, manager of the theatre of Williamsburgh, Va., exhibited fireworks on the King's birthday (16 Jan.)

Annapolis items mention Capt. Lorain, of the ship *Chester*, and Capt. Ingersoll of Salem (16 Jan.)

Peter Ball, of Kent Co., Md., condemned for the murder of his Negro boy, has been pardoned (16 Jan.)

Annapolis item of 28 Dec. reports that on Christmas day, at the house of Joseph Crouch on the north side of Severn, one of said Crouch's legs was accidentally shattered by his son (16 Jan.)

William Archdeken and Samuel Pitt have been convicted in Boston of counterfeiting (16 Jan.)

It is feared that a schooner cast ashore near Cape Ann is that of Thomas Walden from Piscataqua (16 Jan.)

Boston item of 25 Dec. reports that Thomas Chubb and Abraham, a Negro, have been found guilty of manslaughter in the case of the murder of John Crab (16 Jan.)

Boston items of 25 Dec. report that on Thu. last Mr. Dursey of Roxbury, an aged man, was drowned there and that on the same day a child of Mr. Bossom of Roxbury fell into a tub of hot water and the next day died from the scalding (16 Jan.)

New York items of 9 Jan. mention Capts. Nicholls, Waynman and Freeman (16 Jan.)

On 11 Dec. Capt. Ramsey fell in with a wreck in the gulf, the ship *Alexander*, Robert Moody master, of New London (16 Jan.)

Phila. item of 16 Jan. mentions Capts. Mott, Ritchey, Stuart and Arbuckle (16 Jan.)

It is reported from Chester Co. that John Crow, who had been concerned with **Morrison** in robberies, and another man have been committed; they were skulking on land of William Moore (16 Jan.)

Robert Coe will teach the German flute at his house in Third St., next door but one to Joseph Fox's (16 Jan.)

William Stuart, Irish servant, age c. 22, runaway from William Gaa, barber, in Front St. (16 Jan.)

Real estate in Phila., part of the estate of John Shewbert, dec'd, to be sold; apply to Richard Hockley or Isaac Zane (16 Jan.)

Real estate in Fourth St., in the tenure of James Ennis, bounded by land late of Benjamin Clerk, taken at the suit of Thomas Clifford and others, to be sold by Samuel Morris, sheriff, at the house of John Biddle (16 Jan.)

Sugar and rum for sale by John Sayre in Market St. (16 Jan.)

Fulling mill, late of John Harvey, dec'd, in Darby, to be sold by David Davis, fuller, in Darby (16 June)

Louisa, wife of William Leddel, has eloped from her husband (16 Jan.)

Jacob Whitmar, his brother Jacob, and his sisters, Elizabeth and Margaret, came from Switzerland nine years ago and were separated; Jacob wishes them to know that he lives at Harmon Fisher's in Upper Hanover Twp., Phila. Co. (16 Jan.)

Capt. Lyon from Phila. has arrived in London (23 Jan.)

Numerous goods, found buried in Lancaster, near the late house of James M'Connell, are now in the custody of Thomas Smith, Sheriff of Lancaster (23 Jan.)

Louisa Leddel, wife of Dr. William Leddel of Elizabeth-town, brands as false his adv. in the last issue of the paper (23 Jan.)

Thomas Whitton will not pay a bond issued to Jacob Duffield (23 Jan.)

John Jones, smith and farrier, opposite the State House, proposes to take in horses (23 Jan.)

Elizabeth, the wife of Joseph Underwood of Christiana Hundred, has left her husband (23 Jan.)

Maria Catherina, wife of Christopher Westenhever, of Reading, Berks Co., carpenter, has eloped from her husband (23 Jan.)

Message about paper money from Gov. James Hamilton to the Pa. Assembly and reply (30 Jan.)

Capt. Bradford has arrived at Boston with news from London (30 Jan.)

Boston item of 1 Jan. reports that Thu. night the works erected by Mr. Crabb at Rehoboth for making spermaceti candles were destroyed by fire (30 Jan.)

Boston item of 11 Jan. reports sentencing of Thomas Chubb and Abraham (a Negro) for killing John Crabb (a seafaring man), of John and Jonathan Webber of Wells for counterfeiting, and of Sarah Peake for setting fire to the house of her master, Benjamin Brintnal of Chelsea (30 Jan.)

New York items of 15 and 22 Jan. mention Capts. Taylor, Duncan, Fortin, Wilson, Bond, Harrison, Seymour and Richards (30 Jan.)

New York item of 22 Jan. reports that on Fri. last John Farrel was whipped for stealing and on Sat. Richard Roach was sentenced to death for picking the pocket of Theophilus Elsworth (30 Jan.)

Phila. item mentions Capts. Lyon and Mesnard (30 Jan.)

Adv. of Jonathan and John Mifflin at their new store near the drawbridge, opposite Hamilton's wharf (30 Jan.)

John Kearns, cooper, age c. 23, runaway from his bail, Isaac Hersay, of Mill-creek Hundred, Newcastle Co. (30 Jan.)

Horse strayed or stolen from James Russell, coach-maker, on Society Hill (30 Jan.)

Real estate in Pewter-Platter Alley, bounded by land of Thomas Biles, Bernard Eaglesfield and Robert Grace, late the estate of Sarah Read, taken at the suit of John Wallace, to be sold at the house of William Biddle (30 Jan.)

A mare and a horse have been taken from John Pass's door; reward if brought to Joseph Wills, clockmaker, in Third St. (30 Jan.)

Adv. of John Beals, net-maker from London, in Fourth St.; he teaches various musical instruments (30 Jan.)

Adv. of Christopher Marshall, holder of the King's patent for Balsam of Life (30 Jan.)

Samuel Rollston has absconded; his creditors are to appear befor John Scott, Jr., in New-London, Chester Co. (30 Jan.)

Negro wench for sale; enquire of the Widow Rush in Front St. (30 Jan.)

Plantation in Lower Merion for sale; enquire of Uriah White, on the premises (30 Jan.)

William Ratchford, Irish servant, age c. 25, runaway from Daniel M'Neill, living in Salisbury Twp., Lancaster Co. (30 Jan.)

On 14 Jan. the snow Sally, Morton Neal master, with a cargo of rice, came up from the road to stop a leak, according to a Charles-Town, S.C. item (6 Feb.)

Charles-Town, S.C., items of 15 Jan. report that the barn of George Gabriel Powell, Esq., of George-Town was burnt down, along with his crop of rice; that Daniel Horry from Santee made 60 barrels of rice on untended land (6 Feb.)

A Williamsburgh, Va., item of 1 Dec. tells of the loss of some men from a boat belonging to the Hampton, Capt. Wiltshire (6 Feb.)

New York items of 29 Jan. report that about a fortnight ago the house of Capt. Broadhead, near Esopus, N.Y., was destroyed by the explosion of some gunpowder; also that the son of Alexander Macky, near Poughkeepsie, when in delerium from smallpox, got up and disappeared; also that John Parcel, a boatman, lost three of his children by drowning when his boat overset when bound from New York to Hellgate (6 Feb.)

Phila. item tells of the rescue of Capt. Ragg, late commander of the snow Triton, by Capt. Cheesmond (6 Feb.)

Real estate in Germantown for sale; apply to Anthony Newhouse, living on the premises (6 Feb.)

Quitrents are to be paid to Richard Hockley or to Edmund Physick at the Receiver's Office (6 Feb.)

Negroes and time of an English servant for sale; enquire of William Henderson in Market St. (6 Feb.)

Land opposite to Budd's buildings in Phila. to be let by the City of Phila. (6 Feb.)

Meadow in Passyunk Twp. to be let; enquire of Joseph Sims, below the drawbridge (6 Feb.)

Christopher Mier, Dutch servant, age between 40 and 50, runaway from Hugh Linn, of Ashton Twp. (6 Feb.)

Time of an English servant for sale; enquire of Richard Brookbank, baker, in Laetitia Court, Phila. (6 Feb.)

Thomas Ageman, age c. 80, laborer, of Burlington, N.J., is now missing; information of him is sought by his son, William, in care of George Eyre, Esq., in Burlington (6 Feb.)

Thomas Hood has already paid a bond held by James Claypole of Newtown, Md., tanner (6 Feb.)

James Douglass, who came from Ireland last year and has a receipt for his passage from Mr. Knox in Londonderry, age between 30 and 40, runaway from his bail, William M'Camant, of Salisbury Twp., Lancaster Co. (6 Feb.)

New York item of 5 Feb. states that the wife of Mr. Hunt, near the Fish-Kills in Dutchess Co., was delivered of four children; she is said to be a distant relation of the late Gov. Morris (13 Feb.)

New York item of 5 Feb. mentions Capts. William Richards, Barnes, John Sweet and Quereau (13 Feb.)

New York item of 5 Feb. reports that Mon. last the barn of John Ketcham, of Newtown, L.I., was burnt down (13 Feb.)

New York item of 5 Feb. reports that on Tue. last the boat of Mr. Ellis, of South River in the Jerseys, lying at the Old Slip, was robbed; Barnabas Morgan was committed to goal on suspicion (13 Feb.)

New York item of 5 Feb. states that on Tue. last the barn of Mr. Nicholls, tavern-keeper at Stratfield, Mass., was burnt down (13 Feb.)

Last week George Little was found guilty at a court in Lancaster of stealing the pack of Archibald M'Curdy, a pedlar (13 Feb.)

Land and a sawmill in Merion Twp., formerly belonging to David Davis, adjoining land of John Roberts, Robert Jones and David Davis, late the estate of Jacob Simon, taken in execution by Sheriff Samuel Morris, will be sold (13 Feb.)

Benjamin Jackson from London has erected a machine for manufacturing flour of mustard; the flour is sold at William Griffitt's store on Hamilton's wharf (13 Feb.)

Land in Oxford Twp., bounded by land late of John Bood, late in the tenure of Samuel Parr, land of Samuel Sansom and Joseph King, land of John Ross, land of Thomas Kent and land of John Smith, for sale; enquire of Peter Turner in Market St. (13 Feb.)

Anna Maria, wife of Conrad Perlet, of Amity Twp., Berks Co., has eloped from her husband (13 Feb.)

Thomas Ramsey will not pay bonds payable to William Black, of Cumberland Twp., York Co. (13 Feb.)

Any person qualified for keeping school will meet with encouragement by applying to John Luckens, surveyor, Abraham Luckens or Benjamin Cadwalader, living in Horsham Twp. (13 Feb.)

Plantation in Amwell Twp., Hunterdon Co., for sale; apply to John Burcham (13 Feb.)

Memorial to Mayor and Commonalty of Phila., signed by Philip Syng, Hugh Roberts, Joseph Stretch, Jacob Cooper, Joseph Richardson, Charles Jones (city wardens), Thomas Say and Jacob Duche (commissioners), Joseph Lownes, Joseph Watkins, Jacob Lewis, Anthony Morris, Jr., Jeremiah Warder, Thomas Lightfoot (city assessors), Abraham Mitchell, Jacob Shoemaker, Jr., Thomas Clifford and Joseph Howell (commissioners of the poor) (20 Feb.)

Motion presented by Mayor Humphrey Murrey to the Gov. and Council (present Thomas Lloyd, John Simcock, John Delavall, Thomas Duckett, Griffith Owen, William Stockdale and John Bristow, with mention of Jeremiah Elfreth) (20 Feb.)

Petition of Inhabitants of Phila. to Gov. and Council, signed by Humphrey Murrey, John Holme, Samuel Richardson, Robert Ewer, David Lloyd, Albertus Brandt, Philip Richards, Charles Butler, John Murrey, James Fox, Alexander Beardsley, John White, Thomas Budd, William Bradford, Thomas Hooton, Philip Howell, Nathaniel Allen, Christopher Sibthorpe, Abraham Hardyman, William Lee, William Say, John Parsons, William Walker, Andrew Grescom, William Hearne, Francis Cooke, Richard Gove, William Forrest, David Breintnall, Henry Badcock and Isaac Rickets (20 Feb.)

Williamsburgh, Va., item of 8 Dec. reports that Fri. last the play-house there was broken into and Patrick Malony, servant to the company, was seriously wounded (20 Feb.)

Court in Williamsburgh has sentenced the following: Alexander Gauling, for highway robbery, death; John Clifton, for picking a pocket, death; Thomas Aubery, *alias* Smith, for horse-stealing, death; John Robinson, who pleaded guilty to felony, burnt in the hand (20 Feb.)

Annapolis item of 4 Jan. reports that Tue. last Joseph Crouch died there of the gunshot wound inflicted by his drunken son (20 Feb.)

On 2 Jan. the only son of Thomas Ford, age c. 12, was accidentally killed in Baltimore Co. (20 Feb.)

Annapolis item of 1 Feb. reports that on Tue. last died in Calvert Co. Mrs. Alethea Cook, gentlewoman, formerly the wife of the late Walter Smith; her present husband is to be tried for her death (20 Feb.)

Subscriptions for printed lectures on physick to be taken in by Samuel Hazard (20 Feb.)

Horse came to the house of William Levering, tavern-keeper, in Roxburgh Twp., Phila. Co. (20 Feb.)

Mare has been stolen out of the stable of John Beeson in Brandywine Hundred, Newcastle Co. (20 Feb.)

Plymouth, a Negro, age c. 23, runaway from Stephen Williams at Milford Mills in Bucks Co. (20 Feb.)

John Barneby, apprentice, country born, went off with John M'Donald, Irish apprentice of Thomas Pryer's; he is runaway from Joseph Edwards, shoemaker, living in Charles-Town, Cecil Co., Md. (20 Feb.)

Land near Phila., bounded by land of Shute, Hood and Capt. Harris, for sale; apply to John Mifflin in Second St. (20 Feb.)

Boston item of 29 Jan. relates the adventure of the mock Rev. Samuel Hide, a tailor, who was ordained by the lawyer and exhorter Paine (27 Feb.)

On 7 Jan. Deacon Samuel Lilley died at Sutton, Worcester Co., Mass., in his 88th year, leaving 113 progeny (27 Feb.)

Boston item of 5 Feb. reports that William Woodhouse and William Pitty, both of Castle William, were drowned Wed. last when their canoe overset (27 Feb.)

Boston item of 13 Feb. reports that on Wed. last a fire in Marlborough St. burnt the houses of Dr. John Cutler and Dr. Edward Ellis and the barns and blacksmith's shop of Mr. Sellon (27 Feb.)

Boston item of 13 Feb. reports that on Wed. last a Negro man, who belonged to John Brown of Newport, R.I., and whom Dr. Gibbs refused to buy, was finally drowned, after having tried in vain to take revenge on Dr. Gibbs (27 Feb.)

New York items of 12 Feb. mention Capts. Quereau, Sweet, Albuoy, Griffin, Shoals, Mann, Phoenix, Colgan, Smith, Bennet, **Davis,** Furlong, Roome, Jeremiah Leaycraft, Curby, Warren, Manchester, Collins and Holbrook (27 Feb.)

One Hamilton, a seafaring man belonging to the brig Polly, Capt. Badger, on Mon. last fell off the dock and was drowned (27 Feb.)

New York item of 12 Feb. reports that Richard Roche, born in Ireland, age c. 26, was executed on Sat. last, pursuant to his sentence (27 Feb.)

Phila. item of 27 Feb. mentions Capts. Burnet and Hargrave (27 Feb.)

William Dunn, an Irishman, age c. 25, weaver, runaway from his bail, William Wilson, living at Christine Bridge, Newcastle Co. (27 Feb.)

James M'Garrel, Irish servant, age c. 20, runaway from Jonas Seely, living in Reading Town (27 Feb.)

1753

Capt. Deane proposes to sail from New York to London (6 Mar.)

Capt. Devereux has arrived at New York from St. Augustine; he brought Capt. Ball, late of a sloop of New York, and the mate of Capt. Fones of Rhode Island (6 Mar.)

Capt. Ball reports that the following were cast away on 23 Oct. on the Florida shore: Capts. Raymond, Patrick, Dean, Crawford, Edwards, Moodie and Fones; he also mentions Capts. Ramsey and Asa King (6 Mar.)

James M'Donald, shoemaker, is committed to goal in New York on suspicion of picking the pocket of William Duncanson, a sailor, at the house of Mr. Biddle, tavern-keeper (6 Mar.)

At Flatbush on Long Island a farmer named Detmas was run over by his wagon and is not expected to live (6 Mar.)

George Thomas is reported to have been appointed Captain General over all the Leeward and Caribbie Islands (6 Mar.)

The report of the loss of the ship Lucy, Capt. Hargrave, is believed to be false (6 Mar.)

Rowland Evans at Gwynedd gives notice that Christopher Clare has absconded (6 Mar.)

House in Front St. to be sold at public vendue at Jeremiah Smith's, the Sign of the Queen of Hungary; apply to John Denton, carpenter, in Front St. (6 Mar.)

Meadow in Moyamensing (between meadow of Joseph Morris and Joseph House), ground (between lots of Edward Warner and Joseph Oldman) and lot in Wicacoa (between ground of Joseph Wharton and estate of Samuel Hasell, Esq., dec'd) will be sold at public vendue at house of John Biddle in Market St.; enquire of Charles Norris (6 Mar.)

Stallion from Ireland is kept at Chatham ropeyard on Passyunk Road by Edward Caxon, late of the city of York, England (6 Mar.)

House in Germantown where Stephen Benezet lived is to be let; apply to John Wistar in Phila. (6 Mar.)

Grist-mill near Pennypack Meeting House in Lower Dublin Twp. for sale; enquire of George and Peter Eaton (6 Mar.)

Capt. John Minge, of James River, Va., offers reward for recovery of young Negro man who was stolen from him by Joseph Crawford, who took said Negro to Bush River, Baltimore Co., Md., and there sold him to George Lawson, living near the borders of Pa.; the Negro is to be brought to Minge in Va., to Isaac Greenleafe in Phila. or to Isaac Webster of Baltimore Co. (6 Mar.)

Accounts with estate of Matthew Watson, chapman, lately dec'd, to be settled with Matthew and Abraham Usher, admins., at the Green Doors in Walnut St., opposite Rees Meredith's (6 Mar.)

For passage to Dublin in the snow Fanny, Robert Smith master, agree with William Humphries in Walnut St. (6 Mar.)

Robert Sitlinton, Irishman, late schoolteacher in Phila., has run away from his bail; reward for his capture if brought to Quinton Moore in Walnut St. or James Huston in Second St. (6 Mar.)

Real estate for sale by John Spencer at his house in Kensington (6 Mar.)

1753

Tract of land about 3 miles from Phila., bounded on the N.W. by Shute, on the N.E. by Hood and S.E. by Capt. Harrison, for sale; apply to Jonathan or John Mifflin in Front St. (6 Mar.)

Thomas Fitzsimons, next door to the Easy-Chair in Second St., offers reward for recovery of lost pocketbook (6 Mar.)

Reward if strayed or stolen horse is brought to stable of the Widow Ulrick in Second St. or to John Husserd in Whitpain Twp., Phila. Co., or John Chyme, turner, in Germantown (6 Mar.)

Adv. of Andrew Reed, now removed to house of Peter Bard in Water St. (6 Mar.)

Subscriptions for printing work on physick will be taken by Samuel Hazard in Phila. (6 Mar.)

Adv. of Robert Ragg (6 Mar.)

Wines for sale by Joseph Sims, over the drawbridge, and by Buckridge Sims, at the house of Joseph Turner (6 Mar.)

Joseph Boyce, apprentice, age c. 19, runaway from Caleb Evans of Phila.; Edward M'Daniel, Irish servant, age c. 20, formerly servant to Robert Dixon at the Center, runaway from Thomas Bartholomew, tavern-keeper, of Phila.; Joseph Lyon, Irish servant, age c. 20, runaway from Joseph Sinclair, heel-maker, of Phila.; Abraham Ruker, Irish servant, age c. 24, runaway from Benjamin Barton, chair-maker, of Phila. (6 Mar.)

Negro offered for sale by Francis M'Henry at Deep-Run (6 Mar.)

Benjamin Morgan in Moyamensing Twp., Phila. Co., has taken up a mare (6 Mar.)

Mare has been stolen from the stable of John Beeson of Brandywine Hundred, Newcastle Co. (6 Mar.)

Sarah Knox (alias Howard, alias Wilson), convict servant, born in Yorkshire, imported from Whitehaven in the Duke of Cumberland, runaway from David Currie at the Glebe of Lancaster Co., Va. (6 Mar.)

William Rodman will let a grist-mill in Bensalem Twp., Bucks Co. (6 Mar.)

Persons indebted to Randle Mitchell and Co. are to pay debts to Alexander Mitchell in Water St., next door to Samuel Neave (6 Mar.)

The snow Young Lodwick. Capt. Vardil, was driven ashore on a point of rocks at Corlaer's Hook (13 Mar.)

On 25 Feb. arrived at New York Capts. Shoals, Man and Colgan; two Spanish pirate craft were seized by Capt. Griffiths of Bristol; on 12 Jan. the sloop Cedar, Capt. Lawrence, of New York, was cast away on the Grand Key; Capts. Phoenix and Burger left the Bay but there remained in the Bay Capts. Bowen, Furlong, Jones, Stoddard, Green and Guilford; Capt. Robert Leonard of the sloop Diamond was taken by the Spaniards, who released him but kept the following seamen: John Smith, Michael Flanagan and Alexander Horne; Capt. Richey of the ship Beulah, Capt. Barnes and Capt. Campbell have sailed from New York for Newry (13 Mar.)

At Phila. Daniel Shieblie was whipped for receiving goods stolen by a Negro, and John Burns was whipped for a felony (13 Mar.)

1753

On 8 Mar. at Phila. Samuel Austin, James Macky and Thomas Bourne were appointed sworn appraisors (13 Mar.)

Real estate to be sold or let by Joseph House (13 Mar.)

Time of a Dutch servant girl for sale; enquire of William Dakeyn, tanner, near the drawbridge (13 Mar.)

Accounts with estate of Capt. Fobes Briggs, late of Newport, R.I., dec'd, to be settled with Barnet Sisson, of Richmond in Kings Co., R.I., exec. (13 Mar.)

Edward Westward, English servant, blacksmith or lock-maker by trade, and Patrick Gill, Irish servant, bricklayer or mason, runaways from James Few and Nicholas Wilson of Wilmington (13 Mar.)

Richard Jarrad at Spring Garden desires to sell his house in Garden St. (13 Mar.)

Real estate in Gloucester Twp. for rent; apply to Mary Zane or Thomas Clifford in Phila. (13 Mar.)

For freight or passage to London in the snow <u>Sarah</u>, John Mitchell master, agree with John Smith at his wharf in Phila. (13 Mar.)

For freight or passage to London in the ship <u>Lydia</u>, Peter Reeve master, agree with James Pemberton (13 Mar.)

House in Germantown, where Stephen Benezet lived, is to be let; apply to John Wistar in Phila. (13 Mar.)

George Astins, Irish servant, age <u>c</u>. 21, runaway from Douglas Campbell, living in East Nantmel Twp., Chester Co. (13 Mar.)

Patrick O'Hagen, Irish servant, age 30, runaway from Robert Young, near Warwick, Cecil Co., Md. (13 Mar.)

Plantation to be sold by Richard Gabriel of New Providence Twp., Phila. Co.(13 Mar.)

Plantation on Newtown Creek, Gloucester Co., to be sold or let by James Craisbury (13 Mar.)

Adv. of James Smith, brass founder, who has moved from over against the Baptist Meeting-house to Second St., at the Sign of the Founders Arms (20 Mar.)

Barn of Mr. Wheeler, of Dorchester, Mass., was consumed by fire (27 Mar.)

Capt. Striven, arrived at Boston from Swansey in Wales, reports the safe arrival at London of Capts. Trout, Blanchard, Hussey, Holden and Partridge, and of Capt. Francis at Bristol; Capt. Wilson of Boston was forced ashore at Cape Cod in a storm, and Capt. Fadre is ashore near Cape Anne (27 Mar.)

At Westborough, Mass., a lad named Isaac Miller lost his left hand in an accident at Mr. Whipple's mill (27 Mar.)

Items from New York mention Capts. Lewis, White, Lord, Scott Lawrence, Pussey, Gardner, M'Allister and Alexander (27 Mar.)

List of vessels arrived at different ports in various newspapers has been prepared and is published (27 Mar.)

Cornelia, wife of Rev. Gilbert Tennent, died on 19 Mar. (27 Mar.)

House in which Mr. Stoner formerly preached in Sassafras St. is to be sold by Leonard Melker and John Stillwaggon (27 Mar.)

Adv. of John Head, Jr., in Second St. (27 Mar.)

Adv. of Samuel Howell, at the Sign of the Beaver in Chestnut St. (27 Mar.)

James Trotter plans to leave Pa. in a few weeks (27 Mar.)

Adv. of William Grant in Second St. (27 Mar.)

Adv. of Mordecai Yarnall at the Sign of the Handsaw in Second St. (27 Mar.)

Adv. of Joseph Ogden in Chestnut St. (27 Mar.)

Adv. of Edward Penington on south side of Edward Warner's wharf (27 Mar.)

William Glen, Irish servant, runaway from Isaac Janney, who lives in Cecil Co., Md., within 6 miles of Charles-Town (27 Mar.)

John Swayney (or M'Swine), Irish servant, age c. 35, runaway from James Barnes, of West Nottingham, Chester Co. (27 Mar.)

Plantation near Great Timber Creek Bridge, Gloucester Co., West New Jersey, to be let by John Ladd, Esq., near Gloucester (27 Mar.)

Plantation in Bristol Twp., Bucks Co., for sale; apply to Richard Johnson on the premises or Samuel Johnson in Black Horse Alley, Phila. (27 Mar.)

Jacob Parrot, convict servant, formerly servant to Rev. Hugh Jones, and James Jones, servant, runaways from Otho Othoson and John Tree of Cecil Co., Md. (27 Mar.)

Time of servant for sale; enquire of George Young, living at Mr. Lawrence's plantation in Moyamensing Twp., or Anthony Armbruster in Arch St., Phila. (27 Mar.)

John M'Laughlin, Irish servant, age c. 35, who formerly lived with John Spencer near Phila., runaway from Peter Bard, of Phila. (27 Mar.)

Tract of land, late belonging to Samuel Hale, about 2½ miles from Christine Bridge, for sale by David Finney (27 Mar.)

Plantation in Cumru Twp., Berks Co., for sale by Evan Price (27 Mar.)

Lot, being part of Carpenter's Square, between Market and Chestnut Sts., to be sold or let; apply to Joseph Gray in Market St. or George Gray, brewer, in Chestnut St. (27 Mar.)

For freight or passage to Barbados in the sloop Sarah and Ann, John Nicholson master, agree with said master at Fishbourn's wharf (27 Mar.)

Household furniture for sale at house of James Lindsay, next door to William Fishbourn in Front St. (27 Mar.)

Real estate for sale in West New Jersey (some tracts adjoining land of James Logan, Esq.); apply to John Baynton (27 Mar.)

Mr. Dove, English professor at the Academy, has taken Rock Hall (27 Mar.)

Adv. of Donnaldson and Fuller in Walnut St. (27 Mar.)

Adv. of Isaac Jones in Arch St. (27 Mar.)

1753

Adv. of Joseph Saunders, who has removed from his store on Reese Meredith's or Carpenter's wharf to house where Israel Pemberton, Sr., lately lived, next door to James Pemberton's (27 Mar.)

Adv. of Thomas Wharton at his store on Carpenter's wharf, where Joseph Saunders lately kept (27 Mar.)

Adv. of Charles Dutens, jeweller from London, at the Sign of the Ring and Dove in Market St. (27 Mar.)

Adv. of William Wallace in Front St. and Buckridge Sims at the house of Joseph Turner (27 Mar.)

Accounts with estate of Samuel Parr, late of Phila., merchant, dec'd, to be settled with William Parr, attorney-at-law, in Second St. (27 Mar.)

Mill for sale by Robert Lettis Hooper, living in Trenton, N. J. (27 Mar.)

Plantation at Duck Creek Hundred, Kent Co. on Delaware, for sale by John Pennington, living on the premises (27 Mar.)

John Wilcocks offers reward for capture of Richard Cummins, age c. 45 or 50, runaway from the brig Elizabeth, Alexander Katter master, at Reedy Island (27 Mar.)

Anthony Newhouse makes void his adv. concerning his wife Mary (27 Mar.)

Ground in Carter's Alley, late estate of Jane Owen, bounded on N. by Aaron Jenkins and on W. by William Callender, for sale; it was taken in execution by Sheriff Morris; he will also sell at the house of John Cross real estate, late the property of Robert Tims, bounded on the S. by ground of Thomas Boud and Archibald M'Call, taken in execution at suit of William Dowell (27 Mar.)

House in Carlisle, Cumberland Co., for sale; enquire of John M'Callister on the premises (27 Mar.)

Plantation in Cole-Brook Dale, late of Thomas Potts, dec'd, for sale by Thomas Yorke and other execs. (27 Mar.)

Property of Col. Nathan Rigbie, late of Baltimore Co., dec'd, will be sold at his house near Deer Creek by Sabina Rigbie, admin. (27 Mar.)

Water lot on Christian St. for sale; apply to Michael Huling, Peter Keen or Andrew Bankson in Phila. (27 Mar.)

Brigantine, John Huxham master, belonging to Mr. Collins, of Newport, R.I., merchant, has been driven ashore about a mile from Newport (5 Apr.)

Capt. Hyer, in the brig Lark, arrived at New York from Campeachy Bay, gives news of Capts. Hall and Crowell (5 Apr.)

Mary Wilson in New York has been given 31 lashes for stealing a shift (5 Apr.)

Capts. Harrison, Fry, Holwell and M'Allister have arrived at New York; Capt. Schenk of a New York schooner has been arrested and imprisoned at Porto Rico (5 Apr.)

Walter Patterson, Irishman, age c. 28 or 30, who was convicted in London of having been concerned in a conspiracy against Lord Walpole, broke goal and fled to Ireland and thence to Phila. (5 Apr.)

Capt. Mesnard has arrived at Phila. from London (5 Apr.)

John Carr, convicted of theft in Phila., has been sentenced to receive 21 lashes (5 Apr.)

Stray mare has been taken up in Trediffryn; owner is to apply to Dennis O'Neal, living at James Davis's in Trediffryn (5 Apr.)

Daniel Evans, Welch servant, age c. 22, blacksmith, runaway from Thomas Yarnall of Thornbury, Chester Co. (5 Apr.)

James Thompson, formerly silk-dyer for Thomas Green at the house where Michael Brown formerly lived, continues the same business with Sarah Brown (5 Apr.)

William Dawson will open a school in Third St. (5 Apr.)

Treatise has just been published by Christopher Sower, a printer in Germantown, and David Dashler, shopkeeper, in Phila. (5 Apr.)

Alexander Stamper, English servant, age c. 24, runaway from Abraham Sailor of Skippack (5 Apr.)

Real estate in Bristol Twp., bounded by land of Thomas Dowdney, dec'd, of Benjamin Blacklidge and Joseph Smith, late property of Sarah Hooper, admin. of William Hooper, dec'd, taken in execution at the suit of Abraham Bown and wife, to be sold at Patrick O'Hanlin's in Bristol by Sheriff Wm. Yeardley (5 Apr.)

Plantation in Hill Town Twp., Bucks Co., late property of James Steward, bounded by land of Lawrence Growdon, Esq., John Williams, Robert Barnhill and Thomas Jones, taken in execution at suit of Barnard Young, to be sold by Sheriff Wm. Yeardley (5 Apr.)

Plantation of William M'Colock, late of London-Britain Twp., Chester Co., dec'd, for sale; apply to Nathaniel Magee in Arch St., Phila., or Thomas Magee, near the plantation (5 Apr.)

Plantation in Northern Liberties of Phila. for sale; apply to William Adams, Keeper of the Alms-house in Phila. (5 Apr.)

Property, late the estate of Joseph Ellis, situated in Biberry Twp., adjoining lands of Joseph Foster, Daniel and Jonathan Knight, and Benjamin and Joseph Walton, for sale by Sheriff Samuel Morris; the property was taken in execution at the suit of Elizabeth Shewell (5 Apr.)

Mare strayed or stolen from the door of William Roberts of Blockley Twp., Phila. Co.; reward if returned to the owner or to George Ristler (5 Apr.)

Plantation in Ashton Twp., Chester Co., for sale by Joseph Wharton (5 Apr.)

Coffins are sold by John De Nyce in Second St., opposite the Baptist Meeting-house (5 Apr.)

Morris Evans, convict servant, age c. 36, runaway from Nathaniel Scott, of Queen Ann's Co., Md. (5 Apr.)

Plantation and mill for sale by Owen Roberts in New-Britain Twp., Bucks Co. (5 Apr.)

Accounts with estate of Thomas Green, house-carpenter, to be settled with Martha Green, exec. (5 Apr.)

Jane, wife of John Moody of Bethlehem Twp., has eloped from her husband (5 Apr.)

Murtha Dunn, native Irishman, runaway from his bail, Joseph Rotheram and Joseph England, living at Whiteclay Creek, New-Castle Co. (5 Apr.)

House and wharf in the Northern Liberties to be let by William Rakestraw, living at the upper end of Fourth St. (5 Apr.)

Adv. of Thomas Maule at the Sign of the Cross-cut Saw in Second St. (5 Apr.)

Joseph Wood at Back Creek, Cecil Co., Md., has for sale a house and mills (5 Apr.)

Sloop from Casco Bay, Joseph Lunt master, ran upon Newbury Bar; Capt. West in a snow belonging to Boston was wrecked at Jamaica; Capt. Hatch arrived at Boston with news of arrival of Capt. Cullam and Capt. Benjamin Hallowell at Jamaica; Capt. Allen was cast away on the east end of Hispaniola; Capt. Smith was forced ashore on the back of Cape Cod (12 Apr.)

A New York item mentions Capts. Green, Steel, Menzie, Swan, Johnson, Morsley, Cooper, Serjeant, Wyatt, Davis, Dickinson, Clark, Spurrier and Jeremiah Leacraft (12 Apr.)

List of vessels at various ports (12 Apr.)

Capt. Budden was to have sailed from London about 3 weeks after Capt. Mesnard; the snow *Sarah*, Capt. Mitchell, for London, will fall down on Monday (12 Apr.)

At a meeting of Phila. Contributors for insuring houses agt. loss by fire the following were elected directors: Benjamin Franklin, William Coleman, Joseph Morris, Samuel Rhoads, Israel Pemberton, Isaac Jones, Abel James and James Logan; John Smith was chosen treasurer (12 Apr.)

Rev. Peters will preach a sermon at the Academy for benefit of the poor children of Phila. (12 Apr.)

Adv. of Stephen Carmick at his store under Capt. William Spafford's in Market St. (12 Apr.)

William Fulton, Irish servant, age c. 24, runaway from Edward Turner, living at Point-no-Point, Phila. Co. (12 Apr.)

George Palmer, secretary, announces meeting of the Germantown Library Co. at the house of Daniel Macknet, Jr. (12 Apr.)

William Moore intends for London in the *Lydia*, Capt. Reeve (12 Apr.)

Adv. of Benjamin Kendall, at corner of Third St. (12 Apr.)

William Hammer, of Tinnicum Twp., Bucks Co., has absconded; his creditors are to meet at the house of John Wilson in said twp. (12 Apr.)

Cornelius Collins, Irish servant, age c. 22, runaway from Abel Harris in Manington Twp., Salem Co. (12 Apr.)

John Wood in Roxborough Twp. has taken up a stray horse (12 Apr.)

Robert Whitehead, English servant, who has been whipped and branded at Trenton, runaway from John Burroughs of Trenton, Hunterdon Co., N.J. (12 Apr.)

Adv. of Tench Francis, Jr., at store in Front St., opposite to John Armitt's (12 Apr.)

Adv. of Capt. James Child in Water St. (12 Apr.)

1753

Plantation on west side of Sasquehanna for sale by James Silver; enquire of Silver on the premises or Edward Shippen, Esq., in Lancaster (12 Apr.)

Adv. of Thomas and William Lightfoot at corner of Arch and Water Sts. (12 Apr.)

John Mayiam, servant, age c. 19, runaway from Daniel Oliver, of Boston, peruke-maker (12 Apr.)

Adv. of Mrs. Redmond in Chestnut St. (12 Apr.)

Adv. of Thomas Preston, at his store in Second St., next door to Joshua Maddox, Esq. (12 Apr.)

Real estate at Roaringtown in Mill Creek Hundred, New Castle Co., and near White-clay Creek Landing for sale, the whole the property of Walter Thetford, taken in execution by Sheriff George Monro (12 Apr.)

Time of a servant for sale; enquire of Isaac Garrique in Tun Alley (12 Apr.)

David Fitz Gerrald, Irish servant, age c. 26, runaway from his master, William Murray, peruke-maker in King St., Boston (12 Apr.)

House to be sold or let by Henry Marselis, living in Trenton (12 Apr.)

Dennis O'Neal, living at James Davis's in Trediffryn, Chester Co., has taken up a stray mare (12 Apr.)

Peter Green (alias Sparks), convict servant, who speaks West-Country English, age c. 42, runaway from Samuel Read, of Frederick Co., Md. (12 Apr.)

Brick tenement, with malt-house and brew-house, in Northern Liberties to be sold or let; apply to Preserve Brown at his mills in Nottingham, Burlington Co., N.J., or Thomas Clifford in Phila. (12 Apr.)

Real estate, property of the late John Spencer, dec'd, will be sold at his house in Kinsington by Diana Spencer, exec. (19 Apr.)

Griffith Evans, hired servant, born in Wales, age c. 48, runaway from Mary Mitchell, living at the Eastern Branch Ferry; reward if runaway is brought to Thomas Cramphin of Prince George's Co., Md. (19 Apr.)

Stallion from stable of William Hunter in Chester Co., kept three seasons, one by John Hambright in the Great Valley, one by Robert Hopkins at Point-no-Point and one by John Allen, Esq., at Trenton, is now kept by Thomas Bartholomew at the Sign of the White Horse in Elbow Lane (19 Apr.)

The following are the managers of the Delaware Lottery: Reynald Hooper (son of R. Lettice Hooper, Esq.), Joseph Warrell, Jr. (son of Joseph Warrell, Esq.), Joseph Reed, Jr. (son of Andrew Reed, Esq.), Theophilus Severns, Esq., John Allen, Jr. (son of John Allen, Esq.), William Paxton (son of Joseph Paxton, Esq., dec'd) and John Clayton (son of William Clayton, Esq.); tickets are sold at Trenton by Moore Furman, merchant, and at Phila. by Andrew Reed, Esq.; with the money an English and Grammar School is to be built in Trenton under direction of Joseph Reed, Benjamin Yard, Alexander Chambers and John Chambers, all of Trenton (19 Apr.)

Alexander Ray has removed from his store on Hamilton's wharf to the house late of Trotter and Elliot in Front St. (19 Apr.)

Time of a Dutch servant girl to be disposed of by Plunket Fleeson, upholsterer, in Chestnut St. (19 Apr.)

Persons indebted to John Hunt, tavern-keeper, at the Sign of the Ship-a-ground in Water St., are to make prompt payment (19 Apr.)

John Sayre lost his pocketbook under the Courthouse (19 Apr.)

Adv. of Moses Joyce at Mrs. Rankin's in Water St. (19 Apr.)

Elizabeth Neason (called "Lisey"), Dutch servant, runaway from Joseph Beaks, drayman, in Phila. (19 Apr.)

House in Water St., next door to Samuel Shoemaker's, to be let; enquire of Benjamin or Samuel Shoemaker (19 Apr.)

Real estate on Society Hill for sale; apply to Edward Jones at the Vineyard (19 Apr.)

Horse strayed or stolen from Joseph Turner's plantation; reward if brought to the Sign of the Indian King in Market St. or to George Gostalow, living on said plantation (19 Apr.)

Coat and cap stolen from house of Morto Quin in Walnut St. (19 Apr.)

Magdalene Jouvenal, who came last fall with her father from Holland in a ship consigned to James Pemberton, was sold to one Richard Bowman; news of her is sought by her father and should be brought to said Pemberton or Anthony Benezet in Phila. (19 Apr.)

Plantation will be sold by public vendue by Evan Evans at the house of Evan Evans, of Whiteland, Chester Co., near the White Horse Tavern (19 Apr.)

Adv. of Thomas Campbell, about a mile from Phila.; he has erected there a bleaching-green to be run by David Kidd (19 Apr.)

John Duckey, born in Ireland, has escaped from goal in Chester; reward for his capture will be paid by William Hay (19 Apr.)

If James Gibson (son of John Gibson of Sligoe, Ireland), who came to Maryland in 1746, will go to George Gibson of Lancaster he will hear something to his advantage (19 Apr.)

House in Pemberton's New Street will be sold by Leonard Vandegrift (admin. of estate of Peter Granson, dec'd) at the house of William Whitehead in Second St. (19 Apr.)

Adv. of Joseph Borden, Jr., and Joseph Richards about service of the stage boat, Nicholas George master, and shallop, Charles Taylor master (19 Apr.)

In a New York item mention is made of Capts. Amy, Sheldon, Smith, Coffee, Richards, Everson, Kiersted, Gordon and Ray (26 Apr.)

The shallop Rebeccah, Andrew Doz master, overset Thu. last near Gloucester Point (26 Apr.)

Capt. Hall has arrived at the Capes from Jamaica (26 Apr.)

Stallion is kept at Chatham Ropeyard on the Passyunk Road by George Goodwin, late of York, England (26 Apr.)

Adv. of Thomas Gregory, brass founder, in Third St. (26 Apr.)

Tracts of land in Kent Co. on Delaware, late property of Capt. Ebenezer Heathorn, dec'd, for sale by John Vandyke (26 Apr.)

Jacob Shoemaker, at the Sign of the Spinning-wheel in Market St., offers reward for recovery of strayed or stolen horse (26 Apr.)

Philip Cantlon, Iriah servant, age c. 30, runaway from Thomas Rambo, of Mantua Creek, Gloucester Co. (26 Apr.)

Negro named Cuff, who formerly lived with one Scogan (a bricklayer) and then with Anthony Morris, Jr., runaway from Daniel Cooper at the ferry opposite to Phila. (26 Apr.)

House and land of Matthias Millane, of Cresum, dec'd, near the country seat of William Allen, Esq., will be sold at public vendue by John Johnson and Jacob Levering, execs.; plan of land may be seen at house of John Johnson in Germantown (26 Apr.)

Thomas Brown, servant, born near Lancaster, Pa., age c. 25 or 26, runaway from Isaac Conroe, of Burlington, N.J. (26 Apr.)

Accounts with estate of James Tipper, dec'd, to be settled with Ann Tipper, admin. (26 Apr.)

Horse stolen or strayed from John Guy, carter, living in upper end of Walnut St. (26 Apr.)

One John Roberts (*alias* Jones), arrested on suspicion of theft, has escaped, leaving behind his horse (26 Apr.)

John Kean, Irish servant, age c. 20, runaway from Francis Fisher, of East Caln, Chester Co. (26 Apr.)

Brick house below the drawbridge, late property of Robert Toms, taken in execution at suit of William Dowell, will be sold by Sheriff Samuel Morris; land is bounded on south by the property of Thomas Bond and Archibald M'Call; sale will be at house of John Cross (26 Apr.)

Adv. of Andrew Reed, removed to house of Peter Bard in Water St. (26 Apr.)

New York item mentions Capts. Harris, Scot Lawrence, Bussy, Toppam, Gardner and Hunter (3 May)

James M'Daniel, convicted in Phila. of picking the pocket of William Duncason, was sentenced to be whipped (3 May)

Adv. of Cornelius Bradford, pewterer, in Second St. (3 May)

Boot, a Mulatto, age c. 25, runaway from Thomas Hunt of Amwell (3 May)

Plantation in Passyunk Twp., late estate of William Hughes, taken in execution by Sheriff Samuel Morris, will be sold at the house of John Biddle; the plantation is a little above George Gray's and is bounded by lands of Peter Cox and John Sober (3 May)

Shute's plantation in the Northern Liberties will be sold by public vendue at the house of John Biddle (3 May)

Real estate in Lower Merion Twp., late estate of Rees Thomas, taken in execution, will be sold by public vendue at house of Richard Hughes on the Lancaster Road; house borders on land of William Thomas (3 May)

Log house and land in Upper Merion, late estate of John Fletcher, taken in execution at suit of Mary Wilson, adjoining land of one Rees and Joseph Williams, will be sold by Sheriff Morris (3 May)

1753

Charles and Flora, his wife, country-born Negroes, runaways from John Paca of Bush River, Baltimore Md. (3 May)

Real estate in Chestnut St., property of Thomas Peters, late of Phila., shopkeeper, dec'd, for sale; enquire of the Widow Peters (3 May)

House and lot in Phila., part of the estate of John Shewbert, dec'd, to be sold at public vendue at house of John Biddle in High St. (3 May)

House and lot in Reading, Berks Co., late property of Philip Jacob Erpfe, taken in execution at suit of Michael Sauser, will be sold by Sheriff Benjamin Lightfoot (3 May)

House and lot in Reading, late property of Andrew Shock, taken in execution at suit of Samuel Flower & Co., will be sold by public vendue at house of Conrad Bower in Redding (3 May)

Adv. of Joseph Fox in Third St. and John Cox on Market St. Wharf (3 May)

Land and former tavern in Kennet Twp., Chester Co., part of the estate of Abraham Parker, dec'd, formerly property of Elizabeth Ring (alias M'Neal), to be sold by Samuel Gilpen and John Chads, execs. (3 May)

Accounts with estate of John Jackson, dec'd, to be settled with Alexander Moore and John Blackwood, execs. (3 May)

Thomas James, servant, born in or near Phila., who used to drive a team for Bennet Bard in Burlington Co., age c. 19, runaway from Patrick Reynolds of Mount-holly, N.J. (3 May)

John Schluter, Dutch servant, age c. 48, runaway from Jasper Poleson, of Brandywine Hundred, New-Castle Co. (3 May)

Plantation in Maccungle Twp., Northampton Co., late the estate of Christopher Haymaker, taken in execution at suit of Dirk Johnson, will be sold by Sheriff William Craig (3 May)

Mulatto woman for sale by Edward Evans and Thomas Say, execs. of estate of Elizabeth Story, dec'd (3 May)

Samuel Morris, admin. of estate of David Morris, dec'd, will sell share in an iron forge in West N.J.; he will also sell at the house of Richard Waln in Whitemarsh, Phila. Co. (3 May)

Johannes Haas, Dutch servant, age c. 18, runaway from Daniel Lefever, living in Lampeter Twp., Lancaster Co. (3 May)

Jack, a Mulatto, born in Allen-town, Monmouth Co., age c. 22, runaway from Robert Newell, living in Hunterdon Co., East N.J.; reward if he is brought to his master or to James Newell in Allen-town (3 May)

George Palmer announces meeting of the Germantown Library Co. to be held at house of Daniel Mackenet, Jr. (3 May)

Time of a servant lad for sale by Samuel and Thomas Smith in Water St. (3 May)

Account of murder of an Indian near Stockbridge, Mass., by Robert and Stephen Cooke, who have been arrested and committed to goal (10 May)

Capt. Robbins has arrived at Boston from New Providence (10 May)

Capts. Coffy and Viner Leaycraft have arrived at New York (10 May)

John Rian whipped in New York for picking a pocket (10 May)

1753

Account of fight in Kentucky, with mention of Mr. Croghan, John Finley and Michael Tatte (10 May)

Capt. Swaine in the schooner *Argo* seeks the northwest passage (10 May)

On 26 April at York John Swait was found guilty of the murder of John Reily and received sentence of death (10 May)

At Lancaster Catherine Reynolds was sentenced to death for the murder of her bastard child (10 May)

Weston Rakes and one Boyd were tried at Lancaster for the murder of Catherine Shreiner; Boyd was acquitted but Rakes was found guilty of manslaughter (10 May)

Reference to Capts. William Haselton, Coates and Bellamy (10 May)

At a meeting of contributors to the Pennsylvania Hospital the following managers were chosen: Joshua Crosby, Benjamin Franklin, Israel Pemberton, Jr., John Smith, Samuel Rhodes, John Reynell, Samuel Hazard, Isaac Jones, Joseph Morris, Hugh Roberts, William Griffitts and Evan Morgan; Charles Norris was chosen treasurer (10 May)

On 9 May Capt. Reeve in the ship *Lydia* fell down the river for London (10 May)

Adv. of Alexander Lunan, who is removed from the store next door to Capt. Philips in Water St. to that late Mr. Ray's on Hamilton's wharf (10 May)

Bastian Remus, Dutch servant, age upwards of 40, who pretends to be a miller, runaway from Joseph Williams of Lower Merion Twp., Phila. Co. (10 May)

House in Arch St., next door to Lewis Evans, is to be sold by John Hart at public vendue at John Biddle's (10 May)

Accounts with estate of late Caspar Wistar, of Phila., buttonmaker, dec'd, to be settled with Catherine Wistar, David Dainler, Richard Johnston and Richard Wistar, execs. (10 May)

John Ellis, glazier, in Front St., intends to leave the province (10 May)

Mare broke into the pasture of John Shoemaker, Jr. (10 May)

John Devonshire (*alias* Cavin), Irish servant, age c. 20, runaway from James Day of Middletown, Chester Co. (10 May)

Plantation in Lower Milford Twp., Bucks Co., late property of Thomas Christy, taken in execution at the suit of Standish Ford, will be sold by Sheriff William Yeardly; this property is bounded on the W. by land of Richard Roberts, on the N. by Morris Morris, on the E. by Thomas Roberts, on the S. by Charles Maycock (10 May)

Reward for recovery of strayed or stolen mare will be paid by Marcus Hulings, Jr.; the mare is to be brought to Marcus Hulings, living in Easton, or Michael Hulings, shipwright, at the upper end of Phila. (10 May)

Evan Evans of London Britain Twp., Chester Co., offers reward for recovery of watch (maker is Kover), lost between Evan Rice's, of Miln Creek Hundred, and James Alison's of Wilmington (10 May)

Adv. of Edward Penington on S. side of Edward Warner's wharf (10 May)

John Metcalfe, of Patapsco, Md., offers reward for capture of the following four runaway convict servants: John Gingle, farmer, born in west of England; Thomas Brown, brickmaker, age c. 50; Edward Mitchem, age c. 40, who has been a schoolmaster; William Fitch, who was in the army several years (10 May)

Managers of lottery for buying a town clock and cleaning the dock in Annapolis are the following: Benjamin Tasker, Jr., George Steuart, Walter Dulany and Edward Dorsey, Esqrs., Dr. Alexander Hamilton, Robert Swan, Lancelot Jacques, William Reynolds, Samuel Soumaien, Beale Bordley, James Maccubin, James Johnson and Jonas Green; Tickets may be had of them or of John Groves and William Franklin in Phila. (10 May)

Archibald Ewing has absconded; his creditors are to meet John Scott at New London, Chester Co. (10 May)

Johannes Agender, of Aegypta Twp., Northampton Co., has absconded; his creditors are to meet with George Good, auditor, at Easton (10 May)

Plantation in Duck-creek Hundred, Kent Co. on Delaware, for sale; enquire of John Pennington on the premises (10 May)

Lot of ground, part of Carpenter's Square, to be sold or let; apply to Joseph Gray in Market St. or George Gray, brewer, in Chestnut St. (10 May)

Adv. of Thomas Wharton on Carpenter's wharf, where Joseph Saunders lately kept (10 May)

Adv. of Alexander Huston in Second St. (10 May)

Chief Justice Charles Pinckney of South Carolina and family sail for England in the *Edinburgh*, Capt. Russell (17 May)

A schooner, Miles Tedar master, was towed into port by a sloop from Virginia (17 May)

Conner and Grace, captured by Indians, kill their captors and escape to Charles-Town, S.C. (17 May)

Lowe Jackson, of Nansemond Co., was executed 13 Apr. at Williamsburgh, Va. (17 May)

Williamsburgh, Va., item of 20 April mentions Capts. Chip, Kelly and Bedford and Mr. Loveit of Cork (17 May)

Capt. Vallacot in the *Hubbastone* has arrived at Annapolis (17 May)

At Annapolis, Md., Daniel Spinkse and Charles Campbell were convicted of breaking into the store of Edmund Trafford, John Brown of burglary and felony and Thomas Carter of robbing Andrew Rench; the husband of Mrs. Alethea Cook was acquitted of the charge of murdering his wife (17 May)

It is reported that Horatio Sharpe is appointed Gov. of Maryland (17 May)

Capt. Richards has arrived at New York in the ship *Dover* from London; he sailed with Capts. Griffith and Miller of New York and Capt. Budden (17 May)

Capt. Freeman reports at Annapolis that the schooner *Susannah*, Robert Jones master, was cast away near the entrance of Old Top-Sail Inlet (17 May)

Arthur Dobs, Esq., has arrived in Virginia (17 May)

1753

Capts. Edwards and Katter from Phila. have arrived at St. Kitts (17 May)

House and barn of Nicholas Warner, farmer, who lives about 3 miles from Reading, burnt down (17 May)

At Burlington John Shores was committed for stealing a cow (17 May)

Adv. of David Hall at the New Printing Office in Market St. (17 May)

Francis Clayton, English servant, age 24, runaway from Moses Standley of Phila.; Clayton was imported in the ship Sarah, Capt. Tillidge, from Bristol (17 May)

Gov. Robert Dinwiddie of Va. ordered hue and cry after a Negro slave named Plymouth, age c. 28, runaway from John Minge of Charles City Co.; the runaway was clandestinely sold to one George Lawson of Cecil Co., Md.; reward if the slave or news of him is brought to Isaac Greenleafe of Phila. or Isaac Webster in Md. (17 May)

Arthur M'Closky, Irish servant, age c. 35, runaway from Robert Powell, living in Whiteland, Chester Co. (17 May)

James Kelly, Irish servant, and Henry Freeherden, English servant, age 28, runaways from Thomas Underhill, living within 6 miles of Charles-Town, Cecil Co., Md. (17 May)

Charles Damrees, Low Dutchman, a notorious horse-stealer, who speaks French and Indian, has escaped from the goal of Newtown, Bucks Co.; reward offered by Sheriff William Yeardley and Undersheriff Joseph Inslee (17 May)

Connor O'Bryan, Irish servant, age c. 25, runaway from Bryan Connolly, living at Elk River, Md. (17 May)

David M'Ilvaine, Secretary of the St. Andrew's Society, gives notice of a meeting (17 May)

Brigantine Molley, now at Capt. William Attwood's wharf, will be sold at Jones's Coffee-house; apply to Attwood Shute or Capt. Thomas Lauderdale (17 May)

Nathaniel Allen, Jr., in Front St., opposite Joseph Turner, Esq., sells pickled sturgeon, done by the wife of Edward Broadfield, lately arrived in this country and living in Bordentown (17 May)

Saw-mill has lately been erected at Bristol, Bucks Co.; to buy lumber apply to William M'Ilvaine of Phila., merchant, or Alexander Graydon and William Buckly in Bristol (17 May)

Land at Bussel-town, adjoining land of Jacob and Thomas Duffield, late estate of Jacob Duffield, taken in execution at suit of Hannah Leech, will be sold by Sheriff Samuel Morris (17 May)

Plantation on great road from Germantown to Whitemarsh, now in possession of John Gardner, and also a farm called Somerhausen, now in possession of John Grassner, and also a papermill, late the estate of Peter Cock, dec'd, taken in execution at suit of David Vanhorne, will be sold by Sheriff Morris (17 May)

Daniel Miller, Irish servant, age c. 40, runaway from Lazarus Pine, adjoining Benjamin Cooper's ferry (17 May)

Adv. of Robert Robson, farrier, from Yorkshire, England, who lives at Daniel Swan's in Market St. (17 May)

1753

Land in Morris Co., West N.J., late property of William Biddle, for sale; apply to Samuel Smith, William Lawrence or Joshua Fisher in Phila. (17 May)

Merchandize consigned to Alexander M'Douall in Phila. from Liverpool on the Charming Polly, James M'Cullough master; M'Douall, at Capt. William Child's in Chestnut St., has not received advice of the merchandize (17 May)

Richard Dalton, Irish servant, age c. 23, runaway from Peter Sigfriedusalriebs, near Christine Ferry, New-Castle Hundred (17 May)

Gov. Shirley is expected at Boston in June (24 May)

New York item mentions Capt. White of the snow Unicorn, Capts. Stuppard, Ramsey, Albuoy, Spurrier, Mosley, Coverly, Butler, Brown, Davis, Dixon, Weynman, Furlong, and also Capt. Lawrence in the brig Shrewsbury (late Capt. Pattygary, who died in the Bay); Capt. White spoke with Capt. Whipple (24 May)

List of arrivals at different ports (24 May)

News has arrived of the death of son of the Hon. Thomas Penn (24 May)

Prisoners released in France have been brought to America by Capt. Budden (24 May)

On 8 May Hugh Irwin, of Springfield, Bucks Co., was killed by a falling tree; the same day Josiah Wilkinson, of Buckingham, Bucks Co., was accidentally struck with an ax, a blow which will probably be fatal (24 May)

John Denniston, servant, shoemaker, age between 32 and 33, and his wife Hannah, servant, age c. 25, runaways from Daniel Campbell, at the Falls of Rappahannock, Va. (24 May)

John Peele will sell household goods at his house in Arch St. (24 May)

Robert Meade of Phila. intends to depart the province; household goods will be sold by public vendue at his house on Society Hill, next door to Alexander Alexander's (24 May)

Adv. of Samuel Emlen, at the Sign of the Golden Heart, in Phila. (24 May)

Adv. of Wallace and Bryan on Market St. wharf (24 May)

Tract of land on Little-Timber-Creek, about a mile from Gloucester, adjoining ground of William Harrison, for sale by Joseph Hogg, living in Race St., Phila. (24 May)

Negro for sale; enquire at George Morrison's in Second St. (24 May)

Adv. of John Logan, who is removed to William Logan's new house in Second St. (24 May)

Adv. of Samuel Neave in Front St. (24 May)

Adv. of Samuel Howell at the Sign of the Beaver in Chestnut St. (24 May)

Robert Harvey, Englishman, age c. 32, is in goal in Phila. on suspicion of being a runaway; his owner may apply to Edward Collings, goal-keeper (24 May)

Accounts with estate of Thomas Green, dec'd, to be settled with Martha Green, exec., in Phila. (24 May)

Adv. of Thomas Preston in Second St. (24 May)

Medicines for sale by William Chancellor at John Jervis's in Second St. (24 May)

Adv. of Christopher House, peruke-maker, from London, at the Sign of the Valiant Dragoon in Front St. (24 May)

Robert M'Curdy in Springfield Twp., Phila. Co., has taken up a horse (24 May)

Michael Keens, a Dutch lad, was imported into this country a year ago last fall and was sold to Christopher Yust; one Caspar Studer, imported at the same time was sold to the same Yust; John Keens, Michael's father, wishes to see his son and Caspar; John may be heard of at Capt. Coultas's ferry or at one Mislingers below said ferry (24 May)

New York item mentions Capts. Shortess, Moodie, Hodan, Albuoy, Scot Lawrence and Flower (of Phila.), Topham (of R.I.), Sample (of Boston) Kip and Bussey (of N.Y.) (31 May)

Thomas Martin is in prison in New York for stabbing Gilbert King (31 May)

Sat. night a boy of 15, who belonged to the snow Neptune, Capt. Harrison, fell overboard and was drowned according to N.Y. item of 28 May (31 May)

House of William Tufts in Salem, N.J., was burnt by lightning last week (31 May)

Ship Carolina, Capt. Mesnard, will fall down for London tomorrow; the ship Beulah, Capt. Ritchie, of Phila., has arrived at Newry (31 May)

Horse strayed or stolen from plantation of Thomas Rose near Phila. (31 May)

Tract of land within 1½ miles of borough of Wilmington will be sold by William Empson at public vendue at house of Edward Dawes in Wilmington (31 May)

Plantation in Soleberry Twp., Bucks Co., late property of William Satterthwaite, dec'd, now in custody of William Biles, admin., taken in execution at suit of Lawrence Growdon, Esq., will be sold by Sheriff William Yeardley at the house of Joseph Inslee in Newtown; the land is bounded on the N. by Clutter's land and on the S. by land of Stoffel Rose (31 May)

John Leadlie, of Bristol Twp., Phila. Co., has taken up a stray mare (31 May)

House in Sassafras St. in which Mr. Stoner formerly preached will be sold by Leonard Melchor and John Stillwaggon (31 May)

Henry Barlow, English convict servant, age c. 30, broke out of goal of New-Castle; reward for his capture will be paid by Sheriff George Monrow or by William Hodge or Alexander Lunan in Phila. (31 May)

Time of Dutch girl for sale; enquire of James Humphreys in Second St. (31 May)

Time of English servant woman to be sold by William Henderson or Glover Hunt in Market St. (31 May)

Adv. of Matthew and Abraham Usher at the Green Doors in Walnut St. (31 May)

Horse strayed or stolen from Jacob Herse of Cheltenham, Phila. Co. (31 May)

Chaise for sale; enquire of Danial Swan, chaise-maker, near the prison in Phila. (31 May)

Andrew Ramsay, late of Long Island ferry, has revived the Trenton ferry (31 May)

Philip Cantlin, Irish servant, age c. 27, runaway from Thomas Rambo of Mantua Creek, Gloucester Co., West Jersey (31 May)

Williamsburgh item mentions Capt. Elligood of the brig Milcah and Capt. Whitwell of H.M.S. Triton (7 June)

On 16 May Charles Campbell, Daniel Spinkse and John Brown were executed at Annapolis and Thomas Carter was pardoned (7 June)

Sat. last arrived in Patuxent River from London the ship Diamond, Capt. Hutchinson, with James Russell, merchant, on board as a passenger, according to Annapolis item of 24 May (7 June)

Capts. Cockson and Chew were to sail on 20 Apr. from London, with Gov. Sharpe on board the former (7 June)

Boston item mentions arrival at Boston of Capt. Connell in the ship John Galley and of Capt. Davidson from London; an account is given of the killing of Capt. Pennetters and his crew by Indians (7 June)

Capt. Lawrence arrived at New York from Barbados; Capt. Bull from Phila. arrived at Barbados; Capt. Brown reports the safe arrival in Ireland of Capts. Marshal, Boggs, Falls, Campbell, Barns, M'Quoid and Donaldson (7 June)

New York item mentions Capts. Jauncey, Hill, Bowen, Badger and Troy (7 June)

John Swales was executed at York for the murder of John Reily (7 June)

On 30 May the Rev. Cradock from Md. preached in Academy Hall (7 June)

Tue. last in Phila. James Robinson was sentenced to receive 21 lashes for felony and Margaret Hammon 11 lashes for the same crime (7 June)

Plantation in Ashton Twp., Chester Co., to be sold by Joseph Wharton (7 June)

A stranger left two horses at house of Adam Boyer in Hallam Twp., York Co. (7 June)

Richard Norton, of Cecil Co., Md., will not pay debts contracted in future by his wife Unity (7 June)

Sheriff Samuel Morris of Phila. is removed to a house in Second St., a few doors below William Branson's (7 June)

James Hamilton, Esq., of S.C., has obtained a grant of 213,000 acres of land; persons desiring to settle there are to apply to Joseph Shute at the house of Rebecca Steel in Second St. (7 June)

Plantation near S.W. bounds of Phila., belonging to estate of John Kinsey, Esq., dec'd, is to be let; enquire of William Plumsted, Israel Pemberton, Jr., or James Kinsey (7 June)

Accounts with estate of Thomas Shinn, Esq., late of Mountholly, dec'd, to be settled with Henry Paxson and John Woolman, execs. (7 June)

On 28 May Seth Morse of Medfield, Mass., and his two sons, one aged 10 and the other about 7, were drowned in crossing the Charles River (14 June)

New York item mentions Capts. Bayne, Dowell, Taylor, Hill, Jones, Ovens, M'Gee, White, M'Dougall, Allison, Nuttle, Allen, Comrin, Mitchell, Warner, Halloway, Bowen, Rolland, Troy, Ramsey, Spurrier, Waynman, Brown, Furlong, Lawrence, Dickenson, Davis and French (14 June)

At Southole (Southold), Long Island, about three weeks ago, Richard Howell accidentally killed the Rev. John Paine of that place, according to New York item of 11 June (14 June)

Adv. of Augustine Stilman, opposite to James Benezet's in Market St. (14 June)

Adv. of Sarah Brown, living in the house where Michael Brown formerly lived, near Capt. Lyon's house in Sassafras St., near the back part of Edward Warner's house (14 June)

Adv. of Henry Brabazon, dry-scowerer from Dublin, at the house of John Nicholls, carpenter, in Arch St. (14 June)

Richard Hern, English servant, age c. 19, who can speak French, runaway from John Johnson, living in Bert Twp., Lancaster Co.; reward will be paid by said Johnson or Robert Wilson (14 June)

Real estate of Thomas Peters, late of Phila., shopkeeper, dec'd, will be sold by the Widow Peters (14 June)

Isaac Garrison, this country born, age c. 32, runaway from his bail, taking his wife with him; runaway with him is one John Largley; reward will be paid by J. James, Jr., John Lasey or Joseph Garrison (14 June)

Cuff, a Negro, age c. 40, runaway from James Jeans, living on Frankford Road (14 June)

Elizabeth Gollin, Dutch servant, age 14, runaway from Alexander Cruikshank, living in Phila. (14 June)

Con O'Neel, Irish servant, age c. 39 or 40, runaway from Peter Menkens, of Sassafras Neck, Cecil Co., Md. (14 June)

James Dun (alias Dunnebe), Irish servant, age c. 35, runaway from James Scoggin of Alloway's Creek, Salem Co. (14 June)

New York item mentions Capts. Bryant, Ewing, Joseph Hudson, Burchell and Finley (21 June)

It is reported that William Shirley has been appointed Gov. of New York in the room of George Clinton (21 June)

Benjamin Franklin requests observations about the effects of lightning (21 June)

Adv. of John Leacock, goldsmith and jeweller, who is removed into Walnut St. at the Sign of the Golden Cup (21 June)

William Gray, at the Conestogoe-waggon in Market St., seeks the services of a man who understands farming and whose wife understands the management of a dairy (21 June)

Mare strayed or stolen from Richard Jacob of Bebber Twp. on Perkeomen (21 June)

Robert Lettis Hooper has to let a fulling-mill and dye-house in Trenton (21 June)

1753

Samuel Robinson of the parish of Bangar near Belfast, Ireland, blacksmith, came to Pa. about 15 or 16 years ago; John Robinson requests that news of Samuel be brought to Alexander Lunan, merchant, in Phila. or to the printer (21 June)

Adv. of Isaac Thornton in Arch St. at Mrs. Ann Forbes's (21 June)

John Hase, Irishman, sawyer, of Charles-town, Cecil Co., Md., has escaped from Edward Veasey; Hase took with him his English wife Hannah; Johannes Arents offers reward if Hase is brought to the sheriff (21 June)

Augustine Stahl, Dutch servant, age c. 20 or 25, runaway from John Robinson, living in Mill-creek Hundred, New-Castle Co. (21 June)

Ironworks at Cohansie, Cumberland Co., for sale; apply to Samuel Barnes on the premises (21 June)

The following English convict servants, property of Charles Carroll, Esq., and Company, have run away: John Williams, born in Herefordshire, bred a farmer, age c. 30; John Oulton, born in the country but bred mostly in London; reward will be paid by Richard Croxall (21 June)

Henry Whit, Mulatto, age c. 25, who says he served his time with John Linsey, Esq., near Frederick-town, Va., has been committed to goal in Lancaster on suspicion of being a runaway servant; notice inserted by John Clark, keeper of the goal (21 June)

Real estate in Phila. to be sold at public vendue at the house of John Biddle; enquire of Hannah Beasley on the premises (21 June)

Nicholas Gale canes chairs; he is to be spoke with at house of William Cunningham, at the Sign of the Rising Sun in Market St. (21 June)

Richard Jarrad, at Spring-Garden, will let the house in which he now lives (21 June)

Time of a Dutch servant girl, age c. 17, for sale; enquire of Owen Fling in Second St. (21 June)

George Duke offers reward for recovery of his mare, strayed or stolen from the pasture belonging to John Jones (21 June)

Phillis, Negro, age c. 25, runaway from John Jones of Germantown (21 June)

Plantation in Chester Co., between lands of Joseph Eavenson and Robert Mercer, and also tract of land in West Bradford between the Chalfonts land and land of John Leard and Richard Pim and also plantation on Brandywine Creek, adjoining lands of Samuel Taylor and Jonathan Parke, all for sale by John Taylor, exec. of Isaac Taylor, the elder, and admin. of Isaac Taylor, the younger, dec'd (21 June)

John Connor, age c. 25, and Thomas Johnston (who has a wife and little boy), age c. 30, runaways from Thomas Ogle, living near Christiana Bridge in New-Castle Co. (21 June)

Samuel Morris, sheriff, at the house of Benjamin Bagnall in Front St., next door to Dr. Kearsley, will sell household goods and set of watchmaker's tools taken in execution (21 June)

Robert Meade, living on Society Hill, next door to Alexander Alexander's, soon will leave the province (21 June)

Brother of the Rev. Cleveland was recently killed by Indians on Cape Breton (28 June)

New York item of 25 June mentions Capts. Kip, Lewis, Hunter, Cregier, King, Dungam, Thomas White, Nealson, Carlisle and Haselton (28 June)

Ship Duke of Wirtemberg, Daniel Montpelier master, will sail for London (28 June)

Country seat between Moyamensing and Passyunk Road, adjoining land of James Lownes, to be sold by Edward Fitzrandolph (28 June)

Sloop Mayflower, Nathan Solley master, will be sold by public vendue at Market St. wharf (28 June)

John Lewis of Phila. offers reward for recovery of horse that strayed or was stolen from plantation of John Smith of Uuchland, Chester Co. (28 June)

Adv. of James Peller at New-market wharf (28 June)

Stone house near middle of Germantown and a lot of three acres near William Ottinger's in Springfield, near Whitemarsh, to be sold by Anthony Newhouse (28 June)

Hugh Mulvehill, Irish convict servant, runaway from David Clement, living in St. George's Hundred, New-Castle Co. (28 June)

Schoolmaster available; enquire at Samuel Hurford's in Second St. (28 June)

Ship Thames Frigate, James Dobbins captain, and the snow Polly, John Troy captain, with servants sent from London for seven years, have arrived at Annapolis (5 Juny)

Boston item of 25 June mentions Capt. Long, Gov. Shirley and Capt. Montague (5 July)

New York item of 2 July mentions Capt. Seymour from South Carolina, Capts. Lawrence, Brown and Dickson from the Bay of Honduras, Capts. Spurrier and Sergeant of R.I., Capt. Furlong of N.Y., Capts. Sweet, Duncan and Church of R.I., Capts. Davis and Waynman of N.Y., Capts. Tuder, Dunbar, Winthrop, Kiersted, French and Laws (5 July)

Fri. last Capt. Lownes arrived at Phila. from Antigua (5 July)

On 4 July in the Mayor's Court in Phila. Mary Jessop, Catherine Wood and Bridget Burn were convicted of felony and sentenced to be whipped (5 July)

Post Office in Phila. is removed to a house in Third St. by order of William Franklin, Deputy Postmaster (5 July)

Sam, a Negro, age 27, runaway from the brigantine Warren at Clark's wharf; his wife, also Negro, belongs to the Widow Conyers but lives with Capt. Condy; reward if Sam is brought to Henry Elves (5 July)

Michael Walker, Irish servant, age $\underline{c}$. 25, runaway from John Garret of Blockley Twp., Phila. Co. (5 July)

Time of a boy of 15 for sale by Lazarus Lowrie (5 July)

Elizabeth Humphreys, Welch servant, age $\underline{c}$. 25, runaway from Samuel Preston Moore (5 July)

John Hogans, Irish servant, age 20, a good clerk, runaway from James Anderson of Donegall (5 July)

1753

Items belonging to estate of Samuel Hasell, Esq., dec'd, for sale; enquire of Alexander Huston in Second St. (5 July)

Thomas Kelly, Irish servant, age c. 23, and Anthony Clery, Irish servant, age c. 24, runaways from Robert Evans and John Smith, living near the Head of Elk, Cecil Co., Md. (5 July.)

Tract of land in Lower Dublin Twp., extending N.W. by Henry Lycan's land, N.E. by David Fulton's land and S.E. by Benjamin Engle's land, late belonging to Thomas Powell, dec'd, to be sold by Eleanor Powell, Joshua Jones and John Daniel, execs. (5 July)

Two mares broke out of pasture of Joseph Bell, innkeeper, in Third St.; reward if brought to said Bell, George Elly at Camby's ferry or Richard Hains (5 July)

Country seat about ½ mile from upper end of Germantown mainstreet to be sold or rented; apply to Joseph Marks (5 Juny)

Plantation at mouth of Pensouken Creek in Waterford Twp., Gloucester Co., West N.J., to be sold or let by Benjamin Morgan, living on the premises (5 July)

Daniel Johnson, Scotch servant, age c. 25, who has been a drummer in the army, runaway from George Rock, of North East, Cecil Co. (5 July)

John Gordon, Scotch servant, age c. 30, runaway from Andrew Gibson, near Samuel White's tavern in Cecil Co., Md. (5 July)

William Kemp, Scotch servant, age c. 25, runaway from John Glenn, of East Nottingham, Cecil Co., Md. (5 July)

Adv. of Edward Hiley in Front St. (5 July)

Adv. of Thomas Fitzsimmons, next door to the Easy-Chair in Second St. (5 July)

Adv. of Christopher M'Evoy on Mr. Edgar's wharf (5 July)

Tracts of land in Morris Co., part of the estate of David Martin, Esq., dec'd, taken in execution by Sheriff John Ford at the suit of Abraham Bennet, Jr., survivor of Abraham Bennet, dec'd (5 July)

Piece of land in Wicacoa Twp., bounded by lands of Anthony Woodcock, Enoch Flower, Joseph Wharton and late of Samuel Hasell, dec'd, late the estate of John Meredith, taken in execution at suit of William Branson by Sheriff Samuel Morris, will be sold by public vendue at John Biddle's (5 July)

Real estate in Lower Dublin Twp., adjoining lands of Silas Watts, Charles Hassty and Samuel Cooper, late the estate of David Hassty, taken in execution at the suit of Peter Keen, will be sold in Bussel-town; one field is excepted, as it was devised by will to Jacob Hassty (5 July)

Piece of land in Phila., bounded on N. by ground in tenure of Emanuel Rouse and on S. and W. by Alexander Reynold, late the estate of Seth Koyl, taken in execution at the suit of Joseph Galloway by Sheriff Samuel Morris, will be sold at the Boatswain and Call (5 July)

Plantation in Bristol Twp., adjoining land of Griffith Griffith and Thomas Roberts, and lots in said twp., adjoining lands of Thomas Roberts, Robert Whartenby and John Marll, will be sold; plan of the whole may be seen at William Branson's in Phila. (5 July)

Lot on east side of Third St., bounded on N. by ground of Wilcox Phillips, on E. by ground of James Morgotroid, on S. by ground late of Henry Clinton, dec'd, to be sold by public vendue; also another lot in Northern Liberties, which is bounded on N. by lot of William Branson, on S. by lot of Wilcox Phillips, late the estate of Erasmus Stevens, taken in execution by Sheriff Samuel Morris (5 July)

Michael Feltmire, Dutch servant, age c. 17, runaway from Joseph Woollen, of Oxford Twp., Phila. Co. (5 July)

Edward Shannon, Irish servant, age c. 22, runaway from Valentine Honey, living near Collins's mill in Queen Ann's Co., Md. (5 July)

William Iddings, of Reading, has a horse, supposed to stolen, that was taken from one David Damerees, who has been committed to the goal of Berks Co. (5 July)

Gabriel Vanhorn's mare strayed or stolen from his plantation in Middletown, Bucks Co.; reward if mare is brought to him or to Patrick O'Hanlon in Bristol (5 July)

Horse strayed or stolen from house of Valentine Clymer in Rockyhill Twp., Bucks Co.; reward if brought to owner or to Baltis Clymer in Phila. (5 July)

Tract of land in Oley, Phila. Co., bounded on E. by lands late of Abraham Ashman, George Hunter and George Shiers, on S. by land of Caspar Wister, to be sold; enquire of Richard Hockley in Third St., Phila. (5 July)

New York item mentions Capts. Bogart, Badger, Lawrence, Roney and Rawles (12 July)

Letter directed to George Craig at Phila. by Capt. Budden was delivered to a Dutchman at Mr. Kappley's in Phila. to be taken to Lancaster, where Craig now lives; as it has not been received, Craig requests that it be brought or sent to Mr. Stout's in Lancaster (12 July)

Lot in Front St., adjoining lot where Nathaniel Pool formerly lived and also a meadow at Point-no-Point, adjoining Robert Moore's, for sale; apply to Rebecca Wells, living a few doors above the Bank Meeting-house (12 July)

House on W. side of Second St., Phila., adjoining William Branson's, for sale by John Philip Dold (12 July)

Adv. of William Hussey and William Fitzgerald, tailors, at the Hand-and-Shears, next door to John Wood's, clock- and watchmaker in Front St. (12 July)

Two Negro lads for sale; enquire of Andrew Reed in Water St. (12 July)

Lot of ground in Second St., between house where William Clem lives and Simon Siren's, and also part of a lot on York Road, next above Joseph Stinyard's, for sale; apply to William Moode in Chestnut St. or Joseph Hogg in Race St. (12 July)

Joseph Waytes, servant, age c. 18, cooper, runaway from John Garrigues in Phila. (12 July)

Plantation in Hatfield Twp., Phila. Co., adjoining land of James Boyd, Jacob Sudar and Martin Funk, late estate of James Boyd, taken in execution at suit of Martin Funk, will be sold by Sheriff Samuel Morris (12 July)

Plantation in Lower Dublin Twp., bounded by land of Silas Crispin and land of Benjamin Hassty, late estate of Hans Lican, taken in execution at suit of John Petty, will be sold at Busseltown (12 July)

Real estate on the Bank in Phila., bounded on S. by ground of Isaac Zane and on N. by ground of Thomas Green, late estate of Thomas Green, dec'd, taken in execution at suit of William Nicholson and others, will be sold at John Biddle's (12 July)

Joseph Simmons, servant, age c. 19, runaway from Thomas Davis, living at Wright's ferry on Sasquehanna (12 July)

Annapolis item mentions arrival of Capt. John Brown from London, with George Clark, of Charles Co., merchant, a passenger; he informs that Gov. Sharpe will embark on board Capt. Cockson by 1 June (19 July)

Negro lad belonging to Pollard Edmonson of Talbot Co. was drowned a few days ago (19 July)

Letter from England mentions the appointment of Sir D'Anvers Osborne to the government of New York and New Jersey (19 July)

On 18 July in Phila. Christopher Martin and Patrick Ryan attacked and robbed a girl on the highway; the two men were arrested and committed to prison (19 July)

Adv. of Lewis Evans's map (19 July)

Alexander Hamilton, whose store is in Water St., intends to leave the province in October (19 July)

Edward Simons, servant, button-maker, runaway from William Fisher (19 July)

Adv. of James Humphreys, notary public, in Second St. (19 July)

John Vicary at Mrs. Dugdale's, next door to Mrs. Redmond in Market St., draws mortgages, wills, bonds, etc. (19 July)

House in Front St. to be let; enquire of Peter Turner in Market St. (19 July)

Part of house and lot in High St., bounded on E. by ground of Jacob Duchee and on S. by ground of William Hinton, taken in execution at suit of George Shoemaker against goods and chattels of Elizabeth Thompson, to be sold at John Biddle's (19 July)

House and lot in Northern Liberties, bounded on W. by ground of Jonathan Zane, late estate of Richard Murray, taken in execution, will be sold at John Biddle's (19 July)

Real estate in Germantown, adjoining land of Benjamin Shoemaker and John Barge, about ½ mile S. of Joseph Marks's country seat, late the estate of Lawrence Baletz, taken in execution at suit of John Barge and others, will be sold at Daniel Pastorius's in Germantown (19 July)

Michael M'Laughlin, servant, runaway from Alexander Hill of Piles Grove, Salem Co. (19 July)

One half of the snow Mary, Humphrey Clase master, to be sold at Stamper's wharf (19 July)

Hans Peter Kaul, Dutch servant, tailor, runaway from Thomas Lawrence, Esq. (19 July)

1753

Anne Deholly, Dutch girl, age c. 13, runaway from Robert Davis at the Queen's Head in Water St. (19 July)

John Hogans, Irish servant, age 20, runaway from James Anderson of Donegall (19 July)

Plantation in Springfield Twp., Chester Co., for sale; enquire of Benjamin Maddock (19 July)

Melcher Mennig, Dutch servant, age c. 25, runaway from Jacob Wentz, of Worcester Twp., Phila. Co. (19 July)

Matthew Lee, Irish servant, age c. 19, runaway from John M'Nair, living on the Forks of Delaware, Northampton Co. (19 July)

Burlington stage wagon is revived by Jonathan Thomas, John Prigmore, James Wells, John Weggery and Daniel O'Bryant (19 July)

Two lots of land in Water St., adjoining on N. land of Isaac Whitelock, Esq., and on S. a lot late belonging to Edward Smout, Esq., dec'd, to be sold by John Murphey, living in Lancaster (19 July)

Bartholomew Kelly, Irish servant, age c. 45, turner, runaway from Thomas Pain of East Caln, Chester Co. (19 July)

Two pieces of real estate in Water St., bordering N. on land of Anthony Wilkinson and S. on ground of Ann Robbins, to be sold at public vendue at house of William Nicholson in Arch St.; to purchase before the auction, apply to Sarah Wilkinson in Second St. (19 July)

Boston item mentions death at Pembroke on 29 June of the Rev. Daniel Lewis, pastor of the church in that town (26 July)

Boston item of 16 July mentions Capt. Spender (26 July)

Fri. last Samuel Blancher of Weymouth was committed to goal by Justice Stoddard, before whom he was convicted of passing a counterfeit dollar; he admitted that he had cast it of pewter (26 July)

New York item mentions Capts. Stevenson, Harris, Flower, Colgan, Hunter, Cregier, Pepperell, Rash, Sawyer, King, Shannon (26 July)

Sat. last Capt. White arrived at Phila. from Jamaica and yesterday arrived the snow Dispatch, Capt. Heney, from Waterford, with servants (26 July)

Adv. of Andrew Reed in Water St. (26 July)

Plantation near Pennypack Creek, on road to Bristol, whereon a tavern is kept by William Cain at the Sign of the White Horse, to be let by Mrs. Mary Hopkinson in Phila. (26 July)

Ground on Society Hill, adjoining land of William Branson and land of William Annis, dec'd, and also a lot behind house of Anthony Whiteley, for sale; enquire of Josiah Davenport, baker, in Phila. (26 July)

Adv. of Jonathan and John Mifflin near the drawbridge (26 July)

Joseph Davis, English servant, who has sailed out of Phila., and Edward German, English servant, who understands carpentry, runaways from John Nemo and Colin Ferguson, living in George Town, Kent Co., Md. (26 July)

William Holliday, Scotchman, runaway from Deputy Constable Trusdell; reward will be paid by Richard Fry at the Blue Anchor on Great Egg Harbour Road in Gloucester or William Hugg, innkeeper, in that town (26 July)

Adv. of William Clemm in Second St. at the Sign of the Trumpet (26 July)

Sam, Negro, age c. 40, who formerly lived with John Trapnall, of Phila., blacksmith, and James, Negro, age c. 28, who formerly lived with Edward Jones, of Phila., runaways from Reading Furnace; reward offered by Samuel Flower (26 July)

Time of servants for sale by John Leaths at Market St. wharf (26 July)

Thomas Harvey, of Chester Co., has absconded; his creditors are to meet with John Scott (26 July)

John Dosin, Irish servant, age c. 30, who formerly was servant to William Cheeseman in the Jerseys, runaway from James Bonsall (26 July)

Sloop of Stephen Lee of Onslow Co. has been cast away, according to Newbern, N.C., item of 2 June (2 Aug.)

Capt. Freeman from New York came upon a sloop from Bath Town that was sinking; people were all saved (2 Aug.)

New York item mentions Capts. Davis and Waynman from the Bay of Honduras; they mention Capt. Sergeant, of R.I., and Capts. Spurrier, Butler, Phipps, Ruff, Jones and Ovens (2 Aug.)

Capt. Hunter, who arrived at New York from Spanish Town, has news of Capt. Ritchie in a sloop of Phila.; Capts. Quereau and Devereaux of New York have arrived in England on their way to Holland (2 Aug.)

Bolting mills, belonging to estate of Robert Shewell, dec'd, are to be sold; enquire of Joseph Shewell in Front St. (2 Aug.)

Richard Fitz Morris, Irish servant, tailor, age c. 23, who came about 7 weeks ago from Cork with Capt. Brown, runaway from Roger Megrah of New York, tailor (2 Aug.)

Plantation in Oxford Twp., Phila. Co., belonging to estate of Samuel Finney, dec'd, will be sold at Richard Finney's in Oxford Twp. by the execs., Rebecca and Richard Finney and Dan Bristol (2 Aug.)

Adv. of Jonathan Zane, who has removed to the Crown and Canister in Second St. (2 Aug.)

Eleanor Connor, Irish servant, age c. 27, runaway from Timothy Scarth of the Northern Liberties (2 Aug.)

Country seat two miles from Phila., adjoining land of James Lownes, will be sold by Edward Fitzrandolph (2 Aug.)

Plantation in New Britain Twp., Bucks Co., for sale; enquire of Owen Roberts on the premises or Joshua Morris, living in Abington, Phila. Co. (2 Aug.)

Wherry has been taken away from the ferry opposite Gloucester; reward for its recovery offered by Richard Renshaw (2 Aug.)

Morgan Evans, Welsh servant, runaway from Lawrence Debow of Upper Freehold (2 Aug.)

James Lewis, who speaks both Welch and English, being deprived of his reason, went away from his home; reward if he should be brought to Isaac Lewis, living by the Forks of Neshaminey in Bucks Co. (2 Aug.)

Ferdinand Caspar, Dutch servant, age c. 15, runaway from Jonathan Thomas, of Lower Dublin Twp., Phila. Co. (2 Aug.

1753

Henry Clark, Englishman, age c. 30, stocking-weaver by trade, now said to be keeping school in the Lower Counties, has run away from his bail, Joseph Arney, living at Burlington, N.J.; Clark has with him his wife and a son of about 18 or 20 months (2 Aug.)

William Canise, servant, age 27, runaway from David Davis, living in Charles-town, Chester Co. (2 Aug.)

Samuel Cunningham, servant, age c. 16, runaway from Thomas Duffield, of Lower Dublin Twp., Phila. Co.; the lad's mother is named Ruth; his brother, Andrew, is a weaver (2 Aug.)

Henry Coleman, Irish servant, age 21, runaway from John Young, living in Lampeter Twp., Lancaster Co. (2 Aug.)

Fri. last Thomas Green from Northumberland and Henry Bates from New-Kent were executed near Williamsbrgh, according to item of 12 July (9 Aug.)

Sun. last a boat going from Annapolis to Talbot Co. overset, and Mrs. Margaret Fleming, age c. 20, John Gordon (a blockmaker) and a French refugee were drowned; Mr. Fleming, one of his men and a Negro wench were saved, according to item of 22 July (9 Aug.)

Last week Henry Footney, a Dunker, in Frederick Co. was killed by lightning, according to item of 22 July (9 Aug.)

Report that the Gov. of Md. was expected to sail in Capt. Cockson from London (9 Aug.)

Fri. last a Negro lad belonging to Mr. Long, a ship-carpenter, was accidentally killed, according to item of 19 July (9 Aug.)

On 18 July house in Annapolis belonging to Mr. Black of London, a merchant, occupied by Mr. Senhouse, a currier, was burnt to the ground (9 Aug.)

Sat. last the brigantine Swan, Capt. Clarkson, in Swan Creek, Baltimore Co., caught fire and was burnt, according to item of 26 July (9 Aug.)

Sworn declaration of Benjamin Mitchell and Lazarus Noble in Boston on 28 July, before Justices Jacob Wendell and Thomas Hubbard, concerning their trip to Montreal to try to recover their children that had been stolen by an Indian (9 Aug.)

New York item reports rumor of appointment of Capt. Thomas Pitts to be Gov. of South Carolina (9 Aug.)

Capt. Brown informs of arrival of Capt. Jones at New Providence; Capt. Cregier, arrived at New York from St. Thomas, had spoken with Capt. M'Pherson, who sailed from Jamaica in company with Capt. Bradford (9 Aug.)

Robert Smith was committed to goal in New York for having robbed a boat of beaver hats at Hartford, Conn. (9 Aug.)

New York item mentions Capt. Keteltas and also Capt. Deane of the ship John (9 Aug.)

David Smith (who is said to have a wife and family up the North River) was whipped for theft in New York; he went to Norwalk, Conn., and stole there; he has been apprehended in New York and sent to Conn. for punishment (9 Aug.)

On 26 July a horse belonging to Sarah Pearant was struck and killed by lightning at Freehold (9 Aug.)

1753

On 27 July the <u>Shoreham</u>, Capt. Legg, arrived at Charles-Town, S.C., from Antigua; on 26 July Rudeman Robinson arrived in Charles-Town from Phila. (9 Aug.)

Brigantine <u>Addison</u>, Capt. M'Cullough, will sail from Phila. for London (9 Aug.)

Time of a Dutch servant, a baker, for sale; enquire of Michael Holling, baker, in Second St., three doors from William Clemm's (9 Aug.)

Cyder casks for sale at the still-house next door to Joseph Sims's (9 Aug.)

Negro for sale; enquire of John Moland (9 Aug.)

Adv. of Samuel Mifflin, Jr., in Front St., opposite to store of Jonathan and John Mifflin (9 Aug.)

John Coffey, Irishman, age c. 22, who served the latter part of his time with Richard Richison, of Whiteland Twp., Chester Co., runaway from his bail, George Hunter of said twp.; if Coffey is taken, word is to be sent to Robert Dixon, who lives at the Center Phila., or to George Aston, innholder, of Whiteland (9 Aug.)

Cow strayed or stolen from the Phila. Almshouse; reward if cow is brought to William Adams at the almshouse (9 Aug.)

House about a mile from Phila. on Germantown Road for sale; apply to Widow Martha Green on the premises or Joseph Fox or Dr. Sonmans in Phila. (9 Aug.)

John Frederick Gentnen, Dutch servant, age c. 15, a Hanoverian, who came in with Capt. Parish, runaway from Jonathan Lewis, of Phila., merchant; the lad formerly belonged to Jonas Keyler (9 Aug.)

Rum and molasses sold by Capt. Richard Somersall and Lumley Woodyear at Mullin's wharf or at the house of James Cappock in Front St. (9 Aug.)

Mark and Samuel Kuhl will let house in Market St., with or without the cooper's shop, where James M'Creckon dwells, and also a house in Second St., adjoining Englebert Lock's and further a lot of ground in Second St., over against Daniel Stonemitz; Samuel Kuhl sells ship bread (9 Aug.)

Hugh Beaty, servant, age c. 16, runaway from James Gilchrist, of Paxton Twp., Lancaster Co. (9 Aug.)

Accounts with estate of Thomas Sharp, dec'd, to be settled with William Whitehead, sole exec. of John Thomas, dec'd, who was exec. of said Thomas Sharp (9 Aug.)

The following are runaways from the snow <u>Dunlop</u> at the mouth of Severn River at Patapsco, Md.: William White, carpenter, age c. 24; William Smith, Irishman, age 40; Benjamin Wanless, age 22; Alexander Hardy, age 35; reward for their capture will be paid by David Alexander (9 Aug.)

Speech of Gov. James Glen to King Malatchi and other Creeks in South Carolina (16 Aug.)

Boston item mentions Capts. Chandler, Turel, Montgomery and M'Intyre (16 Aug.)

New York item mentions Capts. Samuel Crane, Clarke, Broadhurst, Cosby, Nealson, Magee, Jones and Blair (16 Aug.)

On 12 Aug. William Hill, a sailor, was committed to goal on suspicion of breaking into and stealing from the house of Anthony Sarly, merchant (16 Aug.); Hill was tried and acquitted (23 Aug.)

Letter from New London, Conn., dated 8 Aug., gives account of schemes of Robert Wall and Edward Langford, two rogues; Wall said he was from Brunswick Co., Va.; his age is 21 (16 Aug.)

Phila. item mentions Capts. Haselton, Stiles, Brown, Budden and Gibbon (16 Aug.)

John Lindsay, apprentice, age $\underline{c}$. 20, runaway from John Test, hatter, next door to Franklin and Hall's Printing Office (16 Aug.)

James Smith, servant, a nailor, who served his time in and about Boston, runaway from William Rush, of Phila., blacksmith (16 Aug.)

Frank, a Negro, born in Jamaica, a coachman, runaway from Joshua Crosby of Phila. (16 Aug.)

Abraham Rooker, servant, chair-maker by trade, runaway from Benjamin Barton, of Phila., chair-maker (16 Aug.)

Two Negroes for sale by William Henderson in Market St. (16 Aug.)

John Bleakley intends to leave the province in May (16 Aug.)

Christianus Fredericus Heisterberg, German servant, age $\underline{c}$. 30, runaway from William Nicholson, ship-chandler in New York (16 Aug.)

Joseph Carlisle, this country born, age $\underline{c}$. 30, ship-joiner by trade, runaway from his bail, Thomas Alford, living at Dover, Kent Co. on Delaware (16 Aug.)

Real estate, bounded on W. by land of Henry Trut, on S. by land of William Frames, late the property of Jenkin Philips, taken in execution at suit of John Moland by Sheriff William Yeardley, will be sold by public vendue at house of Samuel Dean in Rockhill Town, Bucks Co. (16 Aug.)

Anne Atkins, servant, age between 20 and 23, runaway from Nicholas Coues, living in Bensalem Twp., Bucks Co. (16 Aug.)

Plantation in Pilesgrove, Salem Co., near Richman's mill, now in the occupation of Barney M'Kinney, to be sold; enquire of Samuel Purveyance, next door to George Mifflin, Jr., in Front St. (16 Aug.)

Paddy M'Laughlin, Irish servant, runaway from John Chestnut, living in Plumsted, Bucks Co. (16 Aug.)

Nathaniel Fitzrandolph of Princetown, N.J., offers reward for recovery of stolen horse (16 Aug.)

Plantation in New-Britain Twp., Bucks Co., for sale; enquire of Owen Roberts on the premises or Joshua Morris, living in Abington, Phila. Co. (16 Aug.)

Notice of arrival in Boston of the Gov. of Mass., who was escorted to the Court House by Col. Pollard's company of cadets (23 Aug.)

Sermon preached by Rev. Cooper in the Old South Meeting-house in Boston; spectators were so numerous that **many compared them** to one of Mr. Whitefield's auditories (23 Aug.)

1753

New York item mentions Capts. Seymour, Ritchie, Stirling and Clark (23 Aug.)

Phila. item mentions Capts. Morrell, Tillidge, Hubbard, Hunt, Hyder, Collins, Blair and Gibbon (23 Aug.)

Gov. Sharp has arrived at Annapolis, Md. (23 Aug.)

George Adams at Christiana Bridge has for sale a pair of millstones (23 Aug.)

Capt. John Sibbald in Second St. has wine and rum for sale (23 Aug.)

Piece of meadow near Phila. to be sold or let by Benjamin Loxley (23 Aug.)

Timothy Linch, Irish servant, age c. 25, runaway from Thomas Hooton, living near Trenton, Burlington Co. (23 Aug.)

William Moore, Irish servant, age c. 30, runaway from Joseph Money, of Robeson Twp., Berks Co., near Reading (23 Aug.)

William Mangles, redemptioner, age c. 27, runaway from John Leaths, who has a parcel of servants for sale at John Parrot's wharf (23 Aug.)

John Clark, goaler, has the following runaway servants in the goal of Lancaster Co.: John Dolin, runaway from James Bonsall in Kingsess; the other, name unknown, belongs either to Robert Alison in Charles-Town or Thomas Archer in Baltimore (23 Aug.)

Robert Carlisle, English or Irish servant, ship-carpenter, runaway from Benjamin Howell of Marcus Hook (23 Aug.)

Thomas Kelly, Irish servant, age c. 24, runaway from Robert Evans, living near the Head of Elk in Cecil Co., Md. (23 Aug.)

John, Giles and Nicholas Hayman (sons of Nicholas Hayman, late of Christiana Bridge, New-Castle Co.), jointly with their brother Peter, by the will of John Hayman of the city of Amsterdam, dec'd, have right to his estate; if alive, they are to appear before the High Sheriff, Aldermen and Justices of Amsterdam to prosecute their claim (23 Aug.)

Lottery to erect a schoolhouse and assist a schoolmaster and for benefit of the poor of the Dutch Reformed Congregation in Phila.; the managers are Henry Bassler, Daniel Bouton, Leonard Melchior, John Goll, Jacob Utrey, John Stillwagon, Jacob Maag, Bernard Lawerswyler, Christopher Geller and John Kempfer (23 Aug.)

Michael Haun, Dutch servant, age c. 19, tailor, runaway from Benjamin Levering of Roxborough Twp., Phila. Co. (23 Aug.)

Stoffel Lym at Point-No-Point has taken up a cow (23 Aug.)

Fri. last arrived at Annapolis the ship Molly, Nicholas Coxen, with Gov. Horatio Sharpe, Rev. Matthias Harris and John Ridout as passengers, according to Annapolis item of 16 Aug. (30 Aug.)

Thirty-month-old son of Henry Jacobs, of Queen Ann's Co., fell into 18 ft. well but was rescued unharmed by a sister (30 Aug.)

Boston item of 20 Aug. mentions Capt. James Young and Capt. Stebbins (30 Aug.)

New York item mentions Capts. Jones, Merand and Haywood (30 Aug.)

At Brunswick to the eastward on 19 July the house of Mrs. Malcom was burnt to the ground and she died 20 July from burns (30 Aug.)

At Superior Court in Cambridge, Mass., John Kemp of Billerica, labourer, pleaded guilty to counterfeiting and passing coins (30 Aug.)

Ship William and Mary, Capt. Peele, from Belfast is in the river at Phila.; Capts. Seymour, Ellis and Trump have sailed from New York for Phila. with Palatines (30 Aug.)

Samuel Morris requests support of voters to re-elect him sheriff (30 Aug.)

Francis Robinson at his house in Walnut St. draws indentures, leases, wills, etc. (30 Aug.)

Ann, wife of Peter Dolon of Phila., has eloped from her husband (30 Aug.)

Adv. of Henry Flower, watchmaker, in Second St. (30 Aug.)

Hull and body of the ship Rebecca, now at Mr. Wharton's wharf, will be sold at public vendue at the Widow Jones's coffeehouse (30 Aug.)

Plantation in Northern Liberties for sale; apply to Edward Richey, living on the premises (30 Aug.)

Sloop to be sold by Joshua Vansant and Mary Carpenter at Holliday's Lower Landing, near Duck-creek town, Kent Co. on Delaware (30 Aug.)

House and land in Princetown, Middlesex Co., for sale; apply to William Mounteer in Trenton or Samuel Horner in Princetown (30 Aug.)

Lottery for purchasing house and lot in Germantown for the minister of the Dutch Lutheran Congregation and a schoolhouse; managers are Sebastine Neff, George Donnenhaver, Jacob Miller, Charles Hay, Jacob Beyerle and Matthias Cainsele (30 Aug.)

John Handley, Irish servant, age 18 or 19, who served part of his time with Robert Armstrong of Paxton, runaway from George Mackrill, living in Leacock Twp., Lancaster Co. (30 Aug.)

Richard Morgan, Welch servant, runaway from Francis Batten of Gloucester Co. (30 Aug.)

John Daniel Digg, Dutch servant, age c. 21, cooper, and John Jacob Pass, Dutch servant, who pretends to be something of a miller, runaways from John Taylor, living in Sadsbury Twp., Lancaster Co. (30 Aug.)

James Lewis, a lunatic, went away from John Griffith, near the Rev. Charles Beaty's meeting-house in Bucks Co.; reward if James Lewis is brought to John Griffith or Isaac Lewis (30 Aug.)

Plantation in Abington, lying on York road, will be sold by Simon Thomas of Lower Dublin at public vendue at the house of William Jenkins in Abington (30 Aug.)

Charlestown, S.C., item mentions the arrival there of Capts. Sch'ermerhorn, Harramond, Hough and Mitchell (6 Sept.)

H.M.S. Port Mahon, Capt. Montague, has sailed from Boston for her station at Newfoundland (6 Sept.)

1753

Boston item of 27 Aug. states that on Thue. last John Kemp the counterfeiter stood in the pillory at Cambridge, had one ear cut off and was whipped 20 stripes (6 Sept.)

New York item of 3 Sept. mentions Capts. Steel, Searle and Smith (6 Sept.)

Amos Jones was committed to goal in Phila., charged with receiving stolen goods; the Grand Jury returned the bill Ignoramus, and Jones was discharged (6 Sept.)

The following captains are mentioned in a Phila. item: Bowes, Nicholson, Noarth, Wright, Keen, Arnott, Ritchie, Stewart, Joy, Stiles, Eve, Power, Morrison, Crathorne, Taylor, Reeve, Murray, Budden, Blake and Wallace (6 Sept.)

Christopher Martin and Patrick Ryan, convicted of felony, are sentenced to be whipped at the cart's tail round two squares in Phila. (6 Sept.)

Observation by Mr. Sherrington of Antigua on the late transit of Mercury over the sun (6 Sept.)

William Kemp, Scotch servant, age c. 24, runaway from John Glen, living in East Nottingham, Chester Co. (6 Sept.)

Samuel Palmer in Third St. has two Negroes for sale (6 Sept.)

Andrew Stevenson, Scotch servant, who has been in the army and pretends to speak French and Dutch, runaway, together with a Scotch woman named Christian Coots, from Samuel Cauldwell, the woman from Thomas Grub, both of Little-Britain Twp., Lancaster Co. (6 Sept.)

Accounts with estate of John Coxe, Esq., late of Trenton, N.J., dec'd, to be settled with William Coxe and Robert Lettis Hooper, execs. (6 Sept.)

Frank, a Negro, born in Jamaica, a young man, who drives a coach, runaway from Joshua Crosby of Phila. (6 Sept.)

Tract of land and house in the Great Valley, Chester Co., for sale; apply to William Griffitts, merchant, or Francis Allison in Phila. or Isaac Davis, Esq., in the Great Valley (6 Sept.)

William Mooney, age c. 21, taken up as a runaway, is in the goal of Chester; he says he came from County Meath, has been in the country 6 years and served 4 years to George Croghan, 6 miles beyond John Harris's ferry, according to notice inserted by Samuel Smith, goal keeper (6 Sept.)

Thomas Scoffield, English servant, age c. 40, weaver, runaway from Nathan Hoopes of East Bradford, Chester Co.; Edward Edwards, English servant, runaway from William Quaintance, also of East Bradford (6 Sept.)

John Stacey, apprentice, age c. 17, runaway from Hugh Durborow, chair-maker, of Phila. (6 Sept.)

Jonathan Stacey, apprentice, age c. 18, runaway from John M' Cullough, cooper, in Front St. (6 Sept.)

Jean M'Clellan, Irish servant, runaway from James Walker, who lives in Mill-creek Hundred, New-Castle Co. (6 Sept.)

Margaret Willey, Irish servant, age c. 18, runaway from Josiah Davenport, of Phila., baker (6 Sept.)

Sanderson Stanford, English servant, who speaks broad Yorkshire, and one Catherine, Irish servant, age c. 30, runaways from James Smith and Thomas Armor of Yorktown (6 Sept.)

1753

Capt. Angier put into Boston to refit (13 Sept.)

Samuel Blancher of Weymouth was found guilty of passing a counterfeit dollar by a jury in Boston (13 Sept.)

At Groton, Conn., Giles Mumford died from injuries caused by a fall from a tree (13 Sept.)

New York item mentions Capts. Heysham, Garrison, Pickeman, Lickly and Jefferson (13 Sept.)

Phila. item mentions Capts. Blair, Mitchell, Henderson, Caldwell, Ellis, Ritchie, Parish, Moore, Mason, Haselton, Duncan, Shirley, Stirling, Wall, Standige and Macilvaine (13 Sept.)

Shop goods to be sold by public vendue at the house late of William Young, next door to Michael Agee's in Second St. (13 Sept.)

Isaac Pearson seeks votes for the office of sheriff (13 Sept.)

Adv. of Charles Willing and Son in Front St. (13 Sept.)

Adv. of Samuel Grisley's wine store below the Jersey Market (13 Sept.)

Plantation on great road from Germantown to Whitemarsh, nine miles from Phila., to be let; apply to Alexander Huston in Phila. (13 Sept.)

Christian Getz, Dutch servant, age c. 20, runaway from Robert Miller, living in East Caln, Chester Co. (13 Sept.)

William Husband, living near the mouth of Octoraro Creek, or Herman Husband, of Baltimore Co., Md., have millstones for sale (13 Sept.)

William Moore, Irish servant, butcher, runaway from Philip Welsh, of Nottingham Twp., Burlington Co. (13 Sept.)

William Deare, sheriff, offers reward for capture of the following prisoners who escaped from Middlesex Co. Goal in Perth Amboy: Benjamin Corle (committed for riot and breach of the peace), age between 40 and 50; Lawrence Ruth (prisoner for debt), age between 30 and 40, a shoemaker; Samuel Cole (prisoner for debt), age between 40 and 50 (13 Sept.)

House in Second St., late property of William Young, opposite to dwelling of Samuel Morris, Esq., will be sold by public vendue at the house of Standish Forde, at the Sign of the George; persons indebted to Young are to make payment to Samuel Neave, Donaldson and Fuller, and Samuel Sanson, assignees (13 Sept.)

Tract of land on Delaware at White-hill in Mansfield Twp., Burlington Co., for sale; enquire of Stacy Potts in Trenton (13 Sept.)

New York item of 17 Sept. mentions arrival of Capt. Jones from the Bay of Honduras; Jones gives news of Capts. Ward, Belston, Sweet, Havens, Guilford, Millar, Porter, Johnson, Ducket, Savage, Dunscomb, Fones, Duncan and Freeborn (20 Sept.)

Capt. Carlisle, who arrived at New York from Jamaica, told of the seizure of the sloop *Fortune*, Michael Hinde master, and its condemnation (20 Sept.)

New York item mentions Capts. Whitney, Bowers, Nathan Simmons, Finley, Bemant and Styles (20 Sept.)

James Elliot (being much in liquor) fell from his horse at Nantmill, Chester Co., and was so dragged and bruised that he soon died (20 Sept.)

1753

Capt. Shirley reports that a daughter has been born to Thomas Penn (20 Sept.)

Phila. item mentions Capts. Mesnard, Mitchell, Reeve, Livingston, Richards, Miller, Harper, Rees, Nicholson, Greenway, Nuttle, Gass, Dingee, Higgs, Lawrence, Kipp, Smith, Russell, Steel, Moore, Lickly, Arnott, Mason, Coatam, Muir, Pitcairn, Tran, Abercrombie, Lyon, Trump, Brown, Crawford, Jones, Caldwell, Simpson, Smith, Duncan (20 Sept.)

Theophilus Grew and Horace Jones will open an evening school at Mr. Atkinson's in Second St. (20 Sept.)

Randle and Alexander Mitchell have removed from their store under Mr. Fishbourn's house, opposite Capt. Philips's, to their house in Water St. (20 Sept.)

Ezekiel Harlan, Jr., late of West Marlborough Twp., a young man, has escaped from Sheriff Isaac Pearson of Chester Co. (20 Sept.)

Adv. of Isaac Jones in Arch St. (20 Sept.)

Adv. of Abel James in Water St. (20 Sept.)

Jonathan Smith, age c. 40, carpenter, who lived near Salem in the Jerseys, has run away from his bail, Thomas Caney in Wilmington (20 Sept.)

Adv. of Joseph Ogden in Chestnut St. (20 Sept.)

Adv. of William M'Ilvaine and Company in Front St. (20 Sept.)

John M'Graw, Irish servant, age c. 28, butcher, Thomas Armstrong, Irish servant, age c. 25 or 26, and James Cooley, Irish servant, age 28 or 30, dyer, runaways from Amos Garrett; John Connor, Irish servant, age c. 22, tailor, servant of David Caldwell, ran away with them; the three first mentioned ran away from Cornwall (alias Grub's) Iron-works in Lancaster Co. (20 Sept.)

Plantation about 3 miles from Phila., on main road to Frankford, adjoining land of George Emlen and bounded with Gunner's Run, late property of Daniel Worthington, dec'd, and other real estate, on which is the up-town vendue house of Daniel Rundle, to be sold; apply to Standish Ford at the Sign of the George in Second St. (20 Sept.)

Arthur M'Closkey, Irish servant, age c. 30, runaway from Robert Powell, living in Whiteland, Chester Co. (20 Sept.)

House and lot in Second St., adjoining William Branson's, and also lot adjoining land of John Moland, Esq., for sale by John Philip Dold (20 Sept.)

Advs. of Charles Meredith, corner of Front and Chestnut Sts., of Robert Ragg in Front St., where Joseph Morris lived and next door to Allen and Turner; of Benjamin Kendall in Chestnut St.; of Solomon Fussell at the Hand and Crown in Second St.; of Samuel Howell at the Sign of the Beaver in Chestnut St.; of Mrs. Anne Redmond in Market St. (20 Sept. (20 Sept.)

Elizabeth Gainsberry, servant of Mr. Suddler's in Queen Anne's Co., gave birth to a bastard child, which she flung over a fence into some bushes; the child was found alive by a Negro and a boy (27 Sept.)

Gov. Hopson has leave to return to England; Col. Lawrence will have command during his absence, according to a Boston item of 17 Sept. (27 Sept.)

Samuel Starke, noted American merchant, has died in London (27 Sept.)

New York item mentions Capts. Philipson, M'Daniel, Lloyd, Lewis (27 Sept.)

Alexander Magenty, an Indian trader, arrived at New York from Montreal and reported that he and the following six traders were captured 26 Jan. at Allegany: James Lowry, Jacob and Jabez Evans, Thomas Hide, David Hendricks and William Powell; after 3 days Lowry escaped; the French general bought both Jacob Evans and Thomas Hide and sent them to Quebec (27 Sept.)

It is reported that Bryan Doran, the third murderer of John Thomas and Eleanor Davis, is in custody in Orange County Goal, N.C. (27 Sept.)

Capt. Beckop from Londonderry has arrived at Newcastle; Capts. Mason, Abercrombie, Muir, Goad, Coatam and Arnott from Rotterdam and Trump from Hamburgh have arrived at Phila. with Palatines, while Capts. Pitcairn, Tran, Lyon and Nevin are expected from Rotterdam (27 Sept.)

Jacob Leeman, Dutch servant, age c. 14 or 15, whose father and mother live in Dunkards Town, runaway from Samuel Read, of Phila., baker (27 Sept.)

Advs. of William Grant in Second St. and of Samuel and Thomas Smith on Market St. wharf (27 Sept.)

William Palmer, servant, born in this country, age c. 21, runaway from Henry Lawrence, of Marple Twp., Chester Co. (27 Sept.)

Mills and plantation of Nathaniel Ware, Esq., 6 miles above Trenton, for sale; apply to William Clayton or William Pidgeon in Trenton (27 Sept.)

Debts owed to Matthew and Abraham Usher are to be paid to Abraham Usher, exec. of Matthew Usher, dec'd; Abraham Usher and James Wharton carry on the business (27 Sept.)

Adv. of Edmund Kearny in Water St. (27 Sept.)

John Headley, servant, age between 16 and 17, runaway from Hugh Mearns, of Warwick, Bucks Co. (27 Sept.)

Harry, Mulatto servant, age c. 22, runaway from Samuel Cookson, living in Carnarvon Twp., Lancaster Co. (27 Sept.)

Horse and colt strayed or stolen from plantation of William M'Afee, of Marple Twp., Chester Co.; reward if animals are brought to the owner or to John Morton, living on Society Hill (27 Sept.)

John Kidd intends for England (27 Sept.)

Accounts with estate of John Parrock, late of Phila., shipwright, to be settled with the admins., James and Mary Parrock (27 Sept.)

Henry Brabazon, scowerer, is removed from Arch St. to the house of William Green, baker, in Second St., near Mr. Levy's (27 Sept.)

Real estate in Kensington will be sold by public vendue at the house of Diana Spencer in Hanover St., Kensington (27 Sept.)

Isaac Brinckerhoff, sheriff, offers reward for capture of the following, who escaped from Dutchess Co. Goal: Joseph Hix, Ebenezer Merick, Ichabod Everil, Edward Lovely and Edward Baily, confined for debt, and Michael Hallingbeck, confined for riot (27 Sept.)

Charles Campbell, Irish servant, and John Steel, English servant, runaways from Joseph Morrison of Lancaster Co. (27 Sept.)

House and lot in Haddonfield, Gloucester Co., will be sold by public vendue on the premises; to view the place apply to Daniel Hilman, Jr., living in Bilingsport, or Daniel Hilman, Sr., living within 2 miles of the premises (27 Sept.)

Samuel Cooper, servant, born in England, age c. 30, blacksmith, and Richard Brown, servant, blacksmith, runaways from Robert Milburn, of Elizabeth Town, Essex Co., N.J., blacksmith (27 Sept.)

Tract of land in Donnegal Twp. for sale; apply to Lazarus Lowrie in Arch St. (27 Sept.)

Capt. Trapp in a snow belonging to R.I., bound to Halifax, was cast away near Cape Negro on 6 Aug. (4 Oct.)

Sir Danvers Osborne will soon embark on H.M.S. *Arundel* for New York (4 Oct.)

New York item of 1 Oct. mentions Capts. Lewis, Maybury, Waite, Deane, Hall, Crowel and William Johnson (mate of Capt. Crowel) (4 Oct.)

Account of capture by Indians of an Italian named John Barry, owner of a small island near Halifax that was presented to him by Gov. Hopson, and his escape from said Indians (4 Oct.)

Elected for Phila. Co. - representatives: Isaac Norris, Edward Warner, Evan Morgan, Joseph Trotter, Joshua Morris, Hugh Evans, Joseph Stretch, Joseph Fox; sheriffs, Samuel Morris, Edward Collins; coroners, William Gray, Thomas James; commissioner, William Foulke; assessors, Derrick Keyser, Robert Thomas, Morris Morris, Daniel Williams, Isaac Jones, North-Wales, John Shrack (4 Oct.)

Elected for Bucks Co. - representatives, Mahlon Kirkbride, Joseph Hamton, Samuel Brown, William Hoge, Griffith Owen, Derrick Hogeland, Jonathan Ingham, William Smith; sheriffs, William Yeardley, Benjamin Chapman; coroners, Evan Jones, Simon Butler; commissioner, Amos Strickland; assessors, Giles Knight, Daniel Palmer, John Kelly, Samuel Foulke, William Morris, Alexander Brown (4 Oct.)

Elected for Chester Co. - representatives, Thomas Cummings, Nathaniel Pennock, George Ashbridge, Joseph Gibbons, Nathaniel Crubb, Peter Dicks, William Peters, Joseph James; sheriffs, Isaac Pearson, Benjamin Davis; coroners, Joshua Thomson, John Kerlin; commissioner, Robert Miller; assessors, Joseph Ashbridge, James Miller, Phineas Lewis, Randle Malin, Jeremiah Brown, William Parker (4 Oct.)

Elected for Lancaster Co. - representatives, Arthur Patterson, James Wright, Calvin Cooper, Peter Worrall; sheriffs, Thomas Smith, James Marshall; **coroners**, John Dougherty, Isaac Whitlock (4 Oct.)

Elected for Newcastle Co. - representatives, William Armstrong, Evan Rees, **Jehu** Curtis, John M'Coole, Jacob Vanbebber, James M'Mechen; sheriffs, George Monroe, William Golden; coroners, Robert Morrison, James Walker (4 Oct.)

Elected for Berks Co. - representatives, Moses Starr; sheriffs, Benjamin Lightfoot, Jacob Morgan; coroners, William Boone, Samuel High; commissioner, Joseph Millard; assessors, Christian Lower, Thomas Wright, Thomas Lee, Sebastian Zimmerman, John Harrison, Nathan Evans (4 Oct.)

Elected for Northampton Co. - representative, William Parsons; sheriffs, Jacob Bachman, Nicholas Scull; coroners, Joseph Scull, John Traxler; commissioner, Christian Rinker; assessors, John Walker, Frederick Shull, George Rex, George Custard, Joseph Everhart, Robert Lisle (4 Oct.)

Elected for the City of Phila. - mayor, Thomas Lawrence; burgesses, Benjamin Franklin, William Callender; assessors, Joseph Watkins, Joseph Lownes, Jacob Lewis, Jeremiah Warder, Thomas Lightfoot, Bartholomew Penrose; wardens, Henry Harrison, Samuel Rhodes (4 Oct.)

Phila. item mentions Capts. Mesnard, Richards, Miller, Livingston, Davis, Reeve, Stirling, Wall, Moore, Stamper, Dowers, Edwards, Arthur, Wright, Trann, Lyon, Pitcairn and Nevin (4 Oct.)

Fri. last Charles Quigg, age c. 15, was murdered by Thomas Ruth, a servant of Mr. Wall's in Strawberry Alley; Ruth was captured and is in a dungeon in Phila. (4 Oct.)

William Dawson will open an evening school in Third St., opposite Mr. Branson's building (4 Oct.)

Adv. of John and Joseph Swift in Water St. (4 Oct.)

A brick house and a bakehouse in Gray's Alley to be sold or let; enquire of Mrs. Weyman in Arch St. (4 Oct.)

Adv. of Cornelius Bradford, pewterer, in Second St. (4 Oct.)

Horses, cows, etc. will be sold by public vendue at the plantation late of John Naglee, dec'd; attendance will be given by Catherine, John and Jacob Naglee (4 Oct.)

Jonas Seely, Chief Ranger of Berks Co., living in Reading, lists strays he has taken up (4 Oct.)

Adv. of Levy and Franks in Second St. (4 Oct.)

John Moore, servant, age c. 22, runaway from Thomas Robertson, of Fogs Manor, Chester Co. (4 Oct.)

Michael Burk, Irish servant, age c. 26, runaway from Arthur Latimer, living in Little-Britain, Chester Co. (4 Oct.)

Con M'Mahon, carpenter, from Carrick M'Cross in Ireland, is desired to come to his brother, Ross M'Mahon, peruke-maker, newly arrived in Phila., or to write to William Dawson in Third St. or Anthony Whitely on Society Hill or Thomas Duff in New-Port, Pa. (4 Oct.)

Reward offered for recovery of a filly strayed or stolen from plantation of Isaac Jones in Montgomery Twp., Phila. Co. (4 Oct.)

Joseph Charnban in Leacock Twp., Lancaster Co., has taken up a mare (4 Oct.)

Adv. of John Ross at Mrs. Deering's in Arch St., near the Sign of Admiral Warren (4 Oct.)

Two tracts of land on Timber Creek in Deptford Twp., Gloucester Co., late property of John Pierce, taken in execution at suit of Mary Conyers and James Lee by Sheriff John Mickle, will be sold by public vendue at house of William Hugg in Gloucester (4 Oct.)

Adv. of James Child in Water St. (4 Oct.)

Real estate in Motherkill Hundred, Kent Co., and at Marshehope in Muspilion Hundred, being estate of Ebenezer Hathorne, late of Kent Co., dec'd, will be sold by public vendue by John Van Dike, admin. (4 Oct.)

Mill in Amwell, Hunterdon Co., West Jersey, and land in Trenton, bounded on W. by land of Thomas Lawrence, Esq., Elijah Bond and John Holder, on N. by land of John Allen, on E. by land of Isaac Conerow and Joseph Green, on S. by land of Cornelius Doude, and also the plantation whereon Thomas Leant dwells in Hanover Twp., Burlington Co., will be sold by Benjamin Smith (4 Oct.)

Notice to Nancy Carson, living in the Forks of Delaware, that her brother, Christopher Dixon, died on board ship when he was coming from Holland and left her goods and money now in the hands of Capt. George Parish; she is to see Thomas Lawrence, Esq., in Phila., who has her brother's will (4 Oct.)

Boston item of 1 Oct. mentions Capt. Warner and Agent Bollan (11 Oct.)

Gov. Sir Danvers Osborne arrived Sat. last at Sandy Hook on board of H.M.S. *Arundel*, Capt. Lloyd, according to New York item of 8 Oct. (11 Oct.)

New York item of 8 Oct. mentions Gov. Clinton (about to embark for London) and Capts. Penny, Braley, Stirling, Walton, Bennet, Greenall, Quereau, Deane, Barrington, Jauncey, Doughty, Bayne and Reese (11 Oct.)

Elected for Kent Co. - representatives, Benjamin Chew, John Brinckloe, John Vining, Andrew Caldwell, John Caten, Vincent Lockerman; sheriffs, John Clayton, Jr., Caesar Rodeney; coroners, French Bartel, Samuel M'Call (11 Oct.)

Elected for Sussex Co. - representatives, Jacob Kollock, Ryves Holt, Benjamin Burton, John Clowes, Josiah Martin, David Hall; sheriffs, Jacob Kollock, Jr., Peter Clowes; coroners, John Spencer, Charles Pratt (11 Oct.)

Elected for York Co. - representatives, John Wright, David M'Conaugby; sheriffs, John Adlin, Abraham Noblit; coroners, Alexander Love, Archibald M'Grew (11 Oct.)

Elected for Cumberland Co. - representatives, Joseph Armstrong, John Armstrong; sheriffs, Ezekiel Dunning, William Parker; coroners, John M'Clure, John Reynolds (11 Oct.)

Capt. Moore from Londonderry reports that the *Isabella*, Capt. Henderson, was to sail on 20 Aug. for Phila. (11 Oct.)

On 12 Oct. Thomas Ruth will be tried in Phila. for the murder of Charles Quigg (11 Oct.)

William Roney, Irish servant, age c. 23, runaway from Moses Black, living in Chestnut Level, Drummore Twp., Lancaster Co. (11 Oct.)

William Foster, of Evesham Twp., Burlington Co., N.J., wishes to engage a schoolmaster (11 Oct.)

Adv. of Adam Klampff, who keeps a stable in Second St. (11 Oct.)

John Pearson, innkeeper in Darby, has a watch taken up between the lower ferry and Darby (11 Oct.)

Real estate in Kennet Twp., joining lands of Benjamin Taylor, William White and others, late property of Joseph Harlan, taken in execution at suit of John Taylor, will be sold at house of John Hannum in Concord, Chester Co. (11 Oct.)

Real estate in Charles-Town, Chester Co., joining lands of David Matthias, William Moore, Esq., and others, late property of Ellis Davis, taken at suit of William Curry by Sheriff Isaac Pearson, and also other real estate in said twp., joining lands of Daniel Walker and Company, late property of Thomas Burch, taken at suit of Thomas Lawrence, Jr., all to be sold at the house of Daniel Goldsmith in Charles-Town (11 Oct.)

John M'Kenally, servant, runaway from John Leaths at Francis Trumble's on Society Hill (11 Oct.)

Adv. of Charles Dutens, jeweller, at the Sign of the Ring and Dove in Market St. (11 Oct.)

Daniel Goodman in Second St., baker, has a cure for the bite of a mad dog (11 Oct.)

Tract of land in York Co., belonging to estate of Edward Smout, Esq., late of the borough of Lancaster, dec'd, for sale; enquire of Elizabeth Smout, Marcus Young and John Hopson, the execs., all living in said borough (11 Oct.)

John Gittins, English servant, who talks broad West Country, age c. 40, runaway from John M'Dermott, living in Frederick Town, Cecil Co., Md. (11 Oct.)

John Hanglin, Irish servant, age c. 26, who has been almost 8 years in the country and served his time with Enoch Roberts in Chester Twp., Burlington Co., West N.J., and has since been servant to Thomas Jarrard at Greenwich, Gloucester Co., runaway from Patrick Porter, living in Chester Twp., Burlington Co. (11 Oct.)

Negro boy for sale; enquire at John De Nyce's in Second St. (11 Oct.)

On 28 Sept. Robert Cooke and Stephen Cooke were tried at Springfield, Mass., for the murder of an Italian; Robert was found guilty of manslaughter, while Stephen was acquitted (18 Oct.)

Thu. last Capt. Grainger arrived at Portsmouth, N.H., in a mast ship from Chatham, England, according to Boston item of 8 Oct. (18 Oct.)

At New York Gov. Osborne was given a dinner on 8 Oct. by the gentlemen of the Council, with George Clinton present; on the 10th the Corporation gave a dinner for Danvers; on the 12th, however, Danvers died and the next day was buried in the chancel of Trinity Church; the government then devolved upon James De Lancey (18 Oct.)

The snow Polly, Capt. Smith, and Capt. Bryant will sail for London (18 Oct.)

Thomas Ruth, convicted of the murder of Charles Quigg, is to be executed in Phila. on Sat. next (18 Oct.)

Phila. item mentions Capts. Stirling, Wall and Brown (18 Oct.)

Advs. of Thomas M'Janett & Co. in Water St., John Bell, Andrew Elliot and Andrew Reed, all in the same street (18 Oct.)

On 17 Oct. at the Mayor's Court in Phila. James Brown was convicted of picking a pocket, Daniel Bachman of stealing goods and Thomas White of horse-stealing, for which each was sentenced to be whipped 21 lashes at the cart's tail (18 Oct.)

House on Society Hill, the Sign of the Phoenix, a noted tavern, is to be let by Philip Halbert (18 Oct.)

- Piece of ground in Germantown Twp., bounded by Dominick Cassner's land, by Nicholas Rous's lane and by a road leading to Joseph Marks's land, late property of Jacob Welckly, dec'd, taken in execution at the suit of one Bealer, will be sold at Daniel Pastorius's in Germantown (18 Oct.)
- Lot of land in Wicacoa Twp., bounded on N. by land of Enoch Flower and on W. and S. by land of William Branson(late of J. Meredith), late the property of Anthony Woodcock, taken in execution by Sheriff Samuel Morris, will be sold at John Biddle's (18 Oct.)
- Joseph Ogden of Phila. offers reward for recovery of a horse (18 Oct.)
- Lydia Humphreys offers reward for recovery of mare stolen from plantation of Samuel Humphreys in Haverford, Chester Co. (18 Oct.)
- An eight day clock to be sold at Taylor Taylor's in Second St., a little above Simon Siron's, shopkeeper (18 Oct.)
- Margaret Wiley, Irish servant, age c. 18, belonging to James White of Phila., runaway from Josiah Davenport of Phila., baker (18 Oct.)
- Plantation and grist mill in Amity Twp., Berks Co., whereon James Kiemer lives, to be sold or let; apply to William Bird of Union Twp. or James Kiemer on the premises (18 Oct.)
- Plantation in Northampton Twp., bounded on N. by land of Samuel Williot, on E. by land of William Carter, dec'd, on S. by land of Philip Dracord, on W. by land of said Williot, late property of Ralph Dracord, taken in execution at suit of Catherine Wistar, David Dashler and other execs. of Caspar Wistar, dec'd, by Sheriff William Yeardley, to be sold at house of John Strickland in Bucks Co. (18 Oct.)
- Plantation in Bristol Twp., adjoining land of John Clawson and one Spencer, late the property of John Towers, dec'd, taken in execution at suit of Langhorne Biles by Sheriff William Yeardley, will be sold at house of Patrick O'Hanlin in the borough of Bristol, Bucks Co. (18 Oct.)
- Address of clergy in New York, signed by Henry Barclay, to Lt.-Gov. James Delancey, with mention of the death of Gov. Osborne, and reply of Delancey (25 Oct.)
- Wed. last died at New Brunswick, N.J., Capt. Henry Cosby, late of H.M.S. Centaur, according to item of 22 Oct. (25 Oct.)
- New York item mentions Capts. Kossler, Seymour, Creighton, Scot Lawrence, Albuoy and Hill (25 Oct.)
- On 3 Oct. James M'Niel, a pedlar, was found murdered within 10 miles of Albany; one Turner was taken upon suspicion and committed to goal (25 Oct.)
- On Wed. last William Rodgers of Middletown, East Jersey, accidentally shot and killed his wife, according to New York item of 22 Oct. (25 Oct.)
- Phila. item mentions Capts. Reeve, Harriot, Gurnay, Wall, Winter, Peter Read, Dowers, Aston, Isaac Cormoran, Kennedy, Arthur, Reese, Edwards and Cookson (25 Oct.)
- The White Horse, a noted tavern, and other real estate in Whiteland, Chester Co., all property of John Hambright, taken in execution at suit of Samuel Flower, Esq., and others, will be sold by Sheriff Isaac Pearson (25 Oct.)

Sat. last Thomas Ruth was executed in Phila. for the murder of Charles Quigg (25 Oct.)

Notice, signed by Benjamin Griffith, Moderator of the Assn. of Baptist Ministers and Elders, concerning Job Parker, an impostor (25 Oct.)

Garden seeds sold by Hannah Duberry, living in the Northern Liberties, next to Capt. Peel's, and by John Bissell in Third St. (25 Oct.)

Adv. of Thomas Preston in Second St., next door to John Maddox, Esq. (25 Oct.)

Adv. of Content Nicholson, who has removed from Chestnut St. to the house in Strawberry Alley wherein Robert Jordan, dec'd, formerly lived (25 Oct.)

Plantation in Whitemarsh Twp., adjoining land of John Morriss, taken in execution at the suit of Andrew Crawford and others, will be sold at the house of Christopher Robins (25 Oct.)

Real estate in Front St., bounded on N. by land of John Reardon, on W. by land of William Shippen and on S. by land of William Branson, late the estate of Jacob Spike, taken at the suit of Abraham Stedman, will be sold at the Boatswain and Call (25 Oct.)

Martha James, servant, age c. 27 or 28, runaway from John Jones of the Manor of Moreland, Phila. Co. (25 Oct.)

Sheriff Samuel Morris will sell at John Biddle's the following real estate: lot in Second St., bounded on N. by land of William Branson and on S. by land of Willcox Philips; lot in Third St., bounded on N. by land of Willcox Philips, on E. by land of James Morgetroid and on S. by land late of Henry Clifton, dec'd; annual rent from ground in tenure of Benjamin Hooton and William Lawrence; rent from lot in tenure of Aquila Jones and John Philip Dold, late the estate of Erasmus Stevens, taken in execution (25 Oct.)

Lot in Main St., Georgetown, between property of George Pickus and that of one Woolery, and another lot in Cross St. will be sold by Sarah Jewell at Miles Town, near Germantown, admin. of Robert Jewell, late of Phila., rope-maker, dec'd (25 Oct.)

Teacher available; enquire of William Bell in Front St. (25 Oct.)

Plantation in East-Town, Chester Co., for sale; apply to Thomas M'Carty, living in Bucks Co., or Standish Ford at the Sign of the George in Second St. (25 Oct.)

The following servants are runaways from John Hall and Jacob Giles in Baltimore Co., Md.: Michael French, age c. 20, who came from Ireland 7 years ago; James Brannon, born in Ireland, age c. 20, who professes to be a schoolmaster; Henry Tedder, age c. 30, born in Essex, England, brought up a gardiner, who has been in the King's service (25 Oct.)

Plantation in Bibury Twp., Phila. Co., late belonging to Crispin Collett, dec'd, will be sold by Mary Collett and Joseph Hart, execs. (25 Oct.)

Henry Hrubb, Dutch servant, age between 30 and 40, stocking-weaver, runaway from William Carnagie of Bedminster Twp., Somerset Co., East N.J. (25 Oct.)

1753

Time of two servants for sale by William Gray at the Sign of the Conestogoe Waggon (25 Oct.)

Plantation in Oxford Twp., Phila. Co., for sale; enquire of Thomas Buzby in Oxford Twp. (25 Oct.)

John M'Cabe, Irish servant, tailor, age c. 23, runaway from Archibald Hamilton of Mannington Twp., Salem Co. (25 Oct.)

Thomas Miller, Welch servant, runaway from George Boyd of Lancaster Co. (25 Oct.)

Address of Upper House, signed by E. Tasker, president, to Gov. Horatio Sharpe of Md.; reply of governor, address of Delegates, signed P. Hammond, speaker, and reply of governor (1 Nov.)

Capts. Miller, Levingston and Shoals have arrived at New York from London (1 Nov.)

Boston item of 21 Oct. mentions Capts. Denn and Bowen (1 Nov.)

New York item mentions Capts. Forsyth, Hopkins, Archer, Gill, Bradford, Shoals, Griffiths, Richards, Walton, Malton, Elijah Goff, Swaine, Livingston, Vardil, Rhodes, Batty, Negat, Owen, Smith, Hall, Stafford, Green, Thompson, Pierce (1 Nov.)

Phila. item of 1 Nov. mentions Capts. Rankin, Gill, Nicholls, Dennison, Vance, Saltus, Godfrey, Mesnard, Gardiner, Dunn and Swaine (1 Nov.)

John Godard, who says he is servant to Loveless Goaset at Chestnut Ridge, Md., is in goal in Trenton, Hunterdon Co., N.J.; William Brown, keeper of the goal, requests that the master fetch said servant (1 Nov.)

Caner's reeds for stay-makers for sale by William Branson in Second St. (1 Nov.)

Subscriptions for engraving of the city and harbour of Phila. by the late George Heap to be received at the office of Nicholas Scull, William Bradford or David Hall in Phila. (1 Nov.)

At the house of Elizabeth Evans at the Sign of the Crown in Market St. will be sold household goods, shop goods and the said house; also at the house of John Biddle will be sold a brick house in Church Alley, adjoining the dwelling of Hugh Roberts, now in the tenure of James Mackey, all to be sold by Evan, Sydney and Sarah Evans (1 Nov.)

Piece of land in Roxborough Twp., Phila. Co., adjoining Robeson's mills, will be sold at the Indian King in Market St. by Sarah Whitpain, admin. of Zechariah Whitpain, dec'd; plan to be seen at the Widow Bingham's or at John Riley's office in Front St. (1 Nov.)

Lot of ground in Wicacoa Twp., bounded on W. by John Parham's ground and on N. by ground of Anthony Duche the younger, late the estate of Patrick Wilson, taken in execution at the suit of Mary Andrews, will be sold at William Bell's near the Drawbridge (1 Nov.)

John Paschall, Richard Lloyd amd John Pearson, auditors, at the house of John Pearson in Darby Twp., Chester Co., will meet the creditors of Robert Dunwodies, late of said county (1 Nov.)

At Salem in Essex Co., Mass., Daniel Giddings, Jr., was indicted (with Charles Boyls) for counterfeiting and passing, to which he pleaded guilty; Thomas Maybee, of Ipswich, fisherman, was found guilty of stabbing a Negro (8 Nov.)

Thu. last a man who came from London as passenger in Capt. Cary and brought with him a quantity of counterfeit halfpence was committed to goal in Boston (8 Nov.)

New York item of 5 Nov. mentions Capts. Drummond, Henry Allen M'Dougall, Savage, Dunscomb, Burger, Menzie, Langdon, Ducket, Stephenson, Crew, Johnson, Porter, Ramsey, Guildford, Dickson, White, Sweet, Morsley, Bristow, Jones, Blake, John Bruen and Rattery and also a Mr. French, mate to Capt. Burger (8 Nov.)

On 30 Oct. the sloop Speedwell, Capt. Sage, of Phila., ran ashore on our cape (8 Nov.)

On 3 and 4 Oct. in a hurricane Capt. Toulon foundered near the Caicos; Capt. Tryon from Conn. ran on the Silver Key (8 Nov.)

The ship Isabella Maria, Capt. M'Pherson, of Phila., has arrived at Dover; the Betty and Sally, Capt. Snead, from Phila., has arrived at Dublin (8 Nov.)

On 31 Oct. the house of John Hanly of Chester was broke open and robbed, apparently by Thomas Brown, who was arrested in Phila.; the house of Mr. Montgomery of Christine has been broke open, and the houses of John Paschall at Darby and of Charles Jenkins at the middle ferry have been attempted (8 Nov.)

Lots of ground fronting the road leading to George Gray's ferry and other real estate to be sold at John Biddle's at the Indian King (8 Nov.)

Tract of land in Passyunk Twp., bounded by land of Peter Cox and John Sober, late the property of William Hughes, taken in execution at suit of Andrew Tranberg, will be sold at John Biddle's (8 Nov.)

Parcel of Irish beef will be sold by George Noarth at Thomas Clifford's wharf (8 Nov.)

Adv. of Thomas Davis in Market in house where Hugh Roberts lately lived (8 Nov.)

William Reiley in Whiteland Twp., Chester Co., has taken up a cow (8 Nov.)

Adv. of Benjamin Kendall in Chestnut St. (8 Nov.)

Boy, age $4\frac{1}{2}$, has gone away from Simon Ruffner, living on the Forks of Delaware; reward if child is brought to said Ruffner or Philip Konnues in Phila. Co., near John Tatel Bowman's (8 Nov.)

Accounts with estate of John Leavering, late of Roxborough Twp., dec'd, to be settled with Abraham and Septimus Leavering, execs. (8 Nov.)

Real estate in Middletown, Bucks Co., six lots on road leading from Newtown to Thomas Jenks's fulling-mill (plan to be seen at William Ashburn's in Newtown) and other lots, being the estate of Thomas Nelson, late of Middletown, dec'd, to be sold by Robert Heaton and William Ashburn, execs. (8 Nov.)

John Osborn, Irish servant, age c. 20, runaway from John Maffett in Ridley Twp., Chester Co. (8 Nov.)

Speech of Lt.-Gov. James De Lancey of New York and addresses to him in regard to the death of Sir Danvers Osborn (15 Nov.)

William Stephens, Esq., lately died in Georgia in his 83rd year (15 Nov.)

1753

Sloop **Sally**, Matthew Santus master, was blown off the coast by a storm; Capts. Elmes, Edmunds, Watson and Alinson suffered in a hurricane (15 Nov.)

New York item of 12 Nov. mentions Capts. Richards, Walton, M'Cleve, Corne, Jones, Francis, Griffiths and Ball (15 Nov.)

H.M.S. **Arundel**, Capt. Lloyd, sailed from Sandy Hook with the late Gov. George Clinton and family on board (15 Nov.)

Phila. item mentions Capts. Charles Swaine, Goff, Read, Stiles, Campbell, Robeson, Flower, Eccles, Vernon, Coxe, Gill, Betaugh, Sage, Ritchie and Shirley (15 Nov.)

Thomas Brown, charged with being concerned in the robbery of Mr. Hanly's house, will be tried in Chester (15 Nov.)

Adv. of John Reily, scrivener; notarial business is transacted at his office by James Humphreys (15 Nov.)

Adv. of Sarah Orr (widow of George Orr, brazier), has removed from Market St. to a house in Front St., opposite to Amos Strettell's, merchant (15 Nov.)

William Derham, Mulatto, age c. 23, mason by trade, runaway from Griffith Griffith, mason, in Bristol Twp. (15 Nov.)

If Alexander Learmonth, carpenter, who left Scotland some years ago, will enquire at the New Printing Office, he will hear something to his advantage (15 Nov.)

Household goods of estate of Mrs. Anne Clawson, dec'd, will be sold at the house of Barnaby Barnes in Second St.; accounts with her estate to be settled with Richard Hockley and Joseph Sims, execs. (15 Nov.)

William Mangles, English servant, age c. 27 (who pretends to be the son of one Mangles, a merchant of London) and an Irish servant named Robert M'Analy, age c. 32, runaways from John Leathes at Francis Trumble's on Society Hill (15 Nov.)

Real estate in Lower-Milford Twp., adjoining land of Joseph Growdon, being the property of William Newman, taken in execution at suit of Morris Morris, Jr., of Phila. merchant, will be sold (15 Nov.)

Lawrence Garrett in Blockly Twp. has taken up a cow (15 Nov.)

Accounts with estate of William Young to be settled with Samuel Neave, Donnaldson and Fuller and Samuel Sansom (15 Nov.)

John Clark, keeper of the goal in Lancaster, has two prisoners taken up on suspicion of being runaway servants, Indian Thomas, who says he served his time with Samuel Lippincut, near Mount-holly Ironworks, and Abigail Allen, who says she served her time with John Rowls in Chester (15 Nov.)

Real estate in Bristol Twp., Phila. Co., opposite to John Ristine, tanner, and near Benjamin Armitage, to be sold by William Wilson (15 Nov.)

Accounts with William M'Carter, of Phila., tailor, to be settled with John Bell, Alexander Houston and Joseph Morris (15 Nov.)

Two Irish servants, Ross Pearsons, age c. 19, and Patrick Fleming, age c. 21, fuller by trade, runaways from on board the **Pembroke** at Clifford's wharf; reward for their capture will be paid by William Griffitts or John Cowan (15 Nov.)

Plantation in Abbington for sale by Richard Treat (15 Nov.)

Samuel Allison, Irish servant, age c. 30 or 40, runaway from David English, living in Mill-Creek Hundred, New-Castle Co. (15 Nov.)

Capt. Comrin arrived 11 Nov. at Boston from Jamaica (22 Nov.)

New York item of 19 Nov. mentions Capts. Tuder, Robert Laton, Downing, Bryson, Lance, Robeson, Hill, Woodlock and Sherman (22 Nov.)

Phila. item mentions Capts. Davis, Bolitho, Burchall, Hunter, Seix and Ritchie (22 Nov.)

Sunday last died at New-Castle the Rev. George Ross in his 74 year (22 Nov.)

Daniel Grant, Irish servant, age c. 19, runaway from Thomas Adams, living in Whitpain Twp., Phila. Co. (22 Nov.)

Lot of land at the Four-Lane-Ends in Middletown, Bucks Co., for sale by James Wildman (22 Nov.)

Lease of mills at Trenton, now let to Andrew Reed, will expire 1 May, and the owner, Robert Lettice Hooper, will let them for a further time (22 Nov.)

Mary Brady, Irish servant, runaway from Alexander Poe, living in Bart Twp., Lancaster Co. (22 Nov.)

Robert Muir, Scotch redemptioner, age c. 18 or 20, tailor, a runaway from John Cameron; reward if brought to James Blair in Phila. or David Finney at New-Castle (22 Nov.)

House in Water St. where John Smith lately lived is to be let (22 Nov.)

James Woods, native Irish servant, age c. 23, runaway from John Smith, living in New London Twp., Chester Co. (22 Nov.)

Adv. of Alexander M'Dougall near the Tun Tavern (22 Nov.)

Patrick Roach, servant, age c. 18, who came from Ireland in the snow *Dispatch*, Capt. Haney, runaway from Josiah and Carpenter (22 Nov.)

Boards and hogsheads are sold by Abraham Carpenter on Pool's Hill in Front St. (22 Nov.)

Votes of the N.Y. Assembly and extract of H.M.'s instructions to Sir Danvers Osborn, copy signed by G. Banyar; addresses to James De Lancey, signed by James Alexander and David Jones (29 Nov.)

Capt. Stewart from Antigua reported in Phila. that Capts. Downy and Joy of Phila. had arrived at Antigua (29 Nov.)

At court in Chester William Tipper pleaded guilty to charge of burning a barn; Thomas Brown broke jail there and escaped before he came to trial for house-breaking (29 Nov.)

Capt. Swaine, though not successful in his attempt to find a northwest passage, is given a handsome present on 23 Nov. (29 Nov.)

William Bradford in Second St. has published a book on the Moravians by Henry Rimius (29 Nov.)

Samuel Jones, of Plymouth, will sell or let 36 lots in Vine St., bounded on N. by land of Thomas Coates and on E. by a new street adjoining other lots of Jones; two lots are on road from Widow Marshall's mill to Phila., 2 miles from the ferry of Stephen Jenkins and 3 from Capt. Coultas's; apply to Joseph Jones, baker, near the Duck in Phila. (29 Nov.)

Sheriff Isaac Pearson offers reward for capture of Thomas Brown, age between 30 and 40, who escaped from goal of Chester Co., to which he was committed for robbing the house of John Hanly (29 Nov.)

Accounts with estate of Reese Peters (who lived in Chestnut St.), dec'd, to be settled with William Savery and William Peters, execs. (29 Nov.)

Joseph Inslee, sub-sheriff, gives notice that Patrick Laning, committed to goal of Bucks Co. in Newtown on suspicion of being Bryan Doran, proves not to be said Doran (29 Nov.)

William Palmer, servant, this country born, age c. 21, weaver, runaway from Henry Lawrence, of Marple Twp., Chester Co. (29 Nov.)

In Baltimore Co. John Barrett was found guilty of the murder of his wife; at the same court John Goldsmith was convicted of breaking into the house of Mrs. Lux (6 Dec.)

The ship Friendship, Capt. John Rattray, arrived at Annapolis with 300 German passengers from Rotterdam (6 Dec.)

The ship Industry, Capt. George Perkins, suddenly sprung a leak and filled with water, according to Annapolis item of 15 Nov. (6 Dec.)

Last week Benjamin Pearce at the head of South River died as result of accidental gunshot wound, according to Annapolis item of 15 Nov. (6 Dec.)

On 30 Nov. at Leicester, Mass., the house of Mr. Earl was struck by lightning (6 Dec.)

Capt. Falis of the ship Prince George reports the death of Capt. Herin at the hands of pirates (6 Dec.)

New York item mentions Capts. M'Laughlin, Alexander Campbell, M'Cleve, Walton, Green, Phoenix, Donaldson and Ross (6 Dec.)

Phila. item mentions Capts. Joy, Clarke and Shearman (6 Dec.)

On 14 Nov. at Reading Jacob Greator was convicted of passing a counterfeit Caroline (6 Dec.)

Fri. last Robert Husband was committed to goal in Phila. on suspicion of horse-stealing (6 Dec.)

Fri. last Daniel Jeffron, a German Newlander, who has lived some years near Frederickstown, Md., was arrested in Phila. for passing counterfeit Maryland bills (6 Dec.)

Tue. last Catherine Jones, convicted in Phila. of felony, was sentenced to be whipped 11 lashes (6 Dec.)

Thomas Brown has been captured in Bristol (6 Dec.)

Jemmy, a Negro, who has been in the country about 16 months, runaway from Stephen Onion's Ironworks in Baltimore Co.; reward offered by Benjamin Welsh (6 Dec.)

Tract of land in Morris Co., N.J., late property of William Biddle, for sale; apply to Samuel Smith, William Lawrence and Joshua Fisher in Phila. (6 Dec.)

Asheton's Ferry, now in the occupation of Joseph Scull, is to be let; enquire of William Asheton at James Humphrey's in Second St. (6 Dec.)

Jacob Matz, Dutch servant, age c. 15, runaway from Elizabeth Smith of the Northern Liberties (6 Dec.)

1753

John Johnston, Irishman, age 22 or 23, who has escaped from the goal of Burlington Co.; reward for his capture offered by Sheriff Samuel Woodward (6 Dec.)

Managers of lottery for building a wharf at Baltimore are John Stevenson, Richard Chase, John Moale, Charles Croxall, William Rogers, Nicholas Rogers, John Ridgely, N. Ruxton Gay, William Lox and Brian Philpot, Jr.; tickets may be had of the managers in Annapolis or of James Stevenson in Water St. in Phila. (6 Dec.)

Speeches of Govs. Robert Dinwiddie and Horatio Sharpe (13 Dec.)

Mon. last in Boston in a quarrel George Kelly (alias William Welsh), a seafaring man, stabbed to death Darby O'Brian, a butcher, according to Boston item of 26 Nov. (13 Dec.)

New York item of 10 Dec. mentions Capts. M'Cleve, Walton, Wanton, Sears, Hubbell, Ducket, Barstow, Wyat, Sweet, Theobalds (on board of whom was John Gill) and Seymour (13 Dec.)

Phila. item mentions Capts. M'Cleve, Lyon and Davis (13 Dec.)

Plantation on White-clay Creek in Newcastle Co. to be sold by Edward Miles, living on the premises (13 Dec.)

Adv. of Alexander M'Douall, next door to Capt. Phillips's in Water St., where Alexander Lunan formerly lived (13 Dec.)

Real estate in and near the town of Reading for sale by Francis Morgan, living in said town (13 Dec.)

Time of English servant girl for sale; enquire at the printing office or at James Smith's, at the Sign of the Founder's Arms in Second St. (13 Dec.)

Horse stolen on 5 Dec. from stable of Jonathan Jones in Phila. (13 Dec.)

On 8 Dec. the following broke goal and escaped from the sheriff of Monmouth in East Jersey: an Irishman named Bryan Dorne; James Wolling, age c. 16 or 17; an Indian named William Pumsher; a servant girl named Catherine Carle, belonging to Thomas Leonard; reward will be paid by Sheriff John Taylor or Thomas Leonard (13 Dec.)

Joseph Chambers, Thomas Barwick and Michael Swoope, auditors, at York Town will sell land in Manchester Twp., York Co., the estate of Simon Heninger, lately absconded, attached at suit of George Keens and Jacob Rudiselly (13 Dec.)

Anthony Cavenaugh (alias Hugh Dougherty), Irish servant, runaway from James M'Cullough of Cecil Co., Md. (13 Dec.)

David Cowpland of Chester has taken up a horse supposed to be stolen from John Johnson (13 Dec.)

Arthur M'Cullough, native Irish servant, age c. 18, runaway from John Black of Fogs Manor, Chester Co. (13 Dec.)

Robert Jones, Welch servant, age c. 24, something of a tailor, runaway from John Morris of Newtown, Chester Co., tavernkeeper (13 Dec.)

Tract of land in the Great Valley, Chester Co,, for sale; enquire of William Griffitts, merchant, or Francis Allison in Phila. or Isaac Davis, Esq., in the Great Valley (13 Dec.)

Sanderson Stanford (alias Emerson), servant, who speaks bad Yorkshire, and Catherine, native Irish servant, age c. 30, runaways from James Smith and Thomas Armor, living in Yorktown, Pa. (13 Dec.)

1753

Phila. item mentions Capts. England, Hubbard, Lake, Rench, Davies, Cathcart, Fadre, Ervin, Waldron, Punter, Keene, Driscall, Allison and White (20 Dec.)

Last week in the goal of Chester Thomas Brown tried without success to hang himself (20 Dec.)

Tue. last fire broke out in the house of Andrew Reed, merchant, in Phila. (20 Dec.)

William Logan offers reward for recovery of a horse strayed from his plantation near Germantown and for another that strayed from George Emlen's plantation near Frankford (20 Dec.)

Piece of ground in Phila., adjoining corner late of Evan Owen's ground and ground now in the possession of Benjamin Loxley, will be sold at William Bell's by Sheriff Samuel Morris (20 Dec.)

Josiah Davenport has opened school in Third St. in the house where the German printing office is now kept (20 Dec.)

Lot of ground in Front St., bounded on N. by lot of Gabriel Wilkinson and on E. by lot of Bartholomew Penrose, late the estate of Thomas Green, dec'd, taken in execution at the suit of Jonathan Mifflin, will be sold by Sheriff Morris at John Biddle's (20 Dec.)

Margaret, wife of John Towers of Phila., has eloped from her husband (20 Dec.)

Mary Hart in Arch St. has a Negro wench for sale (20 Dec.)

John Chalaner (who pretends to be a turner), country born, servant, runaway from Nathan Haines in Evesham, Burlington Co., West N.J. (20 Dec.)

John Miller, Irish servant, age c. 16 or 17, runaway from John Wray, living in Sadsbury Twp., Chester Co. (20 Dec.)

John Hanley, Irish servant, age c. 19 or 20, runaway from George Mackbill, living in Leacock Twp., Lancaster Co. (20 Dec.)

Persons inclined to work on the stone part of the bridge to be built over Darby Creek are asked to meet at John Pearson's in Darby (20 Dec.)

Time of Irish servant girl to be sold by Zacharias Nieman at his house in Almond St. on Society Hill (20 Dec.)

John Parker, Irish servant, runaway from Robert Hart of Elk River Neck, Cecil Co., Md. (20 Dec.)

Plantation in Lower Merion Twp., Phila. Co., late estate of Michael Wills, dec'd, for sale; apply to Thomas Wills on the premises or John Cuthbert or Michael Wills, execs. (20 Dec.)

John Devonshire (alias Cavin), Irish servant, age c. 20, runaway from James Day of Middletown, Chester Co. (20 Dec.)

Real estate in or near Trenton for sale by Thomas Cadwalader at Trenton (20 Dec.)

Capt. Wise has arrived at Charles-Town, S.C. (27 Dec.)

Sat. night the house of the Rev. Andrew Lendrum, Rector of St. George's Parish in Baltimore Co., burned to the ground according to Annapolis item of 29 Nov. (27 Dec.)

1753

Eleven-year-old son of Thomas Cooper, dwelling on the south branch of Potowmack, was carried off by French Indians, as appears by a copy of a letter dated 1 Dec., signed G. Gardiner and directed to a Mr. Green (27 Dec.)

On 5 Dec. at Annapolis died the Hon. Daniel Dulany in his 68 year (27 Dec.)

On the Eastern Shore two Negroes murdered their overseer, a certain Jones (27 Dec.)

Wed. last week John Barret was executed at Joppa for the murder of his wife, according to Annapolis item of 6 Dec. (27 Dec.)

John Goldsmith, condemned in Md. for burglary, has been pardoned by the governor (27 Dec.)

A New York item of 17 Dec. mentions Capts. Hubbel, Pearman, King and Gardner (27 Dec.)

On 12 Nov. a Mr. M'Mea(1?) of Bermuda was murdered by a Negro (27 Dec.)

A Phila. item mentions Capts. Moore, Boatam, Steell, Pitcairn, Russell, Muir, Rowland (all arrived at Charles Town, S.C.), Baker and Allison (27 Dec.)

Fri. last Nathan Levy, an eminent merchant of Phila., died of an apoplectic fit (27 Dec.)

Last week Jacob Viney, of Phila., butcher, killed the largest ox ever raised in Pa. (27 Dec.); the name Viney should have been Odenheimer (8 Jan. 1754)

Mon. night and Tue. morning last in a hurricane Capts. Cowan, Seix and Lowther were driven ashore; Capts. Burrows and M'F(u)n rode out the storm (27 Dec.)

Experiments in electricity are to be conducted at the house of Mr. Kinnersley in Arch St. (27 Dec.)

Horse has strayed from the plantation of John Rowan at Marcus Hook; reward if horse is brought to Thomas Robinson, Esq., at Marcus Hook or John Rowan on Society Hill in Phila. (27 Dec.)

Lease of Asheton's mill in Blockley Twp. and woodland for sale; enquire of James Coultas at the Corporation Ferry or Charles Jenkins at the Lower Ferry (27 Dec.)

Accounts with estate of Thomas Howell, late of Chichester, Chester Co., dec'd, to be settled with Samuel Howell in Phila., exec. (27 Dec.)

Parcel of land in Lower Dublin Twp., bordering on land of Hance Liking and Benjamin Ingle, late estate of Thomas Powell, dec'd, taken in execution at suit of John Holme, will be sold at Bussel-town by Sheriff Samuel Morris (27 Dec.)

Real estate about ½ mile from Marcus Hook for sale; apply to William Howell on the premises (27 Dec.)

Patrick Doran, Irish servant, age c. 20, runaway from Anthony Pritchard of Charlestown, Chester Co. (27 Dec.)

1754

On 21 Nov. last Sarah Bramble was executed at New London in Conn. for the murder of her bastard child (1 Jan.)

Sat. last Capt. Pote arrived at Boston from Liverpool, according to Boston item of 3 Dec. (1 Jan.)

1754

Boston item of 3 Dec. states that on Sat. last Edward Winslow, Esq., who had just entered his 85th year, died in Suffolk Co., Mass. (1 Jan.)

Long list of New York merchants who agree to accept and to pay out British copper halfpence only at the rate of 14 for a shilling (1 Jan.)

Sloop *Polly*, Capt. Houston, outward bound to Antigua, is safe at Marcus Hook (1 Jan.)

Daniel Alexander, Irish servant, age c. 30, runaway from William Boyd, living at Marsh Creek; servant is said to have been 5 years in the country (1 Jan.)

On 18 Dec. Bryan Dorne, James Wolsing, an Indian names William Plumsher and Catherine Carle were committed to goal in Northampton Co., according to notice inserted by Sheriff Nicholas Scull (1 Jan.)

Phila. item mentions Capts. Davis, Budden, Gibbons and Styles (8 Jan.)

Trial of Thomas Brown comes up at Chester on 9 Jan. (8 Jan.)

Adv. of the insurance company office in Water St., Joseph Saunders clerk (8 Jan.)

Charles Coyle, Irish servant, age c. 40, cordwainer, runaway from David Jones, living in East Carnarvin, Berks Co. (8 Jan.)

Grist mill in Wicacoa Twp. for sale by Alexander Crawford, who lives near the corner of Christian St. in Second St. in Wicoaoa (8 Jan.)

Alexander Barclay in Third St. has lost a red cornelian seal; the arms are three crosses and the crest a dove and olive branch (8 Jan.)

John Noah, servant, age c. 18, runaway from Aubrey Harry, who lives in Radnor Twp., Chester Co. (8 Jan.)

Accounts with estate of Margaret M'Carvil, dec'd, to be settled with Frances Holwell, admin., at the Academy (8 Jan.)

Accounts with estate of George Boone, Esq., late of Exeter, Berks Co., dec'd, to be settled with William, Josiah and Jeremiah Boone, execs. (8 Jan.)

Tract of land in Lower Dublin Twp., adjoining land of David Fulton, late estate of Thomas Powell, dec'd, taken in execution at suit of John Holme, to be sold by Sheriff Samuel Morris at Bussel-town (8 Jan.)

Land in Morris Co., West N.J., late property of William Biddle, to be sold at house of John Biddle, the Sign of the Indian King, by Samuel Smith, William Lawrence and Joshua Fisher (8 Jan.)

Capt. Broaders, in a ship belonging to Boston, has been cast away near the Orkneys (15 Jan.)

Thu. last at Weymouth, Mass., were married Ephraim Thair of Braintree, age 85, and Mrs. Mary Kingman, age 78, according to a Boston item of 17 Dec. (15 Jan.)

New York item of 31 Dec. reports that on Thu. last George Harrison was installed as Provincial Grand Master of New York (15 Jan.)

At Chester on Wed. last Thomas Brown was sentenced to death (15 Jan.)

New York item of 31 Dec. reports that on Mon. last Miles Rigs, a boatman, during a gale fell overboard at Peck's slip and was drowned, leaving a wife and eight children (15 Jan.)

New York item of 7 Jan. mentions Capts. Alexander Brown, Elijah Steel, Rodgers, Page, Dixon, Winthrop, Langdon, Waldron and M'Carty (15 Jan.)

John Breton of Middletown, N.J., last week was found frozen to death according to New York item of 7 Jan. (15 Jan.)

A Phila. item mentions Capts. M'Fun, Cookson, Rivers and Murray (15 Jan.)

Lot of ground in Phila. for sale by Deborah and William Claypoole and John Swift, execs. of estate of Abraham Claypoole, dec'd (15 Jan.)

Accounts with partnership of Levy and Franks or with estate of Nathan Levy are to be settled with David Franks (15 Jan.)

Real estate in High St., bounded on W. by property of Abraham Claypoole, dec'd, late estate of James Polegreen, taken in execution at suit of William Bingham, to be sold by Sheriff Samuel Morris at the Indian King (15 Jan.)

Plantation in Passyunk Twp. to be let; enquire of Joseph Sims, below the drawbridge (15 Jan.)

Adv. of Abraham Usher and James Wharton, who carry on the former business of Matthew and Abraham Usher; persons indebted to said Usher are to make prompt payment, as are also persons indebted to the estate of Matthew Watson, dec'd (15 Jan.)

Reward offered for recovery of horse strayed or stolen from Joseph Clark at Pequay, near John Miller's tavern (15 Jan.)

Merchant-mill on Brandywine in East and West Caln Twp. Chester Co., for sale; apply to John Wall on premises (15 Jan.)

Mill in Somerset Co., East N.J., to be let by William Axtell, living in New York (15 Jan.)

Annapolis item of 13 Dec. reports that on Tue. last the body of Daniel Dulany, Commissary-General of Md., was buried in Annapolis (22 Jan.)

Annapolis item of 20 Dec. reports that last week Benjamin Tasker was sworn in as Commissary-General of Md. (22 Jan.)

Capt. White informs that the brig _Charles_, Capt. Jacob Walter, lost the mate, one Robinson, who was washed overboard in a storm (22 Jan.)

Annapolis item of 27 Dec. reports that on Sat. last Daniel Dulany was chosen Recorder of Annapolis in place of his lately dec'd father (22 Jan.)

Boston item of 7 Jan. mentions Capts. Hall and Casneau (22 Jan.)

Proclamation of Lt.-Gov. James De Lancey of New York (22 Jan.)

New York item mentions Capts. Waldron, Langdon, Mann and Thomas (22 Jan.)

Phila. item mentions the loss of the ship _Britannia_, Capt. George Davis, from which James Porter and a Capt. M'Pherson were saved (22 Jan.)

Phila. item mentions Capts. Rees, Collins, Greenway, Cowan, Lowther, M'Fun and Ferguson (22 Jan.)

1754

Israel Pemberton, Sr., died Sat. last in Phila. in his 69th year (22 Jan.)

Farm on Franckfort Creek to be let; apply to Charles Willing, merchant, in Phila. (22 Jan.)

John Floyd of Manor of Moreland has absconded; his creditors are to meet at house of Thomas Fletcher in Abington, Phila. Co. (22 Jan.)

Jonathan Mifflin offers for sale real estate, including house where Richard Swan now lives, next to John Biddle's in Market St., a water lot near Poole's Bridge, bounded by wharf of John Clifton, and land on Germantown Road, opposite to Naglee's brick-kiln (22 Jan.)

John Ermus, or Armus, (alias Huckaback), servant, age c. 28, who can speak Dutch but appears to be this country born; he lived several years about 2 miles E. of Germantown with Thomas Roberts, Jr., runaway from John Ladd of Gloucester Co., N.J. (22 Jan.)

Land in Germantown Twp., adjoining property of George Righter and Henry Dewees, with the moiety of a grist mill in the tenure of John Barge; also real estate adjoining land of Michael Schutz and one Tyson, now in the tenure of John Vandeering, late the estate of Joseph Woollen, taken in execution at suit of John Barge, all will be sold at the house of Daniel Pistorius in Germantown (22 Jan.)

Real estate adjoining land of Anthony Tunes and land of George Rex; also a tract adjoining land of Dennis Strepet, Benjamin Howell and David Reynolds; also a tract adjoining land of Anthony Tunes, John Strepet, Michael Eckart, Cornelius Conrad and the Widow Grotehouse, late the estate of Garrett Dewees, taken in execution at suit of Jacob Luchee, all will be sold at the house of Daniel Pistorius in Germantown (22 Jan.)

Plantation in Marlborough Twp., adjoining lands late of Thomas Maybury, Isaac Sumrie, John Yaglee and George Gargas, late the estate of Adam Kuntz, taken in execution at suit of Alexander Huston and others against Moses Hayman, admin., will be sold at house of George Gargas (22 Jan.)

Lot in Phila. fronting Carter's Alley, estate of Thomas Peters, late of Phila., shopkeeper, dec'd, for sale; apply to the Widow Peters or William Ransted (22 Jan.)

Stones for sale by Phineas Roberts at the Fally Ferry (22 Jan.)

Woodland in Providence Twp. to be sold by John Galbreath, who lives at Springfield meeting-house in said twp. in Chester Co. (22 Jan.)

John Trinder, English servant, age c. 35, runaway from Benjamin Howell of Chichester, Chester Co. (22 Jan.)

Accounts with estate of William Satterthwaite, late of the Falls Twp., Bucks Co., schoolmaster, to be settled with William Biles, admin. (22 Jan.)

John Harry of Whitemarsh Twp., Phila. Co., has taken up a mare (22 Jan.)

Mare strayed or stolen from James Harrison, living at Sasquehannah Lower Ferry in Cecil Co., Md. (22 Jan.)

Plantation in Maiden-creek Twp., Berks Co., for sale; apply to Samuel Pennock, carpenter, in Fourth St., Phila. (22 Jan.)

Daniel Few, near Wilmington, has taken up some horses (22 Jan.)

At Westborough, Mass., on 17 Dec. the house of Alpheus Newton was consumed by fire (29 Jan.)

The snow *Charming Nancy*, Capt. Mallam, of New York, reported lost, is safely arrived at the Downs (29 Jan.)

New York item mentions Capts. Carlisle, Rose, Leake and Reeves (29 Jan.)

On the night of Thu. last in Market St., Phila., a fire broke out; small damage was done to the dwelling of Mr. Snowdon, sadler, and the shop of Mr. Rouse, blacksmith (29 Jan.)

Adv. of Andrew Reed, who is removed to John Smith's house in Water St., opposite to William Callender's (29 Jan.)

Plantation in Oxford Twp. to be sold or let; enquire of Samuel Preston Moore in Third St., Phila. (29 Jan.)

Adv. of James Child in Water St. (29 Jan.)

Meadow in Moyamensing, now in possession of John Ashton, to be let; enquire of William Clark, below the drawbridge (29 Jan.)

Tract of land in Bristol Twp., adjoining lands of Griffith Griffitts and Thomas Roberts, and also woodland, adjoining lands of Thomas Roberts, Robert Whartenby, John Marll and Dr. John Redman, late estate of Erasmus Stevens, taken in execution, to be sold; plan to be seen at Sheriff Samuel Morris's or at William Branson's (29 Jan.)

Two plantations in Passyunk Twp. to be let; one formerly belonged to Richard Roads, on which Andrew Lybert now lives; the other, where Widow Faris dwells, is part of Ramboes land; enquire of John Kearsley, Andrew Hannis or Bartholomew Penrose (29 Jan.)

In Feb. last Benjamin Gibbs obtained a bond from Joseph Gibbs, John Cork and Derrick Williams of Phila. (29 Jan.)

Thomas Berwick, Michael Swoope and John Chambers, auditors, will meet creditors of William Langly, lately absconded, and will sell plantation in Monahan Twp., York Co., adjoining lands of Thomas Hale and William Dodds (29 Jan.)

Mare strayed from plantation of Walter Gilkey of Sadsbury Twp., Chester Co.; reward if mare is brought to said Walter or to James Hope in the Forks of Delaware or to Samuel Gilkey of Whitemarsh (29 Jan.)

Agnes Fee, Irish servant, runaway from Boaz Boyce, of St. George's Hundred in New-Castle Co. (29 Jan.)

Hans Kuhn, High Dutch servant, age c. 28, runaway from Richard Philips of Amwell (29 Jan.)

James Bethell, West-Country servant, age c. 19, runaway from Benjamin Everitt, living near Chester-Town, Kent Co., Md. (29 Jan.)

Real estate in High St., bounded on W. by lot late of Abraham Claypoole, late estate of James Polegreen, taken in execution at suit of William Bingham, will be sold at the Indian King (29 Jan.)

New York public warned against counterfeit bills signed Peter Schuyler, Peter Jay and Stephen Wood (5 Feb.)

New York item of 28 Jan. mentions Capts. Shannon, Arnold, Tudor and Nathaniel Lawrence (5 Feb.)

News comes from Newtown that the following inhabitants were frozen to death when clamming in Jamaica Bay: William Salyar, Amos Roberts, Samuel Leveridge and Thomas Morrel (alias Salyar); one Daniel Smith was frozen to death before he could reach Jamaica (5 Feb.)

New York item of 28 Jan. reports that on Wed. last Mrs. Anne Bockee died at the age of 102 (5 Feb.)

Letter from a gentleman in Va. to a friend in Annapolis, dated 16 Jan. 1754, mentions Mr. Washington, the ambassador to the Indian country (5 Feb.)

Tract in East Nottingham, including house which John Frew lately built, is for sale; enquire of David Finney in New-Castle (5 Feb.)

William Peters in Chestnut St. continues the business of his dec'd father, Rees Peters (5 Feb.)

Persons indebted to the proprietaries are to pay quit-rent to Richard Hockley or Edmund Physick (5 Feb.)

Eleanor Chew, exec. of Joseph Chew, dec'd, will sell plantation on Great Mantua Creek, Gloucester Co., where Archibald Moffett now dwells; to learn terms, apply to Michael Fisher, Esq., living on Great Timber Creek (5 Feb.)

Land in Trediffryn, Chester Co., for sale; apply to Edward Jones or Joseph Tucker in Radnor or John Roberts, miller, in Merion (5 Feb.)

Land in Northampton Co. for sale; apply to Redmond Conyngham, merchant, or John Reily, scrivener, in Front St. (5 Feb.)

Bonds, notes, etc. given to Charles and Alexander Stedman, merchants, are directed by Jacob Frederick Curtius in Lancaster to be settled with Henry Keppley, merchant; said Curtius intends for London in the first ship (5 Feb.)

John Steel, English servant, who served his time with Joshua Yeats in Elk-Ridge, Md., and Charles Campbell, Irish servant, runaways from Joseph Morrison, living in Drummore Twp., Lancaster Co. (5 Feb.)

Plantation in Whiteland Twp., Great Valley, Chester Co., will be sold by William Kinnison (5 Feb.)

Adv. of Thomas Gordon, opposite the Tun Tavern in Water St. (5 Feb.)

New York item of 4 Feb. mentions Capts. Searjant, John Taylor, Manley, Lewis, Stephen Richards and Quinch (12 Feb.)

Phila. item mentions Capts. Alison, Morrison, White, Coatam and Ewing (12 Feb.)

Subscribers to the Pennsylvania Gazette are to pay what is due (for Va.) to William Hunter in Williamsburgh, (for the western shore of Md.) to William Young in Baltimore Co., (for the eastern shore) to Thomas Ringold of Chester Town (12 Feb.)

Two plantations in Bensalem Twp., Bucks Co., for sale; enquire of Robert Greenway in Phila. (12 Feb.)

John Rowan will sell plantation near Marcus Hook (12 Feb.)

Plantation, late the dwelling of Moses Dupui, dec'd, at Mini-
sinks in Lower Smithfield Twp., Northampton Co., will be sold
by Aaron Dupui and Daniel and Ann Shoemaker, admins.; Daniel
Dupui will sell another plantation and Samuel Dupui still
another (12 Feb.)

Lot of ground in Second St. to be sold at public vendue at
John Biddle's; apply to Hermanus Alrichs at the Sign of the
Indian King to know the terms of the sale (12 Feb.)

Plantation in Oiles-grove, Salem Co., now in possession of
John Keen, to be sold by Andrew Tranberg, Adolph Benzel and
Olove Parlin (12 Feb.)

Bryan Reyley, Irish servant, runaway from Jacob Sharpless of
East Bradford, Chester Co, (12 Feb.)

John Wood will sell horses and wagon at public vendue at the
house of Joseph White, next door to the Sign of the Death
of the Fox in Second St. (12 Feb.)

Real estate to be sold by Joseph Talbot, living in Middletown,
Chester Co. (12 Feb.)

Andrew Liburt offers reward for recovery of stallion stolen
from house of Peter Hagner of Passyunk, supposedly by Charles
Perry (12 Feb.)

A mare has been stolen or strayed from John Howard, joiner, of
Phila. (12 Feb.)

Thomas Davis, age c. 21, has been committed to the goal of
Phila.; apply to Edward Callings, keeper of the goal (12 Feb.)

Plantation in Maiden Creek Twp., Berks Co., for sale; enquire
of Samuel Pennock, carpenter, in Fourth St., Phila., or Benjamin Lightfoot, Esq., in Reading (12 Feb.)

Plantation in Lower Merion Twp. for sale; apply to Thomas
Evans of North Wales or Hugh Evans or Robert Roberts, who
live near the premises (12 Feb.)

Jonathan Arnott, English servant, age c. 17, runaway from Samuel Osborne, Esq., on Society Hill (12 Feb.)

Item from Charles-Town, S.C., mentions Capts. Julian Legg,
Thomas Riggs, Witherdon Baker and Archibald Borland (19 Feb.)

A Negro who murdered his master and the master's wife and 3
children in Surrey Co., Va., has been hanged (19 Feb.)

House of Mr. Parran at Patuxent was burnt to the ground (19
Feb.)

On 9 Jan. Capt. William Smith arrived at Annapolis with 52 indented servants (19 Feb.)

Christmas eve one Seth Evans, having crossed the Patuxent in
a canoe, was frozen to death (19 Feb.)

In Queen Anne's Co. one Thomas Watts died of injuries received
at the hands of people at a private tippling-house on Chester
River (19 Feb.)

Capt. Gifford, arrived at New York from Halifax, brought news
of Col. Monkton (19 Feb.)

Mention of Capt. Henry, arrived at Phila. from Coracoa (19 Feb.)

Accounts with estate of John Johnson, late of the Northern Liberties of Phila., dec'd, to be settled with Jacob Dubee and
John Hood, admins. (19 Feb.)

1754

Last week at Phila. David Jession was punished for passing counterfeit Maryland bills (19 Feb.)

Co-partnership between Sankey Hainsworth and Robert Hamilton, of New York City, merchants, is dissolved (19 Feb.)

Mare stolen from Peter Beaker, of Earl Twp., Lancaster Co. (19 Feb.)

House where Martha Green now lives, on Germantown Road, about a mile from Phila., and the house where Timothy Scarth now lives are for sale by Martha Green, exec. of Thomas Green, dec'd (19 Feb.)

Land bounding upon Mr. Inglis's ropewalk and the meadow bounding upon Robert Rawlinson's meadow to the E. and William Shippen's to the S. will be sold by public vendue at John Biddle's (19 Feb.)

Real estate to be sold by Abraham Farrington, living in Bridge-Town, commonly called Mount-holly, in Burlington Co., West N.J. (19 Feb.)

Benjamin Gibbs, sadler, is removed to house almost opposite to James Benezet's and next door to Joseph Baker's (19 Feb.)

Plantation in Plumsted Twp., Bucks Co., late the property of Joseph Brown, dec'd, to be sold by the execs., Alexander Brown and Nathan Preston (19 Feb.)

Real estate in Berks Co. for sale; apply to Benjamin Lightfoot in Reading or Samuel Lightfoot in Pikeland, Chester Co. (19 Feb.)

Accounts with estate of John Hart, late of Phila., dec'd, to be settled with Thomas Hallowell, admin. (19 Feb.)

Plantation in Chester Co., adjoining Goshen Meeting-house, late the property of Isaac Starr, dec'd, for sale by Margaret Starr and Samuel Lightfoot, execs. (19 Feb.)

Plantation in Greenwich Twp. to be sold by Thomas Bickham (19 Feb.)

Tickets for lottery in Conn. for the benefit of the College of New Jersey may be had from John Lloyd, Ephraim Bastwick, Esq., and Dr. Nathaniel Hubbard of Stamford, Conn., David Vanhorne in New York, Samuel Woodruff, Esq., in Elizabethtown, Mr. Sargeant (treasurer of the college) in Newark, John Stockton, Esq., in Prince-town, Rev. Cowell and Messers Reed and Furman in Trenton, Charles Goff, Jr., in Kingwood, John Imley in Bordentown, George Spofford, Andrew Reed, William Grant, John Sayre, Andrew Hodge, William Henry, Hugh M'Cullough and Samuel Hazard in Phila. (19 Feb.)

A schooner's mast, casks, etc. have been taken up; they are supposed to belong to the Elizabeth, Edward Tew master, according to item from Charles-Town, S.C. (26 Feb.)

Capt. Peter Rice died in Marlborough, Mass., on 28 Nov. last in his 100th year (26 Feb.)

On 21 Jan. Capt. Richard in a schooner from Rhode Island ran upon Cohasset Rocks (26 Feb.)

The snow Israel, Capt. Simmon, lies at Parmaceti Cove (26 Feb.)

Pilot boat of Tunis Rivets of New York overset near the West Bank, and two boys, William Bray and Thomas Burdone, were drowned (26 Feb.)

1754

Last week a boat ran upon George's Island; the skipper, one Burt, and a person named Merryman were frozen to death; a lighter from Weymouth ran ashore near Hangman's Island, and the skipper, one Nash, and his Negro survived; two young men from Weymouth, Bernard and Loring, perished; at Newbury a Mr. Flood was frozen to death; Capt. Gill put back to Boston; the above are all Boston items (26 Feb.)

The schooner Katie, Capt. Stewart, was lost on the northwest end of Bermuda on 1 Jan. (26 Feb.)

A Phila. item mentions Capts. Styles, Mason, Arnott and Hayes (26 Feb.)

Printing is done by William Dunlap at Lancaster (26 Feb.)

Accounts with estate of Richard Morrey, late living near Bedminster in the Northern Liberties, dec'd, to be settled with John Baselee, exec. (26 Feb.)

Plantation in Passyunk Twp. for sale by Bartholomew Penrose (26 Feb.)

Adv. of James Chattin, printer and seller of books, next door to Hugh Roberts's in Church Alley, Phila. (26 Feb.)

Lot of ground in Fifth St. to be let or sold; enquire of Robert Tempest (26 Feb.)

Matthew Morrison, servant, age c. 23, who formerly served Nathaniel Grubb in Chester Co., runaway from John Taylor, who lives in Red Lion Hundred, Newcastle Co.; reward will be paid by said Taylor or Alexander Montgomery (26 Feb.)

House in Second St., Phila., for sale by John Snowdon, sadler, living in Market St. (26 Feb.)

John Cory, of Elizabeth-Town, N.J., offers reward for recovery of his son Isaac, age 16, who, disordered in mind, left his parents on 22 Jan. last (26 Feb.)

Plantation in the Great Valley, near the Sign of the White Horse on Lancaster Road, for sale by Malachi Jones (26 Feb.)

George Douglas of Bordentown will not pay debts contracted in future by his wife Athalanah (26 Feb.)

Speech of Gov. Glen of S.C. and addresses of John Cleland and James Michie (5 Mar.)

Punishment of a soldier in Col. Warburton's regiment in Halifax (5 Mar.)

Annapolis item of 7 Feb. reports that last week at the Mayor's Court James Lord was found guilty of stealing and was stood in the pillory and whipped (5 Mar.)

Mon. last Aaron Grace was committed to prison in Annapolis for offering to impose a forged order (5 Mar.)

Sun. last Lord Baltimore entered his 23rd year, according to Annapolis item of 21 Feb. (5 Mar.)

Fri. last the Hon. Benjamin Young died of gout at his seat on Potowmack, according to Annapolis item of 14 Feb. (5 Mar.)

Two houses of Turnor Wootton, High Sheriff of Prince George's Co., near Queen-Anne Town, burned to the ground, and on Sun. last a house owned by Charles Brown of Queen Anne's Co. also burnt down; Capt. Tipple reports the safe arrival of Md. ships; a few days ago house of William Humphreys, near Magothy River, burnt to the ground (5 Mar.)

New York item mentions Capts. Stiles, Jauncey, Spelling and William Dickenson (5 Mar.)

Phila. item mentions Capts. Teague, Godfrey, Budden, Murphey, Stamper, Edwards, Crathorn, Power, Drason, Nabby, Romer, Sage, Arthur, Millar, Greenway, Lawrence, Faulkner, Flower, Cunningham, Brown, Reeve, Rait, Lake, Lownes, Haselton, Winter, Stirling, Wall, Hardy, Hutchinson, Trump, Taylor, Downie and Green (5 Mar.)

Adv. of Benjamin Mifflin, whose store was formerly Anthony Morriss's malt-house, near the drawbridge (5 Mar.)

Houses and lots in Borough of Lancaster for sale by Isaac Whitelock and Thomas Poltany, living in Lancaster; the Sign of the Handsaw, Poltany's shop, is in King St. (5 Mar.)

Animals and farm implements will be sold by Arnold Francis at his house in the Northern Liberties (5 Mar.)

John Hanley, Irish servant, age c. 19 or 20, runaway from George Mackrill, living in Leacock Twp., Lancaster Co. (5 Mar.)

House where Rees Peters lately dwelt, bounded on E, by land late of John Bayley, on N. by land late of Hermanus Alrichs, on W. by land of Rees Peters, part of the estate of Jonathan Dickinson, dec'd, for sale by William Savery and William Peters, execs. (5 Mar.)

House in Bordentown for sale; enquire of John Thorn (5 Mar.)

Speech of Gov. Horatio Sharpe, addresses of B. Tasker and P. Hammond and addresses to Robert Dinwiddie (12 Mar.)

On 4 Jan. Robert Foyle of Augusta Co., his wife and five children were killed by Indians (12 Mar.)

Sat. last Absalom Butler was committed to goal of Baltimore Co. for murder, according to Annapolis item of 28 Feb. (12 Mar.)

A few days ago in Kent Co. Thomas Cartwright beat a servant so severely that he died, according to an Annapolis item of 28 Feb. (12 Mar.)

At Andover, Mass., the roof of the Rev. Philips's meetinghouse was raised from the rafters by a storm (12 Mar.)

New York item mentions Capts. William Dickenson, Duncan, Wilmot, Briggs, Nathaniel Lawrence, Gooding, Hunter, Kip, Edward Menzie, Swan, Burger, Mosley, Kenneway (12 Mar.)

Mon. last the house of Isaac Seixas, of New York, merchant, was broken into; among articles stolen were 2 silver tablespoons, marked IRS (maker's mark MM), 6 teaspoons and a sugar tongs marked RL (12 Mar.)

Sloop belonging to Col. Noble is run ashore on Cape Cod (12 Mar.)

Phila. item mentions Capts. Salter, Canfield, Shirley, Dowers, Sage, Wright and Osborne (12 Mar.)

Adv. of John Pole and Howell (12 Mar.)

Arthur M'Cullough, Irish servant, age c. 18, runaway from John Black in Fogs Manor, Chester Co. (12 Mar.)

Adv. of William Daws, sail-maker from London, who has taken a store on John Pole's wharf (12 Mar.)

Henry Gowmiller, Dutch servant, age c. 37, runaway from Henry Wolff of Alsace Twp., Berks Co. (12 Mar.)

Plantation in Coventry Twp., Chester Co., property of Samuel Meredith, to be sold; apply to Samuel Flower (12 Mar.)

Real estate in South St., including a lot bounded on W. by a lot of George Emlen, Jr., and also land in Lebanon Twp., Lancaster Co., for sale by Conrad Waltacker (12 Mar.)

Letter of Pere Charlevoix concerning M. De Joncaire and the settlement at Niagara; also a note of the late Dr. Douglass of Boston (19 Mar.)

The *Salley*, of Boston, Henry Irving master, foundered at sea south of Bermuda (19 Mar.)

Depositions, sworn to before Capt. Julian Legge, of William Lewis, Allan Stuart and Henry Bull, belonging to the sloop *Elizabeth*, William Mackay master (19 Mar.)

Charles Town, S.C., item mentions Capts. Stevenson, William Blany, Robert Glasgow and Adam Wilson (19 Mar.)

New York item mentions Capts. Codwise, Ebbets, Jones, Koffler, Cozzins, Menzie, Rogers, Ewing, Nicholas Burger and Governors Grenville and Pitts (19 Mar.)

Phila. item mentions Capts. Knox, Blake, Dreson, Stamper, Dowers, Edwards, Hiern, Downie, Houston, Ford, Sibbald, Sage, Rees, Morrison, Albuoy, Vaughan and Currie (19 Mar.)

Plantation in Merion Twp., about a mile from John Roberts's mill, for sale; apply to Richard Lloyd, living in Darby, Chester Co. (19 Mar.)

Peter Patridge, screen-maker, is removed from house of Joseph Saul in Market St. to house of Charles Stow, Sr., at the Sign of the Half Moon (19 Mar.)

Plantation in Little Britain, Lancaster Co., for sale by Emanuel Grubb, Jr., living in Brandywine Hundred, Newcastle Co.; Thomas Grubb on the premises will show the property (19 Mar.)

Thomas Hall, English servant, age c. 21, runaway from Swan Justis, living in Kingsess, Phila. Co. (19 Mar.)

Edmund Nihell in Sixth St. will sell the lease of brewhouse and also lease of a pasture on Moyamensing Road, near Mr. Henis's brickyard; Samuel Carpenter inclines to sell house and brewhouse (19 Mar.)

Copy of letter from Gov. Dinwiddie sent by Major Washington to the commander of the French on the Ohio and the reply of Legardeur de St. Pierre (26 Mar.)

New York item of 18 Mar. mentions Capts. White and Tingley (26 Mar.)

Richard Thorne of Hampstead Bounds on Long Island has brought to New York City two hugh steers he has raised (26 Mar.)

Letter to the printers of the *Gazette* about plays quotes Bishop Burnet, Archbishop Tillotson and Dr. Young (26 Mar.)

Phila. item mentions Capts. Sage, Lowther and Falkner (26 Mar.)

Adv. of Robert Ibison, whose chocolate mill is in Market St. (26 Mar.)

Lectures on electricity; tickets to be had at Mr. Kinnersley's house in Arch St. (26 Mar.)

1754

Lawrence Perkley, Dutch servant, age c. 40, carver in wood and stone, who speaks French and Turkish, runaway from Brian Wilkinson, of Phila., carver (26 Mar.)

Adv. of Wallace and Bryan on Market St. wharf (26 Mar.)

House where Hance Rudolph formerly kept tavern at Christine Bridge in Newcastle Co., now in the tenure of John M'Carty, for sale by William Armstrong and Thomas Rudolph (26 Mar.)

Robert Coe teaches the German flute at his school next door to the Widow Bittle's in Strawberry Alley (26 Mar.)

Tract of land in New London Twp., Chester Co., formerly the property of Robert Allan, dec'd, to be sold by William and David M'Ilvaine (26 Mar.)

John Parrish offers reward if his mare, which strayed from the commons of Phila., is brought to William Gray's, at the Sign of the Conestogoe Wagon in Market St. (26 Mar.)

Plantation in Moyamensing to be let; enquire of Joseph Lawrence in Third St. (26 Mar.)

Adv. of Eleanor Dexter, living in White Horse Alley (26 Mar.)

Letters have been sent by Messers Trent and Gist to Major Washington; they tell of speech made by M. La Force and news from Mr. Croghan; they ask that Washington send them a line by Mr. Stewart (4 Apr.)

Annapolis item mentions Capts. Spencer and Gabrielson and a Mr. Rowland Carnan (4 Apr.)

Annapolis item of 21 Mar. gives the speech of an Indian named Monocatoocha (4 Apr.)

A brigantine, Fortescue Vernon commander and William Harris mate, on 19 Feb. was driven on the rocks at Noman's Island; seven persons were assisted ashore by Mr. Manter, while the others drowned (4 Apr.)

Thu. last a court in Suffolk Co., Mass., found George Kelley, alias William Welch, guilty of the murder of Darby O'Brian in Nov. last, according to Boston item of 11 Mar. (4 Apr.)

New York item of 25 Mar. mentions Capts. Kip (who gave account of robbery of a store of Mr. Frederick on St. Eustatia), Philipson, Devereaux, Bolitho and Kendrick (Kendrick's mate, Francis Healey, was drowned on 21 Feb. (4 Apr.)

Phila. items mention Governors Cornwallis and Pitts and Capts. Southcott, Dowers, Masenet, Middleton, Robinson and Rogers (4 Apr.)

Sloop belonging to Mr. Creagh of Annapolis was seized by the crew, who murdered the captain, one William Curtis, and others; one John Bishop alarmed the Virginia coast (4 Apr.)

Accounts with estate of Daniel Hingston, late of Gloucester Co., dec'd, to be settled with Joseph Sims, admin. (4 Apr.)

Piece of land in the Northern Liberties in Kensington, bounded by land of Anthony Palmer, late the estate of John Ogborne, dec'd, taken in execution, is to be sold by public vendue at the house of James Cusick in Kensington (4 Apr.)

Negro woman for sale by Thomas Duffield in Bussel Town (4 Apr.)

Adv. of Henry Flower, watchmaker, at the Sign of the Dial in Second St. (4 Apr.)

1754

Parcel of land, adjoining lands late of Peter Robinson, late the property of Edward Farmar, dec'd, to be sold at Christopher Robinson's in Whitemarsh; also real estate in Oxford Twp., bounded by land of Thomas Kenton and the road leading to Busby's mill, late the estate of Joseph Woollen, taken in execution, to be sold at the house of James M'Vaugh, a little above Frankford (4 Apr.)

Piece of land on road from Phila. to Darby, bounded on W. by land of Swan Justice, Jr., on N. by land of Mounce Rambo, and on E. by lands of William White and Swan Justice, Jr., late the property of Jacob Lincoln, taken in execution, will be sold at the house of John Crosier, near Cob's Creek Bridge (4 Apr.)

John Frederick Francis Cortine, Dutch servant, age c. 17, who came into the country last fall, runaway from James Stockhouse of Phila., plaisterer (4 Apr.)

Henry Cole, age c. 22, and John Lewis, age c. 22, English servants, runaways from John Wright, of Lancaster, at Sasquehanna Ferry (4 Apr.)

Accounts with estate of John Stow, dec'd, to be settled with Hannah Stow, admin. (4 Apr.)

One Abraham Potts left a horse at the house of John Hanly in Chester (4 Apr.)

John Oulton, an Englishman, convict servant, a labourer, a runaway from the Baltimore Ironworks; he may have an old indenture of one John Williams who lately went away from said works; reward offered by Richard Croxall (4 Apr.)

House where Richard Murray, dec'd, lately dwelt in Vine St., bounded on W. by ground of George Royal and on E. by land of Jonathan Zane, for sale by William Chancellor in Market St. (4 Apr.)

Two tenements in Phila., part of the estate of Seth Koyle, dec'd, and also right claimed by said Seth to real estate which was formerly leased to Emanuel Rouse by Michael Koyle, dec'd, late father to the said Seth, will be sold at the dwelling of William Bell, admin. of Seth Koyle (4 Apr.)

Thomas Deal (or Dean), Irish servant, age c. 36, who says he has been a pedlar, runaway from Peter Jones, at the Lake, in Gloucester Co. (4 Apr.)

Accounts with the estate of John Jones, dec'd, to be settled with Sarah Jones, exec. (4 Apr.)

Edward Linnard, Irish servant, age c. 14, runaway from William Connely at Gilbert's Manor, New Providence Twp. (4 Apr.)

Grist-, fulling- and boulting mill in Shrewsbury, Monmouth Co., East N.J., to be let; apply to John Abbot, near Trenton, or John Williams of Shrewsbury (4 Apr.)

Lot of land in Mill St. in Bridge-town, commonly called Mountholly, in Burlington Co., West N.J., for sale; apply to Zebulon Webb at Mount-Misery sawmill (4 Apr.)

John Oulton, the convict servant who was captured by John Orrick, stabbed Orrick and escaped (11 Apr.)

Widow Vessels, age c. 30 or 35, a few weeks ago was found murdered at her house near Clement's Bay in St. Mary's Co.(11 Apr.)

Boat searching for Mr. Creagh's sloop has returned without finding it (11 Apr,)

At sessions held at Newport, R.I., two men from Conn, Averell and Coggeshall, were convicted of passing counterfeit bills (11 Apr.)

Tue. last George Harrison, Surveyor of Customs at New York, found 150 pounds in counterfeit British halfpence, according to a New York item of 8 Apr., and seized the same (11 Apr.)

The following were elected directors of the Fire Insurance Co.: Hugh Roberts, Samuel Rhoads, Isaac Jones, Joseph Fox, James Pemberton, Abel James, Philip Syng, Evan Morgan, Thomas Crosby, Charles Jones, William Fisher and Buckridge Sims; John Smith was elected treasurer (11 Apr.)

Ship Lydia, Capt. Reeve, for London, will fall down Tue. next (11 Apr.)

Adv. of John Groves, who is removed from store on Carpenter's wharf to house in Front St., opposite Robert Moore's (11 Apr.)

James Lewis, age c. 35, disordered in his senses, went away from Warwick Twp., Bucks Co.; reward for his return will be paid by Isaac Lewis in said twp. (11 Apr.)

Company of comedians in Phila. from London consists of Mr. Malone, Mr. Clarkson, Mr. Rigby, Mr. Singleton, Mr. Adcock, Mrs. Rigby and Miss Hallam (11 Apr.)

Richard Devine, servant from North of Ireland, runaway from Wallace and Bryan in Market St. (11 Apr.)

Abraham Stewart, servant, born in North of England, age not quite 20, runaway from Isaac Zane in Market St. (11 Apr.)

Ebenezer Hopkins directs persons indebted to the Pennsylvania Land Co. to attend at the house of Rebecca and Elizabeth Rawle in Water St. (11 Apr.)

George Burns is removed from New York to Trenton Ferry (11 Apr.)

Samuel Johnson, in Black Horse Alley, has a Negro, a painter, for sale (11 Apr.)

Time of a servant girl for sale; enquire at the German Printing Office in Third St., next door but one to Richard Hockley's (11 Apr.)

Maria Kummenfield, Dutch servant, age c. 26, runaway from John Cuming of Trenton (11 Apr.)

Philip Sinloup, Dutch servant, age c. 40, who pretends to be a mason and plaisterer, runaway from John Potter, living in West Nantmell, Chester Co. (11 Apr.)

Fulling mill in Darby and other real estate for sale by David Davis, living in Cumry Twp.; enquire of Isaac Pearson, Esq., in Cumry Twp. (11 Apr.)

Michael Doyle, native Irish servant, age c. 22, runaway from William Wiley of **Kennet Twp.**, Chester Co. (11 Apr.)

Phila. item mentions Capts. Ainsdel, Benson, Bailey, Wingfield, Mesnard, Hamilton, Magee, Rankin, Duncan, Betaugh, Roberts, Sampson, Gardiner, Dunbar, Moore, Macilvaine, Kenedy, Caldwell, Lee, Boyle, Glentworth, Ritchie, Shirley and Mitchell (18 Apr.)

Adv. of Mrs. Redmond in Market St. (18 Apr.)

John Hart, Indian trader, in Cumberland Co. shot and killed a neighbor named Moreton (18 Apr.)

North Carolina troops are ordered to march to Virginia under Col. Imus for the Ohio expedition (18 Apr.)

Negroes belonging to the estate of Daniel Hingston, dec'd, will be sold by public vendue at John Biddle's in Market St. (18 Apr.)

Barnut Mouran, Dutch servant, age $\underline{c}$. 40, runaway from John Paul of Vincent Twp., Chester Co. (18 Apr.)

Adv. of Richard Farmar, at the Unicorn, in Second St. (18 Apr.)

Adv. of James Child in Water St. (18 Apr.)

Adv. of John Greenleafe in Second St., near Stretch's corner (18 Apr.)

House and lot in Chestnut St. to be sold by Alexander Cruikshank (18 Apr.)

Fire insurance office, lately kept by Joseph Saunders, is now kept by Robert Owen in Mulberry St. (18 Apr.)

Lot in Chestnut St., bounded on W. by lot of E. Wright, and also real estate in Sixth St., bounded on N. by lot of Jasper Carpenter, late estate of Samuel Carpenter, will be sold at house of John Biddle (18 Apr.)

House and lot in Second St., Phila., bounded on W. by land of William Branson and on S. by ground of Aquilla Jones, late the estate of Philip Told, butcher, taken in execution, will be sold at house of John Biddle (18 Apr.)

Adv. of Arent Hassert in Laetitia Court (18 Apr.)

Francis Lolley, servant, a Worcester man, runaway from William Boulton, living near Collins's mill in Queen Ann's Co., Md. (18 Apr.)

John Moll, born in Staffordshire, age $\underline{c}$. 30, and William Faulkner, born in Lincolnshire, age $\underline{c}$. 24, tailor by trade, convict servants, runaways from William Lux and N. Ridgely, who live near Baltimore Town; a convict servant of William Buchanan, of Baltimore Town, is supposed to be in their company (18 Apr.)

John Hogan, Irish servant, age $\underline{c}$. 20, James Adams, Irish servant, age $\underline{c}$. 22, and Martha Suthward, English servant, age $\underline{c}$. 18, runaways from James Anderson, at the ferry on Sasquehanna, Donegall Twp., Lancaster Co. (18 Apr.)

Francis M'Nealis, Irish servant, age $\underline{c}$. 25, runaway from William Smith of Donegall Twp., Lancaster Co. (18 Apr.)

Thomas Fleming (<u>alias</u> Thomas Casedy), Irish servant, age $\underline{c}$. 22, runaway from Nathaniel Grubb of Chester Co. (18 Apr.)

Benjamin Walton offers reward for silver watch lost on the York Road if it is brought to David Rees at the Crooked Billet (18 Apr.)

Barnaby M'Carty, Irish servant, age $\underline{c}$. 46, and James Flin, Irish servant, cooper by trade, age upwards of 30, runaways from Richison and James Williams, living in Whiteland Twp., Chester Co. (18 Apr.)

Thomas Filer, English servant, age $\underline{c}$. 33, who talks West-Country, runaway from Thomas Andrews, living in Evesham Twp., Burlington Co., West N.J. (18 Apr.)

1754

Managers for the Lutheran Lottery for purchasing house and ground in Germantown are Sebastine Neff, George Donnenhaver, Jacob Miller, Charles Hay, Jacob Beyerle and Matthias Gainsele; tickets may be had at Daniel Benezet's and Alexander Huston's (18 Apr.)

On 3 Mar. John Toomer, age c. 28, on the road, about a mile from Charles-Town, S.C., shot and killed William Butler, son of Thomas Butler; both John and William were inhabitants of Prince William's Parish; Gov. James Glen offers reward for the capture of Toomer (25 Apr.)

Thu. last William Welch was executed at Boston, according to Boston item of 15 Apr. (25 Apr.)

New York item mentions Capts. Todd, Hall, Gooding, Stevenson, Steel, Emy; Capt. Gooding reported the execution at St. Eustatia of three Frenchmen for robbing the store of Mr. Frederick (25 Apr.)

Phila. item mentions Capts. Ritchie, Gordon, Jenkins, Thomas, Coatam, Steel, Brown, Mitchell, Nuttle, Magee and Rankin (25 Apr.)

Sun. last Thomas Lawrence, Member of Council, died in Phila. (25 Apr.)

Mills and plantation of Nathaniel Ware, Esq., 6 miles above Trenton on the Delaware, for sale; apply to William Clayton or William Pidgeon in Trenton (25 Apr.)

Catherine, wife of William Johnson, of Worcester, Phila. Co., weaver, has eloped from her husband (25 Apr.)

Adv. of Thomas Wharton at Carpenter's wharf, where Joseph Saunders formerly kept, opposite to Abraham Taylor's (25 Apr.)

Adv. of Stephen Carmick, whose store is under Capt. William Spofford's in Market St. (25 Apr.)

Joseph Bradford, age c. 23, and Mary Chambers (alias Connor), Irish convict servants, runaways from Alexander Baird, living in Kent Co., Md.; they have the pass of one Terence Burns (25 Apr.)

Adv. of Edward Broadfield, who is removed from Bordentown to Trenton, sells kegs of pickled fish; said kegs are also sold by Nathaniel Allen, Jr., in Water St., opposite William Allen, Esq.; William Pancoast of Bordentown has illegally branded kegs with Broadfield's brand (25 Apr.)

Adv. of Redmond Conyngham and also adv. of Benjamin Kendall, both of Phila. (25 Apr.)

Real estate in Phila., bounded on N. by ground late of John Ingram and on S. by land of Dr. Moore and Richard Hill, Jr., for sale; enquire of Charles and Alexander Stedman (25 Apr.)

John Hall has absconded; his creditors are to appear before John Scott in Chester Co. (25 Apr.)

James Allen, Irish servant, age c. 24, runaway from Isaac Janney, living in Cecil Co., Md. (25 Apr.)

Morgan M'Anally, servant, runaway from Thomas England of Phila., tallow-chandler (25 Apr.)

Patrick Dun and Thomas Loyder, servants, runaways from on board the Dursley Galley, William Hamilton master; reward offered by John Rowan on Society Hill (25 Apr.)

1754

Real estate in Newcastle Hundred and in Pencader Hundred, property of the Rev. Timothy Griffith, late of Newcastle Co., dec'd, to be sold by order of the Orphans Court, Richard M'William, clerk; Mrs. Sarah Griffith is admin. of the estate (25 Apr.)

Time of a servant, tailor by trade, for sale; enquire of William Scott in Front St. (25 Apr.)

Adv. of Jacob Shoemaker, Jr., in Market St. (25 Apr.)

Thomas Burk, Irish servant, age c. 36 or 38, runaway from Edward Hughes of Passyunk Twp., Phila. Co. (25 Apr.)

Lot of ground on Society Hill, bounded on E. by house of William Hodge and on W. by house of Mr. Carrell, will be sold by John Perkins at the house of John Thomas(25 Apr.)

Hance Dieder, Dutch servant, age c. 35, runaway from Barnet Vanhorne, living in Northampton Twp., Bucks Co. (25 Apr.)

John Leonard Zembes, Dutch servant, button-maker, runaway from Joseph Carter, miller, of Northampton Twp., Bucks Co. (25 Apr.)

Joseph Davis (alias Williams), Welsh servant, age c. 18, runaway from Pennel Evans, living in Union Twp., Berks Co. (25 Apr.)

Two Negroes for sale, and a house in Fourth St. is to be let by Marcus Kuhl (25 Apr.)

John M'Laughlin, servant, who served part of his time with Joseph Dobbins in Phila., runaway from Amos Grandine, of the Northern Liberties of Phila. (25 Apr.)

Wed. last Thomas Poole, a pilot for some 15 years, was drowned in a gale, as reported in a Charles-Town, S.C., item (2 May)

Col. Joshua Fry, with 300 men, has been sent from Virginia to make a settlement on the Ohio River; Major Washington was sent by Lt.-Gov. Dinwiddie with a letter to the commander of the nearest French fort (2 May)

Williamsburgh item of 29 Mar. mentions Capts. Morris and Daniel Horne (2 May)

At a court held in Baltimore Co. last week Absalom Butler was acquitted of a charge of murder (2 May)

At Assize Court in Annapolis a verdict was found for M. L., a spinster, against P.D., a cooper, for violation of a promise of marriage (2 May)

A widow named Brookes, near Upper Marlborough, fell into the fire and perished, according to Annapolis item of 11 Apr. (2 May)

On 13 Apr. Robert Temple, Esq., died at his home in Charlestown, Mass. (2 May)

Horse of Oliver De Lancey, Esq., in New York, on a wager ran 36 miles in one hour and 47 minutes (2 May)

Thu. last Patrick Creamer in a quarrel struck Martinus Cregier with a pole, knocking him into the water, so that he died within a few minutes, according to a New York item of 29 Apr. (2 May)

New York item mentions Capts. Pell, Nealford, Dorrington, Haviland, Williams, Stevenson, Jones, Thomas, Church, Newbold, Winthrop, White, Dunscomb, Gillford, Serjeant, Alexander, Cathcart, Collum, Adams (2 May)

Phila. item consists of part of a letter that mentions Gov.
Duquesne, M. Morin, Gov. Dinwiddie and Capt. Donahew (2 May)

Thu. last Charles Willing was elected Mayor of Phila. in the
room of Thomas Lawrence, dec'd (2 May)

Phila. item mentions Capts. Swaine, Marsden, M'Clelland, Ross
and Cuzzins (2 May)

Benjamin Price, attorney-at-law, is removed from Front St.
to Joseph Redman's in Market St. (2 May)

Adv. of Rhea and Wikoff at their store on Carpenter's wharf,
from which John Grove, merchant, lately removed (2 May)

Negro man for sale; enquire of Thomas Wills, of Lower Merion,
near John Roberts's mill (2 May)

Adv. of John Head, Jr., in Second St. (2 May)

Adv. of George Smith in Front St. (2 May)

Adv. of James Clulow at the Widow Stanley's in Market St. (2
May)

Lot of ground in Bread St., bounded on N. by land of William
Branson and on S. by land of Aquila Jones; likewise a lot
bounded on N. and W. by land of Richard Hockley; also real
estate in Second St., bounded on N. by land of William Branson and on S. by land of Aquila Jones, all late the estate
of John Philip Told, taken in execution, to be sold at the
house of John Biddle (2 May)

Real estate in High St., Phila., bounded on N. by land of
John Rouse, on E, by land of George Yard, subject to dower
during the life of Ruth Snowden, widow, late the estate of
John Snowden, taken in execution, will be sold at the house
of John Biddle (2 May)

Tract of land in Lower Merion Twp., adjoining lands late of
Richard Harrison, Evan Lloyd and John Lewellin and other
land of the descendants of Hugh Jones, late the estate of
Hugh Jones, taken in execution, will be sold on the premises (2 May)

Adv. of Thomas M'Janett & Co. in Water St. (2 May)

Adv. of Samuel Purviance in Water St., where George Mifflin,
Jr., kept, opposite Richard Edwards's (2 May)

Coat has been taken from house of Joseph Galloway in Market
St. (2 May)

Adv. of Samuel Caruthers in Third St. (2 May)

Time of servants for sale; enquire of William Henderson in
Market St. (2 May)

Accounts with estate of Joseph Webb, late of Phila., house-
carpenter, dec'd, to be settled with Edith Webb, admin.
(2 May)

Two Negro women for sale by James Gilchrist at the Sign of
the Queen of Hungary in Front St. (2 May)

Thomas Ellis, Welch servant, who pretends to be a sailor,
runaway from the sloop _Esther_, belonging to Maryland; reward will be paid by Charles Christie if runaway is brought
to John Biddle's (2 May)

House and lot in Chestnut St. to be sold by Alexander Cruikshank (2 May)

1754

- Plantation called Thomas Rutter's place, near the upper end of Germantown, back of the country seat of William Allen, Esq., for sale; enquire of John Rudolph on the premises (2 May)
- House where Richard Murray, dec'd, formerly dwelt, near the northern bound of Phila., bounded on W. by ground of George Royal and on E. by land of Jonathan Zane, for sale; apply to William Chancellor in Market St. (2 May)
- Speeches of William Shirley and Jonathan Belcher (9 May)
- George Harrison seizes counterfeit British halfpence in New York (9 May)
- Phila. item mentions Major Washington, Mr. Ward, Capt. Trent and Capts. Smith, Kennedy, Rankin, Magee, Wright, Church and Lauderdale (9 May)
- Negroes for sale by Reed and Furman in Trenton and by William Douglass, about 4 miles from Allenstown (9 May)
- House in High St., Phila., bounded on E. by John Ogden's lot and on W. by lot of Marcus Kuhl, for sale; enquire of Hannah Pearson, living in said house, or Thomas Say in Second St. (9 May)
- Adv. of William Clampfer in Second St. (9 May)
- Adv. of Edward Pennington, next door to Edward Cathrall's in Water St. (9 May)
- Daniel Benezet is removed from Front St. to Arch St. (9 May)
- Adv. of James M'Cullough in Front St., where Messieurs Levy and Franks formerly lived and George Mifflin lately removed from (9 May)
- Adv. of Joseph Morris, next door to Robert Rigg in Front-Front St. (9 May)
- Notice of meeting of the Union Library Company of Phila., signed by James Chattin, clerk (9 May)
- Adv. of Patrick Hamilton, whose boat goes between Phila. and Newcastle (9 May)
- Plantation about 1½ miles from Darby to be sold by Swan Boon, living in Darby Twp., Chester Co. (9 May)
- Accounts to be settled with Randle Mitchell or Randle and Alexander Mitchell (9 May)
- Adv. of Thomas Montgomery at John Stamper's wharf (9 May)
- Adv. of Bell and Lawrence in Water St. (9 May)
- Adv. of Charles Dutens, jeweller from London, at the Sign of the Ring and Dove in Market St. (9 May)
- Hugh M'Mahan, servant, age c. 40, cooper, runaway from David Smith (9 May)
- John Adam Herner, Dutch servant, age c. 20, runaway from David Davis, of Charles-Town, Chester Co. (9 May)
- Speech of W. Shirley in Boston; extract from votes of the New Jersey General Assembly, signed by Abraham Clark, Jr., clerk; reply of the governor to message received from Mr. Lawrence and Mr. Hancock (16 May)
- Item of Charles-Town, S.C., mentions Capts. Henry Richard Dubois and Tucker (16 May)

1754

Tue. and Wed. last at Williamsburgh the following criminals were tried: Christopher Bettie from Chesterfield, for felony; Ishmael Drew, Thomas Bryan and Thomas Pendley, from Richmond, for murder; Mary Murray, from Henrico, for felony; Jesse Scott and Randle Gibson, from Charles City, for felony; Ned, *alias* Edward Picket, from Surry, for felony; Edward Dowdle and Edward Davis, both from York, for felony, according to Williamsburgh item of 19 Apr. (16 May)

Boston item mentions Capts. Jacobson and Washington Shirley (16 May)

New York item mentions Father Charlevoix and the Chevalier de Callieres (16 May)

Capt. Mersier gives account of the seizure of the sloop *Thomas*, John Whitesides master, by the slaves; Capt. Mersier and Capt. James tried in vain to take the ship (16 May)

New York item mentions Capts. Langdon, Dudley, Diggs, Miller, Augustine Lawrence, Joseph Wanton, Manchester, Hopkins, Remington, Sheldon, Green, Best, Vardil, Tanner, Mitchell, Shirley, Griffiths and Livingston (16 May)

Joshua Crosby, Benjamin Franklin, Hugh Roberts, Israel Pemberton, John Reynell, Evan Morgan, Joseph Fox, Samuel Rhoads, Isaac Jones, John Smith, Joseph Morris and William Grant have been chosen managers of the Contributors to the Pennsylvania Hospital and Charles Norris has been chosen as treasurer (16 May)

Phila. item mentions Capts. Fowle, Seymour, Carroll, Badger, Vaughan, Harrison, Dubois, Osborne, Eaton, Hamilton, Simpson, M'Fun, Griffith, Alexander Magee, Lisle and Meshard (16 May)

Adv. of Daniel Williams, baker, living near the corner of Second and Walnut Sts. (16 May)

Adv. of Samuel Sanson in Front St. (16 May)

Welch and West Country servants, imported in the *Pearl*, Thomas Griffith master, to be disposed of by Charles Willing and Son (16 May)

Negroes for sale; enquire at Capt. Morrell's on Society Hill (16 May)

English servants, imported in the *Beulah*, to be disposed of by Capt. John Richey at his house in Water St. (16 May)

Adv. of Henry Stocker, on William Fishbourne's wharf, opposite to Joshua Fisher's (16 May)

Adv. of Thomas Clifford in Water St. (16 May)

Philip Ceave, Irish servant, age c. 19 or 20, whose former master was Hugh M'Clelan, of Chester Co., runaway from Jacob Ford, of Morris Co., East N.J. (16 May)

Adv. of Ernst Junkin, living where the German Printing Office is kept (16 May)

House between Poole's Bridge and the Sugar-house is to be let; enquire of Anthony Wilkinson (16 May)

Horse has been stolen, supposedly by one John Hughes, from Henry M'Cay, living at the head of Bohemia in Cecil Co., Md. (16 May)

House and lot in Wicacoa, now in the tenure of Francis Shore, to be sold by Joseph Donaldson, hatter (16 May)

Tenement on Germantown Main St., bounding upon William Allen's country seat, for sale by Conrad Weyttneer (16 May)

Jonathan Belcher, son of Gov. Belcher, is appointed Chief Justice of Nova Scotia (23 May)

Boston item mentions Capts. John Rouse, Inches and William Fleet (23 May)

New York item mentions Capt. Crowell, Robert Livingston and Jonathan Edgecomb of the New London brigantine (23 May)

Phila. item mentions Capts. Shirley, Hood, Oates, M'Cleeve, Joy, Read, Muir, Mason, Arnott, Ewing, Parish, Wilcox, Garret, Spencer, Campbell, Boothby, Galatly, Mitchell, Hamilton, Falkner and Marsden (23 May)

Adv. of John Maxwell Nisbitt in Front St. (23 May)

Accounts with estate of Thomas Lawrence, Esq., dec'd, to be settled with Thomas, John and Mary Lawrence, execs. (23 May)

Plantation in Bensalem Twp., where Thomas Barrow formerly lived, between lands of William Ridge and William Duncan, and tract of land in the same twp., between William Duncan's and Patrick Duncan's, to be sold by Lawrence Growdon (23 May)

Fourth part of the ship American, Fenwick Lyell master, now at James Reynolds's wharf, to be sold at the Widow Jones's Coffee-house by Charles Willing, exec. of the estate of Thomas Lloyd, Dec'd (23 May)

John Stanaland, stone-cutter, is removed from Roxborough to Second St. in Phila., opposite to Mr. Whitebread's; for his services, apply to him in Phila. or to Edward Harding at the Freestone Quarry in Roxborough (23 May)

Adv. of Garrat Noel, bookseller, in New York; catalogues of his books are to be seen at Mr. Biddle's in Market St., Phila. (23 May)

Adv. of Alexander Lunan, Secretary of the St. Andrew's Society (23 May)

Adv. of William Clark in Water St., opposite Fowell's wharf (23 May)

Adv. of Ann Scotton, in Front St., next door to Mr. Read's, baker, and opposite Dr. Sonman's (23 May)

Address to the justices of Lancaster Co. by the following members of the Grand Jury: John Ryers, foreman, Daniel Kenly, Thomas Harris, James Simple, William Wilson, William Simonton, Thomas Black, Timothy Shaw, James Walker, John Rankin, John Smith, Robert Taylor, John Montgomery and Arthur Chambers (23 May)

Adv. of Mr. Nicholson at the Sign of Admiral Warren in Arch St. (23 May)

Accounts with the estate of Ann Haynes, late of Phila., dec'd, to be settled with Judah Foulke, admin. (23 May)

Henry Colesbery and Andrew Tranberg, trustees of the Swedish Congregation in Wilmington, advise persons holding leases from said congregation that arrears must be paid (23 May)

Colin Ferguson, living in George-Town, Kent Co., Md., offers reward for recovery of runaway servant (23 May)

1754

House in Charles-Town, Cecil Co., Md., to be let by John Kirkpatrick, living in said town (23 May)

Speech of Gov. Horatio Sharpe of Md. and addresses to him signed by B. Tasker and P. Hammond (30 May)

Capt. Osbourn from Conn. reports damage to ships from lightning on the coast of Virginia (30 May)

New York item mentions Capts. Bennet, Fowler, Carlisle, Martin and Duncan (30 May)

Phila. items mention Capts. Rees, Lowther, Bowes, Codwise, Condy, Marsden and Mesnard (30 May)

Sat. last John Crow and one Chester were executed at Trenton for house-breaking (30 May)

Fri. last Daniel Kerr was killed at Sadsbury by a falling tree (30 May)

Adv. of Bourne and Jones near Market St. wharf (30 May)

Bancroft Woodcock, goldsmith, has set up his business in Wilmington (30 May)

Adv. of Israel Morris, whip-maker, at the house of Joseph Saul, chair- and spinning wheel maker in Market St. (30 May)

Adv. of Zacharias Nieman in Almond St. on Society Hill, between Capt. Attwood's and Mr. Davey's wharf (30 May)

Adv. of Daniel Rundle in Water St. (30 May)

Negro for sale; enquire of William Jackson in Walnut St. (30 May)

Edward Gilland, of Warwick, Bucks Co., has absconded; his creditors are to meet at the house of Richard Walker (30 May)

Plantation about a mile from Little Elk Meeting-house and 12 from Christiana Bridge for sale; apply to Alexander M'Dowell on the premises (30 May)

Tract of land for sale by Daniel Richard in Kingsess Twp., adjoining the plantation of Capt. Coultas (30 May)

James Murphey, Irish servant, age c. 28, who speaks French, a runaway from John Scott, of Hanover Town, Morris Co., East N.J., who kept him as schoolmaster (30 May)

William M'Analty, Irish servant, age c. 23, runaway from Anthony Whitely, tavern-keeper in New Castle (30 May)

Joseph Clayton, of Biles Island, near Bordentown, makes a lottery for building a church; he appoints as managers William Potts, Thomas Cox, John Imlay and Joseph Borden, Jr. (30 May)

John Bredell, English servant, age c. 40, baker, runaway from Daniel Goodman, of Phila., baker (30 May)

John Clark, keeper of the goal of Lancaster Co., has in custody Edward Dunfield, an Irishman, age c. 25, and Daniel Foley, Irishman, who says he served his time with Adam Hamsour, near the White Horse in Chester Co. (30 May)

On 9 May in Hartford, Conn., Thomas Fitch was chosen governor and William Pitkin deputy-governor (6 June)

On 7 May in Branford, Conn., Col. Russell reviewed the troop of horse commanded by Capt. Allen of Milford and also three companies of militia (6 June)

On the night of 12 May the house of William Luddington of North Branford was burnt to the ground (6 June)

New York items mention Capts. Lowther, Gilford, Dunscomb, Winthorp, Euyvanck, Man, Dudley Diggs, Jackson, John Sawyer and Gov. De Lancey (6 June)

Phila. items mention Capts. Driescall, Cowan, Worsdale, Taylor, Sage, Donnell and Granthum (6 June)

Port wine for sale at the cellars under the house of Buckridge Sims in Water St.; apply to Nathaniel Allen, Jr., at his cooper's shop in Water St. (6 June)

Slator Clay of New-Castle informs that the causeway near New-Castle is repaired and passable (6 June)

Adv. of John Blackwood in Chestnut St. (6 June)

Horse strayed or stolen from Mr. Franklin's stable; reward if brought to David Hall at the Printing Office (6 June)

William Darbey, servant, age c. 19, runaway from Thomas Talman, of Evesham Twp., Burlington Co., N.J. (6 June)

Time of servants for sale; apply to Samuel Ryan in Front St. (6 June)

Tract of land in Burlington Co., about 2 miles from Mountholly, for sale by James Satterthwaite in Phila.; apply to Hugh Hartshorne in Burlington or to Satterthwaite (6 June)

Adv. of John Hickey, late of Dublin, linen stamper and blue dyer, opposite to Mr. Stretch's, watchmaker, in Second St. (6 June)

Thomas Bond offers reward for recovery of horse strayed or stolen from pasture adjoining the Battery in Phila. (6 June)

House where Francis Johnson dwells in Water St., next to Morris Morris's, to be sold or let; apply to Anthony Morris or Joseph Richardson, merchant, in Phila.; any agreement will be confirmed by William Morris (6 June)

Real estate within 3 miles of Dover, Kent Co. on Delaware, and property in George Town, Kent Co., Md., for sale; apply to Patrick Martin, living near Duck Creek Landing in Kent Co. (6 June)

House and lot in Fourth St. for sale; enquire of Ulrick Sherer at the Powder House, near Poole's bridge (6 June)

Accounts with the estate of Dougall Ferguson, Sr., dec'd, to be settled with Samuel Paynter and John Hall, execs. (6 June)

James Murphy, age c. 22, tailor by trade, born in Clonmel, Tipperary Co., Ireland, who says he came from London in the ship *Dogger*, Thomas Brown captain, and landed at Hobb's hole in Virginia, is in custody of Samuel Smith, keepr of the goal in Chester Co. (6 June)

Real estate in Lower Dublin Twp. will be sold by Thomas Ashton (6 June)

Lot of ground in Second St., adjoining house where Mr. Moland lives, to be sold by Thomas Batson; apply to John Banton, who lives in Front St., or William Wisher, living near the premises (6 June)

Fri. last Capt. Dobbins arrived at Annapolis from London, according to Annapolis item of 23 May (13 June)

1754

Wed. last, at the same time that Mrs. Marriott's house in Annapolis was struck by lightning, one Edward Lloyd in Queen Anne's Co. was struck and killed by lightning, according to an Annapolis item of 23 May (13 June)

Fri. last Beale Howard, a young man, was drowned when going to Patapsco in a sloop, according to an Annapolis item of 30 May (13 June)

Henry Cary, a hand on the brigantine Charles, Capt. Walters, in Patapsco, was accidentally killed by a swivel gun on Sat. last, according to Annapolis item of 30 May (13 June)

Fri. last Gov. James De Lancey embarked for Albany, according to New York item of 10 June (13 June)

Wed. last arrived at New York John Penn, Richard Peters, Isaac Norris, Benjamin Franklin, Commissioners from Pennsylvania, and on Thu. Benjamin Tasker and Major Abraham Barnes, commissioners from Maryland, and on 9 June they all embarked for Albany (13 June)

Moses Dimon, Esq., of Fairfield, Conn., was struck by lightning when returning home on horseback; he has recovered but the horse was killed under him (13 June)

New York item mentions Capts. Codwise and Murray (13 June)

Phila. item gives account of how the crew of the sloop Hopewell, belonging to Patrick Creagh of Annapolis, killed the master, William Curtis; the criminals, John Wright (alias William Wilson), John Smith and a Portuguese, were arrested in Charles-Town, S.C. (13 June)

Phila. items mention Capts. Bowes, Nusum, Knox, Katter, Jones and Dorrell (13 June)

William Dunlap and David Hall have published a religious tract by Samuel Delap, a dissenting minister at Letterkenny (13 June)

James Woods, Irish servant, age c. 16, weaver, runaway from Joseph Hudson, living in Whiteland Twp., Chester Co. (13 June)

John Kennedy, apprentice, age c. 16, block-maker, this country born, whose father works in the Jerseys at daily labour, a runaway from Susannah Terry, of Phila., widow of James Terry, block-maker, dec'd (13 June)

John Wilcocks, below the drawbridge in Phila., seeks a house-carpenter to go to the West Indies (13 June)

Tickets for a comedy and pantomime may be had of Mrs. Bridges in Front St. (13 June)

Plantation in the Northern Liberties, bounded by lands of George Springer, Reyneer Custard, Samuel Ashmead and John Ashmead, late the estate of Jacob Schneck, taken in execution, will be sold at the house of Daniel Pistorius in Cermantown (13 June)

Plantation in Bristol Twp., bounded by lands of Bernard Reiser and the Old York Road, late the estate of John Kralft Riestine, taken in execution, will be sold (13 June)

Plantation in Limerick Twp., bounded in part by lands of Joseph Burson and Jonas Potts, late the estate of John Starr, taken in execution, will be sold (13 June)

Matthew Goodman, English servant, age c. 28, and Jacob Hose, Dutch servant, age c. 23, runaways from John Taylor, of Lancaster Co. (13 June)

Plantation in Upper Dublin Twp., on the road from Germantown to Samuel Morris's mill, bounded by lands of Jacob Coleday and Nicholas Scull, late the estate of John Markenderffer, taken in execution, will be sold at the house of William Anderson in Whitemarsh, where Richard Waln lately lived (13 June)

Mare has been stolen from the pasture of Robert Faries of Lower Merion (13 June)

William Hockly, English servant, age c. 35, sawyer, runaway from the ship London, James Shirley captain; reward if the runaway is brought to said Shirley or to John Kidd in Front St. (13 June)

Joseph Holmes, English convict servant, age c. 31 (who will probably change his name to William Yeats), runaway from Abednego Botfield, living near Talbot Co. Court House in Maryland (13 June)

Conrad Hendrick Earns, born in Hanover, servant, age c. 45, runaway from John Leadlie in Bristol Twp. (13 June)

New York items mention Capts. John Jauncey, Hill, French, Johnson, Whitney, Byvanck, Guilford, Winthorp, Ball, Theobalds, Scott, Lawrence, Smith, Harris, Wilson, Tucker, Deane, Bogart, Bryson, Colhoun and Cov. Shirley of Mass. (20 June)

Prologue to play in Phila. was spoken by Mr. Rigby (20 June)

Phila. items mention Capts. Murray, Dunscomb, Lisle, Brown, Vaughan, Mesnard, Pote, Williams, Cowan, Dunn, Cowpland, Keen, Robeson, M'Kenzie, Arthur, Steel, Lee, M'Fun, Miller, Hall, Lawrence and Ford; also Admiral Watson and Mr. Asn, the English consul in Madeira, who died lately (20 June)

Welch servants, imported in the Endeavour, Capt. M'Kenzie, to be disposed of by Charles and Alexander Stedman and Townsend White (20 June)

Plantation in Whitemarsh to be sold by Peter Robeson (20 June)

Adv. of William Rush in Front St., who makes locks, shovels, traps and scale-beams (20 June)

William Haselton on Society Hill has Negroes for sale (20 June)

Hans George Myer, Dutch servant, age 17, runaway from Jacob Duche; he is supposed to be harboured by a sister at the Widow Panebaker's in Skepack Twp. or by another sister at Messieurs M'Calls Ironworks (20 June)

Land in Germantown, opposite to land of William Allen, Esq., to be sold by Jonathan Livezey (20 June)

William Winter, Irish servant, age c. 20, runaway from William Beatey, living in Earl Twp., Lancaster Co. (20 June)

Time of three servants to be disposed of by Samuel Read in Front St. (20 June)

John Kelly, Irish servant, runaway from Joseph Williams, living in Sadsbury Twp., Chester Co. (20 June)

Frederick Wandle, Dutch servant, age c. 20, runaway from Joseph Williams, near the Sign of the Buck on Conestogue Road (20 June)

John Clark, convict servant, gardiner, runaway from W. Buchanan in Baltimore (20 June)

1754

Thomas Erwin, Irish servant, age 24, brick-maker, runaway (supposedly in company of one Hannah Wilson) from Morial Allen, living in London-grove, Chester Twp. (20 June)

Annapolis item of 13 June gives account of some French who were killed or captured; mentioned are Major Washington, Capt. Trent, M. Le Force, M. Jumonville and an ensign, who was killed by Half King (27 June)

Col. Joshua Fry, commander of the forces gone to the Ohio, fell from his horse and died of his injuries at Wills's Creek (27 June)

A schooner, Israel Gross master, and another schooner, one Pike master, were struck by lightning and damaged when at anchor in Cape Cod Harbor on 7 June (27 June)

New York items mention Capts. Everson, Kip, Patten, Gilbert, Stephen Newbold, Dudley Diggs, Livingston, Long, Robert White, Evans, Thompson and Gardiner (27 June)

Farewell epilogue spoken at the theatre in Phila. by Mrs. Hallam on Mon. last (27 June)

Accounts with estate of Joseph Cobourn (who lived in Chestnut St. in Phila.) to be settled with Judah Foulke, admin. (27 June)

Items belonging to the snow *Muggy*, lately lost in Delaware Bay, to be sold by John Meas on Powell's wharf (27 June)

Adv. of John Ord at the corner of Market and Second Sts. (27 June)

Adv. of Standley and Hughes on Carpenter's wharf (27 June)

Adv. of James Eddy, next door to Joseph Trotter's in Second St. (27 June)

Real estate in the Northern Liberties, bounded by lots of William Attmore, Thomas Nevell and James Foster, late the estate of Abraham Gardner, taken in execution, to be sold at Conrad Kemley's in Bedminster (27 June)

Ground in Moyamensing Twp., near or adjoining the property of Joseph Trotter, Joseph Johnson and George Fitzwalter, dec'd, late the estate of Isaac Jones, taken in execution, to be sold on the premises for and during the life of Isaac Jones, blacksmith (27 June)

Real estate in Phila., bounded on the W. by lot of Silas Pryor and on the N. by lot of James Wragg, and another lot, bounded on the N. by ground of Silas Pryor and on the W. by land of Samuel Powell, late the estate of William Ireson, taken in execution, will be sold at the house of John Biddle (27 June)

Piece of land on Frankford Road, adjoining land of George Peter Hillegas, late the estate of John Philip Dold, taken in execution, to be sold at John Biddle's (27 June)

Reward if strayed cow is brought to Andrew Greeble, cooper, in Market St. (27 June)

James Plunket offers reward for recovery of horse strayed from the commons of Phila. (27 June)

Richard Saunders, English servant, age $\underline{c}$. 20, and William Attwood, English servant, age $\underline{c}$. 19, runaways from Christopher Ruth and Henry Williams, both living in Queen Anne's Co., Md. (27 June)

Robert Wharton, English servant, age between 30 and 40, runaway from John Davis, of Queen Anne's Co., Md. (27 June)

In sworn statement before Mayor Charles Willing of Phila. William Rigby brands as totally false a rumor about a bill for services rendered him by Dr. John Plunket (27 June)

Adv. of George Brooks, glazier, plumber and painter, in Front St. (27 June)

John Shaw has absconded; his creditors are to meet John Scott in Chester Co. (27 June)

William Brown, Irish servant, age c. 30 or 40, weaver, runaway from John Jack, living in West Caln Twp., Chester Co. (27 June)

Thomas Miller, servant, age c. 21, runaway from George Boyd, living in Salisbury Twp., Lancaster Co. (27 June)

Addresses to Gov. Horatio Sharpe of Md. and his messages in reply; mention is made of depositions of Sergeant Willis, John Hamwood and William Swallow (4 July)

Charles-Town, S.C., item of 3 May mentions fact that the Harriot, Capt. Borland, from Phila., has put in at Winyaw (4 July)

Williamsburgh item of 6 June records the seizure of two ships by H.M.S. Triton, Capt. Whitwell (4 Juny)

John Wright, John Smith and one Toney, the villains who seized the sloop of Mr. Creagh and murdered William Curtis, the master, have been brought to Virginia (4 July)

Nine French soldiers from the fort delivered up by Ensign Ward have deserted to Major Washington (4 July)

Five cows belonging to Samuel Phipps of Cambridge, Mass., were struck and killed by lightning (4 July)

Sat. last the governor of Mass. embarked for Casco Bay on board the Bourreau, Joseph Inches captain, according to a a Boston item of 24 June (4 July)

New York item mentions Capts. Lewis and Asa King (4 July)

Phila. items mention Capts. Knox, Lowther, Snow, Lownes, Caldwell, Nuttle, Robeson and Dunscomb (4 July)

Capt. Montaur killed some Frenchmen and took others prisoners, as stated in extract of a letter of 24 June from Albany (4 July)

Fri. last an attempt was made to rob the house of Dr. Rowan on Society Hill in Phila. (4 July)

Negro offered for sale by Judah Foulke (4 July)

House, much frequented as a tavern, lately in possession of Joseph Cobourn, dec'd, is to be let; apply to Reese Meredith or Enoch Story (4 July)

Adv. of Matthew **Clarkson** in Arch St. (4 July)

Adv. of James White, upholsterer and undertaker, lately arrived from London, now at Mrs. Bedford's, opposite Mr. Tenant's new church in Third St. (4 July)

Adv. of James Child in Water St. (4 July)

Adv. of Isaac Greenleafe in Second St., near Stretch's corner (4 July)

1754

The owner of boxes that came to Phila. in the London, Capt. Shirley, is to apply to said captain or to John Kidd, merchant in Front St. (4 July)

Plantation in Merion Twp., conveyed to Michael Wills by Joseph Tucker, late the estate of Michael Wills, dec'd, taken in execution at suit of Joseph Tucker, will be sold on the premises, near the mill of John Roberts (4 July)

Tract of land in Whitemarsh Twp., adjoining lands of Thomas York, Christopher Robins, Jacob Coleman and Peter Robeson, late the estate of Edward Farmar, dec'd, taken in execution, will be sold at the house of Christopher Robins (4 July)

Adv. of Thomas Fitzsimmons, lately removed from Second St. to the corner house of Chestnut and Second Sts., opposite to Thomas Stretch's, watchmaker (4 July)

Adv. of Richard Wagstaffe, peruke-maker, in Chestnut St. (4 July)

Mare and colt stolen from Thomas Shipley, of Ridley Twp., in Chester Co.; reward if brought to said Thomas or to William Shipley of Wilmington or Joseph Marriott of Phila. or Thomas Marriott of Bristol (4 July)

Archibald Buchannan of Germantown Twp. has taken up a stray mare (4 July)

Catherine Deimer, at the Sign of the Comb, in Germantown, has a cure for the distemper called The Scald Head (4 July)

Two horses strayed or stolen from William Gladson on Society Hill; reward if brought to Gladson or to Alexander Reynolds or John Fraizer in Front St. (4 July)

John Bowne of Lancaster, tavernkeeper, is removed from his house near the prison to the corner house in the same street (4 July)

Joseph Hewes, living at Christine Ferry, Newcastle Co., has for sale a house and lot in Wilmington (4 July)

Kate, a Negro woman, age c. 28, runaway from John Montgomery, living in Mill-Creek Hundred, Newcastle Co. (4 July)

Philip Sinloup, Dutch servant, age c. 48, mason and plaisterer, runaway from John Potter, of West Nantmill Twp., Chester Co. (4 July)

Two Dutch servants, Nicholas Gardiner, age c. 35, and Conrad Hents, age c. 23, runaways from Stephen Onion's Ironworks on Gunpowder River in Maryland (4 July)

Christian Frits, Dutch servant, age 20, runaway from John Coryell, at his ferry in Amwell, 15 miles above Trenton (4 July)

Thomas Freeman, servant, born in Hertfordshire, England, who has been in Pa. about 4 years, first with Peter Matson of Upper Merion, Phila. Co., and then with James Coultas at the middle ferry on Schuylkill, runaway from Reading Furnace in Chester Co.; reward for his capture will be paid by Samuel Flower or William Branson in Phila. (4 July)

Letter reports that Christopher Cist came from Major Washington's camp with news of a French defeat and the capture of M. La Force; Capt. Dejoinville was killed (11 July)

News contained in a letter for Col. Washington (11 July)

Joshua Fry, colonel of the Virginia regiment, has died; he was born in Somersetshire, studied at Oxford and was first Grammar Master and then Professor of Mathematics at William and Mary College (11 July)

The <u>Shoreham</u>, Capt. Julian Legge, has arrived in Hampton Road, bringing the three convicts who killed the captain of Mr. Creagh's schooner; also arrived in Hampton Road is the <u>Baltimore</u> sloop-of-war, Capt. Suckling commander (11 July)

At a Court of Oyer and Terminer in Williamsburg the following were tried: Godfrey Wall, Jonas Bayley, Patrick Hoggan and John Gowdie, all for felony; they were found guilty and sentenced to death; Dudley Woottin was found guilty of manslaughter, George Dorton of felony and George Burnett also of felony and and all three were burnt in the hand; Mary Gray, accused of murder, and William Sherrin, of felony, were both acquitted (11 July)

Boston item of 1 July reports that on Tue. last died in Boston Thomas Oxnard, Grand Master of the Masons in North America, in his 51st year (11 July)

New York items of 8 July mention Capts. Hill, Price, Easton, Dudley Diggs, Man, Savage, Blunt, Cathcart, Cullum, Adams, Monk, M'Carty, Marshal, Sergeant, Allen, Miller, Ramsey, Furlong, Gordon, Whitesides, Rosse, Philipson, Johnston, Wilmot, Shepherd, Robert Hardy and Vesey (11 July)

Phila. items mention Capts. Stewart, Craig, Lownes, Dowers, Edwards, Riddle, Bane, Foge, Jerrard, Jackson, Eccles and Rankin (11 July)

Guide to psalmody by W. Dawson, writing master, is sold at the Hand and Pen in Third St., at David Chambers's in Arch St., at John Blakeley's in Market St. and at William Henry's in Water St. (11 July)

French is taught by Charles Vignoles at the house of Capt. Palmer, next door to the German Printing Office in Third St. (11 July)

Reward offered by Samuel Rhoades in Phila. for recovery of a strayed or stolen horse (11 July)

Richard Walker gives notice to the creditors of Elijah Matlanachan and Thomas Butler to appear at his house (11 July)

Silver snuff box (maker's initials R.L.) lost in Phila.; reward if box is brought to James Humphrey's in Second St. (11 July)

David Linch, English servant, age $\underline{c}$. 27, runaway from John Cox, of Moyamensing Twp., about 2 miles from Phila. (11 July)

Partnership between Emanuel Josiah and Samuel Carpenter is nearly expired (11 July)

Edward Jerman, English servant, age $\underline{c}$. 25, who pretends to be a ship-carpenter and sawyer, and Joseph Dennis, English servant, age $\underline{c}$. 25, a pretty good scholar, runaways from Colin Ferguson and John Nemo, of George-Town, Kent Co., Md. (11 July)

James Cancanon, servant, age $\underline{c}$. 21, tailor by trade, runaway from Colin Ferguson of George-Town, Kent Co. (11 July)

Horse strayed from pasture of Jacob Shoemaker in Phila. (11 July)

1754

Edward Demsy, born in England, convict servant, age c. 26, barber, runaway from Thomas Chittam of Bladensburg (11 July)

Mon. last Col. Innes arrived at Williamsburg, according to item of 27 June (18 July)

Sun. last one Fell and a 13-year-old daughter of Emanuel Teal were drowned when trying to cross the falls of Patapsco in a canoe, according to an Annapolis item of 11 July (18 July)

A few days before 17 June Obadiah Albee and his brother in a canoe in Sheepscut River were drowned after a struggle with a bear; their companion, a certain Trask, escaped (18 July)

New York items mention Capts. Corne, Keteltas and Heighington (18 July)

Phila. items mention Capts. Hamilton, Simpson, Alexander M'Fun, Joy, Mulford, Harris, Gass, Greenway, Hogg and Badger (18 July)

Negro offered for sale by William Ball, goldsmith, in Front St. (18 July)

William Currie in the Great Valley has for sale two Negro farmers, Glascow (age c. 21) and Quaco (age c. 36), and a Negro woman, Deb (age c. 24, with a child of about 8 mos.) and Moll (age c. 40, with a boy past 4) (18 July)

John Howard in Second St. offers reward for recovery of money stolen from the cabin of a vessel belonging to John Cord, lying at Powell's wharf (18 July)

Horses for sale by John Biddle in Market St. (18 July)

Plantation in Makefield Twp., Bucks Co., for sale by Benjamin Gilbert, living on the premises (18 July)

Negro girl for sale; enquire of George M'Call, below the drawbridge (18 July)

The governor has appointed Thomas Boude as coroner of Phila. in place of Thomas James, Esq., who has left the province (18 July)

William Horn, servant, born in Bucks Co., runaway from David Jones of London Britain Twp., Chester Co., near John Evans's mill (18 July)

Letter from Col. James Innes at Winchester, Va., mentions Gov. Dinwiddie, Col. Washington, Capt. M'Kay and Sasquehanna Jack (25 July)

Articles of capitulation granted by M. De Villier, mentioning Sieur De Jamonville, Jacob Vambram and Richard Stobo (25 July)

Halifax item of 15 June reports that Thu. last Capt. John Wynn (son of Sir Richard Wynn) died in Halifax (25 July)

Capt. Russell informs that Charles Lawrence (Lt.-Col. of Gov. Hopson's regiment) is appointed Governor of Nova Scotia (25 July)

Boston item of 15 July notes the arrival in Boston from Falmouth of Capt. Joseph Inches and reports that Gen. Winslow has gone up Kennebec River to build forts (25 July)

Capt. Starr in the brig *Sea-Horse* from London put in at Newport last week; some chemicals started a fire there when being landed there - both Newport items of 10 July (25 July)

On 7 July John Seymour of New York drowned his infant child (25 July)

New York item of 22 July reports that Thu. last James De Lancey arrived in New York City from Albany (25 July)

On 21 June Richard Peters of Phila. preached in Episcopal Churches in New York City (25 July)

New York items of 22 July mention Capts. Heysham, Nathaniel Magee, Cox, Westlade, Russel, Rush, Frattels, Dixon, Homer, Breestead, Gifford, Crane, Anderson, Jennets, Heyslip and Miller (25 July)

Sun. last Gov. Tinker arrived at Phila. from Providence in the Jamaica, Capt. Dubois (25 July)

Phila. items mention Capts. Smith, Alexander Magee, Crathorn, Rous, Gibbon, Brown, Keane, Hardy, Adams, Gordon and Shettie (25 July)

Margaret, wife of Edward Davis, of Whitemarsh, has eloped from her husband (25 July)

Real estate in Moyamensing, late the estate of Conrad Waltaker, butcher, taken in execution, will be sold at the house of John Biddle (25 July)

Stephen Williams, at Milford mills, Bucks Co., has the time of an English servant and also Negroes for sale (25 July)

Daniel Beekman, a Swede, in custody of William Connor on suspicion of stealing a horse of John Mall of Cumberland Co., has escaped; Ananias Sayre, High Sheriff of Cumberland Co., offers reward for the capture of Beekman (25 July)

Patrick Phlaugherty, Irish servant, age c. 23, runaway from Bryan Connor, living at John Maffet's in Ridgely Twp., in Chester Co. (25 July)

John Dolin, Irish servant, age c. 30, runaway from James Bonsall, living in Kingsess Twp., Phila. Co. (25 July)

Thomas Laitch, Scotch servant, age 40, runaway from Joshua Bisphan (executor of Benjamin Bisphan, dec'd), living in Chester Town, Burlington Co., West N.J. (25 July)

Real estate on Delaware River, near Batchelor's hall, will be sold at the London Coffee House by John Harrison (25 July)

Andrew Lanin, Irish servant, age c. 23, runaway from Philip Fitzgerald of Elsinburgh, Salem Co., West N.J. (25 July)

John Robinson, servant, age c. 24, wig-maker, runaway from John M'Michael of Phila.; the runaway is supposed to have gone in the shallop of Thomas Montgomery to Christine Bridge (25 July)

Adv. of Daniel Rundle in Water St. (25 July)

Speech of Gov. Horatio Sharpe of Md. mentions Col. Washington and Col. Innes; addresses to the governor signed by B. Tasker and P. Hammond (1 Aug.)

Wed. last Col. Washington and Capt. James Maccay arrived in Williamsburgh and gave account of action between them and the French; they mentioned Capt. Van Braam, Mr. Peyronce, Lt. Mercier and Capt. Clark, all according to Williamsburgh item of 19 July (1 Aug.)

Statement in Boston signed by J. Willard, Secretary (1 Aug.)

1754

Boston item of 22 July reports that on Tue. last Thomas Hutchinson arrived at Boston from Albany (1 Aug.)

New York item of 29 July reports that on Thue. last the Rev. George Whitefield arrived at New York from South Carolina (1 Aug.)

New York items mention Capts. Jeffries, Kelly, Westlade and Legge (1 Aug.)

Phila. item mentions Capt. Hamilton, who will bring the baggage of Robert Hunter Morris to Phila. (1 Aug.)

Phila. items mention Capts. Joy, Read, Lowther, Blair, Hudson, Bevansey, Dowers, Jerrard, Edwards and Davis (1 Aug.)

Adv. of Hillborn and Jones in Water St. (1 Aug.)

Jonathan Edwards has taken the ferry on Schuylkill where Joseph Scull formerly lived (1 Aug.)

Jonathan Evans at the corner of Walnut and Front Sts. has for sale a new four-wheel chaise (1 Aug.)

Adv. of James Fagstaffe, tin-plate-worker, at the Lamp and Crown in Second St. (1 Aug.)

Adv. of John Franks, tobacconist and snuff-maker from London, at the corner of Taylor's Alley in Second St. (1 Aug.)

Joseph Allen, English servant, age 38, founder by trade, runaway from James Smith, of Phila., brass-founder (1 Aug.)

Cornelius Darbyson, Irish servant, age c. 25, tailor, runaway from Samuel Webster, of Phila., tailor (1 Aug.)

James Murphy, Irish servant, age c. 25 or 30, tailor, runaway from Samuel Soumain, goldsmith, in Phila. (1 Aug.)

Accounts with estate of George Arnold, late of Phila., dec'd, to be settled with Catherine Arnold (1 Aug.)

House in Morris's Alley, opposite to the Doctors Bonds shop, to be let; apply to Josiah Davenport in Third St. (1 Aug.)

Gelding strayed or stolen from Richard Price, of Bohemia Manor, Cecil Co., Md.; reward if brought to said Price or to John Nelson in Phila. (1 Aug.)

Thomas Hoyd, servant, who says he served his time with Daniel Lawrie, Indian trader in Donegall, Lancaster Co., runaway from Thomas Montgomery, near Christine Bridge, Newcastle Co.; he says he was taken by the French, afterwards got to Liverpool, England, and came from there in the ship *Susanna*, Moses Rankin master, last May (1 Aug.)

William Darbey, servant, this country born, age c. 20, runaway from Thomas Talman, living in Evesham Twp., Burlington Co.; reward if brought to his master or to William Fishbourne in Phila. (1 Aug.)

Morgan James, Welchman, servant, age c. 32, runaway from John Fogwell, living near Chestertown in Kent Co., Md. (1 Aug.)

Reward for recovery of a mare stolen from Hoalman Johnson, of Kent Co., Md., near the head of Chester (1 Aug.)

House in Second St., Phila., in which Lennard Melchior formerly lived, and other real estate for sale; enquire of William Branson (1 Aug.)

Philip Andrew Pitzler, Dutch servant, age c. 28, who speaks English, French and Latin, runaway from Frederick Stone of Lancaster (1 Aug.)

Mare stolen from Thomas Renshaw, living in the Northern Liberties; reward if brought to owner or to Thomas Jervis, at the Sign of the Indian Queen in Market St. (1 Aug.)

The schooner *Two* Friends, John Burgess master, foundered; Sat. last the sloop *Two* Brothers, of New York, John Dunscomb master, put in at Charles Town, S.C., to water, according to Charles Town items of 18 July (8 Aug.)

H.M.S. Mermaid came out with Capts. Comrin and Lewis (8 Aug.)

Gov. Winslow has erected blockhouses on Kennebec River, and Col. Fry is expected there (8 Aug.)

At elections in N.J. the following representatives were chosen: (in Middlesex Co.) Samuel Nevil and John Wetherill; (in Monmouth Co.) Robert Lawrence and Samuel Holmes (John Taylor and John Anderson lost) (8 Aug.)

New York items of 5 Aug, mention Capts. Vardil, Hopkins, Malcom, Johnston, Smith, Goddard, Hawxey, Topham, Nichols, Awl, Benjamin, William Wanton, Low, Sawyer and Badger (8 Aug.)

Phila. items mention Capts. Miller, Edward, Riddle and Read (8 Aug.)

At Dover one Dusset was found guilty of the murder of John Brown (8 Aug.)

Message from freeholders of Hunterdon Co, West N.J., to Joseph Yard and Peter Medah (8 Aug.)

Phila. flour of mustard is manufactured by Benjamin Jackson and is sold at Jonathan Zane's at the Tea Canister in Second St. (8 Aug.)

Thomas M'Kean plans to run for the office of Sheriff of Newcastle Co. upon Delaware (8 Aug.)

Adv. of Francis Trumble, cabinet- and chair-maker in Front St. (8 Aug.)

Creditors of William Biddle and of Biddle and Forbes are to send their accounts to Samuel Smith, Joshua Fisher and William Lawrence (8 Aug.)

Thomas Lucas, clerk, at Pequea, desires members of association to meet in Sadsbury at the house of Robert Sproule (8 Aug.)

Persons indebted to Emanuel Josiah and Samuel Carpenter are to make prompt payment (8 Aug.)

Thomas Hall, English servant, runaway from Thomas Grubb, who lives in Little Britain Twp., Lancaster Co. (8 Aug.)

John Engle, Dutch servant, who pretends to be a miller, runaway from Peter Ten Eick, living upon Rariton River in the Jerseys; reward if man is arrested and the horse he stole is brought to the owner or to John Hambricht at the White Horse in Chester Co. or to Henry Pawling in Phila. Co. (8 Aug.)

Land in Augusta Co., late the property of Major John Pickings, for sale; apply to Thomas Lewis, surveyor, or John Madison, clerk of said county; the owner of the land is Anthony Strother (8 Aug.)

Mare strayed or stolen from John M'Micken, of Point No Point; reward if mare is brought to M'Micken or to Samuel Hastings, ship-carpenter, in Front St. (8 Aug.)

1754

Mary Neal, Irish servant, age c. 20, runaway from James Hicklin, of Christian Hundred, New-Castle Co. (8 Aug.)

Samuel Cox came from Byfield in Northamptonshire, England, about 3 or 4 years ago and went to live with Thomas Messer, in Chester Co.; if alive, he is to apply to David Strattan in Evesham Twp., Burlington Co., in the Jerseys, to hear something to his satisfaction (8 Aug.)

Accounts with the estate of Jonas Kealer, late of Moyamensing, to be settled with Eve Kealer, Henry Kepley and Adam Weaver, execs. (8 Aug.)

Lot in Fifth St., Phila., bounded on the W. by land of Silas Pryor and on N. by land late of James Wragg, and another lot, bounded on the N. by land of Silas Pryor and on W, by land of Samuel Powell, late the estate of William Ireson, taken in execution, will be sold at the house of John Biddle (8 Aug.)

Real estate in Lower Merion Twp., bounded by land of William Thomas, late the estate of Rees Thomas, taken in execution, will be sold (8 Aug.)

Baltus Spackholtz, High Dutch servant, age c. 25, who pretends to be a miller, runaway from William M'Knight, of Upper Freehold, Monmouth Co. (8 Aug.)

Jack, a Negro, age c. 20, runaway from Derrick Aten, of Readens Town, Hunterdon Co., N.J. (8 Aug.)

Two companies will be raised by order of the governor and will march to join the forces of Col. Innes; the governor has commissioned John Ross of Annapolis to enlist men, according to Annapolis item of 8 Aug. (15 Aug.)

John Wright and Toney the Mulatto, indicted for the murder of Capt. Curtis, were executed on 7 Aug.; John Smith, who turned King's evidence, was pardoned (15 Aug.)

On 7 Aug. Capt. Davy arrived at Annapolis from Bristol with indented servants (15 Aug.)

Gov. Winslow is arrived at Treconick on Kennebeck River (15 Aug.)

Sloop bound to Conn., one Patterson master, was cast away about 10 days ago near Marshfield, according to Boston item of 5 Aug. (15 Aug.)

Wed. last Gideon Hawley was ordained at Old South Meetinghouse to be minister to the Mohawk Indians, according to a Boston item of 5 Aug. (15 Aug.)

On 4 Aug. Capt. Joseph Prince arrived at Boston from Cadiz (15 Aug.)

New York items mention Capts. Roome and Julian Legge (15 Aug.)

In Jan. of 1753 four Indian traders, Alexander M'Genty, Jabez Evans, David Hendricks and William Powell, were captured by a party of French Indians; the men were ransomed but the Indians, dissatisfied, sent an insulting letter to Col. Myndert Schuyler; the letter was signed by Ononraguiete and was delivered by Montandre (15 Aug.)

Phila. items mention Capts. Lowther, Dreson, Burrows, Appowiz, Gardner, Rhodes and Reet (15 Aug.)

Preaching schedule of the Rev. George Whitefield (15 Aug.)

Accounts with estate of John Blanchfield, late of Burlington Co., West N.J., yeoman, dec'd, to be settled with Richard Farmar, admin. (15 Aug.)

Bernard Zimmerman, Dutch servant, age c. 17, runaway from Johannes Harpell, living near the Trap in Providence Twp., Phila. Co. (15 Aug.)

Sale of household and shop goods at the house of Capt. Joseph Redmond in Market St. (15 Aug.)

Cow strayed or stolen from Lodowick Cough at William Masters's place between Phila. and Kensington (15 Aug.)

Thomas Miller, born in Wales, age c. 21, who came to Pa. from Bristol about 3 years ago, runaway servant of George Boyd of Sadsbury Twp., Lancaster Co., suspected of having broken into and robbed Boyd's house and stolen a horse of James Keys of the same twp. (15 Aug.)

Persons with demands against Joseph Carbut, late of Phila., coach-maker, are to bring accounts to auditors at the house of John Biddle (15 Aug.)

Real estate in Southampton Twp., Bucks Co., late the property of Ellis Roberts and David Cumming, taken in execution at suit of Charles Norris, to be sold at the house of Joseph Inslee in Newtown (15 Aug.)

Dennis Connell, Irish servant, age c. 23, runaway from Caleb Jackson, living in Leacock Twp., Lancaster Co. (15 Aug.)

John M'Graugh, Irish servant, age 24, runaway from James Love, living in Earl Twp., Lancaster Co. (15 Aug.)

Philip Conner, servant, runaway from Arthur Alexander, living within 2 miles of Charles-town and of North-East (15 Aug.)

Anna Catherina Grobin, Dutch servant, age c. 26, runaway from James Moore, of Newtown, Chester Co. (15 Aug.)

Horse stolen from plantation of Anne Little in Pequea, Lancaster Co. (15 Aug.)

John Hennen, Irish servant, spinning-wheel-maker, and Philip Fitzpatrick, Irish servant, runaways from Thomas Canby and Henry Troth, both living in Wilmington (15 Aug.)

Daniel Yare, Dutch servant, who can speak French, runaway from Hannah Whigam, of West Nantmill Twp., Chester Co. (15 Aug.)

Henry Desell, English servant, age c. 18, upholsterer, runaway from Samuel Forwood, living at Deer-creek, Baltimore Co., Md. (15 Aug.)

Copy of French terms of surrender granted by Capt. Coulon Villier to the English at Fort Necessity (22 Aug.)

H.M.S. Baltimore, Capt. Shutland, has arrived at Boston from Halifax (22 Aug.)

New York items mention Capts. Wardell, Gelston, Adams, Betts, Williams, Griffiths, Crispin, Lawrence, Smith, Leycraft, Broadhurst, Burger, Carlisle and Bennet (22 Aug.)

Letter from Cumberland Co., dated 15 Aug. 1754, reports that steers belonging to one Robert Baker were killed or carried off by the French, who probably killed Alexander Cook, a young man (22 Aug.)

Devout Exercises of the Heart, just published at Lancaster by William Dunlap (22 Aug.)

Household goods will be sold at the house of Thomas Meighan in Second St. (22 Aug.)

Negro boy for sale by Samuel Palmer at his house in Third St., adjoining the house of Mr. Fox (22 Aug.)

James Ryan and Dennis Daley, Irish servants, runaways from James M'Lachlan and Samuel Sloss of Georgetown, Kent Co., Md. (22 Aug.)

Adv. of Matthew Clarkson, who is removed from house in Arch St. to Water St., next door to Samuel Shoemaker (22 Aug.)

Adv. of William Fisher in Water St., where Samuel Hazard recently dwelt (22 Aug.)

Tickets for the Conn. Lottery for the benefit of the College of New Jersey are sold by George Spofford, William Grant, John Sayre, Andrew Hodge, William Henry, Hugh M'Cullough and Samuel Hazard in Phila. (22 Aug.)

Mare stolen from the pasture of Joseph Bell at the Harp and Crown in Third St. (22 Aug.)

Accounts with the estate of Crispin Collett, late of Biberry, yeoman, dec'd, to be settled with Mary Collett and Joseph Hart, execs. (22 Aug.)

Rebecca, wife of Isaac Trueax of New-Castle Co. has eloped from her husband (22 Aug.)

It is reported that a Mr. Atkinson, living in or near Winyah, had a suspicious Indian secured and put on a schooner to be brought to Charles-Town, S.C. (29 Aug.)

Halifax items mention Capts. Rous, Ball and Thomas Martin (29 Aug.)

Jonathan Belcher is appointed Chief Judge of Nova Scotia (29 Aug.)

New York items of 26 Aug. mention Capts. Carlisle, Grant, Coffey and Johnson (29 Aug.)

Tremendous rainfall at Parmus, N.J., on 16 Aug., so that the sawmill of John Hoppe was carried away, Hendrick Hoppe lost his livestock and improvements of Mr. Kingsland suffered greatly (29 Aug.)

Phila. items mention Capts. Low, Collins, Miles, Fitzgerald, Rees, White, Alexander Magee, Hay, Baddely, Borland and Evans (29 Aug.)

Samuel Morris seeks votes of the electors of Phila. Co., as he seeks the office of sheriff (29 Aug.)

Plantation in Lower Merion Twp., touching on land of William Thomas, late the estate of Rees Thomas, taken in execution, will be sold (29 Aug.)

Judah Foulke gives notice for all persons with demands on the estate of Joseph Cobourn to meet at the house of William Whitebread in Second St. (29 Aug.)

Accounts with the estate of William Gray, late of Phila., dec'd, to be settled with Elizabeth Gray, George Gray and George Gray, Jr., admins. (29 Aug.)

Plantation near Burlington, lately in the possession of Isaac Conarro, for sale; enquire of Joshua Crosby in Phila. or of Isaac Conarro on the premises (29 Aug.)

Thomas Lawrence, vendue master, is removed to Second St. (29 Aug.)

1754

John Barge, miller, living at Spruce mill in Germantown Twp., has for sale the following items of real estate: a lot in Germantown near land of Leonard Stoneburner and Derrick Johnson; ten acres adjoining land of Anthony Williams, Justus Revacum and Joshua Harmer; lots in Flower-town, Springfield Twp., adjoining land of Peter Robeson and Appleony Townsand; woodland bordering on land of William Branson and near Christopher Robin's tavern; Paul's mill, now in the occupation of John Vanderin (29 Aug.)

Sawmill in Monmouth Co. for sale by James Hepburn; apply to said Hepburn near Allenstown or Stephen Pangburn, living on the premises (29 Aug.)

Margaret, wife of Thomas Blair of Bethlehem Twp., Hunterdon Co., N.J., has eloped from her husband (29 Aug.)

If Nicholas Lysaght (son of John Lysaght of Hartfordshire, England), who left his father in 1739, will apply to Benjamin Franklin, he will hear something to his advantage (29 Aug.)

Hermanus Haggen, age c. 30, and his wife Catharine, both Dutch servants, runaways from Capt. Robert Harris, of Rocky River, Anson Co., North Carolina; reward will be paid by George Gibson, of Lancaster, or Thomas Harris, of Donnegall (29 Aug.)

Time of a Dutch servant girl to be disposed of; apply to Eleanor Bruce, at the Sign of the Sugar Loaf in Walnut St. (29 Aug.)

Time of a servant, a baker, to be disposed of; enquire of Samuel Read in Front St. (29 Aug.)

James Campbell, weaver, age c. 27, has absconded from his bail; reward for his capture will be paid by John Davidson or Patrick M'Gowon in West Caln Twp., Chester Co. (29 Aug.)

Accounts with the estate of James Russell, late of Phila., coach-maker, dec'd, to be settled with Elizabeth Russell, who carries on the business (29 Aug.)

Mare stolen from the pasture of Christianus Lupardus at Piscataqua in Middlesex Co., N.J. (29 Aug.)

George Hamilton, Scotch servant, runaway from George May, who lives at Egg-Harbour, Gloucester Co. (29 Aug.)

William Denning, English servant, age c. 22, runaway from Thomas Walker, of Phila., victualler (29 Aug.)

Joseph Chambers, tavern-keeper in York-Town, has taken up a stray horse (29 Aug.)

If Patrick Blair (who came to Pa. some years ago from Newtown-Stuart, Tyrone Co., Ireland) will apply to Thomas Lucas at Pequea in Lancaster Co., he will hear something to his advantage (29 Aug.)

Speech of the Hon. James De Lancey mentions Col. Washington and Lt.-Gov. Clarke (5 Sept.)

On 16 Aug. the wife (age c. 70) of Philip Call at Baker's Town, N.H., was killed by Indians (5 Sept.)

Letter of 28 Aug. from a gentleman in Albany to a friend in New York states that he went to Lotteridge's and was informed that the commissioners had taken Hogg's affidavit (5 Sept.)

New York items of 2 Sept. mention Gov. Pitts at the Musqueto Shore and Capts. Ramsey, Furlong, Masterson, Clymer, Crawford, Creighton, Pickeman and Griffiths (5 Sept.)

Gov. Dinwiddie of Va. called his council and assembly about offer to raise 1500 men (5 Sept.)

Rev. Whitefield has arrived in New York (5 Sept.)

Phila. items mention Capts. Stirling, Stewart, Haselton, Rankin, Bartlett, Caldwell, Hamilton, Mitchell, Cameron and Betaugh (5 Sept.)

Wed. last died at Phila. in his 16th year William Thomas Martin, second son of the Hon. Josiah Martin, Esq., of New York, and on Sun. last the Rev. Mr. Smith, Professor of Philosophy at the Academy of Phila., preached a sermon on the death of the young man (5 Sept.)

Plantation in Newtown Twp., Gloucester Co., to be let; apply to Hannah and Jacob Albertson, execs. of the estate of the late William Albertson (5 Sept.)

John Bayly, of Phila., goldsmith, is about to go to London (5 Sept.)

Thomas Byles in Market St. buys and sells pewter (5 Sept.)

Adv. of William Sandwith, who is removed from Chestnut St. to Arch St., next door to William Parr (5 Sept.)

Mary Smith, servant, age between 17 and 18, this country born, now big with child, runaway from Robert Bradshaw of Derry Twp., Lancaster Co. (5 Sept.)

William Webb, servant, born in West of England, sailor, runaway from a vessel in North-East River, Cecil Co., Md.; reward for his capture offered by James Baxter (5 Sept.)

Cow strayed from commons of Phila.; reward offered by Rudolph Fiell, living on George Emlen's place, near the tavern of George Harkness (5 Sept.)

Two tenements on south side of Cedar St. in Phila. to be sold by Henry Dalton, now in possession of the premises (5 Sept.)

Plantation on Oldman's Creek, Greenwich Twp., Gloucester Co., N.J., for sale; enquire of James Talman in Market St., or William Heford on the premises (5 Sept.)

Hugh Morgan, Irish servant, weaver (who has stolen the indenture of one John Peak), runaway from John Forest, living in West Twp., Chester Co. (5 Sept.)

Patrick Hanes, Irish servant, runaway from Lawrence Howard, of Springfield, Chester Co. (5 Sept.)

Tickets for lottery for building a church on Biles Island near Bordentown are sold by William Potts, Thomas Cox, John Imlay and Joseph Borden, Jr. (5 Sept.)

Addresses of Council (Archibald Kennedy, speaker) and of the Assembly (David Jones, speaker) to Gov. James De Lancey of New York and the governor's replies (12 Sept.)

One Hovey, captain of a sloop, fired on a barge from the Vulture sloop-of-war and killed one man; Hovey has been taken to Annapolis Royal and committed to goal by John Duport, Esq. (12 Sept.)

Two cadets, Druillon and Le Force, and 17 privates, prisoners, set out on 22 Aug. from Williamsburg for the French fort at the Ohio; Gen. Innes is preparing to build a fort at Wills's Creek (12 Sept.)

Boston item of 2 Sept. states that on Sat. last John Shirley (son of the governor) arrived at Boston from Falmouth in Casco Bay; he brought news of Gen. Winslow and Lt.-Col. Prebble (12 Sept.)

Capt. Clark, who arrived at Rhode Island from the Musqueto Shore, brought news of Capts. Gordon, Salter, Morrison, Ross, Mr. Pitt, Capt. Ramsey and his mate, Mr. Johnson (12 Sept.)

Phila. items mention Capts. Greenway, Katter, M'Fun and Francis Blair (12 Sept.)

Letter from a gentleman in Virginia, dated 4 Sept., mentions Gov. Dinwiddie and Mr. Gist (12 Sept.)

French have destroyed cattle, horses and grain at the plantation of Vendall Brown in the back parts of Virginia (12 Sept.)

Fri. last at Pequea Mrs. Cowan was accidentally shot and killed; she left a husband and five children (12 Sept.)

Thomas Boude, who was appointed by the governor to succeed Thomas James as coroner of Phila., is running for election to that office; he is opposed by Thomas Bartholomew (12 Sept.)

The Articles of Faith of the Holy Evangelical Church is sold by William Bradford at the corner of Front and Market Sts., by Rev. Brunholtz and Henry Schleydorn in Phila. (12 Sept.)

Piece of ground in Lower Dublin Twp., bounded by lands of Abraham Parsons, Thomas Kent and James Ayr, late the property of Joseph Woollen, to be sold at Busselton; likewise a log house and piece of ground in the Manor of Moreland, bounded by the lands of John Duffield and Thomas Foster, late the property of Daniel Kelly (12 Sept.)

Lot of ground in Gresham Twp., at the upper end of Germantown, bounded by lands of Derrick Johnson and Matthias Adams, late the property of John Mickenderffer, taken in execution, will be sold at the house of Daniel Pistorius in Germantown (12 Sept.)

David Dowderman, near Chestnut Hill in Germantown Twp., has taken up a cow (12 Sept.)

Negroes for sale; enquire of Edward Denny, Jr., at Capt. Arthur's in Walnut St. (12 Sept.)

Pasture to be let; enquire of William Callender in Water St. (12 Sept.)

James M'Laughlin, Irish servant, age c. 19, runaway from Jacobus Hains, at the mouth of Christine Creek, New Castle Co.; it is thought he may use the name Jeremiah Connor (12 Sept.)

Real estate about 26 miles from Phila. for sale; enquire of John Hambright, living at the White-horse tavern on Lancaster Road (12 Sept.)

Lots in Phila. for sale, of which one is divided by an alley from John Emlen's property and another is divided by an alley from property of Robert Rawlinson; apply to Septimus Robinson in Mulberry St., Phila., or James Worrell in Vine St. (12 Sept.)

Robert Cox, servant, born in Northamptonshire or Oxfordshire, age c. 25, George Dale, servant, born in England, age c. 22, John Oulton, servant (who has been in the country about 4 years), age c. 25, Francis Watkinson, servant, born in Darbyshire, age c. 21, and Caesar, a Negro, age c. 25, all runaways from the Baltimore Ironworks in Md., belonging to Charles Carroll, Esq., and Company; Richard Croxall will pay reward if the runaways are captured (12 Sept.)

William Dobbins, Irish servant, age c. 20, runaway from Enoch Fenton (12 Sept.)

Horse strayed or stolen from Thomas Davis of North Wales (12 Sept.)

Speeches of Gov. Dinwiddie of Va. (19 Sept.)

Thu. last arrived at New York H.M.S. *Mermaid*, Washington Shirley commander, having brought Robert Hunter Morris; upon landing, Morris was conducted to the house of James Alexander in Broad St.; Mr. Morris, nephew of the governor, also arrived in the *Mermaid*, according to New York item of 16 Sept. (19 Sept.)

Phila. items mention Capts. Ritchie, Mesnard, Reeve, Stirling, Snead, Cookson, Dunn, Burrows, Ewing, Brown and Head (19 Sept.)

Capt. Adam Stephen of the Virginia Regiment gives an account of the engagement with the French; he mentions Jamonville, Le Force, Ensign Druillon and Col. Washington (19 Sept.)

Imported servants are for sale by William Blair and John Meas on Powell's wharf (19 Sept.)

Riding chair for sale; enquire of Samuel Rhodes at the lower end of Second St. (19 Sept.)

Adv. of Edward Weyman, upholsterer, at the Sign of the Royal Bed, corner of Chestnut and Second Sts. (19 Sept.)

Real estate in Phila., bounded on the E. by property late of Thomas Annis, on the W. by property of Ebenezer Tomlinson and on N. by ground formerly of John Deleval, now of Dr. Zachary, being mortgaged to the Trustees of the General Loan Office by Ann Woods, will be sold at the London Coffee-house (19 Sept.)

John Galohown, Irish servant, age c. 24, who has served a time in Kent Co., runaway from Richard Willmot, living in the Fork of Gun-Powder River, Baltimore Co. (19 Sept.)

Plantation near Timber Creek in West Jersey, now in the tenure of Maham Southwick, to be sold at the house of William Hugg in Gloucester; to view the premises, apply to Henry Woodrow, living at Pooles's bridge, Phila. (19 Sept.)

Two Negroes, each aged c. 35, runaways from Capt. Blair's ship at Lewes-Town; reward if they are taken will be paid by John Spafford in Phila. or Thomas Cooch, miller, on Christine Creek, New Castle Co.; Sam, another Negro, age near 50, is a runaway from said Cooch (19 Sept.)

Mary Smith, born in Manchester, England, servant, age c. 20, and Elizabeth Roach, Irish servant, born in Cork, age c. 22, who both came from Liverpool in the snow *George*, George Rankin master, runaways from Robert Wakely, merchant, in Phila. (19 Sept.)

Adv. of Francis Trumble, cabinet- and chair-maker, at the Sign of the Scrutore in Front St. (19 Sept.)

1754

Reward offered for recovery of lost pocketbook by William Rigden, painter, a little below the drawbridge in Phila. (19 Sept.)

Robert Wharton, English servant, age between 30 and 40, runaway from John Davis of Queen Ann's Co., Md. (19 Sept.)

John Gwin, who says he was born near Dublin and that he worked his passage on the ship Molly from London to Hampton on the James River, is now held in Chester Goal by Samuel Smith, the goaler (19 Sept.)

George M'Donnel, age 26, who says he was born in Dublin, is also being held in the same goal as a runaway (19 Sept.)

Plantation and tanyard in Bristol Twp., the place where Krafft Richstein lately lived, is to be sold or let; apply to Bernhard Reser at said place or to Baltus Reser in Germantown (19 Sept.)

The "Cheese-cake house" in Fourth St. to be let; enquire of Ann Jones at Abraham Mitchell's in Second St. (19 Sept.)

Mon. last the Province sloop, Capt. Saunders, arrived, with Gov. Shirley on board, in Kingroad from Falmouth in Casco Bay, according to Boston item of 16 Sept. (26 Sept.)

New York item mentions Capts. Corne, Everson, Jones and Miller (26 Sept.)

Phila. items mention Capts. Troop, Partridge, Reeve, Ferguson, Mesnard, Budden, Stirling, Russell, Spurrier, Muir and Jackson (26 Sept.)

On 18 Sept. Matthew Wright was robbed on the highway in West New Jersey (26 Sept.)

Sermon was preached by the Rev. Whitefield on Sun. last (26 Sept.)

Samuel Neave intends for England next spring (26 Sept.)

Adv. of John Bell in Water St. (26 Sept.)

Plantation at Burlington, in which Gov. Belcher resided, lately in the possession of Isaac Conarro, is for sale; enquire of Joshua Crosby in Phila. or Isaac Conarro on the premises (26 Sept.)

Writing is taught by Mr. Elphinstone at the Widow Roberts's in Front St., next door to William Ball's, goldsmith (26 Sept.)

Creditors of John Kraft Reistine, late of Bristol Twp., tanner, are to bring their accounts to John Johnson, Derrick Keyser and Christian Lebman, auditors, at the house of Daniel Pistorious in Germantown (26 Sept.)

On 18 Sept. Matthew Wright, of Bethlehem Twp., Hunterdon Co., West N.J., was assaulted and robbed by two men on the road leading from Allen and Turner's Ironworks (26 Sept.)

Accounts with the estate of George Jones, who formerly kept the Sign of the Black Horse, in Black Horse Alley, Phila., are to be settled with Jacob Duche and others, execs. (26 Sept.)

Margaret Ashecraft, English servant, age c. 18, runaway from James Porter of West Nantmill, Chester Co., blacksmith; reward is offered by said Porter, who lives near Dennis Whalen (26 Sept.)

Mare has been stolen from Walter Tolley, living near Joppa in Baltimore Co.; the thief also stole a saddle from Richard Willmott (26 Sept.)

House in the Northern Liberties, about ½ mile from Phila., to be let by Richard Jarard, living on the premises (26 Sept.)

Plantation in White-Marsh, Phila. Co., to be sold by Peter Robeson (26 Sept.)

The brig Prince of Wales at Chester Town on Chester River, Md.; its inventory is to be seen at Capt. James Hopkins's; said Hopkins will sell merchandize, being part of the estate of Capt. John Hopkins, late of Phila. Co., dec'd (26 Sept.)

Coat stolen from the house of Thomas Stackhouse, living in Wrights-Town, Bucks Co. (26 Sept.)

Managers for the benefit of the Academy at Phila. are William Allen, John Inglis, William Masters, Samuel M'Call, Jr., Joseph Turner, Benjamin Franklin, Thomas Leech, William Shippen, Philip Syng, Phineas Bond, Richard Peters, Abraham Taylor, William Plumsted, Joshua Maddox, Thomas White and Thomas Cadwallader (3 Oct.)

Extracts from the Journal of the House of Burgesses in Va. mention Col. Washington, Mr. Walthoe, William Peyronie, Charles Carter, Landon Carter, Capt. Mackay, Major Adam Stephens, Capts. Robert Stobe, Peter Hog, Andrew Lewis and George Mercer, Lieuts. Thomas Wagener, William Polson, John Savage and James Towers, Ensigns William Bronough, John Mercer and James Craig, Mr. Bland, Capt. Matthew Whitwell, George Burnett, and Peyton Randolph (3 Oct.)

Boston items of 23 Sept. mention Gen. Winslow and Col. Washington (3 Oct.)

On 29 Sept. a schooner arrived at New York in which came Capt. Rudyard (3 Oct.)

On Wed. last at the Commencement of the College of New Jersey at Newark orations were delivered by William Shippen and President Burr; the degree of B.A. was conferred upon Benjamin Chapman, John Ewing, Benjamin Hait, Ezra Horton, David Matthews, John Odell, Sylvanus Osborn, David Purviance, William Ramsey, Jacob Reeve, Benajah Roots, Josias Sherman, William Shippen, Thomas Smith, William Thomson and Noah Wadham; Rev. Whitefield was granted the degree of M.A., according to a New York item of 30 Sept. (3 Oct.)

On 3 Oct. Gov. Robert Hunter arrived at Phila. (3 Oct.)

Phila. items mention Capts. Bachop, John Crawford, Noarth, Kennedy, Moore, Russell, Muir, Wier and Spurrier (3 Oct.)

On 2 Oct. Benjamin Franklin and William Callender were chosen burgesses for Phila.; the following were chosen assessors for the city: Joseph Watkins, Jacob Lewis, Joseph Lownes, Thomas Paschall, Thomas Gordon, Richard Wistar; wardens chosen were George Okill and Joseph Morris (3 Oct.)

John and Joseph Swift are removed from Water St. into Grisley's Alley, opposite John Mifflin's (3 Oct.

Adv. of Thomas Lawrence concerning a sale to be held under the courthouse (3 Oct.)

James Rian, Irish convict servant, age c. 23, runaway from Robert Beverlin in Kent Co., Md. (3 Oct.)

Tue. last the following were elected for Phila. Co. -.representatives, Evan Morgan, Isaac Norris, Hugh Evans, Joseph Stretch, Edward Warner, Joseph Fox, Joshua Morris, Joseph Trotter; sheriffs, Samuel Morris, James Coultas; coroners, Thomas Boude, John Biddle; commissioner, Jacob Cooper; assessors, Morris Morris, Derrick Keyser, Daniel Williams, Robert Thomas, Isaac Jones (North Wales) and Peter Pennebaker (3 Oct.)

Tue. last the following were elected for Bucks Co. - representatives, Mahlon Kirkbride, William Smith, Griffith Owen, Derrick Hogeland, Joseph Hamton, William Hoge, Jonathan Ingham, Samuel Brown; sheriffs, William Yeardley, Benjamin Chapman; coroners, Simon Butler, John Story; commissioner, Giles Knight; assessors, Daniel Palmer, Samuel Foulke, John Kelley, William Means, Alexander Brown, Benjamin Courson (3 Oct.)

Tue. last the following were elected for Chester Co. - representatives, George Ashbridge, Joseph Gibbons, Peter Dicks, Thomas Cummings, Nathaniel Pennock, Nathaniel Grubb, Joseph James, William Peters; sheriffs, Isaac Pearson, John Fairlamb; coroners, Joshua Thomson, John Wharton; commissioner, Thomas Pearson; assessors, Joseph Ashbridge, John Meredith, Timothy Kirk, Thomas Pimm, William Parker, Samuel Miller; Charles Willing was re-elected Mayor of Phila. (3 Oct.)

Thomas Jones and John Burridge, servants, runaways from William De Wees of Whitemarsh (3 Oct.)

Plantation in North Wales for sale; apply to Thomas Evans, living on the premises (3 Oct.)

Plantation in Lower Merion for sale; apply to Thomas Evans of North Wales or Hugh Evans or Robert Roberts, living near the premises (3 Oct.)

Address to Gov. Robert Hunter Morris and the reply of the governor, in which he mentions Mr. Hamilton (10 Oct.)

Gov. Arthur Dobbs has arrived in North Carolina (10 Oct.)

Capt. Waddil of the North Carolina Regiment has arrived in Williamsburg; he brought with him M. La Force (10 Oct.)

Troops have marched out of Annapolis for Frederick Co. under the command of Lt. John Forty (10 Oct.)

Capt. Stevens has returned to Annapolis (10 Oct.)

Mon. last second company of Capt. Dagworthy's soldiers left Annapolis under Lt. John Bacon to join the troops in Frederick Co. (10 Oct.)

Boston items of 30 Sept. mention Capts. Trout, Patridge, Jackson, Philips and Saunders and Gen. Winslow (10 Oct.)

New York items of 7 Oct. mention Capts. James White, Nicholls, Jones, Cornelius Livingston, Steel, Leers, Abercrombie, Gilford, Farnando, Bennet, Ramsey, Gordon, Furlong, Creighton, Forsyth, Pounce and Stewart (10 Oct.)

Phila. items mention Capts. Noarth, Simmonds, Taylor, Kennedy and Mesnard (10 Oct.)

John Harrobine was found guilty of publishing two forged deeds and was sentenced to be whipped and set in the pillory in Phila. (10 Oct.)

Notice about postal service by William Franklin, comptroller (10 Oct.)

1754

The following have been elected for Lancaster Co. - representatives, James Wright, Calvin Cooper, Arthur Patterson, Peter Worrall; sheriffs, Thomas Smith, James Marshall; coroners, John Dougharty, Matthias Slough (10 Oct.)

The following have been elected for York Co. - representatives, John Wright, David M'Conaughy; sheriffs, John Audlum, Abraham Noblit; coroners, Archibald M'Grue, William King (10 Oct.)

The following have been elected for Cumberland Co. - representatives, Joseph Armstrong, John Smith; sheriffs, John Potter, William Parker; coroners, John M'Clure, Ezekiel Dunning (10 Oct.)

The following have been elected for Berks Co. - representative, Moses Starr; sheriffs, Benjamin Lightfoot, Jacob Morgan; coroners, William Boone, Samuel Hoy (10 Oct.)

The following have been elected for Northampton Co. - representative, James Burnside; sheriffs, Nicholas Scull, Jacob Baughman; coroners, Jasper Scull, John Traxler (10 Oct.)

The following have been elected for New-Castle Co. - representatives, William Armstrong, Evan Reice, Jacob Vanbibber, James M'Mechen, John M'Cool, William Patterson; sheriffs, William Golden, John M'Kinley; coroners, Robert Morrison, John M'Clughan (10 Oct.)

The following have been elected for Kent Co. - representatives, John Vining, John Brinckle, John Caten, Andrew Caldwell, Benjamin Chew, Thomas Clarke; sheriffs, John Clayton, Caesar Rodney; coroners, French Battle, Peter Brinckle (10 Oct.)

The following have been elected for Sussex Co. - representatives, Jacob Kollock, Benjamin Barton, John Clowes, Benjamin Stockley, Josiah Martin, Ryves Holt; sheriff, Jacob Kollock, Jr. (10 Oct.)

Partnership between James Wallace and George Bryan, of Phila., merchants, will soon determine (10 Oct.)

Animals, farm equipment, etc., will be sold at the plantation late of Andrew Hannis, dec'd (10 Oct.)

Michael Rice and Christian Leybrook have absconded; their creditors are to appear before Hugh Wilson at the Forks of Delaware in Northampton Co. (10 Oct.)

Nicholas Nicholson, servant, from Bradford in Yorkshire, age c. 30, carpenter and joiner, and James Carter, servant, born at Richmond in Yorkshire, age c. 26, carpenter and joiner, runaways from Walter Stirling, commander of the ship Peak-Bay (10 Oct.)

Creditors of Joseph and Ezekiel Harlin are to meet at the house of Amos Harvey in Birmingham, with John Bennet, George Gilpin and Robert Mondenhall, auditors (10 Oct.)

Anne Smith, wife of Hugh Smith, has eloped from her husband (10 Oct.)

Adv. of Samuel Grisley in Market St. (10 Oct.)

Bernard and Jane Colgon, Irish servants, who pretend to be cousins, lately come into this country, runaways from John Simson, living in Londonderry Twp., Chester Co. (10 Oct.)

House in Kensington, bounded on N. by land of Nicholas Cassell, late estate of John Parrock, dec'd, taken in execution, to be sold at John Biddle's (10 Oct.)

George Pearce, convict servant, Englishman, age c. 40, John Jones, Irish convict servant, and Anne Jones, born in Dublin, servant, runaways from William Jenkins, living near Deer Creek, Baltimore Co., Md. (10 Oct.)

Mare strayed or stolen from Thomas Boude, coroner, in Kensington (10 Oct.)

Piece of land in Moyamensing Twp., bounded by land of John Randel and wife and lands of James Lownes and Samuel Wheeler; also another piece of land, adjoining ground late of John Ogden, dec'd, and of Samuel Wheeler, dec'd; also a piece of land near where John Ashton lives, adjoining lands of Samuel Austin, Joseph Lownes, Samuel Wheeler, dec'd; also a lot bounded by land late of William Attwood, dec'd, all pieces late the property of John Ashton, taken in execution; they will be sold at John Ashton's in Moyamensing (10 Oct.)

Real estate in Phila., bounded partly by ground late belonging to Abraham Bickley and by ground of William Till, late the estate of Peter Bard, taken in execution, will be sold at John Biddle's (10 Oct.)

Patrick Wall, Irish servant, who has been in the country 3 months, a slater and plaisterer, runaway from Obadiah Elliot, living at the Red Lion in New-Castle Co. (10 Oct.)

House and lot in Phila., bounded on E. by lot of John Ogden and on W. by lot of Marcus Kuhl, to be sold by Hannah Pearson, living on the premises (10 Oct.)

Timothy Minchan, Irish servant, age c. 20, who has been about 10 weeks in the country, runaway from Capt. William Simpson of Phila. (10 Oct.)

Mare stolen or strayed from Jacob Bruebaker, living in Manheim Twp., Lancaster Co. (10 Oct.)

Proclamation of Gov. Robert Hunter Morris, which mentions Thomas and Richard Penn and is signed by Secretary Richard Peters (17 Oct.)

Speech of Gov. J. Belcher at Perth Amboy (17 Oct.)

At court in Boston Michael Fowler was sentenced to death for burglary, Joseph Severance, Jr., and Eunice Clesson, both of Deerfield, were convicted of incest, and Jedediah Newton was convicted of counterfeiting and passing (17 Oct.)

Capt. Hovey broke goal and escaped a few days before Capt. Bennet sailed from Halifax, according to a New York item of 14 Oct. (17 Oct.)

New York item of 14 Oct. mentions Capts. Paschall and Julian Legge (17 Oct.)

Mon. last Isaac Norris in Phila. was chosen speaker of the General Assembly (17 Oct.)

Tanachrisson, an Indian chief, died 4 Oct. at Harris's Ferry on Sasquehanna (17 Oct.)

Last month in Cumberland Co. Israel, an Indian, killed an Indian trader at the house of one Anthony Thomson (17 Oct.)

Phila. items mention Capts. Budden, Ferguson, Jones, Abercrombie, John Ross, Leslie and Charles Ross (17 Oct.)

Accounts with the estate of Andrew Bartholomew, dec'd, to be settled with Thomas Bartholomew and Jonathan Bebee, execs. (17 Oct.)

Person wishing to dispose of a Negro boy is to enquire of D. Hall at the New Printing Office (17 Oct.)

Man who called himself John Jones came last month to a tavern in Chanceford Twp., York Co., and then fled, leaving behind two mares; owner is desired to claim them at Christian Croll's in York-town (17 Oct.)

Real estate in Market St., between houses of Marcus Kuhl and John Petty, for sale by Hannah Pearson (17 Oct.)

Real estate in the Borough of Bristol, adjoining ground of Israel Pemberton and the late Sampson Cary, late the property of James Murphy, taken in execution at the suit of John Abraham Denormandie, will be sold at the house of Patrick O'Haxlin in Bristol (17 Oct.)

Real estate in Hilltown, Bucks Co., bounded on the N. by land of James Hamilton, Esq., on the E. by land of Thomas Philips, on the S. by land of Lawrence Growdon, Esq., and on the W. by land of Thomas Matthias, late the property of Thomas Philips, taken in execution at the suit of William Coleman and James Pemberton of Phila., merchants, will be sold at the house of John Kelley in Hilltown (17 Oct.)

Real estate in Hilltown, bounded on the N. by land of Philip Hay, on the E. by land of Thomas Morris, on the W. by land of Edward Heaton, late the property of Bartholomew Young, dec'd, will be sold at the house of John Kelley in Hilltown (17 Oct.)

Mare strayed or stolen from the pasture of Matthias Kentzly of Phila.; reward if brought to Christian Sneider or David Shaver in Phila. or John Woodsman in Lancaster (17 Oct.)

Horse strayed from the stable of William M'Ilvaine on Dock St.; reward if brought to owner at his house in Front St. or to Issacher Price, overseer of M'Ilvaine's plantation near Bristol (17 Oct.)

Accounts with the estate of Jonathan Ellis, late of Waterford, Gloucester Co., dec'd, to be settled with Joseph and Mary Ellis, execs. (17 Oct.)

Ann Crotey, Irish servant, age $\underline{c}$. 16, runaway from William Rorrist, at the Sign of the Black Boy and Trumpet in Phila. (17 Oct.)

Thomas Yorke has forge-hammers for sale (17 Oct.)

Negro man and woman, runaways from Benjamin Howell of Marcus Hook (17 Oct.)

Time of three servants, bakers, for sale; enquire of Samuel Read, baker, in Front St. (17 Oct.)

Robert Gordon, Irish servant, age $\underline{c}$. 19, blacksmith, and Philip Pendegraft, Irish servant, age $\underline{c}$. 23 or 24, hatter, runaways from David Offley and Jonathan Wainwright, both living in Phila. (17 Oct.)

Gelding, supposed to have been stolen by Joseph Lacey near Doe Run in Lancaster Co., is now in the custody of Thomas Jarvis at the Indian Queen in Market St. (17 Oct.)

Samuel Bowden, English servant, painter, runaway from Jacob Van Bibber, living in Cecil Co., Md. (17 Oct.)

Catherine Dunsey (Irish), age $\underline{c}$. 30, and Sanderson Stanford (English), servants, runaways from Zachary Stugars, living in York-Town (17 Oct.)

1754

Accounts with estate of Thomas Howell, late of Chichester, Chester Co., dec'd, to be settled with Samuel Howell, exec. (17 Oct.)

Speech of Gov. Robert Hunter Morris and address to him from the Representatives, signed by Isaac Norris, Speaker (24 Oct.)

Lt. Lyon proposed to the French at Fort Duquesne the exchange of M. Druillon and two cadets for Messieurs Stobo and Van Braam (24 Oct.)

Arthur Dobbs, Gov. of N.C., and his son, Capt. Dobbs, arrived Sun. last in Hampton Road in the Garland man-of-war, Capt. Arbuthnot, according to Williamsburg item of 10 Oct. (24 Oct.)

Capt. John Rouse in H.M.S. Success has taken Capt. Donnell of York (24 Oct.)

Rev. Whitefield has preached in Boston (24 Oct.)

Rev. Tennent (with recommendations from Gov. Belcher) has collected 1,000 pounds in Britain for the College of New Jersey (24 Oct.)

New York items mention Capts. Thomas, Jermain, Askin, Morrison, Jones, Clymer, Lyon, Thompson, Nicholls, Frazier, Cotton, Mataseur, Cochran, Pearse, Roome, Heysham, Ketteltas and Quereau (24 Oct.)

Comment on the defeat of Major Washington on the Ohio River (24 Oct.)

Phila. items mention Capts. Swaine, Withy, Taylor, Kelly, Doyle, Ross, Leslie, Coatam, O'Brian, Hardy, Robeson, Stuart, Brown, Arthur, Bane, Wright and Charles Johnston (24 Oct.)

Thomas King, apprentice, age c. 18, runaway from Amos Jones, master of the ship Recovery of Wilmington (24 Oct.)

Jacob Houber, Dutch servant, age c. 25, and John Bragan, Irish servant, age c. 25, who has lived at Mount-holly, N.J., runaways from Isaac Myars and Jacob Rubely, both living in Conestogoe Twp., Lancaster Co. (24 Oct.)

John Jones (late assistant to Mr. Dove in the Academy) has opened a school in Front St., within three doors of Thomas Wells, shipwright (24 Oct.)

House in Second St., between the houses of William Pywell and William Griffitts, is for sale; apply to Jonathan Lewis, who lives on the premises (24 Oct.)

Tract of land in St. George's Hundred, New-Castle Co., part of the real estate of Andrew Peterson, late of New-Castle Co., Esq., dec'd, for sale; apply to David Witherspoon of New-Castle Co. or Jacob Peterson, who lives with Mr. Bond in Phila. (24 Oct.)

Notice to Harmanus Hager (or Heger), who came to Pa. about 5 years ago from Germany, that three of his children, Jacob, Anna Margarietta and Valentine, have come to New York in the ship Sarah Galley, Capt. Thomas Stap; enquire of Philip Livingston at New York (24 Oct.)

Samuel Beverton, travelling without pass, who says he came from Stafford Co., Va., has been committed to goal in Lewistown, Sussex Co. (24 Oct.)

Two horses stolen from Daniel Sexton in Upper Freehold, Monmouth Co., N.J. (24 Oct.)

Plantation at Maiden Creek, Berks Co., 7 miles from Reading, to be sold or let; apply to Samuel Pennock of Phila. or Benjamin Lightfoot, Esq., at Reading (24 Oct.)

Address of Representatives, Robert Lawrence speaker, to Gov. Jonathan Belcher of N.J. (31 Oct.)

Fri. last Capt. Edwards arrived at Boston, with news that Chief Justice Jonathan Belcher had arrived at Halifax, according to Boston item of 21 Oct. (31 Oct.)

New York items mention Capts. Davis, Shaw, Bates, Wardell, Savage, Lawrence, Hunter, Shannon, Sawyer, George Gyon, Thomas, Wallace, Leak and Taylor (31 Oct.)

New York item of 28 Oct. cites a letter from Black River at the Musqueto Shore to the effect that on Fri. last the Rev. Langhorne embarked for Georgia (31 Oct.)

Report of shortage of sarsparilla at Musqueto Shore; only what Mr. Pitts may get from the Spaniards is available (31 Oct.)

Phila. items mention Capts. James Berry, Lownes, Joy, Henderson, Gardner and Broderick (31 Oct.)

Woman of 19, who as a child at her aunt Lydia's was taken a prisoner, is finally released from Canada by order of the Marquis Duquesne; she thinks her father was Richard Tell and that he lived in Phila. (31 Oct.)

James, a Mulatto, who says he belonged to John Sumors at Acomack Co., Md., is in goal at New-Castle; apply to George Monro, sheriff (31 Oct.)

A watch (the maker Robert Barns) is lost out of the house of Widow Farra; reward if brought to David Bevan at the Sign of the Masons Arms in Walnut St. (31 Oct.)

Lots of land and a cart for sale; enquire of Mary Ball or William Ball, goldsmith, in Front St. (31 Oct.)

Letter directed to William Sword, with note in it payable to James Gibbon by George Burnside, was lost last week in Phila. (31 Oct.)

Lot in Moyamensing Twp., bounded on E. by ground of George Emlen, Jr., and on W. by ground of Conrad Waltaker, taken in execution, will be sold at John Biddle's (31 Oct.)

Real estate in Phila., bounded on S. by ground of Samuel Powell and on N. by ground late of John Snowden the Elder, dec'd, late the estate of John Snowden, taken in execution, will be sold at John Biddle's (31 Oct.)

Real estate in Phila., bounded on S. by lot of William Branson and on N. by lot of Willcox Phillips, now in the possession of William Branson, for sale; enquire of Erasmus Stevens (31 Oct.)

Maria Kelcon, Dutch servant, age c. 40, who has been about a fortnight in the country, runaway from John Hopkins, tavernkeeper, at Pequa (31 Oct.)

Patrick Shields, age c. 20, who came into the country about 6 weeks ago in the Hamilton from Derry, runaway from Theophilus Alexander, living on the Main Fresh of Elk River, Cecil Co., Md. (31 Oct.)

Time of servant for sale by Andrew Farrell, tanner, in Chestnut St. (31 Oct.)

House in the Northern Liberties and also a lot on the road from Phila. to Germantown, adjoining plantation of William Vanderspeigle, to be sold at the Sign of the Rising Sun on Germantown Road; attendance by Catherine, John and Jacob Naglee (31 Oct.)

Francis Bibler, of Phila., warns that he will not pay the bond, fraudently obtained from him and Michael Bibler by Conrad Haffner, assigned to George Adam Gaab, of Phila., butcher; Michael Bibler is now dec'd (31 Oct.)

Elizabeth Coates offers reward for recovery of horse strayed from her plantation in East Caln, Chester Co. (31 Oct.)

Addresses of Council and House to Gov. Dinwiddie and of the Gov. to Council and House (7 Nov.)

Boston items mention Capts. Dogget, Benjamin Gorham, M'Daniel and Lewis (7 Nov.)

Elizabeth Canning (whose case with Mary Squires, a **gipsy, in** England is well known) has come to Boston from London (7 Nov.)

Wed. last Anne Hogan was drowned at the mouth of South River, according to Annapolis item of 31 Oct. (7 Nov.)

Snow Beaumont, James Howell captain, foundered last month soon after she left the Capes, with the loss of the captain and all but three on board (7 Nov.)

New York items mention Capts. Burrows, Guilford, Flanagan and Furlong and Mr. Griffiths of Phila., owner of the sloop Polly (7 Nov.)

Phila. items mention Capts. Morrell, Punter, Brown, Ash, Salter, Dings, Atkinson and Ham (7 Nov.)

Rudeman Robeson offers reward for recovery of boat stolen from dock of Abel James in Phila. (7 Nov.)

Hannah Dubre, living in the Northern Liberties, next plantation to Capt. Peel's, has seeds for sale; enquire of John Bissell in Third St. (7 Nov.)

Accounts with estate of James Russell, coach-maker, dec'd, or of Elizabeth Russell, admin. of James Russell, also dec'd, to be settled with Plunket Fleeson and John Palmer, admins. (7 Nov.)

Two silver spoons have been stopped in Noxontown; a lad said he found one of them in Daniel Bryan's field in Kent Co., Md.; apply to John Bayly in Phila. (7 Nov.)

Accounts with estate of George Spafford, dec'd, to be settled with Sarah Spafford (her house is at the corner of Chestnut and Water Sts.) and David Chambers, execs. (7 Nov.)

Wines for sale on Charles Edgar's wharf; apply to Jonathan Evans in Front St. (7 Nov.)

Thomas Caldwell, who says he comes from Rhode Island, is in goal at Easton, Northampton Co. (John Weaver is goaler) on suspicion of being a horse-stealer (7 Nov.)

Thomas Downy, living in Fifth St., has taken up a mare (7 Nov.)

Two tracts of land on Sasquehannah River, adjoining Bear Island, known as Onion's Wilderness and Onion's Fishery, for sale; enquire of Deborah Onion at Onion's Ironworks, near Joppa, Md. (7 Nov.)

Accounts with estate of Thomas Lloyd, dec'd, to be settled with Charles Willing, exec. (7 Nov.)

Purse left at shop of Joseph Richardson, silversmith, in Front St. (7 Nov.)

Fulling mill in Manor of Moreland, near Joshua Morris's gristmill, to be let; apply to Peter Tyson, lime-burner in Abington (7 Nov.)

John M'Cutchin, Scotch servant, age c. 25, tailor, runaway from John Stinson, living in Water St., Phila.; reward if runaway is brought to said Stinson or to Mr. Whitehead, the keeper of the workhouse (7 Nov.)

Thomas Jones, of Horsham, Phila. Co., has taken up a mare (7 Nov.)

House in Water St. where Francis Johnson dwells, next to Morris's, to be sold or let; apply to Anthony Morris or Joseph Richardson, merchant, in Phila. (7 Nov.)

Accounts with estate of George Jones, who formerly kept the Sign of the Black Horse, to be settled with Jacob Duche and others, execs. (7 Nov.)

Plantation in North Wales and another in Lower Merion for sale; apply to Thomas Evans of North Wales or Hugh Evans or Robert Roberts, living near the premises (7 Nov.)

Rev. Whitefield lodged at Col. Royal's at Medford; he later preached at Mr. Hobby's at Reading, at Mr. Leavit's, at Mr. Sparhawk's, at Mr. Rogers's and at Mr. Walley's (14 Nov.)

On 28 Oct. Capt. M'Neal arrived at Boston from New-Castle (14 Nov.)

William Keen, Esq., Judge of the Court of Vice-Admiralty in Newfoundland, was murdered about five weeks ago; his murderers, one Power and his wife, Matthew Holloren (a soldier) and Timothy M'Guire, were convicted and executed (14 Nov.)

On 18 Oct. Eleazer Melven died at Carlisle, Middlesex Co. (14 Nov.)

Phila. items mention Capts. Bedlow, Murray, Shankland, Budden and Wall (14 Nov.)

Tue. last the students in philosophy at the Academy in Phila. delivered exercises; present were John Tinker (governor of Providence) and James Hamilton (our late governor); epilogue was spoken by Master Billy Hamilton, age 9 (14 Nov.)

Real estate in Oxford Twp., formerly belonging to James Street, later in the possession of Griffith Griffith, mason, dec'd, bounded by land of John Edwards, Joseph Griffith, John Huson and James Riche, will be sold; enquire of George Eaton, Thomas Cavell, Isaac Ashton and Daniel Street, execs. of Griffith Griffith (14 Nov.)

Furniture of a person intending for Europe for sale; apply at Capt. Palmer's in Third St. (14 Nov.)

Lot of ground in Second St., adjoining house where Mr. Moland lives, for sale by Thomas Patson (14 Nov.)

Oswald Peel has taken up a colt (14 Nov.)

Samuel Rhoads warns against purchasing the house of Erasmus Stephens in Second St. (14 Nov.)

Chairs caned by the Widow Gale, living opposite William Callender's in Front St. (14 Nov.)

Real estate on the River Delaware in Chichester (called Marcus Hook), now in the tenure of John Webster, for sale; apply to John Karlin in Chichester, Chester Co. (14 Nov.)

Dennis Daley, Irish servant, age c. 24, runaway from Mary Kneesberry, living at the head of Bohemia in Cecil Co., within 1½ miles of David Witherspoon's, Esq. (14 Nov.)

Plantation at Maiden Creek in Berks Co. to be sold or let by Elizabeth Pennock, exec. of Samuel Pennock, dec'd (14 Nov.)

All persons indebted to Alexander Ray, late of Phila., merchant, are to make prompt payment to James Trotter, attorney to said Ray (14 Nov.)

William White, Irish servant, age c. 20, tailor a runaway from William Keyl, of Octerara, Chester Co. (14 Nov.)

Patrick Robinson, servant, age c. 26, shoemaker, runaway from Patrick Dougherty, of Charlestown, Md. (14 Nov.)

Martha Vernor, living in Leacock Twp., Lancaster Co., has taken up a steer (14 Nov.)

Richard Barry has a great coat found near Radnor Meeting-house on the Great Conestogo Road (14 Nov.)

Copper and tin ware and coppersmith's tools, the estate of the late Widow Margaret Young, dec'd, to be sold at Lancaster; attendance by Rev. George Craig, exec., or James Bickham (14 Nov.)

New York item mentions Capts. Pinhorne Duncan, Rawles and Topham (21 Nov.)

Phila. items mention Capts. Wall, Hargrave, Lyell, Murray, Leonard, Leech, Shankland, Garrison, Holdon, Mason, Fairbairn, John Mackay, Thompson and Clark (21 Nov.)

One Newell, of Lynn, was killed by Indians near Ft. Halifax on Kennebeck River (21 Nov.)

Rev. Whitefield preached in Boston (21 Nov.)

Capt. Arnold has arrived at New York from Jamaica; Gov. Knowles has ordered two ships of war to prepare to sail to Musqueto Shore (21 Nov.)

Real estate for sale, including plantation in North Wales, now in possession of John Jones, and a bank house in Front St., Phila., opposite to Joseph Morris; enquire of James Kinsey at Burlington or Edmund Kearny in Phila. (21 Nov.)

Joseph Ono, at the place of the late Edward Warner, at the point, has taken up a steer (21 Nov.)

Adv. of Thomas M'Janet & Company in Water St.; they have for sale works of Rev. John Flavel (21 Nov.)

Margaret, wife of Peter Masters, of Phila., has eloped from her husband (21 Nov.)

Nicholas Scull has for sale copies of perspective view of Phila. at his house in Second St. (21 Nov.)

About a year ago John Hyndshaw, who came passenger in the Cassandra, Capt. Hutchinson, left a blue coat and books with Samuel M'Call, Sr., as security for his note to Hutchinson (21 Nov.)

Adv. of Matthew Clarkson in Water St., next door to Samuel Shoemaker (21 Nov.)

Daniel Swan, of Phila., warns against accepting assignment of a bond that may be offered by Gasper Freder (21 Nov.)

House in King St., where John Hopkins lately dwelt, and another house in Walnut St,, two doors below John Reynell's corner, now in tenure of John Stoops, all being part of the estate of Capt. John Hopkins, dec'd, to be sold; apply to Attwood Shute or Matthew Drason (21 Nov.)

Time of servants for sale; enquire of Thomas Cottringer, staymaker, at the Green Stays in Arch St. (21 Nov.)

Ludwick Hofman, age c. 20, and George Miller, age c. 25, a stocking weaver, German servants, runaways from the ship Recovery of Phila.; reward offered for their capture by Griffith Minshell or Robert Lewis (21 Nov.)

Sun. last Gov. Horatio Sharpe of Md. returned to Annapolis from Virginia, according to Annapolis item of 7 Nov. (28 Nov.)

Speech of Gov. Robert Hunter Morris and address signed by Benjamin Chew, speaker (28 Nov.)

Phila. items mention Capts. Cotton, Arthur, England, Edwards, Gardner, Magee, Stout and Denormandie (28 Nov.)

Horse strayed or stolen; reward if brought to Jonathan Biles in Third St., Phila. (28 Nov.)

Notice concerning the post, signed by William Franklin, comptroller (28 Nov.)

Gilbert Goodridge, Walter Nicholls, age c. 30, and Thomas Hinds, age c. 23, English convict servants, runaways from Edmund Bull, William Johnson and John Love, living near Deer Creek in Baltimore Co., Md. (28 Nov.)

Accounts with Thomas Herbert, dec'd, to be settled with Sarah Herbert, admin. (28 Nov.)

Tract of land at Dover in Kent Co. on Delaware for sale; apply to Patrick Martin at Duck Creek (28 Nov.)

Hanus Outmandorf, Dutchman, a baker, has escaped from Sheriff John Adlum of York Co. (28 Nov.)

Tract of land called Brook's Discovery in Frederick Co., Md., for sale by James Brooke and James Brooke, Jr.; for information, apply to John Everitt, living near the premises (28 Nov.)

Edward Maybe, English servant, age c. 22, runaway from Jacob Hugg, living in Gloucester Twp., Gloucester Co. (28 Nov.)

Accounts with estate of George Emlen, dec'd, to be settled with George Emlen, John Armitt and William Logan (28 Nov.)

Address of Council and House to Gov. William Shirley, signed by J. Willard, Secretary, and T. Hubbard, Speaker, and the reply of the governor (5 Dec.)

Address of the clergy of Virginia to Gov. Robert Dinwiddie, signed by Commissary Thomas Dawson, and the reply of the governor (5 Dec.)

Thu. last one James Gale, a tailor, was committed to goal in New York for the rape of a child of 6 years, according to New York item of 2 Dec. (5 Dec.)

1754

New York items mention Capts. Caldwell, Jauncey, Colgan and Pulling (5 Dec.)

Letter from camp at Wills's Creek mentions Col. Sharpe (5 Dec.)

Sat. last Charles Willing, Mayor of Phila., died in his 45th year, and on 4 Dec. William Plumsted was elected in his place (5 Dec.)

Tue. last Michael Lightfoot, Provincial Treasurer, died in Phila., and on 4 Dec. Samuel Preston Moore was appointed in his place (5 Dec.)

Sat. next a member of the assembly for Phila. will be elected in place of Edward Warner, dec'd (5 Dec.)

Phila. items mention Capts. Arthur, Denormandie, Murdock, Moore and Riddall (5 Dec.)

Preaching of Mr. Whitefield in Boston (5 Dec.)

Nathan Cook offers reward for recovery of a horse strayed or stolen from Cook's lot in Vine St. (5 Dec.)

Hugh M'Donnell almost 1½ years ago bargained with Nicholas Creapel, living in Douglas Twp., Phila. Co., to keep his son for 7 months for 40 shillings. If the boy is not taken away by his father, the lad will be sold, for Creapel is about to leave Pa. (5 Dec.)

Lot of land in Oxford Twp., Phila. Co., for sale by Jacob Duffield, living in Bussel-town (5 Dec.)

Good stabling kept at Cantwell Bridge by Joseph Scull (5 Dec.)

Time of a Dutch servant girl for sale; enquire at Joseph Smith's, brass-founder, in Second St. (5 Dec.)

Henry Walkens, Irish servant, and Robert Faries, servant, age c. 20, runaways from William Smith, living at Christine Bridge (5 Dec.)

Plantation and sawmill in Ridley Twp., Chester Co., for sale; apply to Hugh Ferguson, living on the premises (5 Dec.)

Michael White, Irish servant, age between 25 and 30, tailor, runaway from Henry Baker & Company, of Charles-town, Cecil Co. (5 Dec.)

Margaret, wife of Peter Masters of Phila., has eloped from her husband (5 Dec.)

Tue. last a young man named William Preston was burnt to death in the North Parish of New London, according to Boston item of 25 Nov. (12 Dec.)

Rev. Whitefield has preached, among other places in Mass., at the churches of the following clergymen: Reed, Frost, Weld, Porter, Leonard, Conant, Thatcher, Snow and Bass (12 Dec.)

New York items mention Capts. Carlisle, Howell, Marshall, Syms, Gelston, Dingee, Devereaux, Amory, Waldo and Rivers (12 Dec.)

Phila. items mention Capts. Gardner, Rees, Dowers, Cowie, Sage, Mansfield, Lewis, Ammit, Graham, Price, Shane, Brown, Allison and Simpson (12 Dec.)

List of lectures to be given in Phila. by Ebenezer Kinnersley (12 Dec.)

Sat. last James Pemberton was elected member of the Assembly for Phila. Co. in place of Edward Warner, dec'd (12 Dec.)

Rev. Whitefield was to be at Brunswick yesterday (12 Dec.)

Durham Ironworks to be let; enquire of William Logan at Stenton near Germantown or of Anthony Morris in Phila. (12 Dec.)

Notice, signed by John Brainerd, clerk, that subscriptions for building the College of New Jersey are to be paid to Richard Stockton at Princetown (12 Dec.)

Raft of logs broke loose in Delaware River; reward if the logs are brought to Thomas Cuthbert, mast-maker, in Front St. (12 Dec.)

Henry Seabrand, Dutch servant, age c. 30, runaway from Col. James Gillespie of Lancaster Co. (12 Dec.)

Henry Smith, English servant, of middle age, runaway from William Buckley, of Bristol, Bucks Co.; reward for capture of Smith will be paid by said Buckley or by William M'Ilvaine in Phila. (12 Dec.)

Negro for sale by Alexander Allaire in Sassafras St. (12 Dec.)

Madeira wine for sale by Capt. Sibbald, next door to Mr. Stretch's, watchmaker (12 Dec.)

Michael Copple, next door to John Stillwaggon, has Albany pease for sale (12 Dec.)

Negro boy for sale; enquire of Joseph Greenway in Front St. (12 Dec.)

John Sullivan and John M'Daniel have absconded; their creditors are to appear at the house of Rowland Evans in North Wales (12 Dec.)

Piece of land in Germantownship, bounded by lands of John Barge, Derrick Johnson, Samuel M'Call and Leonard Stoneburner, late the estate of Matthias Ingels, dec'd, taken in execution, to be sold at the house of the Widow Pistorius in Germantown (12 Dec.)

Real estate in Roxborough Twp., bounded by lands of Anthony Newhouse, John Morris, George Wambles, late the estate of Zanas Savage, dec'd, taken in execution, to be sold at the house of William Levering (12 Dec.)

Plantation in Gwinedd (or North Wales) Twp., bounded by lands of Benjamin Davids, Valentine Puff and Charles Hubbs, late the estate of Thomas Wallas, taken in execution, will be sold at the house of Benjamin Davis in North Wales (12 Dec.)

Tract of land in Oxford Twp., bounded by lands of Joseph Ashton, Shalcross and John Kerr, late the estate of John Wilmington, taken in execution, will be sold at the tavern on the great road near the property (12 Dec.)

Thomas Marshall, Scotch servant, runaway from Andrew Leake, of Bridgewater Twp., East N.J. (12 Dec.)

Thomas Long, servant, runaway (supposedly in company with one Richard Dorrel) from Isaac Gibbs, living near Warwick, Cecil Co., Md. (12 Dec.)

Plantation in Gloucester Co. to be let or sold; apply to Samuel Griscom in Combs's Alley, Phila. (12 Dec.)

Messages from Gov. Robert Hunter Morris and replies of the Assembly, Isaac Norris speaker (19 Dec.)

Instructions from freemen in Prince George's Co. to their representatives, Addison, Murdock, Frasier and Hawkins (19 Dec.)

Mr. Whitefield arrived in New York on 11 Dec. (19 Dec.)

Phila. items mention Capts. Miller, Thomas Leech, Palanche, Law, Steel, Hatton and Frisby and a sailor named Alexander Sunbry, who was killed when he fell from a mast (19 Dec.)

Lot of land in Phila., adjoining house of Michael Hillegas, for sale; apply to George Bullock, Joseph Stretch or Edward Brooks, living on the premises (19 Dec.)

George M'Daniel, English servant, age c. 23, and Thomas Wood, English servant, runaways from John Hanly and Samuel Smith, both living in Chester, Pa. (19 Dec.)

Hugh Carberry, Irish servant, age c. 20, runaway from John Thompson, living in New-Castle (19 Dec.)

Furniture to be sold at house of Joseph Clark in Second St. (19 Dec.)

Tract of land in Northampton Co. to be sold; apply to Redmond Conyngham, merchant, in Front St., or John Reily, scrivener, in Chestnut St. (19 Dec.)

Messages from Gov. Morris to Assembly and House and reply from Isaac Norris, speaker (26 Dec.)

New York items mention Capts. Hathorn and Allen (26 Dec.)

Rev. Whitefield has set out for Georgia (26 Dec.)

Notice of Proprietary Land Office in Phila., signed by Richard Peters, secretary (26 Dec.)

Notice, dated Elizabeth-Town, 2 Dec., signed by Cha. Read, Secretary, orders colonels of the militia to send in returns (26 Dec.)

Richard Bull informs that a stray cow has come to the plantation of John Bull in Worcester Twp., Phila. Co. (26 Dec.)

Plantation in Merion Twp., Phila. Co., for sale; enquire of George Bevan in Phila. (26 Dec.)

Plantation in Mill-Creek Hundred, New-Castle Co., for sale; apply to Duncan Drummond (26 Dec.)

Mare has strayed from plantation of Abel Boake in East Bradford, Chester Co. (26 Dec.)

Bake-house of Francis Johnson, baker, next door to Morris Morris, brewer, in Water St., to be let (26 Dec.)

William Lovejoy and William Pitrekin, apprentices, age 16, runaways from the *Friendship*, of Whitby, Charles Ross master (26 Dec.)

Joseph Baker, as agent for William Ashe, collects ashes in Phila. (26 Dec.)

Message from Gov. Morris to the Pa. Assembly and reply of the Assembly, Isaac Norris speaker (31 Dec.)

Adv. of William Collier, tallow-chandler and soap-boiler, to be heard of at John Moore's, blacksmith, in Race St. (31 Dec.)

John or Johannes Manskull, servant, age c. 19, runaway from John Harrison, of Union Twp., Berks Co., near Bird's Ironworks (31 Dec.)

Message from Gov. Hunter to Pa. Assembly and reply, signed by Isaac Norris as speaker (31 Dec.)

1755

Message to Gov. of Pa. from Assembly, with mention of George M'Call and Thomas Robinson (7 Jan.)

Extract from letter from gentleman in Antigua, with mention of Mr. Sharp (agent in England) (7 Jan.)

Gov. Grenville of Barbados has purchased the Island of Tobago (7 Jan.)

Letters from England by Capt. Payne mention Commodore Keppel (7 Jan.)

Speech of Gov. Horatio Sharpe of Md. and answer of the Upper House (B. Tasker president); also Sharpe's address to the House of Delegates and answer (7 Jan.)

Charles-Town, S.C., items mention Capts. Seymour, James Berry, Hood, Don Fernando, Gilford, M'Clelan, Jonathan Waldo, Woodside, Gov. John Reynolds of Georgia, Mr. Buckle, Capts. John Legge and Boyd and Gov. Knowles of Jamaica (7 Jan.)

At Hampton, N.H., on Thu. last Eliphaz Dow struck with a hoe and killed Peter Clough - Boston item of 19 Dec. 1754 (7 Jan.)

At New York Rev. Whitefield was unable to preach charity sermon for prisoner in jail but donates ten pounds (7 Jan.)

The following captains have arrived at South Carolina: Weaver, Smith, Rose, Jacobson, Hornbly, Schermerhorn, Bryson, Fairlie, Drummond, Hunter, Rutgers, Ferguson, Stiles, Higgins, Muir and Gibbon (7 Jan.)

At court in Easton, Northampton Co., in Dec. James Egelson was convicted of horse-stealing and his son John of aiding and abetting him; both were whipped (7 Jan.)

Accounts with estate of Samuel Read, baker, to be settled with Dorothy Read, admin. (7 Jan.)

Plantation in Oxford Twp. to be sold or let; enquire of Samuel Preston Moore in Third St., Phila. (7 Jan.)

House in Fourth St. and another in Vine St. to be sold by Wm. Rakestraw (7 Jan.)

Piece of land in Sassafras St., bounded on N. by ground of Wm. Ball, on E. by ground of Gabriel Rambo, on W. by ground of Samuel Preston Moore, late estate of Thomas Gerrard, taken in execution, to be sold at John Biddle's (7 Jan.)

Mills in Roxborough Twp., bounded by lands of Benjamin Shoemaker and George Wood, and a lot, bounded by lands of Benjamin Shoemaker, George Wood and William Levering, property bounded by lands of John Gorgass and Ruttenbausen, late the estate of Adam Yager, taken in execution, to be sold (7 Jan.)

Real estate in Hill-town, bounded by land of John Vasline, of Evan Matthias, of James M'Callister, of Archibald Hamilton, of Bartholomew Young, late the property of Bartholomew Young, dec'd, taken in execution at suit of Peter Turner, merchant, in Phila., to be sold at house of John Kelly in Hilltown (7 Jan.)

Real estate in Richlow Twp., bounded on N. by land of Robert Penrose and on S. by land of James Morgan, late the property of James Morgan, taken in execution at suit of Mordecai Yarnall, merchant, in Phila., to be sold (7 Jan.)

Accounts with estate of Reese Jones, dec'd, late of Christiana Bridge, Newcastle Co., to be settled with Evan Morgan and his wife and John Watson, admins. (7 Jan.)

1755

Plantation in West Caln, Chester Co., for sale by John Robinson (7 Jan.)

James Sims, servant, age c. 40, runaway from the Castle sawmill; reward if brought to his master, Matthias Vanhorne in Crosswicks, Burlington Co. (7 Jan.)

Land in Radnor Twp., Chester Co., for sale; enquire of Ann Miller at the Sign of the Buck in Haverford (7 Jan.)

Margaret Llewellin, Welch servant, age c. 30, runaway from Edward Lewis, of Phila., labourer (7 Jan.)

Adv. of John White, staymaker, lately arrived from London, at the Sign of the Blue Stays in Front St. (7 Jan.)

Stray colt has been taken up at the plantation of William Coulton in Blockly Twp. (7 Jan.)

Anne M'Gittikin, wife of Bryan M'Gittikin, of the Great Valley in Chester Co., has eloped from her husband (14 Jan.)

Lots of land in Vine St., Phila., for sale; enquire of John Sayre in Market St., Phila., or Andrew Reed in Trenton (14 Jan.)

Various goods, supposed to be stolen, were left in Darby by a strange woman; included was a good hat made by Abraham Mitchell; owner may claim property from William Donaldson (14 Jan.)

Plantation in Bristol Twp. for sale; apply to Thomas Rose, who lives on the premises, or John Luckens, miller, who lives near the premises (14 Jan.)

Plantation on Chestnut Hill in Germantown Twp., Phila. Co. to be sold or let; apply to Edward Scull, living on the premises, or Nicholas Scull in Phila. (14 Jan.)

Plantation in Lower Merion Twp., adjoining land of William Thomas, late the estate of Rees Thomas, taken in execution, will be sold at the house of Richard Hughes (14 Jan.)

Speech of Gov. J. Glen of South Carolina (21 Jan.)

Ship of Capt. Broadhurst foundered at sea east of Antigua - New York item of 13 Jan. (21 Jan.)

Child of John Velzer, of Roxbury, Morris Co., East N.J., a few weeks ago was killed when gunpowder exploded (21 Jan.)

Servant of Matthias Auble, of Roxbury, Morris Co., died a few weeks ago as result of beating at the hands of his master (21 Jan.)

Message from Gov. Robert Hunter Morris to Pa. Assembly and the reply from the Assembly, signed by Isaac Norris as speaker, to be taken to the governor by Joseph Trotter and William Smith; copy of the minutes of the House by William Franklin, Clerk of the Assembly (14 Jan.)

Sat. last the house where Mr. Wallace keeps tavern narrowly escaped burning - Annapolis item of 26 Dec. 1754 (14 Jan.)

New York items mention Capts. Pitcairne, Schermerhorne, M'Daniel and Legge (14 Jan.)

Philip Fitzpatrick, Irish servant, a cooper, runaway from Thomas Canby, living in Wilmington (14 Jan.)

Time of a Dutch servant lad, a leather-dresser, for sale; enquire of Thomas Francis, living in Pewter-platter Alley (14 Jan.)

Amey, wife of Richard Shortall of Phila., has eloped from her husband (14 Jan.)

Horse strayed or stolen from the commons near Phila.; reward if brought to John Butler at the Sign of the Death of the Fox in Second St. (14 Jan.)

Horse stolen from Joseph Curtis of Curtis's Mills, near Bordentown (14 Jan.)

Matthias Schauffele, of Old Cushehoppen, Phila. Co., gave bonds to his father-in-law, Ludowig Lehman, for his plantation, payable to his brother-in-law, Jacob Killer; said Killer now has absented himself and taken the bonds (14 Jan.)

Friendly Indians have come from Mr. Croghan's to Camp Mount Pleasant at Wills's Creek (21 Jan.)

Jacob Bennet, age c. 42, wampum-maker by trade, born in Bucks Co., broke out of goal of Cape May Co.; reward for his capture offered by Sheriff John Shaw (21 Jan.)

Plantation in Kent Co. on Delaware on which Dr. Henry Jaffray lately lived, adjoining Duck Creek Town, for sale; apply to Henry Farsons, living near the premises, or Edmund Kearny in Phila. (21 Jan.)

Land in West Jersey for sale; enquire of John Smith in Phila. (21 Jan.)

Ground in Moyamensing and a lot in Market St., Phila., eastward of where Charles Brockden lives, for sale; enquire of Anthony Morris, Jr. (21 Jan.)

Public vendue to be held at house of Joseph White in Second St.; goods will be stored by Richard Wagstaffe at his house in Chestnut St. (21 Jan.)

Capt. Cornelius Livingston reports in New York that Capt. Dobson of New York has proceeded to Georgia (28 Jan.)

Fri. last arrived at Phila. from Va. Lt.-Col. Ellison of Gov. Shirley's Regt. and Lt.-Col. Mercer of Sir William Pepperell's Regt.; they came over in the Gibraltar and with them Sir John Sinclair, Deputy Quartermaster (28 Jan.)

Benjamin Chew is appointed Attorney General of Pa. in the place of Tench Francis, who lately resigned (28 Jan.)

Phila. items mention Capts. Appowin, Reeve, Punter, Morrell, Wilson, Holbrook, David Stewart, Archibald Stewart, Bogart, Clutsham, Hargrave and Warner (28 Jan.)

Adv. of Richard Footman & Company in Front St. (28 Jan.)

Snow *Nancy*, Samuel Appowen master, built by Cornelius Stout, of Phila., will be sold at the London Coffee-house; inventory to be seen at Thomas Willing's store in Front St. or on the snow at Stamper's wharf (28 Jan.)

Accounts with estates of Charles Willing or Thomas Lloyd, dec'd, to be settled with Thomas Willing, exec. (28 Jan.)

House in Front St. where Thomas Lawrence lately lived is to be let (28 Jan.)

Time of a lad, age c. 16, for sale; agree with James Whitehead, keeper of the workhouse in Phila. (28 Jan.)

Sam, a Negro, age c. 50, runaway from Thomas Cooch, miller, on Christine Creek, New-Castle Co.; reward will be paid by said Cooch or by John Spafford in Phila. (28 Jan.)

Robert Scott, age c. 30, ran away from Cumberland Town, New Kent Co., carrying away effects of great value from Messieurs Campbell and Craig, of King William Co., and Robert Donald, in Hanover, Va.; if Scott is taken in Pa., reward will be paid by John Nelson in Phila. (28 Jan.)

Charles Hamble, Irish servant, age c. 20, weaver, runaway from John Smith, living in East Caln Twp., Chester Co. (28 Jan.)

John Frederick Corn, Dutch servant, age c. 40, runaway from Stephen Carpenter, near Kensington (28 Jan.)

Turrence Magwigin, Irish servant, age c. 27, runaway from William Allen of Chester Twp., Burlington Co., West N.J. (28 Jan.)

Plantation on Raccoon Creek, Greenwich Twp., Gloucester Co., for sale; apply to John Halton, living near the premises (28. Jan.)

Patrick White, Irish servant, age c. 22, runaway from James Duncan, of Vincent Twp., Chester Co. (28 Jan.)

Horse stolen from stable of Edward Hill, living at his ferry in Bensalem, Bucks Co., commonly called Dunks's ferry (28 Jan.)

On 1 Dec. 1754 the sloop Polly, Alexander Innes master, ran ashore on Cape Romain (4 Feb.)

Item from Charles-Town, S.C., mentions Capts. M'Carthy, Joseph Smith and Becket Dewormeaux (4 Feb.)

New York item mentions Capts. William and Robert Dickenson (4 Feb.)

Tue. last Lt.-Cols. Ellison and Mercer set out from Phila. for Boston (4 Feb.)

Tue. last Mr. Pitcher, Commissary of the Musters, arrived at Phila. from New York (4 Feb.)

Wed. last adjutants of Shirley's and Pepperell's Regts. came to Phila. from Va. (4 Feb.)

Phila. items mention Capts. Palmer, Cowpland, Braddock, Menzies, Ross, Edwards, Ritchie, Leslie, Read, Abercrombie, Bolitho and M'Kenzie (4 Feb.)

Adv. of Charles Dutens, jeweller, from London, and David Harper, gold- and silversmith, next door to the Indian King in Market St. (4 Feb.)

Horse, left at the house of Thomas Rice, tavern-keeper in Salem, West Jersey, is now in the possession of Samuel Tylar of the same place (4 Feb.)

John Tucker, age c. 45, ship-carpenter, broke out of the county goal at Joppa, Baltimore Co., Md.; William Young is sheriff (4 Feb.)

Quit-rents are to be paid to Richard Hockley or Edmund Physick (4 Feb.)

Partnership of James Wallace and George Bryan is now dissolved (4 Feb.)

Adv. of Trustees of the London Coffee-house, George Okill, William Grant, William Fisher and Joseph Richardson; mention is made of cash paid to William Bradford (4 Feb.)

Brick house in Second St. to be sold by John Snowdon, living in Market St. (4 Feb.)

Plantation in Bensalem Twp., Bucks Co., where Stephen Gordon lives, bounded by lands of Stephen Williams, James Rue, Gilbert Hicks and land late of Samuel Hassell; also plantation where Thomas Stone lives, bounded by lands of William Duncan, Nicholas Vansandt, William Ridge and Henry Pointer; also a piece of land lying between lands of William, Edmund and Patrick Duncan and Nicholas Vansandt, all to be sold at Newtown, Bucks Co., by Lawrence Growdon; also to be sold by said Growdon is a tract of land in Hilltown, adjoining property of Thomas Jones Taylor; to view the same, apply to William Williams near the premises (4 Feb.)

Cows, horses and farming utensils to be sold at the plantation late of John Lassell, dec'd, near Fairhill Meeting-house, adjoining land of Isaac Norris, Esq.; attendance at the vendue will be given by Enoch Flower and Evan Morgan, execs. (4 Feb.)

Real estate in Phila., opposite to Samuel Rhodes's, bounded on E. by George Fitzwalter's ground, on S. by ground of George Davis, on N. by land of William Pyewell, to be sold at John Biddle's; household goods to be sold at house of Jonathan Lewis in Second St.; also to be sold is Jonathan Lewis's right to two lots on west side of alley leading from Chestnut St. to Joseph Howell's tanyard, bounded on S. by ground late of John Breintnall, dec'd, on W. by ground of George Emlen, on N. by ground of said Breintnall, taken in execution at suit of Peter Keene (4 Feb.)

Real estate in Germantown, bounded by lands of Adam Hitner and George Damhower, to be sold at house of the Widow Pastorius (4 Feb.)

James Cosgrave, who lately taught for Mr. Dove, has opened a school in Second St., in the house of Joseph Clark, baker (4 Feb.)

Cap, a Negro, age c. 36, country born, and a Negro woman named Rane, age c. 40, runaways from Richbell Mott, living near Dover, Kent Co. on Delaware (4 Feb.)

James Poilloin has a mare that was left at the Sign of the Blue Ball, near Marcus Hook, by one James Magee (4 Feb.)

About a fortnight ago Mr. Gullison, shipwright, at Kingston in Plymouth Co., died after falling from a stage - Boston item of 20 Jan. (11 Feb.)

Tue. last in the Mayor's Court a jury found for the plaintiff, Mrs. Frances Dupuy, a widow, in action of slander against John Perot - New York item of 3 Feb. (11 Feb.)

On 21 Jan. a sloop belonging to Norwalk, Conn., James Hoit master, was driven ashore off Guilford (11 Feb.)

Wed. last John Gains stood an hour in the pillory for assaulting and abusing a child of six years - New York item of 3 Feb. (11 Feb.)

Information from Winchester about Sir John Sinclair, Gov. Sharpe, Lt.-Col. Stephens and Gen. Braddock (11 Feb.)

Capt. David Stewart, off the west end of Hispaniola, spoke with the brigantine *Thistle*, Capt. Murray, of Phila., bound for Jamaica (11 Feb.)

Man wanted to manage plantation about 5 miles from Phila.; enquire of James Coultas at the Corporation Ferry on Schuylkill (11 Feb.)

Roger O'Dougherty, Irish servant, runaway from John Elder, who lives in Hanover Twp., Lancaster Co.; the servant stole a horse of Benjamin Wallace (11 Feb.)

The <u>Original</u> <u>Constitution</u> <u>of</u> <u>East</u> <u>and</u> <u>West</u> <u>Jersey</u> will soon be published; subscriptions will be taken in Phila. by William Bradford; in New York by Hugh Gaine; in Sussex on Delaware by Rives Holt and William Shankland; in New-Castle by George Monroe; notice inserted by Aaron Leaming and Jacob Spicer (11 Feb.)

Household goods and carpenter's shop and tools, late property of Thomas Nevel, taken in execution, will be sold at shop next to the house of Richard Murray, dec'd, in Vine St., near Bedminster (11 Feb.)

Plantation, estate of Joseph Brown, dec'd, in Plumsted Twp., Bucks Co., to be sold by Alexander Brown and Nathan Preston, execs. of the estate of said Joseph (11 Feb.)

Plantation in Falls Twp., Bucks Co., to be sold by Daniel Burgess, living on the premises (11 Feb.)

Walter Welsh, Irish servant, age $\underline{c}$. 18, runaway from Robert Jamison, living in Warwick Twp., Bucks Co. (11 Feb.)

Deborah, wife of John M'Clelland, of Phila., mariner, has run her husband into debt (11 Feb.)

Speech of Gov. Arthur Dobbs of North Carolina (18 Feb.)

Proclamation of fast by Gov. Robert Dinwiddie of Va. (18 Feb.)

Extract of letter from Wills's Creek, dated 27 Jan., mentions Sir John St. Clair and Gov. Sharpe (18 Feb.)

Mon. last James Pitcher, commissary, came to Annapolis and is now gone to Va. (18 Feb.)

New York items mention Capts. Ebbits and Morsley and Gov. Knowles (18 Feb.)

House and lot on northwest side of Jones's Alley, bounded on E. by ground of John Fordham, now in possession of George Harding's estate, and on W. by ground formerly of James Poultis, to be sold at the London Coffee-house (18 Feb.)

Two houses for sale on Society Hill; apply to Isaac Lincon (18 Feb.)

Horse has broken out of lot of Valentine Bouyers in Phila.; David Hayes will pay reward if horse is brought to Bouyers or John Hannums in Concord, Chester Co. (18 Feb.)

St. Andrew's Society will meet at Masons Lodge in Second St.; notice is signed by Thomas M'Janet, secretary (18 Feb.)

Land in Great Valley, Chester Co., part of the Welsh Tract, for sale; apply to Thomas Robinson at Naaman's Creek or to John Reily, conveyancer, in Chestnut St. (18 Feb.)

B. Hands and John Williamson, justices of the peace for Kent Co., Md., offer reward for apprehension of the following felons and robbers: Edward Price (servant to William Ringold near Chester Town), a young fellow, blacksmith, an Englishman; Thomas ... (servant to John Gleaves), miller by trade, West of England man, who broke into the store of Capt. Nathaniel Mash of Chester Town; a letter may be directed for William Ringold at the Post Office in Phila. (18 Feb.)

William Conrad, Dutch servant, age $\underline{c}$. 18, runaway from Peter Young, of Rockanixom Twp., Bucks Co. (18 Feb.)

Mills and plantation of Nathaniel Ware, Esq,, six miles above Trenton on the Delaware River in West Jersey, for sale; apply to William Clayton or William Pidgeon in Trenton (18 Feb.)

New-born male child was placed at the door of James Burnside, of Little Cot, Northampton Co., on 31 Jan.; reward will be paid by George Gray, Overseer of the Poor of Allen Twp., if the name of the mother of the child is revealed to the justices of the county (18 Feb.)

James Hamilton, Irish lad, age c. 18 or 19, is committed to the goal of Lancaster Co. (John Clark goaler); he says he belongs to Moses Rankin, master of the ship William, from Londonderry (18 Feb.)

Stone house near the Four-Lane Ends in Bucks Co. for sale; enquire of George Dunn, tavern-keeper at said Four-Lane Ends (18 Feb.)

Accounts with estate of Jonas Kealer, late of Moyamensing Twp., dec'd, or estate of Eve Kealer, dec'd, widow of said Jonas, to be settled with Henry Keppele and Adam Weaver, admins. (18 Feb.)

Plantation on Chestnut Hill, Germantown Twp., Phila. Co., to be sold or let; apply to Edward Scull, living on the premises, or Nicholas Scull in Phila. (18 Feb.)

Accounts with estate of Daniel Pastorius, late of Germantown, dec'd, to be settled with Sarah Pastorius and George Shoemaker, execs. (18 Feb.)

Land in Franconia, Phila. Co., to be sold by Sarah Pastorius and George Shoemaker, execs.; apply to them or Abraham Lucken, living on the premises (18 Feb.)

Plantation in the Northern Liberties of Phila., opposite the Rising Sun, for sale; apply to Edward Jones of the Vineyard plantation; a mare and a stallion have been taken up there; apply to Edward Jones, ranger (18 Feb.)

At Braintree, Mass., on 19 Jan., when William Wild, Jr., and his wife were at public worship, their sons, aged 8 and about 6, fell through the ice and were drowned (25 Feb.)

Wed. last Robert M'Keen, of Litchfield, N.H., tried to pass counterfeit bills in Boston, Mass.; he is now confined in goal - Boston item of 3 Feb. (25 Feb.)

New York item mentions Capts. Benjamin and Matthew Dickenson (25 Feb.)

On 7 Feb. the shop of Mr. Doalittle, clockmaker, in New Haven, was consumed by fire (25 Feb.)

On 24 Feb. Capts. Edwards, Reeve and Moncrief arrived at Phila. from Charles-Town, S.C., bringing message of Gov. James Glen to the Assembly (Henry Middleton speaker) and a resolution of the House signed by Childermas Croft (25 Feb.)

Phila. items mention Capts. Hood, Suckling and Ford and Commodore Kepple (25 Feb.)

On Mon. last Rev. George Whitefield arrived in Phila. (25 Feb.)

Meeting of contributors to the Pennsylvania Hospital called by Joshua Crosby, president (25 Feb.)

One William Horne is in custody of Joseph Inslee, sub-sheriff, in the goal of Newtown, Bucks Co., on suspicion of being a runaway (25 Feb.)

- Adv. of Joshua Howell, who has removed to the store where Edward Pennington kept, being south side of stores lately belonging to Edward Warner, dec'd, and adjoining to William Fisher's; Howell has mackrel to sell at store in Water St. where John Pole, dec'd, lately dwelt (25 Feb.)
- William Thomson, Irish servant, runaway from John Marlet, of Mansfield Twp., Sussex Co. (25 Feb.)
- Robert Philips, Irish apprentice, age c. 22, runaway from Thomas Marshall, of Phila., cooper (25 Feb.)
- Plantation in North Wales for sale; apply to John Jones, living on the premises (25 Feb.)
- Negro wench for sale by Josiah Appleton, living in Trenton (25 Feb.)
- William Spafford is removed to house in Front St. on Society Hill (25 Feb.)
- James M'Daniel and Robert Barry, Irish servants, runaways from James Martin and William Woodcock, both living near Blackbird Creek, New-Castle Co. (25 Feb.)
- Hans Boch, Dutch servant, runaway from Thomas Hall, of Concord, Chester Co. (25 Feb.)
- House in Front St., just above Pool's Bridge, to be let; enquire of Anthony Wilkinson (25 Feb.)
- Speech of Gov. Horatio Sharpe to Upper and Lower Houses of the Maryland Assembly (4 Mar.)
- Report from Halifax that Capt. Taggart lay ready for sailing (4 Mar.)
- Thu. last at Portsmouth, N.H., Eliphaz Dow was found guilty of the murder of Peter Clough of Hampton - Boston item of 10 Feb. (4 Mar.)
- Extract from a gentleman in Annapolis mentions Major Carlisle and Gen. Braddock (4 Mar.)
- Adv. of Benjamin Loxley, living near the drawbridge in Phila. (4 Mar.)
- George Jacob Crodal left sundry goods at the house of David Kinsey in Bucks Co. last Dec. (4 Mar.)
- David Franks has removed his store to the house of the late Thomas Lawrence, Esq., in Water St. (4 Mar.)
- William Moore intends to go to England next fall (4 Mar.)
- Goods and effects of Robert Cochran, who has absconded, have been attached; his creditors are to appear before John Scott in New London, Chester Co. (4 Mar.)
- Household goods will be sold at the house of Andrew Bartholomew, dec'd, in Chestnut St., by Thomas Bartholomew and Jonathan Beebe (4 Mar.)
- Adv. of George Bryan, who has removed to house in Front St. in which Mr. Conyngham lately dwelt (4 Mar.)
- Plantation on Delaware River, 2 miles from Phila., to be let by Mary Ball in Front St., Phila. (4 Mar.)
- Real estate in Whitemarsh, about 12 miles from Phila., for sale by Thomas Yorke (4 Mar.)
- Adv. of John Julius Sorge from Germany, now at John Barge's, at the Sign of the White Lamb in Market St. (4 Mar.)

1755

Lot of land in Sassafras St., bounded by land of Alexander Allair, late the estate of Jacob Groff, dec'd, for sale; apply to Jacob Groff and Blasius Daniel Mackenet (4 Mar.)

Accounts with Thomas Nevill, house-carpenter, to be settled with William Rush and William Dawson; said Dawson has a cellar to let under the house where Mr. Vidal kept school (4 Mar.)

At Slator Clay's, the Sign of the King's Head in New-Castle, a pair of silver spurs was exchanged by mistake with another pair (4 Mar.)

Address of German Protestants of Phila. Co. to Robert Hunter Morris (11 Mar.)

New York item mentions Capts. Green, Shoals, French and Fossay and Gov. Knowles (11 Mar.)

Capt. Lane from Dublin and Capt. Baker from London have arrived in York River; in one came the Rev. Samuel Davies (11 Mar.)

The *Grantham*, Capt. Miller, was lost on New Year's Day (11 Mar.)

Commodore Keppel, Capt. Barrington and Capt. Proby have arrived; Gen. Braddock, Capt. Orme and Mr. Shirley came with Capt. Barrington in the *Norwich* - Williamsburg item of 28 Feb. (11 Mar.)

Williamsburg items mention Capts. Arbuthnot, Spry and Coxen (11 Mar.)

Gov. Charles Knowles of Jamaica dissolved his Assembly on 24 Jan. (11 Mar.)

William M'Ilvaine desires to let the house where he lives in Front St., opposite to Anthony Morris, Jr. (11 Mar.)

Managers of the lottery for benefit of the college, academy and charity school in Phila. are the following: William Allen, John Inglis, William Masters, Samuel M'Call, Jr., Joseph Turner, Benjamin Franklin, Thomas Leech, William Shippen, Philip Syng, Phineas Bond, Richard Peters, Abraham Taylor, William Plumsted, Thomas Cadwallader and Alexander Stedman (11 Mar.)

Plantation where Thomas Montgomery lately lived in East Jersey, between Brunswick and Kingston, to be sold; enquire of Thomas Lawrence, John Lawrence, William Masters and wife, execs. of Thomas Lawrence, Esq., dec'd (11 Mar.)

Accounts with estate of John Lassell, late of Phila., glazier, dec'd, to be settled with the execs., Evan Morgan and Enoch Flower (11 Mar.)

Horse and saddle stolen from inclosure of Robert Lewis in Wilmington; reward if intelligence of horse is sent to Robert Lewis or to Joseph Way, innkeeper, in Phila. (11 Mar.)

House and tanyard in the Northern Liberties, bounded on N. and W. by land of Philip Halbert, late the estate of Andrew Houck, taken in execution, to be sold at the Rising Sun (11 Mar.)

Real estate in Gwined Twp., adjoining lands of Thomas Davis, John Jones, Methusalem Evans and Benjamin Davis, late estate of Thomas Wallace, taken in execution, will be sold at house of Benjamin Davis on the North Wales Road (11 Mar.)

Lots in Vine St. for sale; enquire of John Sayre in Market St., Phila., or Andrew Reed in Trenton (11 Mar.)

Accounts with estate of Stephen Onion, dec'd, late of Baltimore Co., Md., ironmaster, to be settled with Deborah Onion, exec. (11 Mar.)

Accounts with estate of John Pole, dec'd, to be settled with his execs., William Callender, Edward Cathrall and John Smith; executors will sell house and lot in Burlington, now in the tenure of John Tylee (11 Mar.)

A flat that can carry eight cords of wood is to be sold by Thomas Williams, boat-builder, in the Northern Liberties (11 Mar.)

Plantation in Haverford Twp., Chester Co., for sale by David Llewelyn (11 Mar.)

John O'Bryan, Irishman, weaver, and John Cudwell, servants, runaways from Edward Worrell and John Mecaulle, of Kent Co., Md. (11 Mar.)

Speech of Gov. Jonathan Belcher of N.J. and address of Representatives (Robert **Lawrence** speaker) to the governor (18 Mar.)

Boston items mention Capts. Hunt, Rogers and Hodges (18 Mar.)

Thu. last Lt.-Col. Mercer of Sir William Pepperell's Regt. arrived at New York - New York item of 10 Mar. (18 Mar.)

Warrant from Gov. Morris to Collector and Naval Officer of Port of Phila. (18 Mar.)

John Bell of Phila. intends for England next summer (18 Mar.)

Engraving of east prospects of Phila. taken from the Jersey shore to be sold by Nicholas Scull in Second St. (18 Mar.)

Hay for sale at plantation of William Callender, four miles from Phila. (18 Mar.)

Members of the Phila. contributionship for insuring houses from loss by fire are to meet to choose a treasurer and 12 directors; notice signed by Robert Owen, clerk (18 Mar.)

Adv. of Standley and Hughes on Lloyd's wharf (18 Mar.)

List of Joseph Scattergood's books remaining unsold at Burlington (18 Mar.)

Accounts with estate of James Parroke, dec'd, to be settled with Jeremiah Elfreth and William Callender, execs. (18 Mar.)

Partnership between Emanuel Josiah and Samuel Carpenter will expire in May (18 Mar.)

Store in Water St., between Joseph Richardson's and Joseph Sims's, fifth part of right of woodland in Blockley Twp., about 3 miles from Ashton's ferry, joining to land of James Jones, fifth part of ground rent payable to Attwood Shute, Caleb Ransted and James Koppock, all for sale by Samuel Carpenter (18 Mar.)

Patrick Gile, bricklayer, and Philip Fitzpatrick, Irish servant lads, runaways from Thomas Canby and Nicholas Wilson, both of Wilmington, New-Castle Co. (18 Mar.)

Notice of land to be granted by Gov. of Va., signed by N. Walthoe, clerk (18 Mar.)

Jack, generally known as John Powell, a young Mulatto slave, a cooper by trade, runaway from Mordecai Moore in New-Town, Chester Co. (18 Mar.)

Robin, a Negro, age $\underline{c}$. 19, runaway from John Price in Chichester Twp., Chester Co. (18 Mar.)

Speech of Gov. John Reynolds of Georgia to Council and House and their addresses in reply; Patrick Graham signs for the Council and David Douglas for the House (25 Mar.)

1755

Address of Upper House (B. Tasker president) and of Lower House (H. Hooper speaker) to Gov. Horatio Sharpe of Md. and reply of the governor (25 Mar.)

On 5 Mar. the Gov. of Va. received a letter from Sir John St. Clair at Alexandria (25 Mar.)

Capts. William Tipple, Crookshanks, Rawlings, Curling, Nevin, Terry, Wright, Burton, Judd, Brown, Boynton, Hall, Johnson, Miller and Montgomery have arrived at Va. (25 Mar.)

Last Mon. in a storm Capt. Hatch was forced on the rocks near Cohassee - Boston item of 10 Mar. (25 Mar.)

New York items mention Capts. Bennet, Leacraft, Edward Gay, Broadhurst, Miller, Nicholls, Fry, Pierce, Ingraham, Smith, Thompson, Ford, Brown, Dolliver, Chievers, Carr, Green, Wadham, Hopkins, Newton, Roads, Stoddard, Leavens, Elliot, Vardil, Lassells and Tucker (25 Mar.)

Phila. items mention Capts. Fortin, Moore, Negus and Sir William Pepperill (25 Mar.)

Brick house and lot in Phila., bounded on E. by ground late of Jane Harding, on S. by ground of Samuel Powell, on W. by ground of John Newman and Edward Nicholas, dec'd, late the estate of Andrew Bartholomew, dec'd, taken in execution, to be sold at house of John Biddle (25 Mar.)

House and lot in Phila., bounded on N. by ground of William Rakestraw and on S. by ground of Samuel Abbot and Jervis Byewater, late the estate of Ulrick Sharer, taken in execution, to be sold at house of John Biddle (25 Mar.)

Lot of ground in Phila., bounded on E. by property of Francis Knowles, on S. by ground of Henry Badcock and on W. by land of Samuel Rhodes, late the estate of William Knight, dec'd, taken in execution, to be sold at house of John Biddle (25 Mar.)

Third part of tract in Phila., bounded on S. by ground of John Jackson, dec'd, and on N. by ground of Mary Gordon, late the estate of Lambert Emmerson, taken in execution, to be sold at house of John Biddle (25 Mar.)

All of the right of Erasmus Stephens (the reversion of the premises upon decease of William Branson) to brick building and lot in Phila., bounded on S. by ground of William Branson and on N. by ground of Wilcox Philips, late the estate of Erasmus Stephens, dec'd, to be sold at John Biddle's (25 Mar.)

Various goods and chattels to be sold by Daniel Stewart at his plantation in Oxford Twp. (25 Mar.)

Plantation in Mill-Creek Hundred, New-Castle Co., to be sold by William Geddes, living on the premises (25 Mar.)

William Dawson will open an evening school in Phila. for young ladies (25 Mar.)

Plantation in Middletown, Bucks Co., for sale; apply to Robert Heaton, of Byberry Twp., Phila. Co., or William Ashburn, of Newtown, near the premises, being the estate of Thomas Nelson, late of Middletown, dec'd (25 Mar.)

Plantation in Germantown, near De Wees's mill, to be sold by Benjamin Howell on the premises (25 Mar.)

Ferry at Schuylkill, now in tenure of James Coultas, to be let; apply to Mayor William Plumsted (25 Mar.)

1755

Land in Radnor, the premises adjoining the public road which leads from Conestogoe by Humphreys's mill to Phila., to be sold by Ann Miller at her house in Haverford (25 Mar.)

Robert Rouze, Irish servant, age 21, runaway from Roger Hiffernan, chocolate grinder, living in Front St., Phila. (25 Mar.)

John Ross, age c. 19 or 20, tailor, who says he came in with Capt. M'Carty from Dublin to New-Castle almost 5 years ago in vessel consigned to Mr. Wakely in Phila., is now in the goal of Lancaster Co. (John Clark goaler) on suspicion of being a runaway servant (25 Mar.)

James Francis, age c. 26, indented English servant, who speaks West Country dialect, and Toby, a Mulatto slave, age c. 26, runaways from James Ringgold of Eastern Neck in Kent Co., Md. (25 Mar.)

House and lot in High St., Burlington, for sale; apply to Daniel Bacon, living on the premises, or Hugh Hartshorne and Daniel Smith, Jr., of said city (25 Mar.)

Plantation in Merion Twp., Phila. Co., about a mile from John Roberts's mill, to be sold by Richard Lloyd, living in Darby, Chester Co. (25 Mar.)

Thu. last the snow *Thetis*, Capt. Jay, from St. Kitts, arrived at Charles-Town, S.C.; five of the crew had seized the ship but they were eventually overpowered and killed - Charles-Town item of 20 Mar. (3 Apr.)

Rev. Whitefield will embark soon at Charles-Town for England in the *Friendship*, Capt. Ball (3 Apr.)

Two snows, masters' names Montgomery, that sailed from Boston, were overtaken by a storm; Capt. Robert Montgomery, whose snow was wrecked on the back of Cape Cod, got ashore with his crew (3 Apr.)

A sloop, John M'Fadden master, was driven ashore at Cape Cod; the captain, crew and five passengers were found frozen to death 1½ miles from the vessel (3 Apr.)

Capt. James Nickles has arrived safely at Boston from Halifax (3 Apr.)

A small schooner, bound from Marblehead to Ispwich, was cast away on 9 Mar.; two passengers, John Rogers and John Boardman, were frozen to death (3 Apr.)

New York items mention Capts. Proby, Drumgold, Lewis, Harris, Brasher, Scot Lawrence, R. Thomas, Hill, Wright, Emott, Heysham, Albouy, Tudor, Donaldson, Jones, Byvank, Masterson, Strange, Burger and Fry (3 Apr.)

House of David Smith, Jr., of Goshen, Orange Co., N.Y., in Feb. was burnt to the ground, with two of his small children inside (3 Apr.)

Wife of Thomas Stubs, of Goshen, having lately turned Separatist, cut her throat and died immediately - New York item of 24 Mar. (3 Apr.)

Tue. last the shop of Mrs. Alexander in New York was broken open and robbed of some 200 pounds in gold, silver and paper money - New York item of 24 Mar. (3 Apr.)

Phila. items mention Capts. Troy, Lyon and Mesnard (3 Apr.)

Store of Dennis Whalen in Nantmill Twp., Chester Co., was broken open and robbed (3 Apr.)

Adv. of Thomas Riche, whose store is in Water St., where Thomas Clifford lately lived (3 Apr.)

Thomas Campbell has opened a bleaching-green about one mile from Phila., where work will be done by David Kidd (3 Apr.)

Real estate in Fourth St., bounded on S. by ground of Ulrick Sipple and on N. by ground of Thomas Coates, late the estate of Patrick Bard, taken in execution, to be sold at the house of John Biddle (3 Apr.)

Plantation in Merion Twp., conveyed to Michael Wills by Joseph Tucker, late the estate of Hugh Jones, taken in execution at suit of Joseph Tucker, to be sold at the premises, near to John Roberts's mill (3 Apr.)

Yearly rent issuing out of bank and water lot in Wicacoa, bounded on N. by ground of Joseph Knowles; also another lot in Wicacoa, bounded on N. by ground of John Parham, late the estate of Anthony Duche, taken in execution, to be sold at house of John Biddle (3 Apr.)

Stephen Hall, a New Englandman, and Thomas Dunning, Englishman, age c. 20, a schoolmaster, broke out of goal of Newtown, Bucks Co. (Joseph Insle goaler); reward will be paid by Insle or William Yeardley, sheriff (3 Apr,)

Real estate in New-Britain Twp., adjoining land of Simon Matthews, land late of George Fitzwater, dec'd, near land of Keltoe and Griffith Owens, late of Lewis Roberts and John Davis, being late the property of Mary Little, taken in execution at suit of John Frazer, to be sold (3 Apr.)

House and lot in Middletown Twp., near the house of George Dunn, bounded by land of Jesinah Vansant, Jeremiah Langhorn, dec'd, John Vansant and land la.ely of Charles Plumley, dec'd, late the property of James Vansant, taken in execution, will be sold at house of George Dunn, at the Four Lane Ends (3 Apr.)

Keeper of the workhouse of Chester Co. is lately dec'd; person desiring said position is to apply to John Mather or to Thomas Morgan, Esquires, at Chester (3 Apr.)

Accounts with estate of Thomas Lacey, baker, dec'd, to be settled with Benjamin Britton, exec. (3 Apr.)

Land in West-town, Chester Co., between lands of Joseph Hunt and John Haynes, for sale; enquire of John Taylor, Esq., near said land, or of Joseph Parker, Esq., in Chester (3 Apr.)

John Row, who hired a mare of Joseph Hough, of the Falls Twp., Bucks Co., never returned (3 Apr.)

House, with a malt- and brew-house, to be sold or let at Spring Garden by Richard Jerrard (3 Apr.)

Real estate in Second St., Phila., adjoining land of Richard Dickenson, Frederick Becker and Israel Pemberton, to be sold by Christopher Brean, living opposite the Sign of the Ship on Frankford Road (3 Apr.)

Thomas Mason, Irish servant, age c. 23, who knows something of the shoemaker's trade, runaway from William Runshey, of Salisbury Twp., Lancaster Co. (3 Apr.)

Accounts with estate of Patrick Orr, dec'd, late of Leacock Twp., Lancaster Co., storekeeper, to be settled with James Caldwell, admin., at John Huston's in Pequea; Daniel Orr, blacksmith, formerly of Chester Co., is desired to apply to said Caldwell (3 Apr.)

1755

Letter signed by Thomas Clarke, William Ogilvie, Simeon Soumain, Richard Miller, William Spearing and Alexander Colhoun, dated at Fort Cumberland, Wills's Creek, 12 Mar. 1755, mentions Capt. Clarke, James De Lancey, Mr. Spearing, Capt. Digges, Capt. Rutherford, Gov. Dinwiddie, Archibald Kennedy, Jr., Col. Hunter, Col. Washington, Capt. Maccoy, Dr. Colhoun, Mr. Carlisle, Lt. Ogilvie and Col. Innes (10 Apr.)

On 26 Mar. Capt. Clinton arrived at New London from St. Martins (10 Apr.)

New York items mention Capts. Heysham and Augustine Lawrence and General Pepperell (10 Apr.)

Tue. evening Govs. William Shirley and James De Lancey arrived in Phila. and the next day they left with Gov. Morris for Annapolis (10 Apr.)

Capts. Dowers, Arthur and Bowes have arrived at Phila. (10 Apr.)

Tract of land in Passyunk Twp., late of Israel Cox, and other real estate to be sold by Benjamin Mifflin, near the drawbridge (10 Apr.)

Three Dutch servants, Leonard Yanawine, a wheelwright, Christian Fistmire, age c. 23, and Andrew Golden, age c. 20, runaways from Benjamin Flower and Benjamin Bartholomew, living at Reading Furnace, Chester Co. (10 Apr.)

Tract of land in Quohocken Twp., West N.J., bounded by land of Robert Strettell and Biles, for sale; enquire of John Rickey in Trenton or Moses Coates, Jr., in Charlestown, Chester Co. (10 Apr.)

Accounts with estate of Mary Webb, dec'd, to be settled with Nathaniel Allen, Sr., admin.; her furniture will be sold at her house in Second St., opposite to Mary Lisle's (10 Apr.)

Lydia Waterman, age c. 20, this country born, mantle-maker, who says she has a step-father named Thomas Horner in Byberry Twp.; she learned her trade in Phila. with one Augustine Sti(l)man; she was committed to goal of Lancaster Co. (John Clark goaler) on suspicion of being a runaway servant (10 Apr.)

Horse strayed or stolen from John Preston, living in Vine St., Phila. (10 Apr.)

Plantation in Union Twp., Berks Co., for sale by John Godfrey, living on the premises (10 Apr.)

Adv. of Edward Broadfield, removed from Bordentown to Trenton (10 Apr.)

Selling of whisky to troops is forbidden by Capt. John Rutherford, Commandant at Fort Cumberland; no liquor to be sold there except by two persons, one to be appointed by Capt. Demene and one by Capt. Peyrenie, at rate of one gill a day to each man (10 Apr.)

The following deserted from the company of Capt. John Rutherford: William Marshall, born in Pa., age 23, and William Moore, an Englishman, age c. 22; John Brodie, a Scotchman, deserted from Capt. William Peyronie's company of Va. (10 Apr.)

Fulling mill and land in Darby, Chester Co., late property of David David, taken in execution at suit of Samuel Bunting and Isaac Peatson, to be sold by Joshua Thomson, coroner (10 Apr.)

Plantation in Whiteland Twp., Chester Co., and other real estate to be sold by John Hambrecht (10 Apr.)

Real estate near William Allen's summer seat in Germantown Twp. for sale; also for sale is tract of land in Cresham in Germantown Twp., bounded by land belonging to Peter Rittenhausen, to be sold; apply to Conrad Weittner, living near Mr. Allen's (10 Apr.)

John Lownes, master of the brigantine Cumberland, has two lots of ground to let, lying on Moyamensing Road, lately rented by John Biddle; enquire of John Lownes in Third St., Phila. (10 Apr.)

Daniel Carty, apprentice, age c. 21, born in Manor of Moreland, Phila. Co., runaway from Benjamin Corson, of Northampton, Bucks Co. (10 Apr.)

Real estate in Twp. of Cumrie and Heidelberg, Berks Co., late property of Hans Zimmerman, taken in execution, to be sold (10 Apr.)

Lot of ground in town of Reading, late property of Leonard Ruport, taken in execution, to be sold (10 Apr.)

Jacob Bernhard, who speaks French better than Dutch, and Christina Bernhard, age 20, runaway servants of Michael Bens, who lives in Earl Twp., Lancaster Co. (10 Apr.)

Lot and tenement on the Bank, where John Dennis, barber, lives, for sale by Samuel Rhodes, carpenter, in Phila. (10 Apr.)

Plantation in Middletown, Bucks Co., for sale; apply to Robert Heaton, of Byberry Twp., Phila. Co., or William Ashburn, of Newtown, being the estate of Thomas Nelson, late of Middletown, dec'd; Heaton and Ashburn are execs. of Nelson's estate (10 Apr.)

William Anderson of Whitemarsh has taken up a mare (10 Apr.)

John Levetru, Dutch servant, and his wife Mary, runaways from Robert Andrews, living in Strasbourgh Twp., Lancaster Co. (10 Apr.)

Goods and chattels of James M'Cullough, late of Chester Twp., Chester Co., dec'd, to be sold by William Evans and Martha his wife (administratrix) by order of the Orphan's Court, of which Henry Hale Graham is clerk (10 Apr.)

Lot of ground in Wicacoa, bounded on S. by land of James Reynolds, and other ground belonging to the estate of Andrew Hannis, to be sold; also another lot, bounded on the E. by land of James Reynolds and on S. by ground belonging to Peter David and wife; said lots to be sold by Joseph Trotter, Isaac Zane and Joseph Stretch, execs. of Andrew Hannis (10 Apr.)

ABBOT, John 278; Samuel 331
ABERCROMBIE, - Capt. 146, 147, 195, 251, 252, 308, 310, 324; James, 63
ABRAHAM, Isaac 88
ACTON, William 180
ADAIR, Edward 157; James 192, 194
ADAMS, - Capt. 57, 168, 205, 206, 282, 294, 296, 300; Daniel 67; George 3, 15, 45, 136, 157, 158, 247; James 9, 63, 179, 280; John 59; Matthias 304; Robert 104; Thomas 262; William 162, 175, 180, 224, 245
ADAMSON, - Capt. 3; John 183
ADCOCK, - Mr. 279
ADDISON, - 320
ADLIN, John 255
ADLUM/AUDLUM, John 199, 309, 317
AGEE, Michael 250
AGEMAN, Thomas 216; William 216
AGENDER, Johannes 231
AIKEN, David 207
AIKING, - Capt. 21
AINSDEL, - Capt. 279
AITKINS, - Capt. 14
ALBEE, Obadiah 295
ALBERTSON, Gilbert 53; Hannah 303; Jacob 303; Jane 53; William 72, 84, 303
ALBIN/ALBINE/ABLINE, - Capt. 2, 9; James 122
ALBUOY/ALBOUY, - Capt. 212, 218, 233, 234, 257, 276, 332
ALBURTIS, Benjamin 121
ALEXANDER, - Capt. 221, 282; Mrs. 332; Alexander 90, 120, 174, 233, 237; Arthur 300; Daniel 267; David 245; Ebenezer 176; James 159, 262, 305; Jedediah 13; John 20; Theophilus 313
ALFORD, - Col. 208; Thomas 246
ALFREE, Paul 4
ALGERUS, Lawrence 120
ALINSON, - Capt. 261
ALL, William 118
ALLAIRE/ALLAIR, Alexander 65, 77, 91, 124, 152, 319, 329; Hennretta 124
ALLBRECHT, George 177, 179
ALLEE, Abraham 31, 103; Jacob 16
ALLEN/ALLAN, - and Strettell 83; and Turner, 50, 97, 191, 206, 251, 306; - 183; Capt. 21, 117, 225, 236, 287, 294, 320; Mr. 10, 58, 74, 111; Aaron 57, 78; Abigail 261; Charles 118; David 178; George 202; Henry 260; James 7, 281; Jeremiah 7; John 6, 11, 93, 96, 119, 133, 134, 138, 191, 226, 255; John, Jr. 226; Joseph 297; Morial 291; Nathan 62; Nathaniel 10, 26, 42, 97, 146, 173, 217; Nathaniel, Jr. 12, 232, 281, 288; Nathaniel, Sr. 334; Nehemiah 28, 49; Patrick 173; Richard 47, 85, 105; Robert 168, 277; Samuel 97; Sarah 62; Susanna 7; William 1, 18, 27, 42, 45, 46, 56, 77, 79, 83, 101, 106, 125, 130, 146, 187, 195, 208, 210, 228, 281, 284, 286, 290, 307, 324, 329, 335
ALLEY, Thomas 128
ALLISON/ALISON, - Capt. 71, 212, 236, 265, 266, 271, 318; Francis 181, 249, 264; James 30, 33, 230; John 102, 153; Joseph 205; Patrick 33; Robert 8, 56, 247; Samuel 202, 262; William 13, 38, 150, 153
ALLMOND, John 11
ALRICHS/ALLRICHS/ALLRICKS, Hermanus 103, 272, 275; Peter 53; Peter Sigfridus 131; Samuel 4
AMBLER, - Capt. 18
AMBRUST, Matthias 190
AMES, - Capt. 194
AMMIT, - Capt. 318
AMORY, - Capt. 2, 4, 21, 148, 154, 157, 202, 204, 318
AMY, - Capt. 227
ANCTS, Henry 66
ANDERSON, - Capt. 42, 56, 61, 156, 296; Mr. 171; Archibald 2, 194; Enoch 21; Hezekiah 113; James 13, 107, 242, 280; John 39, 185, 238, 298; Katherine 22; Lawrence 132; Randell 8; Robert 2; Samuel 13, 20; William 66, 151, 290, 335
ANDREWS/ANDREW, - Mrs. 74, 77; John 75; Mary 34, 70, 92, 103, 157, 161, 259; Robert 335; Thomas 280
ANGIER, - Capt. 250
ANKS, Henry 40
ANNIS, Thomas 305; William 61, 198, 242
ANSLOW, Thomas 121
ANTES, Fredrick 44
ANTHONY, - Capt. 26; Stephen 60
ANTIG, William 163
ANTIL, - Mr. 186
ANTRAM, John 27
APPLETON, - Capt. 141; Josiah 328; Samuel 137
APPLEWHAITE, Thomas 56
APPOWIN/APPOWEN/APPOWIZ, - Capt. 113, 194, 299, 323; Samuel 323
ARBUCKLE, - Capt. 213; James 32
ARBUTHNOT/ARBUTHNOTT, - Capt. 80, 81, 312, 329; Lt. 131
ARCHDALL, Reily and 81; Thomas 62, 141, 155
ARCHDEKEN, William 213
ARCHER, - Capt. 259; Adam 165; Thomas 247
ARENTS, Johannes 237
ARIS, John 138
ARMBRUSTER, Anthony 201, 222; George 32; Godhart 4
ARMITAGE, Benjamin 101, 261
ARMITT, John 41, 112, 225, 317; Stephen 133, 137
ARMOR, Thomas 249, 264
ARMSTRONG, - Capt. 139; Col. 20; Abel 9, 48; Alexander 9, 13; Archibald 13; James 13; John 63, 199, 255; Joseph 103, 199, 255, 309; Robert 248; Thomas 9, 251; William 7, 11, 31, 61, 102, 150, 197, 253, 277, 309
ARNETT, David 188
ARNEY, Joseph 244
ARNOLD, - Capt. 15, 26, 206, 271, 316; Catherine 297; George 297; John George 152; Valentine 182
ARNOT/ARNOTT, - Capt. 28, 59, 147, 194, 249, 251, 252, 274, 286; Jonathan 272
ARROWSMITH, - Capt. 27, 77
ARTHUR, - Capt. 24, 58, 102, 254, 257, 275, 290, 304, 312, 317, 318, 334; Joseph 35, 207; Robert 25; Thomas 115
ARTIS, Tarver 23
ASH/ASHE, - Capt. 170, 314; Mr. 290; Henry 75, 108; William 320
ASHBRIDGE, George 30, 61, 102, 149, 172, 189, 197, 253, 308; Joseph 68, 197, 253, 308
ASHBURN, William 260, 331, 335
ASHECRAFT, Margaret 306
ASHFIELD, Lewis 134
ASHFORD, John 84
ASHLEY, - Mrs. 154; Mr. 154
ASHMAN, Abraham 154, 240

ASHMEAD, John 289; Samuel 52, 289
ASHTON/ASHETON, - 19, 82, 145, 208, 263, 266, 330; Benjamin 156; George 2; Isaac 5, 70, 198, 315; John 33, 103, 131, 148, 154, 170, 270, 210; Joseph 319; Peter 78, 205; Ralph 59, 82; Susanna 59; Thomas 288; William 263
ASHWELL, John 128
ASKEW, - Capt. 29; Thomas 185
ASKINS/ASKIN, - Capt. 76, 312; Vincent 19
ASLEMAN, Jacob 37
ASPAY, John 71; Thomas 71
ASPDEN, Matthias 42
ASPINWALL, John 149
ASTINS, George 221
ASTON, - Capt. 257; George 7, 87, 96, 103, 245; Nicholas 106; Peter 125, 128; Samuel 68, 101
ATEN, Derrick 299
ATKINS, Anne 246; John 33, 163, 165, 169, 177, 183; John Jr. 13; John Sr. 13
ATKINSON, - Capt. 314; Mr. 195, 251; John 159; Matthew 101; Samuel 126; William 43
ATTMORE, William 86, 291
ATWOOD/ATTWOOD, - 147, 208; Capt. 129, 287; William 96, 108, 203, 232, 291, 310
AUBERY, Thomas (alias of Thomas Smith) 217
AUBLE, Matthias 322
AUCHMUTY, Robert 81
AUSTIL, - Capt. 13
AUSTIN/AUSTEN, - Mr. 43; John 1; Nicholas 29; Robert 158; Samuel 22, 146, 221, 310
AVERELL, - 279
AWL, - Capt. 298; Robert 2
AX, John Frederick 7, 9
AXTELL, William 268
AYR, James 304
AYRES/AYERS/AYRS, Edmund (alias Grievous) 65; John 148; Obadiah 89, 139, 184
AYSCOUGH, John 187

BABB, - Capt. 205; John 204
BABCOCK, Joshua 120
BACCHUS, John 129
BACHMAN, Daniel 256; Jacob 254
BACHOP, - Capt. 198, 307
BACLOW, - Capt. 77
BACON, - 147; Daniel 332; John 308

BADCOCK, Henry 217, 331
BADLEY/BADDLEY/BADDELY, - Capt. 195, 301; John 204
BADGER, - Capt. 75, 130, 178, 218, 235, 240, 285, 295, 298
BAGNALL, Benjamin 53, 115, 146, 153, 210, 237; Benjamin, Jr. 95
BAILEY/BALEY/BAILY/BALE/BAYLEY/BAYLY/BEALEY, - Capt. 144, 279; Mr. 85; Daniel 157, 170, 199; Edward 252; Elizabeth 157, 170; George 42, 82; John 3, 14, 172, 195, 275, 303, 314; Jonas 294; Joseph 77
BAIRD, Alexander 281; Evan 12; Patrick 23, 115, 122, 134
BAISER, John 77
BAKER, - Capt. 76, 205, 266, 329; Justice 89; Bartholomew 187; George 80; Henry 87, 179, 318; Jacob 41; John 28, 51, 55, 60, 65, 129, 137, 156, 208; Joseph 273, 320; Mary 122, 185; Michael 77; Nathan 113; Nehemiah 140; Robert 13, 300; Witherdon 272
BALDWIN, James 6, 212; John 22
BALETZ, Lawrence 241
BALL, - Capt. 219, 261, 290, 301; Widow 51; Andrew 20; Edward 191; Mary 6, 9, 161, 313, 328; Peter 209, 213; William/Wm. 180, 185, 295, 306, 313, 321
BALLENDINE, James 62
BALLET, - Capt. 20, 31, 57
BALLINGER, Henry 181
BALTIMORE, Lord 151, 274
BAMBER, William 153
BAMBRIDGE, James 59
BANDY, Andrew 9; Richard 9
BANE, - Capt. 294, 312
BANES, John 89
BANKS, William 27
BANKSON, Andrew 223
BANNISTER, John 133
BANTON, John 288; Peter 112
BANYAR, G. 262
BARBER, James 5
BARCLAY, Alexander 161, 202, 267; James 54; John 53; William 135
BARD, - 136; Mr. 174; Bennet 92, 229; Dinah 15; Patrick 333; Peter 7, 15, 37, 52, 58, 61, 69, 75, 107, 128, 149, 156, 157, 159, 176, 180, 192, 196, 207, 220, 222, 228, 310

BARGE, John 3, 20, 76, 241, 269, 302, 319, 328; William 136
BARICRAFT, John 168
BARKLEY, Elizabeth 4; John 4, 13
BARLOW/BARLO, Henry 234; Thomas 165
BARNEBY, John 217
BARNES/BARNS, - Capt. 47, 200, 209, 212, 216, 220, 235; Abraham 289; Barnaby 261; James 222; Joseph 109; Margaret (alias hopping Peg) 1; Robert 164, 313; Samuel 140, 186, 237; Theophilus 201
BARNET, Jacob 156; William 14
BARNHILL, Robert 224
BARNSLEY, - Capt. 91
BARR, Zachariah 194
BARRETT/BARRET, John 263, 266; Richard 193
BARRINGTON, - Capt. 255, 329
BARROW, Thomas 286
BARRY, John 253; Richard 187, 316; Robert 328; William 171
BARSTOW, - Capt. 264
BARTEL, French 255
BARTELO, - Capt. 81
BARTHOLOMEW, Andrew 25, 126, 156, 310, 328, 331; Benjamin 334; John 120; Joseph 31, 61; Thomas 138, 142, 151, 220, 226, 304, 310, 328
BARTLET/BARTLETT, - Capt. 303; John 144
BARTOLETT, John 154
BARTON, Benjamin 220, 246, 309; Thomas 16, 53; Woolsey 31
BARTOW, Thomas 114
BARTRAM, John 135
BARWICK, Edward 83, 135; Thomas 264
BASCOME/BASCUM, George 45, 63; Robert 47
BASKELL, William 13
BASS, - Rev. 318
BASSET, Martha (alias Catcham) 164
BAST, Lawrence 104
BASTLER, Henry 211, 247
BASTWICK, Ephraim 273
BATE, Henry 109
BATES, - Capt. 313; Daniel 136; Henry 207, 244
BATHO, Charles 25, 86, 96, 116
BATSON, Thomas 288
BATTAGEN, - Capt. 144
BATTEN, Francis 248
BATTER, - Mr. 101; John 198
BATTLE/BATTELT, French 199, 309
BATTY, - Capt. 259

337

BAUGHMAN/BAUMAN, Jacob 309; Michael 116; Titer 145
BAXTER, - Mr. 113, 198; James 303
BAYARD, Peter 123
BAYER, Valentine 77
BAYERLEY, Jacob 68
BAYNE, - Capt. 212, 236, 255
BAYNTON, John 22, 60, 65, 144, 183, 192, 203, 213, 222; Mary 22; Peter 22, 60, 65
BEACH, Edmund 122
BEADY, John 73
BEAKER, Peter 273
BEAKS, Joseph 227; Nathan 42
BEAL, Benjamin 27
BEALER, - 257
BEALS, John 43, 166, 215
BEAR/BEARE, John 80; Thomas 211
BEARD, Archibald 188
BEARDSLEY, Alexander 217
BEARS, Andrew 211
BEASLEY/BEEZLEY, - Widow 200; Hannah 237
BEATH, - 59
BEATY/BEATEY, Charles 248; Hugh 245; William 290
BEAUCHAR, - Capt. 180
BEAUMONT, John 119
BEEBE/BEBEE, Jonathan 310, 328
BECKER, Frederick 333
BECKET, - Capt. 110
BECKFORD, Richard 178
BECOP, - Capt. 252
BECKTEL, John 17
BEDDOME, Joseph 38, 88, 137
BEDFORD, - Capt. 231; Mrs. 292
BEDLOW, - Capt. 171, 315
BEEKMAN, Charles 153; Daniel 296
BEELER, Joseph 62
BEERS, Jonathan 59
BEESON, John 217, 220
BEHM, John 55
BEKERS, Frederick 93
BELCHER, - Gov. 112, 286, 306, 312; Alexander 169; Gov. J. 310; Jonathan 74, 78, 120, 284, 286, 301, 313, 330
BELDEN, John 16
BELDING, Aaron 25
BELFORD, James 177
BELL, - and Lawrence 284; Capt. 55; Mr. 72, Widow 97; George 167; James 202; John 44, 54, 87, 101, 125, 143, 149, 153, 174, 256, 261, 306, 330; Joseph 208, 239, 301; Tom 59, 191, 197, 198; William 7, 50, 63, 77, 108, 162, 173, 258, 259, 265, 278

BELLAMY, - Capt. 230
BELLEC, Peter 81
BELLY, Mary 198
BELSTON, - Capt. 250
BEMANT, - Capt. 250
BENEZET/BENEZETT, - Mr. 179; Anthony 149, 227; Daniel 8, 27, 87, 94, 186, 281, 284; James 27, 30, 49, 52, 69, 78, 95, 180, 196, 236, 273; Philip 36, 127; Stephen 219, 221
BENGER, Elliott 132
BENJAMIN, - Capt. 298, 327
BENNET/BENNETT, - Capt. 13, 20, 23, 123, 162, 198, 218, 255, 287, 300, 308, 310, 331; Mr. 126; Abraham 239; Abraham, Jr. 239; George 4; Jacob 62, 323; James 97, 122; Jane 162, 175; John 309; Dr. Parker 119, 120; Richard 64, 68; Thomas 4, 67; William 20
BENNING, William 86, 181
BENS, Michael, 335
BENSON, - Capt. 279; Benjamin 54
BENTLEY, George 9; Thomas 22
BENZEL, Adolph 272
BERESFORD, - Mr. 204, 205
BERGEAU, Abraham 45
BERNARD, - 274
BERNHARD, Christina 335; Jacob 335
BERRIAN, John 21, 41, 134
BERRY, Charles 177; James 313, 321; John 158, 164, 167
BERWICK, Thomas 270
BEST, - Capt. 285; John 210
BESTOCK, - Capt. 183
BETAUGH/BETAGH, - Capt. 172, 197, 261, 279, 303
BETHELL, James 270
BETTIE, Christopher 285
BETTS, - Capt. 300
BEVAN, - Mr. 110; Aubrey/ Aubry 62, 71, 140, 149; David 313; George 320; John 106; Richard 47, 138; Thomas 142, 148
BEVANSEY, - Capt. 297
BEVERLIN, Robert 307
BEVERS, Sarah 122, 126
BEVERTON, Samuel 312
BEWLEY, Nathan 180
BEYERLE, Jacob 248, 281
BIBBING, Thomas 125
BIBLER, Francis 314; Michael 314
BICKER, Martin 19
BICKHAM, James 316; Martin 22, 115; Sarah 115; Thomas 273

BICKLEY, Abraham 310; Mary 116
BIDDLE/BITTLE, - Forbes and 173, 298; Mr. 219, 286; Widdow 277; John 23, 44, 47, 49, 69, 79, 88, 118, 123, 133, 138, 155, 158, 161, 163, 171, 176, 187, 188, 214, 219, 228, 229, 230, 237, 239, 241, 257, 258, 259, 260, 265, 267, 269, 272, 273, 280, 283, 291, 295, 296, 299, 300, 308, 309, 310, 313, 321, 325, 331, 333, 335; Joseph 18, 58; William 100, 111, 176, 202, 205, 215, 233, 263, 267, 298
BIGGER/BIGGAR, Michael 8; Peacock 202, 209, 212
BIGLEY, James 12
BILES; see also BYLES, - 334; Benjamin 82, 94, 108, 191; Elizabeth 50, 61, 157; Jonathan 317; Langhorne 5, 257; Thomas 215; William 234, 269
BILL, - Capt. 24, 25, 72, 76; Benajah 114; James (alias of James Bradford) 141
BIMPSON, Henry 196
BINGHAM, - Widow 259; James 56; William 268, 270
BIRD/BURD, - 320; Mr. 114, 129; James 10, 14, 27, 47, 48, 104, 142, 148, 152, 153, 161; William 97, 137, 146, 257
BIRK, John 128
BIRNEY, William 209
BISHOP, Henry 121, 146; Hester 119; John 277; Robert 111; William 208
BISPHAM/BISPHAN, Benjamin 296; Joshua 147, 296
BISSELL, John 258, 314
BLACK, - two brothers 185; Mr. 244; Hance 181; John 124, 264, 275; Moses 255; Robert 38; Thomas 286; William 216
BLACKBURN, - Col. 176
BLACKFORD, Richard 166
BLACKHAM, Richard 35, 129
BLACKLIDGE, Benjamin 224
BLACKSHIRE, Robert 14
BLACKSTONE, - Mr. 29; William 31
BLACKWELL, Jacob 40; Thomas 36
BLACKWOOD, John 229, 288

BLAIR, - Capt. 68, 80, 113, 245, 247, 250, 297, 305; Alexander 200; Arthur 150; David 103; Francis 304; James 85, 149, 153, 156, 262; Margaret 302; Patrick 302; Thomas 16, 161, 302; William 32, 39, 57, 93, 100, 103, 203, 305
BLAKE, - Capt. 18, 249, 260, 276; William 200
BLAKELEY/BLEAKLEY/ BLEAKLY, - 202; John 11, 65, 69, 76, 91, 160, 246, 294
BLAKENEY, - Gen. 6
BLAKER, John 184
BLAKISTON, William 103
BLANCHARD, - Capt. 221
BLANCHER, Samuel 242, 250
BLANCHFIELD, John 300
BLAND, - Gen. 6; Mr. 307
BLANY, Benjamin 117; William 276
BLILER, John 92
BLISS, Samuel 55
BLIVAN, - Capt. 66
BLOWS, William 46, 60
BLUE, Uriah 121
BLUMFFIELD, William 128
BLUNT, - Capt. 294
BOAH, John 128
BOAKE, Abel 320
BOARD, John 11
BOARDMAN, John 332
BOAT, William 22
BOATAM, - Capt. 266
BOCH, Hans 328
BOCKEE, Anne 271
BODINE, John 36
BOGART, - Capt. 189, 212, 240, 290, 323; Cornelius 188; Jacob 9
BOGDEN, William 69
BOGGS, - Capt. 129, 235; Ezekiel 35; Samuel 132, 182; William 206
BOGLE, - Capt. 19
BOHAM, John 211
BOLITHO, - Capt. 262, 277, 324
BOLLAN/BOLLEN, - Agent 255; William 53, 56, 60
BOLTON, Isaac 159
BOND, - Capt. 214; Dr. 101; Doctors 297; Mr. 312; Elijah 11, 72, 102, 119, 134, 140, 172, 255; Elisha 115; John 5; Phineas 34, 48, 307, 329; Thomas 34, 91, 94, 99, 135, 158, 228, 288
BONDLEY, Matthias 172
BONNER, Reuben 9
BONNIN, - Mr. 47
BONSALL, Abraham 172; James 243, 247, 296; Obadiah 34
BOOD/BOUDE/BOUD, - Widow 70; Gertrude 18;

John 18, 47, 70, 78, 85, 91, 152, 161, 185, 216; Thomas 223, 295, 304, 308, 310
BOOKINS, Henry 24
BOOKMAN, Samuel 45
BOONE/BOON, - 72, 83; George 50, 267; Jeremiah 267; Josiah 267; Swan 50, 284; William 197, 253, 267, 309
BOORE/BOOR, Andrew 105; Joseph 105, 120
BOOTHBY, - Capt. 286
BOOTMAN, George 71; Mary 71
BORADILL, Arthur 17
BORDEN, Joseph 210; Joseph, Jr. 11, 101, 122, 134, 227, 287, 303
BORDLEY, Beale 231; John 193
BORLAND, - Capt. 292, 301; Archibald 272
BOSCAWEN, - Admiral 117
BOSE, John 74
BOSWELL, Thomas 14
BOSWORTH, - Capt. 61
BOTFIELD, - Mrs. 109; Abednego 109, 290; Meshech 109; Shadrach 109
BOUCHER, James 34, 59, 162; John 109
BOUDINOT, - Mr. 195; Elias 25
BOUL, Edward 173
BOULTON, William 280
BOURGOIN, Joseph 36
BOURJEAU, - Capt. 44
BOURNE, - and Jones 287; - 164; James 156; John 40; Thomas 14, 221
BOURTCHIER, Thomas 98
BOUTON, Daniel 77, 247
BOUYERS, Valentine 326
BOWDEN, Samuel 311
BOWEN, - Capt. 189, 195, 220, 235, 236, 259; John 144; Stephen 41; Thomas 131; William 150
BOWER/BOWERS, - Capt. 7, 250; Conrad 229; Cornelius 34
BOWES, - Capt. 249, 287, 289, 334; Francis 1, 2, 17, 72; Rachel 72
BOWLING, Lucy 28
BOWMAN/BOMAN, - 28, 146, 178, 205; Widow 29; Jacob 29; John Tate1 260; Joseph 17; Margaret 17; Richard 227
BOWNE/BOWN, - Capt. 13, 17; Abraham 224
BOWS, Thomas 124
BOWSER, Nathaniel 37, 72, 78
BOYCE, Boaz 132, 270; John 135; Joseph 220
BOYD, - 85, 230; Capt. 117, 205, 206, 321; Alexander 143; Anne 72; George 259, 292, 300; Hannah 58; James

74, 199, 240; John 3; William 6, 8, 126, 267
BOYDEN, James 69; John 24; Mary 24
BOYER, Adam 235; Valentine 32
BOYLE, - Capt. 279; James 11, 206; Robert 22, 96
BOYLES/BOYLS, Charles 259; James 201, 207
BOYNTON, - Capt. 331
BRABAZON, Henry 236, 252
BRABSTON, Thomas 209
BRACE, - Capt. 195
BRAD, - Capt. 72
BRADBURY, - Capt. 33
BRADDOCK, - Capt. 324; Gen. 325, 328, 329
BRADFORD, - 110; Capt. 214, 244, 259; Dr. 83, 198; Cornelia 65, 176; Cornelius 228, 254; Hugh 2, 5, 7; James (alias of James Bill) 141; Joseph 281; William 29, 43, 57, 180, 217, 259, 262, 304, 324, 326; William, Jr. 41
BRADSHAW, Robert 303; William 128
BRADT, Johannes 190; John A. 24
BRADY, John 197; Mary 262
BRAGAN, John 312
BRAINARD/BRAINERD, David 105; John 319
BRAISER, Francis 114
BRAKEN, William 131
BRALEY, - Capt. 255
BRAMBLE/BRAMBEL, Sarah 266; William 193
BRAME, John 42
BRANDT/BRAND, Albertus 217; Michael 67
BRANNON/BRANNEN/ BRANNIN, James 258; Michael 138; Timothy 86
BRANSON, - 98, 143; Mr. 125, 153, 254; William 69, 102, 133, 164, 198, 235, 239, 240, 242, 251, 257, 258, 259, 270, 280, 283, 293, 297, 302, 313, 331
BRASHER, - Capt. 332
BRASLAM, Hugh 13
BRATTEN, George 138
BRAY, William 273
BREACH/BREECH, John 12, 24; Peter 24; Simon 24
BREADING, - Capt. 147
BREAN, Christopher 333
BREDELL, John 287
BREESTEAD, - Capt. 296
BREINTNALL/BRINTNAL, Benjamin 214; David 217; John 325
BREME, - Capt. 41
BRENNAR, George 8

BRETON, John 268
BREWER, Richard 182
BRICK, John, Jr. 115; John, Sr. 115; Joseph 174
BRICKWLL, Richard 192
BRIDGES, - Mrs. 289
BRIGGS/BRIGS, - Capt. 142, 275; Fobes 221; John 110
BRIGHT, - Widow 64, 156
BRINCKERHOFF, Isaac 252
BRINCKLE/BRINKLE/ BRINCKLOE, John 31, 255, 309; Peter 309
BRINGHURST, Anna 179; George 124, 179; John 10, 198, 203
BRINKLEY, John 199
BRINTON, Edward 95, 102; Moses 100
BRISTOL, Dan 243
BRISTOW, - Capt. 260; John 144, 217
BRITT, Daniel 138, 140
BRITTON/BRITTIN, Benjamin 20, 51, 81, 85, 135, 195, 333; Mary 195; William, Sr. 109
BRITTKIRLL, Joseph 196
BROADERS, - Capt. 267
BROADFIELD, Edward 232, 281, 334
BROADHEAD, - Capt. 215
BROADHURST, - Capt. 144, 245, 300, 322, 331
BROCKDEN/BROGDEN, Charles 37, 44, 88, 152, 154, 170, 188, 204, 323
BRODERICK, - Capt. 313
BRODIE, John 334
BROMWICH, William 153, 209
BRONON, John 55
BRONOUGH, William 307
BROOKBANK, Richard 93, 216
BROOKE, James 317; James, Jr. 317
BROOKS/BROOKES, - Capt. 109; Widow 282; Ann 62; David 55; Edward 320; George 56, 137, 292; John 156
BROOM, Elizabeth 85; James 85, 112; Thomas 85, 112
BROTHERSON, - Mr. 63
BROTHERTON, - Mr. 68; Peter 67
BROUGHTON, John 21, 41, 176, 180; Nathaniel 163; William (alias of William Williams) 15; William (alias of William Evans) 115
BROWN, - 74; - alias of one Jones 130; Capt. 28, 58, 193, 207, 233, 235, 236, 238, 243, 244, 246, 251, 256, 275, 281, 290, 296, 305, 312, 314, 318, 331; Dr. 54; Alexander 102, 116, 149, 197,
253, 268, 273, 308, 326; Amos 46; Charles 274; David 204; Ebenezer 104; George 8, 151; Jacob 116; James 45, 73, 170, 256; Jeremiah 102, 197, 253; Jeremiah, Jr. 149; John 46, 60, 62, 97, 158, 178, 183, 218, 231, 235, 241, 298; John Michael 123; Joseph 208, 273, 326; Margaret 49; Matthew 157; Michael 16, 125, 131, 163, 224, 236; Patrick 50; Preserve 23, 168, 213, 226; Preserve, Jr. 70, 171, 178; Preserve, Sr. 171, 178; Richard 253; Samuel 25, 149, 197, 253, 308; Sarah 92, 96, 125, 163, 224, 236; Thomas 9, 73, 78, 150, 166, 228, 231, 260, 261, 262, 263, 265, 267, 288; Thomasine 199; Timothy 54; Vendall 304; William 25, 52, 259, 292
BROWNING, Thomas 211
BROWNLOW, Samuel 63
BRUCE, - Capt. 21; Eleanor 302
BRUEBAKER, Jacob 310
BRUEN, - Capt. 162, 201; John 260
BRUNHOLTZ, - Rev. 304
BRUNSON, Barefoot 20, 148; Mary 20, 148
BRUSHFORD, Richard 182, 186
BRYAN, - Wallace and 189, 192, 195, 207, 233, 277, 279; Charles, Sr. 11; Daniel 314; George 309, 324, 328; James 53; Nathaniel 26; Thomas 285
BRYANT, - Capt. 78, 148, 154, 157, 194, 197, 202, 204, 206, 207, 236, 256; James 167; Valentine 135
BRYSON, - Capt. 262, 290, 321
BUBB, Jacob 187
BUCHANAN/BUCHANNAN, - Dr. 190; Mr. 190; Widow 208; Archibald 293; George 73; William 5, 280, 290
BUCKER, Ambrose 182
BUCKLE, - Mr. 321
BUCKLEY/BUCKLY, - 153; Thomas 103; William 186, 232, 319
BUCKMASTER, George 175
BUDD, - 215; John 11; Thomas 30, 217
BUDDEN, - Capt. 5, 21, 27, 66, 71, 124, 149, 193, 195, 205, 225, 232, 233, 240, 246, 249, 267, 275, 306, 310, 315; Richard 27, 98

BUFFINGTON, John 212; Peter 77
BULL, - Capt. 235; Edmund 317; Henry 276; John 320; Richard 103, 320; Thomas 3; William 137; William, Jr. 131
BULLERT, Thomas 100
BULLINGHAM, Elisha 54
BULLOCK, George 209, 320
BULMAN, - Capt. 205; John 204
BUNTING, Samuel 168, 334
BURCH, Thomas 256
BURCHAM, John 216
BURCHALL/BURCHELL, - Capt. 236, 262; William 137, 171
BURD; see BIRD
BURDONE, Thomas 273
BUREY, John 21
BURGAN, Sutton 134
BURGE, Samuel 63, 98, 108, 119, 164
BURGER, - Capt. 133, 195, 220, 260, 275, 300, 332; John 177; Nicholas 276
BURGESS, - Capt. 18; Daniel 326; Jervis 16; John 298; Thomas 16, 86
BURK/BURKE, - Capt. 5, 17; Benjamin 8; Edward 6; John 6, 196; Mary 31; Matthew 93; Michael 254; Patrick 19; Richard 158; Thomas 282
BURN, Alice 143; Bridget 238; John 23; Thomas 183
BURNET/BURNETT, - Bishop 276; Capt. 218; George 189, 294, 307
BURNS, Edward 171; George 279; James 89; John 220; Ned 198; Terence 281
BURNSIDE/BURNSIDES, George 313; James 199, 309, 327
BURR, - Capt. 189; President 307
BURRIDGE, John 308
BURRMAN, William 75
BURROUGHS/BURROWS, - Capt. 45, 209, 266, 299, 305, 314; Arthur 3, 26; Isaac 26; John 225; Michael 150, 186; Samuel 74
BURSON, Joseph 289
BURT, - 274
BURTON, - Capt. 331; Anthony 108; Benjamin 150, 199, 255; Woolsey 63, 103
BUSBY, - 278; Thomas 163
BUSH, - Capt. 20; Charles 5, 198; David 170; George 5
BUSSEY/BUSSY, - Capt. 221, 228, 234

BUTCHER, Samuel 151;
  Zach. 149
BUTLER, - Capt. 198,
  233, 243; Absalom
  275, 282; Benjamin 6;
  Charles 217; Edmund
  188; Gamaliel 125;
  John 178, 323; Sarah
  104; Simon 6, 253,
  308; Simon, Jr. 197;
  Thomas 281, 294; William 281
BUZBY, Thomas 259
BUZER, John 179
BYAM, William 41
BYARLEY/BYERLEY, Jacob
  193; Thomas 52
BYERS/BYARS, Blass 199;
  John 101
BYEWATER, Jervis 331
BYLES; see also Biles,
  Mr. 64; Daniel 134;
  Thomas 180, 203, 303
BYRN, James 182
BYVANCK/BUYVANCK/BYVANK,
  - Capt. 288, 290, 332

CADDLE, James 210
CADMAN, Anthony 173
CADOGAN, John 171
CADWALADER, - Dr. 141,
  178; Benjamin 216;
  John 125; Thomas 82,
  94, 159, 193, 203,
  265, 307, 329
CAIN, John 172, 183;
  William 242
CALDER, James 73
CALDWELL/CAULDWELL/
  CALWELL, - Capt. 250,
  251, 279, 292, 303,
  318; Andrew 31, 103,
  150, 199, 255, 309;
  David 251; Henry 168;
  James 333; Samuel
  249; Thomas 314
CALL, Philip 302
CALLENDER/CALLENDAR, -
  Mr. 10; Benjamin 89,
  94, 123; William 5,
  30, 89, 94, 116, 117,
  163, 166, 223, 254,
  270, 304, 307, 316,
  330
CALLEY/CALE, - Capt. 37,
  45, 114
CALLINGS, Edward 272
CALLISTER, Henry 213
CALLOW, Robert 89
CALVERT, Benedict 177,
  190
CALVIN, Hans Michal 75
CALVIN (or COLPEN), Malashiah or Melchior
  94
CAMBY, - 239
CAMERON, - Capt. 303;
  Dougal 16; John 153,
  156, 262
CAMNEY, - Capt. 137
CAMP, Joseph 114
CAMPBELL, - and Craig
  324; Capt. 143, 185,
  195, 220, 235, 261,
  286; Alexander 263;
  Ann 183; Archibald 28;
  Charles 221, 235, 253,
  271; Daniel 233;
  Douglass/Douglas,
  164, 221; Duncan 25;
  Francis 203; James
  145, 302; John 67,
  176, 198, 210; Mungo
  144, 177; Peter 190;
  Thomas 30, 38, 55,
  135, 166, 183, 227,
  333
CANADA, - Mr. 114
CANBY, Benjamin/Benjamine 42, 108; Thomas
  300, 322, 330
CANCANON, James 76, 294
CANDOUR/CANDOR, Joseph
  1, 13
CANE, Miles 186
CANEY, Thomas 251
CANFIELD, - Capt. 275
CANISE, William 199,
  244
CANNER, Frank 24
CANNING, Elizabeth 314
CANNON, Francis 124; Jacob 6; William 32
CANTLON/CANTLIN, Philip
  228, 235
CANTWELL, Edward 181;
  Richard 181
CANTZ, Adam 70
CAPPES, John 106
CAPPOCK, James 245
CARAHAN, John 204
CARBERRY, Hugh 320
CARBUT/CARBUTT, Joseph
  153, 300
CARDERY, Hugh 183
CARDMAN, Joseph 201
CARIO, Michael 10
CARLE, Catherine 264,
  267
CARLETON, Edward 205
CARLISLE/CARLILE, - Capt.
  120, 156, 238, 250,
  270, 287, 300, 301,
  318; Major 328; Mr.
  334; Joseph 246; Robert 247
CARMAN, John 205
CARMICK, Stephen 84, 94,
  225, 281
CARNAGHAN, James 8
CARNAGIE, William 258
CARNAN, Christopher 51;
  John 51; Rowland 277
CARNEY; see KEARNEY,
  Patrick 147; Thomas 68
CARPENTER, - JOSIAH and
  262; - 53, 83, 88, 91,
  104, 107, 112, 117,
  127, 136, 168, 185,
  190, 195, 222, 223,
  231, 279, 281, 291;
  Capt. 144; Abraham 39,
  86, 109, 118, 175, 192,
  210, 262; Jasper 90,
  280; John Read 183;
  Mary 248; Samuel 100,
  133, 276, 280, 294,
  298, 330; Stephen 137,
  324
CARR/CAR, - Capt. 7, 15,
  32, 193, 197, 331; Anthony 182; Benjamin
  121; James 90, 92, 142;
  John 52, 208, 224; Samuel 128
CARRICK, John 118
CARROLL/CARRELL, - Capt.
  285; Mr. 282; Catherine 82, 101; Charles
  208, 237, 305; Robert
  50; Thomas 101
CARRUTHERS/CARUTHERS,
  James 133; Samuel 283
CARSON/CARSSON, - DAVEY
  and 66, 151; Hamilton
  204; John 147; Nancy
  255; William 3
CARTER, - 156, 162, 204,
  223, 269; Charles 307;
  Jacob 118, 181; James
  309; Joseph 118, 181,
  282; Landon 307; Thomas 120, 124, 231,
  235; William 123, 257
CARTWRIGHT, Thomas 275
CARTY, Daniel 131, 335;
  Darby 184; Enos 82,
  89, 122
CARVELL/CARVEL/CARVILL/
  CARVIL, Thomas 7, 21,
  27, 36, 46, 95
CARVER, Isaac 177; Jacob
  153; John 131; John,
  Jr. 177
CARWAY, James 140
CARY, - Capt. 260; Henry
  289; Sampson 311; Samuel 93, 108
CASDORP, Henry 45; Jacob 45, 104
CASEDY, Thomas (alias of
  Thomas Fleming) 280
CASEY, Gideon 189, 201;
  James 14; John 188;
  Mark 92; Michael 92
CASH, Thomas 30, 159
CASNEAU, - Capt. 268
CASPAR, Ferdinand 243
CASSEL/CASSELL, Michael
  56; Nicholas 309
CASSNER, Dominick 257
CASTLE, Nicholas 135
CATCHAM, Martha (alias
  of Martha Basset) 158,
  164
CATEN, John 255, 309
CATHCART, - Capt. 265,
  282, 294
CATHRALL/CATHERALL, Edward 31, 150, 284, 330
CATLIN, Robert 20
CATRINGER/CATTHRINGER/
  CATERINGER/CATHERINGA/
  COTRINGER/COTTRINGER,
  - Mr. 188; Elizabeth
  3; John 68, 87; Thomas
  3, 6, 91, 99, 317
CATTELL, - Mr. 205
CATTON/CATON, John 20,
  150, 199; Thomas 39,
  106
CAULFIELD, Francis 212
CAULK, Jacob 9
CAVELL, Thomas 315
CAVENAUGH/CAVANACH, Anthony (alias of Hugh
  Dougherty) 264; James
  20
CAVIN, John (alias of
  John Devonshire) 265
CAW, - Dr. 204
CAWLEY, James 93

CAXON, Edward 219
CAZIER, Philip, Jr. 159
CEAVE, Philip 285
CELY, John 121
CHACE, - Capt. 81
CHADS, John 229
CHAFFEN/CHAFIN, Henry 110; James 76
CHAIN, Matthew 31
CHALANER, John 265
CHALFANT/CHALFONT, - 237; Henry 204
CHALKLEY, Thomas 89, 94, 117
CHAMBERLAIN, an *alias* 127
CHAMBERLIN, John 39
CHAMBERS, Alexander 226; Arthur 286; Benjamin 8, 125; David 26, 108, 161, 294, 314; George 168; James 51; John 8, 51, 226, 270; Joseph 264, 302; Mary (*alias* Mary Connor) 281; Robert 8, 212
CHANCE, Alexander 4
CHANCELLOR, William 234, 278, 284
CHANDLER, - Capt. 245; Jacob 200; Reuben 76; Thomas 30, 31, 61, 102, 105, 149
CHANNEL, John 101
CHAPMAN, - Mrs. 33; Abraham 30, 102, 149, 197; Benjamin 253, 307, 308; George 204; John 61; Joseph 67; Michael 104; Nathan 12; William 30
CHARLES, Robert 53; William 74
CHARLEVOIX, -Pere/Father 276, 285
CHARLTON/CHARLETON, Thomas 5, 13, 16, 65; William 59, 187
CHARNABAN, Joseph 254
CHASE, - Capt. 141; Humphry 170; Jeremiah 107; Richard 264; Thomas 106
CHATTIN, Abraham 57; Abraham, Jr. 84; James 106, 120, 167, 175, 201, 274, 284
CHEESEMAN/CHEASMAN, - 76; Thomas 28; William 243
CHEESMOND, - Capt. 215
CHERRYHOME, William 91
CHESTER, - 287
CHESTNUT, James 210; John 246; Thomas 190
CHEW, - Capt. 235; Anne 10; Benjamin 103, 150, 199, 255, 309, 317, 323; Edward 174; Eleanor 271; Joseph 271; Nathaniel 10, 134
CHICHESTER, Jeremiah 136
CHICK, John, Jr. 84; Joseph 88
CHIEVERS, - Capt. 331

CHILD, - 135; Capt. 57, 66, 71, 73, 193; Mr. 205; Cephas 30; Elizabeth 169; James 1, 31, 35, 141, 189, 225, 254, 270, 280, 292; Katherine 100; Thomas 170; William 233
CHIP, - Capt. 231
CHISHOLM, John 168
CHITTAM, Thomas 295
CHRISTIE/CHRISTY, - Widow 87; Charles 283; Thomas 230
CHUBB, - 207; Sarah 24; Thomas 213, 214; Vioeall 24
CHURCH, - Capt. 160, 238, 282, 284; Anne 18; Daniel 18; John 155, 191
CHURCHILL, John 76, 141
CHURCHMAN, - Capt. 151; Henry 151
CHYME, John 220
CISTI, John 145
CLAYBORNE, Thomas 28
CLAMPFER/CLAMPSTER, Adam 77, 211; William 211, 284
CLAPHAM, - Capt. 59, 80, 81
CLARE, Christopher 219; John 47, 70, 203
CLARK/CLARKE, - 238; Capt. 57, 225, 245, 247, 263, 296, 304, 316, 334; Lt.-Gov. 302; Mrs. 167; Abraham, Jr. 284; Charles 86; George 241; Henry 244; Hugh 73, 96; James 67, 205; John 36, 55, 88, 104, 122, 144, 158, 173, 182, 206, 237, 247, 261, 287, 290, 327, 332, 334; Joseph 212, 268, 320, 325; Mary 164, 166; Sarah 158, 164; Thomas 9, 64, 103, 204, 309, 334; William 46, 50, 270, 286
CLARKSON, - Capt. 244; Mr. 279; Matthew 292, 301, 317
CLARY, Mary 166
CLASE, Humphrey/Humphry, 119, 241
CLAWSON, Anne 261; John 257
CLAXON, - Mr. 145
CLAXTON, James 47, 62
CLAY, Slator 288, 329
CLAYPOOLE/CLAYPOLE, - Mr. 208; Abraham 10, 15, 99, 121, 125, 160, 203, 268, 270; Deborah 121, 125, 160, 268; James 55, 71, 146, 216; William 268
CLAYTON, Francis 14, 232; John 31, 226, 309; John, Jr. 103, 199, 255; Joseph 141, 287; Mary 131; Parnell 22; Thomas 14, 95; William

14, 22, 69, 204, 226, 252, 281, 327
CLEAR, Thomas 169
CLEARA, Andrew 129
CLEARWATER, Peter 141
CLEARY/CLERY, Anthony 239; Robert 200
CLEAVE, Isaac 158
CLEAVER/CLEVER, Derrick 86; Martin 55; Peter 86
CLEIM, Michael 55
CLELAND, John 274
CLEMM/CLEM, William 77, 101, 145, 174, 176, 240, 243, 245
CLEMENT, David 238
CLERK, Benjamin 214
CLESSON, Eunice 310
CLEVELAND, - Rev. 238
CLIFFORD, - 261; Thomas 81, 140, 213, 214, 217, 221, 226, 260, 285, 333
CLIFTON/CLIFFTON, Henry 133, 258; John 4, 11, 23, 31, 34, 41, 102, 104, 133, 140, 143, 217, 269; Sarah 196; William 196
CLINE; see KLEIN, Michael 111; Susannah 111
CLINTON, - Capt. 20, 334; Gov. 255; George 236, 256, 261; Henry 240; William 11
CLOATH, Carberry 21
CLOUD, Joseph 42
CLOUGH, Peter 103, 110, 321, 328
CLOVE, John 149
CLOWES/CLOWS, John 31, 63, 103, 199, 255, 309; Peter 31, 63, 255
CLUCK, John 122
CLULOW, James 43, 283
CLUTSHAM, - Capt. 323
CLUTTER, - 234
CLUTTON, - CORBYN and 158
CLYMER, - Capt. 303, 312; Baltis 240; Valentine 240; William 30, 69, 77, 102, 116, 127; William, Jr. 20; William, Sr. 1
COALE, - Capt. 201
COATAM, - Capt. 58, 146, 147, 194, 251, 252, 271, 281, 312; Thomas 98, 145
COATES/COTES/COATS, - 100, 119, 196; Capt. 230; Elizabeth 314; John 107; John, Jr. 45; Mary 38, 55; Moses, Jr. 334; Samuel 38, 55; Thomas 262, 333; Timothy 192; William 6, 196; William, Jr. 45; William, Sr. 45
COBB, - Capt. 80, 107, 119, 142; James 76
COBURN/COBOURN, Joseph 32, 163, 182, 195,

COBURN/COBOURN (cont'd) 212, 291, 292, 301
COCHRAN/COCKREN, - Capt. 312; Cuddie 156; James 8; Robert 328; Samuel 11
COCK, Peter 232
COCKBURN, Joseph 21
COCKLIN, John 202
COCKSON, - Capt. 235, 241, 244
CODWISE, - Capt. 276, 287, 289
COE, Robert 214, 277
COFFEE/COFFEY/COFFY, - Capt. 227, 229, 301; Daniel 175, 187; John 245; Mary 143
COFFERY, Edward 177
COFFIN, - Capt. 37
COFFING, Abraham 53
COGER, - Capt. 75
COGGESHALL, - 279
COLBOURN, Joseph 75, 92, 135
COLCOCK, - Capt. 206; Isaac 205
COLDEN, Cadwalleder 97, 110; John 97
COLDREN, James 186
COLE, - Mr. 148; Charles 137, 138, 142; Henry 278; Samuel 250
COLEDAY, Jacob 290
COLEMAN, Henry 200, 244; Jacob 293; John 67; Roger 119; William 1, 14, 27, 36, 55, 57, 60, 87, 115, 121, 125, 142, 160, 168, 225, 311
COLES, Samuel 32, 34
COLESBERY/COLEBERRY, Henry 9, 286
COLGAN/COLGON, - Capt. 218, 220, 242, 318; Bernard 309; Jane 309
COLHOUN, - Capt. 290; Dr. 334; Alexander 334
COLLARD, Thomas 95
COLLETT, Crispin 106, 258, 301; Mary 258, 301
COLLIER/COLLEAR, - Capt. 173; Samuel 10; William 320
COLLINS/COLLINGS, - 240, 280; Capt. 194, 218, 247, 268; Mr. 223; Cornelius 213, 225; Edward 1, 31, 73, 102, 140, 143, 152, 165, 233, 253; Edward the Elder 152; Francis 45; John 24; Michael 32; Peter 111; Thomas 35, 66
COLLISON, Margaret 134; Mary 134; Robert 134
COLLUM, - Capt. 282
COLPEN (or CALVIN), Malashiah (or Melchior) 94
COLVILL/COLVIL, - Col. 113; Lord Alexander 88, 135, 137, 180,

197; Thomas 68
COMBES, - Capt. 21; Ann 98
COMERIN, - Capt. 178
COMINGS, James 62
COMISH, - Capt. 2
COMELY/COMLY, Joseph 27, 188; Walter 57, 120, 174
COMPTON, John 37
COMRIN, - Capt. 236, 262, 298
CONANT, - Rev. 318
CONAROW/CONARRO/CONROE/ CONEROW, Isaac 112, 228, 255, 301, 306
CONDON, Janet 11
CONDY/CONDE, - Capt. 238, 287; Adam 24
CONN, Hugh 188
CONNELL, - Capt. 235; Dennis 300
CONNOLIN, Patrick 138
CONNOLY/CONNOLLY/CONNALY/ CONNELY, - Capt. 28; Bryan 232; Edmund 34; James 130; Mary 83; Patrick 198; Thomas 146; William 278
CONNOR/CONNER, - 126, 231; Mr. 126; Capt. 205; Bryan 296; Charles 110, 113, 121, 140, 142, 169; Eleanor 243; Jeremiah (see James M'Laughlin) 304; John 142, 144, 237, 251; Marks 116; Mary (alias of Mary Chambers) 281; Morris 114; Nathaniel 122; Patrick 3; Philip 300; Roger 142, 199; Terence 201, 207; William 296
CONRAD, Cornelius 269; William 326
CONTER, Peter 69
CONWAY, Withers 141
CONYERS, - Capt. 116; Widow 238; Clement 63, 102, 136; Joseph 63, 95; Mary 254
COOCH, Thomas 37, 305, 323
COOK/COOKE, - 82; Alethea 217, 231; Alexander 181, 300; Francis 217; John 201; Nathan 318; Robert 11, 229, 256; Stephen 229, 256; William 62
COOKSON, - Capt. 257, 268, 305; Charles 106, 178, 206; Elizabeth 178; Samuel 252; Thomas 13, 80, 99
COOLEY, James 251
COOMS, - 161, 169; Ann 80; William 125
COON, - Capt. 204
COONEY, Christopher 113
COOPER, - 65, 132, 177; Capt. 209, 225; Rev. 246; Benjamin 232; Calvin 61, 82, 102, 150, 199, 253, 309; Daniel 126, 127, 139,

151, 189, 228; David 30, 133; Isaac 153, 164; Jacob 1, 102, 149, 170, 217, 308; James 133; John 158; Joseph 6, 63, 112; Samuel 239, 253; Thomas 266; William 126
COOTS, Christian 249
COOZAR, Jacob 152
COPE, George 199
COPPLE, Michael 319
COPYTHORNE, - Capt. 205
CORAN, Isaac 57, 176
CORBYN, - and CLUTTON 158
CORD, John 295
CORDAVA, - Mr. 170
CORDERY/CORDRAE, Hugh 86, 192
CORK, John 270
CORLE, Benjamin 250
CORLOP, - Capt. 162
CORMORAN, Isaac 257
CORN, John Frederick 324
CORNE/CORNEE, - Capt. 78, 148, 154, 176, 180, 197, 202, 204, 261, 295, 306
CORNISH, - Capt. 24, 25; Joseph 196
CORNWALLIS, - Col. 52, 54; Gov. 55, 60, 78, 81, 125, 128, 277; Edward 205
CORREY/CORRY/CORY, Isaac 274; John 107, 166, 167, 170, 274; William 107
CORSAN, Cornelius 19; Samuel 205
CORSEN/CORSON, Benjamin 48, 335
CORTINE, John Frederick Francis 278
CORTNEY, Ann 187
CORYELL, John 293
COSBY, - Capt. 144, 153, 197, 245; Henry 257;
COSGRAVE, James 325
COSSAR, Jacob 146; Margaret 146
COSTELOE, John 34
COSTIGIN, Francis 134
COTTNAM, George 22
COTTON, - Capt. 312, 317
COUCH, William 167
COUES, Nicholas 246
COUGH, Lodowick 300
COUGHMAN, John 180
COUGLER, Michael 156
COULSON, John 171
COULTAS, - Capt. 33, 107, 184, 234, 262, 287; James 29, 43, 55, 140, 210, 266, 293, 308, 325, 331
COULTER, Hugh 14
COULTON, William 322
COUNSILL, Henry 158
COURSON, Benjamin 308
COVERLY, - Capt. 233
COWALT, Nicholas 50
COWAN, - Capt. 266, 268, 288, 296; Mrs. 304; John 128, 261; Patrick

COWAN, Patrick (cont'd) 139, 184
COWARD, - Capt. 197
COWARDIN, Abraham 122
COWELL, - Rev. 273
COWGILL, Edward 209
COWIE, - Capt. 318; James 36
COWIN, George 152
COWPLAND/COUPLAND, - Capt. 290, 324; Caleb 101, 198; David 45, 199, 264; Hugh 19
COX/COXE, - Capt. 209, 261, 296; Andrew 83, 145; Daniel 134; Israel 334; John 40, 54, 86, 97, 146, 148, 152, 173, 229, 249, 294; Peter 228, 260; Robert 305; Samuel 14, 299; Sarah 58; Thomas 287, 303; William 119, 132, 134, 183, 210, 249
COXEN, - Capt. 329; Nicholas 247
COYLE, Charles 267
CRABB/CRAB, - Mr. 214; John 207, 213, 214; William 132
CRADDOCK/CRADOCK, - Mr. 177; Rev. 235
CRAIG, CAMPBELL and 324; Capt. 294; George 240, 316; James 307; Thomas 7, 133; William 9, 199, 229
CRAIGIE/CRAIGE, - Capt. 47, 69, 178
CRAMPLIN, Thomas 226
CRAMPTON, John 126
CRANE, - Capt. 296; John 114; Samuel 245
CRANFIELD, Michael 65
CRASSWELL, Anne 106; William 106
CRATHORN/CRATHORNE, - Capt. 249, 275, 296; Jonathan 151
CRATOR, Melchior 77
CRAVEN, James 203; Thomas 36
CRAWFORD, - Capt. 67, 219, 251, 303; Mr. 170; Alexander 267; Andrew 211, 258; Daniel 129; David 187, 188; John 13, 307; Joseph 219; Richard 83; Samuel 8; William 20
CREAGH, - Mr. 128, 277, 279, 292, 294; James 61; Patrick 289
CREAMER, Patrick 282
CREAPEL, Nicholas 318
CREGIER, - Capt. 238, 242, 244; Henry 204; Martinus 282
CREIGHTON, - Capt. 212, 257, 304, 308; William 186
CRESAP, Thomas 49
CRESSON, John 1, 100, 172
CREST, Frederick 36

CREVET, John 211
CREW, - Capt. 260
CRIPPEN, William 18
CRISPIN, - Capt. 300; Silas 241; Thomas 10
CROCKET, Robert 157, 173
CRODAL, George Jacob 328
CROFT, Childermas 327
CROGHAN, - Mr. 230, 277, 323; George 54, 58, 249
CROLL, Christian 311
CROMPTON, William 156
CROMWELL, Isaac 49
CRONEY, Philip 174
CROOK, Valentine 116
CROSBY, - Capt. 137; Daniel 84; John 133; Joshua 135, 176, 184, 192, 230, 246, 249, 285, 301, 306, 327; Mary 86; Richard 133; Thomas 116, 170, 279; William 118
CROSDALE, William 93
CROSIER/CROZIER, John 278; James 187
CROSON, Henry 6
CROSS, Edward 156; John 33, 108, 122, 223, 228; Thomas 147
CROSSMAN, William 206
CROSTHWAITE, William 6, 48, 53
CROTEY, Ann 311
CROUCH, Joseph 213, 217
CROW, - Capt. 20; George 196; John 112, 114, 115, 132, 213, 287
CROWELL/CROWEL, - Capt. 206, 223, 253, 286; Thomas 77
CROWNINGSHIELD, - Capt. 82
CROXALL, Charles 264; Richard 237, 278, 305; R./Robert 46, 208
CROXFORD, William 37
CROYAL, Emanuel 29
CRUIKSHANKS/CROOKSHANKS/ CRUIKSHANK, - Capt. 331; Alexander 69, 236, 280, 283
CUBBIN, Thomas 96
CUDWELL, John 330
CUFFY, - Capt. 76
CULBERSON, John 26; William 26
CULBERTSON, Andrew 175; John 8
CULBIN, Thomas 81
CULLAM/CULLUM, - Capt. 225, 294
CULLY, William 109
CUMMINGS/CUMMINS/CUMMING/ CUMING, David 82, 300; John 279; Matthew 202; Richard 223; Robert 18, 20; Thomas 76, 84, 99, 102, 149, 197, 253, 308; William 5
CUNNINGHAM/CONYNGHAM, - and GARDNER 14, 35, 42, 48, 51, 100, 109, 141, 188, 191, 209; Capt. 150, 275; Mr. 101, 328; Alice 163,

165; Andrew 244; Archibald 163, 165; Daniel 6; John 5, 36; Redmond 41, 271, 281, 320; Ruth 244; Samuel 244; William 13, 47, 167, 237
CUNRADS, Dennis 48
CURAINS, Nicholas 100
CURBY, - Capt. 218
CURLING, - Capt. 331
CURRAN, Nicholas 87
CURRIE/CURRY, - Capt. 70, 276; Rev. 6; David 220; Ebenezer 2, 26, 36, 40; James 196; Thomas 70; William 3, 10, 15, 19, 58, 64, 202, 256, 295
CURTIS, - Capt. 299; Jehu 31, 61, 102, 150, 197, 253; Joseph 323; William 277, 289, 292
CURTIUS, Christian Henry 154; Jacob Frederick 271
CUSICK, James 277
CUSSENS, - Capt. 46, 162
CUSTARD/CUSTORD/COSTARD, Arnold 34; George 199; John 152; Reiner/Reyneer 179, 289
CUTHBERT, - Capt. 130; John 3, 207, 265; Thomas 319
CUTHBERTSON, John 2
CUTLER, John 218
CUZZINS/COZZINS, - and SMYTER 23, 34, 46, 104; Capt. 276, 283

DAGWORTHY, - Capt. 308; John 107; John, Jr. 134
DAINLER, David 230
DAIRS, Gabriel 7
DAKEYN, William 221
DALE, George 305
DALEY, Dennis 301, 316; James 19; Owen 82
DALTON, Henry 303; Richard 233
DAMHOWER, George 325
DAMERES/DAMREES, Charles 232; David 240
DAMOOD, Henry 39
DANFORD, - Capt. 20; William 9
DANIEL, John 239
DARBEY, William 288, 297
DARBYSON, Cornelius 297
DARDING, John 45
DARDID, Catherine 143; Michael 143
DARLINGTON, William 2
DARRELL, - Mr. 29; Sampson 139
DARVIL, William 12, 27, 42, 80
DASHLER, David 224, 257
DAVENPORT, Isaac 166; Josiah 67, 101, 129, 142, 147, 180, 189, 242, 249, 257, 265, 297

DAVEY/DAVIE, - and CAR-
SON 66, 151; Mr. 287;
David 174; Hugh 64
DAVID/DAVIDS - Mr. 32;
Benjamin 319; David
334; Evan 147; Han-
nah 79; James 19, 35,
44; Mary 147; P. 201;
Peter 140, 335; Ste-
phen 79
DAVIDSON, - Capt. 33,
66, 235; Alexander
174; Catherine 73;
James 111; John 302
DAVIES/DEVIES, - Capt.
265; James 13, 199;
Richard 201; Samuel
329; Thomas 53
DAVIS, - Capt. 16, 37,
43, 59, 129, 202,
206, 210, 212, 218,
225, 233, 236, 238,
243, 254, 262, 264,
267, 297, 313; Widow
81; Alexander 161;
Ann 101; Badem 55;
Benjamin 3, 4, 7, 30,
74, 92, 109, 132,
197, 253, 319, 329;
Daniel 140; David 1,
13, 17, 42, 67, 79,
89, 139, 196, 199,
214, 216, 244, 279,
284; Edward 7, 126,
127, 212, 285, 296;
Eleanor 189, 192, 194,
198, 200, 201, 202,
205, 206, 208, 210,
252; Ellis 256; Eze-
kiel 104; George 268,
325; Hugh 182, 190;
Isaac 30, 249, 264;
James 224, 226; John
30, 40, 45, 66, 91,
98, 100, 110, 121,
199, 306, 333; Joseph
41, 110, 156, 242;
Joseph (alias Williams)
282; Joshua 101; Lewis
49, 76, 110; Lydia 13;
Margaret 127, 296;
Mary 54, 199; Mathu-
salah 95; Nathaniel 2;
Philip 196; Robert 2,
5, 115, 193, 242; Tho-
mas 5, 36, 175, 207,
208, 241, 260, 272,
305, 329; Walter 8;
William 5, 85, 89,
118, 178, 182, 212
DAVISON, William 179
DAVY, - Capt. 299; Isaac
2
DAWS/DAWES, Abraham 4,
109; Edward 167, 234;
William 275
DAWSON, - Widow 84;
Charles 91, 94, 132;
John 182; Mary 183;
Thomas 77, 317; Wil-
liam 224, 254, 294,
329, 331
DAY, - Capt. 25; Humph-
rey 24; James 92, 230,
265; John 172
DEAL, Michael 172
DEAL (or DEAN), Thomas
278

DEAN/DEANE, - Capt. 112,
143, 176, 180, 212,
219, 244, 253, 255,
290; Edward 151; Ralph
20; Samuel 246;
DEARE, William 140, 250
DEARN, - Lt. 24
DEATO, Michael 179, 185
DEAVER, Mary 74; Richard
74
DEBOW, Lawrence 243
DE CALLIERES, - Cheva-
lier 285
DE COW, Isaac 120; Jo-
seph 120
DEEING, - 44
DEERING, - Mrs. 254
DE GRAAF, Klaas A. 24
DEHAVEN, - Capt. 17; Ab-
raham 7, 99
DEHOLLY, Anne 242
DEIMER, Catherine 293
DEIRS, James 153
DE JAMONVILLE/JAMONVILLE,
- Sieur 295, 305
DE JERSEY, - Capt. 110
DEJOINVILLE, - Capt.
293
DE JONCAIRE, - M. 276
DELAGE, - and READ 113;
Mr. 112; Peter 72, 140,
196
DE LANCEY/DELANCEY, -
Gov. 288; James 256,
257, 260, 262, 268,
289, 296, 302, 303,
334; Oliver 282
DELAP, Samuel 289
DELEVAL/DELAVALL, John
217, 305
DELIGNY, - M. 106
DE LOPEZ, Vincent 18, 22
DEMENE, - Capt. 334
DEMING, - 114
DEMSY, Edward 295
DE NAVARETTA, Don Mel-
chior 195
DENE, Thomas 47
DENN, - Capt. 259
DENNING, William 302
DENNIS, John 61, 199,
335; Joseph 294; Ri-
chard 165; Thomas 116;
William 189
DENNISON, - Capt. 259
DENNISTON, Hannah 233;
John 233
DENNY, Benjamin 196; Ed-
ward, Jr. 304; S. 105;
Trent 124; Walter 22
DENORMANDIE/DENORMANDY,
- Capt. 317, 318;
Anthony 5; Daniel 211;
John 8, 33; John Ab-
raham 7, 61, 108, 190,
192, 201, 311
DENT, - Justice 180
DENTON, John 219
DE NYCE/DENYCE, - and
MASON 151; John 105,
152, 153, 164, 224,
256
DE PREFONTAINE, Peter
Papin 179
DERHAM, William 261
DERNIN, Nicholas 158

DE ST. PIERRE, Legardeur
276
DESELL, Henry 300
DESHLAR, David 183
DESSNER, William 68
DETMAS, - 219
DEVEREUX/DEVEREAUX/
DAVERAUX, - Capt. 45,
71, 219, 243, 277, 318;
Edward 118
DE VILLIER, - Mr. 295
DEVINE, Richard 279
DEVONSHIRE, John (alias
CAVIN) 230, 265
DEWAR, - Capt. 195, 204,
205, 208, 210; David
211
DE WEES/DEWEES/DEWEESE,
331; Cornelius 180;
Garret/Garrat 120, 180,
269; Henry 269; Wil-
liam 75, 96, 308
DEWER, Andrew 75
DEWORMEAUX, Becket 324
DEXTER, Eleanor 277
DEY, Derrick 114
DEYERMAN, Catherine 26
DICKIE/DICKEY, Moses 3,
147
DICKINSON/DICKENSON, -
35, 103, 115, 127;
Capt. 63, 123, 128,
142, 225, 236; George
99; Ja. 141; Jonathan
52, 70, 275; Joseph 38;
Matthew 327; R. 141;
Richard 333; Robert
324; William 275, 324
DICKS, Peter 102, 116,
128, 149, 197, 253,
308
DICKSON, - Capt. 202,
238, 260
DIDGER, Francis 202
DIEDER, Hance 282
DIEL, Michael 77
DIEMER, Catherine 145;
John 81
DIGG, John Daniel 248
DIGGS/DIGGES, - Capt.
285, 334; Mr. 126, 169;
Dudley/Dudly 204, 288,
291, 294
DILL, Matthew 8
DILLAND, James 176
DILLON, James (alias of
James Rice) 198, 200,
202, 209
DILWORTH, Jacob 191
DILWIN/DILWYN, - 157;
John 82; Sarah 85; Su-
sanna 82
DIMMITTI, James 93
DIMON, Moses 289
DINGEE, - Capt. 251, 318
DINGS, - Capt. 314
DINSDALE, - Dr. 30
DINWIDDIE/DUNWIDDIE/DIN-
WODIES/DUNWODY, - Gov./
Lt.-Gov. 276, 282, 295,
303, 304, 305, 314,
334; John 187; Robert
142, 232, 259, 264, 275,
317, 326
DIVERS, Christopher 14
DIXEY, John 133

DIXON/DIXSON, - Capt. 182, 233, 268, 296; Christopher 255; Henry 84; John 36; Joseph 79, 202; Nancy 255; Robert 56, 67, 72, 138, 220, 245
DOALITTLE, - Mr. 237
DOANE, Elisha 194, 198; Hezekiah 194
DOAREN, Patrick 125
DOBBINS/DOBBIN, - 110; Capt. 288; James 15, 132, 176, 238; John 11, 73; Joseph 282; William 128, 305
DOBBS/DOBS, - Capt. 312; Arthur 231, 308, 312, 326
DOBSON, - Capt. 323
DOCKERY, Matthew 84
DODD, - Widow 59; Alice 202
DODDS, William 270
DODSON, - Dr. 126
DODSWORTH, William 171
DOGGET, - Capt. 141, 314
DOGHARTY, James 11
DOLD, John Philip 240, 251, 258, 291
DOLIN, John 247, 296
DOLLIVER, - Capt. 331
DOLON, Ann 248; Peter 248
DONAHEW, - Capt. 283
DONALD, Robert 324
DONALDSON, - and FULLER 180, 222, 250, 261; Capt. 235, 263, 332; Hugh 115; Joseph 57, 80, 137, 286; Thomas 121; William 57, 62, 137, 322
DONDORSE, David 65
DONESON/DONESAN, John 64, 66
DONNEL/DONNELL/DONNAL, - Capt. 62, 288, 312; John 8
DONNELLY, Michael 186
DONNENHAVER, George 248, 281
DONNOGHON/DONNOHON, John 75, 84
DORAN/DORON, Brian/Bryan 75, 104, 198, 201, 205, 208, 209, 252, 263; Patrick 266
DORE, Jonathan 54
DORNE, Bryan 264, 267
DORRELL/DORREL, - Capt. 56, 58, 189; Richard 319
DORRINGTON, - Capt. 205, 282
DORSEY, Edward 231
DORSIUS, Jane 19; Peter Henry 19
DORTON, George 294
DOSIN, John 243
DOTTON, - Capt. 201
DOUDE, Cornelius 255; George 56
DOUGHERTY/DOUGHARTY/DOUGHART, Edward 88; Hugh (alias of Anthony Cavenaugh) 264; John 13, 88, 139, 253, 309; Patrick 81, 316; Walter 120, 173
DOUGHTY, - Capt. 255; Thomas 209; William 42
DOUGLASS/DOUGLAS, - Dr. 276; Archibald 114; Athalanah 274; David 330; George 274; James 216; William 50, 59, 78, 82, 94, 102, 202, 284
DOVE, - Capt. 88; Mr. 128, 144, 161, 222, 312, 325; David James 109
DOW, Eliphaz 103, 110, 321, 328
DOWD, Michael 183
DOWDERMAN, David 304
DOWDLE/DOWDALL, Edward 285; Elizabeth 126; James 195, 206; Richard 19
DOWDNEY, Thomas 224
DOWELL, - Capt. 27, 76, 236; William 204, 223, 228
DOWERS, - Capt. 59, 119, 254, 257, 275, 276, 277, 294, 297, 318, 334; Mr. 12; Edward 1, 15, 32, 57, 69, 136, 143, 204
DOWLING, Michael 210
DOWNES, William 134
WOWNING/DOUNING, - Capt. 262; John 121; Sarah 12, 45
DOWNY/DOWNIE, - Capt. 262, 275, 276; Thomas 314
DOYLE, - Capt. 312; Brian (alias of William Bride) 188; John 204; Michael 279; Philip 12
DOZ, Andrew 227
DRACORD, Philip 257; Ralph 257
DRACY, - Capt. 25
DRAKE, William Francis 24
DRASON/DRESON/DRESSON, - Capt. 18, 275, 276, 299; Matthew 199, 317
DREW, Ishmael 285
DRISCALL/DRIESCALL, - Capt. 265, 288
DRUGAN, Edward 174
DRUILLON, - Ensign/M. 304, 305, 312
DRUMGOLD, - Capt. 332
DRUMMOND, - Capt. 260, 321; Duncan 320
DRURY, Edward 197; Edward (error for Edward Ruby) 166, 167
DRY, - Capt. 31
DUBEE, Jacob 272
DUBERRY, Hannah 258
DUBOIS, - Capt. 38, 285, 296; Henry Richard 284
DUBRE, Hannah 314
DUCHAR, - Capt. 114
DUCHE/DUCHEE, - Mr. 109; Anthony 162, 188, 333; Anthony, Jr. 259; Jacob 23, 31, 72, 132, 197, 203, 217, 241, 269, 290, 306, 315
DUCKET/DUCKETT, - Capt. 250, 260, 264; Thomas 217
DUCKEY, John 227
DUDLEY, - Capt. 285; William 52
DUER, Joseph 208
DUFF, Thomas 254
DUFFIELD, Benjamin 39; Edward 140; Jacob 214, 232, 318; John 304; Joseph 13; Thomas 232, 244, 277
DUFFY, Frances 53
DUGALL, Robert 87, 179
DUGDALE, - Mrs. 241
DUGUD, Margaret 134
DUKE, George 237
DULANY, D. 15; Daniel 266, 268; Walter 231
DULBY, - Capt. 156
DUNBAR, - Capt. 66, 136, 238, 279; David 134; John 82
DUNBIBIN, - Capt. 63
DUNBLASS, David 105
DUNCAN, - Capt. 152, 214, 238, 250, 251, 275, 279, 287; Edmund 325; George 97, 100; James 324; Patrick 286, 325; Pinhorne 316; William 5, 286, 325
DUNCANSON/DUNCASON, William 219, 228
DUNCKS/DUNKS/DUNK, - 66, 84, 125, 324
DUNDAS/DUNDASS, David 20; James 69
DUNFIELD, Edward 287
DUNGAM, - Capt. 238
DUNGON, Thomas 203
DUNLAP/DUNLOPE, - Capt. 195; James 126; Samuel 77; William 192, 274, 289, 300
DUNN/DUN, - Capt. 3, 129, 194, 259, 290, 305; Andrew 211; Catherine 2; George 327, 333; James (alias DUNNEBE) 236; John 103; Murtha 225; Patrick 174, 281; Philip 184; Ralph 4; Robert 5; Thomas 106, 172; William 218
DUNNING, Ezekiel 150, 199, 255, 309; Robert 8; Thomas 333
DUNNIVIN, John 158
DUNNODY, John 175
DUNNOGHON, John 68
DUNSCOMB, - Capt. 250, 260, 282, 288, 290, 292; John 298
DUNSEY, Catherine 311
DUPORT, John 303
DUPUY/DUPUE/DUPUI, Aaron 272; Daniel 51, 87, 272; Frances 325; Samuel 149, 272

DUQUESNE, - Gov./Marquis 283, 313
DURANT, Nathan 130
DURBOROW, Daniel 49; Hugh 249; John 35, 84, 118; Joseph 89; Mary 100, 183
DURELL, Jonathan 18, 190
DURHAM, James 175; Stephen 175
DURSEY, - Mr. 213
DURYEE, Abraham 212
DUSHANE/DUSHAN, Isaac 6, 25, 184; Jerome 6; Valentine 17, 46, 65; Valentine, Jr. 9
DUSSET, - 298
DUSTEN, Samuel 154
DUTENS, Charles/Charles J. 146, 152, 170, 187, 223, 256, 284, 324
DUTHY, - Capt. 131
DUVALL, Benjamin 22
DYMOND, James 66
DYRE, Henry 4; Mary 14; Samuel 14
DYSART/DYSSARD, James 8

EAGLESFIELD, Bernard 215
EARLE/EARL, - Mr. 263; Michael 68, 176
EARNS, Conrad Hendrick 290
EASTBOURNE/EASTBURN, John 31, 125; Robert 7; Samuel 61
EASTLAND, Thomas 23
EASTON, - Capt. 294
EATON, - Capt. 285; George 219, 315; Peter 189, 219; Revell 10
EAVENSON, Joseph 237
EBBETS/EBBITS, - Capt. 276, 326
EBTHORP/EBTHARP, Thomas 91, 175, 186
ECCLES/ECLES/EACLES, - Capt. 261, 294; George 127, 178
ECKART, Michael 269
EDDY, James 291
EDGAR, - NIXON and 17; Capt. 53, 149; Mr. 329; Charles 51, 69, 102, 186, 198, 314
EDGE, Andrew 43, 48, 73
EDGECOMB, Jonathan 286
EDGELL/EDGILL, Rebecca 28, 90, 91, 118; William 42, 64, 184
EDINGWOOD, - Capt. 22
EDMONSON, Pollard/241
EDMONSTON, James 195
EDMUNDS, - Capt. 261
EDWARDS/EDWARD, - 188; Capt. 18, 81, 126, 138, 209, 219, 232, 254, 257, 275, 276, 294, 297, 298, 313, 317, 324, 327; Justice 153; Mr. 204; Squire 50; Alexander 106; Cony 107; David 155; Edward 7, 97, 112, 249; James 20 John 31, 61, 102, 116, 315; Jonathan 297; Joseph 217; Joshua 64; Richard 107, 202, 283; Thomas 155; William 30, 61, 102
EDWELL, William 127
EGBERGEN, Peter 171
EGBERTSON, James 4
EGBURTS, James 187
EGE, Michael 63, 172
EGELSON, James 321; John 321
EGLINGTON, John 36
EGONSONS, John 103
EICHOLTZ, Jacob 135
EIRIS, John 184
ELBERSON, - Capt. 45
ELDER, David 153; John 326
ELDRED, Ezekiel 153
ELDRIDGE, James 36; Obadiah 65
ELFRETH, Jeremiah 105, 217, 330
ELKINS, - MORGAN and 85
ELLET, Thomas 81
ELLIGOOD, - Capt. 235
ELLIOT/ELLIOTT, - TROTTER and 226; Capt. 331; Andrew 10, 26, 42, 58, 108, 149, 256; Charles 129; Enoch 76; James 189, 250; Obadiah 92, 190, 310; Thomas 204, 205
ELLIS, - Capt. 248, 250; Mr. 116, 216; Catherine 30; Edward 218; Ever 33; Isaac 114; John 230; Jonathan 17, 311; Joseph 33, 46, 224, 311; Josiah 88; Mary 311; Robert 7, 37, 77, 78, 96, 123; Samuel 210; Thomas 91, 283; Umphry 30; William 68
ELLISON, - Lt.-Col. 323, 324
ELLIT, John 49
ELLWELL, - Capt. 39
ELLY, George 239
ELMES, - Capt. 261
ELPHINSTON/ELPHINSTONE, - Capt. 152; Mr. 306
ELSEY, John 186
ELSWORTH, Theophilus 207, 214
ELTINGE, Cornelius 43
ELTON, Revel 11
ELVES, Henry 15, 52, 69, 157, 161, 180, 196, 203, 238
EMERSON/EMMERSON, - 207; Caleb 10, 16; Lambert 331
EMEY/EMY, - Capt. 20, 281
EMLEN/EMLIN, Caleb, Jr. 41; George 141, 148, 152, 185, 251, 265, 303, 317, 325; George, Jr. 8, 23, 104, 276, 313, 317; 304; Joshua 40, 41, 81, 194; Samuel 28, 79, 233
EMLEY, Elisha 174; John 115, 174; John, Jr. 174; William 174

EMMIT, John 8
EMOTT, - Capt. 197, 332
EMPSON, William 234
END, Theobald 72
ENGELHART, Andrew 105
ENGLAND, - Capt. 201, 265, 317; Daniel 122; Joseph 225; Thomas 2, 281
ENGLE, Benjamin 26, 239; John 298
ENGLISH, David 262
ENNIS, James 214
ENCCHS, Henry 121
ENOS, Abraham 6
ENTERKIN, George 67, 211
ERDEN, Christian 77
ERMUS (or ARMUS), John (alias Huckaback) 269
ERPFE, Philip Jacob 229
ERVIN, - Capt. 265
ERWIN, - Mr. 143; James 82; John 36, 52, 60, 75, 87, 108, 135, 191; Joseph 8; Robert 25; Thomas 291
ESCHULLION, Morris 14
EUGENE, John 88
EVAN, Lott 104
EVANS, - Capt. 291, 301; Widow 45, 96, 180; Abner 175; Caleb 220; Daniel 224; David 19, 200; Edward 16, 75, 150, 157, 164, 182, 229; Eleazar 98;Elizabeth 259; Evan 69, 119, 227, 230, 259; George 10, 32; Griffith 226; Hugh 30, 61, 102, 149, 197, 253, 272, 308, 315; Jabez 252, 299; Jacob 252; Jane 67; John 121, 205, 207, 295; Jonathan 33, 127, 153, 181, 196, 297, 314; Lewis 31, 41, 42, 70, 77, 187, 230, 241; Martha 335; Methusalem 329; Morgan 243; Morris 224; Musgrave 84; Nathan 197, 253; Owen 30, 61, 102; Pennel 282; Peter 72, 179; Richard 138; Robert 36, 155, 239, 247; Rowland 219, 319; Samuel 34; Sarah 259; Seth 272; Stephen 148; Sydney 259; Thomas 76, 97, 135, 272, 308, 315; William 100, 335
EVE, - Capt. 173, 249; Oswald/Oswall 88, 155
EVELEIGH, - Mr. 204
EVERHART, Joseph 199, 254
EVERIL, Ichabod 252
EVERITT, Benjamin 270; John 317
EVERSLEY, Jacob 33
EVERSON, - Capt. 142, 164, 197, 227, 291, 306; Nicholas 127
EVERTSON, Jonathan 130
EVES, John 164; Mary 48
EWER, Robert 217

EWING, - Capt. 173, 174, 195, 236, 271, 276, 286, 305; Archibald 231; John 307
EYRE, George 216; John 61, 105
FADRE, - Capt. 221, 265
FAGEN, Francis 135; Mary 135
FAIL, Samuel 79
FAIRBAIRN, - Capt. 316
FAIRBANKS, Jonathan 199
FAIRFAX, Thomas, Lord 88
FAIRLAMB, John 61, 149, 197, 308
FAIRLIE, - Capt. 321
FALCONER, - Capt. 60
FALES, Nathaniel 138
FALIS, - Capt. 263
FALKINGHAM, - Capt. 116, 144
FALLS, - Capt. 129, 235
FARIES, Robert 290, 318
FARIS, - Widow 270; David 20; Helen 44; John 161, 195; Samuel 44; William 13, 161
FARISH, Richard 111
FARLER, - Capt. 21
FARMER/FARMAR, - 57; Edward 4, 5, 278, 293; Richard 2, 29, 48, 88, 157, 280, 300; Samuel 136
FARNANDO, - Capt. 308
FARNSWORTH, Nicholas 29
FARRA, - Widow 313; William 173
FARREL/FARRELL, Andrew 28, 40, 51, 54, 118, 313; John 214; Patrick 142; William 95
FARRINGTON, Abraham 30, 273
FARSONS, Henry 323
FAULK, John 29
FAULKNER/FALKNER, - Capt. 43, 171, 207, 212, 275, 276, 286; Thomas 107; William 280
FEAGON, Henry 166
FEARTLOUGH, - Capt. 205
FEDDEMON, Henry 208
FEE, Agnes 270
FEGHAN, Francis 86
FEHL, Catherine 132; Philip 132
FELL, - 295; Capt. 175; William 93
FELTMIRE, Michael 240
FEMEL, John 37
FENTON, Enoch 305
FERDINANDO, John 38
FEREE, Isaac 83
FERGUSON, - Capt. 59, 268, 306, 310, 321; Colin 242, 286, 294; Dougall, Sr. 288; Hugh 318; Patrick 28
FERLON, John 102
FERMOR, Juliana 155
FERNANDO, - Don 321
FERRISS, David 155
FEW, Daniel 198, 270; James 221
FIELD, Benjamin 74, 79; Robert 163, 167; Sarah 74, 79
FIELDING, - Capt. 43; Thomas 58, 60, 62
FIELDS, Philip 107
FIELL, Rudolph 303
FILER, Thomas 280
FILLING, James 45
FINCH, Abraham 182
FINLEY, - Capt. 236, 250; Andrew 8; Archibald 6, 168; John 230; Samuel 64
FINN, Michael 171
FINNEY, David 194, 222, 262, 271; James 13; Rebecca 243; Richard 203, 243; Samuel 243; William 5, 203
FISHBOURN/FISHBOURNE, - 26, 86, 96, 97, 98, 113, 130, 202, 222, 251; William 96, 222, 285, 297
FISHER, - and FUSSELL 48, 98, 111, 160; PIERCE and 136; Francis 228; Frederick 205; George 23; Harmon 214; Hendrick 114; John 72, 75, 169; Joshua 116, 170, 233, 263, 267, 285, 298; Maria 105; Melchior 105; Michael 271; Samuel 8, 82, 97, 158; William 116, 241, 279, 301, 324, 328
FISTMIRE, Christian 334
FITCH, John 23; Thomas 112; William 231
FITZ, John 107
FITZ GERALD/FITZGERALD/ FITZ GERRALD, - HUSSEY and 173; Capt. 301; David 226; James 156, 186; John 47; Philip 296; William 127, 240
FITZHUGH, William 58
FITZ MORRIS, Richard 243
FITZPATRICK, Dennis 100; Peter 3; Philip 300, 322, 330; Richard 132
FITZRANDOLPH, Edward 4, 238, 243; Nathaniel 246
FITZSIMMONS/FITZSIMONS, Patrick 82; Thomas 156, 220, 239, 293; William 156
FITZWATER/FITZWALTER, George 87, 99, 168, 291, 325, 333; Joseph 105; Thomas 34
FLANAGAN/FLANNAGAN/ FLANAGEN, - Capt. 314; John 194; Michael 220; Roger 69
FLANNAKIN, William 182
FLAVEL, John 316
FLEESON, Plunket 227, 314
FLEET, William 286
FLEMER, Hannah Gertrude 79
FLEMING, - Mr. 244; Gilbert 114, 125; John 32, 33; Margaret 244; Patrick 261; Thomas 139, 280
FLETCHER, - 104; John 228; Thomas 10, 90, 162, 269
FLIN, James 280
FLING, Edward 116; George 30, 47, 163, 179, 184; Owen 79. 179, 184, 237
FLINT, - Capt. 119
FLOOD, - Mr. 274; Dennis 1
FLOWER, - Capt. 143, 144, 159, 160, 234, 242, 261, 275; Benjamin 164, 334; Enoch 239, 257, 325, 329; Henry 248, 277; Richard 140; Samuel 2, 110, 229, 243, 257, 276, 293
FLOYD, John 269
FOLEY/FOELY, Daniel 287; Michael 140
FOGE, - Capt. 294
FOGWELL, John 297
FOLGER, - Capt. 131, 165
FOLKES, Thomas 168
FOLWELL, Edward 39
FONES, - Capt. 47, 128, 178, 206, 219, 250
FOOTMAN, Richard 323
FOOTNEY, Henry 244
FORBES, - and BIDDLE/ BIDDLE and 173, 298; Alexander 7, 38, 76, 115, 153, 166; Ann 166, 237; Hugh 40
FORD/FORDE/FOARD, - Capt. 276, 290, 327, 331; Elizabeth 172; Jacob 115, 285; James 111; John 239; Robert 207; Standish 98, 110, 134, 154, 157, 171, 200, 104, 230, 250, 251, 258; Thomas 217; William 172
FORDER, John 81
FORDHAM, Jon 326
FOREMAN/FORMAN, Alexander, Jr. 62; Charles 83
FORREST/FOREST, John 303, William 217
FORRESTER, - Capt. 194; George William 60
FORSTER, Arthur 37
FORSYTH, - Capt. 259, 308; Matthew 54
FORTEY/FORTY, Ann 10; John 10, 308
FORTIN, - Capt. 214, 331
FORWOOD, Samuel 300
FOSS, - Capt. 105
FOSSAY, - Capt. 329
FOSSET, Renard 44
FOSTER, - Capt. 27, 52, 55, 125; Bazaleel 185; Edward 89; Henry 23; James 291; Joseph 224; Mary 174; Samuel, Jr. 181; Thomas 13, 304; William 65, 174, 255

FOULKE, John 204; Judah 95, 96, 99, 119, 144, 149, 175, 191, 197, 286, 291, 301; Samuel 149, 197, 253, 308; William 30, 61, 253
FOWELL, - 286
FOWLE, - Capt. 141, 285
FOWLER, - 174; Capt. 287; Mr. 213; Michael 310
FOX, - Mr. 301; James 187, 217; John 130; Joseph 31, 102, 116, 178, 182, 214, 229, 245, 253, 279, 285, 308
FOY, Daniel 111; John 175
FOYLE, Robert 275; Samuel 22
FRAMES, William 246
FRANCIS, - Capt. 31, 221, 261; Mr. 183; Widow 54; Arnold 136, 275; James 332; John 51; Rees 54; Tench 23, 99, 102, 323; Tench, Jr. 225; Thomas 15, 33, 57, 85, 118, 322
FRANKLAND, - Capt. 3, 20
FRANKLIN, - and HALL 176, 246; Mr. 288; Benjamin 1, 33, 39, 41, 62, 68, 85, 92, 105, 110, 117, 127, 135, 136, 149, 172, 176, 197, 203, 225, 230, 236, 254, 285, 289, 302, 207, 329; Peter 42, 43; William 134, 181, 231, 238, 308, 317, 322
FRANKS, - LEVY and 17, 27, 67, 90, 93, 98, 127, 135, 155, 156, 168, 169, 254, 268, 284; - Mr. 181; David 4, 79, 119, 268, 328; John 297
FRASEY, - Capt. 21
FRATTELS, - Capt. 296
FRASIER, - 320
FRAZER/FRAIZER, John 172, 195, 293, 333; Joseph 87
FRAZIER, - Capt. 312; Joseph 182
FREAME, - Mrs. 129; Thomas 129
FREDER, Gasper 317
FREDERICK, - Mr. 277, 281
FREE, Jacob 3
FREEBORN, - Capt. 250; Isaac 101; William 100, 173
FREEHERDEN, Henry 232
FREEMAN, - Capt. 27, 213, 231, 243; Isaac 28; Thomas 293; William 159, 207
FREEMILLER, Joseph 74
FRENCH, - Capt. 236, 238, 290, 329; Mr. 260; John 124; Michael 258; Philip 35
FREW, John 8, 9, 19, 159, 161, 168, 271

FRIEND, Gabriel 18
FRISBY, - Capt. 320
FRITH, - Capt. 20
FRITS, Christian 293
FROST, - Rev. 318
FRY, - Capt. 109, 223, 331, 332; Col. 298; Joshua 282, 291, 294; Richard 242
FULLER, - DONALDSON and 180, 222, 250, 261; Benjamin 157
FULLERTON, William 98
FULTON, David 239, 267; Francis 166; William 225
FUNK, Martin 240
FUNSTON, John 136
FURLONG/FURLOW, - Capt. 130, 189, 218, 220, 233, 236, 238, 294, 303, 308, 314
FURMAN, - REED and 273, 284; - 184; Moore 107, 152, 226; Thomas 191
FURNELL, Peter 41
FURNIS, Anthony 171, 177
FURYE, Peregrine 53
FUSSELL, - FISHER and 48, 98, 111, 160; Solomon 251

GAA, William 214
GAAB, George Adam 314
GABRIEL, Richard 221
GABRIELSON, - Capt. 277
GAINE, Hugh 326
GAINS, John 325
GAINSBERRY, Elizabeth 251
GAINSELE, Matthias 248, 281
GALATLY, - Capt. 286
GALBRAITH/GALBREATH/ GALBRETH, James 12, 40, 44; John 13, 269
GALE, - Widow 316; James 317; Nicholas 237
GALLACHER, Bridget 59
GALLOP, - Capt. 66; Samuel 151
GALLOWAY, Joseph 122, 239, 283; Peter 84
GALOHOWN, John 305
GAMBLE, William 74
GAMMON, William 119
GANO, George 4
GANTHONY, Peter 73, 85, 112
GARRAGAN/GARAGAN, Peter 72, 92
GARDNER/GARDINER, - CUNNINGHAM/CONYNGHAM and 14, 35, 42, 48, 51, 100, 109, 141, 188, 191, 209; Capt. 221, 228, 259, 266, 279, 291, 299, 313, 317, 318; Abraham 291; Francis 2; G. 266; John 207, 232; Joseph 185; Nanny 154; Nicholas 293; Peter 18, 20; Theophilus 41, 143
GARDY, Daniel 123
GARGAS, George 269
GARNER, John 11

GARRAWAY/GARROWAY, - and WRIGHT 127; Charles 183
GARRET/GARRETT/GARRAT, - and PARKER 73, 98, 139; Capt. 286; Amos 2, 129, 251; Isaac 43; John 238; Joseph 187; Lawrence 261
GARRETSON, - Capt. 58
GARRICK, - Mr. 59
GARRIGUE/GARRIGUES/ GARRIQUE, Francis 82, 110, 127, 208; Isaac 226; John 240
GARRISON, - Capt. 47, 143, 197, 202, 207, 250, 316; Isaac 236; John 134; Joseph 236
GASS, - Capt. 21, 160, 251, 295
GASSNER/GASNER/GESNER, Dominicus 12, 27, 43, 49, 163
GATCHELL, Isaac 61; Elisha, Jr. 30
GAULING, Alexander 217
GAVIN, Joseph 25
GAY, Edward 331; N. Ruxton 264
GEBHARD/GEBBARD, John 77, 135
GEDDES, William 331
GEHR, Conrad 36
GEIGER, Matthias 61
GELLER, Christopher 247
GELSTON, - Capt. 300, 318
GENTNEN, John Frederick 245
GEORGE, David 84, 139; Elizabeth 128; Nicholas 210, 227; Richard 102
GERMAN, Edward 242
GERRARD/GERARD; see JERRARD - M 77; Samuel 161; Thomas 321
GETZ, Christian 250
GHISLIN/GHISELIN, William 87, 156
GIBBONS/GIBBON, - Capt. 246, 247, 267, 296, 321; James 174, 313; Joseph 30, 61, 102, 149, 197, 253, 308; Nicholas 115; Thomas 162
GIBBS, - Capt. 55; Dr. 218; Benjamin 270, 273; Benjamin, Jr. 46; Dorothy 201; Isaac 319; Joseph 270
GIBSON, - Capt. 71; Andrew 239; George 38, 54, 69, 94, 98, 99, 116, 227, 302; James 227; John 159, 227; Nathan 16; Randle 285; William 159
GIDDENS, George 76
GIDDINGS, - Capt. 178; Daniel, Jr. 259
GIFFORD, - Capt. 78, 143, 177, 272, 296

GILBERT, - 85, 169;
   Capt. 291; Benjamin
   133, 295; Ephraim 30;
   Henry 134; James 141;
   John 50; Thomas 127,
   196
GILCHRIST/GILCREAST,
   James 8, 245, 283
GILES/GILE, - Capt. 189;
   Jacob 74, 156, 258;
   Patrick 330
GILKEY, Samuel 270; Walter 270
GILL, - Capt. 259, 261,
   274; Elizabeth 190;
   John 264; Patrick 221;
   Robert 34
GILLAND, Edward 287
GILLESPIE/GILLESPY/
   GILESPY/GALLASPY, Hugh
   11; James 8, 20, 319;
   John 48, 51
GILLEYLEN/GILLELYN, -
   Mr. 10; John 85, 125
GILLIAM, William 36
GILMAN, - Major 52, 64
GILMORE, - HINSHELWOOD
   and 194
GILPIN/GILPEN, George
   309; Samuel 229
GINGLE, Isaac 198; John
   231
GINNENS, John 145
GIRAUDET, Julian 81
GIRTIE, Simon 123
GIST, - Mr. 277, 304;
   Christopher 293
GITTINS, John 256
GIVIN, - Capt. 71
GLADSON, William 293
GLASFORD, Henry 8
GLASGOW, Hugh 88; Robert 276
GLAZIER, - Lt. 22
GLEAVES/GLEAVE, Isaac
   120, 165; John 326
GLENN/GLEN, - Gov./Gov.
   J. 274, 322; Jacob,
   Jr. 24; James 245,
   281, 327; John 239,
   249; John, Jr. 53;
   William 222
GLENTWORTH, - Capt. 169,
   279
GLOVER, - Capt. 22; Widow 89; Richard 175,
   190
GOAD, - Capt. 252
GOASET, Loveless 259
GODDARD/GODARD, - Capt.
   298; John 259
GODDEN, - LAWRENCE and
   110
GODFREY, - Capt. 259,
   275; Benjamin 98, 130;
   Cesar 109; John 334;
   Thomas 69
GOFF, - Capt. 261; Charles, Jr. 273; Elijah
   259; Peter 110
GOLDEN, Andrew 334; Anthony 9; Samuel 102;
   William 197, 253, 309
GOLDING, Samuel 197
GOLDSMITH, Daniel 129,
   133, 256; John 263,
   266; William 87

GOLL, John 247
GOLLIN, Elizabeth 236
GOLOCHAR, Eleanor 163
GOM, Stephen 211
GOMEZ, Benjamin 51, 53
GOOD, Christian 146;
   George 231
GOODING, - Capt. 275,
   281; Col. 20; Jacob
   8; John, Sr. 13
GOODMAN, - 209; Capt.
   31, 75, 99; Mr. 64;
   Daniel 160, 256, 287;
   Matthew 289; Nathaniel
   11; Stephen 108; Walter 44, 90; William
   19, 36
GOODRIDGE, - Capt. 22;
   Gilbert 317
GOODS, John 80
GOODSHIUS, John 50, 150
GOODWIN, - Capt. 201;
   George 227; Lyde 75
GOOL, John 77
GORDON, - HUTTON and 51;
   Capt. 207, 208, 227,
   281, 294, 296, 304,
   308; George 85; James
   52; John 239, 244;
   Lewis 159, 165; Mary
   331; Robert 30, 311;
   Stephen 325; Thomas
   57, 61, 85, 94, 102,
   105, 174, 271, 307;
   Walter 212
GORE, - Capt. 205;
   George 204
GORGASS, John 321
GORHAM, - Capt. 37, 71,
   80; Col. 29, 52, 54,
   55, 60, 64, 79, 137;
   Lt. 81; Benjamin 314;
   John 170; Joseph 62,
   131
GORRELL, James 31, 103;
   Ruth 193
GOSLING, John 164; Sylvanus 164
GOSTALOW, George 227
GOUCHER, Richard 130
GOULD, Benjamin 14
GOURLEY, John 145
GOVAN, John 33
GOVE, Richard 217
GOWDIE, John 294
GOWMILLER, Henry 276
GRACE, - 231; Aaron
   274; John (alias John
   Jones) 40; Robert 3,
   11, 203, 215; William 85
GRACEY, - Capt. 167
GRADY, James 182
GRAEF, John 58
GRAEME/GREAMS, - Dr. 39,
   150, 157, 173; Mrs.
   150; Thomas 7, 48, 83,
   198
GRAFF, Barbary 213;
   Matthew 213
GRAHAM, - Capt. 318;
   Col. 56; Dr. 154; Mr.
   61; Arthur 77; Francis 3, 114; Henry
   Hale/Henryhale/Henry
   Hall 30, 169, 335;
   James 2, 13, 46, 207;

John 132; Patrick 330;
   William 106
GRAINGER, - Capt. 201,
   256
GRAISBURY, James 221
GRANDINE, Amos 282
GRANSON, Peter 227
GRANT, - Capt. 301; Daniel 262; John 32, 186;
   William 178, 204, 222,
   252, 273, 285, 301, 324
GRANTHUM, - Capt. 288
GRASSNER, John 232
GRAVELL, Aylmer 40
GRAVES, Sarah 147; William 147
GRAY/GREY, - 65, 95, 99,
   101, 155, 180, 189,
   254; - Capt. 20; Rev.
   119; Anne 158; Elizabeth 301; George 9, 42,
   50, 51, 57, 127, 184,
   222, 228, 231, 260,
   301, 327; George, Jr.
   301; Harrison 127; James 150; Joseph 26, 31,
   34, 39, 44, 222, 231;
   Mary 294; Samuel 124;
   Thomas 54, 102; William 12, 45, 60, 79,
   84, 103, 104, 109,
   120, 125, 129, 142,
   145, 152, 189, 197,
   200, 236, 253, 259,
   277, 301
GRAYDON, Alexander 5, 8,
   10, 16, 51, 88, 94,
   144, 186, 192, 194,
   232
GREATOR, Jacob 263
GREEBLE, Andrew 291
GREEK, John 73
GREEN, - and WHITLOCK
   160, 207; Capt. 21,
   25, 30, 220, 225, 259,
   263, 275, 285, 329,
   331; Mr. 266; Widow
   170; Anne 49; Elizabeth 152; James 92,
   94, 118; John 212; Jonas 106, 231; Joseph
   255; Martha 224, 233,
   245, 273; Matthew 211;
   Peter (alias SPARKS)
   226; Pyramus 16; Sarah
   177, 179; Thomas 42,
   58, 60, 92, 114, 124,
   131, 133, 154, 184,
   204, 224, 233, 241,
   244, 265, 273; William 82, 192, 252
GREENAL/GREENALL/GRENALL,
   - Capt. 1, 202, 255
GREENLEAFE, Isaac 73,
   111, 128, 205, 219,
   232, 292; John 280;
   Stephen 48
GREENWAY/GREENAWAY, -
   and RUNDLE 106, 150;
   Capt. 251, 268, 275,
   295, 304; John 150;
   Joseph 118, 136, 319;
   Robert 18, 32, 85,
   203, 271; William 17
GREENWOOD, David 211;
   James 19
GREFF, Jacob 187

351

GREGG/GREGGE, - Capt. 194; Andrew 20; Harmon 138; James 85; John 168; Robert 199; William 35
GREGORY, - Widow 94, 152; Elizabeth 65; Thomas 227
GRENVILLE/GREENVILLE, - Gov. 276, 321; Mr. 106
GRETELL, Thomas 25
GREVILL/GREVELL, Jane 100, 136
GREW, Theophilus 38, 129, 155, 195, 251
GRIFFEY, Timothy 146
GRIFFIN, - Widow 99, 127; Elizabeth 99; George 89, 131; Joannah 107; John 141; Peter 169
GRIFFITHS/GRIFFITH/ GRIFFITTS, - NORRIS and 3, 26, 35, 118, 130; 172; Capt. 59, 189, 200, 202, 220, 231, 259, 261, 285, 300, 303; Mr. 314; Abraham 8; Abraham, Jr. 127; Benjamin 258; David (alias of David Smith) 206; Evan 83; Griffith 6, 102, 174, 239, 261, 270, 315; Isaac 9, 96, 102, 111, 117, 127, 135, 136, 144, 149, 165, 168, 169, 171; John 100, 248; Sarah 282; Thomas 83, 87, 100, 118, 141, 168, 182, 285; Timothy 13, 42, 131, 282; William 37, 90, 176, 202, 216, 230, 249, 261, 264, 312
GRIGG, - Capt. 128
GRIMES, Francis 41
GRIMORE, Henry 173
GRINDY, William 176, 180
GRISCOM/GRESCOM, Andrew 217; Samuel 319; Tobias 116
GRISLEY, - 307; Samuel 169, 250, 309
GROBIN, Anna Catherina 300
GROFF, Joseph 157, 329
GROLL, Christian 168
GROSS/GROSE/GROCE, - Capt. 66; Israel 291; Jos. 150; Michael 116, 146
GROTEHOUSE, - Widow 269
GROVE, - Capt. 201; John 283
GROVER, John 174
GROVES, - Capt. 144; John 2, 26, 28, 40, 231, 279; Norton 74
GROWDON, Joseph 261; Lawrence 81, 101, 150, 224, 234, 286, 311, 325
GRUBB/GRUB, - 132, 251; Emanuel, Jr. 276;
Nathaniel 16, 49, 61, 102, 149, 175, 197, 253, 274, 280, 308; Peter 115; Thomas 3, 249, 276, 298
GRUMBLE/GRUMLEY, Honor Yerack/Hanis Yarick 72, 84
GUILFORD/GUILDFORD/ GILLFORD/GILFORD, - Capt. 220, 250, 260, 282, 288, 290, 308, 314, 321
GUION/GYON, George 51, 313
GULLISON, - Mr. 325
GUNN, Samuel 23
GURNEY/GURNAY, - Capt. 257; Thomas 123
GUTHERY, James 54
GUY, John 138, 228
GWIN, Hannah 30; John 306; Morris 141, 205, 212; Owen 30; Reese 70

HAASE/HAAS, Hans Yerrick 75; Johannes 229
HACK/HACKE, John 85; Tunstall 201
HACKET/HACKETT, - Dr. 208; John 171, 208; William (alias of Brian Doron) 104
HACKNEY, Joseph 172
HADDEN, Abigail 40; John 40
HADDON, - Capt. 21
HADLEY, Joseph 185
HAFFNER, Conrad 314
HAGAN, James 26; John 113
HAGEMAN, - Capt. 38
HAGER, Anna Margarietta 312; Harmanus 312; Jacob 312; Valentine 312
HAGGEN, Catherine 302; Hermanus 302; Wolfgang 184
HAGIE/HAGY, Jacob 16, 123, 131, 137, 140, 150, 194
HAGNER, Peter 272
HAINES/HAYNES/HAINES/ HANES, Ann 286; Arthur 17; Christina 124; Enoch 186; Henry 124; Hugh 17; Jacobus 304; John 46, 333; Nathan 265; Patrick 303; Richard 239
HAINEY, - 43
HAINLY, Sigismund 151, 156
HAINSWORTH, Sankey 273
HAISTINS, David 35
HAIT, Benjamin 307
HAKE, Thomas 36
HALBERT, - Mr. 51, 54; Philip 125, 256, 329
HALE, Samuel 194, 222; Thomas 270
HALL, FRANKLIN and 176, 246; Capt. 24, 40, 55, 206, 223, 227, 253, 259, 268, 281, 290, 331, 332; Mr. 192;
Widow 174; Aquila 113; D./David 10, 15, 16, 124, 134, 135, 136, 140, 161, 172, 180, 199, 200, 206, 232, 255, 259, 289, 311; Hugh 1, 87; Jacob 1, 5, 17, 69, 73, 203; John 13, 16, 17, 102, 159, 160, 176, 186, 188, 190, 258, 281, 288; Lawrence 188; Matthew 118, 123; Richard 43, 184; Samuel 53, 130; Stephen 333; Theodorus 176; Thomas 276, 298, 328; William 28, 173
HALLAM, - Miss 279; Mrs. 291; Mr. 213; Thomas 155
HALLING, Michael 163
HALLINGBECK, Michael 252
HALLOWAY, - Capt. 236; Mary 1
HALLOWELL, Benjamin 74, 225; John 40, 64; Thomas 273
HALTHOM, John 173
HALTON, John 324
HAM, - Capt. 314
HAMAN, William 64
HAMBLE, Charles 324
HAMBRICHT/HAMBRECHT/ HAMBRIGHT/ HAMBRYGHT/ HAMBRYGT/HAMBRITH, Henry 213; John 3, 50, 54, 131, 213, 226, 257, 298, 334
HAMILTON, - 26, 37, 40, 52, 72, 81, 87, 95, 101, 110, 142, 149, 150, 162, 174, 179, 196, 201, 215, 218, 226, 230; Capt. 15, 129, 279, 285, 286, 295, 297, 303; Col. 116; Lt. 71; Mr. 308; Alexander 36, 49, 83, 90, 92, 97, 100, 119, 153, 174, 231, 241, 259; Andrew 18, 35, 46; Archibald 321; Billy 315; Charlotte (alias Charles) 186; Francis 22, 140; George 302; Hance 63, 131, 150, 151; Hugh 5; James 17, 35, 38, 125, 132, 189, 209, 214, 235, 311, 315, 327; John 60, 103, 161, 168, 172, 182, 190, 195, 202, 212; Malcom 168; Patrick 194, 284; Robert 273; William 82, 120, 136, 156, 191, 281
HAMMER, Elizabeth 101; William 225
HAMMON, Margaret 235
HAMMOND, - Capt. 55; John 91, 98; P. 259, 275, 287, 296
HAMPTON/HAMTON, Joseph 30, 61, 102, 149, 197, 253, 308
HAMSOUR, Adam 287

HAMWOOD, John 292
HANCE, John 12
HANCOCK, - Mr. 284; William 23, 115
HANDFIELD, Bill 71
HANDLEY, John 248; William 107
HANDS, B. 326
HANEY, - Capt. 262; Andrew 34, 65
HANGLIN, John 256
HANKINSON, William 18
HANLEY/HANLY, John 95, 260, 261, 263, 265, 275, 278, 320; Dudley 147, 171, 189
HANLIN/HANLON, Patrick 117, 152; Thomas 147
HANNIS, Andrew 76, 166, 270, 309, 335; John 76
HANNOTEAU, Don Joseph 20
HANNUM/HANNUMS/HANNAMS, John 45, 255, 326; Robert 210
HARBORTH, Elizabeth 121
HARBOTTLE, - Capt. 123
HARBURY, - Mr. 122
HARDING, Edward 286; Elizabeth 63; George 32, 52, 63, 326; John 3, 15, 23, 50, 331; John. Jr. 3, 15
HARDTMAN, Isaac 33
HARDWICH, Coles 57
HARDY, - Capt. 275, 296, 312; Alexander 245; Robert 294
HARDYMAN, Abraham 217
HARGRAVE, - Capt. 22, 218, 219, 316, 323
HARGROVES, George 192
HARKER, Ephraim 68
HARKNESS, George 4, 5, 303
HARLAN/HARLIN, Ezekiel, Jr. 251, 309; Joseph 144, 255, 309
HARLEY/HARLY/HARLEE, Manus 116; William 162, 172
HARMAN, Daniel 152
HARMER, Joshua 302
HARPELL, Johannes 300
HARPER, - Capt. 251; David, 324; Joseph 2; Robert 90; Thomas 68, 69, 80, 90, 102, 111, 117, 124, 138, 139, 143, 152, 165, 171, 179, 185
HARRAMOND, - Capt. 248
HARRAWAY, William 6
HARRIOT, - Capt. 257; Daniel 41
HARRIS, - 174; Capt. 22, 45, 217, 228, 242, 290, 295, 332; Mr. 54; Abel 213, 225; David 25; James 35; John 13, 50, 112, 150, 201, 249; Leech 66; Matthias 247; Richard 29; Sapience 64; Robert 302; Thomas 13, 19, 180, 286, 302;
William 277
HARRISON, - Capt. 214, 220, 223, 234, 285; George 267, 279, 284; Henry 26, 32, 63, 147, 157, 203, 254; James 57, 269; John 11, 19, 26, 140, 144, 146, 156, 196, 253, 296, 320; Philip 95; Richard 283; Samuel 115; William 132, 233
HARROBINE, John 308
HARRY, Aubrey 267; Henry 19; John 211, 269; Samuel 116
HART/HARTT, Elizabeth 95; George 95; James 130; John 30, 61, 102, 116, 126, 198, 230, 273, 280; Joseph 6, 77, 108, 123, 148, 149, 173, 258, 301; Mary 68, 115, 265; Robert 265; Samuel 175; Thomas 68, 71, 83, 187
HARTLEY, Hannah 71, 94; William 71, 94
HARTMAN, Henry 124; Theophilus 129, 141
HARTSHORNE, Hugh 288, 332; Robert 102
HARVEY/HARVIE, - Capt. 205, 206; Amos 309; James 200; Job 168, 196; John 164, 214; Joseph 139; Robert 123, 233; Thomas 200, 243
HASE, Hannah 237; John 237
HASELL/HASSELL/HAZELL, Ann 137; Matthew 24; Samuel 1, 25, 88, 111, 121, 125, 137, 160, 168, 176, 219, 239, 325
HASELGASER, Jacob 154
HASKELL, Andrew 18
HASSER, Frederick 125
HASSERT, Arent 43, 84, 130, 280
HASTINGS, Samuel 203, 298; Thomas 171, 189
HASSTY/HASTY, - Capt. 38; Benjamin 241, Charles 239; David 21; Jacob 239
HATCH, - Capt. 181, 225, 331
HATHERLY, Benedict Leonard 126; Benjamin 126; Elizabeth 126; John 122, 126
HATHORN/HATHORNE/HEATHORN, - Capt. 320; Daniel 67; Ebenezer 199, 227, 255
HATTON, - Capt. 320; George 147; Jane 30; Lucy 97; Thomas 30, 52, 70, 191
HAUN, Michael 247
HAUSSE, Christopher 62; Regina 62
HAVARD, William 161, 168
HAVENS, - Capt. 250
HAVILAND, - Capt. 110, 190, 282
HAWKE, - 59; Admiral 2; Serjeant 14; Andrew 63
HAWKINS, - 320; Widow 78; John (alias of John Hawksford) 2; Phebe 82; William 58, 82
HAWKSFORD, John (alias John Hawkins or Oxford) 2
HAWLEY, Gideon 299
HAWORD, John 60
HAWTHORN, Jonathan (alias of Maxwell M'Cormick) 186
HAWXEY, - Capt. 298
HAY, - Capt. 301; Charles 248, 281; Philip 311; William 136, 168, 174, 211, 227
HAYES/HAYS, - Capt. 274; Adam 8; Andrew 144; David 326; Dennis 198; James 68; Judah 116, 130; Richard 40
HAYHURST, Cuthbert 46, 79
HAYMAKER, Christopher 229
HAYMAN, Giles 188, 247; John 188, 247; Moses 269; Nicholas 188, 247; Peter 188, 247
HAYWOOD, - Capt. 247
HAZARD/HAZZARD, - 88; Jupiter 133; Robert 82; Samuel 21, 23, 37, 61, 66, 69, 77, 83, 88, 105, 125, 128, 135, 168, 174, 176, 177, 217, 220, 230, 273, 301
HASELTON/HAZELTON, - Capt. 78, 238, 246; James 147; William 230, 290
HEAD, - Capt. 305; Andrew 163; John, Jr. 222, 283
HEADLEY, John 252
HEADON, Daniel 148
HEALEY, Francis 277
HEANY, Patrick 50
HEAP, George 27, 61, 85, 101, 102, 117, 124, 136, 147, 154, 180, 196, 259; Samuel 169
HEARNE, William 217
HEATH, James Paul 73
HEATHBOURN, Benjamin 157
HEATHCOAT, John 147
HEATON, - 71; Edward 311; Robert 49, 131, 260, 331, 335; William 59
HEBERT, Lawrence 140
HERBERT, Sarah 317; Thomas 317
HEDGES/HEDGE, Rebecca 73; William 73, 102, 114
HEFLIKEFER, Jacob 100
HEFORD, William 303
HEIGHINGTON, - Capt. 295
HEISTERBERG, Christianus Fredericus 246
HENCHY, Joseph 179

353

HENDERSON, - Capt. 68, 110, 114, 198, 200, 250, 255, 313; John 18, 113, 142; Joseph 26, 31; William 3, 76, 191, 215, 234, 246, 283
HENDRICK, Edward 25
HENDRICKS, David 252, 299; Tobias 8, 150, 199
HENDRY, Darby 97
HENEY, - Capt. 242
HENINGER, Simon 264
HENIS, - Mr. 276
HENKE, Jacob 82
HENLEY, Margaret 107
HENMAN, Daniel 97
HENNEN, John 300
HENNING, Philip 143
HENRY, - Capt. 272; Darby (alias of Jeremiah Henry) 66 80; George 179; Jeremiah (alias of Darby Henry) 66; Michael 29; William 273, 294, 301
HENTS, Conrad 293
HEPBURN, James 302
HERBERT, Elizabeth 117; Elizabeth (alias of Elizabeth Linn) 195; Lawrence 16; Philip 198; William 195
HERD, William 185
HERIN, - Capt. 263
HERITAGE, Benjamin 25
HERLAN, William 183
HERMAN, Leonard 104
HERN, Richard 236
HERNER, John Adam 284
HERON, - Col./Lt.-Col. 32, 204
HERRING, - 33; Capt. 205
HERSEY/HERSAY/HERSE, - Mr. 155; Isaac 215; Jacob 234
HESSY, Robert 41
HEWES/HEWS, Joseph 155, 293; Moses 177, 188
HEWIT, John 171
HEYSHAM, - Capt. 1, 59, 90, 121, 250, 296, 312, 332, 334
HEYSLIP, - Capt. 296
HICKEY, John 288
HICKLIN, James 299
HICKMAN, Francis 166, 197
HICKS/HIX, - 27; Augustine 23, 191; Edward 79; Gilbert 121, 181, 325; Joseph 252; Thomas 40
HIDE, Samuel 217; Thomas 252
HIDEGGAR, - Gov. 212
HIDNER, George 33
HIERN, - Capt. 276
HIFFERNAN, Roger 332
HIGGINS, - Capt. 321; Jedediah 67; John (alias of John Pepperdine) 174; Patrick 48
HIGGS, - Capt. 251
HIGH, Samuel 253

HILDRETH, Joseph 74
HILEY, Edward 239
HILL, - Capt. 76, 90, 206, 235, 236, 257, 262, 290, 294, 332; Alexander 241; Edward 66, 71, 84, 90, 125, 324; John 99; John (alias John Seale) 128; Richard 134; Richard, Jr. 149, 281; Stephen 67; William 42, 246
HILLARD, James 178
HILLBORN/HILLBOURN, - and JONES 297; Widow 145
HILLEGAS/HELLEGAS, George Peter 291, Michael 22, 24, 37, 45, 61, 90, 110, 320
HILLIER, William 90
HILMAN, Daniel, Jr. 253; Daniel, Sr. 253
HILTON, - Capt. 17
HINCHMAN, James 177
HINCKES, Anthony 106
HINDE, Michael 250
HINDS, Thomas 317
HINES, John 106; Thomas 180
HINGSTON, Daniel 277, 280
HINCKEL/HINKELS, Anthony 10, 80
HINSDALE, - Col 24
HINSHELWOOD, and GILMORE 194
HINSON, Charles 29
HINTON, - Capt. 155, 156, 158; William 241
HIRONS, Mark 14; Simon 163; William 14
HIRST, John 46, 60
HITCHMAN, William 100
HITE, Jacob 105
HITNER, Adam 325
HOBART, Enoch 98
HOBBS, - Capt. 23
HOBBY, - Mr. 315
HOBSON, - Gov. 50, 54, 78; John 176
HOCKLEY/HOCKLY, Henry 61, 102, 149; Richard 49, 96, 99, 119, 154, 163, 214, 215, 240, 261, 271, 279, 283, 324; William 290
HODAN, - Capt. 234
HODGE, Andrew 41, 44, 179, 200, 273; 301; Samuel 25, 32; William 234, 282
HODGES, - Capt. 330
HODGSON, Peter 107
HODSON, Joseph 20
HOFMAN, Ludwick 317
HOGAN/HOGGAN, Anne 314; John 174, 280; Michael 186; Patrick 294; William 90
HOGANS, John 238, 242
HOGE, William 197, 253, 308
HOGELAND, Derrick/Derick 19, 30, 197, 253, 308; Jane 19

HOGG/HOG, - 302; Capt. 295; Joseph 193, 233, 240; Peter 307; Thomas 192
HOIT, James 325
HOLBORN, - Commodore 116
HOLBROOK, - Capt. 218, 323
HOLCOMB/HOLCOMBE, Jacob 29; Mary 29; Thomas 84, 90, 93, 103, 104
HOLDEN/HOLDON, - Capt. 221, 316
HOLDER, John 199, 255
HOLE, Matthias 162
HOLLAND, - MILLER and 161; Capt. 13, 115; James 136; Richard 40; Samuel 187
HOLLIDAY/HOLLYDAY, - 248; William 108, 242
HOLLING, Michael 245
HOLLINGSWORTH, Zebulon 38, 181
HOLLINSHEAD, Francis 136; John 65; Joseph 29
HOLLIS, - Mr. 154
HALLOREN, Matthew 315
HOLLOWAY/HOLAWAY, Manchester 19, 36; Robert 156; Thomas 207
HOLLY, - Capt. 142
HOLME, James 139; John 139, 217, 266, 267
HOLMES/HOLMS, - Capt. 49; John 34, 117; Jonathan 8; Joseph 290; Samuel 298
HOLSTEIN, Frederick 3, 202; Matthias 3, 114
HOLSTON, John 145
HOLT, Elizabeth 196; James 45; John 158, 165; Rives/Ryves 31, 63, 103, 150, 199, 255, 309, 326; Samuel 196
HOLTHAM, John 101; Joseph 4
HOLWAY, Thomas 60
HOLWELL, - Capt. 206, 223; Frances 267
HOMER, - Capt. 296
HOMEWOOD, - Mr. 190
HONEY, Valentine 240
HONNOR, - Capt. 206
HONYMIN, James 91
HOOD/HOODT, - 217, 220; Capt. 286, 321, 327; James 84, 107; John 130, 272; Thomas 84, 112, 171, 216
HOOK/HOOKE, George 129, 135; William 114
HOOMES, William 182
HOOPER, H. 331; Reynald 226; Robert Lettice/ Robert Lettis 114, 134, 151, 184, 223, 226, 236, 249, 262; Sarah 224; William 224
HOOPE/HOOPES/HOOPS, Adam 103, 206; Nathan 249
HOOTON, Benjamin 258;

HOOTON (cont'd) Thomas 94, 217, 247
HOPE, - Capt. 76; James 149, 270; John 62; Thomas 9, 205; William 191
HOPKINS, - Capt. 259, 285, 298, 331; Ebenezer 279; Gerard 190; Hannah 182; James 307; John 78, 138, 149, 190, 199, 307, 313, 317; Patrick 9; Robert 80, 226
HOPKINSON, Mary 193, 203, 242; Thomas 1, 36, 63, 68, 120, 155, 193, 203
HOPPE, Hendrick 301; John 301
HOPPER, - Capt. 84
HOPSON, - Gov. 251, 253, 295; John 256
HOPTON, - Gov. 190
HORNBLY, - Capt. 321
HORNE/HORN, Alexander 220; Daniel 282; Peter 189; William 295, 327
HORNBROOK, Thomas 176, 180
HORNER, John 65; Robert 16; Samuel 248; Tho,as 334
HORRY, Daniel 215
HORTON, - Major 32; Ezra 307
HOSE, Jacob 289; William 139
HOSKIN, - Capt. 201
HOUBER, Jacob 312
HOUCK, Andrew 329
HOUGH, - Capt. 248; Henry 194; Jonathan 20; Joseph 190, 333
HOULSE, Silas 182
HOULT, John 172
HOUSE, - 153; Christopher 234; George 30, 59, 102, 185; Joseph 72, 219, 221
HOUSTON, - Capt. 267, 276; Alexander 261; John 125
HOUTON, Edward 74
HOVEY, - Capt. 303, 310
HOW, - Capt. 195, 110, 119
HOWARD, Beale 289; Gideon 167; Gordon 142, 148; John 39, 53, 158, 167, 272, 295; John Grinef 190; Joseph 150; Lawrence 303; Matthew 112; Rachel 142, 148; Sarah (alias of Sarah Knox) 220; Thomas 39
HOWELL/HOWEL, - POLE and 146, 184, 202, 204, 275; Capt. 318; Mrs. 60, 160; Widow 21; Benjamin 93, 127, 247, 269, 311, 331; Daniel 47; David 8; Isaac 4; Jacob 45, 197; James 314; John 4, 11, 27, 32; Joseph 4, 217, 325; Joshua 328; Philip 6, 217; Richard 236; Samuel 158, 222, 233, 251, 266, 312; Thomas 53, 62, 127, 266, 312; William 6, 266
HOWLES, Robert 158
HOY, Samuel 197, 309
HOYD, Thomas 297
HRUBB, Henry 258
HUBBARD, - Capt. 247, 265; Nathaniel 273; T./Thomas 244, 317
HUBBEL/HUBBELL, - Capt. 264, 266
HUBBERT, Thomas, Jr. 20 319; Joseph 48; Lucy 163; Robert 163
HUBER, Jacob 17, 56
HUBLEY, Bernard 91
HUDE, James 69
HUDSON, - Capt. 297; John 48; Joseph 236, 289; William 1
HUFF, Francis 181
HUGG, Jacob 317; William 242, 254, 305
HUGHES/HEWES, - STANDLEY and 291, 330; Capt. 17; David (alias David Luellin) 19; Edward 69, 282; Elisha 172; Ferdinand/Ferdinando 72, 152; George 9, 136; Griffith 124; John 3, 32, 66, 121, 125, 285; Martin 167; Mary 167; Matthew 8; Moses 173; Richard 115, 161, 228, 322; Thomas 118; William 42, 74, 228, 260
HULINGS/HULING, Marcus 230; Marcus, Jr. 230; Michael 223, 230
HUMPHREYS/HUMPHRYS/ HIMPHREY/HUMPHRIES/ HUMPHRES/HUMPHRIS, Abraham 46; Catherine 109; Charles 33, 132; Edward 193; Elizabeth 238; James 32, 59, 70, 82, 131, 162, 203, 234, 241, 261, 263, 294; Joshua 148, 182; Lydia 257; Samuel 109, 257; Solomon 28; William 53, 80, 100, 113, 219, 274
HUNLOCK/HUNLOCKE, - Widow 22; Bouman 163
HUNN, John 14
HUNNEWELL, - Capt. 172
HUNT, - 46; Capt. 212, 247, 330; Mr. 216; Charles 76; Glover 181, 234; John 31, 36, 54, 60, 174, 227; Jonathan 31; Joseph 333; Mary 93; Michael 162, 173; Roger 2, 61, 86; Thomas 93, 228; Wilson 26, 31, 71
HUNTER, - Capt. 42, 58, 228, 238, 242, 243, 262, 275, 313, 321
Col. 334; Alexander 8, 179; Benjamin 184; George 154, 240, 245; James 5, 122, 191; John 31; Robert 307; Thomas 184; William 226, 271
HURFORD, Samuel 238
HURLEY, Daniel 205, 206, 207
HURST, Thomas 120
HUSBAND, Herman 250; Robert 263; William 250
HUSE, - 6; William 195
HUSES, Ferdinando 60, 62
HUSK, - Capt. 193
HUSON, John 315
HUSSERD, John 220
HUSSEY, - and FITZGERALD 173; Capt. 60, 221; John 188; Nathan 68; Timothy 212; William 127, 240
HUSTLER, William 191
HUSTON, - Capt. 143, 174; Alexander 93, 160, 176, 231, 239, 250, 269, 281; James 6, 190, 219; John 19, 36, 176, 333; Peter 22
HUTCHINS/HUTCHINGS, - Capt. 71, 205
HUTCHINSON, - Capt. 1, 109, 147, 202, 275, 316; John 59; Joseph 123; Michael 62, 123, 206; Randel 123; Thomas 297
HUTCHISON, - Capt. 52, 235
HUTTON, - and GORDON 51
HUXHAM, John 223
HYAM, Joshua 52, 70
HYAT, John 5
HYDE, John 37
HYDER, - Capt. 247
HYER, - Capt. 223
HYNDSHAW, John 316
HYNE, Thomas 203
HYNSON, - Mr. 70

IBISON, Robert 276
IDDINGS, William 240
IDEN, John 64
ILIFF, Edmund 78
IMLEY/IMLAY, John 273, 287, 303
INCHES/INCH, - Capt. 286; Mr. 190; Joseph 292, 295
INGELADO, - Capt. 41
INGELS, Matthew/Matthias 121, 319
INGERSOLL, - Capt. 213
INGHAM, - Capt. 133; Jonathan 11, 48, 253, 308
INGLE, Benjamin 266
INGLEHART, Michael 37
INGLIS/INGLES, - Mr. 162, 273; James 155; John 2, 23, 40, 62, 97, 148, 171, 182, 307, 329

INGRAM/INGRAHAM, - Capt. 331; John 22, 281; Margaret 30
INHAVEN, Edward 28
INNES, - Capt. 200; Col. 295, 296, 299, 334; Gen. 304; Alexander 324; James 295
INSKAPE, John 7
INSLEY/INSLEE/INSLE, Joseph 5, 49, 77, 91, 103, 123, 154, 232, 234, 263, 300, 327, 333
ION, Richard 152
IRELAND, - Capt. 123
IRESON, William 202, 291, 299
IRONS, Thomas 151
IRVING, Henry 276
IRWIN, Hugh 233; Samuel 4, 5
ISELSTINE, Matthias 139, 184
ISEN, Frederick 130
ISRAEL, Michael 18, 33, 76, 99

JACK, James 8; John 292
JACKMAN, Joseph 185
JACKSON, - Capt. 193, 288, 294, 306, 308; Mr. 208; Benjamin 205, 216; Caleb 300; James 108, 205; John 108, 157, 173, 229, 331; Joseph 74, 95, 103; Lovell 124; Low/Lowe 108, 128, 231; Samuel 53; William 69, 120, 123, 124, 210, 287
JACOBS/JACOB, Henry 247; Israel 134; Job 53; John 134; Martha 23; Matthias 178; Michael 156; Richard 236; Samuel 212; Thomas 23
JACOBSON, - Capt. 285, 321
JACQUES, Lancelot 231
JACQUET, Peter 9
JADCOCKS, Tho. 41
JAFFRAY, Henry 323
JAMES, - SMITH and 25, 28, 46, 150, 158; - 71, 72, 82, 88, 90, 106, 120, 125, 137, 141, 146, 157, 161, 175, 177, 180, 183, 185, 192, 193, 196, 201, 202, 203; Capt. 25, 58, 73, 285; Abel 61, 62, 77, 80, 95, 102, 140, 157, 168, 169, 172, 182, 187, 225, 251, 279, 314; Daniel 79; George 6; J., Jr. 236; James 20, 98, 121; Joseph 30, 181, 198, 253, 308; Lewis 91, 206; Martha 258; Michael 59; Morgan 297; Rachel 189; Thomas 13, 29, 43, 91, 128, 149, 197, 206, 229, 253, 295, 304; Thomas, Jr. 43, 48, 145; William 132, 204, 206
JAMISON/JEMISON, Robert 11, 36, 326; Samuel 8
JANNEY, Isaac 222, 281
JANUARY, Thomas 136
JANVIER, Isaac 177
JAQUES, Samuel 132
JARRARD/JARARD/JARRAD, Richard 221, 237, 307; Thomas 256
JARVIS/JERVIS, - 208; John 88, 146, 234; Thomas 132, 298, 311
JASPAR, - Capt. 195
JAUNCEY, - Capt. 52, 235, 255, 275, 318; John 290
JAY, - Capt. 332; Peter 270
JEANS, James 236
JEBB, John 190
JEFFERSON, - Capt. 163, 250
JEFFREY/JEFFERY/JEFFRIES/JEFFERIS, - Capt. 147, 297; John 11; Richard 151; Robert 22
JEFFRON, Daniel 263
JEKYLL, - Mrs. 59; Widow 65
JENKINS, - 180; Capt. 281; Aaron 55, 223; Charles 19, 197, 260, 266; Elizabeth 164; John 77, 88, 166; Philip 124; Stephen 262; Thomas 20; William 68, 85, 248, 310
JENKISON, William 155
JENKS, Thomas 260
JENNETS, - Capt. 296
JENNINGS, John 159
JERMAIN, - Capt. 312
JERMAN, Edward 294; John 104, 197
JERRARD; see GERRARD, - Capt. 294, 297; Richard 333
JESSION, David 273
JESSOP, Mary 238; Robert 150
JEVON, William 14, 86
JEWELL, Robert 44, 258; Sarah 44, 258
JILLET, William 206
JOEL, - Capt. 59
JOHN, Daniel 87; David 47; Evan 130; Nathaniel 87
JOHNS, Isaac 209; Robert 204
JOHNSON, - Capt. 55, 58, 178, 205, 225, 250, 260, 290, 301, 331; Mr. 304; Widow 125; Catherine 281; Daniel 239; Derrick 302, 304, 319; Dirk 229; Francis 22, 108, 134, 288, 315, 320; Hoalman 297; Humphrey 116; James 58, 60, 62, 231; John 5, 83, 85, 124, 139, 228, 236, 264, 272, 306; Joseph 291; Margaret 64; Nathaniel 21; Obadiah 106; Richard 222; Samuel 222, 279; Thomas 46; William 40, 158, 253, 281, 317
JOHNSTON, - Capt. 129, 294, 298; Alexander 32, 68; Charles 312; David 206; Gabriel 192; Henry 104; Jacob 46; Jane 104; John 100, 134, 264; Mary 27; Richard 183, 230; Thomas 237
JOLLY/JOLLEY, - Capt. 21; Andrew 167; Richard 15
JONES, - BOURNE and 287; HILLBORN and 297; SMITH and 60; - 118, 128, 130, 131, 138, 144, 232, 266, 326; Capt. 119, 186, 189, 195, 220, 236, 243, 244, 245, 247, 250, 251, 260, 261, 276, 282, 289, 306, 310, 312, 332; Widow 55, 122, 173, 248, 286; Abel 94, 109; Amos 114, 142, 192, 249, 312; Ann/Anne 306, 310; Aquila 203, 258, 280, 283; Catherine 263; Charles 61, 149, 157, 197, 217, 279; David 6, 121, 123, 148, 156, 182, 262, 267, 295, 303; David, Jr. 71; Edward 6, 9, 16, 17, 42, 52, 70, 102, 106, 117, 129, 134, 227, 243, 271, 327; Evan 103, 149, 197, 203, 253; Francis 52, 70; George 132, 306, 315; Gerard 213; Griffith 42; Henry 11; Horace 195, 251; Hugh 83, 179, 222, 283, 333; Isaac 14, 27, 42, 95, 96, 149, 160, 165, 176, 197, 222, 225, 230, 251, 253, 254, 279, 285, 291, 308; Jacob 159; James 30, 61, 83, 222, 330; John 5, 18, 20, 31, 41, 54, 62, 70, 76, 81, 83, 92, 100, 108, 112, 134, 153, 178, 192, 200, 205, 212, 214, 237, 258, 278, 310, 311, 312, 316, 328, 329; John (alias of John Grace) 40; Jonathan 41, 96, 264; Joseph 65, 100, 262; Joshua 188, 239; Lewis 36, 41, 202; Malachi 274; Mary 54; Nathaniel 130;

JONES (Cont'd), Oliver 115; Owen 102, 182; Peter 278; Rees 5, 67, 94, 321; Reuben 124; Richard 108; Robert 14, 118, 205, 216, 231, 264; Samuel 262; Sarah/Sara 18, 278; Sylvanus 40; Thomas 18, 64, 75, 171, 202, 224, 308, 315; William 41, 60, 102, 130, 141, 195
JONQUIERE, - M. 62
JORDAN, Adam 193; Anne 198; Robert 258
JOSEPHSON, W. 146
JOSIAH, - and CARPENTER 262; Emanuel 100, 133, 193, 294, 298, 330
JOSLYNE, Joseph 208
JOUVENAL, Magdalene 227
JOWLES, - 52
JOY, - Capt. 25, 249, 262, 263, 286, 295, 297, 313
JOYCE, Moses 227
JUDD, - Capt. 107, 167, 331
JUMONVILLE, - M. 291
JUNG, Ann Margaret 58; Mark 58; Matthew 58
JUNKIN, Ernst 285
JUQUAT, John 91
JUSTICE/JUSTIS, John 34, 99; Mary 99; Neils 99; Swan 276; Swan, Jr. 278; Swethen 99

KABE, Hans William 130
KANE, Margaret 16
KAPPLEY, - Mr. 240
KARIN, Patrick 202
KARLIN, John 316
KARNEY, Patrick 19
KARR, William 11
KASEL, Nicholas 136
KASTNER, George 111
KATERA, Thomas 85
KATTER/KATTUR, - Capt. 41, 90, 110, 232, 289, 304; Alexander 160, 223
KAUL, Hans Peter 241
KAY, - 180
KEALER, Eve 299, 327; Jonas 299, 327
KAPPOCK, James 56
KEARNEY/KEARNY; see CARNEY, - Lt. 57; Edmund 125, 252, 323; Patrick 36
KEARNS/KEARN, John 215; Patrick 198, 208, 209
KEARSLEY, - Dr. 237; John 1, 34, 48, 117, 166, 203, 270; John, Jr. 48, 65
KEBLER, Jonas 33
KEEF, John 182
KEEMER, James 137
KEEN/KEENE/KEAN/KEANE, - Capt. 249, 265, 290, 296; John 91, 188, 228, 272; Matthias 2, 156, 189, 210; Mounce 121; Peter 1, 223, 239, 325; William 315
KEENS, George 264; John 234; Michael 234
KEEPERS, William 129
KEFFER, Leonard 37
KEITH, - Capt. 18; Thomasine/Thomasin 56, 65
KELCON, Maria 313
KELL, John 22
KELLOG/KELLOGG, - Capt. 67, 154
KELLY/KELLEY, - Capt. 231, 297, 312; Bartholomew 242; Daniel 304; Elizabeth 180; George 96; George (alias William Welsh/Welch) 264, 277; Hugh 32, 88, 148; James 193, 232; John 74, 157, 168, 170, 197, 253, 290, 308, 311, 321; Luke 212; Margaret 25; Mary 182; Patrick 54, 59, 180; Robert 67; Thomas 7, 119, 192, 198, 206, 207, 208, 209, 210, 239, 247
KEMBLE, Peter 20, 21, 23, 41
KEMLEY, Conrad 291
KEMP, - Mr. 113; John 248, 249; William 239, 249
KEMPER, Jacob 111
KEMPFER, John 247
KEMPLER, Andreas 145; Susanna 145
KENDALL, Benjamin 40, 61, 73, 98, 165, 225, 251, 260, 281; Thomas 103; William 95
KENDRICK, - Capt. 277; Henry 205
KENEY, John 115
KENLY, Daniel 143, 286
KENNEDY/KENEDY, - Capt. 257, 279, 284, 307, 308; Archibald 303; Archibald, Jr. 334; James 73; John 207, 289; Samuel 24, 35; William 169
KENNEWAY, - Capt. 195, 275
KENT, J. 33; John 3; Richard 15; Thomas 185, 216, 304
KENTON, Thomas 69, 278; William 69
KENTZLY, Matthias 311
KEORON, James 178
KEPPLE/KEPPEL/KEPPELE/KEPPLEY/KEPLEY, - Commodore 103, 109, 111, 321, 327, 329; Henry 64, 104, 106, 207, 271, 299, 327
KERBY, Joseph 6
KEREVAN, Michael 195
KERLIN, John 62, 197, 253; Matthias 95
KERR, - Capt. 147; Daniel 287; George 158; James 110; John 319; William 165, 166, 201
KETCHAM, John 216
KETELTAS/KETTELTAS, - Capt. 24, 70, 71, 244, 295, 312; Abraham 43
KEY, - 143
KEYL, William 316
KEYLER, Jonas 245
KEYS, James 300
KEYSER, Derrick/Dirk 17, 29, 46, 102, 121, 149, 197, 253, 306, 308
KHOLER, Jonas 27
KIDD/KID, David 227, 333; John 49, 91, 130, 157, 171, 252, 290, 293; Robert 91
KIDNEY, William 100
KIEMER, James 257
KIERSTEDE/KIERSTED, - Capt. 87, 227, 238
KIEVE, Philip 159
KIFF, Edmond 39
KILLER, Jacob 323
KIMBLE, Peter 134
KIMPLER, Andrew 81
KINCHLOW, Matthew 97
KINDLE, William 8
KING, - family 90; Capt. 164, 238, 242, 266; Asa 194, 219, 292; Gilbert 234; James 4, 70; John 155; Joseph 185, 216; Nathaniel 4; Thomas 312; William 309
KINGMAN, Mary 267
KINGSLAND, - Mr. 301
KINLY, John 58
KINNARD, Anthony 44; Esther 110; John 44
KINNENMOUTH, Alexander 52
KINNERSLEY/KENNERSLEY, - Mr. 266, 276; Ebenezer 13, 194, 318
KINNEY, - Capt. 122
KINNISON, William 271
KINSEY, David 328; James 235, 316; John 1, 6, 23, 30, 42, 52, 61, 72, 82, 86, 94, 125, 235
KINSING, Christian 55
KIPP/KIP, - Capt. 21, 46, 74, 234, 238, 251, 275, 277, 291
KIRK, John 100; Patrick 68; Timothy 308
KIRKBRIDE, Joseph 29; Mahlon 25, 29, 30, 34, 61, 102, 109, 149, 197, 253, 308; Sarah 29
KIRKPATRICK, Catherine 122; Hugh 5; John 191, 287
KITCHEN, William 200
KITE, Edward 132
KITTERA, Thomas 65
KITTS, - Capt. 195
KITZMILLER, Jacob 169, 204; Martin 169, 204
KLAMPFF, Adam 255
KLEIN; see CLINE, Henry 8
KLINGENMEYER, Conrad, Jr. 200; Conrad, Sr. 200

357

KNAGE, Hans 182
KNEESBERRY, Mary 316
KNIGHT, Daniel 224; Giles 30, 61, 102, 149, 197, 253, 308; John 55, 160; Jonathan 224; Joseph 69; Nicholas 142; Peter 7; William 331
KNILL, John 208
KNODLE, Anna Maria 55; Frederick 55
KNOT, Peter 17
KNOWLES, - Admiral 33, 197; Gov. 316, 321, 326, 329; Charles/Cha. 3, 59, 329; Elizabeth 7; Francis 211, 331; John 7, 17; John (alias of John Smith) 22; Joseph 333; Mary 188; Robert 128;
KNOWLTON, Peter 53
KNOX, - Capt. 289, 292; Mr. 216; James 34, 153; John 160; Sarah (alias Howard, alias Wilson) 220; Victor 152, 153
KOCK, - 45; Anne 198; Peter 69, 198
KOFFLER, - Capt. 276
KOLGHLESER, Emanuel 178
KOLLOCK, Cornelius, Jr. 104; Jacob 31, 34, 58, 63, 79, 103, 150, 199, 255, 309; Jacob, Jr. 255, 309; Shepard 63, 103, 150
KONNUES, Philip 260
KOOL, Johannes 15
KOPPOCK, James 330
KOSSLER, - Capt. 257
KOSTER, John 130
KOVER, - 230
KOYL/KOYLE, Michael 25, 68, 92, 278; Seth 239, 278
KROFT, Jacob 120
KUHL, Marcus/Mark 3, 16, 43, 54, 65, 89, 122, 173, 174, 187, 245, 282, 284, 310, 311; Samuel 245
KUHN, Adam Simon 116; Hans 270
KUISEY, Caleb 74
KUMMENFIELD, Maria 279
KUNTZ, Adam 269

LACEY/LACY/LASEY, Joseph 311; John 236; Thomas 135, 195, 333
LADD/LAD, John 180, 222, 269
LA FORCE/LE FORCE, - M./Cadet 277, 291, 293, 304, 305, 308
LAITCH, Thomas 296
LA JANQUIERE, - M. 173
LAKE, - Capt. 36, 208, 265, 275; Thomas 115
LAMB, Andrew 32, 64, 92; Anthony 40; Samuel 155
LAMEY, Matthias 36, 42
LAMPLUGH, Samuel 105
LANCASTER, Sarah 54
LANCE, - Capt. 262; John 198
LANE, - Capt. 329; Mr. 56; Edward 6, 81; James 33; Samuel 129; Thomas 177, 201; Thomas (alias Thomas Lyons) 133
LANG, Alexander 26, 41, 42; Regina 62; Thomas 56
LANGDALE, John 1, 108
LANGDON, - Capt. 71, 142, 260, 268, 285
LANGFORD, Edward 246
LANGHORN/LANGHORNE, - Rev. 313; Jeremiah 56, 333
LANGLY, John 109; William 270
LANIN, Andrew 296
LANING, Patrick 263
LANNAN, John 190
LANPHIER, Thomas 84
LANTZELL, Johannes 150
LARDNER, Lynford/Lynford 4, 41, 47, 105, 195
LARGE, Ebenezer 40, 95, 181; Samuel 95, 169
LARGLEY, John 236
LARY, Cornelius 12; Katherine 12
LASCOM, William 58
LASHER, Adam 73
LASSELL/LASSELLS, - Capt. 331; John 12, 27, 178, 325, 329
LATIMER, Arthur 254
LATON, Robert 262
LAUDERDALE, - Capt. 155, 284; Thomas 232
LAUFERSWEILER/LAWERSWYLER, Bernard 77, 247
LAUGHLEN, Philip 118
LAW, - Capt. 320; Jonathan 108
LAWELL, David 5, 151
LAWLER, Mary 17
LAWLESS, John 144
LAWRENCE, - BELL and 284; and GODDEN 110; Capt. 165, 220, 221, 233, 235, 238, 240, 251, 275, 290, 300, 313; Col. 119, 133, 135, 251; Major 81; Mr. 222, 284; Augustine 285, 334; Charles 295; David 148; Elisha 134; Giles 83; Henry 139, 181, 252, 263; John 45, 132, 169, 286, 329; Joseph 277; Mary 286; Nathaniel 165, 195, 271, 275; Robert 62, 114, 298, 313, 330; Scot 171, 228, 234, 257, 332; Thomas 1, 5, 20, 27, 42, 61, 65, 68, 72, 146, 148, 159, 161, 203, 206, 241, 254, 255, 281, 283, 286, 301, 307, 328, 329 ; Thomas, Jr. 1, 175,
176, 188, 207, 256; William 148, 233, 258, 263, 267, 298
LAWS, - Capt. 238
LAWSON, - Capt. 26, 29; Mr. 167, 212; Alexander 15, 46; George 32, 46, 219, 232; William 100, 119
LEACOCK, John 134, 210, 236; Mary 210
LEAYCRAFT/LEYCRAFT/LEACRAFT, - Capt. 180, 218, 300, 331; Jeremiah 217, 225; Viner 204, 229
LEADLIE, John 40, 49, 234, 290
LEAKE/LEAK, - Capt. 113, 195, 204, 270, 313; Andrew 319; John 59
LEAMING, Aaron 115, 326
LEANT, Thomas 255
LEARD, John 95, 237
LEARMONTH, Alexander 261
LEAVENS, - Capt. 331
LEAVIT, - Mr. 315
LE BLANC, Francis 22
LEBMAN, Christian 306
LE CORNE, - M. 105
LE CRAS, - Capt. 88
LEDDEL, Louisa 214; William 214
LEDITE, Benjamin 137
LEE, - Capt. 141, 279, 290; Benjamin 89; Danaiel 102, 153; Edward 184, 187; Francis/ Fr. 12, 48; George 65; Isaac 30, 61, 102; James 254; John 76; Matthew 242; Richard 65; Robert 121; Stephen 243; Thomas 85, 108, 109, 253; William 217
LEECE, Thomas 92
LEECH, - 127, 140; Capt. 316; Widow 11, 97, 164, 170; Abraham 1, 73; Ephraim 209; Francis 185; Hannah 232; Jacob 3, 20, 84, 90, 104, 164, 170; John 169, 210; Joseph 97; Mary 77, 169, 181; Rebecca 17, 25, 211; Thomas 1, 5, 31, 61, 68, 100, 203, 307, 320, 329
LEEDS, - Capt. 157
LEEMAN, Jacob 252
LEERS, - Capt. 308
LEFEVER/LEFAVER, Daniel 229; John 7
LEFFERTS, Derrick 186, 198
LEGAY, Jacob 94
LEGGE/LEGG, - Capt. 245, 297, 322; John 321; Julian 272, 276, 294, 299, 310
LE GROS, - Capt. 59, 75, 90
LEHMAN, Christian 49, 186; Christopher 198; Ludowig 323
LEIDENBURG, Aaron 60

LEIDICH/LEYDICH, John
  Philip 67, 211
LEITHS/LEATHS/LEATHES, -
  Capt. 138; John 140,
  243, 247, 256, 261
LEMON, Isaac 39
LENDRUM, Andrew 265
Lennord, Christopher
  153
LENNOX/LENOX, James
  137, 184; Janet 210;
  Margaret 210
LENSE, Mathias 66
LEONARD, - Capt. 316;
  Rev. 318; Robert 220;
  Thomas 264
LESAR, John 8
LESLIE, - Capt. 310, 312,
  324; George 38
LETTIMORE, John 162
LEVAN, Abraham 197
LEVANT, Abraham 30, 61;
  Isaac 149
LEVERIDGE, Samuel 271
LEVERING/LEAVERING,
  Abraham 260; Benjamin
  24,; Jacob 37, 67,
  228; John 260; Sep-
  timus 260; William
  217, 319, 321
LEVETRU, John 335; Mary
  335
LEVIS, John 110; Joseph
  83
LEVY, - and FRANKS 17,
  27, 67, 90, 98, 127,
  135, 155, 156, 168,
  169, 254, 268, 284;
  Mr. 252; Widow 57;
  Nathan 17, 141, 144,
  266, 268
LEWIS, - 129; Capt. 76,
  171, 221, 238, 252,
  253, 271, 292, 298,
  314, 318, 332; Adam
  67; Andrew 307; Daniel
  242; David 37, 191;
  Edward 322; Eunus 161;
  Henry 6, 37, 75, 205;
  Isaac 243, 248, 279;
  Jacob 39, 149, 151,
  197, 217, 254, 307;
  James 20, 133, 154,
  243, 248, 279; John
  23, 67, 80, 238, 278;
  Jonathan 245, 312;
  325; Joseph 5, 80;
  Nathan 107; Phineas
  31, 61, 102, 149, 197,
  253; Robert 50, 317,
  329; Samuel 124; Tho-
  mas 35, 55, 185, 191,
  212, 298; William 149,
  276
LEYBROOK, Christian 309
LIBURT, Andrew 43, 272
LICKLY, - Capt. 250, 251
LIDDLE, Jonathan 120
LIGHTBORNE, Richard 186
LIGHTFOOT, Benjamin 125,
  197, 229, 253, 272,
  273, 309, 313; Michael
  318; Samuel 125, 273;
  Thomas 14, 31, 41,
  107, 114, 197, 226,
  254; William 170, 226
LIKING, Hance 266

LILLEY, Samuel 218
LINCOLN/LINCON, Isaac
  326; Jacob 278
LINDSAY/LINSEY, - Capt.
  174; David 24, 76; Ja-
  mes 157, 222; John
  237, 246; Susannah 198
LINN, Adam 107; David
  159, 161; Elizabeth
  (alias Hebert) 195;
  Hugh 216; John 86,
  180
LINNARD, Edward 278
LINTHICUM, Francis 126
LINTON, - Mr. 43; Widow
  94; Benjamin 46; John
  46, 69; Joseph 46;
  Martha 69
LIPPINCOTT/LIPPINCUT,
  Samuel 12, 261
LISCHY, Jacob 211
LISLE, - Capt. 7, 200,
  285, 290; Mary 105,
  127, 334; Robert 254
LISTER, Thomas 159
LITLER, William 2
LITTLE, Anne 185, 300;
  Archibald 105; George
  153, 216; John 118;
  Mary 333; Nathaniel 13;
  Nicholas 45; Otis 47
LITTLEJOHN, David 169
LIVEZEY/LIVESAY/LIEVEZEY,
  - Mr. 127; David 111;
  Jonathan 111, 125,
  290; Jonathan, Jr.
  106; Thomas 111, 157,
  171
LIVINGSTON/LEVINGSTON, -
  Capt. 251, 254, 259,
  291; Cornelius 308,
  323; Peter Vanbrugh
  69; Philip 149, 312;
  Robert R. 144, 286
LLEWELLIN/LLEWELYN/
  LEWELLIN/LUELLIN, Da-
  vid 330; David (alias
  of David Hughes) 19;
  John 283; Margaret
  322; Morris 69, 106
LLOYD, -WILLING and 115;
  - 60, 101, 151, 153,
  170, 175, 192, 330;
  Capt. 8, 47, 252, 255,
  261; Mrs. 109; David
  217; Edward 289; Evan
  283; Hannah 215; John
  18, 273; Mary 15, Na-
  thaniel 207; Peter
  120; Richard 65, 259,
  276, 332; Robert 147;
  Thomas 15, 20, 25, 38,
  77, 184, 192, 217,
  286, 315, 323
LOCK, Englebert 245; Me-
  verell 118
LOCKERMAN/LOOCKERMAN,
  Nicholas 64; Vincent
  80, 172, 199, 255
LOCKHART, Alexander 86
LOFTUS, Ralph 71
LOGAN, - Mr. 114; Bar-
  tholomew 88; David
  132; George 30, 49;
  James 1, 44, 144,
  153, 154, 213, 222,
  225; John 198, 233

William 1, 13, 28, 77,
  233, 265, 317, 319
LOGUE, John 146; Mana-
  seth 12
LOLLEY, Francis 280
LOLOR, Mark 73
LONE, Abraham 25
LONG, - Capt. 238, 291;
  Mr. 244; Joseph 81;
  Thomas 319
LONGSTREET, Stophel 151
LORAIN, - Capt. 160, 213
LORD, - Capt. 221; Abra-
  ham 111; James 274
LORING, - 274
LOTTERIDGE, - 302
LOUTTIT, James 110, 142,
  153
LOVE, Alexander 150,
  199, 255; James 95,
  100, 300; John 317;
  Samuel 2
LOVEGROVE, John 81
LOVEJOY, William 320
LOVELY, Edward 252
LOVERING, John 89
LOVIT/LOVEIT, - Mr.
  231; John 122
LOW/LOWE, - Capt. 298,
  301; John 50
LOWDER, Samuel 15
LOWER, Christian 253
LOWNES, - Capt. 238,
  275, 292, 294, 313;
  Benanuel 153; George
  90; James 2, 238,
  243, 310; John 173,
  335; Joseph 5, 71,
  149, 197, 217, 254,
  307, 310; Mary 49
LOWRIE/LOWRY/LAWRIE, -
  Capt. 212; Daniel
  297; James 252; Laza-
  rus 20, 35, 198, 238,
  253
LOWRING, Hezekiah 39
LOWTHER, - Capt. 266,
  268, 276, 287, 288,
  292, 297, 299
LOX, William 264
LOXLEY/LOXLY, Benjamin
  77, 139, 155, 247,
  265, 328
LOYDER, Thomas 281
LUCAS, - Capt. 197; One-
  siphorus 135, 137;
  Thomas 298, 302
LUCKEN/LUCKENS, - 177;
  Abraham 216, 327; John
  216, 322
LUDDINGTON, William 288
LUDGATE, John 140
LUDLAM, Joseph 196
LUNAN, - Mr. 198; Ale-
  xander 230, 234, 237,
  264, 286
LUNT, Joseph 41, 225
LUPARDUS, Christianus
  302
LUSBY, Joseph 130
LUSHING, Christopher 76
LUSK, - Capt. 206
LUTTREL, - Major 144
LUX, - Mrs. 263; Darby
  93; William 280
LYBERT, Andrew 270

LYCAN/LICAN, Hans 36, 241; Hance, Sr. 78, 85; Henry 239; Nicholas 36, 78, 85; Peter 11
LYELL, - Capt. 209, 316; Fenwick 286
LYM, Stoffel 247
LYNCH/LINCH, David 294; James 44; Samuel 56; Timothy 213, 247
LYNDVIL, Jos. 155
LYNE, James 21, 41
LYNN, David 29; Jacob 203; Joseph 39; William 88
LYON, - Capt. 37, 166, 170, 171, 172, 214, 215, 236, 251, 252, 264, 312, 332; Lt. 312; Charles 137; John 131; Joseph 106, 194, 220
LYONS, Thomas (alias of Thomas Lane) 133
LYSAGHT, John 302; Nicholas 302
LYTTON, James 63

M'AFEE, William 252
M'ALLISTER/M'ALISTER/ M'CALLISTER, - Capt. 221, 223; James 321; John 223; Patrick 155; Richard 103
M'ANALLY/M'ANALY, Morgan 281; Robert 261
M'ANALTY, William 287
M'AULIFF/M'CAULEFD, Dennis 170; John 122, 123
MECAULLE, John 330
MACKBILL, George 265
M'BRIDE/M'BRID/ MACKBRIDE, Daniel 57; James 100; John 175, 186
M'BROOM, Andrew 65; Eleanor 65
M'CABE, John 259
M'CALL, - 202; Mr. 179; Archibald 169, 223, 228; George 2, 98, 295, 321; Jasper 2; John 35; Magdalene 2; Samuel 2, 46, 98, 113, 255, 319; Samuel, Jr. 23, 33, 40, 61, 113, 121, 145, 307, 329; Samuel, Sr. 1, 2, 11, 13, 26, 28, 42, 49, 50, 79, 124, 142, 158, 169, 179, 183, 199, 316
M'CAMANT, William 216
M'CANN, James 178
M'CARMISH/M'CAMISH, Patrick 38, 98
M'CARTER, - Capt. 16; William 133, 261
M'CARTNEY, George 136; Michael 209
M'CARTY/MACARTY/MACARTIE/McCARTHY, - Capt. 15, 63, 92, 97, 98, 138, 170, 268, 294, 324, 332; Barnaby 280; Daniel 92, 137, 150; Florence 194; James 114; John 277; Sheeley 100; Thomas 258
M'CARVIL, Margaret 267
M'CASHEN, Alexander 118
M'CAY/MACCAY/MACKAY, Henry 285; James 296; William 79, 276
M'CLEAN, - Capt. 200; Archibald 209; James 192
M'CLELLAN/M'CLELAN, - Capt. 321; Hugh 285; Jean 249
M'CLELLAND, - Capt. 283; Brice 51; Deborah 326; John 326
M'CLELENT, Hugh 159
M'CLEMENT, Andrew 9
M'CLENACHAN, - Rev. 201
M'CLEVE, - Capt. 142, 261, 263, 264, 286
M'CLOSKY, Arthur 175, 232, 251
M'CLUE/MACCLUE/M'CLEW, Bernard 25; Catherine (alias Catherine Moore) 56; Robert 15
M'CLUGHAN, John 309
M'CLURE, David 13; John 255, 309; Thomas 179
M'COLOCK, William 224
M'COMB, John 92
M'CONAUGHBY/M'CONAUGHY, David 199, 255, 309
M'CONCKY, William 145
M'CONNELL, - Capt. 163; Esther 159, 204; Francis 209; James 78, 204, 214; Mary 159; Susannah 158
M'COOL/M'COOLE/M'COOLL, Adam 124; John 2, 31, 61, 102, 150, 197, 253, 309; Walter 126, 139, 199
M'COOMBS, - 77, 119
M'CORMICK/MACCORMICK, Edward 149; Henry 138; ; John 8; Maxwell 186; Rachel (alias of Rachel Mahorne) 210
M'COY/MACCOY, - 112; Capt. 334; Francis 111, 114, 115; John 68, 206; Mary 112, 114; Samuel 206
M'CRACKAN/M'CRACKKEN/ M'CRECKON, James 245; William 159, 165
M'CREA, - Major 20; Samuel 93; William 3, 11, 196
M'CREARY, James 91; Mary 91
M'CREE, Richard 104
M'CROSS, Carrick 254
MACCUBBIN, James 164, 231
M'CULLOUGH, - Capt. 245; Arthur 264, 275; David 14; George 5; Hugh 273, 301; James 56, 99, 233, 264, 284, 335; John 106, 167, 169, 249; Thomas 13
M'CUNE, Bryan 209
M'CUNN, - Capt. 105; John 110; Susanna 110; William 22
M'CURDY, Archibald 153, 216; Robert 36, 234
M'CURRY, James 196
M'CUTCHIN, John 315
M'DANIEL, - Capt. 32, 205, 252, 314, 322; Daniel 65; Edward 220; Francis 184; Garret 174; George 320; James 228, 328; John 99, 110, 193, 319; Nicholas 156; Timothy 205
M'DEARMON, John 36
M'DERMOT/M'DERMOTT, John 123, 256; Margaret 202, 209;Philip 202, 208, 209
MACDID, Cornelius 54; James 54
M'DONALD/MACDONALD/ M'DONNALD, Alexander 156; Daniel 50; Edmund 135; James 83, 219; John 211, 217; Richard 8; William 26
M'DONNELL/M'DONNEL, Alexander 186; George 306; Hugh 318
M'DONOUGH, Thomas 75
M'DOUGALL, - Capt. 209, 212, 236, 260; Alexander 262
M'DOWELL/MACDOWELL/ M'DOWAL/M'DOUALL, - Capt. 176; Alexander 181, 233, 264, 287; Andrew 5, 9; Joseph 105; Thomas 3
MACELHAGA, James 31
M'ELVENEY, James 48
M'EVOY, Christopher 239
M'FADDEN, John 332
M'FALL, James 78; John 109; Neal 145
M'FARLAN, Joseph 31
M'FARLAND, Andrew 186; Edward 110
M'FELLY, Robert 186
MACFERRAN, Samuel 191
M'FUN, - Capt. 201, 266, 268, 285, 290, 304; Alexander 295
M'GARREL, James 218
M'GEE/MAGEE/M'GHEE, - Capt. 164, 236, 245, 279, 281, 284, 317; Abraham 62, 104; Alexander 285, 296, 301; James 325; John 39; Nathaniel 3, 4, 81, 224, 296; Thomas 224; William 126
M'GENTY/MAGENTY, Alexander 252, 299
M'GILL/MACGILL/MAGILL, Andrew 103, 185; Charles 8; James 160
M'GILLIVRAY, - Capt. 205; Alex. 204
M'GINNESS, Arthur 12
M'GITTIKIN, Anne 322; Bryan 322

359

M'GLEW, Bryan (or Barnabe) 38
M'GOWON, Patrick 302
M'GRAW/M'GRAUGH/MEGRAH, John 251, 300; Roger 243
M'GREW/M'GRUE, Archibald 255, 309
M'GRIGER, Duncan 174
M'GUIRE/MACGUIRE/MAGUIRE/MAQUIRE, Bartholomew 67, 76, 114; Bartle 62; Hugh 202, 208; James 192; John 82, 196; Michael 120; Patrick 77; Peter 182; Timothy 315
MACHAFFY/MAHAFFY, Hugh 122; Hugh, Jr. 82, 89; Margaret 82, 89
M'HARGE, Thomas 173
M'HENRY, Francis 220
M'HUGH/MACHUGH, - 112; Capt. 148; Mrs. 112
M'ILVAINE/MACILVAINE, - Capt. 141, 250, 279; David 27, 110, 122, 159, 160, 161, 168, 179, 183, 191, 192, 205, 232, 277; James 185; John 109, 183; Robert 103, 150; William 27, 51, 94, 110, 122, 144, 159, 160, 161, 168, 175, 179, 192, 232, 251, 277, 311, 319, 329
M'ILVEEN, Arthur 158
M'ILWAINE, Archibald 205
M'INTYRE, - Capt. 245; Mr. 117
M'JANET/M'JANETT, - and M'MURPHY 204; Thomas 149, 256, 283, 316, 326
M'KAY/MACKAY, - Capt. 295, 307
M'KEDDIE, Daniel 22
M'KEE, Robert 104, 113, 168; Thomas 13
M'KEEN/M'KEAN, Robert 327; Thomas 88, 112, 159, 206, 298
McKELVAIN, John 101
MACKEN, James 5
M'KENALLY, John 256
MACKENET/MACKNET. Blasius Daniel 329; Daniel 177; Daniel, Jr. 225, 229
M'KENNIE, Donald 126, 128
M'KENZIE, - Capt. 290, 324
MACKEY/MACKY/MACKAY, - Capt. 30, 32, 67, 119, 199; Alexander 215; James 55, 58, 83, 221, 259; James, Jr. 132; James, Sr. 132; John 51, 316; Robert 9
MACKELLIEK, James 50
M'KINLEY/M'KINLY, John 5, 90, 309
M'KINNEY, Barney 246

MACKLEREATH, - Capt. 24
MACKLEVAIN , John 39
M'KNEEL, - 115; Mrs. 115; Daniel 92
M'KNIGHT , James 112; William 2, 299
M'KNOWN, John 13
M'KOWN, - Capt. 117
MACKRILL, George 248, 275
M'LANE, Archibald 183
M'LAUGHLIN/MACLAUGHLIN/ M'CLAUGHLIN/M'LACHLAN, - Capt. 263; Cornelius 212; Hugh 50; James 13, 301, 304; John 192, 205, 222, 282; Michael 241; Paddy 246
M'LEAN, John 121
M'MAHAN/M'MAHON, Con 254; Hugh 284; Hugh (alias of Hugh Matthews) 136; Ross 254
M'MANEMEN, Richard 212
M'MANUS, James 175
M'MEA (?), - Mr. 266
M'MECHEN/M'MECHAN/ MACMECHAN/M'MEKEN, - Capt. 20; James 9, 31, 61, 83, 102, 150, 155, 197, 253, 309; John 83, 104; William 29
M'MICHAEL , John 77, 122, 296
M'MICKEN, John 298
M'MULLEN/MACMULLIN, Neal 129; Robert 7; William 13
M'MURPHY, - M'JANET and 204
M'MURRAY, - 130
MACKNAB, John 160
M'NAIR, John 242
M'NAMARA/MACNAMARA, - 139; Capt. 189
M'NEAL/M'NEIL/M'NIEL/ M'NEILL/MACNEELL, - Capt. 177, 315; Daniel 215; Francis 121; James 208, 257; John 149; John (alias John Oneal) 53; William 47
M'NEALIS, Francis 280
M'NELLY, Adam 122
M'PHERSON, - Capt. 244, 260, 268; John 174
M'QUILLIN, Alexander 85
M'QUOID, - Capt. 235
M'SEER, James 8
M'SWAIN, Grace 12
M'VAUGH, James 278
M'VEY, Owen 19
MACWHAN, John 100
MAGWIGIN, Turrence 324
M'WILLIAM, Richard 11, 155, 193, 282

MAAG, Jacob 77, 247
MACE, - Capt. 201
MACHET, - Capt. 137, 143, 200
MACK, Adam 24
MADDEN, Dennis (alias Duncan Woods) 87
MADDOCK, Benjamin 242; Mordecai 120
MADDOX, Daniel 54; John 258; Joshua 1, 5, 46,
116, 226, 307
MADISON, John 298
MAFFET/MAFFETT, John 260, 296
MAGAHEY, Catherine 191; Nicholas 191
MAHAR, Thomas 185
MAHORNE, Rachel (alias Rachel M'Cormick) 210
MAHR, Jost 143
MAISTERSON, - Capt. 87
MAILEY, John 178
MAJOR, - Capt. 106; Christopher 99, 114
MALCOLM/MALCOM/MALCOMB, - Capt. 298; Mrs. 248; John 59, 80, 130, 196
MALGER, John 74
MALIN, Randle/Randal 149, 253
MALL, John 296
MALLAM, - Capt. 181, 270
MALONE, - Mr. 279; John 140
MALONEY/MALONY, James 145; Patrick 217
MALTON, - Capt. 259
MANN/MAN, - Capt. 17, 189, 195, 212, 218, 220, 268, 288, 294
MANCHESTER, - Capt. 116, 218, 285
MANGLES, - 261; William 247, 261
MANIFFEE, William 128
MANLEY/MANLY, - Capt. 133, 271; Richard 204
MANNY, Francis 85
MANSFIELD, - Capt. 318
MANSKULL, John/Johannes 320
MANTER, - Mr. 277
MANYPENNY, - Capt. 147
MARCHANT, John 37
MARIER, James 151
MARINES, Johan 24
MARKENDERFFER/MICKENDERFFER, John 290, 304
MARKHAM, John 128
MARKS, Joseph 51, 88, 131, 177, 210, 211, 239, 241, 257
MARL/MARLL, John 133, 179, 239, 270
MARLET, John 328
MARLEY, Adam 157
MAROT, Philip 104
MARPLE, Alice 64; George 52, 57; Richard 64
MARRIOTT, - Mrs. 289; Isaac 34; Joseph 293; Thomas 9, 25, 34, 293
MARSDEN, - Capt. 283, 286, 287
MARSELIS, Henry 226
MARSH, Thomas 99
MARSHALL/MARSHAL, - Capt. 147, 166, 235, 294, 318; Widow 262; Abraham 107, 167; Christopher 11, 27, 37, 62, 72, 98, 130, 206, 215; James 132, 253, 309; John 70, 90, 167; Joseph 133; Thomas 319, 328; William 146, 334
MARSTON, Nathaniel 136

361

MARTIN, - 53, 140; Capt. 21, 287; Alexander 41; Christopher 241, 249; David 92, 134, 159, 166, 239; Edward 165; George 16; James 8, 118, 328; John 14, 26, 54, 202; Josiah 255, 303, 309; Mary 81, 86, 143, 152, 165; Patrick 288, 217; Richard 9, 143, 152; Samuel 11, 23; Sarah 86; Susannah 81; Thomas 114, 172, 183, 234, 301; William 4, 109; William Thomas 303
MASCARENE, - Gov. 55
MASENET, - Capt. 277
MASH, Nathaniel 326
MASLEY, White 173
MASON, - DENYCE and 151; Capt. 13, 22, 59, 146, 147, 197, 250, 251, 252, 274, 286, 316; Mr. 162; Abraham 198; Benjamin 213; John 3, 102;Thomas 333; William 152, 163
MASSACRE, Adam 151
MASSEY, - Turner and 66; Samuel 186
MASTERS, - Mr. 43, 164, 171, 196; Margaret 316, 318; Peter 316, 318; William 1, 38, 97, 119, 173, 193, 300, 307, 329
MASTERSON, - Capt. 55, 303, 332
MATASEUR, - Capt. 312
MATHER, James 5, 92; John 2, 5, 333
MATHIAS, Thomas 99
MATLACK, Timothy 4, 45, 89, 118, 133, 143
MATLANACHAN, Elijah 294
MATSON, Peter 293
MATTHEWS/MATHEWS, - Capt. 21, 33, 147; Dr. 198; Gen. 190, 200; Abraham 19; David 307; Edward 169; George 32, 150; Hugh 50, 169, 195, 204; Hugh (alias Hugh M'Mahon) 136; John 152, 153, 158, 204; Peter 206; Robert 188; Simon 333
MATTHIAS, David 256; Evan 321; Thomas 311
MATZ, Jacob 263
MAUGER, - Capt. 142
MAUGRUDGE, William 16
MAULE, Joseph 183; Thomas 47, 55, 110, 120, 126, 225
MAXWELL, - Capt. 64, 181; William 8
MAY, - Capt. 184; Daniel 52, 70; George 302
MAYBEE/MAYBE, Edward 317; Thomas 259

MAYBURY/MAYBURRY/MAYBERRY, - 208; Capt. 1, 253; Mrs. 47; Sophia 12, 24; Thomas 12, 24, 269
MAYCOCK, Charles 230
MAYCUM, John 84
MAYIAM, John 226
MEADE, Robert 28, 123, 133, 233, 237
MEANS, Edward 28; William 197, 308
MEARNS, Hugh 252; William 95
MEAS, John 33, 81, 291, 305
MECOMB, John 63
MEDAH, Peter 298
MEEK, Robert 8
MEGOUND, Edmund 140
MEIGHAN, Thomas 301
MELCHIOR/MELCHOR/MELKER/MELCHOIR, Leonard/Lennard 77, 222, 234, 247, 297; William 132
MELDRUM, Hannah 195; John 100
MELENBERGH, - Parson 91
MELLEN/MELLIN, Randle 102, 197
MELVEN, Eleazer 315
MENDENHALL/MENDINGHALL/MONDENHALL, George 111, 121; Robert 30, 309; Samuel 79; Sarah 111, 121
MENELY, Adam 106
MENG, Christopher 17
MENKENS, Peter 236
MENNIG, Melcher 242
MENZIE/MENZIES, - Capt. 25, 192, 225, 260, 276, 324; Edward 275
MERAND, - Capt. 247
MERCER, - Lt.-Col. 323, 324, 330; John 307; Robert 237
MERCIER, - Lt. 296
MERCY, John 45
MEREDITH - 25; Charles 143, 154, 161, 168, 251; Hugh 118; J. 257; James 6; John 163, 239, 308; Rees/Reese 11, 24, 27, 32, 82, 89, 121, 166, 168, 171, 219, 223, 292; Samuel 276
MERICK, Ebenezer 252
MERONE, William 99
MERRYMAN, - 274
MERSIER/MERSEYER, - Capt. 180, 285
MESNARD, - Capt. 8, 22, 26, 58, 75, 76, 80, 126, 137, 166, 180, 215, 223, 225, 234, 251, 254, 259, 279, 285, 287, 290, 305, 306, 308, 332; Stephen 26, 32, 106
MESSER, Thomas 299
METCALF/METCALFE, John 178, 198, 231
MEULE, Thomas 8

MEYER, Abraham 134
MICHENER, John 34, 174
MICHIE, James 274
MICK, John 210
MICKLE, John 30, 129, 164, 189, 254; Letitia 30; Samuel 80, 189; William 115
MIDDLETON, - Capt. 277; Mr. 113; George 72; Henry 327; Thomas 28
MIER, Christopher 216
MIFFLIN, - 73, 94, 201, 203; Capt. 57; Benjamin 42, 81, 275, 334; George 14, 27, 202, 284; George, Jr. 246, 283; Hannah 170; John 11, 14, 27, 32, 49, 77, 86, 98, 162, 181, 184, 215, 217, 220, 242, 245, 307; John, Jr. 80, 113, 170, 185; Jonathan 15, 41, 91, 99, 118, 162, 185, 215, 220, 242, 245, 265, 269; Samuel 130; Samuel, Jr. 245
MILAN, Matthias 176, 178
MILBURN, Robert 253
MILES, - Capt. 301; Edward 77, 188, 264; James 148
MILHOUS, John 167
MILL, John 144
MILLANE, Matthias 228
MILLARD, Joseph 197, 253; M. 62
MILLBY, Robert 29
MILLER/MILLAR, - and HOLLAND 161; - 207; Capt. 66, 129, 130, 202, 206, 209, 231, 250, 251, 254, 259, 275, 285, 290, 294, 296, 298, 306, 320, 329, 331; Alexander 200; Andrew 8, 168; Ann 322, 332; Benjamin 136; Catherine 66; Daniel 166, 232; Ebenezer, Jr. 42; George 39, 66, 130, 187, 317; Henry 83, 104, 106, 118; Hugh 9; Isaac 221; Jacob 248, 281; James 102, 149, 197, 253; John 5, 8, 9, 108, 265, 268; John (alias John Stogdal) 84; Joseph 204; Patrick 35, 95; Paul 11; Richard 334; Robert 159, 250, 253; Samuel 308; Thomas 143, 146, 259, 292, 300; William 16
MILLIBELL, John 8
MILLS, - Capt. 206; John 205
MILNE, James 84; William 107, 151
MILNER, Samuel 128; Thomas 195
MILTON, - Capt. 179, 183; Robert 182
MINCHAN, Timothy 310

MINEHEX, Joshua 187
MINES, William 199
MING, Christopher 29
MINGE, John 219, 232
MINOT, Amos 204, 206;
  James 154
MINSHALL/MINSHELL, Griffith 50, 212, 317;
  John 6; Joshua 190;
  Moses 50; Thomas 190
MIRICK, Simeon 114
MISLINGER, - 234
MITCHELL/ MITCHEL, -
  Capt. 129, 141, 172,
  193, 225, 236, 248,
  250, 251, 279, 281,
  285, 286, 303; Mr.
  81, 113; Abraham 57,
  217, 306, 322; Alexander 157, 220, 251,
  284; Benjamin 244;
  Eben. 23; Henry 7, 23,
  40; Hugh 157; John 8,
  57, 109, 151, 221;
  Joseph 165; Mary 226;
  Patrick 20; Randle 54,
  83, 92, 101, 112, 123,
  157, 166, 183, 220,
  251, 284; Richard 30,
  44, 89; Sarah 141;
  Thomas 13; William
  13, 105
MITCHELSON, Samuel 164
MITCHEM, Edward 231
MOALE, John 264
MOCK, John 143
MOFFETT, Archibald 271
MOLAND, - Mr. 288, 315;
  John 2, 133, 245, 246,
  251
MOLL, John 280
MONCRIEF, - Capt. 327
MONEY, Joseph 247; Thomas 91
MONK, - Capt. 294; James 176
MONKTON, - Col. 272; Dr. 59
MONNINGTON, - Mr. 95
MONROE/MONROW/MONRO,
  George 88, 128, 150,
  183, 197, 210, 226,
  234, 253, 313, 326;
  John 188, 203; Margaret 188; Rowland
  123
MONTAGUE, - Capt. 60,
  238, 248
MONTAUR, - Capt. 292
MONTGOMERY, - Capt. 54,
  245, 331, 332; Mr.
  260; Widow 127;
  Alexander 274; Archibald 51; Hugh 22;
  James 3, 8; John 155,
  286, 293; Robert 104,
  332; Thomas 71, 83,
  284, 296, 297, 329
MONTPELIER/MONTPELLIER,
  - Capt. 151, 200,
  201; Daniel 154, 238
MOODY/MOODIE/MOODE/
  MUDIE, - Capt. 53,
  219, 234; Alexander 3,
  84, 107; Jane 224;
  John 224; Robert 213;
  William 12, 31, 35,
82, 159, 196, 208,240
MOONEY, William 45, 249
MOORE/MOOR, - Capt. 19,
  31, 129, 195, 250, 251,
  254, 266, 279, 307,
  318, 331; Dr. 281;
  Aaron 166; Alexander
  37, 229; Ambrose 98;
  Andrew 100; Benjamin
  147, 166; Catherine
  (alias of Catherine
  M'Clue) 56; Charles
  5; David 210; Ephraim
  171; Guyan 2; Hamill
  182; James 19, 68,
  100, 147, 189, 205,
  300; Janet 210; John
  7, 79, 148, 154, 211,
  254, 320; Joseph 108,
  126, 136, 137; Mary
  193; Mordecai 330;
  Patrick 197, 206;
  Quinton 219; Robert
  48, 63, 78, 93, 139,
  240, 279; Samuel Preston 2, 41, 48, 134,
  238, 270, 318, 321;
  Thomas 154, 164; Thomas, Jr. 120; Walter
  84, 90, 104; William
  2, 19, 27, 32, 33, 35,
  133, 181, 195, 213,
  225, 247, 250, 256,
  328, 334
MORARTY, Sylvester 183
MORELAND, - Capt. 205
MORETON, 280
MORGAN, - and ELKINS 85;
  203; Abel 64; Abev.
  106; Alexander 73;
  Barnabas 216; Benjamin
  17, 21, 27, 28, 42, 80,
  105, 146, 163, 205,
  220, 239; Cadwalader
  89, 183; David 84;
  Evan/Even 1, 7, 18,
  21, 22, 27, 37, 42,
  61, 77, 80, 102, 121,
  135, 140, 146, 149,
  172, 189, 197, 203,
  205, 230, 253, 279,
  285, 308, 321, 325,
  329; Evan, Jr. 12, 23,
  27; Francis 264; Hugh
  303; Jacob 197, 253,
  309; James 128, 321;
  John 5, 6, 46, 54, 85;
  Katharine 21, 27;Lydia
  212; Mary 85; Morris
  37, 114, 192; Richard
  248; Thomas 30, 37, 77,
  129, 333
MORIN, - M. 283
MORN, John (or John
  Moore) 148
MORNINGTON, John 200
MORREL/MORRELL, - Capt.
  130, 181, 191, 247,
  285, 314, 323; Robert
  2; Thomas (alias Thomas Salyar) 271
MORREY, Richard 274
MORRICE, Daniel 132;
  John (or John Morrison) 112
MORRIEL, Jeremiah 117
MORRIS/MORRISS, - 45,
  115, 129, 186, 297;
  Capt. 282; Gov. 65,
  216, 320, 330, 334;
  Mr. 194, 305; Sheriff
  223, 228, 232, 265;
  Anthony 79, 98, 130,
  142, 197, 275, 288,
  319; Anthony, Jr. 8,
  35, 44, 115, 123, 133,
  141, 151, 171, 217,
  228, 315, 323, 329;
  Benjamin 38; Charles
  173; David 229;
  Eleanor 212; Elizabeth 104, 117; Isaac
  153; Isabella 172;
  Israel 131, 197, 287;
  James 7, 30, 61, 78,
  83, 97, 106, 115;John
  30, 61, 87, 111, 114,
  115, 119, 211, 258,
  264, 319; Joseph 38,
  83, 115, 135, 176,
  182, 219, 225, 230,
  251, 261, 284, 285,
  307, 316; Joshua 103,
  149, 197, 243, 246,
  253, 308, 315; Lewis
  172; Luke 35, 68, 90;
  Mark 145; Morris 73,
  94, 122, 134, 149,
  197, 230, 253, 288,
  308, 320; Morris, Jr.
  261; Robert Hunter
  148, 204, 297, 305,
  308, 310, 312, 317,
  319, 322, 329; Samuel
  31, 57, 61, 65, 66,
  73, 94, 102, 117,
  130, 182, 189, 197,
  202, 211, 214, 216,
  224, 228, 229, 232,
  235, 237, 239, 240,
  248, 250, 253, 257,
  258, 265, 266, 267,
  268, 270, 290, 308;
  Thomas 311; William
  57, 87, 94, 253, 288;
  William, Jr. 50
MORRISON, - 213; Capt.
  4, 41, 193, 195, 197,
  249, 271, 276, 304,
  312; George 233; John
  67; John (or John Morrice) 112; Joseph 253,
  271; Lot 191; Matthew
  274; Robert 190, 197,
  253, 309
MORROW, Charles 8
MORSE, Moses 77; Seth
  236
MORSLEY, - Capt. 225,
  260, 326
MORTIMER/MORTIMORE/
  MORTEMOR, - Capt. 72,
  115; Mr. 205; John 88
MORTON, - Capt. 28, 162;
  Abigail 130; John252
MOSCHELL, George 150,
  157
MOSLEY, Capt. 233, 275
MOSS, Hannah 53, 88,
  130; Matthew 53, 88
MOSSON, James 140
MOTT/MOTTE, - Capt. 213;
  Mr. 204; Asher 84;

MOTT (cont'd) Richbell 325; William 115
MOULDER, Robert 204
MOUNCE, Luke 11
MOUNTEER, William 248
MOURAN, Barnut 280
MUCKLEROY, Mary 12
MUIR, - Capt. 146, 147, 195, 251, 252, 266, 286, 306, 307, 321; Robert 262; William 67
MUIRHEAD, - Rev. 129; James 39
MULFORD, - Capt. 295
MULHALL, Henry 156
MULLAN, Thomas 51
MULLIN, - 30, 245
MULLOCK/MULOCK, Joshua 13, 22, 30
MULVEHILL, Hugh 238
MUMFORD, Giles 250
MURDOCK, - 320; Capt. 318
MURFIN, William 95
MURGATROYD/MORGATROYD/MORGETROYD/MORGOTROYD, James 13, 123, 202, 240, 258
MURNHAN, Thomas 34
MURPHY/MURPHEY/MURFEY/MURPHYS, - Capt. 275; Bryan 145; Daniel 183; James 93, 287, 288, 297, 311; John 36, 70, 123, 242; Morgan 54, 151, 189, 195
MURRAY/MURREY/MURRY, - Capt. 194, 249, 268, 289, 290, 315, 316, 325; Alexander 50; David 190; Humphrey 217; John 217; Joseph 52; Mary 285; Richard 39, 194, 241, 278, 284, 326; Robert 190; Sarah 25, 87, 93; Sebastian 87, 93; Thomas 16, 19, 36; William 30, 61, 226
MURRELL, - Capt. 100; William 72
MUSGRAVE, Thomas 100
MYARS, Isaac 312
MYER, - Capt. 171; Caspar 187; Hans George 290; Michael 69

NABBY, - Capt. 275
NAGLEE/NAGLE/NEGLEE/NEGLEA, - 269; Catherine 153, 173, 254, 314; Jacob 2, 20, 28, 39, 153, 173, 198, 254, 314; James 36; John 2, 28, 39, 109, 153, 166, 173, 187, 198, 209, 254, 314
NANNA, Abraham 7; Jacob 7; Margaret 43; Rees 7
NAPIER, James 41
NASH, - Capt. 274
NEAL/NEILL, John 31, 63, 150; Mary 299; Morton 215; Thomas 59
NEALEY, James 159
NEALFORD, - Capt. 282
NEALIS, Francis 30

NEALSON, - Capt. 238, 245
NEASON, Elizabeth 227
NEAT/NEATE, - and SMITH 10, 21, 26
NEAVE, Samuel 27, 110, 121, 129, 140, 169, 220, 233, 250, 261, 306; Thomas 10
NEFF, Sebastine 248, 281
NEGAT, - Capt. 259
NEGUS, - Capt. 331
NEISLEY, George 191
NELLIS, Francis 33
NELSON, - Capt. 177; James 69; John 2, 15, 297, 324; Thomas 260, 331, 335
NEMO, John 198, 242, 294
NESMAN, Gabriel/Gabriele 49, 67, 112, 182
NESMITH, Thomas 4
NEVIL/NEVILL/NEVELL/NEVEL, Samuel 114, 187, 210, 298; Thomas 291, 326, 329
NEWBERRY, Joseph 72
NEWBOLD, - Capt. 282; Stephen 291
NEWCOMB, John 161
NEWELL/NEWEL, - 316; James 229; Mary 151; Robert 229
NEWGAR, Peter 110, 169
NEWHOUSE, Anthony 49, 136, 175, 194, 209, 215, 223, 238, 319; Mary 209, 223
NEWLAND, John 12
NEWMAN, - Widow 32; John 331; William 261
NEWTON, - 118, 128, 130, 131, 138, 144; Capt. 331; Alpheus 270; Jedediah 310; William 190
NICE, Anthony 21
NICHOLAS, Anthony 145; Edward 3, 10, 22, 331; John 108, 145; William 130
NICHOLS/NICHOLLS, - Capt. 198, 213, 259, 298, 308, 312, 331; Mr. 216; Abington 105; Eleazer 205; James 207; John 69, 236; Joseph 9; Thomas 64; Walter 317
NICHOLSON, 149; Capt. 206, 249, 251; Mr. 286; Content 62, 258; George 69; John 222; Nicholas 309; William 39, 90, 130, 136, 161, 169, 175, 241, 242, 246
NICKLES, James 332
NICOLL, - Capt. 118
NIEMAN, Zacharias 265, 287
NIHELL/NIHILL, Edmund 2, 100, 112, 133, 177, 276; Maurice

100, 133, 183
NIMMS, - Capt. 193
NISBET/NISBITT, Albert 178; John Maxwell 286
NEVIN/NEVEN, - Capt. 37, 252, 254, 331; Margaret 155; Richard 155; Robert 48
NIXON, - and EDGAR 17; 27; Richard 23; William 17, 172
NOAH, John 156, 267
BOBLE, - Col. 275; Abel 203; Anthony 161, 163; John 8; Lazarus 244; Samuel 113, 153, 154; William 203
NOBLIT, Abraham 255, 309; William 83
NOEL, Anthony 22; Garrat 286
NOLAND, Roger 121
NORBURY, - Capt. 25
NORRIS, - and GRIFFITHS/GRIFFITH/GRIFFITTS 3, 26, 35, 118, 130; - 51, 75, 95, 99, 120, 129, 159; Mr. 163; Anthony 12; Charles 132, 135, 176, 182, 219, 230, 285, 300; Isaac 15, 28, 30, 37, 61, 67, 90, 94, 102, 103, 135, 149, 151, 197, 200, 253, 289, 308, 310, 312, 319, 320, 322, 325; James 100; John 102; Joseph 125; Mary 15
NORTH/NOARTH, - Capt. 119, 249, 307, 308; George 86, 135, 141, 260; Joshua 186;Roger 7, 192; Robert 10
NORTON, Richard 48, 235; Unity 235
NORWOOD, John 33, 52, 69, 152, 180, 196
NOXON, Benjamin 167
NOYER, Jane 47
NOYES, Thomas 114
NUGENT, John 156
NUSUM, - Capt. 289
NUTT, - Mrs. 30
NUTTLE, - Capt. 236, 251, 281, 292
NUTUS, John 127; Thomas 127
NYGH, Peter 46

OAKFORD, William 138
OATES, - Capt. 286
OBLINE, - Capt. 1
OBORN, Joseph 24
O'BRIAN/O'BRYAN, - Capt. 312; Catherine 182; Christopher 29; Connor 232; Darby 264, 277; Eleanor 29; James 84, 109; John 109, 330; Thomas 109
OBRYANT, Daniel 122, 242
O'CAIN, Richard 8
OCHTERLONY/OUCHTERLONY, - Capt. 118, 197; Patrick 90; Robert 207
ODELL, John 307

ODENHEIMER, Jacob 266
ODIORNE, Jotham 57
O'DONNEL, May 48
O'DOUGHERTY, Roger 326
O'FARREL, Dennis 166
OFFLEY, David 311
OGBORNE/OGBURN, John 172, 277
OGDEN/OGDON, David 114; John 39, 284, 310; Joseph 73, 98, 159, 222, 251, 257; Robert 114
OGILBY, Patrick 99
OGILSBY, - Capt. 209
OGILVIE, - Lt. 334; James 153; William 334
OGLE, Martha 150; Samuel 151, 177, 180; Thomas 9, 150, 237
O'HAGEN, Patrick 221
O'HANLIN/O'HANLON/O'HAXLIN, Patrick 123, 176, 194, 224, 240, 257, 311
OKILL, George 6, 48, 53, 69, 147, 167, 188, 200, 201, 307, 324
O'LANSHAHIN, Teddy 25
OLDMAN, - 126, 147; Joseph 16, 20, 28, 80, 98, 112, 122, 219
OLIFF, Edward 73
OLIPHANT, Ephraim 141
OLIVE, Edward 32
OLIVER, - Capt. 194; Daniel 226
O'MURRY, Bryan 31
O'NEAL/ONEAL/ONEIL/O'NEILL/O'Neel, Charles 23; Con 236; Dennis 224, 226; John (alias of John M'Neal) 50; Patrick 116
ONION, - 314; Deborah 314, 329; Stephen 135, 169, 263, 293, 329
ONO, Joseph 316
ORD, John 86, 163, 291
ORME, - Capt. 329
ORMSBY, John 213
ORR, Daniel 333; George 212, 261; Patrick 333; Sarah 261
ORRICK, John 278
OSBORN/OSBORNE/OSBOURN, - Capt. 275; Sir Danvers/Gov. 241, 253, 255, 256, 257, 260, 262; John 260; Joseph 2, 5; Peter 167; Samuel 272; Sylvanus 307; William 56
OSTLEY, Daniel 191
OSWALD, Andrew 206
OTHOSON, Otho 222
OTTEN, William 144
OTTINGER, William 49, 238
OUKE, William 114
OULTON, John 237, 278, 305
OUTERBRIDGE, - Capt. 18
OUTMANDORF, Hanus 317
OVE, Jacob 94
OVENS, - Capt. 236, 243
OVEREND, Thomas 106, 177
OVERPACK, George 16
OWEN/OWENS, - Capt. 259

David 205; Evan 265; George 164, 167; Griffith 7, 61, 102, 149, 197, 217, 253, 308, 333; Jane 223; John 30, 61, 102, 126, 149, 161, 164, 167; Keltoe 333; Owen 89, 139; Robert 280, 330
OXFORD, John (alias of John Hawksford) 2
OXLEY, - 89, 94; John 117
OXNARD, Thomas 294

PACA, John 229
PACKER, John 114
PADMORE, John 204
PAGE, - Capt. 268; John 55
PAINE/PAIN; see also PAYNE, - 217; Jane 175; John 236; Thomas 242
PAINTER/PAYNTER, Peter 17; Samuel 288
PALANCHE, - Capt. 320
PALMER, - Capt. 18, 178, 202, 294, 315, 324; Anthony 1, 56, 65, 77, 91, 152, 277; Daniel 30, 61, 102, 149, 197, 253, 308; Eliakim 47, 56; Elizabeth 56; George 225, 229; John 35, 142, 177, 314; Samuel 65, 81, 148, 166, 249, 301; Thomas 24, 56; William 52, 80, 181, 252, 263
PALMO, - Don 206
PANCH, Francisco 178
PANCOAST, William 281
PANEBAKER/PENNEBAKER, - Widow 290; Peter 308
PANGBURN, Stephen 302
PANKES, John 135
PARCEL, John 215
PARE, Edward 51
PARHAM, John 57, 110, 259, 333; Margaret 110
PARISH, - Capt. 150, 204, 245, 250, 286; George 207, 255
PARK/PARKE, Jonathan 95, 237; Joseph 8; Thomas 13, 95, 103, 145, 150
PARKER, - and GARRETT 73, 98, 139; - 139, 160; Capt. 151; Mr. 64, 170; Widow 75, 133; Abraham 133, 229; Alexander 24, 57, 76; James 42, 115, 134, 187, 196; Job 258; John 265; Joseph 45, 195, 333; Nathaniel 134, 169, 188; Richard 178; William 18, 38, 48, 71, 85, 90, 110, 253, 255, 308, 309
PARKINSON, Jane 158; John 5, 158
PARKS, David 109; Richard 103
PARLIN, Olove 272
PARR, - 198; John 49;

Nathaniel 205; Samuel 34, 63, 65, 75, 112, 140, 177, 185, 208, 216, 223; William 112, 177, 208, 223, 303
PARRAN, - Mr. 272
PARRISH, John 277; Robert 157
PARROCK/PARROKE, James 57, 252, 330; John 9, 114, 252, 309; Mary 252
PARROT/PARROTT, Jacob 83, 179, 222; John 105, 247
PARRY, David 2; Jane 49; John 138, 178; Rowland 7; Stephen 49; Thomas 49
PARSONS, - Capt. 205; Abraham 304; John 217; William 254
PARTRIDGE/PATRIDGE, - Capt. 60, 154, 221, 306, 308; Peter 132, 276; Richard 47, 53
PARVIN, Silas 98, 103
PASCHALL, - Capt. 310; Lt. 81; Elizabeth 55; John 72, 259, 260; Jonathan 72, 164; Stephen 119; Thomas 307; William 160
PASHASHEE, George 172
PASS, John 7, 215; John Jacob 248
PASSMORE, John 146
PASTORIUS/PISTORIUS/PISTORIOUS/PISTORUS/PISTORAS, - Widow 319, 325; Daniel 11, 121, 139, 152, 163, 176, 177, 178, 241, 257, 269, 289, 304, 306, 327; Sarah 327
PATESHALL, - Lt. 141
PATRICK, - Capt. 219; Hugh 3; John 53
PATSON, Thomas 315
PATTEN, - Capt. 291
PATTERSON, - Capt. 299; Lt.-Col. 20; Andrew 58; Arthur 31, 61, 102, 150, 199, 253, 309; James 13; Walter 223; William 8, 11, 69, 71, 79, 158, 168, 309
PATTING, Elisha 76
PATTISON, Joseph 131
PATTYGARY, - Capt. 233
PAU, Christina 110; Hans Michael 110
PAUL, - 302; John 280; Joseph 9
PAWLING/PAWLIN, - Capt. 17; Henry 5, 103, 149, 298; John 7
PAXTON/PAXSON, Henry 72, 235; Joseph 112, 226; Mary 112; Thomas 61; William 25, 30, 34, 109, 149, 226
PAYNE; see also PAINE, - Capt. 321
PEAK/PEAKE, John 303; Sarah 214
PEARANT, Sarah 244

365

PEARCE, Benjamin 263; George 310
PEARMAN, - Capt. 266
PEARNE/PEARN, Richard 8, 14, 106, 114
PEARSE, - Capt. 55, 56, 312; Thomas 72
PEARSELL/PIERSAL, Jeremiah 48; Richard 81
PEARSON/PEARSONS, Hannah 52, 89, 173, 284, 310, 311; Isaac 61, 70, 90, 167, 168, 193, 197, 250, 251, 253, 256, 257, 263, 279, 308; John 108, 255, 259, 265; Joseph 181; Robert 134; Robert Isaac 30; Ross 261; Samuel 99; Thomas 61, 70, 90, 102, 149, 167, 197, 308; William 87
PEATSON, Isaac 334
PEDWEOW, Abigail 112; Philip 114
PEDIN, Hugh 89
PEDNORE, Ulrick 163
PEELE/PEEL, - 106, 119; Capt. 248, 258, 314; Anthony 200; John 30, 99, 233; Oswald 1, 30, 61, 63, 65, 167, 200, 315
PELL, - Capt. 130, 282
PELLER, James 55, 98, 161, 238
PEMBERTON, - 227; Catherine 132; Ebenezer 132; Israel 9, 19, 71, 100, 103, 120, 158, 182, 225, 285, 333; Israel, Jr. 39, 66, 79, 102, 106, 135, 176, 203, 230, 235; Israel, Sr. 31, 61, 168, 223, 269, 311; James 1, 22, 26, 86, 92, 106, 115, 142, 149, 150, 168, 173, 177, 221, 223, 227, 279, 311, 319; John 28, 56, 59
PENDER/PENDOR, Arnold 143, 205
PENDERGRASS/PENDERGRAFT, - 71; Philip 311
PENDLEY, Thomas 285
PENN, John 207, 209, 289; Juliana 155; Richard 132, 209, 310; Thomas 132, 155, 193, 233, 251, 310; William 129, 207
PENNETTERS, - Capt. 235
PENNEL/PENNELL/PENNILL, John 40, 175; William 50, 80, 187
PENNIMAN, James 185
PENNINGTON/PENINGTON, - Edward 158, 170, 183, 222, 230, 284, 328; John 189, 223, 231
PENNOCK, Elizabeth 316; Joshua, Sr. 75; Nathaniel 61, 102, 149, 197, 253, 308; Samuel 75, 269, 272, 313, 316
PENNY, - Capt. 255; Abraham 178
PENROSE, Bartholomew 5, 34, 149, 166, 254, 265, 270, 274; Robert 321; Thomas 84, 100, 142
PEPPERDINE, John (alias John Higgins) 174
PEPPERELL/PEPPERILL, - Capt. 242; Col. 324; Gen. 334; Sir William 323, 330, 331
PERKESON, Robert 129
PERKINS, - 144, 148, 195; Capt. 1, 162; George 263; John 282
PERKLEY, Lawrence 277
PERLET, Anna Maria 216; Conrad 216
PEROT, John 325; Richard 189, 192, 194, 198
PERRIN, - Capt. 29
PERRY, - Capt. 15; Arthur 141; Charles 272; James 208; Mary 196, 201, 209; Thomas 93, 184, 187
PESHLEY, William 206
PETERS, Mr. 88; Rev. 160, 225; Widow 229, 236, 269; Joseph 172; Moses 147; Rees/Reese 43, 179, 263, 271,275; Richard 1, 13, 103, 105, 113, 135, 189, 193, 203, 289, 296, 307, 310, 320, 329; Thomas 43, 229, 236, 269; William 54, 86, 116, 135, 136, 186, 194, 197, 253, 263, 271, 275, 308
PETERSON, Andrew 312; Jacob 312; John 153; Luloff 11; Swain 14
PETTON, Benjamin 61
PETTY, - 139, 184; Capt. 143; James 36; John 71, 78, 85, 241, 311
PEW, David 76
PEYRONCE, - Mr. 296
PEYRONIE/PEYRENIE, - Capt. 334; William 307, 334
PHENIX/PHAENIX/PHOENIX, - Capt. 43, 52, 76, 212, 218, 220, 263
PHILIPS/PHILLIPS/PHILIPPS, - Capt. 54, 74, 83, 87, 135, 230, 251, 264, 308; (Col.) 52; Justice 130, 166; Gen. 80; Lt.-Gen. 22; Rev. 275; Daniel 92; Eleazer 112; Jenkin 72, 246; John 15, 49, 161, 173, 185, 186; Margaret 36; Richard 270; Robert 328; Thomas 7, 311; Wilcox/Willcox 240, 258, 313, 331
PHILIPSON, - Capt. 252, 277, 294
PHILPOT, Brian, Jr. 264; Mary 107; William 163

PHIPPS, - Capt. 243; John 49; Joseph, Jr. 205; S. 114; Samuel 292; William 119
PHLAUGHERTY, Patrick 296
PHYSICK, Edmund 215, 271, 324
PICKEMAN, - Capt. 197, 200, 250, 303
PICKET, Ned (alias Edward) 285
PICKFORD, Thomas 134
PICKINGS, John 298
PICKUS, George 258
PIDGEON/PIGEON, William 103, 119, 134, 138, 252, 281, 327
PIERCE, - and FISHER 136; Capt. 201, 259, 331; Edward 2; John 254; Robert 13
PIERCY, John 143
PIESLEY, Francis 200
PIGGOT, - Capt. 205
PILLAR, James 47
PIMM/PIM, Richard 237; Thomas 35, 308; William 95, 111
PINCKNEY, Charles 231
PINE, Lazarus 232
PITCAIRN/PITCAIRNE, - Capt. 204, 251, 252, 254, 266, 322
PITCH, Thomas 287
PITCHER, - Mr. 324; James 326
PITKIN, William 287
PITREKIN, William 320
PITT/PITTS, - Gov. 276, 277, 303, 313; Mr. 304; Samuel 213; Thomas 244
PITTY, William 217
PITZLER, Philip Andrew 297
PLACE, Aaron 92
PLAIN, William 20
PLAISTED, Edward 166
PLASKET, William 42
PLATT, John 208
PLIM, George 192
PLUMLEY, Charles 333; George 44, 75, 76, 133, 156, 159; John 131
PLUMSHER/PUMSHER, William 264, 267
PLUMSTEAD/PLUMSTED, - 28, 178; Mary 72, 73; William 23, 72, 88, 102, 106, 125, 140, 172, 235, 307, 318, 329, 331
PLUNKET, James 291; John 292
POAK, Archibald 162
POCE, George 15
POCKLENTON, Margaret 44
POCOCK, - Capt. 17; Daniel, Sr. 190
POE, Alexander 262; Patrick 103
POILLOIN, James 325
POKE, Charles 166
POLE, - and HOWELL 146, 184, 202, 204, 275

POLE (contin'd) - 42, 43; John 23, 41, 75, 119, 146, 175, 275, 328, 330
POLESON/POLSON, Jasper 229; William 196, 307
POLEGREEN/POLGREEN, James 150, 268, 270; Thomas Bickley 153, 181
POLLARD, - Col. 246
POLLOCK, James 143
POLTANY, Thomas 275
POMFRET, Earl of 155
PONEO, Gabriel 66; Mary 66
PONEY, Thomas 135
POOLE/POOL, - 81, 86, 109, 118, 150, 170, 192, 193, 194, 262, 269, 262, 269, 285, 288, 305, 328; Nathaniel 240; Thomas 282
POOLLEY/POLLEY, George 50, 165
POOR, - 42
PORTEOUS, George 17
PORTER, - Capt. 20, 250, 260; Rev. 318; Alexander 4; Anthony 152, 153; Charles 98; James 268, 306; Patrick 256; Robert 187, 188; Walter 39; William 9
POSTLETHWAITE, John 80
POTE, - Capt. 266, 290
POTTER, Henry 93; John 8, 103, 279, 293, 309; Matthew 44
POTTS, - and YORKE 101; Capt. 121; Abraham 75, 278; John 21, 145, 162, 167, 196, 202; Jonas 289; Joshua 19; Magdalene/Magdalen 162, 196; Nathaniel 151; Stacy 250; Stephen 49, 75, 133; Thomas 86, 162, 167, 196, 223; Thomas, Sr. 34, 167; William 287, 303
POULTIS, James 326
POULTNEY, Thomas 100
POUNCE, - Capt. 308
POWELL, - 50, 57, 94, 95, 100, 105, 127, 133, 161, 291, 195, 305; Mr. 194; Eleanor 239; George 14; George Gabriel 215; James 67, 176, 180; John 110; John (alias of Jack, a Negro) 73, 330; Mary 164; Nicholas 64; Robert 175, 232, 251; Samuel 8, 22, 118, 132, 179, 185, 191, 299, 313, 331; Samuel, Jr. 1, 27, 31, 55, 115, 142; Simeon 213; Thomas 108, 239, 266, 267; William 252, 299
POWER, - Capt. 249, 275; Mrs. 315; Mr. 315; Peter 212;

William 183
PRALL, Peter 29
PRATHER, Thomas 54
PRATT, - Widow 65, 67, 99, 138; Charles 255; Henry 31; Joseph 120
PREBBLE/PREBLE, - Capt. 37; Lt.-Col. 304
PREDMORE, John 139, 184
PRESCOTT, - Mr. 142
PRESTON, - 190; John 334; Nathan 273, 326; Thomas 9, 171, 226, 233, 258; William 30, 89, 318
PRESTWOOD, Richard 46
PRICE, - Capt. 294, 318; Benjamin 70, 283; David, Sr. 106; Edward 326; Evan 78, 197, 222; Issacher 311; John 103, 330; Jonathan 142; Joseph 144; Richard 163, 297; William 32, 34
PRIDE, William 188
PRIEST, John 90, 99, 127, 162; Robert 99
PRIGG, John 78
PRIGMORE, John 242
PRINCE, Joseph 299
PRITCHARD, Anthony 79, 266; John 83; Rees 6; Robert 112; Samuel 206
PROBART, William 125
PROBY, - Capt. 329, 332; John 23
PROCTOR, - Capt. 131; George 18
PROGER, Edward 185
PROSSER, William 212
PROVOST, - Mrs. 70; David 114
PROWELL, James 187
PRYOR/PRIOR, - Widow 177; Silas 291, 299; Thomas 46, 217
PUFF, Valentine 319
PUGH, Joseph 31; Michael 193
PULLING, - Capt. 318
PUMMELL, James 42
PUNTER, - Capt. 265, 314, 323
PURFIELD, John 35
PURRIERS, John 13
PURRY, - Mr. 205
PURVEYANCE/PURVIANCE, David 307; Samuel 246, 283
PUSEY, Caleb 89, 186; John 61
PUTTIN, Daniel 163
PYE, - Capt. 147; Commodore 190
PYEWELL/PYWELL, William 325

QUAINTANCE, William 249
QUEREAU, - Capt. 216, 218, 243, 255, 312
QUICK, Anne 79; Cornelius 56, 173; John 79
QUIGG, Charles 254, 255, 258
QUIN, Morto 227
QUINCH, - Capt. 271

QUINCY, John 127
QUINTON, John 34

RABLING, Thomas 52
RAFEUR, Conrad 11
RAGENNAS, John 51
RAGG, - Capt. 204, 215; Robert 100, 146, 147, 180, 220, 251
RAIN, Timothy 152
RAINER, Mary 199
RAIT/RAITT, - Capt. 275; Mr. 141; Robert 106
RAKES, Weston 230
RAKESTRAW, William/Wm. 47, 225, 321, 331
RAMADGE, - Capt. 111, 123, 147
RAMBO/RAMBOES, - 270; Andrew 10, 16; Gabriel 321; Mounce 278; Thomas 228, 235
RAMSAY/RAMSEY, - Capt. 213, 219, 233, 236, 260, 294, 303, 304, 308; Mr. 55; Andrew 235; Anthony 139; Robert 31; Samuel 95; Sarah 151; Thomas 216; William 9, 307
RANDLE/RANDEL, - Capt. 59, 130; John 310
RANDOLPH, Isham 11; Peyton 307
RANKIN, - Capt. 259, 279, 281, 284, 294, 303; Mrs. 227; George 32, 305; John 286; Moses 297, 327; Robert 205
RANSTED, Caleb 330; William 269
RAPER, - Mr. 204
RAPPALIE, Derrick 85
RASH, - Capt. 242
RATCHFORD, William 215
RATTERY, - Capt. 260
RATTRAY, - Mr. 205; John 263
RAW, Thomas 11
RAWISTON, James 199
RAWLE, Benjamin 44, 111, 130; Elizabeth 279; Rebecca 279
RAWLES, - Capt. 240, 316; Francis 109
RAWLINS/RAWLINGS, - Capt. 331; Moses 158; Mary (alias of Mary Baker) 185
RAWLINSON/RAWLISON, John 138, 145; Robert 273, 304
RAY, - Capt. 227; Mr. 230; Alexander 201, 226, 316; David 171; James 35; John 31, 180
RAYMOND, - Capt. 219
RAZWELL, Thomas 189
REACE, Edward 119
READ, - DELAGE and 113; Capt. 261, 286, 297, 298, 324; Andrew 17, 69, 72, 134; Betsy 212; Charles/CHA. 52, 57, 320; Dorothy 321; James 1, 117, 171;

READ (cont'd), John 71, 143, 158, 164, 171, 192; Michael 197; Peter 257; Samuel 48, 52, 226, 252, 290, 302, 311, 321; Sarah 176, 180, 203, 215
READINGTON, Gregory 79
REAGAN, William 195
REALY, Edward 162
REARDON, John 96, 196, 258; Martin 131
REAVERDY, Daniel 106
REDDING, Michael 66
REDFIELD, - Capt. 171
REDFORD, John 108, 114
REDMAN/REDMON, Ann 177; Henry 145; John 60, 270; Joseph 60, 61, 69, 96, 203, 283; Penelope 10, 90; Thomas 10, 90, 171
REDMOND, - Capt. 33; Mrs. 195, 226, 241, 279; Anne 251; Joseph 26, 210, 300
REED, - and FURMAN 273, 284; Rev. 318; Adam 13; Andrew 1, 152, 169, 201, 207, 220, 226, 228, 240, 242, 256, 262, 265, 270, 273, 322, 329; Charles 176, 190; Hugh 36; Joseph 16, 152, 226; Joseph, Jr. 226; Samuel 39; William 9
REES/REESE/REICE, - 288; Capt. 20, 101, 208, 209, 251, 255, 257, 268, 276, 287, 301, 318; David 162, 280; John 14, 20, 123, 125, 203; William 4
REET, - Capt. 299
REEVE/REEVES, - Capt. 225, 230, 249, 251, 254, 257, 270, 275, 279, 305, 306, 323, 327; Jacob 307; Peter 86, 149, 221
REGAN, Timothy 146
REID, John 8
REIFF, Jacob 67
REILY/REILEY/REILLY/ RILEY/ REYLEY/RYLEY, - and ARCHDALL 81; Ambrose 110; Bryan 272; Hugh 169; James 169; John 34, 62, 117, 120, 162, 198, 230, 235, 259, 261, 171, 320, 326; Miles 159; William 93, 260
REISER/REIZER/RESER, Baltus 179, 306; Bernard/Bernhard 289, 306
REISTINE/RISTINE/ RIESTINE/RICHSTEIN, John 261; John Kraft/ John Krallft 289, 306; Krafft 306
REMINGTON, - Capt. 285
REMUS, Bastian 230
RENCH, - Capt. 110, 265; Andrew 231

RENDELS, Hugh 41
RENNER, Michael 184
RENNICKS, Henry 13
RENSHAW, John 52, 106, 126, 131; Richard 57, 61, 72, 127, 162, 243; Thomas 126, 298
REUCH, Peter 15
REVACUM, Justus 302
REX, George 254, 269
REYNELL, John 95, 112, 119, 135, 143, 170, 176, 230, 285, 317
REYNOLDS/REYNOLD/ RENALDS/RENNALS, Alexander 239, 293; Catherine 230; David 47, 269; James 21, 174, 286, 335; John 255, 321, 330; Patrick 128, 229; William 44, 231
RHEA, - and WIKOFF 283
RHODES/RHOADS/ RHOADES/ ROADS/RODES, - 43; Capt. 259, 299, 331; James 164, 167; Jonah 43; Richard 270; Samuel 28, 69, 98, 235, 141, 151, 176, 225, 230, 254, 279, 285, 294, 305, 315, 325, 331, 335
RICE/REICE, Evan 11, 150, 197, 230, 309; James (alias James Dillon) 198, 200, 202, 206, 208, 209, 210; Michael 309; Peter 273; Thomas 324; William 66
RICHARDS/RICHARD, - Capt. 40, 76, 130, 137, 152, 174, 178, 197, 202, 206, 209, 214, 227, 231, 251, 254, 259, 261, 273; Daniel 287; James 97; Joseph 2, 55, 89, 90, 122, 127, 227; Mary 2; Philip 217; Stephen 271; William 51, 216
RICHARDSON , - Mr. 141, 155; Widow 101; Aubrey/AWBRAY 129, 158; Francis 87, 119, 148, 168; Henry 107; John 161; Joseph 64, 87, 100, 160, 182, 197, 217, 288, 315, 324, 330; Richard 79, 129, 158; Samuel 217; William 212
RICHEY/RICHIE/RICHE/ RICHY, - Capt. 43; 220; Edward 248; James 6; John 93, 198, 210, 285; Thomas 333
RICHISON, Richard 3, 19, 23, 24, 35, 44, 90, 141, 245
RICHMAN, - 246
RICHMOND, Matthew 113
RICKETS, - Col 86; Isaac 217
RICKEY, John 334; Thomas 104

RIDDLE/RIDDALL, - Capt. 74, 294, 298, 318; Francis 195
RIDGE, William 286
RIDGELY/RIDGLEY, Charles 11, 187; John 20, 264
RIDGEWAY, John 16
RIDOUT, John 247
RIEGER, Jacob 18; John Bartholomew 67
RIETZ, Anthony 8
RIGBY/RIGBIE/RIGBEE, - Mrs. 279; Mr. 279, 290; John 187, 190; Nathan 56, 187, 190, 223; Sabina 223; William 292
RIGDON/RIGDEN, William 52, 306
RIGG, Robert 284
RIGGABY, Thomas 138
RIGGS/RIGS, Miles 268; Thomas 272
RIGHTER, George 269; Peter 37
RIMIUS, Henry 262
RING, Elizabeth (alias Elizabeth M'Neal) 229
RINGOLD/RINGGOLD, James 332; Thomas 271; William 326
RINKER, Christian 254
RISE, William 25
RISPHAM, John 114
RISTLER/RISLER, George 128, 224
RITCHIE/RITCHEY, - Capt. 38, 119, 155, 171, 172, 195, 213, 234, 247, 249, 250, 261; 262; 279, 281, 305, 324
RITTENHAUSEN, Peter 335
RIVEN, - Capt. 70
RIVERS, - Capt. 67, 268
RIVETS, Tunis 273
ROACH, Edward 78; Elizabeth 305; John 51; Patrick 262; Richard 207, 214
ROAN, - Dr. 29; John 156
ROBASS, James 59
ROBINS/ROBBINS, - Capt. 17, 193, 229; Ann 242; Christopher 4, 5, 7, 54, 154, 211, 258, 293, 302
ROBBS, Thomas 165
ROBERDEAU, Daniel 173, 192
ROBERTS/ROBERDS, - Capt. 18, 279; Justice 89; Mrs./Widow 18, 21, 28, 38, 70, 72, 82, 84, 86, 100, 104, 113, 118, 120, 306; Amos 197, 271; Aubrey 165; Daniel 103; Ellin 165; Ellis 148, 300; Enoch 256; Evan 99; Hugh 77, 116, 128, 132, 135, 140, 149, 165, 170, 176, 178, 197, 208, 217, 230, 259, 260, 274, 279, 285; Hunn 43; Isaac 13, 121,

ROBERTS, Isaac (cont'd) 124, 132; James 156; John 5, 12, 18, 128, 164, 207, 216, 271, 276, 283, 293, 332, 333; John (alias John Jones) 228; Joshua 211; Lewis 333; Mary 130, 137, 150; Owen 5, 69, 224, 243, 246; Phineas 123, 200, 269; Richard 230; Robert 154, 272, 308, 315; Samuel 51; Thomas 102, 230, 239, 270; Thomas, Jr. 269; Timothy 146; William 69, 128, 224
ROBERTSON, Peter 56, 67; Thomas 211, 254; William 118
ROBESON/ROBISON, - 37, 44, 124, 259; Capt. 43, 44, 72, 74, 94, 261, 262, 290, 292, 312; Andrew 38; Jonathan 4, 5, 132, 208; Magdalene 38; Maurice 141; Peter 3, 4, 5, 11, 31, 136, 169, 290, 293, 302, 307; Rudeman 47, 314; Samuel 7, 48; Septimus 46; William 53
ROBINSON, - 179, 268; Capt. 105, 277; Andrew 116; Elizabeth/ Betty 112, 114, 115; Christopher 278; Francis 248; James 50, 235; John 117, 142, 217, 237, 296, 322; Jonathan 111; Joseph 192; Patrick 316; Peter 278; Rudeman 245; Samuel 237; Septimus 36, 78, 105, 123, 190, 304; Thomas 9, 18, 190, 200, 266, 321, 326
ROBOTHAM, George 88
ROBSON, Robert 232; Thomas 11
ROCHE, John 68; Richard 218
ROCK, - Justice 89; Mr. 113; George 84, 92, 99, 151, 239
ROCKHILL, Ann22; Edward ?2, 151; John 141
ROCQUET, - Capt. 172
RODDAM, - Capt. 86; Lucy 111; Robert 111
RODGER/RODGERS, - Capt. 205, 268; William 257
RODMAN, John 128; William 220
RODNEY/RODENEY, - Capt. 144; Caesar/CESAR 255, 309; John 199
ROE, John 118, 175
ROG(?)ES, Andrew 13
ROGERS, - Capt. 195, 276, 277, 330; Mr. 315; Elisha 116; John 332; Margaret 202; Mary 55; Nicholas 264; Samuel 11; Thomas 211;
William 264
ROLLAND, - Capt. 236
ROLLINSON, Robert 189
ROLLSTON, Samuel 215
ROMER, - Capt. 275
RONEY, - Capt. 34, 240; Hercules 133, 157; John 49; Patrick 165; William 255
ROOKER, Abraham 246
ROOME, - Capt. 180, 218, 299, 312
ROOTS, Benajah 307
RORKE, Morgan 164
RORRIST, William 311
ROSE, - Capt. 270, 321; Richard 121; Stephen 164; Stoffel 234; Thomas 111, 234, 322
ROSS/ROSSE, - 160; Capt. 90, 166, 263, 283, 294, 304, 312, 324; Charles 201, 310, 320; David 15, 125; George 196, 262; James Isaiah 156; John 21, 27, 43, 58, 64, 112, 184, 185, 216, 254, 299, 310, 332
ROTHERAM, Joseph 71, 225
ROTHWELL, Charles 147; Jerrard 4
ROUNDTREE, George 41
ROUNSAVALL, Benjamin 23
ROUSE/ROUS/ROUZE, - Capt. 47, 52, 54, 55, 56, 80, 81, 88, 286, 296, 301; Mr. 270; Emanuel 25, 239, 278; John 87, 155, 283, 312; Nicholas 257; Robert 332
ROW, Jacob 179; John 333
ROWAN/ROWEN, - Dr. 292; John 36, 57, 59, 62, 191, 266, 271, 281
ROWLAND, - Capt. 266; David 13; James 91; Samuel 39; William 8
ROWLEY, Bartholomew 147
ROWLS, John 261
ROYAL; see RYALL, - Col. 315; George 278, 284
RUBELY, Jacob 312
RUBY, Edward 167
RUCH, Jacob 55
RUDISELLY, Jacob 264
RUDOLPH, Hance 177; John 10, 80, 284; Thomas 277
RUDYARD, - Capt. 307
RUE, James 325; John 28; Lewis 13; Lydia 28
RUFF, - Capt. 206, 243
RUFFNER, Simon 260
RUGGLES, - Capt. 76
RUKER, Abraham 220
RUMNEY, Edward 108
RUMSEY, William 52, 209
RUNDLE, - GREENWAY and 106, 150; Daniel
127, 173, 251, 287, 296
RUNSHEY, William 333
RUPORT, Leonard 335
RUSH, - Capt. 296; Mr. 58; Widow 186, 215; Barbara 111; Hannah 152; John 111, 152, 177; Joseph 45; Mary 193; Samuel 193; Thomas 45, 139; William 51, 91, 152, 167, 169, 246, 290, 329; Wilmot 177
RUSSELL/RUSSEL, - Capt. 59, 146, 147, 194, 231, 251, 266, 295, 296, 306, 307; Col. 287; Clement 161; Edward 45; Elizabeth 302, 314; James 51, 97, 127, 215, 235, 302, 314; William 134
RUSTON, Job 8, 19, 89, 93
RUTGERS, - Capt. 321
RUTH, Christopher 291; Lawrence 250; Thomas 254, 255, 256, 258
RUTHERFORD, - Capt. 171, 334; Rev. 201; James 162; John 334
RUTTENBAUSEN, - 321
RUTTER, Susanna 136; Thomas 155, 171, 284
RYALL; see ROYAL, George 48, 142
RYALLS, Samuel 20
RYAN/RIAN, - 141; Capt. 40, 143; Dennis 5; James 301, 307; John 229; Patrick 241, 249; Samuel 288; Thomas 121, 146; William 186
RYERS, John 286
RYERSON, Martin 29
RYKER, Jacob 56
RYLAND, Nicholas 63

SACKEL, David 104
SACKETT/SACKET, James 10, 12, 26, 34, 109, 124, 130; Joseph 96; Thomas 156
SADBROOK, - 196
SADLER, John 114
SAGE, - Capt. 260, 261, 275, 276, 288
SAILOR, Abraham 224
ST. CLAIR, Sir John 326, 331
ST. LOE/ST. LO, - Capt. 80, 81
SALMON, George 11
SALTER, - Capt. 194, 275, 304, 314
SALTONSTALL, - Col. 157
SALTUS, - Capt. 144, 259
SALYAR, Thomas (alias of Thomas Morrell) 271; William 271
SAMPLE, - Capt. 234; James 13
SAMPSON, - Capt. 279; Mark 171

SANDELANDS, David 47
SANDERS, - Capt. 146
SANDIFORD, Ralph 42
SANDWITH, William 303
SANSOM/SANSON, Samuel 86, 177, 185, 203, 216, 250, 261, 285
SANTIA, Domingo 165
SANTINO, Isaac Rodriquez 82
SANTUS, Matthew 261
SARLY, Anthony 246
SARVER, Ralph 70, 101
SATTERTHWAITE, James 288; William 234, 269
SAUER/SOWER, Christopher 63, 224
SAUL, Joseph 44, 132, 153, 197, 276, 287
SAUNDERS, - Capt. 88, 90, 306, 308; Mr. 176, 177; Isaac 31; Joseph 24, 89, 101, 117, 168, 182, 223, 231, 267, 280, 281; Richard 291; Samuel 123
SAUNDERSON, George 151
SAUSER, Michael 229
SAVAGE, - Capt. 250, 260, 294, 313; Asanus 175; Deliverance 136, 175; George 19; John 307; Joseph 119; Robert 152; Zanas/Zeanus 136, 319
SAVERY, William 263, 275
SAWER, Ralph 21
SAWYER, - Capt. 110, 242, 298, 313; John 288
SAY/SAYE, Thomas 45, 58, 72, 102, 129, 149, 173, 182, 217, 229, 284; William 217
SAYRE, Ananias 39, 296; John 146, 152, 214, 227, 273, 301, 322, 329
SCANLIN, William 19
SCANNELL, Timothy 24
SCANTON, William 36
SCARLET, John 35, 168
SCARTH/SCARF, Timothy 52, 124, 154, 243, 273
SCATTERGOOD, Joseph 130, 210, 330
SCHAUFFELE, Matthias 323
SCHEETZ, Alexander 154
SCHENCK/SCHENK, - Capt. 223
SCHERMERHORN/SCHERMERHORNE, - Capt. 38, 248, 321, 322
SCHERP, Johannes 15
SCHLAUGH, Jacob 105
SCHLEYDORN, - Mr. 17; Henry 4, 27, 75, 97, 175, 304
SCHLUTER, John 229
SCHNECK, Jacob 289
SCHOLDFIELD, John 190
SCHOONMAKER, Jacob, Jr. 49

SCHREIBER, Elias 194; George 194
SCHROCK, John 197
SCHUTZ, Michael 269
SCHUYLER, - Mr. 186; Dirck 41; Myndert 299; Peter 270
SCOFFIELD, Thomas 249
SCOGAN/SCOGGAN/SCOGGIN, - 228; James 236; John 7, 132; Mary Anne 7
SCOTT/SCOT, - Capt. 81, 221, 290; Mr. 204; Alexander 26; David 191; Ely 23; Henry 66; James 2, 21, 113, 188; Jesse 285; John 15, 211, 231, 243, 281, 287, 328; John, Jr. 215; Jonathan 66; Nathaniel 66, 224; Robert 191, 324; Samuel 87, 89, 119, 150; William 31, 282
SCOTTON/SCOTEN, Ann 10, 286
SCROOP/SCROOPE, - Capt. 116, 126
SCULL, - 81; Edward 179, 322, 327; Jasper 309; Joseph 7, 16, 25, 52, 55, 57, 68, 82, 90, 145, 208, 254, 263, 297, 318; Nicholas 4, 78, 116, 180, 196, 254, 259, 267, 290, 309, 316, 322, 327, 330
SCURLOCK, - Capt. 18
SEABRAND, Henry 319
SEAGER, John 19
SEAL/SEALE, John (alias of John Hill) 128; Thomas 55
SEANT, Thomas 170
SEARLE/SEARLS, - Capt. 249; John 111, 171
SEARS/SEERS, - Capt. 264; Joseph 205; William 132
SEAVERNS, Daniel 121
SEDGWICK, Richard 154
SEEKEL, George David 46
SEELY, Ephraim 29, 148; Jonas 218, 254; Samuel 171
SEILER, Hance Ulrich 104
SEIRES, - Capt. 29
SEIX, - Capt. 262, 266
SEIXAS, Isaac 275
SELKIRK, - 139
SELLERS, James 167; Samuel 55; William 96, 104
SELLON, - Mr. 218
SEMMES, Joseph Milburn 129
SENHOUSE, - Mr. 244
SERGEANT/SERJEANT/SARGEANT/SEARJANT, - Capt. 144, 225, 238, 271, 282, 294; Mrs. 154; Mr. 273; John 178
SERRILL, James 61
SETON, John 26

SEVERANCE, Joseph, Jr. 310
SEVERNS, John 5; Theophilus 171, 192, 226
SEWELL/SEWALL, - Mr. 162, 175; Rev. Dr. 144; Jane 126; Richard 28, 30, 31, 58, 61, 67, 69, 93, 95, 99, 177
SEXTON, Daniel 312
SEYMOUR/SEAMOUR, - Capt. 21, 147, 192, 214, 238, 247, 248, 257, 264, 285, 321; Daniel 147; John 296; William 144
SHAGHNESEY, Michael Coleman 5
SHAFTER, Henry 39
SHAKLETON, William 185
SHALCROSS, - 319
SHANE, - Capt. 318
SHANKLAND, - Capt. 315, 316; William 31, 63, 103, 150, 199, 326
SHANNON, - Capt. 242, 271, 313; Edward 240
SHANO, Isaac 93, 149
SHARER, Ulrick 331
SHARP/SHARPE, - Col. 318; Gov. 235, 241, 247, 325, 326; Mr. 321; Horatio 231, 247, 259, 264, 275, 287, 292, 296, 317, 321, 328, 331; Solomon 160; Thomas 90, 139, 175, 245
SHARPLESS, Benjamin 108; Jacob 272; John 182
SHARSWOOD/SHARWOOD, George 59, 182
SHARTS, Jacob 16
SHAVER, David 311
SHAW, - Capt. 313; Major 17; Widow 210; Ann/Anne 93, 181; John 18, 48, 292, 323; Samuel 5, 16, 93, 181; Thomas 86, 93, 181; Timothy 286
SHEA, Walter 65, 200
SHELDON, - Capt. 163, 227, 285
SHELLENBERG/SHELLEBERG, Abraham 177, 179; Henry 187
SHELLEY, Abraham 84, 140, 187
SHEPHERD/SHEPHARD/SHEPPARD, - Capt. 294; John 10, 48, 79, 120
SHERBURNE, - Capt. 171
SHERER, Ulrick 288
SHERMAN/SHEARMAN, - Capt. 262, 263; Josias 307
SHERRIN, William 294
SHERRINGTON, - Mr. 249
SHERWOOD/SHEERWOOD, Henry 187; Henry Francis 164; John 112
SHETTIE, - Capt. 296
SHEVERS, - Capt. 21
SHEWBART/SHEWBERT, John 214, 229; Mary 163
SHEWELL, Elizabeth 117, 146, 224; Joseph 117, 243; Richard 52;

SHEWELL (cont'd) Robert 43, 117, 119, 243; Stephen 117
SHIEBLIE, Daniel 220
SHIELDS, Patrick 313
SHIERS, George 49, 154, 188, 240; Hannah 49, 188
SHINN, Caleb 65; Thomas 235
SHIPLEY, Thomas 293; William 293
SHIPPEN, - Dr. 134; Edward 1, 23, 62, 77, 79, 96, 114, 129, 148, 161, 163, 180, 201, 202, 226; Joseph 29, 114; William 48, 69, 76, 114, 163, 258, 273, 307, 329
SHIPPEY, Deborah 16; John 16
SHIRLEY, - Capt. 81, 96, 109, 129, 150, 170, 250, 261, 275, 279, 285, 286, 293; Col. 51, 201, 324; Gov. 38, 193, 233, 238, 251, 290, 306, 323; Mr. 329; George 39; James 290; John 304; Washington 285, 305; William/W. 3, 236, 284, 317, 334
SHITERS, Samuel 9
SHOALS, - Capt. 162, 189, 218, 220, 259, 329
SHOCK, Andrew 229
SHOCKLEY, John 182
SHOEMAKER, - 88, 155; Ann 272; Benjamin 1, 3, 14, 31, 45, 93, 97, 102, 178, 197, 199, 209, 227, 241, 321; Daniel 272; George 241, 327; Isaac 138, 139; Jacob 27, 93, 164, 170, 228, 294; Jacob, Jr. 60, 65, 170, 217, 282; John 139; John, Jr. 230; Peter 139; Samuel 1, 3, 14, 26, 31, 32, 93, 97, 102, 147, 169, 183, 209, 227, 301, 317
SHOPPLEY, John (alias John Williams) 86
SHORE, Francis 286
SHORES, John 232
SHORTALL, Amey 323; Richard 323
SHORTES/SHORTESS, - Capt. 141, 234
SHOURT, - Capt. 163, 165, 190; Oliver 75
SHOUT, Philip 130
SHRACK, John 253
SHRINER/SHREINER, Catherine 230; George 67
SHUGAR, Thomas 104
SHULL/SHUL, Frederick 199, 254
SHULTZ, David 104
SHURMER, Benjamin 64
SHURTLEFF, - Capt. 185

SHUTE, - 217, 220; Atwood/Attwood 110, 121, 140, 145, 169, 232, 317, 330; Joseph 235; Thomas 178
SHUTLAND, - Capt. 300
SHUTZMAN, John 184
SHWYTSER, Lawrence 63
SIBBALD, - Capt. 110, 276, 319; John 136, 247
SIBTHORPE, Christopher 217
SICKMAN, John Henry 145
SIDDAL, James 124
SIEGEL, Jacob 92
SIEVEN, James 109
SIGFRIEDUSALRIEBS, Peter 233
SILSBY, Samuel 31, 61, 102
SILVENE, William 193
SILVER, James 8, 226
SIM, John 74; William 71
SIMCOCK, John 217
SIMINTON, Robert 75, 84; Theophilus 75
SIMKINS/SIMKIN, Daniel 73; John 143; Margaret 73
SIMMONS/SIMMONDS/SIMONS/SIMON, - Capt. 204, 273, 308; Edward 241; Jacob 216; Joseph 172, 211, 241; Nathan 250; Richard 36
SIMONTON, Robert 64, 68; William 286
SIMPLE, James 286
SIMPSON/SIMSON, - Capt. 210, 251, 285, 295, 318; John 38, 309; Samuel 20; William 310
SIMS/SYMS/SYMES, - 27; Capt. 318; Buckridge 26, 65, 94, 98, 220, 223, 279, 288; James 322; James (alias of James Williams) 147; Joseph 21, 22, 23, 25, 27, 33, 64, 90, 94, 113, 118, 119, 135, 141, 160, 167, 216, 220, 245, 261, 268, 277, 330; Richard 86; William 185, 186, 211
SINCLAIR, Sir John 323, 325; Joseph 194, 220
SINGLETON, - Mr. 279; John 171
SINLOUP, Philip 279, 293
SIPPLE, Ulrick 333
SIRON/SIREN, Simon 9, 240, 257
SISOM, Thomas 43
SISSON, Barnet 221
SITLINTON, Robert 219
SKEELES, William 116
SKELDEN, Nathaniel 142
SKERRETT, James 159
SKINNER, Matt. 186; Richard 198, 209
SKULLY, Patrick 198
SLADE, - Capt. 126, 130; Jonathan 127
SLAIN, John 51

SLAINEY, Michael 147
SLATER/SLAYTER/SLATTER, Michael 63, 67, 77, 161, 211
SLAUGHTER, Catherine 98; John 98
SLEIGH, Joseph 14
SLEMONS, Thomas 159
SLEVAN, Patrick 191
SLIPPER, Thomas 119
SLOAN, Alexander 209
SLOSS, Samuel 301; Thomas 172
SLOUGH, Matthias 309
SLUMAN, - Capt. 206, 212
SMELT, - Capt. 50, 118
SMITH, - and JAMES 25, 28, 46, 150, 158; and JONES 60; NEATE/NEAT and 10, 21, 26; Capt. 83, 95, 102, 128, 129, 134, 147, 170, 173, 177, 212, 218, 225, 227, 249, 251, 256, 259, 284, 296, 298, 300, 321, 331; Rev. 303; Alethea 217; Andrew 16, 103, 176; Anne 309; Benjamin 170, 255; Cornelius 171; Daniel 82, 114, 172, 184, 271; Daniel, Jr. 332; David 244, 284; David, Jr. 332; David (alias Griffith Smith) 206; Edward 19, 36; Elisha 78; Elizabeth 263; George 38, 47, 63, 95, 99, 182, 283; Gideon 76; Henry 23, 319; Hugh 189, 309; James 13, 22, 114, 131, 196, 210, 221, 246, 249, 264, 297; Jeremiah 98, 118, 119, 135, 142, 154, 177, 191, 219; Johanna 189; Johannes 137; John 9, 10, 13, 17, 30, 46, 62, 76, 77, 79, 80, 81, 91, 94, 96, 102, 105, 109, 113, 135, 149, 165, 166, 171, 176, 177, 185, 197, 200, 211, 216, 220, 221, 225, 230, 238, 239, 262, 270, 279, 285, 286, 289, 292, 299, 309, 323, 324, 330; John (alias John Knowles) 22; Jonathan 251; Joseph 8, 11, 132, 180, 224, 318, 324; Margaret 142; Mary 303, 305; Maurice 154; Nathan 198; Richard 23, 123, 138, 156; Richard, Jr. 114; Robert 13, 173, 219, 244; Samuel 69, 89, 139, 207, 229, 233, 249, 252, 263, 267, 288, 298, 306, 320; Thomas 128, 133, 138, 139, 199, 204, 207, 214, 229, 252, 253,

SMITH, Thomas (cont'd) 397, 309; Thomas (alias of Thomas Aubery) 217; Timothy 197; Walter 217; William 8, 47, 61, 99, 102, 149, 170, 172, 180, 245, 253, 272, 280, 308, 318, 322; William Peartree 69, 162
SMOUT, Edward 29, 44, 176, 242, 256; Elizabeth 176, 256
SMYTER, - CUZZINS and 23, 46, 104; Capt. 9, 36; Charles 10, 14
SNEAD, - Capt. 260, 305 Edward 123, 160, 165
SNYDER/SNIDER/SNEIDER, Arons Raff 129; Barbara 21; Christian 156, 311; Jacob 21
SNODGRASS, James 20; John 20
SNOW, - Capt. 138,140, 292; Rev. 318; Peter 51; Prince 67
SNOWDEN/SNOWDON, - Mr. 270; Isaac 179; Jedediah 40, 56, 93; John 40, 56, 93, 155, 179, 274, 283, 313, 324; John, Sr. 313; Ruth 283; William 85
SOBER, John 23, 73, 118, 228, 260
SOBERT, - Mr. 14
SOHIER, - Capt. 140
SOLLEY/SOLLY, Nathan 64, 238
SOMERS, Adam 129
SOMERSALL, Richard 245; Stafford 56
SOMMERS, Samuel 54
SOMMET, Leonard 187
SONMANS/SONMAN, - Dr. 245, 286; Peter 48, 144, 173
SOOY, Joseph 94
SOUMAIN/SOUMAIEN, Samuel 231, 297; Simeon 334
SOUTHCOTT, - Capt. 277
SOUTHWICK, Maham 305
SPACKHOLTZ, Baltus 299
SPAFFORD, George 69, 108, 138, 314; John 105, 113, 305, 323; Sarah 314; William 24, 26, 42, 51, 64, 177, 225, 328
SPARHAWK, - Mr. 315
SPARKS, John 187; Peter (alias of Peter Green) 226
SPARLING, John 53
SPEAR, - 190; William 88
SPEARING, - Mr. 334; William 334
SPELLING, - Capt. 275
SPENCELY, John 138
SPENCER, - 171, 177, 257; Capt. 205, 277, 286; Adam 128; Diana 226, 252; John 89,
219, 222, 226 255; Samuel 89; Thomas 113
SPENDER, - Capt. 242
SPICER, Jacob 326; John 115; Samuel 65
SPIKE, Jacob 258
SPINKSE, Daniel 231, 235
SPITZER, - Dr. 25
SPOFFORD, - Capt. 202; George 99, 146, 273, 301; William 281
SPOFFORTH, Samuel 81
SPRIGGS, George 74
SPRINGER, George 289
SPROULE, Robert 298; Samuel 118
SPROUT, - Capt. 166
SPRUCE, John 51
SPRY, - Capt. 329
SPURRIER, - Capt. 146, 147, 202, 209, 225, 233, 236, 238, 243, 306, 307
SPYCKER/SPYEKER, Peter 37, 138
SQUIRES, Mary 314
STACKHOUSE/STOCKHOUSE, James 278; Samuel 108; Thomas 307
STACY/STACEY, Edmund 57; John 249; Jonathan 249
STADLEMAN, William 177, 179
STAFFORD, - Capt. 259
STAHL, Augustine 237
STALKER, - WARREN and 16
STALTZ, Abraham 37; Matthias 37; Wendle 37
STAMER, Anna Magdalena 159
STAMPER, - 63, 241,323; Capt. 8, 25, 146, 170, 254, 275, 276; Alexander 224; John 11, 27, 32, 284; Thomas 3, 41, 170
STANALAND, John 170, 286
STANDIGE, - Capt. 250
STANFORD, Sanderson 249, 264, 311
STANLEY/STANDLEY/STANDLY, - and HUGHES 291, 330; Widow 43, 283; John 53, Mary 38; Moses 176, 185, 195, 232; Richard 38; Thomas 176; Volantine 38; William 88, 137, 158, 176, 185
STANNARD, Thomas 192
STANT, James 27
STANWORTH, Henry 158
STAP, Thomas 312
STAPLER, John 119
STAPLES, John 196
STARK, Jonathan 74
STARKE, Samuel 252
STARR, - Capt. 295; Isaac 273; John 134, 199, 289; Margaret 273; Moses 8, 197, 253, 309
STEBER, John 93
STEBBINS, - Capt. 247
STEDMAN, Abraham 258;
Alexander 14, 28, 59, 63, 67, 80, 95, 97, 98, 129, 134, 145, 271, 281, 290, 329; Charles 14, 28, 59, 63, 67, 95, 97, 98, 129, 134, 145, 203, 271, 281, 290; John 126; Joseph 103; Mary 122
STEEL/STEELE/STEELL, - Capt. 146, 201, 225, 249, 251, 266, 281, 290, 308, 320; Mrs. 112; Alexander 148; Elijah 268; Hugh 95; James 50, 80, 117; John 253, 271; Jonas 178; Joseph 138; Rebecca 61, 103, 117, 185, 199, 235; Robert 127, 173
STEEN, - Widow 120; Andrew 166; Nehemiah 166
STEER, Joseph 73, 100; Nicholas 100
STEINMAN, Christian 3
STEINMITZ/STONEMETZ/ STONEMITZ/STONEMAT, Daniel 77, 105, 135, 245
STERRAT, James 7
STEVENS/STEPHENS/STEPHEN, - Capt. 19, 47, 143, 192, 206, 212, 308; Lt.-Col. 325; Mrs. 142; Adam 105, 305, 307; Cornelius 86; Erasmus 102, 148, 240, 258, 270, 313, 315, 331; Isaac 12; John 72, 82, 88, 134, 147, 156; Margaret 82; Philip 35; Phineas 123; Robert 12, 145; William 260
STEVENSON/STEPHENSON, - Capt. 57, 94, 98, 192, 242, 260, 276, 281, 282; Andrew 249; George 6, 64, 99, 120, 143, 155; Henry 169; James 264; John 264; Nicholas 156, 190
STEWARD, Hugh 175;James 22, 34, 35, 37, 90, 96, 127, 224; John 36; Robert 37; William 183
STEWART/STEUART, - Capt. 73, 80, 249, 262, 274, 294, 303, 308; Mr. 277; Abraham 279; Archibald 100, 150, 210, 323; Daniel 331; David 323, 325; George 231; Hannah 155;James 72, 155; Philip 45; Robert 50, 61, 102, 150; Thomas 73, 191; William 104
STILES/STYLES, - Capt. 44, 151, 210, 246,249, 250, 261, 267, 274, 275, 321; Benjamin 23; Edward 136, 139; Joseph 127; Richard 180
STILLMAN/STILMAN, Augustine 99, 145, 236, 334

STILLWAGON/STILLWAGGON, John 222, 234, 247, 319
STILLWELL, Thomas 198
STINE, Elias 178
STINSON, John 10, 21, 52, 97, 112, 114, 117, 173, 315
STINYARD, Joseph 240
STIRLING, - Capt. 150, 195, 204, 205, 247, 250, 254, 255, 256, 275, 303, 305, 306; Walter 72, 149, 309
STOBE/STOBO, Richard 295, 307, 312
STOCKDALE, William 217
STOCKER, Anthony 73, 93, 118; Henry 285
STOCKLEY, Benjamin 309
STOCKS, William 143
STOCKTON, John 273; Richard 319
STODDARD/STODDERT, - Capt. 194, 220, 331; Justice 242; Benjamin 92
STOGDAL, John (alias of John Miller) 84
STOKES, Edward 158; John 35; Samuel 168
STONE, Frederick 297; Lodowick 116; Thomas 325
STONEBURNER, Leonard 46, 61, 302, 319
STONEMAN, Christian 134
STONER, - Mr. 222, 234
STOOP/STOOPS, John 25, 58, 317
STORMER, Elizabeth 5
STORY, Elizabeth 40, 182, 229; Enoch 40, 182, 292; John 308
STOUT, - Capt. 193, 317; Mr. 240; Cornelius 323; Joseph 193
STOVELL, - Capt. 24
STOW, Charles 43, 137, 195, 204; Charles, Jr. 141; Charles, Sr. 276; Hannah 278; John 55, 156, 169, 278
STOWN, John 29
STRACHAN, - Capt. 64; John 85
STRANGE, - Capt. 332
STRATTAN, David 299
STRAWBRIDGE, - Capt. 20
STREET, Daniel 315; James 315
STREPET, Dennis 269; John 269
STRETCH, - 111, 144, 280; Mr. 32, 199, 288, 319; Joseph 61, 102, 149, 170, 197, 217, 253, 308, 320, 335; Peter 91; Thomas 293
STRETTELL, - ALLEN and 83; Amos 12, 33, 66, 85, 86, 108, 184, 261; Robert 1, 12, 33, 66, 83, 85, 86, 108, 149, 334
STRICKER/STRICKERS, John 168, 173

STRICKLAND, Amos 30, 93, 123, 140, 253; John 77, 91, 145, 170, 257; Miles/Myles 42, 134, 145, 170
STRICKLER, Adam 77
STRIDHAM, Lucas 70; Jonas 70; Peter 70
STRIKER, John 153
STRIVEN, - Capt. 221
STROAP, - 115
STRONG, Valentine 53, 88
STROTHER, Anthony 298
STROUD, Jacob 165
STRUTTON, John 149
STUARD, James 13
STUART, - Capt. 18,213, 312; Allan 276; David 6; Thomas 155; William 214
STUBS, Thomas 332
STUDER, Caspar 234
STUGARS, Zachary 311
STUPART/STUPPARD, - Capt. 47, 50, 86, 233
STURGISS, Stephen 81
SUCKLING, - Capt. 294, 327
SUDAR, Jacob 240
SUDDLER, - Mr. 251
SUGAR, Elizabeth 29; Thomas 29
SULLIVAN, - 103, 126, 199; Mr. 87; Cornelius 12, 18, 58; David (alias Daniel Sullivan) 126, 128; Jeremiah 146; John 319; Owen 100, 193; Patrick 154; Timothy 171
SUMORS, John 313
SUMRIE, Isaac 269
SUNBRY, Alexander 320
SURBER, Rudolph 187
SURRELL, Daniel 186
SUTHER, Samuel 63
SUTHWARD, Martha 280
SUTTON, - Mr. 122; Thomas 152; W. 131, 142
SWAINE, - Capt. 230, 259, 262, 312; Charles 261, 283
SWAINY/SWAYNEY, Hannah 35; John 222
SWAIT, John 230
SWALES, John 235
SWALLOW, William 292
SWAN, - Capt. 157, 225, 275; Daniel 137, 232, 235, 317; Richard 269; Robert 15, 231
SWANSON, - 163, 201
SWEAT, - 115
SWEATING, Martha 139; William 139
SWEENEY, George 61
SWEET, - Capt. 218, 238, 250, 260, 264; John 216
SWEETING, - Capt. 89
SWIFT, Jeremiah 122, 126, 128; John 79, 104, 121, 125, 160, 193, 195, 203, 254, 268, 307; Joseph 254, 307; Samuel 13, 29, 69, 109, 188
SWIGARD, Peter 166

SWIKEHAUSER/SWICHEHAUSER, Conrad 46, 108
SWINNY/SWINNEY, Edward 145; Terence 176
SWOOPE, Michael 264, 270
SWORD, William 313
SYNG, Philip 15, 16, 23, 44, 87, 101, 108, 116, 117, 150, 170, 217, 279, 307, 329

TAGGART, - Capt. 328
TALBERT, Joseph 5
TALBOT, - Capt. 193; James 198; Joseph 272
TALMAN, James 303; Thomas 288, 297
TANNER, - Capt. 59, 285; Cornelius 17
TARR, George 85
TASKER, - Capt. 76; Col. 151; B./Benjamin 259, 268, 275, 287, 289, 296, 321, 331; Benjamin, Jr. 231
TATE/TATTE/TEATE, - Capt. 28; Andrew 87; Anthony 5; Joseph 87; Michael 230; William 129
TATNAL/TATNALL/TATNELL, Anne 7; Robert 183; Thomas 7
TAYLOR, - 71, 297; Capt. 214, 236, 249, 275, 288, 308, 312, 313; Col. 17; Mr. 135, 175, 186; Abraham 1, 23, 32, 87, 92, 203, 281, 307, 329; Benjamin 76, 144, 165, 255; Charles 227; Christopher 76; Edward 113; Frederick 129; George 2, 31, 82; Hathorn 35; Isaac 69; Isaac, Jr. 237; Isaac, Sr. 237; James 57; John 95, 114, 149, 183, 237, 248, 255, 264, 271, 274, 289, 298, 333; Robert 286; Samuel 95, 111, 237; Taylor 257; Thomas Jones 325; William 27, 121, 205
TEAGUE, - Capt. 275
TEAL, Emanuel 295
TEDAR/TEDDER, - Capt. 205; Henry 258; Miles 231
TEDMAN, Hendrick Theodorus 188
TELL, Richard 313
TEMPEST, Robert 274
TEMPLE, Robert 282
TEN EYCK/TEN EICK, Widow 138; Peter 298
TENNENT/TENNANT, - Rev. 83, 292, 312; Cornelia 221; Gilbert 4, 5, 6, 60, 221
TENNIS, John 116; Samuel 116; William 116
TERRY, - Capt. 331; James 196, 289; Susannah 289; Thomas 160
TEST, John 246
TEW, Edward 273

THAIR, Ephraim 267;
  Mary 267
THARP, John 207, 209;
  Moses 125
THATCHER, - Rev. 318;
  Richard 81
THETFORD/THEADFORD, Walter 73, 148, 226
THEOBALDS, - Capt. 264,
  290
THOMAS, - Capt. 57, 268,
  281, 282, 312, 313;
  Benjamin 183; Daniel
  106; George 219; John
  90, 139, 145, 175,
  186, 189, 192, 194,
  198, 200, 202, 205,
  206, 208, 210, 245,
  252, 282; Jonathan
  78, 92, 113, 242,
  243; Joshua 10, 16;
  Lewis 64, 70, 90,
  167; Margaret 12; Morris 14; Moses 45, 140;
  Nathaniel 11; Philip
  16; Capt. R. 332;
  Rees/Reas 54, 228,
  299, 301, 322;Richard
  35, 139, 168; Robert
  30, 61, 84, 90, 102,
  104, 149, 157, 171,
  176, 195, 197, 253,
  308; Simon 248; Thomas 12, 104, 130;
  William 228, 299, 301,
  322
THOMPSON/THOMSON, -
  Capt. 18, 70, 259,
  291, 312, 316, 331;
  Misses 54; Adam 34,
  108, 110, 117;
  Anthony 310; Elizabeth 241; J. 210;
  James 34, 189, 224;
  John 8, 195, 320; Joseph 148; Joshua 149,
  197, 253, 308, 334;
  Moses 207; Robert 87,
  116, 182; William 53,
  62, 178, 307, 328
THORN/THORNE, John 275;
  Richard 276
THORNBRUGH/THORNBROUGH,
  Thomas 71, 99
THORNTON, Isaac 237;
  James 139; John 170;
  Thomas 151, 199
TIAS, John 100
TIBB, Henry 65
TILBURY, Thomas 44, 74,
  81, 93, 154, 168, 198
TILDEN, Marmaduke 86
TILL, William 1, 52,
  63, 183, 310
TILLA, John 201, 202
TILLIDGE/TILLAGE, -
  Capt. 76, 232, 247
TILLOTSON, - Archbishop
  276
TILLYER, Philip 107;
  William 107
TIMS, Bartholomew 75;
  Robert 223
TINDALL, Thomas 182
TINGLEY, - Capt. 68,
  107, 202, 276
TINKER, - Gov. 296;

John 315
TIPPER/TIPPAR, Ann 228;
  James 104, 143, 154,
  228; William 262
TIPPLE, - Capt. 274;
  William 331
TISE, Michael 182
TITCOMB, Enoch 114
TODD, Henry 182
TOL, Darfiel 24
TOLD, John Philip/Philip
  133, 280, 283
TOLFORD, James 188
TOLLEY, Walter 307
TOMKINS, Edward 78
TOMLINSON, Ebenezer 30,
  69, 99, 104, 182, 305
TOMS, Robert 228
TONAT, George 157
TOOL, Patrick 186
TOOMER, John 281
TOOTELL, - Dr. 185
TOPPAM/TOPHAM, - Capt.
  10, 16, 80, 98, 228,
  234, 298, 316
TOULON, - Capt. 260
TOWERS, James 307; John
  41, 257, 265; Margaret 265; Robert 176
TOWNSEND/TOWNSAND, -
  Commodore 181; Appleony 302; John 168
TRACY/TRACEY, James 128;
  Laughlin 22
TRAFFORD, Edmund 231
TRAIN, James 103, 150
TRANN/TRAN, - Capt.
  251, 252, 254; Arthur
  205
TRANBERG, Andrew 75,
  260, 272, 286
TRAPNALL, John 243
TRAPP, - Capt. 253
TRASK, - 295
TRAXLER, John 254, 309;
  Peter 102, 149, 199
TREASURY, Christiana
  108
TREAT, Richard 261
TREE, John 222
TRELAWNY/TRELAWNEY, -
  Gov. 212; Edward 21
TREMBLE, William 105
TRENT, - Capt. 91, 284,
  291; Mr. 277; William
  150
TRESS, Andrew 99
TRIGO, James 23
TRINDER, John 269
TROTH, Henry 300
TROTMAN, James 187
TROTTER, - and ELLIOT
  266; Capt. 70; Mrs.
  185; Ann 166; Benjamin 77; James 36, 47,
  73, 96, 171, 181,
  222, 316; Joseph 30,
  43, 61, 100, 102,
  112, 149, 197, 253,
  291, 308, 322, 335;
  Nathan 151; Spencer
  149; Thomas 107; William 102, 146, 149
TROUP/TROOP, - Capt. 1,
  12, 121, 143, 148,
  169, 171, 173, 306;
  Alexander 15; Robert

24, 29, 181
TROUT, - 121; Capt. 221,
  308
TROY, - Capt. 235, 236,
  332; John 112, 115,
  238
TRUAX/TRUEAX/TRUEAXE, -
  Mr. 68; Isaac 24,
  301; Rebecca 301
TRUMAN, James 69
TRUMBLE, Francis 91, 98,
  256, 261, 298, 305
TRUMP, - Capt. 248, 251,
  252, 275; John 6, 92,
  178
TRUSDELL, - Deputy Constable 242
TRUT, Henry 246
TRYON, - Capt. 260
TUBB, George 194
TUCKER, - Capt. 90, 125,
  133, 141, 205, 284,
  290, 331; Col. 64;
  John 324; Joseph 271,
  293, 333; Nicholas 188;
  Thomas 159; William 52
TUDOR/TUDER, - Capt. 192,
  212, 238, 262; Stephen
  212; Walter 148
TUETT, - Mr. 61
TUFTS, William 234
TUITE, - Mr. 82, 94
TULLEY, - 118, 175
TUMEY, Joseph 27, 46
TUNIS/TUNES, Anthony 34,
  119, 269
TUPPEN, John 204
TUREL, - Capt. 245
TURNER, - ALLEN and 50,
  97, 191, 206, 251,
  306; - and MASSEY 66;
  - 81, 97, 100, 129,
  257; Capt. 21, 171;
  Edward 225; John 110;
  Joseph 1, 18, 23, 26,
  94, 98, 148, 206, 220,
  223, 227, 232, 307,
  329; Peter 27, 91,
  203, 216, 241, 321;
  Samuel 176
TUSSEY, William 161
TUTTE, - Rev. Dr. 141
TWERD, Robert 153
TWINING, John 203, 209
TYLEE, John 330
TYLER/TYLAR, Edward 93;
  Samuel 324
TYRANT, - Capt. 21
TYRREL, - Capt. 20
TYSON, - 269; Derrick
  38; Peter 315; Reiner
  86

ULRICK, - Capt. 37;
  Widow 220; Caspar 136
UNDERHILL, John 175;
  Thomas 193, 232
UNDERWOOD, Elizabeth
  214; John 76; Joseph
  214; Samuel 137
URIE, Alexander 12
USHER, Abraham 13, 16,
  88, 95, 189, 199,
  219, 234, 252, 268;
  Matthew 88, 95, 189,
  199, 219, 234, 252,
  268
UTREY, Jacob 247

VALENTINE, John 83, 85, 96
VALLACOT, - Capt. 231; Samuel 141
VALLET, Peter 211
VAN ANTWERPEN, Daniel 24; J.P. 24
VAN BIBBER/VANBIBBER/VAN BEBBER/VANBEBBER, Adam 103; Henry 44; Jacob 8, 13, 146, 253, 309, 311
VAN BRAAM/VAMBRAM, - Capt./Mr. 296, 312; Jacob 295
VAN BUSKIRK, Lawrence 6, 114
VANCE, - Capt. 25, 26, 259; John 6, 31,100, 102, 150, 197; Patrick 41
VANCLEAVE, John 138
VAN CULIN, John 9; William 9
VAN DAM, Rip 74
VANDEERING, John 269
VANDEGRIFT, Leonard 71, 227
VANDEN BOGART, Francis, Jr. 24
VANDERIN, John 302
VANDER KRUYT/VANDER KLUYT, Matthias a Brackel 36, 41, 46
VANDERSPEIGLE, - Mr. 91, 94; William 314
VANDEVER, John 157
VANDYKE/VAN DIKE/VANDIKE, Charles 210; Frederick 66, 91; John 6, 31, 61, 102, 227, 255
VAN EECKELEN, Johannes 64
VAN ERDEN, Christian 101
VANHORNE/VANHORN, Barnet 282; Bernard 9, 20; David 232, 273; Gabriel 240; Matthias 322; Richard 13
VAN MIDDLESWORTH, John 114
VAN NESTE/VANESTE, - Mr. 212; Jacob 212
VAN SLYKE, Adrian 24
VAN WAGENEN, - Dr. 212
VANWINKLE, John 16
VANSANDT/VANSANT/VANZANT, Garret/Garrett/Gerret 5, 61, 102, 149, 203; Isaiah 6; James 333; Jesinah 333; John 333; Joshua 248; Nicholas 325
VARDIL, - Capt. 90, 220, 259, 285, 298, 331
VASLINE, John 321
VASS, - Capt. 168; William 152
VASTINE, Abraham 30, 61, 102
VAUGHAN/VAHAN, - Capt. 276, 285, 290; James 19; John 205; John, Jr. 2; William 93, 95, 127

VAULX, Robert 19
VAUNCE, John 61
VAVASOR, John 77
VEDDER, Albert John 24
VELZER, John 322
VENABLE, Thomas 117
VERHULST, Stanford 137
VERNON, - Capt. 261; Fortescue 277
VERNOR, John 38, 193; Martha 316
VERPLANK, Gulian 155
VERREE, James 140, 181; Rachel 140, 181
VESEY/VEASEY/VEAZY, - Capt. 294; Mr. 113; Edward 237; William 10
VESSELS, - Widow 278
VICARY, John 241
VIDAL/VIDALL, - Mr. 112, 152, 329; Stephen 55, 200
VIELEN, Cor., Jr. 24
VIGNOLES, Charles 294
VIGOE, Francis 178
VILETT, Stephen 185
VILLIER, Coulon 300
VINEY, Jacob (error for Jacob Odenheimer) 266
VINING, John 13, 150, 193, 199, 255, 300
VISCOUNT, - Capt. 195
VOGAN, William 162
VONDERWITE, Jacob 7
VOTO, Paul Isaac 88, 208
VROMAN, John S. 24; Peter 24

WADDEL/WADDIL, - Capt. 78, 308
WADE, - Capt. 42; Zebulon 107
WADHAM, - Capt. 180, 331; John 99; Noah 307
WADLEY, - Capt. 114
WAGENER, Peter 19; Thomas 307
WAGGAMAN, Henry 184
WAGSTAFF/WAGSTAFFE, James 118, 297; Richard 92, 195, 293, 323
WAINWRIGHT, Jonathan 311
WAIT/WAITE, - Capt. 110, 253
WAKEFIELD, - Capt. 172; John 208
WAKELY, - Mr. 332; Robert 305
WALBER/WALBERT, Nicholas 103, 145; Peter 103
WALBURTON, Robert 112
WALDEN, Thomas 213
WALDO, - Capt. 162, 318; Jonathan 321
WALDRON, - Capt. 205, 265, 268
WALES, North (?) 253
WALKENS, Henry 318
WALKER, - Capt. 144, 204; Abel 132; Andrew 64; Daniel 121, 256; Edward 164; Hannah 165, 203; James 11, 209, 249, 253, 286

Job 203; John 199, 254; Michael 238; Moses 183; Ralph 165; Richard 5, 61, 102, 149, 172, 197, 210, 287, 294; Robert 5, 157, 168; Thomas 60, 203, 302; William 6, 211, 217
WALL, - 199; Capt. 51, 250, 254, 256, 257, 275, 315, 316; Mr. 254; Godfrey 294; Gurnay 206; Jacob 40; John 40, 268; Joseph 40; Martin 73; Patrick 137, 146, 310; Richard 196; Robert 55, 246
WALLACE/WALLAS. - and BRYAN 189, 192, 195, 207, 233, 277, 279; Capt. 137, 185, 201, 249, 313; Mr. 322; Benjamin 326; James 81, 96, 127, 138, 164, 192, 309, 324; John 36, 63, 01, 93, 135, 215; Sarah 62; Thomas 319, 329; William 26, 98, 202, 223
WALLEY, - Mr. 315; Joseph 77, 91
WALN/WALLN, Richard 4, 86, 142, 178, 229, 290; Richard, Jr. 109; Robert 80, 83, 203
WALPOLE, Lord 223
WALTAKER/WALTIKER, Conrad 172, 187, 204, 276, 296, 313; Margaret 204
WALTER/WALTHER/WALTERS, - Capt. 289; Jacob 98, 130, 211, 268
WALTHOE, - Mr. 307; N. 330
WALTON, - Capt. 255, 259, 261, 263, 264; Benjamin 224, 280; Joseph 224; Nathaniel 99
WAMBLES, George 319
WAMPALT, George 126
WAMSLEY, John 105
WANDLE, Frederick 290
WANLESS, Benjamin 245
WANTON, - Capt. 66, 264; Joseph 285; William 298
WARBURTON, - Col. 78, 143, 274; Robert 97
WARD, - Capt. 250; Ensign 292; Mr. 284; James 95; William 191
WARDELL, - Capt. 300, 313
WARDER, Jeremiah 112, 137, 197, 217, 254
WARDROP, - Mr. 127; Henry 162
WARE, John 155; Nathaniel 103, 252, 281, 327
WARMER, George 115
WARNE, Stephen 41
WARNER, - 66; Capt. 236, 255, 323; Edward 16, 30, 61, 87, 93, 98, 100, 102, 136, 149, 163, 183, 185, 197,

WARNER, Edward (cont'd) 219, 222, 230, 236, 253, 308, 316, 318, 319, 328; Isaac 74, 165; John 82, 90; Joseph 206; Nicholas 232; Oliver Ring 191; Veronica 74, 81
WARREN, - and STALKER 16; Admiral 3; Capt. 218; Lady 3; Jacob 197; Sir Peter 56, 154, 200; Robert 69, 70, 108, 117, 134
WARRICK, Jacob 212
WARTIN, Jack 8
WASDALE, William 179
WASHINGTON, - Col. 293, 295, 296, 302, 305, 307, 334; Major 198, 276, 277, 282, 284, 291, 292, 293, 312; Mr. 271; Lawrence 29
WATERHOUSE, - Capt. 59
WATERMAN, Ann 31; Lydia 334; Thomas 31
WATERS, Anthony 48; Elizabeth 157, 170
WATKINS, Anne 27; Joseph 48, 73, 149, 197, 217, 254, 307; William 190
WATKINSON, Francis 305
WATMAUGH, - Lt. 81
WATSON, - Admiral 290; Capt. 90, 181, 195, 201, 261; Alexander 21; Bethel 31; David 86; James 70; John 30, 321; Joseph 197; Mark 29, 109; Matthew 219, 268; Nathan 113; Richard 66
WATTS/WATT, Mary 109; Robert 101; Samuel 127; Silas 239; Thomas 272
WAUGH, Henry 37; William 77
WAY, Elizabeth 155; James 48, 92; Joshua 99, 155, 167, 329
WAYMAN/WEYMAN, - Mrs. 189, 254; Widow 180; Edward 94, 305
WAYN, Anthony 175
WAYNMAN/WEYNMAN, - Capt. 23, 206, 212, 213, 233, 236, 238, 243
WAYTES, Joseph 240
WEAS, K. 163
WEATHERBY, Benjamin 5, 53
WEATHERS, Archibald 21
WEAVER/WEVER, - Capt. 321; Adam 7, 299, 327; John 314; Joseph 57, 120, 174
WEBB, - Dr. 126; Edith 283; James 31, 60, 72, 102; Mary 334; William 46, 303; Zebulon 278
WEBBER, John 204, 214; Jonathan 204, 214; Thomas 166
WEBSLEY, John 136

WEBSTER, Isaac 219, 232; John 60, 62, 158, 159, 162, 174, 175, 176, 204, 316; Michael 74; Samuel 297; Thomas 72
WEDHAM, - Capt. 60
WEEKS/WEEKES, - Mr. 70; Elizabeth 5
WEGGERY, John 242
WEINEMER, Philip 104
WEIS, Anna 103; Johannis 103
WEISER, - Mr. 1; Caleb 42; Conrad 22, 44, 56
WEISS, George Michael 67
WEITTNER/WEYTTNER, Conrad 286, 335
WELCH, John 46, 52, 158; Thomas 46; William 107, 281
WELCKLY, Jacob 257
WELD, - Rev. 318
WELLEN, Dennis 48
WELLS, David 166; Ezekiel 199; Harry (alias Bond's Harry) 20; James 242; Rebecca 240; Richard 13; Samuel 165; Thomas 57, 69, 172, 195, 312
WELSH, Benjamin 263; Edward 173; Francis 165; Mary 105; Nicholas 105; Philip 250; Walter 326; William (alias of George Kelly) 264
WEMP, Ryer 24
WENDELL, Jacob 244
WENTZ, Jacob 242
WENWICK, Thomas 182
WESCOTT, George 140
WEST, - Capt. 170, 225; Charity 54; James 79, 143; Jonathan 50; Thomas 105; William 54, 82
WESTENHEVER, Christopher 214; Maria Catherina 214
WESTLADE, - Capt. 296, 297
WESTWARD, Edward 221
WETHERELL/WETHERILL, John 114, 298; Samuel 125
WETHERSPOON, David 9
WEYNANT, John 39
WHALEN, Dennis 306, 332; Luke 183
WHARTENBY, Robert 239, 270
WHARTON, - Mr. 248; James 252, 268; John 23, 308; Joseph 23, 45, 88, 93, 104, 112, 125, 163, 219, 224, 235, 239; Robert 292, 306; Thomas 223, 231, 281;
WHEATLEY, John 191
WHEATON, Solomon 124; Timothy 124
WHEELER, - Mr. 221; Samuel 310
WHEELWRIGHT, Nathaniel 192
WHIGAM, Hannah 300

WHINEMORE, Philip 14
WHIP, Hans Martin 191
WHIPPLE, - Capt. 233; Mr. 221; Rev. 76
WHIT, Henry 237
WHITAKER, Edward 95
WHITCOM, Joseph 24
WHITE, - Capt. 12, 18, 24, 76, 190, 194, 212, 221, 233, 236, 242, 260, 265, 268, 271, 276, 282, 301; Col. 59; James 84, 96, 292, 308; John 9, 29, 44, 60, 76, 147, 158, 201, 217, 322; Joseph 272, 323; Lawrence 209; Lydia 190; Michael 318; Patrick 144, 324; Philip 205; Robert 174, 291; Samuel 14, 157, 239; Thomas 4, 26, 28, 31, 39, 58, 92, 107, 115, 238, 256, 307; Townsend/Townshend 10, 47, 63, 96, 113, 140, 290; Uriah 215; William 245, 255, 278, 316
WHITEBREAD, - Mr. 286; William 15, 64, 139, 158, 169, 175, 301
WHITEFIELD, - 174; Capt. 155; Rev./MR. 23, 159, 175, 246, 303, 306, 307, 312, 315, 316, 318, 319, 320, 321, 332; George 160, 174, 297, 299, 327
WHITEFORD, Hugh 13
WHITEHEAD, - Mr. 178, 315; James 40, 49, 115, 194, 206, 323; Robert 225; William 227, 245
WHITEHILL, James 20
WHITELY/WHITELEY/WHITLEY, Anthony 26, 50, 93, 142, 161, 174, 183, 198, 242, 254, 287; Frederick 53
WHITELOCK/WHITLOCK, -GREEN and 160, 207; Isaac 95, 116, 139, 242, 253, 275
WHITESIDES, - Capt. 285, 294
WHITMAR, Elizabeth 214; Jacob 214; Margaret 214
WHITNEY, - Capt. 250, 290
WHITPAIN/WHIPAIN, Sarah 259; Zechariah 259
WHITSITT, Ralph 56
WHITTAL, William 110
WHITTEN/WHITTON, Yhomas 39, 214
WHITWELL, - Capt. 235, 292; Matthew 307
WICKREY, James 50
WIDDIFIELD, Peter 13
WIDMORE, Charles 15
WIEDMAN, Jacob 77
WIER, - Capt. 147, 307; James 150
WIGLAY, John 65

WIKOFF, - RHEA and 283
WILCOX/WILCOCKS, - Capt. 286; John 26, 58, 61, 182, 223, 289; Robert 31, 150
WILD, William, Jr. 327
WILDMAN, James 262
WILEY/WILLEY, Margaret 249, 257; William 279
WILKEY, James 8
WILKIN, David 83
WILKINS, William 183
WILKINSON, Anthony 2, 124, 150, 170, 194, 242, 285, 328; Brian/ Bryan 36, 45, 81, 185, 277; Gabriel 101, 193, 265; John 185; Josiah 27, 233; Sarah 101, 179, 193, 242; William 53
WILKS, Jonathan 12
WILL, Isaac 145
WILLAN, Robert 66
WILLARD, J. 296, 317
WILLIAMS, - Capt. 19, 171, 193, 211, 282, 290, 300; Anthony 302; Charles 22; Daniel 149, 150, 187, 197, 253, 285, 308; Derrick 270; Ennion 43, 103, 194; Henry 291; Hugh 48; Isaac 91, 95, 143, 154; James 280; James (alias of James Symes) 147; John 100, 102, 119, 120, 201, 202, 224, 237, 278; John (alias of John Shoppley) 86; Joseph 89, 148, 228, 230, 290; Joseph (alias of Joseph Davis) 282; Matthew 129; Owen 74; Rees 45, 64; Richison 280; Robert 59; Stephen 11, 35, 217, 296, 325; Thomas 3, 56, 58, 72, 83, 84, 91, 101, 107, 108, 122, 123, 143, 330; Walter 107; William 7, 68, 325; William (alias William Broughton) 15
WILLIAMSON, John 5, 326
WILLING, - and LLOYD 115; Charles 1, 10, 14, 20, 31, 33, 37, 40, 56, 62, 86, 93, 98, 99, 104, 143, 151, 171, 193, 203, 208, 250, 269, 283, 285, 286, 292, 308, 315, 318, 323; Thomas 323
WILLIOT, Samuel 257
WILLIS, - Sergeant 292; John, Jr. 46
WILLOCK, William 167, 307
WILLS, Daniel 13; Henry 131; Joseph 215; Margaret 13; Michael 207, 265, 293, 333; Thomas 77, 207, 265, 283
WILMER/WILMORE, Simon 183, 202
WILMINGTON, John 319
WILMOT/WILLMOT, - Capt. 275, 294; Richard 305, 307
WILSON, - Capt. 20, 81, 214, 221, 290, 323; Mr. 176; Adam 276; Anthony 117; David, Jr. 72; George/G. (alias Newton, alias Jones) 130, 131, 142, 148, 177, 180; Hannah 291; Hugh 309; James 66, 80, 97, 108, 139, 184; James (alias Scotch James) 113; John 13, 16, 106, 225; Joseph 8, 54, 68, 212; Mary 223, 228; Matthew 162; Nicholas 221, 330, Patrick 259; Robert 161, 236; Sarah (alias of Sarah Knox) 220; Thomas 184, 199; William 153, 218, 261, 286; William (alias of John Wright) 289
WILTSHIRE, - Capt. 215
WILY, John 66
WINDSOR, Jacob 134
WINEY, Thomas 58
WINGFIELD, - Capt. 279
WINNIET, Alex. 71
WINSLOW, - Capt. 172; Gen. 295, 304, 307, 308; Gov. 298, 299; Lt. 81; Edward 267; John 128
WINTER, - Capt. 257, 275; John 85; William 290
WINTHROP/WINTHORP, - Capt. 206, 212, 238, 268, 282, 288, 290
WISE, - Capt. 265; John 100
WISEHART, Ninian 21
WISEMAN, Isaac 171
WISENDEN, Robert 139
WISHER, William 288
WISTAR/WISTER, Caspar 146, 154, 183, 230, 240, 257; Catherine 183, 230, 257; John 179, 219, 221; Richard 183, 188, 230, 307
WITHERILL, Thomas, Jr. 212
WITHEROW, John 150
WITHERSPOON, David 58, 131, 193, 312, 316
WITHY, - Capt. 312
WITT, Christopher 48
WITTEN, Moses 173
WITTER, - Capt. 40, 133
WOLCOTT, Roger 112
WOLFF, Henry 276
WOLLING/WOLSING, James 264, 267
WOOD, Abraham 39; Ann 108; Catherine 238; George 108, 321; Hannah 108; James 170, 179, 187; Jeremiah 60; John 225, 240, 272; Joseph 16, 58, 103, 147, 200, 225; Joshua 78; Robert 98; Stephen 270; Thomas 211; William 188
WOODALL, Abraham 126
WOODCOCK, Anthony 239, 257; Bancroft 287; William 328
WOODEN, - Widow 126
WOODHOUSE, William 218
WOODLOCK, - Capt. 262
WOODMAN, Jonathan 140, 141, 146
WOODROP/WOODROPE, - 151; Capt. 44; Mr. 114, 129, 208
WOODROW, Henry 305
WOODRUFF, Samuel 69, 273
WOODS, Ann/Anne 141, 305; Duncan (alias of Dennis Madden) 87; Fortunatus 141; James 8, 262, 289
WOODSIDE, - Capt. 76, 321; John 13; William 80, 92
WOODSMAN, John 311
WOODWARD, Elizabeth 153, 178; Samuel 115, 264; William 191
WOODYEAR, Lumley 245
WOOLCOMB, Joseph 34
WOOLERY, - 258
WOOLFORD, - 208; Capt. 110
WOOLLEN, Joseph 240, 269, 278, 304
WOOLEY/WOOLLEY, Rebecca 65; Thomas 26, 62, 79
WOOLMAN, John 235
WOOLSEY, John 11
WOOLSTON, John 30, 61, 102, 149
WOOTON/WOOTTON/WOOTTIN, - Capt. 201; Dudley 294; Turnor 274
WORK, Andrew 102
WORMELSDORF, Daniel 25
WORMS, Daniel 154
WORRELL/WORREL/WORRALL/ WARRELL, Edward 330; Isaiah 4, 6; Jacob 127; James 304; Joseph 88, 226; Joseph, Jr. 226; Peter 31, 50, 61, 100, 150, 199, 253, 309; Robert 99, 111, 157, 171; Samuel 111, 157, 171
WORRICK, Andrew 61
WORSDALE, - Capt. 4, 288
WORTH, Thomas 30
WORTHINGTON, Daniel 251
WRAGG, James 202, 291, 299
WRAY, John 265
WRIGHT, - GARRAWAY and 127; - 241; Capt. 194, 249, 254, 275, 284, 312, 331, 332; Mr. 204; Anthony 13; Barrack 46;

WRIGHT (cont'd) Daniel 123; E. 280; Elizabeth 158; Fretwell 139, 184; Henry 21, 79, 176; Hinson 76; Hugh 195; Isaac 68; James 61, 102, 150, 172, 199, 253, 309; John 31, 41, 44, 63, 91, 107, 143, 150, 158, 172, 187, 199, 255, 278, 292, 299, 309; John (alias William Wilson) 289; Joshua 126, 168; Matthew 306; Thomas 107, 197, 253
WROTH, Kinvin 193
WYAT/WYATT, - Capt. 225, 264
WYERMAN, William 34
WYNKOOP/WYNCOOP, Abraham 103, 150, 199; Garret 4
WYNN, John 295; Sir Richard 295
WYRICK, Nicholas 25
WYSHE, George 190

YAGER, Adam 321
YAGLEE, John 269
YANAWINE, Leonard 334
YARD, Benjamin 226; George 283; Joseph 1, 298; Mary 17; William 17, 171, 194
YARDLEY/YEARDLY, Thomas 42, 194; William 42, 149, 197, 224, 230, 232, 234, 246, 253, 257, 308, 333
YARE, Daniel 300
YARLY, Thomas 45
YARNALL, Abigail 66; Francis 30; John 66; Mordecai 13, 43, 94, 128, 205, 222, 321; Nathan 9, 66; Philip 66; Thomas 224
YEATS/YEATES, George 11; John 197; Joshua 271; William (possible alias of Joseph Holmes) 290
YELDHALL/YELDALL/YALDMALL, Anthony 96, 161, 173
YORK/YORKE, - POTTS and 101; Lt.-Col. 17;Thomas 3, 10, 16, 21, 22, 26, 32, 78, 145, 149, 162, 196, 223, 311, 328
YOUNG, - Capt. 14, 190; Dr. 276; Archibald 158; Barnard 224; Bartholomew 311, 321; Benjamin 274; Eleanor 48; George 222; Hugh 48; James 67, 147; John 13, 200, 244; Joseph 75, 77, 78; Marcus 176, 256; Margaret 316; Matthew 49, Peter 326; Robert 48, 88, 221; William 123, 250, 261, 271, 324

YUST, Christopher 234
ZACHARY, - Dr. 88, 305; Lloyd 48
ZANE/ZEAN, Isaac 84, 93, 100, 163, 214, 241, 279, 335; Jonathan 30, 34, 61, 93, 116, 142, 154, 241, 243, 278, 284, 298; Mary 221
ZEMBES, John Leonard 282
ZIMMERMAN, Bernard 300; Hans 335; Sebastian 253
ZISLAND, Nicholas 15

No Surname
(Indians, Slaves, etc.)
Abraham 213, 214
Andrew 71
Apollo 22
Bess 93
Bill 97
Bob 113
Booner (alias Mooner) 47
Boot 228
Boss 32
Bristow 26
Caesar 11, 67, 89, 138, 305
Cap 325
Catherine 84, 249, 264
Cato 15
Charles 185, 229
Chillawlee 32
Cuff 132, 151, 228, 236
Cuffee 180
Dan 43
Deb 295
Dick 60, 65, 113, 132, 172
Dick (or Harry) 9, 46
Dove 24
Flora 229
Frank 47, 93, 181, 256, 249
George 52, 57, 64, 129
Glascow 295
Gloucester 35
Gregg 199
Half King 291
Harry 252
Harry (or Dick) 9, 17
Bond's Harry (alias of Harry Wells) 20
Israel 310
Jack 35, 50, 229, 299
Jack (alias of John Powell) 73, 330
Jacob 89
James 16, 58, 132, 243, 313
Jehu 184
Jemmy 263
Capt. Job 71
Joe 113, 116, 135, 201
John 21, 137
Judith 1
Kate 24, 293
Lilly 85
Lot 94, 119, 140
Madockawando 71
Malatchi 245
Martha 158
Mary 131
Michael 35, 37
Moll 295
Mona 24

Monocatoocha 277
Montandre 299
Mooner (alias of Booner) 47
Nasey 54
Ned 24, 186
Ononraguiete 299
Pat 158
Hopping Peg (alias of Margaret Barnes) 1
Peter 50, 71
Phil 93
Phillis 124, 237
Plymouth 217
Quaco 295
Rane 325
Robin 97, 330
Sam 91, 98, 238, 243, 305, 323
Sampson/Samson 56, 161
Saracy 71
Sarah 116, 130
Sasquehanna Jack 295
Scaiohady 1
Scipio 16, 54, 65
Sharper 126
Sib 60
Stephen 54
Swilli 22
Tanachrisson 310
Thomas 57, 326
Indian Thomas 261
Tobey/Toby 83, 332
Tom 20, 23, 29, 98, 103, 127
Toney 29, 292, 299
Toxus 71
Will 95, 99, 129, 198

377

www.ingramcontent.com/pod-product-compliance
Lightning Source LLC
Chambersburg PA
CBHW070058020526
44112CB00034B/1473